AQA GCSE History

UNDERSTANDING THE MODERN WORLD

David Ferriby

Dave Martin

Ben Walsh

Approval message from AQA

This textbook has been approved by AQA for use with our qualification. This means that we have checked that it broadly covers the specification and we are satisfied with the overall quality. Full details of our approval process can be found on our website.

We approve textbooks because we know how important it is for teachers and students to have the right resources to support their teaching and learning. However, the publisher is ultimately responsible for the editorial control and quality of this book.

Please note that when teaching the *AQA GCSE History* course, you must refer to AQA's specification as your definitive source of information. While this book has been written to match the specification, it cannot provide complete coverage of every aspect of the course.

A wide range of other useful resources can be found on the relevant subject pages of our website: www.aqa.org.uk.

HODDER
EDUCATION
AN HACHETTE UK COMPANY

The Publishers would like to thank the following for permission to reproduce copyright material.

Photo credits: See inside back cover

Acknowledgements:

John Traynor: Extracts from 'Europe 1890-1990' (Nelson, 1991; **Victoria J. Barnett:** Extract from 'The Role of the Churches: Compliance and Confrontation' *Dimensions*, Vol 12, No. 2 (1998) ; **General Peter Wrangel:** Extract from Always with Honour'; Online extracts from 'Marxists Internet Archive' (https://www.marxists.org); **Heinrich Metelmann:** Extract from 'Through Hell for Hitler' (Spellbound Publishers, 2002); **John Daborn:** extract from *Russia: Revolution and Counter-Revolution, 1917–1924* (CUP 1991); **Robert Service:** Extract from 'A History of Modern Russia: From Nicholas II to Putin' (Penguin, 2003); **Alexander Solzhenitsyn:** Extract from 'One Day in the Life of Ivan Denisovitch' (Penguin Modern Classics, 2000); **U. Alam:** Extract from 'Stalin' (USA, 1973); Online extracts from 'Marxists Internet Archive' (https://www.marxists. org); **V. Ryabov:** Extracts from 'The Great Victory' (Official Press Agency of the USSR, 1975); **W.E. Leuchtenberg:** Extract from 'The Perils of Prosperity' (University of Chicago Press, 1958); **James T. Patterson:** Extract from 'America in the Twentieth Century' (Cengage Learning, 1976); **Craig Mair:** Adapted extract from *Britain at War* (John Murray, 1982); **Richard Holmes:** Extract from 'Tommy: The British Soldier on the Western Front' (HarperCollins, 2004); **Martin Middlebrook:** Extract from 'The First Day of the Somme' (Penguin, 1971); **Nigel Jones:** Extract from 'The War Walk' (Robert Hale, 1983); **Gary Sheffield:** Extract from *BBC History Magazine* (July 2011); **Chris Page:** 'The British Experience of Enforcing Blockage' from *Facing Armageddon: The First World War Experience* (Leo Cooper, 1996); **Neil DeMarco:** Tables from 'The Great War' (Hodder, 1997); **Margaret Macmillan:** Extracts from 'Peacemakers: Six Months that Changed the World' (John Murray, 2003); **Susan Pedersen:** Extract from 'Back to the League of Nations' from *The American Historical Review* Vol. 112, No. 4 (Oct., 2007); **Ralph Manheim:** Extracts from translation of Hitler's 'Mein Kampf' (Hutchinson, 1969); **Laszlo Beke:** Extracts from 'A Student's Diary: Budapest October 16-November 1, 1956' (Hutchinson, 1957); Extract from the *St Louis Post-Dispatch* (3 May 1970); **Daniel Hallin:** Online extract from 'Vietnam on Television' (http://www.museum.tv/eotv/vietnamonte.htm); Extract from blog 'Warbird's Forum'; Extract from *Newsweek* (1973)

Note: The wording and sentence structure of some written sources have been adapted and simplified to make them accessible to all students while faithfully preserving the sense of the original.

Every effort has been made to trace all copyright holders, but if any have been inadvertently overlooked, the Publishers will be pleased to make the necessary arrangements at the first opportunity.

Although every effort has been made to ensure that website addresses are correct at time of going to press, Hodder Education cannot be held responsible for the content of any website mentioned in this book. It is sometimes possible to find a relocated web page by typing in the address of the home page for a website in the URL window of your browser.

Hachette UK's policy is to use papers that are natural, renewable and recyclable products and made from wood grown in well-managed forests and other controlled sources. The logging and manufacturing processes are expected to conform to the environmental regulations of the country of origin.

Orders: please contact Hachette UK Distribution, Hely Hutchinson Centre, Milton Road, Didcot, Oxfordshire, OX11 7HH. Telephone: +44 (0)1235 827827. Email education@hachette.co.uk. Lines are open from 9 a.m. to 5 p.m., Monday to Friday. You can also order through our website: www.hoddereducation.co.uk

ISBN: 978 1 471862946

© David Ferriby, Dave Martin, Ben Walsh 2016

First published in 2016 by
Hodder Education,
An Hachette UK Company
Carmelite House
50 Victoria Embankment
London EC4Y 0DZ
www.hoddereducation.co.uk

Impression number   11

Year   2021

Reprinted with revisions 2019

Cover photo © vario images & GmbH Co. KG / Alamy Stock Photo

Illustrations by DC Graphic Design Limited

Typeset in ITC Giovanni Std Book 9.5/12pt by DC Graphic Design Limited, Hextable, Kent.

Printed in Italy

A catalogue record for this title is available from the British Library.

CONTENTS

How this book will help you in AQA GCSE History

HOW THIS BOOK WILL HELP YOU IN AQA GCSE HISTORY

It will help you to learn the content

Is your main worry when you prepare for an exam that you won't know enough to answer the questions? Many people feel that way. And it is true you will need good knowledge of the main events and the detail to do well in this study. This book will help you acquire both the overview and the detail.

The **text** explains all the key content clearly and thoroughly. It helps you understand each period, and each topic and the themes that connect the topics.

The **Factfiles** and **Profiles** are packed with facts and examples to use in your own work to support your arguments.

We use lots of **diagrams** and **timelines**. These help you to visualise, understand and remember topics. We also encourage you to draw your own diagrams – that is an even better way to learn.

It's full of brilliant **sources**. This course deals with some big issues but sources can help pin those issues down. History is at its best when you can see what real people said, did, wrote, sang, watched, laughed about, cried over, and got upset about. Sources can really help you to understand the story better and remember it because they help you to see what each development or event meant to people at the time.

Think questions direct you to the things you should be noticing or thinking about. They also practise the kind of analytical skills that you need to improve in history. **Activities** are included as more creative approaches to learning the content.

Key words – every subject and topic has its own vocabulary. If you don't know what these words mean you won't be able to write about the subject. So for each chapter we have provided a key word list. These are the kind of words or terms that could be used in sources or an exam question without any explanation so you need to be able to understand them and use them confidently in your writing. They are all defined in the **glossary** on page 371. But we also want you to create your own key word list. In a notebook or on your phone, write down each word with your own definitions.

Finally there is a **Topic Summary** at the end of each of the three parts of each chapter. This condenses all the content into a few points, which should help you to get your bearings in even the most complicated content. Some people say it is good to read that summary before you even start the topic to know where you are heading!

It will help you to apply what you learn

The second big aim of this book is to help you apply what you learn, which means to help you think deeply about the content and develop your own judgements about the issues, and make sure you can support those judgements with evidence and relevant knowledge. This is a difficult skill that you will need to practise.

The main way we help you with this is through the **Focus Tasks**. These are the big tasks that appear at various points in each chapter.

Most Focus Tasks have tips that help you get started – for example, highlighting a couple of key points that you can use in your answers.

It will help you prepare for your examination

If you read all the text and tackled all the Focus Tasks in this book we are sure you would also find you were well prepared for the challenges of Paper 1 of the exam, but you will probably also want something more exam-focused. So on the next two pages we explain how the content in this book will be assessed and how you can prepare yourself for the assessment.

Additionally:
- Dotted throughout the chapters you will find **Practice Question** boxes – offering practice questions.
- At the end of each chapter is an **Assessment Focus** specific to that topic which analyses different question types and uses sample answers to help you to see how to improve your own performance.

How the period studies will be assessed

Section A of this book includes all four period studies from the specification. You only have to answer questions on one. This will be examined in Section A of Paper 1. The questions could be on any part of the content so you need to know it all. It will test three of the assessment objectives:
- AO1 – knowledge and understanding
- AO2 – explanation and analysis
- AO4 – interpretations

Questions 1–3 will focus on interpretations, for example:
- comparing interpretations and explaining why they differ
- asking you to evaluate each interpretation – for instance saying how convincing the interpretation is. This means you have to compare what the interpretation says against your own knowledge.

Interpreting history

Interpretations can often look like sources, but there is one big difference. Interpretations are created after the events they describe. Sometimes they can be a short time afterwards. They could be memoirs or memorials or a foreign newspaper article. Sometimes interpretations are created many years after the event e.g. a textbook, films, statues. The key issue is that they usually have a purpose – to justify, to celebrate or to put forward evidence that goes against the accepted version of an event.

FOCUS TASK

How did the Depression affect the League of Nations?

Look back at the Focus Task on page 256.

1 Using the information on pages 258–59, add another speech bubble for each of the two diplomats to sum up their views of the League now that the world has been affected by the Depression.
2 Add a speech bubble for each diplomat to explain their views on the future of the League.

PRACTICE QUESTION

Which of the following was the more important reason why the Mormons travelled to Salt Lake City:
- Religious persecution
- The leadership of Brigham Young?

Explain your answer with reference to both reasons.

How does Interpretation B differ from Interpretation A about …?
(4 marks)

Why might the authors of Interpretations A and B have a different interpretation about …?
(4 marks)

Which interpretation gives the more convincing opinion …?
(8 marks)

> Describe two problems
> faced by …
> (4 marks)

> In what ways was X
> affected by …?
> (8 marks)

> Which was the more important
> reason why …?
> (12 marks)

Question 4 will ask you to describe two key features or characteristics of a period. This is a pure 'knowledge' question but you will need to select the knowledge that is relevant to the question, write in clear language and include plenty of relevant detail to support your answer.

Question 5 is about change. You will need to use your knowledge to explain how a particular group or people were affected by an event or a development.

Question 6, which carries the highest marks, is an essay question in bullet-point format. The two bullets will give structure to your answer. You need to consider each of them and reach a conclusion. You need to know your topic well to write an essay but equally importantly you also need to think clearly because the best answers will be those that develop a clear, coherent and relevant argument from the start and carry it through the whole essay.

You will get plenty of practice thinking about these issues and practising different question types throughout the study. Then there are some sample questions and answers with teacher feedback and analysis at the end of each period study:

How the wider world depth studies will be assessed

These will be examined in Section B of Paper 1. The exam will include all the depth studies but remember you only need to answer questions on one–make sure it is the one that you have actually studied!

The questions could be on any part of the content so you need to know it all. It will test three of the assessment objectives:

- AO1 – knowledge and understanding
- AO2 – explanation and analysis
- AO3 – source analysis

There will also be marks for spelling, punctuation and grammar (SPAG).

Questions 1 and 2 are the source-based questions:

- The first will usually present a visual source from the period. Use the source and your knowledge to back up the statement that you are given about the source.
- The second question will ask you to compare two sources (written, visual or both) and evaluate how useful they are for a given investigation.

> Source A opposes X. How do
> you know? Explain your answer
> by using the source and your
> contextual knowledge.
> (4 marks)

> How useful are the two sources to
> an historian studying …?
> (12 marks)

Question 3 asks you to write an account of an event from the depth study.

Question 4 is another essay question. You will be presented with a statement and you need to write clearly and coherently about how far you agree with it. This is less structured than the period study essay but the expectations are similar. To prepare to answer these kind of questions you need to revise the content but also think about it and learn how to present an argument and support it. The best answers will be those that do that and develop a clear, coherent and relevant argument. This is the question which carries extra marks for correct use of spelling, punctuation and grammar.

> Write an account of …
> (8 marks)

> 'The main reason for … was …'
> How far do you agree?
> (16 marks)

You will get plenty of practice thinking about these issues and practising different question types throughout the depth study. Then there are some sample questions and answers with teacher feedback and analysis at the end of each depth study.

America 1840–1895: Expansion and Consolidation

This period study focuses on the development of America during a turbulent half century of change. It was a period of expansion and consolidation – the expansion to the West and the consolidation of the United States as a nation.

You will be studying the development of the United States from various perspectives:

- Political developments such as the growth of the United States, the power of the federal government versus the power of individual states and the tensions that nearly broke the Union.
- Economic developments such as the spread of cattle ranching on to the Great Plains and the bridging of the continent by the new railroads.
- Social and cultural developments such as the destruction of the Plains Indian way of life and culture.
- The role of ideas in influencing change such as Manifest Destiny, differing perspectives on land and slavery and the religious beliefs of a group like the Mormons.
- The role of key individuals and groups in shaping change and the impact the developments had on them such as Abraham Lincoln, Brigham Young, Jefferson Davis, John Brown, George Armstrong Custer and Red Cloud; and African Americans, homesteaders, the Mormons and the Plains Indians.

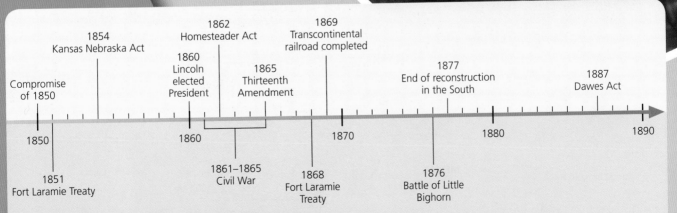

Compromise of 1850

1851 Fort Laramie Treaty

1854 Kansas Nebraska Act

1860 Lincoln elected President

1861–1865 Civil War

1862 Homesteader Act

1865 Thirteenth Amendment

1868 Fort Laramie Treaty

1869 Transcontinental railroad completed

1876 Battle of Little Bighorn

1877 End of reconstruction in the South

1887 Dawes Act

1850 1860 1870 1880 1890

1.1 Expansion: Opportunities and challenges

SOURCE 1

Major Stephen Long, of the Army Corps of Engineers, described the Great Plains after crossing them in 1820. His expedition was for the United States government which was exploring its boundaries with Spanish California and British Oregon.

In regard to this extensive section of country, I do not hesitate in giving the opinion that it is almost wholly unfit for cultivation, and of course uninhabitable by a people depending upon agriculture for their subsistence [producing enough food to live on]. Large areas of fertile land are occasionally to be found, but the scarcity of wood and water will prove an impossible obstacle in the way of settling the country.

FOCUS

In 1840 the United States of America was made up of 27 states, most of them east of the Mississippi River. To the west were the Great Plains. To the nomadic Plains Indians these were home. To the citizens of the United States they were 'the Great American Desert'; but change was coming.

In 1.1 you will study these changes, and in particular:

- The geography of North America and how attitudes towards the Great American Desert changed.
- Why the early settlers went west and the challenges they faced.
- How the Plains Indians adapted their lives to the Great Plains and how their culture was at odds with American culture.

FIGURE 2

The geography of North America.

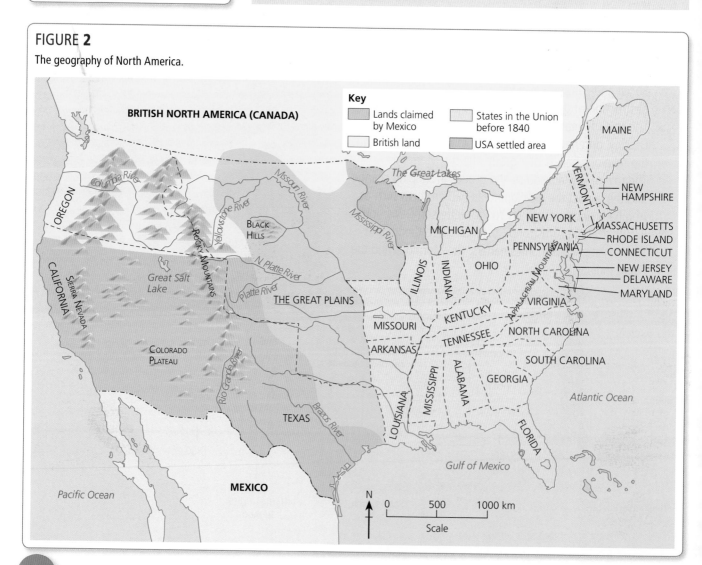

FIGURE **3**
The Great Plains.

● Attitudes to the Great American Desert

In 1840 the people of the United States were not interested in the Great Plains. They were simply dismissed as the Great American DESERT although some journeys of exploration were supported by the government. That attitude, however, would be changed by a number of developments.

The 27 United States were not alone on the continent of North America. To their north was British Canada and to the south and west was Mexico, including California. During the early 1800s Americans had travelled to and peacefully traded with California, while from the 1820s others had settled in the Mexican STATE of Texas. These Texas SETTLERS were originally encouraged by the Mexican government. However, they tended to be southern farmers who brought slaves with them for their cotton PLANTATIONS and after the Mexican government abolished SLAVERY in 1829 it tried to stop them. These tensions eventually led to rebellion and Texas declared itself a REPUBLIC in 1836. Meanwhile by the 1840s Americans were beginning to settle the good farming land in California.

In 1845 the United States took over Texas. It became the 28th state of the Union. This led to the Mexican–American War 1846–48 which ended in complete defeat for Mexico. By the Treaty of Guadalupe Hidalgo, the United States gained the Rio Grande as the southern boundary for Texas, all of California and a large area of land that was to become the future states of Arizona, Colorado, New Mexico, Nevada, Utah and Wyoming.

THINK

Look at Source 1. Why does Major Long say the West is not suitable for farming?

FACTFILE

The Mexican–American War, 1846–48

The Mexican-American War had its roots in the tussle for control of Texas and was triggered in 1846 by the annexation of Texas, including land south of the Rio Grande. Negotiations failed and after Mexican troops attacked US troops in Texas open war broke out. The Mexicans were driven out of Texas. Then US armies occupied New Mexico and California. Finally in 1847 the US armies advanced deep into Mexico, winning the Battle of Buena Vista, capturing Mexico City and forcing Mexico to sign the Treaty of Guadalupe Hidalgo.

SOURCE 4

A close-up of a Shako cap worn by US soldiers during the Mexican-American War. The cap shows an eagle spreading its wings, the symbol of Manifest Destiny.

SOURCE 5

Extract from the column written by John L. Sullivan in *New York Morning News* on 27 December 1845.

And that claim is by the right of our manifest destiny to overspread and to possess the whole of the continent which Providence has given us for the development of the great experiment of liberty and federated self-government entrusted to us.

The belief in 'Manifest Destiny'

In the north-west the newly opened Oregon Trail c.1840, brought new American settlers to Oregon Country in British Canada. Many Americans began to believe that their country should occupy the entire continent from coast to coast. This idea of expansionism was captured by the journalist John L. Sullivan who coined the phrase 'MANIFEST DESTINY'. To many Americans it was God's will that as they occupied these new lands they should bring with them their ideas and beliefs of Christianity, freedom and DEMOCRACY. They believed they would use these lands more effectively than their existing occupants, whether these were the Mexican Hispanic people in California and Texas, who some viewed as lazy and slow, or the Plains Indians, who some viewed as savages. Furthermore the Americans believed that this made it right for them to go to war if necessary to achieve that destiny. For a time it seemed that Britain and the United States might go to war but the boundary dispute was settled by negotiation. By the Oregon Treaty in 1846 the United States gained the land which was to become the future state of Oregon.

FOCUS TASK

Why did attitudes to the Great American Desert change after the Mexican–American War?

1 Copy and complete the following table to show how attitudes to the Great American Desert changed before and after the Mexican–American War.

Attitudes before the war	Attitudes after the war	Reasons for change

2 Now, use your notes from the table to prepare a podcast (no longer than one minute, so around 200 words) to explain how victory in the war against Mexico and the Americans' belief in Manifest Destiny changed the attitude of Americans to the Great American Desert.

Why the early settlers went west and the challenges they faced

FOCUS TASK

Part 1: Why did the settlers go west?

1 Create three 'gingerbread' figures, like the one shown here, to represent the following groups:

- Pioneer farmers like the Knight family
- Mormons
- Gold miners

As you read pages 5–8, annotate these figures. *Inside* the figures write their motives for going west and on the *outside* write those factors that influenced them.

2 In pairs, discuss what reasons were common between the three groups and highlight them in one colour on your gingerbread figures.

3 In the same pair, choose a second colour and highlight one reason for each figure which was unique to that group.

Part 2: What challenges did settlers face?

1 On the back of each figure, use pages 5–8 to write the challenges this particular group faced *inside* the figure, and around the *outside* write how they dealt with these challenges.

2 In pairs, discuss how successful you think the settlers to the Plains were during this period.

The pioneer farmers and their journey west

The first group of Americans to travel west across the Great Plains and into the Rocky Mountains were fur trappers. Fur hats became very fashionable in the eastern United States and in Europe in the '1820s and 30s' and there was money to be made. The trappers came to be known as 'mountain men'. Following them came thousands of pioneer farmers who went west in the 1840s for a variety of reasons. For some it was the pull of good farming land, a better climate or simply the excitement of the new. Others were pushed by the effects of the ECONOMIC DEPRESSION in the eastern states that began in 1837 and led to wage cuts, increased unemployment and the loss of savings when banks collapsed. This depression also had a negative impact on farmers in the Mississippi Valley as crop prices fell, leading some of them to move further west for a new start in the fertile farmlands of Oregon and California. Whatever the reason, it had to be a strong one as the four-month journey was long and hazardous, as Source 6 shows.

SOURCE 6

An edited diary entry by Amelia Stewart Knight on the Oregon Trail.

Saturday, May 14th - We see very few Indians. We are now in the Sioux country. Travelled 2 miles and were obliged to stop and camp on the prairie near a large pond of water, on account of the high winds. Winds so high that we dare not make a fire, impossible to pitch the tent, the wagons could hardly stand the wind.

PRACTICE QUESTION

Describe two problems faced by the pioneers on the Oregon Trail.

FIGURE 7

Map showing the journey to the West.

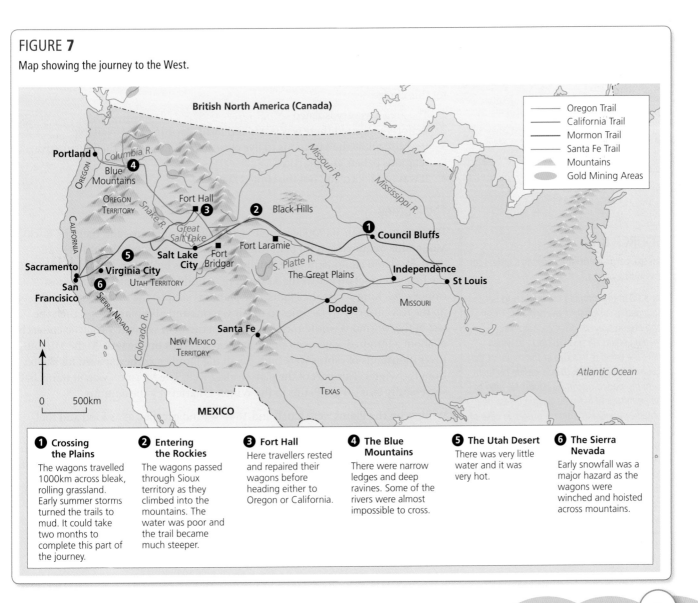

1 Crossing the Plains
The wagons travelled 1000km across bleak, rolling grassland. Early summer storms turned the trails to mud. It could take two months to complete this part of the journey.

2 Entering the Rockies
The wagons passed through Sioux territory as they climbed into the mountains. The water was poor and the trail became much steeper.

3 Fort Hall
Here travellers rested and repaired their wagons before heading either to Oregon or California.

4 The Blue Mountains
There were narrow ledges and deep ravines. Some of the rivers were almost impossible to cross.

5 The Utah Desert
There was very little water and it was very hot.

6 The Sierra Nevada
Early snowfall was a major hazard as the wagons were winched and hoisted across mountains.

SOURCE 8

An extract from Brigham Young's orders for the journey west.

At 5.00 in the morning the bugle is to be sounded as a signal for every man to arise and attend prayers. Then cooking, eating, feeding teams till seven o'clock, at which time the camp is to move at the sound of the bugle. Each teamster to stay beside his team, with his loaded gun in his hands. No man to be permitted to leave his wagon unless he obtains permission from his officer. In case of an attack from Indians, the wagons to travel in double file. The order of encampment to be in a circle with the mouth of the wagon to the outside, and the horses and stock tied inside the circle. At 8.30 the bugle to be sounded again at which time all to have prayers in their wagons and to retire to rest by nine o'clock.

Brigham Young and the Mormons

Brigham Young became leader of the MORMONS in 1845 after the murder of the religion's founder Joseph Smith. Since their religion began, the Mormons had faced hostility and violence from non-Mormons or GENTILES. They worked hard and were successful, which aroused the envy of some. Their belief that they were God's chosen people and that they were against slavery angered others.

They had already been driven out of Kirtland and Missouri before they settled at Nauvoo in Illinois. Here they were allowed to build their own independent city state with its own armed forces and their numbers grew. But things changed significantly after Joseph Smith announced that God had told him men could have more than one wife (POLYGAMY). This led to divisions among the Mormons themselves and non-Mormons were shocked. They believed polygamy was a sin. Some feared it would lead to a Mormon population explosion. When in 1844 Smith announced that he was standing for president it sparked trouble. In the turmoil that followed Smith was arrested and jailed in the town of Carthage. On 27 June 1844 a mob attacked the jail and Smith was murdered.

In September 1845 Brigham Young took the crucial decision that the Mormons would never be allowed to practise their religion and to live peacefully within the United States alongside non-Mormons, so they should leave. He decided not to go to California or Oregon as there were already many American settlers there and the Mormons believed that the same problems would resurface.

Brigham Young therefore decided that the Mormons should move to the area around the Great Salt Lake, east of the Rocky Mountains. There were four reasons for this choice:

1 The area was very isolated.
2 Reports suggested there was water and fertile farming land available.
3 It would allow the Mormons to live close together to retain their distinctive religious beliefs and practices.
4 It was in Mexico and not the United States.

The journey

To move more than 16,000 Mormons across the Great Plains, and then the Rocky Mountains, required careful planning. During the winter months of 1845–46 oxen, food and equipment were bought and wagons built. Then, in February 1846, the first group set off across the Mississippi to build the first of a chain of rest camps stretching across the Plains. The plan was simple: the first groups would set up the rest camps with facilities to repair wagons and also plant crops, then the rest of the Mormons would travel in a steady stream of separate WAGON TRAINS, each of about a hundred wagons stopping at the rest camps on the way. At the Missouri River thousands of cabins were built for all the families as they arrived for shelter from the winter. This part of the plan worked well. The Mormon wagon trains had successfully crossed the Plains to the Winter Quarters by the autumn.

Winters on the Plains were harsh and 1846 was no exception. As food and fuel supplies ran low and disease spread, over 700 died in the Winter Quarters. But the rest survived and in the spring Brigham Young led a 'Pioneer Band' onwards through the South Pass in the Rockies to the Great Salt Lake, clearing a path for the rest of the wagons to follow.

SOURCE 9

'The Mormons' Winter Quarters' by C. C. A. Christensen.

SOURCE 10

Group statue of a Mormon family with a handcart outside the Mormon Trail Centre. Later groups of Mormons were too poor to afford ox-drawn wagons. They used handcarts instead.

Settling Salt Lake

The success of the crossing of the Plains consolidated Young's position as leader of the Mormons and this helped to ensure the success in settling Salt Lake. First Young was able to ensure that the church allocated land to people and families according to their needs. At the centre of the new city was the temple and the main square. Leading off from this were planned streets lined with plots of land for homes and gardens as well as farms for larger families. Access to water was managed by a system of IRRIGATION ditches and a timetable for when individuals could draw off water for their own plots. By this co-operative working the Mormons were able to feed themselves.

Deseret

The Mormons had succeeded in building a new life for themselves in Mexico, but with the end of the Mexican–American War they found themselves back in the United States. Brigham Young wanted to found a new state called 'Deseret', the 'land of the honey bee', and for it to be admitted into the Union but the US government refused. Instead a compromise was negotiated. The TERRITORY of Utah, smaller than Deseret, was created and Young was appointed as its first governor.

In the final phase of Young's plan the Mormons established towns and settlements in those parts of Utah where farming was possible and on the borders of the territory: such towns as Carson City and Las Vegas. They also tried to start an iron and linen industry to become even more self-sufficient, although these initiatives were unsuccessful. Finally, as more Mormon settlers were needed, missionaries were sent to Europe and South America to gather more converts to the Mormon religion. These tended to come from the poorer sections of society and so, in a final step, a PERPETUAL EMIGRATING FUND was established to pay for their travel to Utah. Their journey was organised by ship to America and then by wagon or handcart across the Plains using the existing resting stations. In this way the population of Utah grew, the Mormons became almost self-sufficient and they hoped to be able to live in peace.

SOURCE 11

A description of Salt Lake City by a US government surveyor in 1850.

A city has been laid out upon a magnificent scale. Through the city itself flows an unfailing stream of pure, sweet water, which, by an ingenious mode of irrigation, is made to travel along each side of every street whence it is led into every garden-spot, spreading life, and beauty, over what was a barren waste.

The houses are built, principally, of sun-dried brick, which make a warm comfortable dwelling, presenting a very neat appearance.

PRACTICE QUESTION

Which of the following was the more important reason why the Mormons travelled to Salt Lake City:

● Religious persecution
● The leadership of Brigham Young?

Explain your answer with reference to both reasons.

The miners

The fourth group of Americans to go west were the 'FORTY-NINERS'. They were not seeking the solitary lifestyle of the mountain men, the fertile farmland of the settlers or the freedom from persecution of the Mormons. They sought wealth.

In 1848 a carpenter building a saw mill in the foothills of California's Sierra Nevada mountain range discovered gold.

News of this discovery spread slowly at first until it was picked up by a San Francisco newspaper. Then it spread rapidly across the USA and beyond. The first miners to arrive were locals. Two-thirds of the able-bodied men in Oregon joined the Gold Rush in the months that followed. By 1849 miners were arriving from around the world. Those who could afford it came by sea. Others took the slower route by wagon train across the Great Plains. The population of California rocketed from roughly 15,000 in the summer of 1848 to nearly 250,000 by 1852.

All that the earliest miners needed was a pick and shovel and a washing pan. In the washing pan water would carry away the lighter soil and gravel, leaving the heavier gold in the bottom. Later on the cradle was developed, a box that did the same job as the washing pan but for larger quantities.

THINK

1. List the items of equipment the miners in this picture appear to have.
2. If you were to use one word to describe this scene, what would it be?

SOURCE 12

Miners using washing pans and cradles in a Californian stream bed.

Mining towns grew out of the mining camps and they were lawless places. Tensions and violence arose because there were:

- no organised forces of law and order; the area was still under military control following the Mexican–American War
- disputes between miners and the local Californians
- disputes between miners over mining CLAIMS.

PRACTICE QUESTION

Which of the following was the more important reason why white Americans travelled across the Great Plains in the 1840s and 1850s:

- Religion
- Economic opportunity?

Explain your answer with reference to both reasons.

This was made worse by racial tensions between Americans and Hispanics (Mexicans, Chileans and Peruvians), the Californian Indians and the thousands of Chinese who arrived as labourers for Chinese merchants, as mining came to be dominated by large companies. Added to this mix were ex-convicts from Australia, free African Americans and slaves brought with them by ex-plantation owners from the southern United States. These slaves were not allowed to stay. When California was admitted to the Union in 1850 it was as a free state. This again illustrates that slavery was an issue in the United States.

By 1852 the Gold Rush was over and many miners moved on to search for gold in the Rocky Mountains.

● Dealing with a different culture

Attitudes to the Plains were greatly influenced by early travellers such as Major Long (see page 2). It would be many years before outsiders began to see the farming potential of the Plains. In the 1830s all they could see were the problems – the harsh weather, the lack of trees, the wind, the absence of water. The Indians of course had a very different view. They were not farmers but NOMADIC hunters who moved across the Plains following the buffalo herds. The Plains were perfect for this nomadic way of life.

The Plains Indians' way of life

Homes

The TIPI (also called a lodge or tepee) was the home of each Indian family. It was made from 10 to 20 buffalo skins sewn together and supported by a frame of wooden poles arranged in a circle. It was the responsibility of the women. They made it, owned it, put it up and moved it. It could be taken down and packed for transport in ten minutes. This made it an ideal home for people who were frequently on the move.

At the top of the *tipi* there were two 'ears', or flaps, that could be moved to direct the wind so that the smoke from the fire inside could escape. In summer the *tipi* bottom could be rolled up to let air in. In winter it could be banked with earth to keep the *tipi* warm. The *tipi*'s conical shape made it strong enough to resist the strong winds on the Great Plains. Sioux *tipis* were decorated by the men with geometric patterns and scenes recording their bravery in the hunt and in battle.

Inside, a fire would always be burning at the centre to provide heat and for cooking. The floor was covered with furs.

Everybody had their place in the *tipi*. Because the space was small there were strict rules about behaviour. For example, it was rude to pass between another person and the fire.

Family life

Indians spent most of the year travelling, hunting and camping with their band. This would consist of between 10 and 50 families, each with their own *tipi*. Within the family there were different roles. The men were responsible for hunting, looking after the horses and protecting the band. They were judged by their skills as hunters, WARRIORS and horsemen. Women were responsible for the *tipi*, for preparing food and fetching water, and for making clothing and other items. They were judged by their skill at crafts and as homemakers.

Most men had one wife but rich men could have several wives – known as polygamy. Polygamy made sense in a situation where there were more women than men, and this was often the case because of the dangers of hunting and warfare.

THINK

Describe how the *tipi* design solved the following problems facing Indians living on the Plains:

● The lack of wood
● The strong winds
● The extremes of temperature
● The need to move frequently.

FIGURE 13

A modern artist's drawing of a *tipi*.

SOURCE 15

George Catlin, *Manners, Customs and Condition of the North American Indian*, 1841. Catlin's writings and the hundreds of paintings he made of scenes from Indian life have had a great influence on the way people think about the Plains Indians.

The lodges are taken down in a few minutes by the women and easily transported to any part of the country where they wish to camp. They generally move six to eight times in the summer, following the immense herds of buffalo. The manner in which a camp of Indians strike [take down] their tents and move them is curious. I saw a camp of Sioux, consisting of six hundred lodges, struck and everything packed and on the move in a very few minutes.

SOURCE 16

Extract from Colonel Dodge's book *Hunting Grounds of the Great West* (1877), based upon his experience serving in the army in the West before and after the Civil War.

I cannot say exactly how these powers and duties of these three governmental forms [i.e. chiefs, councils and warrior societies] blend and concur … and I have never met an Indian or white man who could satisfactorily explain them. The result, however, is fairly good, and seems well suited to the character, needs and peculiarities of the life of the Plains Indians.

Indian society and political organisation

To survive on the Great Plains the members of an Indian band had to co-operate and be well organised as they moved following the buffalo. Sometimes bands would meet to camp and hunt together. At least once a year the bands would meet as a NATION.

Chiefs

Indian chiefs were not elected, nor did they inherit power. They became chiefs because of their wisdom, their spiritual power or 'medicine', and their skills as hunters and warriors. Only great chiefs like Red Cloud and Sitting Bull were able to persuade the warriors of many bands and even of different nations to follow them.

Councils

Important decisions were taken in council. The advice of the MEDICINE MEN, chiefs and elders would be listened to with respect, but these men would not tell the others what to do. Normally, the council members would keep talking until everyone agreed. While they talked they smoked a ceremonial pipe, believing that the smoke would inform the spirit world and help them to make good decisions.

When bands met, the council of the nation would meet. It could take important decisions, such as deciding to go to war, but the bands were not bound to agree with the council's decision. As a result, some bands might be at war while others were at peace. Later this was a source of confusion for the settlers when conflict broke out. Was a band at war or not? Were all its members peaceful, or just some?

Warrior societies

All the men of a band belonged to a warrior society, such as the Kit Foxes of the Sioux. They were responsible for supervising hunting and travelling, and for protecting the village.

SOURCE 17

A Sioux Council, a painting by George Catlin, 1847.

The importance of the buffalo to the Plains Indians

Buffalo Dances

The Plains Indians did not farm the buffalo; they hunted them. Before setting out to hunt, they would hold a ceremonial Buffalo Dance which could last for many days (see Source 18). The purpose of the dance was to call upon the spirit world for help in their hunting and to call the buffalo herd closer to them. Plains Indians believed this would bring them good luck and ensure a successful hunt.

The buffalo hunt

Once they had horses, Plains Indians were able to kill greater numbers of buffalo. The hunt was organised and policed by the warrior societies. They ensured that the buffalo were not scared away before all was ready and that not too many animals were killed. Two or three successful buffalo hunts a year were sufficient to feed and shelter the band.

SOURCE 18

Buffalo Dance of the Sioux, painted by George Catlin.

SOURCE 19

Buffalo Hunt, Chase, painted by George Catlin.

SOURCE 20

Black Elk, a Sioux Indian, born c.1863, describes the preparations for a hunt.

Then the crier shouted, 'Your knives shall be sharpened. Make ready, make haste; your horses make ready! We shall go forth with arrows. Plenty of meat we shall make!'

Then the head man went around picking out the best hunters with the fastest horses, and to these he said, 'Young warriors, your work I know is good; so today you will feed the helpless. You shall help the old and the young and whatever you kill shall be theirs.' This was a great honour for young men.

THINK

Study Source 18, *Buffalo Dance of the Sioux*. Explain what roles the men are playing and what they are re-enacting. Thinking about what they are wearing and carrying should help you.

THINK

Study Source 19, *Buffalo Hunt, Chase*. What are the dangers of the hunt for the Indians and what skills do they need?

FIGURE 21

A hundred uses? How the Plains Indians used every part of the buffalo.

Horns were used for arrow-straighteners, cups, fire-carriers, head-dress ornaments, ladles, spoons, toys and quill-flatteners.

The **skull** was used in religious ceremonies. The **brain** was used for tanning the hides.

Rawhide was used for bags, belts, containers, horse harnesses, lashings, masks, sheaths, shields, snow-shoes, string and travois lashings.

Tanned hide was used for bags, bedding, blankets, clothes, dolls, dresses, drums, leggings, mittens, moccasins, pouches, robes, saddle and *tipi* covers.

The **flesh** was cooked, or dried and mixed with fat and wild cherries to preserve it as pemmican.

Sinews were used for bowstrings and thread.

The **tongue** was used as a hairbrush and also eaten raw as a delicacy.

Fur was used for decoration on clothes, as stuffing for saddles and pillows, and to make mittens and rope.

The **heart** was cut from the body and left on the ground to give new life to the herd. The buffalo was sacred, man's relative who gave his life so that the people could live. The heart might also be eaten raw so that the warrior could take the strength and power of the buffalo.

The **tail** was used for fly swats, ornaments and whips.

The **bladder** was used for food bags.

Gall was used to make yellow paint. The **liver** was eaten raw as a delicacy.

Intestines were used for buckets and cooking vessels.

Dung was used for fuel (buffalo chips) and smoked by men in special ceremonies.

Fat was used for cooking, to make soap and as hair grease

Bones were used for arrowheads, dice, game counters, jewellery, knives, needles, paint brushes, saddle frames, shovels, sledge runners, tools and war clubs.

Hooves were used to make glue and also to make rattles and tools.

PRACTICE QUESTION

Describe two ways in which the buffalo was important to the life of the Plains Indians.

After the hunt

Once the buffalo was dead, it was butchered by the women and children. The meat was eaten or preserved. The hides were processed. First they were pegged out to dry and scraped to remove all the flesh. This made RAWHIDE. Some hides were then tanned, using the animals' brains, and worked to make them soft and pliable. They were then ready to be made into clothing or *tipi* covers.

The importance of the horse to the Plains Indians

The horse was vital to the Plains Indians. They used it to hunt, as a means of transport for home and family, and in war. The horse enabled warriors to raid over much longer distances and gave a new reason for warfare – stealing horses. It also changed the way that individuals actually fought. It led to war skills and horsemanship becoming an important measure of bravery and status in Plains society.

The horse was so vital to life on the Plains that individuals counted their wealth by the number of horses they owned.

Indian warfare

Warfare to the Sioux was a series of raids by relatively small groups of warriors. Plains Indians went on these raids for a number of reasons: to steal horses, to seek revenge or to destroy their enemies. They did not want to conquer land in the way that the settlers did. Plains Indians did not believe that anyone could own land. But there was rivalry for hunting and living space.

Wars happened in the summer when the Plains Indians had built up their food supplies. Some historians have argued that the warfare helped to keep the bands together. Certainly, by 1840 the Sioux nation had traditional enemies, the Crow and the Pawnee, and traditional allies, the Cheyenne.

Counting coup

The arrival of the gun on the Great Plains could have made war far more destructive. Yet it did not, because war was made into a ritual with the idea of 'counting COUP'. It was considered braver to touch an enemy – to count coup – than to kill him and that it was foolish to fight if outnumbered. Casualties were relatively low. Between 1835 and 1845 the Sioux were at war with their eastern neighbours, the Ojibwa. In that decade the Sioux lost 88 people, their enemies 129. More men were probably lost as a result of hunting accidents than through fighting.

Taking scalps

Plains Indians took SCALPS as evidence of their successes in battle. The scalps were dried and hung as trophies outside their *tipis*. The Plains Indians believed that if a warrior lost his scalp he could not go into the afterlife. You scalped your enemy so that he would not be there to fight you when you died. This was also the reason for the MUTILATION of dead enemies: to leave them disabled in the afterlife.

FOCUS TASK

Part 1: How did the Plains Indians adapt their lives to the Great Plains?
It is 1840. Use the information and sources on pages 9–12 to make notes under the following headings:

- The Indians' nomadic lifestyle
- Indian homes and society
- The importance of the buffalo
- The importance of the horse.

Using your notes, write a newspaper article describing the Plains Indians for an audience back east. Your opening sentences could be:

'The Great Plains, which have been described as the Great American Desert, are home to the Plains Indians. What makes their way of life so well adapted?'

Part 2: In what ways was Plains Indians' culture different?
Your article should now go on to explain to readers how Plains Indians' culture was so very different from American culture, and what problems you can see this may cause in the future.

Your article should tell readers about:

- the importance of the spirit world
- their attitudes to land ownership, war and horse stealing
- the fact that every band makes its own separate decisions.

SOURCE 22
Sioux war song first written down in the nineteenth century.

See them prancing.
They come neighing,
They come a Horse Nation.
See them prancing,
They come neighing,
They come.

Crow Indian
You must watch your horses.
A horse thief,
Often,
Am I.

SOURCE 23
Extract from *Native Americans: the Sioux* by Richard Erdoes, 1982.

For young braves the main purpose of making war was to 'count coup', that is, to gain war honours, which was the way to fame and advancement. There was comparatively little prestige in killing an enemy. After all, a coward could shoot a man from ambush without any danger to himself. But to ride or walk up to a foe while he was still alive and armed, touching him with one's hand or one's special coup stick brought great honours, because a man risked his life doing it. Stealing horses right under the enemy's nose was also counted as a fine 'coup'.

THINK
Which part of Source 22 supports Richard Erdoes' view of Sioux warfare in Source 23?

PRACTICE QUESTION
Which of the following two animals was the more important in enabling the Plains Indians to live as nomads on the Great Plains:

- the horse
- the buffalo?

Explain your answer with reference to both animals.

Early American government policy towards the Plains Indians

From the very beginnings of its founding colonies the people of the United States of America had encountered the original inhabitants, the Indian nations. The early history of this relationship varied from friendship and co-operation to hostility and open war. To begin with, the Indians were treated as SOVEREIGN NATIONS to be negotiated with but, over time, they became increasingly seen as a barrier. In 1824 the Bureau of Indian Affairs was set up within the US War Department to manage this relationship.

The Permanent Indian Frontier

In 1830 the Indian Removal Act was passed. This did two things:

- It established a Permanent Indian Frontier in the West, across the Mississippi.
- It allowed the removal of the south-eastern Indian nations so that their lands would then be available for settlement.

These Indians were no longer seen as separate nations but rather as people under the control of the United States and they were moved to lands beyond the Permanent Indian Frontier in what became known as Indian Territory. This measure was described as being for their protection although thousands died during the forced removal known as 'The Trail of Tears'. This removal process was completed by 1838.

The situation changed in the 1840s when the Great Plains became a barrier to cross for the settlers moving to California and Oregon, to the miners heading for California and to the Mormons heading for Salt Lake City. Figures vary but between 1840 and 1848 it is estimated that 11,500 Americans took the overland trail to Oregon and 2,500 to California. During this great movement of people there were few violent incidents between travellers and the Plains Indians but a change in attitude was happening.

Indian Appropriations Act, 1851

By the 1850s, more travellers were crossing the Great Plains and settlers were moving beyond the Permanent Indian Frontier onto the eastern edges of the Plains. This westward movement was something that the US government encouraged, but it made the Plains Indians' need for protection more pressing. Meanwhile in 1849 the Bureau of Indian Affairs had been moved from the War Department to the Department of the Interior. US government policy focused on trying to 'civilise' the Indians by confining them to RESERVATIONS and setting up schools. The outcome of this policy was the Indian Appropriations Act of 1851. This set up legally recognised reservations intended to protect Indians from westward expansion.

The Americans were beginning to see the land of the Great Plains from the point of view of ownership and settlement but the Plains Indians believed that no one could own the land. At the core of their religious belief was the circle of life and death and the circle of nature. They believed that they were a part of nature, that they came from the earth just like all animals and plants and when they died they returned to the earth. As well as a clash over land, at the heart of the later conflict between the Plains Indians and the United States was a clash of cultures, with neither side fully understanding the other.

SOURCE 24

Crowfoot, a Blackfoot Chief responding to an offer of money for tribal land from the US government.

Our land is more valuable than your money. It will last forever. It will not perish as long as the sun shines and the rivers flow, and through all of the years, it will give life to men and beasts. We cannot sell the lives of men and animals, and so, we cannot sell the land. It was put here by the Great Spirit and we cannot sell it because it does not really belong to us. You can count your money and burn it with the nod of a buffalo's head but only the Great Spirit can count the grains of sand and the blades of grass on these plains.

THINK

1   The attitudes and beliefs expressed by Crowfoot in Source 24 are typical of the Plains Indians. How could a US government treaty negotiator trying to buy land for settlement, trails and railroad links respond to this?

2   Study the Topic Summary. If you were asked to identify one key reason for the expansion of the United States, which would you choose?
   a)   Belief in Manifest Destiny
   b)   Victory in the Mexican–American War.

TOPIC SUMMARY

Expansion: Opportunities and challenges

- At the start of the 1840s the Great Plains was seen as the Great American Desert.
- The Great Plains was the home of the Plains Indians whose nomadic lifestyle was perfectly suited to the challenges of life on the Plains.
- Early American pioneer farmers, guided by the mountain men, began to cross the Plains in the 1840s in order to settle Oregon and later California.
- The United States annexed Texas from Mexico in 1845.
- In 1846 the Mormons crossed the Great Plains to escape from the United States.
- Victory in the Mexican–American War that ended in 1848 doubled the size of the United States and brought the Mormons back into the United States.
- Differing beliefs were a significant factor in destabilising peace in North America – Manifest Destiny helped to drive the expansion of the United States and it came into conflict with Mexico, Britain and the Plains Indians; religious differences prompted the Mormons to try to leave the United States; and arguments over the existence of slavery were already creating divisions within the United States.
- The discovery of gold in California in 1848 led to a Gold Rush, with thousands travelling to California hoping to get rich quick.
- Initially, Plains Indians were seen as nations who could be negotiated with to ensure free passage for settlers, miners and other travellers across the Plains.
- Once their lands were wanted for settlers, the Plains Indians became increasingly seen as a problem to be resolved.

1.2 Conflict across America

FOCUS

By 1850 the United States had won a war against Mexico and gained vast areas of land stretching to the Pacific Ocean. It had gained further land in Oregon through its negotiations with Britain. Its citizens had begun to settle these new lands and as they did so they came into conflict with others and with each other.

In this part of the topic you will study the following:

- How and why conflict was increasing on the Plains.
- The background to the Civil War and why war broke out in 1861.
- Coming to terms with the Mormons and the reasons why the US government found it hard to deal with them.

● Increasing conflict on the Plains

Fort Laramie Treaty, 1851

While the Americans were simply crossing the Great Plains there was very little actual conflict with the Plains Indians. But with the numbers increasing, the US government felt it needed to take action. The first FORT LARAMIE TREATY between the US government and representatives of the Plains Indian nations (the Arapahoe, Cheyenne, Crow and Sioux) was signed on 17 September 1851. The Plains Indians promised not to attack settlers travelling on the Oregon Trail and to allow the building of some roads and forts in their territory. In return each nation had its agreed hunting area and was promised an annual SUBSIDY.

This policy of 'concentration' seemed to solve the 'Indian problem' and pleased the 'negotiators' – those people who wanted a negotiated solution to the Indian problem. These were mainly people living in the East. They did include some Westerners, such as government officials who, as Indian agents working with the Indians, had gained some understanding of them and their way of life. The 'negotiators' believed that responsibility for Indian affairs should be kept within the Bureau of Indian Affairs.

THINK

Study Source 1, *Fort Laramie*. What does the building of this fort tell you about the attitude of the US government to the Plains Indians?

SOURCE 1

Fort Laramie, Wyoming in 1837, painted from memory by Alfred Jacob Miller.

Not everyone was pleased with this. Some Plains Indian nations, notably the Crow, did not feel bound by the treaty. But more significantly another group existed who had very different ideas about the Plains Indians. Termed the 'exterminators', this group believed that the Indians were savages, and that the 'Indian problem' required a military solution. Their aim was to use the army to wipe out the Plains Indians – a solution that today we would call GENOCIDE. These 'exterminators' were mainly people living in the West – the settlers, ranchers and miners and the soldiers sent to protect them. They also included some who profited by selling beef and other supplies to the US army. They were both the people with most to gain if the Plains Indians were removed and those most likely to have suffered from Indian hostility.

THINK

Write a paragraph to explain the key differences between the negotiators and the exterminators.

Failure of the policy of concentration

Although some nations never received the goods promised as payments, the Fort Laramie Treaty was followed by a period of peace. The historian John D. Unrah's research showed that between 1840 and 1860, while over 250,000 travellers followed the California and Oregon Trails, fewer than 400 were killed. Of these, 90 per cent were killed west of South Pass, that is, not on the Great Plains. However, this peace on the Great Plains was broken by four developments:

- In 1858 gold was discovered in the Rocky Mountains and the Colorado Gold Rush began. In the three years to 1861, roughly 100,000 settlers and miners poured into parts of Colorado and Kansas looking to get rich quick. They were moving on to Indian lands in breach of the treaty but the US government chose not to enforce it.
- Nor did the government do anything to stop a second development, the movement of settlers on to the plains of Kansas and Nebraska from 1854 onwards.
- The third development was the start of organised transport links across the Plains. In 1858 Butterfield's overland mail coaches began to run regularly from St Louis, Missouri, to San Francisco, California. Meanwhile railroad surveyors began searching for the best routes across the Plains.
- Fourth and finally, while the chiefs of the Indian nations might have agreed to the peace treaty, the nature of Plains Indian society meant that there would always be warriors or bands who would not feel bound by that agreement.

FIGURE 2

A map showing the developments that undermined the Fort Laramie Treaty.

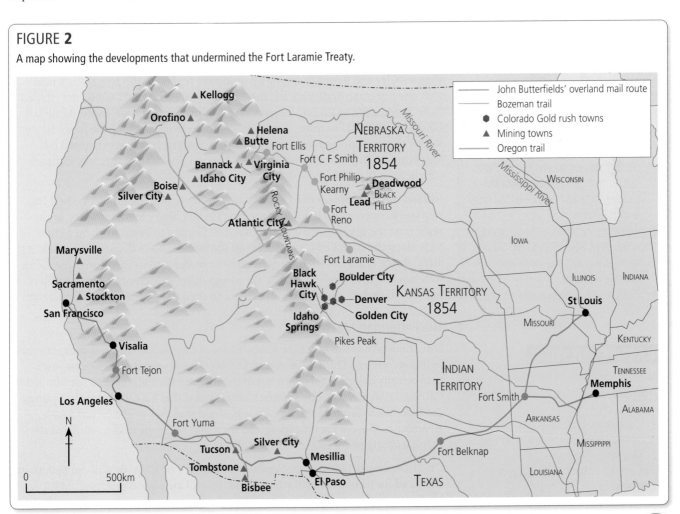

FOCUS TASK

Why did conflict increase on the Plains, 1851–68?

1 Create a timeline for the period 1851–68 to explore the idea that conflict was increasing on the Plains.
2 Underneath the timeline, note the treaties, acts and actions of the USA and its citizens.
3 Above the timeline, note the years when the Cheyenne and the Sioux were at war together with any notable incidents.
4 Does your completed timeline show increasing conflict?

PRACTICE QUESTION

Which of the following was the more important reason for conflict with the Plains Indians?
– Discoveries of gold
– Settlers travelling to California and Oregon.
Explain your answer with reference to both reasons.

The Indian Wars, 1863–68

Cheyenne War, 1863–67

In 1861 the Cheyenne and Arapahoe began making serious attacks on the miners, travellers and railway surveyors on their lands and by 1863 full-scale war had broken out on the Southern Plains. This was at the same time as many regular soldiers had been withdrawn to fight in the CIVIL WAR back east so local volunteer forces, such as the Colorado MILITIA, were raised. The fighting continued with Indian attacks on RANCHES and small settlements. In 1864 some Cheyenne came to an agreement to move on to a new, smaller reservation. Among these were Black Kettle and his followers. They were camped at Sand Creek when they were attacked by Colonel Chivington and his Colorado militia. Initially hailed as a victory, this came to be known as the Sand Creek Massacre as it emerged in a government enquiry that most of the approximately 150 Indian dead were women, children and the elderly.

After the peace agreement, although many Cheyenne lived peacefully on their reservation, others continued to fight. On 6 January 1865, over one thousand Arapaho, Cheyenne and Sioux warriors attacked Julesburg. The garrison of only 60 soldiers were able to hold out but the area was plundered and the Indians took away cattle and horses. Later in 1867 another Cheyenne band living off the reservation were attacked and defeated by General George Armstrong Custer at the Battle of Washita, itself a controversial event see (page 45). Others continued to live off the reservation, continued raiding and later still could be found fighting in Red Cloud's War.

Sioux or Red Cloud's War, 1865–68

Red Cloud's War had similar causes to the Cheyenne War. In 1862 gold was discovered in the Rocky Mountains in Montana. New mining towns such as Virginia City and Bannack sprang up as miners rushed to the area along a new trail, the Bozeman Trail. This left the Oregon Trail near Fort Laramie and crossed Sioux lands, once again breaking the terms of the Fort Laramie Treaty. Again the US government did nothing to stop these miners from breaking the peace treaty. Rather they encouraged them as by 1865 the country, finances exhausted by four years of Civil War, needed the gold. The reaction of the Sioux was to attack travellers on the trail.

In 1866 the government tried a negotiated settlement to the problem. Their first step was to open peace talks with the Sioux leader, Red Cloud. However, at the same time the government also ordered the US army to begin work on a chain of forts along the trail. Red Cloud broke off the peace talks in disgust and attacked the army. By the winter of 1866 the soldiers were under SIEGE in their forts. The Sioux were not strong enough to capture the forts, which were equipped with artillery, but they did attack wood-cutting parties and tried to lure the soldiers into a trap.

The Fetterman Massacre

Fort Phil Kearney was commanded by Colonel Carrington who was inexperienced in Indian warfare. During the autumn of 1866 there were frequent skirmishes between any troops that he sent out of the fort and the Indians who surrounded it. Carrington took a cautious approach and insisted that his officers did not pursue the Indians too far from the fort. He was afraid that they might be lured into an ambush. Most of his officers agreed with him but some under estimated the fighting ability of the Sioux and their allies.

On 21 December 1866 a detachment of 80 men led by Captain William Fetterman was lured into a trap set by the Sioux and were all killed and mutilated. Who was to blame is still disputed by historians.

Red Cloud's achievement

Since the superior firepower of the soldiers prevented the capture of Fort Phil Kearney, Red Cloud made sure that it was surrounded by his warriors. The army could not move safely outside the fort and travellers could not use the Bozeman Trail. This was the major achievement of Red Cloud: that he kept together a force of several Sioux bands, plus their Arapaho and Cheyenne allies. He managed to keep them fighting through the winter months. He also had the vision to try to persuade the Crow, traditional enemies of the Sioux, to fight with him. Although he was unsuccessful in this, he kept the US army on the defensive.

The Peace Treaty

In 1868 the government was forced to admit defeat and change its policy. The government realised that the Sioux and their allies could not be defeated militarily. At the same time an alternative route to the gold-mining areas had been opened. So the government agreed to withdraw from the forts and under the terms of the second Fort Laramie Treaty the Great Sioux Reservation was created (see page 43). No non-Indian settlers were to ever be allowed to enter this land. Red Cloud agreed to this treaty. When the soldiers withdrew, the Sioux moved in and burned the forts to the ground. The Sioux had won – or had they?

For Red Cloud it marked the end of his fighting against the US army. From this point on he lived peacefully on the Sioux reservation. However, not all the Sioux agreed with the peace treaty. Red Cloud's power decreased and many of the Sioux went on to follow younger, more militant leaders such as Sitting Bull and Crazy Horse.

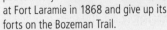

Red Cloud

- Born near the forks of the Platte River c.1819.
- War leader of the Sioux by the 1860s.
- Forced the US government to negotiate a peace treaty at Fort Laramie in 1868 and give up its forts on the Bozeman Trail.
- Lived as a respected councillor on the Sioux reservation after 1868.
- In 1880 he successfully exposed the corruption of the Indian agent running the Sioux reservation but earlier was unable to prevent the government actions that precipitated the Great Sioux War 1876–77.
- Died in 1909 at the Pine Ridge Reservation.

PRACTICE QUESTIONS

Interpretation A From *John Burnett's Story of the Trail of Tears*, written in 1890 by a US soldier who served during the Cherokee removal of 1838

As a boy and young man I often went on long hunting trips. On these trips I met and became acquainted with many of the Cherokee Indians, hunting with them by day and sleeping around their camp fires by night. I learned to speak their language, and they taught me the arts of trailing and building traps and snares …

Some years later and as a man in the prime of my life, I became a Private soldier in the American Army… (I) witnessed the execution of the most brutal order in the History of American Warfare - the removal of Cherokee Indians from their life long homes in the year of 1838. I saw the helpless Cherokees arrested and dragged from their homes, and driven at the bayonet point… the sufferings of the Cherokees were awful.

Interpretation B From the *Memoirs of General George Armstrong Custer*, published in 1874. Custer fought against the Indians in the wars of the 1860s. He fought them again after the American Civil War and was killed fighting the Sioux in 1876. In this extract he is writing about the wars in the 1860s.

First came a deployed line of horsemen, followed in rear, as we could plainly see, by a reserve, also mounted and moving in compact order. It required no practised eye to comprehend what was happening. The parties advancing in this precise and determined manner upon us were doing so with hostile purpose, and evidently intended to charge into our camp unless defeated in their purpose. We had often heard of the high perfection of some of the Indian tribes in military evolutions and discipline, but here we saw evidences which went far to convince us that the red man was not far behind his more civilized brother in the art of war. Certainly no troops of my command could have advanced a skirmish line or moved a reserve more accurately than was done in our presence that morning.

Read Interpretations A and B and answer Questions 1–3.

1 How does Interpretation A differ from Interpretation B about the Indians?

  Explain your answer based on what it says in Interpretations A and B.

2 Why might these two historians have different interpretations about the Indians?

  Explain your answer using Interpretations A and B and your own contextual knowledge.

3 Which interpretation gives the more convincing opinion about the Indians?

  Explain your answer based on your contextual knowledge and what it says in Interpretations A and B.

The background to the American Civil War, 1861–65

Victory in the Mexican–American War brought vast new territories into the United States, and the question of how they should be run brought into focus existing divisions within the country.

When the United States first became a country after defeating the British in 1774 they adopted a FEDERAL model of government and the individual states formed the Union. In this federal model power is shared between the federal (or central) government, and state governments, and from the beginning there were debates about how much power the federal government should have over the lives of the people and the separate states in which they lived.

FIGURE 3

Map showing states and territories in 1854.

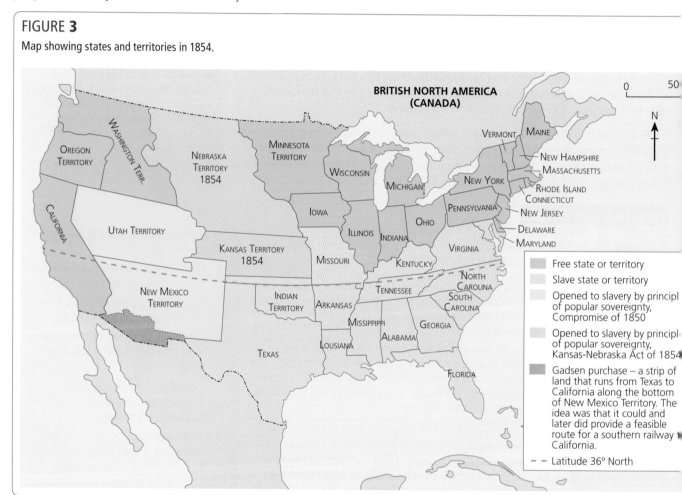

Differences between North and South

There were significant differences between the Northern and Southern states, which grew wider during the period 1800–40. These differences had their origins in the geography and climate of North America. The Southern states were more suitable for plantation agriculture, growing rice, tobacco and particularly cotton. Supplying the cotton industries of Britain and Europe made the South rich and this is where investors in the South, including in the new lands in the south-west towards Texas, put their money. Crucially the plantation system relied upon slave labour. Roughly a quarter of the South's population was economically dependent on slavery; but there was also arable and food crop farming so the South could feed itself.

In comparison, the Northern states industrialised, with towns and cities developing alongside agriculture. It was to the Northern states that the many immigrants to America came and stayed. They arrived in the North because that was where the shipping lines ran to and they stayed because they did not want to try and compete with slave labour.

Meanwhile in the North slavery was disappearing. The last Northern state to end slavery was New Jersey in 1804. At the same time an ABOLITIONIST movement, working for the total end to slavery, developed in the Northern states.

Differences aside, historians argue that the two economies of North and South complemented each other so in that respect the Union worked well. But the fact that they had different interests meant that the Northern and Southern states sometimes disagreed on federal government policy. For example when regulating trade with Britain, the main market for Southern cotton, the Southern states wanted open trade while the Northern ones wanted protection for some of their industries. When such disagreements arose the equal numbers of Northern free and Southern slave states balanced each other, neither could vote down the other's interests so everyone was forced to look for a compromise.

PRACTICE QUESTION

Describe two differences between the Northern and Southern states in the 1840s.

Abolitionism

Formal organised opposition to slavery in the USA began as early as 1817 when the American Colonisation Society began work. It bought land in West Africa and worked to resettle freed slaves there in what was to eventually become the country of Liberia. This gradual approach gathered only limited support from white and black Americans. Only about 12,000 freed slaves had been helped to migrate to Liberia by 1860.

In the meantime the wider anti-slavery movement that emerged in 1831 demanded an immediate end to slavery. The Anti-Slavery Society was set up in 1832 and gained momentum after slavery was abolished throughout the British Empire in 1833. It also went further in demanding equal civil and religious rights for freed slaves. Unsurprisingly it was far stronger in the Northern states. The issue of slavery therefore became part of the political debate in the United States and part of the argument between the Northern and Southern states.

Westward expansion

When the USA expanded westwards the federal government divided the land into new territories. As each territory was settled and its population grew, the people within it could apply for full statehood. They would then be admitted as a state into the Union. As the free states of Ohio, Indiana and Illinois entered the Union so too did the slave states of Louisiana, Mississippi and Alabama, thus maintaining the voting balance between North and South. But when in 1819 Missouri was ready to enter as a slave state, the Northern states initially opposed this. In the end the Missouri Compromise, 1820, was reached by which Missouri could enter as a slave state while Maine entered as a non-slave state, but no more slave states were to be allowed north of the line of latitude 36 degrees north.

The Compromise of 1850

After 1848, as the United States expanded into the vast new territories captured from Mexico, it still contained an equal number of free and slave states, 15 of each. The political debate over the new territories was whether slavery should be allowed to continue there, and this threatened to break up the Union. While many in the South wanted to allow the expansion of slavery, many Northerners, known

Uncle Tom's Cabin

In 1851 *Uncle Tom's Cabin* by Harriet Beecher Stowe was published. Her hero, Uncle Tom, a long-suffering slave, is torn from his family when he is sold separately from them. Tom goes on to rescue the daughter of his new master and is well treated as a reward. When his master dies Tom is sold by the cruel widow to an evil owner who whips poor Tom to death. Stowe's portrayal of slavery as an evil institution that destroyed the family was enormously popular and sold 1.2 million copies by 1853, going on to become the best-selling novel of the century. How far it increased anti-slavery feeling in the Northern states is open to debate. One historian David Potter suggested that Northern attitudes were 'never quite the same' after *Uncle Tom's Cabin*. Meanwhile to some Southerners, Stowe was 'a vile wretch in petticoats'.

sometimes as FREE-SOILERS, did not. In 1850 a new compromise, the Compromise of 1850, was reached, including the following points:

- California would be admitted to the Union as a free state, breaking the balance of free and slave states.
- The decision whether to permit slavery in the new south-west territories would be taken by their own governments.
- A more effective Fugitive Slave Act was passed making it easier for slave catchers to recapture runaway slaves in the Northern states and return them to their owners in the South.

This compromise kept the peace between North and South, but the possibility of the two breaking apart was growing stronger. Increasingly Southerners were considering secession (that is, leaving or breaking away) from the Union. Meanwhile the Fugitive Slave Act made the institution of slavery very visible to Northerners and so anti-slavery feeling grew even stronger there.

The Underground Railroad

From 1786 runaway slaves were helped to escape northwards along a secret route, by a secret network. In the period 1840–60, an estimated 50,000 slaves were helped to escape and settle in the Northern states or in Canada. One notable individual associated with this was Harriet Tubman, born c.1822 and died 10 March 1913, Auburn, New York State. She was born a slave, escaped and made many trips back into the South to help others to escape too. She helped John Brown recruit men for his raid on Harpers Ferry (see page 24), was a Union spy during the Civil War and afterwards worked for women's SUFFRAGE. At the time of writing she is one of the female candidates to be on a ten-dollar bill. The statue pictured stands as a memorial in Harlem, New York.

Kansas–Nebraska Act 1854

Within four years the Union was threatened again. This time the trigger was a disagreement over the route of a TRANSCONTINENTAL railroad. The Southerners were behind Secretary of War Jefferson Davis' favoured Southern route and encouraged the Gadsden Purchase – the buying of a barren stretch of land through what is today New Mexico and Arizona – from Mexico for $10 million.

The alternative proposal was for a line further north through Nebraska and this prompted the creation of two new territories, Nebraska and Kansas. To gain Southern support for this, they were not to be free territories and eventually free states. Instead, as in 1850, the issue of slavery was to be left open to popular sovereignty – that is for the people of the territories to decide for themselves.

Compare the contributions of the two Harriets, Stowe and Tubman, to the emancipation of slaves in the USA. Which woman would you put on the ten-dollar bill and why?

The breakdown of the Missouri Compromise

At the same time it was agreed that this new Kansas–Nebraska Act meant that the Missouri Compromise had been superseded or that it no longer applied. So new states north of the Missouri Compromise line could potentially become slave states even though this was unlikely. This decision changed the nature of US politics for good. Instead of the two old political parties whose members were split between pro- and anti-slavery, and who gained support in both Northern and Southern states, a new political party emerged, the REPUBLICANS, whose supporters were in the Northern states and who were anti-slavery.

THINK

Study Figure 4. How does this map help to explain the increasing importance of slavery in US politics?

FIGURE 4

The spread of cotton growing using slave labour between 1839 and 1860.

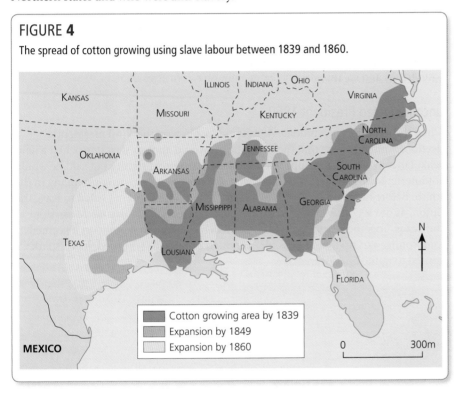

Cotton growing area by 1839
Expansion by 1849
Expansion by 1860

0   300m

Bleeding Kansas

Most people agreed that Nebraska would never be a slave state but in Kansas it was a different matter. Both those for and those against slavery began to encourage like-minded settlers to move to Kansas in an attempt to gain control of the government of the state. Then they believed they could win the vote on whether it would become a slave or a free state. By 1856 Kansas had two opposing governments, both illegally formed, and as the prospect of a political solution faded both sides armed. In 1856, 700 pro-slavery supporters entered the free-state town of Lawrence and smashed newspaper presses, stole property and burned buildings, although there was only one fatality. The 'sack' of Lawrence prompted a free-soiler, John Brown, to lead four sons and three other men to attack the Potawatomie Creek pro-slavery settlement. There they killed five men in front of their families. In the months that followed the violence spread and there were more raids across Kansas that left roughly 200 killed (including one of Brown's sons) and much property destroyed. After federal government involvement, a political decision was eventually reached in 1858 that Kansas would be a free state.

PRACTICE QUESTION

In what way did the United States' westward expansion make the disagreements between the North and South worse in the 1840s and 1850s? Explain your answer.

John Brown and Harpers Ferry

Following Potawatomie, John Brown kept a low profile although he was still involved in fundraising and recruiting for the abolition of slavery. He came back to national attention on the night of 16 October 1859 when with a band of 19 followers he seized the federal arsenal at Harpers Ferry, Virginia. This is believed to have been an attempt to arm a slave rebellion but it failed. Instead the townspeople and local troops surrounded the building and then it was recaptured by a force of US Marines led by Army Lieutenant-Colonel Robert E. Lee. Several men were killed, including more of Brown's sons. Brown himself was tried for treason against Virginia and hanged.

Initial Southern reaction was that Brown was a mad fanatic but, as his links with Northern abolitionists emerged and some Northern abolitionists made a martyr of him, opinion changed. To some Southerners his raid was proof that the North intended to destroy them.

Lincoln elected President 1860

When the Republican candidate Abraham Lincoln won the 1860 presidential election, Southern fears that the Republicans would abolish slavery reached a new peak. Lincoln was a strong opponent of the expansion of slavery but said he would not interfere with it where it existed. That was not enough to convince many in the South. Before he was even sworn in as President, South Carolina voted to leave the Union, as did six other states: Alabama, Florida, Georgia, Louisiana, Mississippi and Texas. Together they formed the Confederacy. From that point on it seemed compromise was no longer possible, although politicians still tried. Just a spark was needed to ignite open war.

PROFILE

Abraham Lincoln

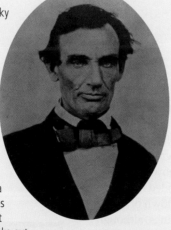

- Born in Hodgenville, Kentucky in 1809.
- Early career as a lawyer before entering politics. He returned to legal practice after opposing the Mexican–American War.
- Re-entered politics in 1854 and became a leader of the new Republican Party. In 1858, while running for CONGRESS, he took part in a series of high-profile debates with his Democrat opponent Stephen A. Douglas and spoke out against the expansion of slavery.
- In 1860 he successfully ran for President and his election convinced many in the South of the need to secede from the Union.
- His Emancipation Proclamation in January 1863 was a key move towards ending slavery.
- In July 1863 his Gettysburg address given at the battlefield cemetery clearly identified the Civil War as a war against slavery.
- ASSASSINATED by John Wilkes Booth just six days after the Confederacy had surrendered in 1865.

PROFILE

Jefferson Davis

- Born in Fairview, Kentucky in 1807 or 1808.
- Early career as a soldier. Later ran a plantation and became a slave owner before entering politics.
- He fought and was wounded in the Mexican–American War.
- After that war he returned to politics with a seat in Congress and went on to become Secretary of War.
- As the split between North and South widened he was a supporter of states' rights but argued against secession.
- Elected the President of Confederacy in 1861.
- After the Civil War he was imprisoned for two years but then released.
- Died in New Orleans in 1889.

PRACTICE QUESTIONS

Read Interpretations A and B and answer Questions 1–3.

Interpretation A Thomas Johnson, from his book, *Twenty-Eight Years a Slave*, published in 1909. Johnson was born a slave in Virginia where he was bought and sold several times. After the Civil War he was freed and moved north where he became a church minister and eventually a missionary in Africa.

In 1860, there was great excitement over the election of Mr Abraham Lincoln as President of the United States. The slaves prayed to God for his success because we knew he was in sympathy with the abolition of slavery. The election was the signal for a great conflict in which the question was: Shall there be slavery? The South said: Yes. All the coloured people that I spoke to believed that if the North gained victory they would have their freedom.

Interpretation B Jefferson Davis, from his memoirs, *The Rise and Fall of Confederate Government*, written in 1881. Davis was the son of a plantation owner who, in 1845, entered Congress for the state of Mississippi. When Mississippi and six other states left the Union and set up their own Confederate government in 1861, Davis was elected as President.

The Confederates fought for the defence of a fundamental right to withdraw from a Union which they had, as independent communities, voluntarily entered. The existence of slavery was in no way the cause of the conflict but was only a minor issue.

1 How does Interpretation B differ from Interpretation A about what the conflict between North and South was about in the American Civil War?

Explain your answer based on what it says in Interpretations A and B.

2 Why might the authors of Interpretations A and B have a different interpretation of what the conflict between the North and South in the American Civil War was about?

Explain your answer using Interpretations A and B and your contextual knowledge.

3 Which interpretation gives the more convincing opinion about what the conflict between North and South in the American Civil War was about?

Explain your answer based on your contextual knowledge and what it says in Interpretations A and B.

FOCUS TASK

Why did the Civil War break out in 1861?

Here is a list of long- and short-term causes of the Civil War:

- Differences between North and South
- Abolitionism
- Westward expansion
- The spread of cotton growing
- Publication of *Uncle Tom's Cabin*
- The underground railroad
- Transcontinental railroad
- Bleeding Kansas
- John Brown and the Harpers Ferry Raid
- The election of Lincoln as President

1 For each write down one example of why it made war more likely.
2 Give each a mark out of 10 for its importance in bringing about war, with 1 being the most important.
3 Choose what you think are the five most important causes and write a short paragraph on each, explaining why you have chosen it.
4 If you took away any of those causes, would war still have broken out in 1861?

The social and economic impact of the American Civil War

Recruitment and conscription

At the start of the Civil War volunteers rushed to join the armies of both sides. Local recruiting offices were set up and volunteer regiments tended to be composed of men from a particular area. Initially officers up to the rank of colonel were elected by other officers and enlisted men, and uniforms varied between units. People expected a short war but it quickly became apparent that that would not be the case and soon the volunteers were not enough.

The Confederacy introduced CONSCRIPTION first in April 1862. All able-bodied men between 18 and 35 were required to serve for three years. By the end of the war this had been extended to all men between the ages of 17 and 50. The Union introduced conscription in March 1863 for all able-bodied men between the ages of 20 and 45. In the South there were exemptions for planters with 20 or more slaves. In both North and South those unwilling to fight could provide a substitute not of draft age or pay a fee $300 or $500, respectively. There was widespread opposition to conscription in both the North and South, which limited its enforcement.

Emancipation

On 1 January 1863 President Lincoln signed the Emancipation Proclamation. This was a key moment. Up to then Lincoln had insisted that the war was to restore the Union and not to free the slaves, but growing numbers of slaves began to turn up in Union army camps. The question then was should they be freed. In the end Lincoln decided that emancipation was necessary for three reasons:

1   It would give the North a moral cause, public opinion was moving in that direction already and he felt this would boost morale.
2   Slave labour was propping up the Confederate war effort with slaves working in MUNITIONS works and army camps.
3   Making the war into one against slavery would remove any danger of France or Britain supporting the Confederacy.

One immediate effect of emancipation was that African Americans could enrol in the armed forces. Moves were made to form all-black units and by mid-1863 they were involved in the fighting. They did not always receive equal treatment and there were no black officers. Initially black soldiers received lower pay than white soldiers, but this was changed in June 1864. When some were captured by the Confederates they were not treated as prisoners of war but were returned to slavery in the state they came from or in some instances executed. Over 38,000 had died by the war's end.

THINK

1   Which cause of the Civil War can you see evidence of in both posters?
2   In what different ways do the posters try to persuade men to enlist?

SOURCE 6
Recruitment poster designed to encourage African American men to enlist in the Union army.

SOURCE 7
Recruitment poster designed to encourage Virginians to enlist in the Confederate army, May 1861.

Head Quarters, Virginia Forces,
STAUNTON, VA.

MEN OF VIRGINIA, TO THE RESCUE !

Your soil has been invaded by your Abolition foes, and we call upon you to rally at once, and drive them back. We want Volunteers to march immediately to Grafton and report for duty. Come one! Come ALL! and render the service due to your State and Country. Fly to arms, and succour your brave brothers who are now in the field.

The Volunteers from the Counties of Pendleton, Highland, Bath, Alleghany, Monroe, Mercer, and other Counties convenient to that point, will immediately organize, and report at Monterey, in Highland County, where they will join the Companies from the Valley, marching to Grafton. The Volunteers from the Counties of Hardy, Hampshire, Randolph, Pendleton, Greenbrier, and other Counties convenient, will in like manner report at Beverly. And the Volunteers from the Counties of Upshur, Lewis, Barbour, and other Counties, will report at Philippi, in Barbour County. The Volunteers, as soon as they report at the above points, will be furnished with arms, rations, &c., &c.

Action! Action! should be our rallying motto, and the sentiment of Virginia's inspired Orator, "Give me Liberty or give me Death," animate every loyal son of the Old Dominion! Let us drive back the invading foot of a brutal and desperate foe, or leave a record to posterity that we died bravely defending our homes and firesides,—the honor of our wives and daughters,—and the sacred graves of our ancestors!

[Done by Authority.]

M. G. HARMAN, Maj. Comm'g
at Staunton.
J. M. HECK, Lt. Col. Va. Vol.
R. E. COWAN, Maj. Va. Vol.

May 30, 1861.

Economic impact on the North

As the pre-war economies of North and South were complementary the war was inevitably going to damage some industries. The Northern shoe industry lost a big part of its market which was in the South. It was noticeable that the Confederate army was never short of munitions but was short of boots for its men! The cotton textile industry lost access to its raw materials – Southern cotton. Other industries directly related to the war flourished, such as the manufacture of arms and uniforms and the railroads that moved men and munitions.

It was the wealthy manufacturers and traders who tended to profit most from the war. Ordinary workers found their wages lagging behind prices as wartime taxes and INFLATION pushed them up. This was made worse by the presence in the workplace of women and boys replacing men. They were happy to accept lower wages as this represented an improvement for them. When workers pushed for wage increases they were accused of being unpatriotic and in 1864 troops were diverted from the battlefield to put down protests in war industries.

By the end of the war the industries of the North were ready for rapid growth.

Economic impact on the South

If the effect of the war in the North was mixed, it was an economic disaster in the South. The war destroyed the railroad system as Union troops tore up tracks, bent rails and burnt rolling stock. Cotton growing was badly disrupted by the Union advances. Production fell from 4 million bales in 1861 to 300,000 bales in 1865. The only industries to grow were those associated with the war effort, such as munitions.

Food shortages became a major problem in the South towards the end of the war as agricultural crop yields fell due to manpower shortages, as the men were in the army. But there were food riots in some cities as early as 1863. Meanwhile, some plantation owners continued to grow cotton in search of profits rather than listening to their government's appeals to grow food. In one respect cotton growers did help the South. They were cut off from Britain and their European markets by the Union naval BLOCKADE but they were able to trade for food with the North, which was itself desperate for supplies for its cotton industry. So even during the fighting there was some trade across the lines.

The South also suffered from terrible inflation. The Confederate government at first tried to fund the war through new taxes but was so unsuccessful in collecting them that it resorted to printing more money. This led to HYPERINFLATION and the more money the government printed the worse it became.

Social impact

During the war, as men went off to fight, many women volunteered as unpaid nurses while thousands took on new roles as farmers, plantation managers and munitions-plant workers. While many returned to their traditional roles when the war ended, the experience had changed the status of women. Moreover the high numbers of casualties created a generation of widows, spinsters and wives of disabled husbands. Immediately after the war, however, an appeal for the vote for women as well as for black males received little support.

FACTFILE

Army nationalities

Both Confederate and Union armies frequently organised units along community and ethnic lines. The Union army had French, German, Irish, Scandinavian and Scottish Highlander units. The Confederate army had German, Mexican–Texan and Creek and Cherokee nation units. Towards the very end of the war the Confederacy was so desperate for men that it passed a law allowing the arming of 300,000 slave soldiers, although this was too late for any plan to be put into action.

FIGURE 8

Rising inflation in the Confederacy.

1861	12%
1862	70%
1863	190%
1864	250%
1865	500%

*Figures for May each year, although it should be noted that inflation rose still higher and then fell back between May 1863 and May 1864 when the Confederate government controlled the money supply.

PRACTICE QUESTIONS

1 Describe how the Civil War damaged the Southern economy.
2 Describe how the lives of African Americans were affected by the Civil War.

Coming to terms with the Mormons

Just as the lives of the Plains Indians were disturbed by the westward movement of travellers, settlers and miners, so too were those of the Mormons in Utah. Travellers on the Oregon and California trails complained that the Mormons charged very high prices for supplies. Moreover the conversion of some Indians to the Mormon faith raised new fears about the Mormons plotting to kill all Gentiles. Meanwhile the federal government were concerned that the Mormon practice of polygamy was illegal and that the Mormon leaders' control of Utah was actually a theocracy – a state ruled by a religion.

In July 1857 a new non-Mormon governor, along with 2,500 troops, was sent to Utah to replace Brigham Young. Although the governor's orders were not to start any hostilities, the Mormons did not trust the peaceful intentions of this expedition. Instead Brigham Young mobilised defence forces, the Nauvoo Legion. The Mormon strategy was to harass the army's advance into Utah and make it difficult for them to gather supplies. This was so successful that the troops had to spend the winter at Fort Bridger.

Mountain Meadow Massacre

With neither side wanting to engage in full-scale fighting, the Mormon War of 1857–58 was unlikely to result in many casualties. By its end about 150 had died but most of these casualties occurred in a single incident. In early September a wagon train of families bound for California camped at Mountain Meadows and was attacked either by Paiute Indians or Mormon militia. Who started the trouble is still a matter of debate.

Historians also disagree on why the trouble started. Some point to the tensions in Utah because of the presence of what was seen as an invading US army, or the fact that in August Brigham Young had declared martial law and that he had instructed Mormons not to trade with non-Mormons. Others note that the migrants were from Arkansas and that a Mormon leader had been murdered in that state. Still others suggest that the migrants had been behaving badly and provoking either the Mormons or the Paiute Indians.

That trouble occurred is not in dispute. The first attack on the wagon train was repelled and a five-day siege ensued. When it became obvious that the migrants knew that Mormons were involved, the local Mormon militia leader took the decision to kill everyone so there would be no witnesses. After the travellers were tricked into leaving the protection of their wagons, all were killed except for 17 children under the age of 7 who were taken into Mormon homes. As part of the cover-up that followed, the Mormons spread the story that Indians had been responsible, but this was not believed. The investigation that eventually followed was hampered by the Mormons and did not result in any charges until 1874. In the end just one Mormon, a militia leader named John Lee, was convicted and executed for the crime in 1877.

News of the massacre inflamed public opinion against the Mormons back in the East and the federal government sent more troops. In response thousands of Mormon families packed up their homes to flee from the expected attack. This turned public opinion back in their favour.

In the end a peaceful settlement was negotiated. In April 1858 the Mormons were pardoned, a non-Mormon governor was installed and the US army entered Utah peacefully.

Utah becomes a state

Utah was not allowed to enter the Union as a state until it banned polygamy. This finally happened in 1896.

FOCUS TASK

Why did the US government find it hard to come to terms with the Mormons?

1 Using page 28, make notes on the reasons why the US government found the Mormons hard to deal with under the following headings:
   - Hostility to their idea of being God's chosen
   - Envy of their economic success
   - Their armed resistance to a new governor
   - Their practice of polygamy.
2 In groups, use your notes to discuss which of these reasons was the most important in explaining why the US government found it hard to come to terms with the Mormons.

ACTIVITY

Write a paragraph to describe the events of the Mormon War. Include your judgement on whether it deserves to be labelled a war.

FACTFILE

The Stars and Bars

The Stars and Bars is the flag that today represents the Confederacy. To some it is a symbol of southern pride, to others it is a racist symbol. This can be seen in the decision of some southern states in 2015 to remove it from their state flag and to no longer fly it over official buildings.

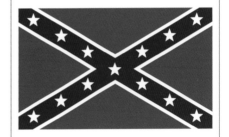

TOPIC SUMMARY

Conflict across America

- The westward spread of the United States resulted in conflicts with the Cheyenne in 1863 and the Sioux 1865–68.
- The discoveries of gold in Colorado and later in Montana in the Rocky Mountains were very disruptive events for the Plains Indians.
- The debate over the spread of slavery, together with the growth of the abolitionist movement, widened the split between the Northern and Southern states.
- The debate about slave and free states brought to the forefront of politics the question of the balance of power between federal and state government.
- Political disagreements turned into violence in Kansas and the actions of extremists such as John Brown made war more likely.
- The American Civil War 1861–65 was a devastating event in American history. Roughly 3 million men fought in the armies and with roughly 620,000 deaths it remains the bloodiest conflict in American history. It also led to great destruction across the Southern states and changed American society forever.
- The war may have begun as a war over states' rights but by the end it was a war over slavery. This has led to a disputed history of the Confederacy which still continues and which is evident in the debates over the message conveyed by its flag to this very day.
- Westward expansion also led the United States into conflict with the Mormons in 1857–58 although a political solution was eventually reached.

1.3 Consolidation – forging the nation

FOCUS

By 1865 the fighting in the American Civil War was over and the challenge facing politicians was how to rebuild the nation. While the war was over, the battle for equality for African Americans was just beginning. Meanwhile the end of the war led to a flood of settlers and soldiers onto the Great Plains. This led to more fighting, although on a much smaller scale, which was only ended by the defeat of the Plains Indians and their confinement to reservations.

In this part of the topic you will study the following:

- The aftermath of the American Civil War and the extent to which reconstruction was achieved.
- The continued settlement of the West and the extent to which the homesteaders successfully made a life for themselves there.
- The resolution of the 'Indian problem' after 1865 and the factors involved in this.

● The aftermath of the American Civil War

When the war ended the key task facing the United States was RECONSTRUCTION. The Union needed to be restored and the defeated South needed to be reintegrated. There were a number of questions to consider, foremost of which were how the Confederacy's leaders and soldiers should be treated and what should happen to the 3.5 million former slaves.

The balance of federal and state powers

Closely linked with the problem of the former Confederates and former slaves was the issue of the balance of federal and state powers. During the struggles of the reconstruction period the federal government was in conflict with the Southern states over the freedom and equality of African Americans, and had to intervene in matters such as the rights of CITIZENS, which those states considered were their concerns only. It was for this reason that Section 2 of the Thirteenth Amendment (see Source 1) was added and that the word 'State' was explicitly included in the Fourteenth Amendment (see Source 4).

Presidential reconstruction under Andrew Johnson

Political arguments about how reconstruction should be carried out began well before the war itself ended. As the Union armies advanced, Southern states came back under Union control. President Lincoln's policy was to give these Southern states military governors to begin with and then they were allowed to form civil state governments with a view to them rejoining the Union. This brought Lincoln into conflict with some Republicans in Congress who wanted a slower process that would bar many ex-Confederates from political life. As the war ended Lincoln was assassinated so the task of reconstruction fell to President Andrew Johnson.

Under Johnson's plan all seven Southern states still without reconstruction governments – Alabama, Florida, Georgia, Mississippi, North Carolina, South Carolina and Texas – could return to the Union. Almost all Southerners who took an oath of allegiance would be pardoned and have their property returned. Of course their slaves could not be returned because there were now no slaves. These Southerners could then take part in the political process of elections.

SOURCE 1

The Thirteenth Amendment, 1865.

Section 1. Neither slavery nor involuntary servitude, except as a punishment for crime whereof the party shall have been duly convicted, shall exist within the United States, or any place subject to their jurisdiction.

Section 2. Congress shall have power to enforce this article by appropriate legislation.

Those excluded were ex-Confederate civil government officials and military officers and those with taxable property worth $20,000 (Johnson was hostile to rich plantation owners). In practice those excluded were able to apply for a pardon and Johnson granted over 13,000.

The Thirteenth Amendment

The Thirteenth Amendment abolished slavery and gave Congress the power to enforce this. To make doubly sure of this the new state governments in the South had to ratify the Thirteenth Amendment. They had to formally agree that slavery could not exist in the United States. Furthermore, to make sure that the Confederacy was dead and buried, these Southern states had to REPUDIATE the loans that the Confederacy had built up during the Civil War. Only then could they rejoin the Union. When elected, some state governments refused to do this. In some Southern states little seemed to have changed since before the war. The presidential dispute with the Republicans in Congress over reconstruction worsened.

Black codes

Moreover all seven Southern states passed 'black codes'. Under these laws freed slaves could marry, own property, make legal contracts and testify against other black Americans in court, but most prohibited racial intermarriage, jury service by black Americans and testimony in court by blacks against whites. They also contained provisions for annual contracts between black Americans and landowners. In effect, while the ex-slaves were free, they were not fully free. The status of black Americans in the Southern states thus became a major political issue. The Republicans in Congress believed that the Southern states would not deal fairly with black Americans unless they were forced to do so.

Civil Rights Act

In 1866 Congress passed the Civil Rights Act which President Johnson vetoed. Congress overrode his VETO and by ratifying it as the Fourteenth Amendment ensured it could not easily be overturned. The Act was intended to protect the rights of ex-slaves by making them citizens. It could not guarantee black suffrage but tried to ensure this by threatening that Southern states would have reduced representation in the federal government if they refused to give black men the vote. This was the first attempt by the federal government to limit state control of civil and political rights. This amendment also disqualified from political office all those pre-war officers, both in civil government and the military, who had supported the Confederacy. Their disqualification could be removed by Congress if two-thirds voted for it. So they were not permanently excluded from political life.

> **SOURCE 4**
>
> Extract from the Fourteenth Amendment, 1866.
>
> *All persons born or naturalised in the United States … are citizens of the United States and of the State wherein they reside.*

> **THINK**
>
> 1 How does the passing of the black codes support the argument that the Civil War was a war fought over slavery?
> 2 After reading pages 30–31, explain why the word 'State' was inserted into the Fourteenth Amendment.

> **FIGURE 2**
> The legislative process in the United States.
>
> *All legislation begins as a **bill** in Congress.*
>
> ▼
>
> *When a bill is passed it goes to the President for approval. If the President approves it, it becomes an **Act**.*
>
> ▼
>
> *The President can veto a bill to stop it becoming a law.*
>
> ▼
>
> *Congress can overrule a Presidential veto.*

> **FIGURE 3**
> Separation of government powers under the US Constitution.
>
> *Congress, the Legislature makes the law.*
>
> ▼
>
> *The President, the Executive carries out the laws passed by Congress.*
>
> ▼
>
> *The Supreme Court, the Judiciary decides cases and controversies.*
>
> ▼
>
> *Having the three separate parts of government is known as the system of checks and balances.*

Reconstruction in the South, 1866–77

President Johnson and the Republican Party in Congress remained in dispute over reconstruction. Essentially the Republicans wanted to ensure the vote for African Americans and wanted to keep ex-Confederates out of power until there was no longer a danger of a new rebellion. In 1867 Congress passed a new Act which overturned the state governments formed under the Lincoln and Johnson plans. The Act divided the South into five temporary military districts each run by a General. New elections of state governments were to be held in which all black Americans, and those whites not barred by the Fourteenth Amendment, could vote. Once the state had rewritten its constitution and approved the Fourteenth Amendment it could be re-admitted to the Union and political reconstruction would be complete.

FIGURE 5

Reconstruction of the Southern states.

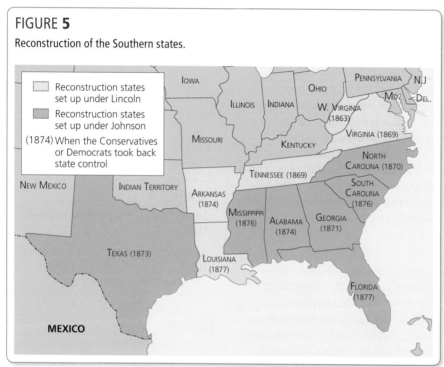

Johnson vetoed the Act but again Congress overrode his veto and the Act became law. However, in order to put Congressional reconstruction into effect, military power was needed and Johnson hindered this by replacing military officers who were sympathetic to the idea.

Impeachment crisis, 1868

The political battle now moved to the power of the president. The Republicans in Congress passed two new laws that limited the power of the president. In particular they did not want the Secretary of War, Henry Stanton, removed as they needed his support to enforce their Reconstruction Acts. After Johnson removed Stanton for a second time in 1868 the Republicans IMPEACHED him. The charges were that Johnson had exceeded his powers as president and had not enforced the Reconstruction Acts. At the end of his trial the vote was against Johnson by 35 votes to 19, just short of the two-thirds majority required to remove him from office. So Johnson continued to serve out the remaining period of his term in office.

The Fifteenth Amendment, 1869

The final reconstruction objective of the Republicans was to guarantee black male suffrage in both the Northern and the Southern states. This led to the Fifteenth Amendment, whose key provision was that the vote could not be denied on the basis of race or colour or previous enslavement. The Democrats' argument against this was that it violated states' rights by denying them the right to decide who could vote. The Republicans won and the Amendment was passed. However, there were loopholes in the legislation as it did not prohibit restrictions on voting such as property requirements or literacy tests, which were two ways in which Southern states stopped African Americans voting. Meanwhile efforts to win the vote for women were unsuccessful.

In 1869 Ulysses S. Grant was elected President, by 1870 all the Southern states had been re-admitted to the Union and the struggle over political reconstruction was at an end.

FACTFILE

Impeachment of a President

Under the United States Constitution the President can be removed from office through the process known as impeachment. The grounds for impeachment are 'treason, bribery or other high crimes and misdemeanours'. If a case can be made then the upper house of Congress, the Senate, holds a trial. This needs to find the president guilty by a two-thirds majority vote. If it does the President can be removed from office. So far in its history no US President has been removed from office.

FIGURE 6

Reconstruction Amendments to the United States Constitution.

Date	Amendment	Main provisions
January 1965	Thirteenth	Prohibited slavery in the United States.
June 1866	Fourteenth	Defined citizenship as including all people born or naturalised in the United States.
February 1869	Fifteenth	Prohibited the denial of the vote because of race, colour or previous servitude.

Reconstruction in the South – the struggle continues after 1870

As the individual Southern states were re-admitted to the Union, political life could begin again. In each there was the same struggle over the role of African Americans, between the conservative old order, the Democrats, and the Republican new order. It was a struggle in which African Americans themselves played an important part. Although many freed slaves were uneducated and destitute there were others who had been born free and those who had served in the Union army. Military veterans' service in the army had given them experience of leadership, opportunities for education, a sense of national pride and a strong desire for freedom from white control.

The most obvious evidence of this was the establishment of independent black churches across the South. The Baptist Church, with its decentralised structure, was most popular and by 1890 there were over a million black Baptists in the South. These churches were also important in the development of black education through funding the building of schools and the payment of teachers. Freed African Americans also organised thousands of mutual-aid clubs and societies.

SOURCE 7

Group portrait of the first coloured senator and representatives, 1872.

PRACTICE QUESTION

Describe two ways in which African Americans helped themselves in the aftermath of the Civil War (or during reconstruction).

Carpetbaggers and scallywags

Many African Americans entered politics. Over 600 served in state governments and a few served in Congress. However, the leading roles in state governments were played by white Republican politicians. Most influential were those originally from the North. They were committed to black rights. These included former Union soldiers who came South in search of business opportunities in land, factories and railroads; and professionals such as lawyers, teachers and preachers. They were CARICATURED by Southern Democrats as 'carpetbaggers' – Northern opportunists who came south for money and power with so few possessions that they could be stuffed into a travelling bag made of carpet material.

The other group of white Republicans were Southerners, mostly poorer farmers from the mountain regions of the Southern states. They were not part of the old plantation-owning elite, had tended to support the Union during the war and did not own slaves themselves. They were even more hated than the carpetbaggers and were called 'scallywags'. They were accused of being opportunists out to make money for themselves. They held the most political offices during reconstruction although they tended to drift back to supporting the Democrats as they were not deeply concerned about black rights.

Reconstruction government achievements

While the Republicans remained in control they managed a number of significant achievements. They established the first state school systems with 600,000 black pupils in schools by 1877. They ensured that African Americans achieved lasting rights to an education. They also ensured that in principle African Americans had equality before the law, the right to own property, to set up businesses and to enter the professions.

They repaired and rebuilt roads, buildings and bridges. There was corruption in some states, but then that was true in some Northern states too. So Republican reconstruction achieved some lasting benefits. However, by 1877 the conservative forces of the Democrats had regained power in all Southern states, bringing reconstruction to an end. This happened for four reasons:

- The drift of Republicans, both Southern and Northern, to the DEMOCRATIC views of their neighbours: it had been difficult holding views that were in conflict with their friends and associates.
- The loss of Republican morale due to the actions of the KU KLUX KLAN (see page 35).
- Vote rigging such as ballot stuffing where extra voting papers are added to the ballot box or simply by miscounting the votes cast.
- The lack of political will of the federal government to support black rights. The government was tired of the Southern struggle and focused instead upon other issues such as westward expansion and the Indian Wars.

THINK

1   Study Source 8. Look at the figure on the left of the picture. Who does he represent and how do you know this?
2   What sort of bag is he carrying and what does he have in it?
3   What sort of house or property is shown on the right of the picture?
4   Using these details and anything else you can see, explain what message the artist is trying to convey.

The Ku Klux Klan

Most white Southerners remained hostile to the idea of freedom and equality for African Americans and this lay behind political opposition to Republican reconstruction. It also gave rise to terrorism. The Ku Klux Klan began in 1866 in Tennessee and spread rapidly across the South. It drew members from all walks of Southern society. Klansmen hiding their identity behind white robes carried out acts of terrorism, including whippings and murders, to intimidate blacks and white Republicans. The federal government passed Enforcement Acts to protect black voters. These included making illegal: the wearing of disguises, conspiracies, resisting officers of the law and intimidating officials. In 1871 President Grant targeted an area of South Carolina for mass prosecutions and this broke the power of the Klan. It did not, however, stop intimidation by PARAMILITARY groups such as the White League and the Red Shirts. These continued into the twentieth century.

Share cropping

Once freed, many ex-slaves moved away from the plantations. Some left for the south-west, such as Texas, where planters paid higher wages; more moved into towns and cities. Some spent years reuniting with their families that had been separated by sale. With little money or technical skills, freed slaves faced the prospect of becoming wage labourers, but many turned to share cropping. Under this system the landowner provided the land, housing, tools and seed and a local merchant provided food and supplies on CREDIT. At harvest time the share cropper received a share of the crop for their labour with the landowner taking the rest. The share cropper then used their share to pay off their debt to the merchant. The advantage to the white landowner was that their land was being worked and for the freed slaves they had more control over their own lives and the lives of their families. But the system was inefficient and the share croppers were in continual debt.

Exodus to Kansas

Thousands of African Americans began migrating west to Kansas. They became known as 'EXODUSTERS' as they were looking for freedom from the racism and poverty of the post-war South just as the Israelites fled from Ancient Egypt. They became farmers, ranchers and cowboys.

FOCUS TASK

How successful was Republican Reconstruction in the South?

Read these two statements:
- 'Republican reconstruction was a failure.'
- 'Republican reconstruction was a success.'

1 Create a table with two columns using these statements as headings. Now note down the points or examples from the text that support each side.
2 Use your table to write a speech by either:
   – Jefferson Davis (see page 24), who was still alive in 1877, entitled 'Republican reconstruction is a failure'.

   Or
   – A Republican supporter, entitled 'Republican reconstruction is a success.

PRACTICE QUESTION

Describe two reasons why slaves turned to share cropping.

SOURCE 9

The new town of Nicodemus, established by black Americans in Kansas in 1877.

SOURCE 10

The Shores family, who settled in Custer County, Nebraska, in 1887.

FIGURE **11**

Decade	Immigrants
1841–50	1,713,000
1851–60	2,598,000
1861–70	2,315,000
1871–80	2,812,000
1881–90	5,247,000

THINK

Study Source 12 carefully.

1 What clothes were the Bentley family wearing?
2 What sort of house did they live in?
3 What tools did they use?
4 What work might they have done?
5 They are all members of the same family. Can you work out what their relationships might be?
6 Look at their faces. What sort of life do you think the Bentleys lived?

● The continued settlement of the West

While the Civil War raged there were still some who went West, but this trickle turned into a flood when the war was over, as they came from both victorious North and defeated South.

The homesteaders

Thousands of people moved onto the Plains – onto land occupied by the Plains Indians. These people sold their homes, left their friends and families and travelled, in some cases for thousands of miles, to settle on the Great Plains.

Why the homesteaders went west

Reason 1: The actions of the US government

The US government recognised the need to populate the West and to help achieve this the Homestead Act was passed in 1862. It was intended to encourage people to settle in the West by allowing each family 160 acres of land. This land was given to them free, provided they lived on it and farmed it for five years. Two later Acts also encouraged settlers. These were:

- **The Timber Culture Act, 1873:** This gave settlers a further 160 acres of free land, provided they planted 40 acres with trees.
- **The Desert Land Act, 1877:** This gave settlers the right to buy 640 acres cheaply in areas where lack of rainfall was a particular problem.

The effect of these three Acts was to make millions of acres of land available for HOMESTEADERS to settle. Thousands of men and women seized this opportunity and became homesteaders.

Reason 2: The end of the American Civil War

The end of the Civil War marked a turning point in American history. Thousands of DEMOBILISED soldiers and their families were looking to rebuild their lives. Thousands of newly freed black slaves were looking for new beginnings. The eastern states where they had grown up did not seem to be the best place to do this, so they looked towards the West. They became the homesteaders, cowboys, miners, soldiers and railroad-builders who transformed this area.

Reason 3: The building of the transcontinental railroads

The US government had long wanted to build a transcontinental railroad to link east and west. In the 1860s two companies started building the Northern route, one from the east, the other from the west. Eventually they met at Promontory Point in Utah in 1869. This had three main effects: now it was easy for homesteaders to get to the Plains; it was also cheap to buy land, as the railroad companies sold off the land on either side of the line at low prices; and finally the railroad could bring new machinery quickly to the Plains.

So land was cheap, travel was easy and there were plenty of people looking for a new life. The result was a flood of homesteaders onto the Plains.

SOURCE **12**

The Bentley family, homesteaders, proudly photographed outside their sod house in Custer County, Nebraska, in 1887. Remember that when people had their photographs taken at this time they had to keep perfectly still in the same pose for much longer than we do today. So they couldn't smile for the camera, in case they couldn't hold the smile for long enough! Look at the bushes in the photo. They are blurred. This is because they moved in the breeze that must have been blowing at the time.

FIGURE 13

Routes of the transcontinental railroads.

A map of the United States showing the routes of the transcontinental railroads. Key features include:
- Major railroads
- Kansas Pacific RR
- Union Pacific RR
- Central Pacific RR
- Northern buffalo herd
- Southern buffalo herd

Cities marked: Helena, Bismarck, Chicago, Promontory Point, Salt Lake City, Denver, Kansas City, Dodge City, San Francisco, Los Angeles, Adobe Walls, Fort Worth, New Orleans. MEXICO and Atlantic Ocean are labelled. Scale: 0 – 1000km. North arrow shown.

SOURCE 14

A railroad land sale poster, 1875.

LARGE DISCOUNTS FOR CASH.
BETTER TERMS THAN EVER!
BUY BEFORE JULY 1st, 1875, and Secure these Terms.
PRODUCTS will PAY for LAND and IMPROVEMENTS.
THE BEST
PRAIRIE LANDS
IN
IOWA AND NEBRASKA
ARE FOR SALE BY THE
Burlington & Missouri River Railroad Co.
10 Years' Credit. LOW PRICES 6 Per Cent. Interest.
ONLY THE INTEREST PAYMENT DOWN.
PAYMENTS ON PRINCIPAL BEGIN THE FOURTH YEAR.
BUY LAND EXPLORING TICKETS,
LAND COMMISSIONER B. & M. R. R.,
PREMIUMS FOR IMPROVEMENTS.

As well as the general reasons, each group of homesteaders had its own special reasons for moving West.

FIGURE 15

The 'push' and 'pull' factors that encouraged people to move West.

PULL FACTORS

← The offer of free land.
← The chance of a new start/adventure.
← Advertising by the railroad companies and by the territories and states.
← Letters home from those who had already gone West, and who were successfully farming, encouraged people to move.

ENABLING FACTORS

← The early homesteaders travelled by wagon, by riverboat or on foot.
← Later homesteaders travelled on the new railroads.
← The Indians were cleared from these lands, defeated by the US army and confined to reservations or pushed further west.

PUSH FACTORS

Europe

← Scandinavians wanted good farming land that was no longer available at home.
← English, Germans, Irish, Russians and Scots were looking to escape from poverty and unemployment at home.
← Jews and other religious groups, such as the Amish and Mennonites, were looking to escape from religious persecution at home.
← Thousands of EMIGRANTS left Europe to settle in Iowa, Minnesota and the Dakotas.

The eastern states

← Ex-soldiers from both sides in the Civil War saw a lack of opportunity when they returned to their homes.
← Other easterners wanted farming land or opportunities to get on that were no longer available in the settled eastern states.

The Southern states

← The after-effects of the Civil War: black ex-slaves were persecuted in the South and many Southerners lost their land and income.
← Serious economic problems, when crops failed and people went hungry.
← Ex-slaves, Exodusters, from the Southern states mainly went to Kansas. In 1879, the peak year of migration, up to 40,000 went west.

The problems of living on the Great Plains

The journey of the homesteaders to their new farms might not have been quite as demanding as that of the early pioneers but once they arrived they faced significant problems.

Water shortages

In many places water was scarce. In such places it was difficult for people to keep either themselves or their clothing clean.

Extremes of weather

The extreme weather, hot in summer and cold in winter, with a low rainfall, made life on the Great Plains very uncomfortable. The nomadic Indians moved with the seasons but the homesteaders remained rooted on one spot. Many grew to hate the fierce winds that howled around their houses for days on end.

Fuel

There was no wood to burn for heating and cooking. Instead homesteaders used buffalo or cow 'chips' – dried dung.

Building materials

Homesteaders who settled in river valleys might be able to use wood for building homes, and wood was also transported from the East to the small number who could afford it. But for the vast majority the only material available for house-building was earth. Blocks of earth (sods) were cut out by hand or with a special plough. These were then used as building bricks to construct the house walls. Windows and doors were fitted. Then the house was roofed with boards, grass and more sods. Finally, the outside walls were plastered with clay-like mud. Such houses were very cheap to build. They could be warm in winter and cool in summer if well-built but it was very difficult to stop water leaking in when it rained.

Dirt and disease

SOD HOUSES with earth floors, walls and roofs were very difficult to keep clean. They harboured all sorts of pests, such as bed bugs, fleas, mice and snakes. Living in such conditions it was difficult for people to keep clean, especially where a shortage of water was also a problem. It was all too easy for disease to develop and illness was common among homesteaders, particularly children.

The problems of farming on the Plains

To simply live on the Plains the homesteaders overcame many problems but there were more problems to be surmounted if they were to farm successfully.

Water shortages

The shortage of water was a major problem. It could lead to the total failure of crops. This would lead in turn to bankruptcy or starvation. For the Mormons of Salt Lake City, irrigation was a solution but out on the Great Plains there were no rivers or lakes from which to draw water. Wells were a possible solution but digging a well was expensive and gave no guarantee of finding water.

Extremes of weather

The extremes of weather were a major problem. Drought in summer and cold in winter could damage or destroy crops. In Kansas, for example, no rain fell between January 1859 and November 1860.

Ploughing

The Great Plains had never been farmed before. So the first task for the homesteader was to plough the land. The grasses had dense, tangled roots and the early cast-iron ploughs needed constant repairs. Ploughing was a slow, back-breaking task.

Protecting crops

There was no wood for fencing so there was nothing to protect growing crops from buffalo or straying cattle. Nor was it possible to mark land boundaries clearly, and this could lead to disputes.

Growing crops

The homesteaders planted the crops they had always grown, such as maize and soft winter and spring wheats. These were not well suited to the weather conditions on the Great Plains.

Natural hazards

In the summer, when the grass was so dry, it was easy for prairie fires to start. If they were too big for the people to fight then their crops would be destroyed. The plagues of grasshoppers which swept across the Plains in 1871, 1874 and 1875 were another natural hazard. The insects descended on the land in columns 240 km wide and 160 km long. Hundred-acre cornfields vanished in a few hours.

Living and farming on the Great Plains: solutions to problems

Despite the many problems of living and farming on the Great Plains, the majority of homesteaders stayed on after their first year. Not all of them were successful. One crucial factor was the exact location of their land. Some parts of the Great Plains were less fertile than others. A second factor was the adaptability of homesteaders. The Great Plains required them to adapt their farming to the conditions. Those who did not adapt failed. A third factor outside their control was the weather. The severe droughts of the 1870s and 1880s forced thousands into bankruptcy. For example, approximately 11,000 homesteads were REPOSSESSED in Kansas between 1889 and 1893. Those who survived and prospered were helped by a number of inventions and developments.

Windmills

As you have already seen, a lack of water was a major problem on the Great Plains. There were two solutions to this. The first was developed in 1874, when Daniel Halliday invented a self-governing windmill: it always kept in line with the wind so that it did not get damaged by the strong winds. This windmill could be used to pump water from underground. First, a high-powered drill was used to get down to the water. Then the wind pump was fitted. It would pump water night and day for people to use in their homes and to irrigate their crops.

	Problems	Solutions
Homesteaders living on the Plains		
Homesteaders farming on the Plains		

2 Begin by listing the problems faced by homesteaders living on the Plains and those faced by homesteaders working on the Plains.
3 Now write a few words to give further explanation where it is needed.
4 Next complete the third column by matching the solutions to the problems.
5 Were there any problems for which there was no solution?
6 Now highlight those solutions that were helped by the building of the railroads.

In what ways were the lives of homesteaders on the Great Plains affected by the arrival of the railroads?

Explain your answer.

Dry farming

The second solution was dry farming. Farmers ploughed their land when there had been heavy rain or snow. This left a thin layer of dust over the surface, which trapped and preserved the moisture in the soil. The land was then left fallow ready for the following year's crop.

Growing a surplus

In their early years on the Great Plains homesteaders would plough enough land to grow food to feed their family. In later years they could plough more land and grow more crops. This would produce a surplus that they could sell. With this money they could buy better equipment and increase their surplus.

Hard winter wheat

Homesteaders recognised that wheat was a more suitable crop than corn. Those who settled on the high Plains realised that it was better to keep animals – sheep and cattle – rather than just to grow crops.

Russian Mennonite immigrants introduced hard winter wheat (Turkey Red wheat). The climatic conditions on the Great Plains were similar to those on the Russian steppes, so these crops flourished and homesteaders who grew it were successful. The Russians accidentally brought Russian weeds mixed in with the wheat seed. These also flourished, notably the tumbleweed (Russian thistle) seen in so many Westerns.

Barbed wire

In 1874 Joseph Glidden invented barbed wire. This provided a cheap and effective solution to the problem of fencing and protecting crops.

Sod-buster

John Deere invented a particularly strong plough which could deal with the tough grass roots. This was known as a 'sod-buster', the nickname sometimes given to homesteaders by the cowboys.

Other machinery

From the 1880s other new farming machinery was developed. This included reapers, binders and threshers. These could be easily transported by railroad to the Great Plains and were affordable. The machines increased the area that a homesteader could manage to farm and were well suited to the wide open spaces of the Great Plains.

Hard work

By the 1890s a combination of all these inventions and developments had helped the homesteaders to solve the problems of farming on the Great Plains. The Great Plains became a fertile area for wheat production and the majority of homesteaders prospered. Their success can be explained by their determination, hard work and adaptability. They were supported by the railroads which took them there, brought them equipment and carried their crops to market.

The resolution of the 'Indian problem' after 1865

The movement of homesteaders onto the Plains had an increasing impact on the Plains Indians. So too did the cattle drives that had started at the end of the Civil War northwards from Texas to the new railroads. All this disrupted the buffalo herd migration routes and led to increasing tension. The influx of people meant that the small reservations policy that underlay the second Fort Laramie Treaty 1868 was destined to fail. This was because:

- not all Plains Indian bands had ever agreed to live on the reservations
- whenever there was a conflict between preserving the Indian reservations and the interests of cattle drivers, railroad engineers, miners or settlers, the United States government favoured the latter group.

Attitudes to the Native Americans

Since the forced removal of the eastern Indian Nations to Indian territory, the view of the United States government had changed from seeing the Plains Indians as nations to be negotiated with on equal terms, to simply Americans subject to the rule of the United States government. Meanwhile the old debate between negotiators and exterminators still continued.

The US army

With the end of the Civil War the US army was better prepared to campaign in the West.

- **New troops**: Many seasoned troops became available so the army had far superior numbers and if it lost men they could be quickly replaced. Not so the Indians.
- **Forts**: The army benefited from the network of forts built to protect the overland routes and to keep watch over reservations. These served as a base from which soldiers could patrol and watch. Although Plains Indians attacked forts on a number of occasions, they never managed to capture one. The combination of men and artillery, sometimes protected by walls, was too strong.
- **'TOTAL WAR'**: Officers also brought new strategies to the Indian Wars – the first was that of 'total war'. This had been successfully used by Generals Sherman and Sheridan during the Civil War. 'Total war' meant waging war against a whole enemy population, not just against the fighting troops. It did not mean the killing of women and children. Instead it meant destroying all the food, shelter, clothing, possessions and animals of the Plains Indians. This left them with a choice between starvation, or else going into the reservation and surrendering. This strategy demoralised the Plains Indians and strengthened the arguments of those in favour of peace.
- **Winter campaigns**: The second strategy was that of winter campaigns. With the heavy snow and sub-zero temperatures on the Plains it was the time of year when the Plains Indians needed to stay in one place and conserve food supplies and the strength of their ponies. Defeat at such a time could be devastating. The US army were able to campaign in the winter months.

The combination of all four factors ensured that the army would be able to defeat the Plains Indians if war broke out, and break out it did for two reasons. The first was associated with the new railroads and the buffalo, and the second was gold again.

SOURCE 18

Figures for buffalo hides shipped east by railroads, 1872–74. These figures are from Colonel Dodge's book, *Hunting Grounds of the Great West.*

Year	Hides carried
1872	497,163
1873	754,329
1874	126,867

THINK

1. Study Source 18. What pattern can you see in these figures?
2. How would you explain this pattern?
3. Read Sources 19 and 20. Which key point do Tall Bull and General Sheridan agree on?

PRACTICE QUESTION

In what ways did the destruction of the buffalo affect the lives of the Plains Indians?

Explain your answer.

War on the Southern plains

As the new railroads were constructed across the Plains their workforce needed feeding and buffalo hunters were employed. This disrupted buffalo herd movements but a new development in 1871 led to a dramatic increase in buffalo hunting. This was the discovery by an eastern tannery of a process to produce high-quality leather from buffalo hides. The price of buffalo hides shot up and now that the railroads had reached the Great Plains the hides could easily be transported back east to the tanning industry. The buffalo hunting industry was centred on Dodge City and Fort Worth. Hunters flooded onto the Southern Plains, shooting buffalo for their hides. The carcasses were left to rot.

The hunting method used could not have been more different from that of the Indians. who only killed what they could use. These hunters were armed with powerful long-range rifles. They would take up a position some distance from the buffalo and first shoot the leading animal. They would then shoot individual animals one at a time. If each shot killed the buffalo instantly then the rest of the group would not be alarmed and the hunter could stay in position and continue the killing. This was known as a stand. By the end of 1875 the Southern buffalo herd was destroyed.

The Indians who depended upon the buffalo for their survival were not blind to what was happening. In the summer of 1874, in an attempt to force the hunters from the Southern Plains before the last of the herds vanished, 700 Arapahos, Cheyennes, Comanches and Kiowas attacked the buffalo hunters based near Adobe Walls. The Indians launched repeated attacks against the settlement, but they were no match for the defending hunters with their powerful buffalo guns.

SOURCE 19

Tall Bull, a Cheyenne (dog soldier) chief, talking to General Winfield Scott Hancock, 1867.

The buffalo are diminishing fast. The antelope, that were plenty a few years ago, they are now thin. When they shall all die we shall be hungry; we shall want something to eat, and we will be compelled to come into the fort.

SOURCE 20

General Philip H. Sheridan in a speech to the Texas legislature in 1873.

These men [the buffalo hunters] have done more in the last two years, and will do more in the next year to settle the vexed Indian question, than the entire regular army has done in the last 30 years. They are destroying the Indians' food supply … Send them powder and lead if you will; but for the sake of a lasting peace, let them kill, skin and sell until the buffalos are exterminated.

The Great Sioux War, 1876–77

The destruction of the buffalo affected the Sioux too but it was the discovery of gold in the Black Hills that triggered the most serious fighting. In 1874 an expedition of the Seventh Cavalry led by George Armstrong Custer was sent into the Black Hills. They were there to protect railway surveyors and to find out if there was gold in the area. This expedition broke the Fort Laramie Treaty signed six years earlier.

Custer reported that the hills were filled with gold 'from the grassroots down' and from that moment the Black Hills were invaded by miners. In 1875 General Crook found over 1,000 miners there. The US army was unable to prevent this influx of miners, and the government was unwilling to do so. Some miners were attacked by the Sioux.

The government then made an offer of $6,000,000 to buy the Black Hills or $400,000 a year for the mineral rights. This was a ridiculous offer to the Sioux: to them the Black Hills were sacred as the place where their nation began. The government offer was rejected. At this point, relations between the Sioux and the government were very poor.

In December 1875 all Sioux were ordered to return to their reservation. In winter it was impossible for them to obey this order even if they wished to. There were approximately 7,000 Indians with Sitting Bull and Crazy Horse in the Powder River country, mainly Sioux but also Arapaho and Cheyenne. This number shows two things: the strength of the Indians' anger over the Black Hills, and Sitting Bull's great reputation as a leader. He had been consistently hostile to outside authorities and refused to live on the reservation. Many Sioux had turned to his leadership.

Sheridan's plan

By February 1876 the army was instructed to treat all Indians outside the reservation as hostile. General Philip Sheridan planned and ordered a three-pronged campaign. It involved three columns co-ordinating their movements. General George Crook would lead a column of 1,049 cavalry and infantry northwards from Fort Fetterman. Colonel Gibbon would lead a column of 450 infantry eastwards from Fort Shaw. General Terry, accompanied by Custer, would lead a column of 1,000 cavalry, infantry and GATLING GUNS westwards from Fort Abraham Lincoln. The three would trap the Indians between them.

THINK

Study Figure 21. Roughly how far apart are the three columns at the start of the campaign? What problems might this lead to?

FIGURE 21

A map showing the plan of General Sheridan's campaign.

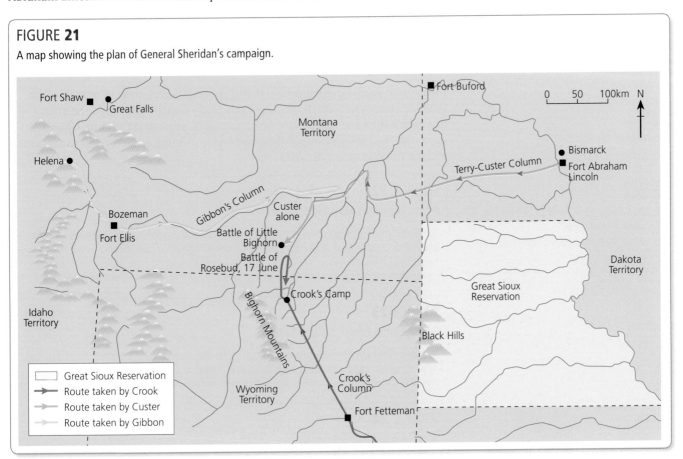

The plan's weaknesses

This plan had two major weaknesses. First, there was no effective liaison between Terry and Crook. Second, there was no serious attempt to find out how many Indians they might be facing. It was wrongly assumed that the Indians would number approximately 800 warriors, which any one of the three columns could have defeated. This estimate was based upon information from the Bureau of Indian Affairs, whose job it was to supervise the Sioux reservation.

The Battle of the Rosebud

The campaign started well. However, on 17 June 1876 it began to go wrong. General Crook's column was halted for a coffee break on the Rosebud Creek. While the officers were playing a game of whist, Crazy Horse led a full-frontal attack with about 1,500 warriors. By the end of the day Crook had lost 28 men killed and 63 wounded, and had fired 25,000 rounds of ammunition. He retreated southwards towards Fort Fetterman.

Meanwhile, Crazy Horse took his forces to join Sitting Bull on the Little Bighorn. His losses were 36 killed and 63 wounded. These were terribly high casualties for the Sioux.

Terry divided his forces

Four days later Gibbon and Terry joined forces on the Yellowstone River. General Terry again divided his forces. This time the infantry was to march along the Yellowstone towards the Little Bighorn. Custer was ordered to follow the Indian trail found by Major Reno – which was, in fact, the trail left by Crazy Horse – and approach the Little Bighorn from the south. He was offered 180 extra men from the Second Cavalry and Gatling guns, but refused them.

Custer rode south but then deliberately disobeyed orders. Instead of circling the Wolf Mountains he rode straight across them. By marching through the night and driving his men and horses hard he succeeded in arriving at the Little Bighorn a day early. The Indians camped there were not expecting an attack. But Custer's men and their horses were exhausted.

THINK

1   Do Sources 22, 23 and 24 all have the same view of Custer?
2   What faults do they accuse him of having?

SOURCE 22

Private Theodore Ewert, Seventh Cavalry.

The hardships and danger to his [Custer's] men, as well as the probable loss of life were worthy of but little consideration when dim visions of a star [indication of rank] floated before our Lieutenant Colonel.

SOURCE 23

Corporal Jacob Horner, Seventh Cavalry.

He [Custer] was too hard on the men and horses. He changed his mind too often. He was always right. He never conferred enough with his officers. When he got a notion, we had to go.

SOURCE 24

Major Marcus Reno, Seventh Cavalry.

Well sir, I had known General Custer a long time and I had no confidence in his ability as a soldier.

The Battle of the Little Bighorn, 1876

On the afternoon of 25 June Custer reached the camp of Sitting Bull and Crazy Horse on the Little Bighorn. Despite the warnings of his scouts he decided to attack. One scout, Mitch Bouyer, warned, 'If we go in there we will never come out.' Custer may have been afraid that the Indians would escape. He wanted a glorious victory. He supposedly said: 'The largest Indian camp on the North American continent is ahead and I am going to attack it.'

Having taken the decision to attack, Custer then split his forces. He sent Major Reno with 125 men to attack the southern end of the Indian camp. Captain Benteen, with 125 men, was sent to the south. Captain McDougall took charge of B Company and the pack train. Custer himself took 260 men further north to cross the river to attack the Indian camp.

Major Reno's attack was stopped by the Sioux and he retreated across the river, where he took up a defensive position. Reno was then joined by Benteen and his men. For the rest of the day they were surrounded and suffered many casualties. They had received an order from Custer to support him but did not do so. In the enquiry that took place after the battle, they argued that they were unable to follow Custer's last order because they were under attack.

What happened to Custer and his men is not clear as there were no survivors from his force. The evidence pieced together from archaeological excavations and the oral accounts of Indians indicates that Custer failed to cross the river. He turned back and made for higher ground but was overwhelmed by Crazy Horse's attack. Without the support of Reno and Benteen his force was totally outnumbered. Some of Custer's men may have panicked and tried to surrender or run away. Others fought together to the end. The only survivor was Curley, a Crow Indian scout, who disguised himself as a Sioux warrior.

FIGURE 25

A map showing the events of the Battle of the Little Bighorn.

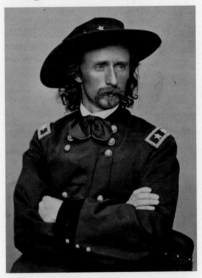

PROFILE

George Armstrong Custer

- Born 5 December 1839 in New Rumley, Ohio.
- Attended West Point Military Academy and on graduating went straight into the Union army.
- Served with distinction during the Civil War and went into the army in the West when it ended.
- Highly ambitious and controversial figure.
- Defeated Cheyenne at Battle of Washita, although some now view this as an attack on a village rather than a battle. He split his forces and some were cut off and killed
- Defeated and killed at the Battle of the Little Bighorn on 25 June 1876.

The Indians had the advantage of vastly superior numbers, 2,000 against 600. Some of them were better armed than the cavalrymen. These warriors had Winchester repeating rifles, which had been supplied to them by traders, while the cavalrymen were armed with Springfield single-shot rifles. While half the Indian forces defended their camp, Crazy Horse led the rest to surround Custer and his men. For Indians to fight a pitched battle was entirely new. Their normal tactic was to fight a delaying action while the women and children escaped and then withdraw themselves. This change reflected the leadership qualities of Crazy Horse.

ACTIVITY

Who was responsible for the defeat of the US army at the Battle of the Little Bighorn?

From the evidence on pages 42–46 write a paragraph on each of the following to explain how their actions contributed to the defeat of the US army at the Battle of the Little Bighorn:

● Custer
● His subordinates Reno and Benteen
● His superiors Terry, Crook and Sheridan
● The Sioux and their allies
● Crazy Horse.

Then write a final paragraph explaining which person or persons you think were most responsible for the defeat.

The aftermath

News of the defeat reached the rest of America on 4 July – the hundredth anniversary of the USA's independence. The public reaction was one of great shock. No effort was spared in supporting the army campaign that followed. Two new forts were built on the Yellowstone River and 2,500 reinforcements were sent west.

After the Battle of the Little Bighorn, the Indians split up into their bands. These bands were followed and attacked throughout the autumn and winter. One by one, the bands gave in and returned to the reservation. By the autumn most were back. On 5 May 1877, Crazy Horse and his followers rode into the reservation and surrendered. The day before, Sitting Bull and his followers had escaped over the border into Canada. The armed resistance of the Sioux was over.

With the Sioux defeated and the Northern Pacific Railroad having reached Bismarck, the destruction of the Northern buffalo herd began. By 1882 an estimated 5,000 hunters and skinners were at work, and by 1883 the Northern herd was destroyed.

Thereafter the government followed a deliberate policy of destroying all aspects of Indian culture. Through a series of laws the Sioux were forced to sell the Black Hills, the Powder River country and the Bighorn Mountains and were put under military rule. Eventually the reservation itself was split up into smaller reservations which split up the Sioux into smaller groups. Finally, their horses and weapons were taken. Never again were the Sioux able to fight in any great numbers against the army.

At first, rations on the reservations were given to the chiefs to distribute. Later, this policy was changed. Heads of families were encouraged to collect their own rations. This weakened the political power and authority of chiefs. In 1885 the government took control of all legal matters. Indians had lost any power to judge and punish members of their bands.

THINK

After studying both the battle and its aftermath do you think the Battle of the Little Bighorn should be seen as an Indian victory or defeat?

The Dawes General Allotment Act, 1887

In 1887 the DAWES GENERAL ALLOTMENT ACT was passed. This allowed the communal reservation lands to be broken up into individual plots. This was intended to completely destroy the power of chiefs and the tribal structure. Individual Indians who accepted a plot would become land-owning farmers and citizens of the United States. They would no longer need to go to their chiefs, or even see them, as they became self-sufficient. The Act also allowed any land left over to be sold to non-Indian farmers. It was another opportunity for land-grabbers to make money.

The ban on the Sioux leaving their reservations to hunt or make war on their enemies destroyed the economic foundations of their society. There was no buffalo meat for food, no buffalo hides for *tipis*, clothing and 97 other uses; and no opportunity to increase their wealth by stealing horses.

Feasts, dances and ceremonies, such as the Sun Dance, were banned. The power of the medicine men was undermined. There was little need for young men to seek visions to give them power in war and in the buffalo hunt. This spiritual 'gap' was then filled by the arrival of Christian missionaries.

Children, girls and boys, were taken from their parents and sent away to boarding school. There they were to be prepared for life in 'the white man's world'. One boarding-school founder defined his aim as to 'kill the Indian in him and save the man'. Children in the schools were not allowed to speak their own language and were punished if they did. They lived under military conditions and were taught to have no respect for their traditional way of life. By 1887, 2,020 Indian children were in the 117 boarding schools and 2,500 in the 110 day schools. The Sioux were unable to prevent their children being taken. If they resisted their rations were stopped until they had to give in. When the children returned from boarding school they often found that they fitted neither the Sioux world nor the world of other Americans.

SOURCE 26

Three Sioux boys at the Carlisle Indian School in Pennsylvania. The boys are photographed as new arrivals and again six months later.

THINK

Study Source 26. Look at the before and after photographs. What would have been the likely reaction of the boys' family to the changes? What would have been the likely reaction of the school's founder?

PRACTICE QUESTIONS

1 Describe two ways in which the Dawes Act contributed to the destruction of Plains Indian society.
2 Which of the following was the more important reason for the destruction of the Plains Indians' way of life on the reservations?
 ● Banning feasts, dances and ceremonies
 ● Forcing children to be sent away to boarding schools.
 Explain your answer with reference to both reasons.

PROFILE

Sitting Bull

- Born at Grand River, South Dakota, in around 1834.
- He became an important chief of the Sioux after Red Cloud made peace in 1868.
- Refused to live on the Great Sioux Reservation.
- After the Battle of the Little Bighorn he led his followers to safety in Canada.
- By 1881 hunger forced him and his followers to return to live on the reservation. He was still widely respected among the Sioux.
- On his return from Canada he took part in Buffalo Bill's Wild West Show for a while but returned to the reservation when there was a government attempt to take more Sioux lands.
- He became involved in the Ghost Dance Movement and was shot and killed by Indian police sent to arrest him on 15 December 1890.

The Battle of Wounded Knee

The effect of all these measures was to damage tribal structures and to weaken the Indians' self-belief. All the problems on the reservations led to an atmosphere of despair, and it was in that atmosphere that the final tragedy was played out. Just before dawn on New Year's Day 1889, a Paiute holy man called Wovoka received a vision. An Indian Messiah was coming. If the Indians remained peaceful and danced the Ghost Dance, then a new world would come. All the whites would disappear, the buffalo would return and all the dead Indians would come back to life. This Ghost Dance religion spread rapidly across the reservations in the West and reached the Sioux in 1890. It coincided with a time of great hunger on the reservations. The Sioux rations had been cut by the government and the drought in the summer of 1890 led their crops to fail. In this climate of hunger and despair the Ghost Dance held great appeal and it spread quickly among the Sioux.

The Indian agents were seriously worried. They tried to ban the Ghost Dance. When that failed they called in the army to help. The army treated it as a war situation. An attempt by Sioux Indian police was made to arrest Sitting Bull because of his involvement. His followers tried to prevent this, a scuffle broke out and Sitting Bull was shot dead by one of the Sioux policeman. Many of his followers fled to join the band of Big Foot, another of the chiefs leading the dance, whom the army were also moving to arrest.

On 28 December soldiers of the Seventh Cavalry caught up with Big Foot and his band. They were then taken under guard to camp at Wounded Knee. Next morning the soldiers obeying orders moved to disarm the Sioux. At least one Sioux warrior resisted and in the confusion that followed firing started. Were the Seventh Cavalry looking for a chance to revenge the Little Bighorn? Regardless of who was to blame, the soldiers were ready for trouble. They opened fire with repeating rifles and four Hotchkiss cannon. By the time the firing stopped 146 Indians and 25 soldiers were dead. The Indian dead were 102 adult men and women, 24 old men, 7 old women, 6 boys aged between five and eight years and 7 babies under the age of two. As one soldier said, 'It was a thing to melt the heart of a man, if it was not stone, to see those little children with their bodies shot to pieces.' Afterwards, the many Indian wounded were taken to the agency church. This awful massacre marked the end of the Plains Wars.

The end of the Indian Wars

Following the ending of the Indian Wars the western territories were settled. Once their governments were organised they were able to apply to join the Union. By 1890 Colorado, North Dakota, South Dakota, Montana, Washington, Idaho and Wyoming had all achieved statehood. Utah would have qualified for admission too but for the failure to make polygamy illegal there.

In 1889, the federal government opened up 2 million acres in Oklahoma for settlement. This was reservation land that had been occupied by the Creek and Seminole Indian nations. Before the opening date, many settlers, known as 'Sooners' because they were too soon, tried to sneak across the boundary to claim the best sites. Most were removed by the army, showing this could be done peacefully if the federal government possessed the will. At noon on 22 April 1889, a starting gun signalled that the territory was open for settlement. An estimated 50,000 settlers crossed the boundary, racing to claim the best land. By the end of the year Oklahoma had a population of 60,000.

SOURCE 28

Custer's Last Stand by Edgar Paxson, 1893.

THINK

What impressions do you think Source 28 is intended to give about Custer's Last Stand?

PRACTICE QUESTIONS

Interpretation A From *The Memoirs of General Philip Henry Sheridan of the US Army,* published in 1888. Sheridan had a long and distinguished career in the army fighting against Indians in the 1850s and 1860s, then in the American Civil War and then against Indians again in the 1870s and 1880s.

In those days the Plains were filled with so called "Indian scouts," whose common boast was of having slain scores of redskins, but the real scout—that is, a 'guide and trailer knowing the habits of the Indians—was very scarce. One of the best was Mr. William F. Cody ("Buffalo Bill"), whose renown has since become world-wide. On one occasion Cody brought me information about Indian villages from which Indian warriors were marauding against white settlements. I decided to move on them about the 1st of November. Many severe fights occurred between our troops and these marauders, and before November 1 over a hundred Indians were killed, yet from the ease with which the escaping savages would disappear only to fall upon remote settlements with pillage and murder, the results were by no means satisfactory.

Interpretation B John Burke, the manager of Buffalo Bill's Wild West Show. Burke had been a major in the Army and left around 1870. He was making a speech in 1909 in support of a campaign to build a monument to the American Indian race.

America owes the Indians at least an apology for the actions of civilized man and his greed in appropriating the red man's land. Of course, we must remember that this was all done in the name of progress. God had foreordained that it should be so. But that does not mean we should forget the Red Man. Let us build this monument as a lasting tribute to a dying race.

1 How does Interpretation A differ from Interpretation B in its attitude towards Indians?

Explain your answer based on what it says in Interpretations A and B.

2 Why might the authors of Intepretations A and B differ in their attitudes towards Indians?

Explain your answer using Interpretations A and B and your own contextual knowledge.

3 Which interpretation gives the more convincing opinion in its attitudes towards Indians?

Explain your answer based on your contextual knowledge and what it says in Interpretations A and B.

The closing of the frontier

In 1890, the US Census Bureau announced the end of the frontier. There was no longer a frontier line in the West. Nor were there any large areas of unsettled land. In 1893, Frederick Jackson Turner wrote an influential essay, 'The Significance of the Frontier in American History'. He claimed that American history had been a continual process of expansion and settlement of a series of 'wests': the west beyond the Atlantic Coast, over the Appalachian Mountains, the Mississippi Valley, onto the Great Plains and across the Rocky Mountains to the far west. He claimed that this had a great influence on the character of the American people. What Turner did not write about though was the experience of the Native Americans confined to reservations or those Hispanic Americans who had once lived in Mexico. Nor did he discuss the changes for African Americans. In 1895 all of these groups still had frontiers to cross.

FOCUS TASK

Which factors explain the resolution of the 'Indian problem'?

The resolution of the 'Indian problem' involved their military defeat, confinement to reservations and the destruction of their way of life.

1   Place each one of the following factors which played a part in this on a hexagon card. Write a brief summary on the back of each card.
    – US government policy
    – Manifest Destiny
    – Gold
    – The development of homesteading
    – The transcontinental railroads
    – The end of the American Civil War
    – The US army
    – Indian society and organisation
    – Indian tactics and weapons
    – The destruction of the buffalo
    – Reservations
    – Sioux beliefs about land
    – Total war
    – The Dawes Act.
2   Now arrange the factor hexagon cards until they fit together into the best explanation of how this happened.

TOPIC SUMMARY

Consolidation: Forging the nation

- The end of the Civil War in 1865 was a turning point in American history.
- After the Civil War a long process of reconstruction in the South took place.
- Black equality was not achieved due to the re-establishment of conservative white rule by 1877 in all Southern states and the failure of the federal government to fully enforce measures.
- The Indian Wars ending in 1877 saw the Plains Indians confined to reservations, the buffalo herds gone, and their way of life destroyed by government measures such as the Dawes Act of 1887.
- Meanwhile the population of the United States was swelled by massive immigration. Fourteen million people arrived between 1840 and 1890.
- Thousands flooded onto the Great Plains as homesteaders, encouraged by government legislation. There they solved the problems of living and farming and as their population grew the western territories became states and were admitted to the Union.
- By 1890 the US Census could announce that the frontier was closed.

KEY WORDS

Make sure you know what these terms mean and are able to define them confidently:
- Civil war
- Congress
- Conscription
- The Dawes Act
- Exodusters
- Federal
- Fort Laramie Treaty
- Forty-niner
- Immigration
- Ku Klux Klan
- Manifest Destiny
- Mormon
- Nation
- New Deal
- Perpetual Emigrating Fund
- President
- Reconstruction
- Reservation
- Settler
- Slavery
- Sod house
- State
- Territory
- Total War
- Veto
- Vigilante

ASSESSMENT FOCUS

Key

Focus words

Command words

Interpretation/knowledge reminder words

Your exam will include six questions on this topic. The question types will be the same every year, but the questions could be on any content from the specification, so you need to know it all!

We have provided one example of each kind of question. For questions based on interpretations we have used interpretations that you have already come across in this chapter. We have analysed each of the questions to highlight what you are being asked to do and written a sample answer with comments on how it could be improved.

Read Interpretations A and B and then answer questions 1–3. Interpretation A is Interpretation A, page 25. Interpretation B is Interpretation B, page 25.

Q1 How does Interpretation B **differ** from Interpretation A about what the conflict between the North and the South was about in the American Civil War?

Explain your answer **based on what it says in Interpretations A and B**. (4 marks)

- This answer provides a basic comparison between Interpretations A and B, but it needs to provide more detailed evidence.
- You need to be able to *explain* the differences in the content of the interpretations.
- *What extra evidence could you add to highlight the differences more completely?*

Sample answer

Interpretation A says that the American Civil War was fought over slavery. Interpretation B says that it was fought over the right to withdraw from the Union and that slavery was only a minor issue.

Q2 Why might the authors of Interpretations A and B have **a different interpretation** of what the conflict between the North and South in the American Civil War was about?

Explain your answer using **Interpretations A and B** and your **contextual knowledge**. (4 marks)

Sample answer

Interpretation A comes from a book written by a man who was a slave. Interpretation B is taken from the memoirs of the President of the Confederacy who is bound to be biased.

- This answer provides a good basis for development, but it would benefit from more analysis of the provenance. For example, you could explain how the impact of the Civil War on the two men's lives were so different, one freed from slavery and the other driven from political office, and how this would be likely to create differences. So make sure you think about the writers' viewpoints.
- Also think about the purpose of Interpretation B. This was written many years after the Civil War ended, after the end of Southern Reconstruction too, and Davis wanted to justify his actions.
- *Write two sentences for each interpretation on the provenance of each. You should focus on the purpose and attitudes of the two authors.*

Q3 Which interpretation gives the **more convincing opinion** about what the conflict between the North and the South in the American Civil War was about?

Explain your answer based on your **contextual knowledge** and what it says in **Interpretations A and B**. (8 marks)

Sample answer

Interpretation A is right to say that the American Civil War was a war over slavery and certainly that is how many Americans would have viewed it by the end of the century. On the other hand, in Interpretation B, while the writer downplays slavery as a minor issue, he does have a point. For many people in the Confederacy it was a war to defend the power of the individual states against their being taken over by the federal government.

However, after Lincoln's Emancipation Proclamation in 1863 it certainly did become a war fought for the abolition of slavery. So Interpretation A is more convincing as an explanation.

- This answer provides a basic analysis of the two interpretations through the use of some factual knowledge. Ideally you could extend it further to argue in more depth.
- However, it is important that the knowledge is used as part of the analysis of the content of the interpretation, rather than being 'free-standing' as 'what I know about the topic'.
- *Think about the tone and language of each interpretation. What words and phrases could you use to describe them? Does one seem more objective than the other?*

Q4 Describe two problems faced by the Mormons in settling at **Salt Lake**.

(4 marks)

Sample answer

The Mormons faced the problem of a lack of water when they arrived in the area of the Great Salt Lake under their leader Brigham Young. They also had to decide how to divide up the land.

> – This brief answer introduces two problems, but they are only stated, and so need to be more fully described.
>
> – *List TWO details that you could add to EACH of the two short sentences above in order to make the description more precise for each.*

Q5 **In what ways** were the lives of the Plains Indians affected by the arrival of the railroads on the Great Plains from the **1870s** onwards?

Explain your answer. (8 marks)

Sample answer

Plains Indians suffered great changes in their lives from the 1870s onwards. The railroads disturbed the buffalo and brought the buffalo hunters. The railroad companies sold land to the homesteaders who flooded onto Indian lands. The railroads also shipped cattle back east from the cattle ranches. When the Indians were at war with the US army the railroads could quickly bring reinforcements.

> – This answer mentions several aspects of how Plains Indians were affected. However, they could be presented with much more factual detail, rather than just a list.
>
> – *Write a list of evidence that could be included to support each of the sentences in the answer.*

Q6 **Which** of the following was the **more important reason** why homesteaders flooded onto the Great Plains in the 1860s and 1870s?
- The ending of the Civil War 1865
- The actions of the US government

Explain your answer with reference to **both reasons**. (12 marks)

Sample answer

The end of the Civil War in 1865 was an important point in the settlement of the West. Thousands of soldiers were demobilised. Many of them were unable to settle back into their old lives and they wanted to head west to start a new life.

In the Southern states many ex-slaves wanted an escape from the poverty of share cropping and from prejudice and persecution. They too went west in search of a new life. In the 1880s many of them, the 'Exodusters', went to Kansas.

The end of the Civil War also meant that the capital and labour (including ex-soldiers) were available to build the transcontinental railroads. Railroad companies took prospective settlers out onto the Plains, sold them the land and supported them by bringing the materials they needed to farm successfully.

> – This answer evaluates both bullet points in turn. It reaches a judgement based on precise arguments. The relationships between the two bullet points are explored.
>
> – *Working backwards, read through the essay again and write out the plan that it must have been based on. You can then look at the plan and see why it was the starting point for this comprehensive answer.*

Finally, the end of the Civil War meant that the civilian militias could be replaced by seasoned soldiers who were able to protect the settlers from attack by the Plains Indians.

On the other hand, the US government played an important part too. The Homestead Act passed in 1862 was deliberately intended to encourage settlement. Each family could claim 160 acres of free land. All they had to do was settle on it, build a home and farm it for five years. Not only did this encourage the ex-soldiers to become homesteaders but also thousands of the immigrants who arrived in the United States of America from Europe. Later Acts, the Timber Culture Act and the Desert Land Act encouraged the settlement of less fertile areas too.

It was also the US government that gave the railroad companies great grants of land to help finance the building of the transcontinental railroads that were so important to the homesteaders.

Therefore, both were important in explaining why homesteaders flooded onto the Great Plains in the 1860s and 1870s. The ending of the Civil War freed up the manpower and money but it was the actions of the government that were crucial. Without the attraction of free land provided by the Homestead Act and the aid of the railroads made possible by government land grants and support, the settlement would not have taken place at anything like the rate it did. Therefore it can be argued that the actions of the US government were more important.

> Now write your own answers to the questions on pages 51–52 using the teacher's feedback to help you.

Germany 1890–1945: Democracy and Dictatorship

This period study focuses on the development of Germany during a turbulent half century of change. It was a period of democracy and dictatorship – the development and collapse of the Weimar Republic and the rise and fall of Nazi Germany.

You will be studying the following aspects of this development of democracy and dictatorship:

- The political aspects of a changing country, as Germany shifted from the rule of an autocratic Kaiser, to a Republic with a President, and finally to a dictatorship.
- The economic aspects of a country which saw times of progression and depression across the period.
- The social and cultural reflection of Germany's development, in the form of shifting ideas on freedom of expression.
- The role of ideas in influencing change, such as nationalism before the First World War and Nazism between the wars.
- The role of key individuals and groups in shaping change, and the impact the development of Germany had on them, for example, Kaiser Wilhelm II, Stresemann, and Hitler.

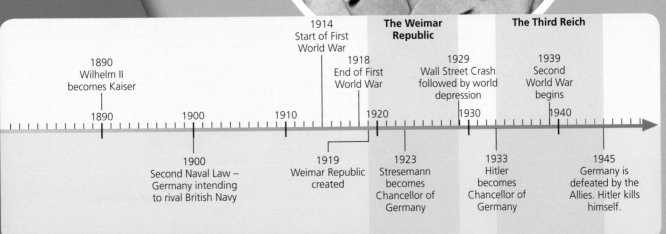

1890 Wilhelm II becomes Kaiser

1900 Second Naval Law – Germany intending to rival British Navy

1914 Start of First World War

1918 End of First World War

1919 Weimar Republic created

The Weimar Republic

1923 Stresemann becomes Chancellor of Germany

1929 Wall Street Crash followed by world depression

The Third Reich

1933 Hitler becomes Chancellor of Germany

1939 Second World War begins

1945 Germany is defeated by the Allies. Hitler kills himself.

In the quarter-century before the First World War, Germany was ruled by Kaiser Wilhelm II. This was at a time when Germany, as a new nation, was ambitious and keen to increase its power and expand its territory. In 1918 Germany faced the consequences of defeat and in the 1920s a period of attempted recovery.

In this part of the topic you will study the following:

- Kaiser Wilhelm II, the difficulties of ruling Germany and the strength of autocracy by 1914.
- The impact of the First World War and the extent to which Germany was altered by 1918.
- The Weimar Republic: Economic and political challenges and its condition by 1929.

2.1 Germany and the growth of democracy

● Kaiser Wilhelm II and the difficulties of ruling Germany

Germany had only been a united country since 1871. Before that what we call Germany had been made up of several independent states, the most important of which was Prussia.

This new empire was created in 1871 after victory against France in 1870. Berlin, the capital of Prussia, became the capital of the empire. The KAISER (Emperor) had complete control over the appointment of the Chancellor, the chief minister of Germany. The Chancellor had power over policies and appointments and was answerable only to the Kaiser. There was a parliament – the REICHSTAG – but this had very limited power and could be ignored by the Chancellor.

FIGURE 1

The German Empire, 1871.

In the 1870s and 1880s, Otto von Bismarck was Chancellor, and in practice wielded more power than the Kaiser, Wilhelm I. Bismarck had done much to unify the country, by introducing a national coinage, postal service, law system, railway network and army. Bismarck also attempted to assimilate ethnic minority groups within the new empire, such as the Poles in the east, the Danes in the north and the French in Alsace-Lorraine in the west. However, he was less successful in making these other nationalities adopt German IMPERIAL ambitions.

Germany wanted an empire, like Britain, and therefore wanted to expand its territory in Europe and in other continents.

Wilhelm I's son, Frederick III, reigned for just ninety-nine days before succumbing to a long-standing illness. He was succeeded by his son, Wilhelm II. Unlike his grandfather, Kaiser Wilhelm II was determined to control German affairs himself rather than the Chancellor. Indeed, none of his four Chancellors could rival the power that Bismarck had enjoyed. Wilhelm II's youthful optimism seemed to match well the ambitions of the new empire.

However, Wilhelm II's character did not suit his position as Kaiser. He was somewhat unstable in mood and prone to violent rages. It has also been suggested that he was a repressed homosexual. He had been born with a withered left hand and was acutely aware of this defect, especially in his capacity as Commander-in-Chief of the armed forces. Historians are not in full agreement about his character, but they all agree that he lacked the ability to govern effectively or command the army.

Kaiser Wilhelm II was determined not to rule Germany in the same way as Bismarck. He wanted Germany to adopt a new course with the focus on its international position and status. He wanted a world policy (WELTPOLITIK). He believed that with Germany's industrial growth, rising population and nationalist ambition, it could achieve its 'place in the sun'. He had seen the European powers seize colonies in Africa (the so-called 'Scramble for Africa'), and wanted Germany to join in – to build an overseas empire in Africa and elsewhere, for example in the Far East. To achieve this he believed that Germany needed a navy to match Great Britain's and an army that could defeat all other powers in Europe. Many Germans agreed with him.

SOURCE 2

From a letter to Philip Eulenburg, Wilhelm's close friend, from von Bülow shortly after he became Chancellor in 1900.

I place my faith increasingly in the Emperor. He is so impressive! He is the most impressive Hohenzollern [family name] who has ever lived. In a manner which I have never seen before, he combines genius – the most genuine and original genius – with the clearest good sense.

SOURCE 3

From a secret letter written by Eulenburg to Bülow, during the Kaiser's North Sea cruise in 1903.

His [Wilhelm's] face is completely distorted by rage … There can no longer be any question of self-control … I predict a breakdown of the nerves.

SOURCE 4

From *Kaiser Wilhelm II, New Interpretations* by J. G. C. Rohl, 1982.

There were periods when Wilhelm II became totally obsessed with one idea to such a degree that everything touching upon it even remotely produced in him a violent rage … It was at this stage, surely, with his utterly relentless pursuit of one goal and angry determination to brook no opposition, that Kaiser Wilhelm's personality had the greatest impact on policy making.

FACTFILE

Wilhelm II's European relations

A complicating factor in Germany's foreign policy was the inter-relationship of the royal families of Europe. Wilhelm was a grandchild of Queen Victoria, and therefore her eldest son, Bertie, who became Edward VII in 1901, was his uncle. He resented his uncle (a mere heir to the throne!) treating him, not as Kaiser, but just as a nephew. He was a first cousin of Bertie's eldest son who became George V in 1910. He was also a cousin of Nicholas who became Tsar Nicholas II of Russia in 1894 and also a cousin of his wife, Alexandra. He was also related to other royal families in Norway, Spain and Greece. Wilhelm's character did not endear him to many of the royal family members who found him overbearing and arrogant. Nevertheless, Wilhelm stayed on close terms with Queen Victoria, and was at her bedside when she died in January 1901. However, this relationship did not prevent the two countries going to war against each other in 1914.

THINK

1   Study Sources 2–4. For each of the three sources, summarise what is said about the character of Kaiser Wilhelm II.
2   In what ways do the sources agree or disagree?

The growth of parliamentary government

The Kaiser had extensive powers. He alone had the right to appoint and dismiss the Chancellor and his State Secretaries, completely independently of any views in the Reichstag. Government ministers were answerable only to the Kaiser. No major decision could be taken without the Kaiser's agreement.

The Reichstag could discuss, amend and vote on new legislation, but it could not decide on the topics in question. That was totally under the control of the Kaiser and his ministers. Even if it had had more powers, the Reichstag would have been limited in its decision-making.

Yet, at the same time as the Kaiser dominated decision-making, political parties developed in terms of organisation and importance. There were several main political parties, but never in the years 1871–1914 did any one of them come close to gaining a majority. In the early years of Wilhelm II's reign, the RIGHT-WING conservative parties usually joined together to pass government laws. However, by 1914 these parties had declined in influence. Others gained support, especially the more LEFT-WING SOCIAL DEMOCRAT PARTY, which appealed to Germany's growing numbers of industrial workers.

Each of Germany's 25 states had control over their own domestic matters. However, this control diminished as the national government passed legislation in areas such as communications, expansion of the army and navy, and social insurance schemes.

This meant that, while all men were eligible to vote, in practice the direction of government policy was controlled almost entirely by the Kaiser and his ministers. Many members of the middle class were happy with this right-wing dominated government because they were afraid of the growing political strength of the industrial workers. This meant that the people in power were mostly nationalist in their views. They were also traditionally hostile to the Jews. This is known as anti-Semitism.

Industrialisation

The industrial strength of Germany increased rapidly under Wilhelm II. For example, in 1880 Germany had only been producing half the amount of steel produced by Britain, but by 1914 was producing more than twice as much. By 1914 Germany was producing one-third of the world's electrical goods. Its telephone system was more advanced than that of any other country. Germany led the world in the chemical and steel industries. The engineering firms of Bosch and Siemens were known worldwide. Foreign trade flourished as exports rose rapidly.

SOURCE 5

A photograph from the Krupp Steel Works in the 1880s. It shows Bessemer converters in action. The process was the first cheap method for MASS PRODUCTION of steel.

The population grew from just over 40 million in 1871 to nearly 68 million in 1914. This rapid increase helped to provide manpower for the growing industrial cities. By 1914 only one-third of the labour force still worked in agriculture, and as a result food imports rose quickly, reaching about one-fifth of Germany's needs by 1914.

Social reform and the growth of socialism

German society was dominated by the traditional ruling classes – both in the cities and on the land. AUTHORITARIANISM was accepted by most as the norm in society as a whole. In particular, the middle-class elements in society supported the social structure of the empire, happy to thrive in its developing wealth and power. Thus most political parties, both right-wing and centre, accepted the authoritarian nature of German rule.

However, the growing numbers of industrial workers did pose a possible threat to the traditional structure of society based on a land-owning aristocracy – as they did in other European countries. The ruling classes were afraid of the socialist movement that was growing in strength. Successive governments had tried to pacify socialist demands by enacting social reforms, such as the introduction of old age pensions in 1889 – 20 years before their introduction in Britain. Sickness and accident insurance schemes were also introduced at the same time, and by 1911 this covered nearly 14 million Germans. However, many workers remained dissatisfied and this led to a continued growth in support for the Social Democrat Party (SPD), whose socialism encompassed the COMMUNIST ideology of Karl Marx. In 1912 the Social Democrats gained nearly one-third of the seats in the Reichstag.

The influence of Prussian militarism

Prussia was by far the most important of the 25 states within Germany. It had two-thirds of the population and over half the territory. Prussia had a proud tradition of military activity and the army swore an oath of allegiance to the Kaiser. The influence of the military chiefs often determined German foreign policy which was concerned with expansion. Long-established countries on Germany's borders were often viewed with suspicion. This special status of the army did not help the development of DEMOCRATIC systems of government. Indeed, the government and many civilians admired the army and what it stood for in this newly created country.

The domestic importance of the Navy Laws

To Wilhelm II a large powerful navy was essential to his ambitions for Germany. In addition to expanding the size of the German army, he wanted to develop a navy that could match the British Royal Navy. It was Admiral von Tirpitz who argued that Germany needed large battleships that could compete with those of Britain. Success over the British navy would ensure that Germany could achieve world power for itself. A large ship-building programme would frighten the British government which would then be more amenable to Germany gaining colonies and trade overseas. Thus, after Tirpitz became State Secretary of the Navy in 1897, several laws were passed. These had a profound effect on Anglo-German relations, as well as affecting the lives and attitudes of millions of Germans.

The First Navy Law was passed in 1898, in spite of opposition from the Conservative Party and the Social Democrat Party. The law allowed for the addition of seven battleships, which would be built in the next three years in addition to the twelve Germany already possessed. These extra battleships would not be enough to match either the British or the French navies, but this law marked a turning point in German foreign policy.

FIGURE 6

Germany's foreign trade (in millions of marks).

Year	Marks
1880	2,977
1890	3,410
1900	4,753
1910	7,475
1913	10,097

FACTFILE

Karl Marx and Communism

Karl Marx (1818–83) was a German writer. He believed that history was dominated by class struggle – that is, conflict between the different classes in society. Those who believed in his theories believed that the middle classes would take over from the aristocracy and monarchy, and then a further revolution would result in rule by the working classes.

Marx is regarded as the founder of modern COMMUNISM.

In 1900, during the Boer War conflict in South Africa, the Second Naval Law was passed. The German government took the opportunity to sympathise with the Boers, who were fighting against the British. This Second Naval Law doubled the size of the fleet to 38 battleships. It was clear that the German navy was not just patrolling its coastlines; it saw its primary objective as rivalling the British navy. In Germany the policy had the effect of encouraging imperialist attitudes and a fear of British ambitions.

In the early 1900s , more Naval Laws were passed in the Reichstag, increasing the size of the navy slightly and illustrating its importance. International crises (see Chapter 5, page 210) encouraged the belief among many Germans that Britain had ambitions to be even more powerful and that its policy was to deny German ambitions to become a colonial empire. Therefore, from 1902 onwards an Anglo-German naval ARMS RACE developed.

The Kaiser was an enthusiastic supporter of naval expansion. He believed that it was the key to fulfilling his ambitions for the creation of a more powerful German Empire. Meanwhile, traditional military leaders argued that it would be the army that would be the key to success in future conflict, and therefore the armed forces also needed to be maintained ready for any conflict.

FOCUS TASK

How strong was autocratic rule in Germany by 1914?

1   Create your own spider diagram to assess the strength of autocratic rule in Germany. In the centre of your page write the following statement: 'Strength of traditional, autocratic rule'

2   On one side of your diagram, in one colour, add points that show that the Kaiser had full control and that AUTOCRACY was strong in Germany. On the other side, in a different colour, note the factors that were threatening to weaken autocracy.

3   Once you have completed your diagram, write a paragraph to sum up the strength of autocratic rule in Germany by 1914.

SOURCE 7

SMS Rhineland, launched in 1908. This battleship was 146 metres long, it could travel at 20 knots and could carry over 1,000 men. It had 40 guns of different sizes and 5 torpedoes.

PRACTICE QUESTIONS

Interpretation A King Edward VII describing Kaiser Wilhelm II in the early 1900s. Edward was the Kaiser's uncle. At the time tension and rivalry was building between Britain and Germany.

Wilhelm is the most brilliant failure in history. He is highly talented but superficial, a neurotic braggart and romantic dreamer, a militaristic poseur and passionate slaughterer of wild animals. I recall Bismarck said of him that he wanted every day to be his birthday. Another wit remarked that he wanted to be the bride at every wedding, the stag at every hunt, and the corpse at every funeral.

Interpretation B Count Bernard von Bulow writing in his memoirs about serving in Kaiser Wilhelm's government in the 1890s and 1900s. Bulow held several important offices in the Kaiser's government, including Reich Chancellor. Bulow died in 1929 and his memoirs were published in 1931.

As I worked with the Kaiser I grew fonder and fonder of him. He is the greatest of his family line to have ever lived. He combines genius with good sense. His vivid imagination lifts me above the petty detail of government, yet he could judge soberly what is or is not possible and attainable. And what vitality! And how quick and sure his understanding was!

Read Interpretations A and B and answer Questions 1–3.

1   How does Interpretation A differ from Interpretation B about the Kaiser? Explain your answer based on what it says in Interpretations A and B.

2   Why might these two historians have a different interpretation of the Kaiser?

   Explain your answer using Interpretations A and B and your own contextual knowledge.

3   Which interpretation gives the more convincing opinion about the Kaiser? Explain your answer based on your contextual knowledge and what it says in Interpretations A and B.

The impact of the First World War

In 1914 the Germans were a proud people. Their Kaiser, virtually a dictator, was celebrated for his achievements. Their army was probably the finest in the world. A journey through the streets of Berlin in 1914 would have revealed prospering businesses and a well-educated and well-fed workforce. There was great optimism about the power and strength of Germany.

Four years later a similar journey would have revealed a very different picture. Although little fighting had taken place in Germany itself, the war had still destroyed much of the old Germany. The proud German army was defeated. The German people were surviving on turnips and bread. A flu epidemic was sweeping the country, killing thousands of people already weakened by rations.

FIGURE 8

War weariness, economic problems and defeat in 1918.

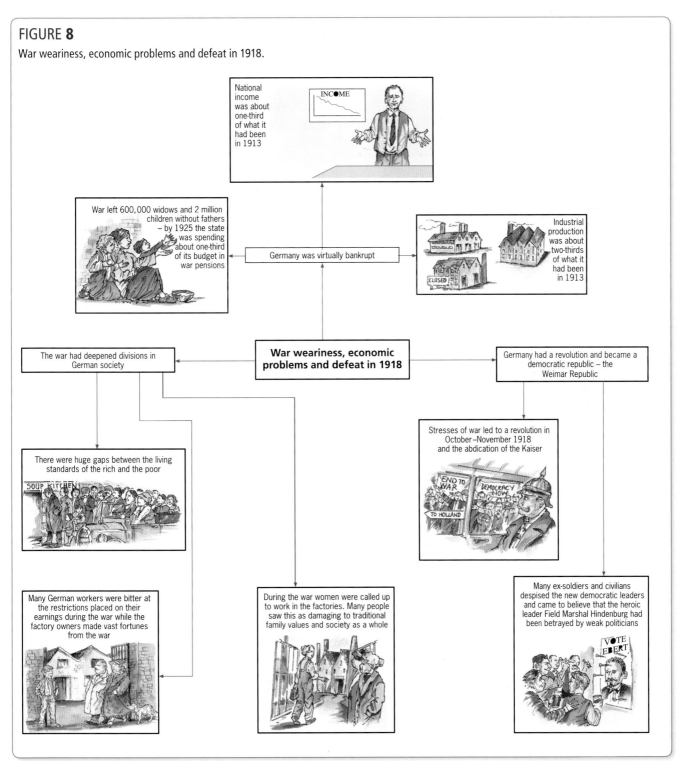

SOURCE 9

A cartoon from *Punch* magazine, 1919.

GIVING HIM ROPE?

GERMAN CRIMINAL (*to Allied Police*). "HERE, I SAY, STOP! YOU'RE HURTING ME! [*Aside*
IF I ONLY WHINE ENOUGH I MAY BE ABLE TO WRIGGLE OUT OF THIS YET."

The end of the monarchy, November 1918

In autumn 1918 the Allies had clearly won the war. Germany was in a state of chaos, as you have seen in Figure 8. The Allies offered Germany peace, but under strict conditions. One condition was that Germany should become more democratic. When the Kaiser refused, sailors in northern Germany mutinied and took over the town of Kiel. This triggered other revolts. The Kaiser's old enemies, the Socialists, led uprisings of workers and soldiers in other German ports. Soon, other German cities followed. In Bavaria an independent Socialist REPUBLIC was declared. On 9 November 1918 the Kaiser, realising he had little choice, abdicated his throne and left Germany for the Netherlands.

Post-war problems in Germany

Germans felt betrayed. The end of the war had come suddenly and unexpectedly; their Kaiser had run away; the new government had to face all the problems that existed – political uncertainties, economic problems, and a crisis in German society. In addition, a devastating outbreak of flu had swept across western Europe and killed many Germans who were suffering from malnourishment and had little resistance to germs.

German reparations

At the end of any conflict, the victorious countries sought compensation from those NATIONS responsible for starting the war. At the conclusion to the First World War, Germany's REPARATIONS were spelt out in the Treaty of Versailles, decided upon by the British, American and French leaders.

The details of this are covered in Chapter 6 on pages 245–50, but the main terms are given in the Factfile here.

Financial reparations were also enforced by the treaty. The bill, announced in April 1921, was set at £6,600 million, to be paid in annual instalments. This was 2 per cent of Germany's annual output. The Germans protested that this was an intolerable strain on the economy, which they were struggling to rebuild after the war, but their protests were ignored.

The invasion of the Ruhr

The first instalment of £50 million was paid in 1921, but in 1922 nothing was paid. Ebert, Socialist leader and German Chancellor, did his best to play for time and to negotiate concessions from the Allies, but the French in particular ran out of patience. They too had war debts to pay to the USA. So in January 1923 French and Belgian troops entered the Ruhr, an industrial area of Germany near the French border. This was quite legal under the Treaty of Versailles. They began to take what was owed to them in the form of raw materials and goods.

The results of the occupation of the Ruhr were disastrous for Germany. The government ordered the workers to carry out passive resistance, which meant to go on strike. That way, there would be nothing for the French to take away. The French reacted harshly, killing over 100 workers and expelling over 100,000 protesters from the region. More importantly, the halt in industrial production in Germany's most important region caused the collapse of the German currency.

FACTFILE

Treaty of Versailles terms

As a result of the terms of the Treaty of Versailles, signed in June 1919, Germany:

- was blamed for the war (WAR GUILT clause)
- lost its overseas empire
- lost some territory in Europe
- was forbidden to join with Austria
- could not join the League of Nations
- was limited in its armed forces.

As a result of the Treaty of Versailles, Germany lost:

- approximately 10 per cent of its territory
- 12.5 per cent of its population
- 16 per cent of its coal fields and almost half of its iron and steel industry.

SOURCE 10

A 1923 German poster discouraging people from buying French and Belgian goods, as long as Germany is under occupation.

SOURCE 11

The memories of Jutta Rudiger, a German woman living in the Ruhr during the French occupation.

There was a lot of official harassment. There was widespread hunger, squalor and poverty and – what really affected us – there was humiliation. The French ruled with an iron hand. If they disliked you walking on the pavement, for instance, they'd come along with their riding crops and you'd have to walk in the road.

FOCUS TASK

How had the war and post-war settlement changed Germany?

Use the information on pages 53–60 and your own research to complete the following task.

1 Use the map on page 54 to draw a simple outline of Germany in 1914. Annotate your map in one colour with words and images to indicate the situation in Germany at that time. Include who was in charge, the population of Germany, its main industries, etc.

2 Now annotate your map in a similar way, using a second colour, to show how things have changed by 1919. Shade in any areas of land which have been removed, and cross out any resources which have been lost. Add words and drawings to indicate the situation by 1919.

3 Now write a paragraph under your map to summarise the main changes which have taken place in Germany between 1914 and 1919.

PRACTICE QUESTIONS

Read Interpretations A and B and then answer Questions 1–3.

Interpretation A The imposition of reparations on the Weimar Republic. This was written in 1976 by Egon Larsen, who had been a German journalist in the 1920s.

As the terms of peace became known, we came to realise what it meant to lose a war against two dozen countries. The cost of reparations, to be paid by a Germany which had lost its economic power, was shattering.

Interpretation B British politician Winston Churchill writing in 1948. Churchill had been a member of the British government in 1919 when the Versailles Treaty and reparations were negotiated.

The economic clauses of the Treaty were malignant and silly to an extent that made them obviously futile. Germany was condemned to pay reparations on a fabulous scale. The multitudes remained plunged in ignorance of the simplest economic facts, and their leaders, seeking their votes, did not dare to undeceive them. The triumphant Allies continued to assert that they would squeeze Germany "till the pips squeaked". All this had a potent bearing on the prosperity of the world and the mood of the German Race. In fact, however, these clauses were never enforced. On the contrary, whereas about £1,000 million of German assets were appropriated by the victorious Powers, more than £1,500 millions were lent a few years later to Germany principally by the United States and Great Britain, thus enabling the ruin of the war to be rapidly repaired in Germany.

1 How does Interpretation B differ from Interpretation A about the impact of reparations on Germans in the early 1920s?

Explain your answer based on what it says in Interpretations A and B.

2 Why might the authors of Interpretations A and B have a different interpretation about the impact of reparations on Germans in the early 1920s?

Explain your answer using Interpretations A and B and your contextual knowledge.

3 Which interpretation gives the more convincing opinion about the impact of reparations on Germans in the early 1920s?

Explain your answer based on your contextual knowledge and what it says in Interpretations A and B.

FIGURE 12

The rising cost of a loaf of bread in Berlin.

Date	Number of marks
1918	0.63
1922	163
January 1923	250
July 1923	3,465
September 1923	1,512,000
November 1923	201,000,000,000

FIGURE 13

The exchange rate value of the mark in pounds.

1921   £1 = 500 marks

Nov 1923   £1 = 14,000,000,000,000 marks

SOURCE 14

E. Dobert, *Convert to Freedom*, 1941.

Billion-mark notes were quickly handed on as though they burned one's fingers, for tomorrow one would no longer pay in notes but in bundles of notes … One afternoon I rang Aunt Louise's bell. The door was opened merely a crack. From the dark came an odd broken voice: 'I've used 60 billion marks' worth of gas. My milk bill is 1 million. But all I have left is 2,000 marks. I don't understand any more.'

THINK

1   Use Figure 12 to work out how much bread a one-billion mark banknote could buy in July 1923 and November 1923.
2   Use the sources and figures on this page to describe in your own words how ordinary Germans were affected by the collapse of the mark.

PRACTICE QUESTION

Which of the following was the more important reason for the collapse of the German economy by 1923?

- The harshness of the Treaty of Versailles, including reparations payments.
- The hyperinflation that had developed by 1923.

Explain your answer with reference to both reasons.

Hyperinflation

SOURCE 15

A photograph taken in 1923 showing a woman using banknotes to start her fire.

Because it had no goods to trade, the government simply printed more money. For the government this seemed an attractive solution. It paid off its debts in worthless marks, including war loans of over £2,200 million. The great industrialists were able to pay off all their debts as well.

This set off a chain reaction. With so much money in circulation, prices and wages rocketed, but people soon realised that this money was worthless. Wages began to be paid daily instead of weekly. Workers needed wheelbarrows to carry home their wages. The price of goods could rise between joining the back of a queue in a shop and reaching the front!

Poor people suffered, but the greatest casualties were the richer Germans – those with savings. Prosperous middle-class families would find that their savings in the bank, which might have bought them a house in 1921, by 1923 would not even buy a loaf of bread. Pensioners found that their previously ample monthly pension would not even buy a cup of coffee.

It was clear to all, both inside and outside Germany, that the situation needed urgent action. In August 1923 a new government under Gustav Stresemann took over. He called off the passive resistance in the Ruhr. He called in the worthless marks and burned them, replacing them with a new currency called the Rentenmark. He negotiated to receive American loans under the Dawes Plan. He even renegotiated the reparations payments (see page 69). The economic crisis was solved very quickly. Some historians suggest that this is evidence that Germany's problems were not as severe as its politicians had made out.

It was also increasingly clear, however, that the HYPERINFLATION had done great political damage to the Weimar government. Right-wing opponents had yet another problem to blame the government for, and the government had lost the support of the middle classes.

● Weimar Germany

The day after the Kaiser fled, Friedrich Ebert became the new leader of the Republic of Germany. He immediately signed an ARMISTICE with the Allies. The war was over. He also announced to the German people that the new Republic was giving them freedom of speech, freedom of worship and better working conditions. A new constitution was drawn up (see Factfile and Figure 16).

The success of the new government depended on the German people accepting an almost instant change from the traditional, AUTOCRATIC German system of government to this new democratic system. The prospects for this did not look good.

Weimar democracy

The reaction of politicians in Germany was unenthusiastic. Ebert had opposition from both right and left. On the right wing, nearly all the Kaiser's former advisers remained in their positions in the army, judiciary, civil service and industry. They restricted what the new government could do. Many still hoped for a return to rule by the Kaiser. A powerful myth developed that men such as Ebert had stabbed Germany in the back and caused German defeat in the war. On the left wing there were many Communists who believed that at this stage what Germany actually needed was a Communist revolution just like Russia's in 1917.

Despite this opposition, in January 1919 free elections took place for the first time in Germany's history. Ebert's party won a majority and he became the President of the Weimar Republic. It was called this because, to start with, the new government met in the small town of Weimar rather than in the German capital, Berlin. Even in February 1919, Berlin was thought to be too violent and unstable.

THINK

Study the Factfile on the Weimar Constitution and Figure 16.

1   What aspects of the Constitution made Weimar Germany seem very democratic?
2   What aspects might suggest the possibility of either weak government or one person being able to take charge?

FIGURE 16

The Weimar Constitution.

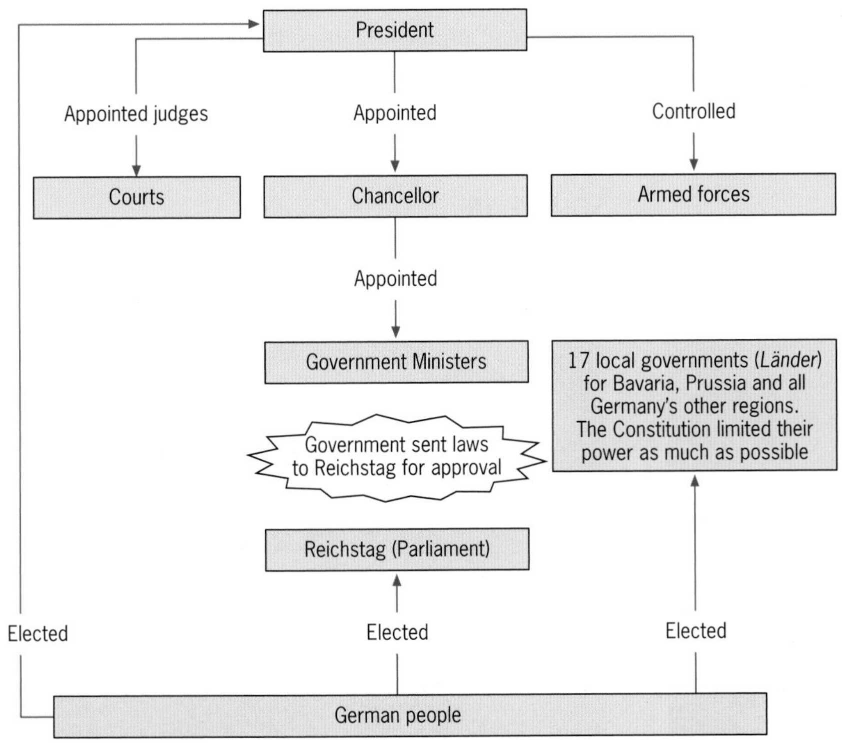

FACTFILE

The Weimar Constitution

- Before the war Germany had had no real DEMOCRACY. The Kaiser was virtually a dictator.
- The Weimar Constitution, on the other hand, attempted to set up probably the most democratic system in the world where no individual could gain too much power.
- All Germans over the age of 20 could vote.
- There was a system of PROPORTIONAL REPRESENTATION – if a party gained 20 per cent of the votes, they gained 20 per cent of the seats in the Parliament (Reichstag).
- The Chancellor was responsible for day-to-day government, but he needed the support of half the Reichstag.
- The Head of State was the President. The President stayed out of day-to-day government. In a crisis he could rule the country directly through Article 48 of the Constitution. This gave him emergency powers, which meant he did not have to consult the Reichstag.

Weimar Germany: Political change and unrest, 1919–23

From the start the new government had to establish itself at a time of political unrest as well as economic and social problems.

The threat from the Left: The Spartacists

One left-wing group was a Communist party known as the SPARTACISTS. They were led by Karl Liebknecht and Rosa Luxemburg. Their party was much like Lenin's BOLSHEVIKS, who had just taken power in Russia. They argued strongly against Ebert's plans for a democratic Germany. They wanted a Germany ruled by workers' councils or soviets.

Early in 1919 the Spartacists launched their bid for power. Joined by rebel soldiers and sailors, they set up soviets in many towns. Not all soldiers were on the side of the Spartacists, however. Some anti-Communist ex-soldiers had formed themselves into VIGILANTE groups called *FREIKORPS*. Ebert made an agreement with the commanders of the army and the *Freikorps* to put down the Spartacist rebellion. Bitter street fighting followed between the Spartacists and *Freikorps*. Both sides were heavily armed and casualties were high. The *Freikorps* crushed the rebellion and Liebknecht and Luxemburg were murdered. The Spartacists had failed, but another Communist revolt was soon to follow.

This time it emerged in Bavaria in the south of Germany. Bavaria was still an independent socialist state led by Kurt Eisner, who was Ebert's ally. In February 1919 he was murdered by political opponents. The Communists in Bavaria seized the opportunity to declare a soviet republic there. Ebert used the same tactics as he had against the Spartacists. The *Freikorps* moved in to crush the revolt in May 1919 and around 600 Communists were killed.

In 1920 there was more Communist agitation in the Ruhr industrial area. Again police, army and *Freikorps* clashed with Communists, resulting in 2,000 casualties.

Ebert's ruthless measures against the Communists created lasting bitterness between them and his Socialist Party. However, it gained approval from many in Germany. Ebert was terrified that Germany might go the same way as Russia (at that time rocked by bloody CIVIL WAR). Many Germans shared his fears. Even so, despite these defeats, the Communists remained a powerful anti-government force in Germany throughout the 1920s.

SOURCE 17

Spartacists – the Communists who felt that Germany was ready to follow Russia's example of Communist revolution.

SOURCE 18

The *Freikorps* – ex-servicemen who were totally opposed to Communism.

The threat from the right: The Kapp Putsch

Ebert's government also faced violent opposition from the right. His right-wing opponents were largely people who had grown up in, and benefited from, the successful days of the Kaiser's rule. As a result they preferred Germany under a dictatorial-style government, than under a democracy; they wanted a strong German army in order for Germany to expand its territory, and to regain the empire lost through the Treaty of Versailles; and they were proud of Germany's powerful industry.

In March 1920 Dr Wolfgang Kapp led 5,000 *Freikorps* into Berlin in a rebellion known as the Kapp PUTSCH ('Putsch' means rebellion). The army refused to fire on the *Freikorps* and it looked as if Ebert's government was doomed. However, it was saved by the German people, especially the industrial workers of Berlin. They declared a general strike which brought the capital to a halt with no transport, power or water (see Source 19). After a few days Kapp realised he could not succeed and left the country. He was hunted down and died while awaiting trial. It seemed that Weimar had support and power after all. Even so, the rest of the rebels went unpunished by the courts and judges.

Ebert's government struggled to deal with the political violence in Germany. Political ASSASSINATIONS were frequent. In the summer of 1922, Ebert's Foreign Minister Walther Rathenau was murdered by extremists. Then, in November 1923, Adolf Hitler led an attempted rebellion in Munich, known as the Munich Putsch (see page 67). Both Hitler and the murderers of Rathenau received short prison sentences. Strangely, Hitler's judge at the trial was the same judge who had tried him two years earlier for disorder. Both times he got off very lightly. It seemed that Weimar's right-wing opponents had friends in high places.

PRACTICE QUESTIONS

1 Describe two ways in which the *Freikorps* disagreed with the policies of the new Weimar government.
2 In what ways were the Spartacists a problem for the Weimar government in the early 1920s? Explain your answer.

THINK

1 Why might right-wingers dislike the Weimar Constitution (see Factfile on page 63)?
2 From reading pages 64–65, what differences can you see between the treatment of left-wing and right-wing extremists? Can you explain this?

SOURCE 19

Workers being bussed to work privately during the 1920 general strike.

The beginnings of the Nazi Party

Adolf Hitler – the early years, 1889–1919

- Born in Austria in 1889.
- He got on badly with his father but was fond of his mother.
- At the age of 16 he left school and went to Vienna to pursue his ambition of becoming an artist. However, things went wrong for him and between 1909 and 1914 he was virtually a 'down and out' on the streets of Vienna.
- During this period he developed his hatred of foreigners and Jews.
- When war broke out in 1914, Hitler joined the German army and served with distinction, winning the Iron Cross.
- Hitler found it very hard to accept the armistice and was completely opposed to the terms of the Treaty of Versailles.
- He despised Weimar democracy and like many Germans looked back to the 'glorious days' of the Kaiser.
- Hitler stayed in the army after the war, working in Munich for the intelligence services. It was in this job that he came across the DAP or German Workers' Party led by Anton Drexler. He liked the ideas of the party and joined in 1919.

FACTFILE

The 25-Point Programme of the Nazi Party

The most important pledges of the Programme were:

- the abolition of the Treaty of Versailles
- union of Germany and Austria
- only 'true' Germans to be allowed to live in Germany; Jews in particular were to be excluded
- large industries and businesses to be nationalised
- generous provision for old age pensioners
- a strong central government in Germany.

Germany faced another crisis in 1923. The Nazi Party (National Socialist German Workers' Party) had been formed in 1920. It had a 25-point programme (see Factfile) which combined right-wing and left-wing policies in an attempt to appeal to as many Germans as possible. In 1921 Hitler became its leader.

SOURCE 20

American intelligence report on political activities in Germany, 1922.

The most active political force in Bavaria at the present time is the National Socialist Party … It has recently acquired a political influence quite disproportionate to its actual numerical strength … Adolf Hitler from the very first has been the dominating force in the movement and the personality of this man has undoubtedly been one of the most important factors contributing to its success … His ability to influence a popular assembly is uncanny.

SOURCE 21

A person who went to Nazi meetings describes the impact of Hitler's speeches. From *A Part of Myself: Portrait of an Epoch*, by C. Zuckmayer.

Hitler knew how to whip up those crowds jammed closely in a dense cloud of cigarette smoke – not by argument, but by his manner: the roaring and especially the power of his repetitions delivered in a certain infectious rhythm … He would draw up a list of existing evils and imaginary abuses and after listing them, in higher and higher crescendo, he screamed: 'And whose fault is it? It's all … the fault … of the Jews!'

Hitler had a clear and simple appeal. He stirred nationalist passions in his audiences. He gave them SCAPEGOATS to blame for Germany's problems: the Allies, the Versailles Treaty, the 'November Criminals' (the Socialist politicians who signed the Treaty), the Communists and the Jews.

His meetings were so successful that his opponents tried to disrupt them. To counter this, he set up the SA, also known as the storm troopers or brownshirts, in 1921. These hired thugs protected Hitler's meetings but also disrupted those of other parties.

By 1923 the Nazis were still very much a minority party, but Hitler had given them a high profile.

The Munich Putsch, 1923

By November 1923 Hitler believed that the moment had come for him to topple the Weimar government. The government was preoccupied with the economic crisis. Stresemann had just called off Germany's passive resistance in the Ruhr (see page 62). On 8 November, Hitler hijacked a local government meeting and announced he was taking over the government of Bavaria. He was joined by the old war hero Ludendorff.

Nazi storm troopers began taking over official buildings. The next day, however, the Weimar government forces hit back. Police rounded up the storm troopers and in a brief exchange of shots 16 Nazis were killed by the police. The rebellion broke up in chaos. Hitler escaped in a car, while Ludendorff and others stayed to face the armed police.

Hitler had miscalculated the mood of the German people. In the short term, the Munich Putsch was a disaster for him. People did not rise up to support him. He and other leading Nazis were arrested and charged with treason. At the trial, however, Hitler gained enormous publicity for himself and his ideas, as his every word was reported in the newspapers.

In fact, Hitler so impressed the judges that he and his accomplices got off very lightly. Ludendorff was freed altogether and Hitler was given only five years in prison, even though the legal guidelines said that high treason should carry a life sentence. In the end, Hitler served only nine months of the sentence and did so in great comfort in Landsberg castle.

This last point is very significant. It was clear that Hitler had some sympathy and support from important figures in the legal system. Because of his links with Ludendorff, Hitler probably gained the attention of important figures in the army. Time would show that Hitler was down, but not out.

SOURCE 22

Leading Nazi Otto Strasser recalls a conversation with Hitler in the early 1920s.

'Power!' screamed Adolf. 'We must have power!' 'Before we gain it,' I replied firmly, 'let us decide what we propose to do with it.'

Hitler, who even then could hardly bear contradiction, thumped the table and barked: 'Power first – afterwards we can act as circumstances dictate.'

SOURCE 23

Hitler declares the revolution, 8 November 1923.

The Bavarian Ministry is removed. I propose that a Bavarian government be formed consisting of a Regent and a Prime Minister invested with dictatorial powers … The government of the November Criminals and the Reich president are declared to be removed … I propose that, until accounts have been finally settled with the November Criminals, the direction of policy in the National Government be taken over by me …

SOURCE 24

Hitler at his trial in January 1924.

I alone bear the responsibility but I am not a criminal because of that … There is no such thing as high treason against the traitors of 1918 … I feel myself the best of Germans who wanted the best for the German people.

ACTIVITY

It is 1923. Use the information and sources on pages 66–67 to write a newspaper article about the rise of Hitler and the Nazi Party. Your opening sentences could be:

'In recent months, a new force seems to be arising in German politics. Adolf Hitler and the Nazis have hit the headlines with their meetings, banners and radical ideas. What makes this man successful? …'

Your article should tell readers about:
- Hitler's background
- his qualities
- what he and the Nazis believe.

THINK

What can you learn from Sources 22–24 about Hitler's attitude towards attempting to seize power in 1923?

Gustav Stresemann

- Born in 1878.
- University educated.
- Politician – tending towards right-wing beliefs.
- August 1923 appointed Chancellor.
- In 1923–29 served as foreign minister, but dominated the government.
- Awarded Nobel Peace Prize in 1926.
- Died in October 1929, just before the Wall Street Crash.

FIGURE 25

Support for the main political parties in Germany, 1919–28.

Date	Number of MPs elected
1919	350 left wing supporting the Republic
	60 right wing opposed to the Republic
May 1924	60 left wing opposed to the Republic
	200 left wing supporting the Republic
	160 right wing opposed to the Republic
1928	50 left wing opposed to the Republic
	250 left wing supporting the Republic
	140 right wing opposed to the Republic

The extent of recovery during the Stresemann era, 1924–29

In the later 1920s Germany appeared to be recovering from the political and economic crises of the early 1920s. Life in Germany was getting back to normal. There was less support for political parties that wanted to destroy the Weimar Republic. Yet at the same time there were still underlying problems in society that were exposed when the WALL STREET CRASH occurred in 1929. At the same time, Germany was gradually being accepted within Europe with various agreements and treaties (see Chapter 6, page 257).

Political achievements under Stresemann

Politics became more stable. There were no more attempted revolutions after 1923. Figure 25 shows that the parties that supported Weimar democracy did well in these years. By 1928 the moderate parties had 136 more seats in the Reichstag than the radical parties. Hitler's Nazi Party gained less than 3 per cent of the vote in the 1928 election. Just as important, some of the parties who had co-operated in the revolution of 1918 began to co-operate again. The Socialists (SPD), Catholic Centre Party, German Democratic Party (DDP) and the German People's Party (DVP) generally worked well together in the years 1924–29.

Political problems under Stresemann

Despite the relative stability of Weimar politics in this period, both the Nazis and Communists were building up their party organisations. Even during these stable years there were four different Chancellors and it was only the influence of party leaders that held the party coalitions together.

More worrying for the Republic, despite increased support for more moderate parties, was that around 30 per cent of the vote regularly went to parties opposed to the Republic. Most serious of all, the right-wing organisations which posed the greatest threat to the Republic were quiet rather than destroyed. The right-wing Nationalist Party (DNVP) and the Nazis began to collaborate closely and make themselves appear more respectable. Another event which would turn out to be very significant was that the German people elected Hindenburg as President in 1926. He was opposed to democracy and wrote to the Kaiser in exile for approval before he took up the post! It was clear that the Weimar Republic had not yet won the loyalty of all sections of German society.

The Nazi Party in the late 1920s

After the failed Munich Putsch, Hitler used his time in prison to write a book, *Mein Kampf* (*My Struggle*). It set out at great length his ideas about how the Nazis should develop as a party. He came to the conclusion that trying to seize power by force was a mistake. The Nazi Party would have to work within the democratic system to achieve power, but once they had achieved it, this system could be destroyed.

Once out of prison, Hitler copied the Communist Party by seeking to strengthen the party, for example, by setting up youth organisations and recruitment drives. Hitler was encouraged that the Nazi Party gained 32 seats in the Reichstag elections of 1924. However in 1928 the Nazis gained only 12 seats. The party was gaining little support from the industrial workers who were more inclined to support the Communist groups. Therefore he decided to focus much more on other groups in society.

Economic developments: The new currency and the Dawes and Young Plans

Although Chancellor for only a few months, Stresemann was a leading member of every government from 1923 to 1929. He was a more skilful politician than Ebert, and, as a right-winger, he had wider support from business interests. He was also helped by the fact that through the 1920s the rest of Europe was gradually coming out of its post-war DEPRESSION. Slowly but surely, he built up Germany's prosperity again. First he called in the worthless marks and replaced them with a new currency called the Rentenmark. This provided confidence and stability.

After the crisis of 1923 the American government stepped in to offer financial support for Germany. It was in the USA's interest for Germany to be able to build up her international trade again. Under the Dawes Plan of 1924, reparations payments were spread over a longer period of time, and the USA provided 800 million marks in loans.

Some of the money went into German industry, replacing old equipment with the latest technology. Some of the money went into public works like swimming pools, sports stadiums and apartment blocks. As well as providing facilities, these projects created jobs.

By 1927 German industry seemed to have recovered very well. In 1928 Germany finally achieved the same levels of production as before the war and regained its place as the world's second greatest industrial power (behind the USA). Wages for industrial workers rose and for many Germans there was a higher standard of living. Reparations were being paid and exports were on the increase. The government was even able to increase welfare benefits and wages for state employees.

The impact of international agreements on recovery

Stresemann worked hard to improve Germany's international reputation during this period. In 1925 the Locarno Treaties were agreed in which Germany promised to respect its existing borders with France and Belgium. Consequently, in 1926, Germany was admitted into the League of Nations. This in turn aided German recovery, as trade between the increasingly trusted and respected Germany, and other countries, increased.

In 1929, under the Young Plan, German reparations payments were to be reduced to £2.2 billion, and the country given longer to pay. In the event, the Wall Street Crash destroyed the intentions of this plan, and in 1932 the Allies agreed to cancel reparations payments altogether.

Stresemann: A balance sheet

Although many of Stresemann's actions strengthened the German economy, the picture was mixed. The economic boom in Weimar Germany was precarious as US loans could be called in at short notice, which would cause ruin in Germany.

The main economic winners in Germany were big businesses (such as the steel and chemical industries) which controlled about half of Germany's industrial production. Other winners were big landowners, particularly if they owned land in towns – the value of land in Berlin rose by 700 per cent in this period. The workers in the big industries gained as well. Most Weimar governments were sympathetic towards the unions, which led to improved pay and conditions. However, even here there were concerns as unemployment began to rise – it was 6 per cent of the working population by 1928.

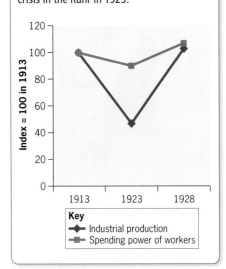

FIGURE 26

Comparison of aspects of the German economy in 1913, 1923 and 1928. The figures show how badly industrial production was harmed by the economic crisis in the Ruhr in 1923.

Key
- Industrial production
- Spending power of workers

THINK

What factors helped Germany's economy to recover?

PRACTICE QUESTIONS

1 Describe two reasons why Germany was able to improve relations with other countries in the later 1920s.

2 In what ways did the Dawes Plan and the Young Plan help the lives of German people under Stresemann? Explain your answer.

SOURCE 27

A Nazi election poster from 1928, saying 'Work, freedom and bread! Vote for the National Socialists!'

FOCUS TASK

How strong was the Weimar Republic by 1929?

Work in pairs.

1 One of you take a small note card and write the heading 'The Weimar Republic – in good health' at the top.
2 Add five bullet points and list evidence of the strengths of the Weimar Republic.
3 The other person should take another card and write the heading 'The Weimar Republic – in poor health' at the top.
4 Add five bullet points and list evidence of the weaknesses of the Weimar Republic.
5 Now share your findings with each other and discuss whether you think the Weimar Republic was in good or poor health by 1929.

THINK

Explain how Source 27 is trying to get more support for the Nazi Party.

The main losers were the peasant farmers and sections of the middle classes. The peasant farmers had increased production during the war. In peacetime, they found themselves overproducing. They had mortgages to pay but not enough demand for the food they produced. Many small business owners became disillusioned during this period. Small shopkeepers saw their businesses threatened by large department stores (many of which were owned by Jews). A university lecturer in 1913 earned ten times as much as a coal miner. In the 1920s he earned twice as much. These people began to feel that the Weimar government offered them little.

Weimar culture

During the 1920s there was also a cultural revival in Germany. In the Kaiser's time there had been strict censorship, but the Weimar Constitution allowed free expression of ideas. Writers and poets flourished, especially in Berlin. Artists in Weimar Germany turned their back on old styles of painting and tried to represent the reality of everyday life, even when that reality was sometimes harsh and shocking. Artists like George Grosz produced powerful paintings like Source 29, which criticised the politicians of the Weimar period. Other paintings by Grosz showed how many soldiers had been traumatised by their experiences in the war. Otto Dix produced paintings which highlighted the gaps between the rich and poor in Germany at the time.

SOURCE 28

The Bauhaus design college in Dessau, built between 1925 and 1926.

The famous Bauhaus style of design and architecture developed. Artists such as Walter Gropius, Paul Klee and Wassily Kandinsky taught at the Bauhaus design college in Dessau. The Bauhaus architects rejected traditional styles to create new and exciting buildings. They produced designs for anything from houses and shops to art galleries and factories. The first Bauhaus exhibition attracted 15,000 visitors.

The 1920s were a golden age for German cinema, producing one of its greatest ever international stars, Marlene Dietrich, and one of its most celebrated directors, Fritz Lang. Berlin was famous for its daring and liberated night life. Going to clubs was a major pastime. In 1927 there were 900 dance bands in Berlin alone. Cabaret artists performed songs criticising political leaders that would have been banned in the Kaiser's days. These included songs about sex that would have shocked an earlier generation of Germans.

SOURCE 29

Pillars of Society by George Grosz, 1926. Grosz criticised Weimar Germany because he felt too many leading figures in society still believed in the ideals of the Kaiser's Germany. In this painting you can see that the civilians still dream of military glory.

SOURCE 30

Poster for one of Marlene Dietrich's films.

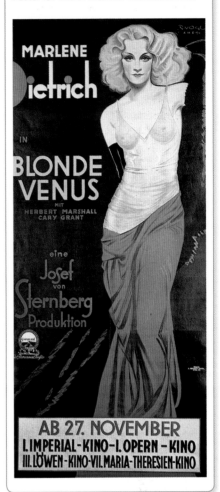

The Weimar culture was colourful and exciting to many. However, in many of Germany's villages and country towns, the culture of the cities seemed to represent a moral decline, made worse by American immigrants and Jewish artists and musicians. As you have read, the Bauhaus design college was in Dessau. It was situated there because it was forced out of Weimar by hostile town officials.

Organisations such as the Wandervogel movement were a reaction to Weimar's culture. The Wandervogel wanted a return to simple country values and wanted to see more help for the countryside and less decadence in the towns. It was a powerful feeling which the Nazis successfully harnessed in later years.

SOURCE 31

A Wandervogel camp in the 1920s.

PRACTICE QUESTIONS

Read Interpretations A and B and then answer Questions 1–3.

Interpretation A American journalist, William Shirer, who was in Germany in the 1920s and was forced to flee when the Nazis came to power in the 1930s. This extract is from a book he wrote and published in the 1960s.

A wonderful ferment was working in Germany . .. most Germans one met struck you as being democratic, liberal, even pacifist [peace loving]. One scarcely even heard of Hitler or the Nazis except as jokes.

Interpretation B From *Goodbye to Berlin* by the British writer Christopher Isherwood. Isherwood lived in Germany in the 1920s. As a homosexual and a foreigner he was hounded out of Germany. This book was published in 1939. Here he describes a summer holiday in the mid 1920s.

There are now a good many summer visitors to the village. The bathing-beach by the pier, with its array of banners, begins to look like a medieval camp. Each family has its own enormous hooded wicker beach-chair, and each chair flies a little flag. There are the German city-flags – Hamburg, Hanover, Dresden, Rostock and Berlin, as well as the National, Republican and Nazi colours. Heil Hitler! Many of these are also decorated with the Nazi swastika. The other morning I saw a child of about five years old, stark naked, marching along all by himself with a swastika flag over his shoulder and singing 'Deutschland über alles'.

1   How does Interpretation B differ from Interpretation A about the impact of the Nazis in Germany in the 1920s?

    Explain your answer based on what it says in Interpretation A and B.

2   Why might the authors of Interpretations A and B have a different interpretation about the impact of the Nazis in Germany in the 1920s ?

    Explain your answer by using Interpretations A and B and your contextual knowledge.

3   Which interpretation gives the more convincing opinion about the impact of the Nazis in Germany in the 1920s?

    Explain your answer based on your contextual knowledge and what it says in Interpretations A and B.

TOPIC SUMMARY

Germany and the growth of democracy
- Wilhelm II became Kaiser of Germany in 1890. His character was likely to pose problems.
- In the period 1890–1914, the new German government was increasingly dominated by militarism and nationalism.
- In the decades before the First World War Germany was becoming more industrialised.
- Germany suffered badly in the First World War, with civilians in cities experiencing food and fuel shortages.
- In November 1918, days before the end of the war, Kaiser Wilhelm II abdicated.
- In 1919 the Treaty of Versailles punished Germany, setting out severe reparations terms.
- The Weimar Republic was established in 1919, but it faced political and economic problems arising from the chaos in Germany after the war.
- In 1923 the French occupied the Ruhr to try to claim their reparations payments.
- The same year also saw the economic crisis caused by hyperinflation and Hitler's attempt to seize power (the Munich Putsch).
- From 1924 onwards Stresemann was the leading minister, and Germany began to recover economically and improve its relations with other countries.
- In October 1929 the Wall Street Crash shattered the German recovery.

2.2 Germany and the Depression

● The impact of the Depression

SOURCE 1

Upper Silesia in 1932: unemployed miners and their families moved into shacks in a shanty town because they had no money to pay their rent.

SOURCE 2

An eyewitness describes the unemployed vagrants in Germany in 1932.

No one knew how many there were of them. They completely filled the streets. They stood or lay about in the streets as if they had taken root there. They sat or lay on the pavements or in the roadway and gravely shared out scraps of newspapers among themselves.

The Depression was a worldwide problem. It was not just Germany that suffered. Nor was the Weimar government the only government grappling with the problem of unemployment. However, because Germany had been so dependent on American loans, and because it still had to pay reparations to the Allies, the problems were most acute in Germany.

In addition, it seemed that the Weimar Constitution, with its careful balance of power, made firm and decisive action by the government very difficult indeed (see Factfile, page 63).

Thus all sections of society were affected in different ways – from business leaders to industrial workers. The effects were not just economic. The recently gained mood of optimism vanished, and the defects of Weimar Germany, mostly hidden in the later 1920s, suddenly became glaringly obvious.

ACTIVITY

Draw a diagram to show how the Wall Street Crash could lead to miners losing their jobs in Silesia.

PRACTICE QUESTION

Describe two economic problems for Germans caused by the Wall Street Crash.

FIGURE 3

Support for the Nazis and Communists, and unemployment, 1928–32.

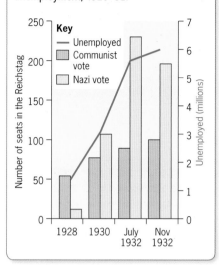

Growth in support for extremist parties, 1928–32

The effects of the Wall Street Crash, leading to economic depression in Germany, convinced many Germans that the government of the Weimar Republic had failed. Therefore many turned to the Communists who promised a workers' revolution, or they looked to the right-wing parties, especially the Nazis with their promises of a return to strong rule and the restoration of Germany's status in the world.

The appeal of the Nazi Party

Hitler's ideas now had a special relevance:

- Is the Weimar government indecisive? Then Germany needs a strong leader!
- Are reparations adding to Germany's problems? Then kick out the Treaty of Versailles!
- Is unemployment a problem? Let the unemployed join the army, build Germany's armaments and be used for public works like road building!

The Nazis' 25-Point Programme (see page 66) was very attractive to those most vulnerable to the effects of the Depression: the unemployed, the elderly and the middle classes. Hitler offered them culprits to blame for Germany's troubles – the Allies, the 'November Criminals' and the Jews. None of these messages was new but they had not won support for the Nazis in the Stresemann years. The difference now was that the democratic parties simply could not get Germany back to work.

In the 1930 elections the Nazis won 107 seats. In November 1932 they won 196 seats. They did not yet have an overall majority, but they were now the biggest single party.

SOURCE 4

Albert Speer, writing in 1931. Later, he was to become an important and powerful Nazi leader.

My mother saw a storm trooper parade in the streets of Heidelberg. The sight of discipline in a time of chaos, the impression of energy in an atmosphere of universal hopelessness seems to have won her over.

Why did the Nazis succeed in elections?

The Nazis came to power because Hitler and his supporters made promises that appealed to many people. Hitler's PROPAGANDA chief, Joseph Goebbels, simplified the main policies put forward by the Nazi Party so that they could be easily understood by everyone.

The use of propaganda

The promises made by the Nazi Party during this period were generalised statements of their beliefs:

- They talked about a return to traditional values.
- They criticised the democratic system of the Weimar Republic and its failure to solve the nation's economic problems.
- They promised employment and economic strength.
- They cited the Jews, Communists, Weimar politicians and the Treaty of Versailles as the root causes of Germany's problems.

Because these were expressed as generalised beliefs, rather than detailed policies, it was difficult to criticise them, and they appealed to large sections of society. When the Nazis were criticised over a specific policy, they were very likely to drop it. This happened when their plans to nationalise industry were criticised by industrialists.

There is no doubt that Nazi campaign methods were modern and effective. Goebbels understood how effectively propaganda could be used and the Nazis' posters and pamphlets could be found everywhere. Their rallies impressed people with their energy, enthusiasm and sheer size.

SOURCE 5

A Nazi Party rally in Frankfurt in 1932.

The role of the SA

The Nazi Party was also seen as a party of order, in a time of chaos. During this period there were frequent street battles between Communist gangs and the police. In contrast, the SA and SS gave an impression of discipline and order. Many people welcomed the fact that the SA were prepared to fight the Communists (page 76). The SA were better organised and usually had the support of the police and army when they beat up opponents and disrupted meetings and rallies.

Hitler's appeal

The Nazis' greatest campaigning asset was Hitler. He was a powerful speaker who was years ahead of his time as a communicator. Hitler ran for president in 1932, winning 13 million votes to Hindenburg's 19 million. Despite Hitler's defeat, the campaign raised his profile hugely. Using films, radio and records he brought his message to millions. He travelled by plane on a hectic tour of rallies all over Germany. He appeared as a dynamic man of the moment, the leader of a modern party with modern ideas. At the same time, he was able to appear to be a man of the people, someone who knew and understood the Germans and their problems.

FACTFILE

The SA

This military group was important in the Nazi rise to power. It protected Nazi rallies and disrupted the meetings of political opponents. Although the organisation gave the impression of order, its members were not always strictly disciplined and were not fully under Hitler's control. They were known as the Brownshirts.

The SS

Originally part of the SA in the 1920s, but the organisation became separate under Heinrich Himmler. The SS swore total loyalty to Hitler, were tightly disciplined, and were known as the Blackshirts.

SOURCE 6

A Nazi election poster from July 1932. The Nazis proclaim 'We build!' and promise to provide work, freedom and bread. They accuse the opposing parties of planning to use terror, corruption, lies and other strategies as the basis for their government.

SOURCE 7

Hitler speaking at an election rally, July 1932.

Our opponents accuse us National Socialists, and me in particular, of being intolerant and quarrelsome. They say that we don't want to work with other parties. They say the National Socialists are not German at all, because they refuse to work with other political parties. So is it typically German to have thirty political parties? I have to admit one thing – these gentlemen are quite right. We are intolerant. I have given myself this one goal – to sweep these thirty political parties out of Germany.

SOURCE 8

An eyewitness account of one of Hitler's meetings in the 1920s.

He began to speak and I immediately disliked him. I didn't know then what he would later become. I found him rather comical, with his funny moustache. He had a scratchy voice and a rather strange appearance, and he shouted so much. He was shouting in this small room, and what he was saying was very simplistic. I thought he wasn't quite normal. I found him spooky.

'Negative cohesion'

Not everyone was taken in by Nazi campaigning methods and Hitler's magnetism (see Source 8). But even some of the sceptics supported the Nazis. The historian Gordon Craig believed that this was because of something he called 'negative cohesion'. This meant that people supported the Nazis not because they shared Nazi views (that would be positive cohesion) but because they shared Nazi fears and dislikes. In what was seen as a modern, decadent culture, the Nazis could count on the support of those who felt traditional German values were under threat.

The SOCIAL DEMOCRATIC PARTY made a grave mistake in thinking that German people would not fall for these vague promises and accusations. They underestimated the fear and anger that German people felt towards the Weimar Republic.

The Communist threat

As the crisis deepened, Communist support was rising too. The Nazis turned this to their advantage. 'Fear of Communism' was another shared negative. The Communist Red Fighting League broke up opposition party meetings, just like the SA. They fought street battles with police. So, out on the streets, the Nazi SA storm troopers met Communist violence with their own violence.

Many middle-class business owners had read about how the Communist Party in the USSR had discriminated against people like them. The owners of the big industries feared the Communists because of their plans to introduce state control of businesses. The industrialists were also concerned about the growing strength of Germany's trade unions. They felt the Nazis would combat these threats and some began to put money into Nazi campaign funds.

All farmers were alarmed by the Communists. They had read about Communist farming policies in the USSR where the Soviet government had taken over all of the land. Millions of peasants had been killed or imprisoned in the process. In contrast, the Nazis promised to help Germany's desperately struggling small farmers.

SOURCE 9

'Little Adolf tries on the spiked moustache' – a cartoon by a British cartoonist, commenting on Hitler's ambitions, 27 September 1930.

THINK

What is the cartoon (Source 9) trying to say to the British public in early 1933?

● The failure of Weimar democracy

Perhaps the biggest negative factor that explained the popularity of the Nazis was a shared dislike of democracy in Weimar Germany. Politicians seemed unable to tackle the problems of the Depression. When the Depression began to bite in 1930 the Chancellor, Heinrich Brüning, pursued a tough economic policy. He cut government spending and welfare benefits. He urged Germans to make sacrifices. Some historians think that he was deliberately making the situation worse in order to get the international community to cancel reparations payments. Other historians think that he was afraid of hyperinflation recurring as in 1923. In protest, the SPD (still the main party in the Reichstag) pulled out of the government. To get his measures passed, Brüning relied on President Hindenburg to use his powers under Article 48 (see Factfile, page 63) to bypass the Reichstag.

Brüning and Hindenburg decided to call new elections in 1930. This was a disastrous decision, as it gave the Nazis the opportunity to exploit the fear and discontent in Germany and make the gains you have seen in Figure 3 on page 74. The new elections resulted in another divided Reichstag, and the problems continued into 1931 and 1932. The impression was that democracy involved politicians squabbling over which job they would get in the Cabinet. Meanwhile, they did nothing about the real world, where unemployment was heading towards 6 million and the average German's income had fallen by 40 per cent since 1929. The Reichstag met fewer and fewer times (for only five days in 1932). Brüning had to continue to rely on Hindenburg using his emergency powers, bypassing the democratic process altogether.

PRACTICE QUESTION

Which of the following was a more important reason for Hitler and the Nazis coming to power in Germany in 1933:

● The Wall Street Crash
● Nazi propaganda?

Explain your answer with reference to both reasons.

Why did people support the Nazis?

Do you agree with Goebbels' view that people rallied to support Hitler for positive reasons, or do you think that Gordon Craig was right that people supported the Nazis out of fear and disillusionment? Work through Questions 1–4 to help you make up your mind.

1 Look carefully at Figure 3 and Sources 2, 4, 5 and 6 on pages 73–75. For each, write two sentences explaining whether you think it is evidence that:
   - supports Goebbels' view
   - supports Craig's view
   - could be used to support either interpretation.
2 Now work through the text and other sources on this page. Make a list of examples and evidence that seem to support either viewpoint.
3 Decide how far you agree with each of the following statements and give them a score on a scale of 1–5, with 1 meaning you totally agree.
   - Very few people fully supported the Nazis.
   - The key factor was the economic depression. Without it, the Nazis would have remained a minority fringe party.
   - The politicians of the Weimar Republic were mainly responsible for the rise of the Nazis.
4 Write a short paragraph explaining your score for each statement.

SOURCE 10

S. Williams, in *The Rise and Fall of Hitler's Germany*, published in 1986, assesses the reasons for Hitler's success.

The majority of Germans never voted for the Nazis.

The Nazis made it clear they would destroy democracy and all who stood in their way. Why then didn't their enemies join together to stop Hitler? … Had the Communists and Socialists joined forces they would probably have been strong enough both in the Reichstag and on the streets to have blocked the Nazis. The fact was that by 1932–33 there were simply not enough Germans who believed in democracy and individual freedom to save the Weimar Republic.

Look at the last sentence of Source 10. Write a list of reasons why this might be true.

How Hitler became Chancellor: The role of Papen and Hindenburg

After the Reichstag elections of July 1932 the Nazis were the largest single party (with 230 seats) but not a majority party. Hitler demanded the post of Chancellor from the President, the old war hero Hindenburg. However, Hindenburg was suspicious of Hitler and refused. He allowed the current Chancellor Franz von Papen (an old friend of Hindenburg) to carry on as Chancellor. He then used his emergency powers to pass the measures that von Papen had hoped would solve the unemployment problem.

However, von Papen was soon in trouble. He had virtually no support at all in the Reichstag and so called yet another election in November 1932. The Nazis again came out as the largest party, although their share of the vote fell.

Hitler regarded the election as a disaster for the Nazis. The signs were that the Hitler flood tide had finally turned. The Nazis started to run out of funds. Hitler is said to have threatened suicide.

Hindenburg again refused to appoint Hitler as Chancellor. In December 1932 he chose Kurt von Schleicher, one of his own advisers and a bitter rival of von Papen. Von Papen remained as an adviser to Hindenburg. Within a month, however, von Schleicher too was forced to resign. By this time it was clear that the Weimar system of government was not working. In one sense, Hindenburg had already overthrown the principles of democracy by running Germany with emergency powers. If he was to rescue the democratic system, he needed a Chancellor who actually had support in the Reichstag.

Through January 1933 Hindenburg and von Papen met secretly with industrialists, army leaders and politicians. And on 30 January, to everyone's great surprise, they offered Hitler the post of Chancellor. Why did they do this? With only a few Nazis in the Cabinet and von Papen as Vice Chancellor, they were confident that they could limit Hitler's influence and resist his extremist demands. The idea was that the policies would be made by the Cabinet, which was filled with conservatives like von Papen. Hitler would be there to get support in the Reichstag for those policies and to control the Communists. So Hitler ended up as Chancellor not because of the will of the German people, but through a behind-the-scenes deal by some German aristocrats. Both Hindenburg and von Papen were sure that they could control Hitler. Both were very wrong.

FOCUS TASK

How did Hitler become Chancellor in 1933?

Here is a list of factors that helped Hitler come to power.

Nazi strengths

- Hitler's speaking skills
- Nazi propaganda campaigns
- The Nazis' violent treatment of their opponents
- Nazis' criticisms of the Weimar system of government
- Nazi policies
- Support from big business

Opponents' weaknesses

- Failure to deal with the Depression
- Failure to co-operate with one another
- Attitudes of Germans to the democratic parties

Other factors

- Weaknesses of the Weimar Republic
- Scheming of Hindenburg and von Papen
- The impact of the Depression
- The Treaty of Versailles
- Memories of the problems of 1923

1 For each factor, write down one example of how it helped Hitler.
2 Give each factor a mark out of 10 for its importance in bringing Hitler to power, with 1 being the most important.
3 Choose what you think are the five most important factors and write a short paragraph on each, explaining why you have chosen it.
4 If you took away any of those factors, would Hitler still have become Chancellor in 1933?
5 Were any of those five factors also present in the 1920s?
6 If so, explain why the Nazis were not successful in the 1920s.

SOURCE 11

The Reichstag Fire.

THINK

Some people suggest that the Nazis burnt down the Reichstag themselves. Explain why the Nazis might have wanted to do this.

The establishment of Hitler's dictatorship

It is easy to forget, but when Hitler became Chancellor in January 1933 he was in a very precarious position. Few people thought he would hold on to power for long. Even fewer thought that by the summer of 1934 he would be the supreme dictator of Germany. He achieved this through a clever combination of methods – some legal, others dubious. He also managed to defeat or reach agreements with those who could have stopped him.

The Reichstag Fire and the March 1933 election

Once he was Chancellor, Hitler took steps to complete a Nazi takeover of Germany. He called another election for March 1933 to try to get an overall Nazi majority in the Reichstag. Germany's cities again witnessed speeches, rallies, processions and street fighting. Hitler was using the same tactics as in previous elections, but now he had the resources of state media and control of the streets. Even so, success was in the balance. Then on 27 February there was a dramatic development; the Reichstag building burned down. Hitler blamed the Communists and declared that the fire was the beginning of a Communist uprising. A young Dutch Communist, named Marinus van der Lubbe, was arrested at the scene and was said to have confessed to starting the fire. Hitler demanded special emergency powers to deal with the situation and was given them by President Hindenburg. The Nazis used these powers to arrest Communists, break up meetings and frighten voters.

There have been many theories about what caused the fire, including that it was an accident, the work of a madman, or a Communist plot. Many Germans at the time thought that the Nazis might have started the fire themselves.

PRACTICE QUESTIONS

Interpretation A: One view about the Reichstag Fire, February 1933. It comes from an account written in 1950 by Rudolph Diels, a Nazi and head of police in Berlin in 1933.

I think van der Lubbe started the Reichstag Fire on his own. When I arrived at the burning building, some police officers were already questioning him. His voluntary confession made me think that he was such an expert arsonist that he did not need any helpers. Why could not one person set fire to the old furniture, the heavy curtains and the bone-dry wood panelling? He had lit several dozen fires using firelighters and his burning shirt, which he was holding in his right hand like a torch when he was overpowered by Reichstag officials.

Interpretation B: Another view of the Reichstag Fire. It comes from the records of the Nuremberg War Crimes Trial, 1945. General Halder, Chief of the German General Staff, was asked about the fire.

At a luncheon on the birthday of the Führer in 1942, the conversation turned to the topic of the Reichstag building. I heard with my own ears when Goering interrupted the conversation and shouted: 'The only one who really knows about the Reichstag is I, because I set it on fire!'

Read Interpretations A and B and then answer Questions 1–3.

1 How does Interpretation B differ from Interpretation A about the cause of the Reichstag Fire?
  Explain your answer based on what it says in Interpretations A and B.

2 Why might the authors of Interpretations A and B have a different interpretation about the cause of the fire?
  Explain your answer using Interpretations A and B and your contextual knowledge.

3 Which interpretation gives the more convincing opinion about the cause of the fire?
  Explain your answer based on your contextual knowledge and what it says in Interpretations A and B.

The Enabling Act, March 1933

In the election of early March 1933, the Nazis won their largest-ever share of the votes and, with the support of the smaller Nationalist Party who got 52 seats, Hitler had an overall majority. He could use this to destroy the Constitution of the Weimar Republic.

Using the SA and SS, Hitler then intimidated the Reichstag into passing the Enabling Act which allowed him to make laws without consulting the Reichstag. Only the SPD voted against him. Following the election, the Communists had been banned. The Catholic Centre Party decided to co-operate with the Nazis rather than be treated like the Communists. In return, they retained control of Catholic schools. The Enabling Act made Hitler a virtual dictator. For the next four years if he wanted a new law he could just pass it. There was nothing President Hindenburg or anyone else could do.

FIGURE 12

Election results from March 1933 compared to the previous election in November 1932.

Party	Number of seats	Seats in 1932
Nazi Party	288	196
Social Democrats (SPD)	120	121
Communist Party	81	100
Catholic Centre Party	73	70
Others	85	97

The elimination of political opposition in 1933

Within six months of Hitler becoming Chancellor, all political opposition had been silenced:

30 January   Hitler appointed Chancellor.

27 February   Reichstag Fire. Arrest of 4,000 Communists.

28 February   Emergency Decree issued by Hindenburg.

5 March   Reichstag elections – Nazis gained 44 per cent of votes.

  With support of Nationalist Party, Nazis had 52 per cent of votes.

13 March   Goebbels took control of all media.

24 March   Enabling Act – Hitler could pass decrees without the President being involved.

April   Civil service, law courts and education purged of opponents of the Nazis.

2 May   Trade unions banned. All German workers to belong to new German Labour Front.

14 July   Law Against Formation of New Parties. Germany becomes a one-party state.

20 July   Concordat (agreement) between state and Catholic Church.

The Night of the Long Knives, June 1934

Hitler was still not entirely secure, however. The leading officers in the army were not impressed by him and were particularly suspicious of Hitler's SA and its leader, Ernst Röhm. The SA was a badly disciplined force and, what's more, Röhm talked of making the SA into a second German army. Hitler himself was also suspicious of Röhm. Hitler feared that Röhm's control over the 4 million SA men made him a potentially dangerous rival.

Hitler had to choose between the army and the SA. He made his choice and acted ruthlessly. On the weekend of 29–30 June 1934 squads of SS men broke into the homes of Röhm and other leading figures in the SA and arrested them. Hitler accused Röhm of plotting to overthrow and murder him. Over the weekend Röhm and possibly as many as 400 others were executed. These included the former Chancellor von Schleicher, a fierce critic of Hitler, and others who actually had no connection with Röhm. Although the killings took place over the whole weekend, this purge came to be known as the Night of the Long Knives.

Hindenburg thanked Hitler for his 'determined action which has nipped treason in the bud'. The army said it was well satisfied with the events of the weekend.

The SA was not disbanded afterwards. It remained as a Nazi PARAMILITARY organisation, but was very much subordinate to the SS and never regained the influence of 1933. Many of its members were absorbed by the army and the SS.

Der Führer, August 1934

Soon after the Night of the Long Knives, Hindenburg died and Hitler took over as Supreme Leader (*Führer*) of Germany. On 2 August 1934 the entire army swore an oath of personal loyalty to Adolf Hitler as Führer of Germany. The army agreed to stay out of politics and to serve Hitler. In return, Hitler spent vast sums on REARMAMENT, brought back CONSCRIPTION and made plans to make Germany a great military power again. Hitler had total control, in theory, over the government and the armed forces.

FOCUS TASK

How did Hitler establish his dictatorship, 1933–34?

1   Study the information and sources on pages 78–80. Make a list of examples of:
    – Nazis using force against their opponents
    – Nazis making deals with their opponents
    – Nazis combining these two methods.
2   Explain why the Enabling Act was so important to Hitler.
3   Why might Hitler have executed people such as von Schleicher who were nothing to do with the SA?
4   Why do you think Hitler chose the support of the army over the support of the SA?

TOPIC SUMMARY

Germany and the Depression

- In 1929 the STOCK MARKET collapse in Wall Street, New York, USA, led to economic chaos across the world.
- There were worsening economic problems in Germany in 1930–32.
- Extremist parties gained more support – the Nazis and the Communists.
- In May 1932 Hitler stood for President, but was defeated by Hindenburg. However, the Nazis were the largest party in two successive Reichstag elections.
- In January 1933 Hitler was invited to be Chancellor, with von Papen as Vice-Chancellor.
- The Reichstag Fire in February 1933 gave Hitler the excuse to act against the Communists.
- In March 1933 the Reichstag passed the Enabling Act, which gave Hitler the ability to pass his own laws.
- In April 1933 all civil servants and teachers who were not Nazi supporters were removed from their posts.
- In May 1933 no political party other than the Nazis was allowed. Trade unions were banned.
- Hitler saw the SA as a possible threat to his power, and in the Night of the Long Knives, June 1934, leading SA members were killed.
- Hitler became Führer in August 1934 after the death of President Hindenburg.

FOCUS

This section explains how a fundamental change affected the lives of Germans, both in the 1930s and during the Second World War. Democracy had been replaced by dictatorship. Personal freedoms were lost. Initially, many people were pleased to see the Nazis in charge – creating order and restoring the economy. However, by 1939 many saw the dark side of Nazi rule, and this became obvious to all, within and outside Germany, during the Second World War.

In this part of the topic you will study the following:

- Economic changes in peacetime and war and their effects on German society.
- Social policy and practice and its effects on:
  - women
  - youth
  - the Churches
  - ethnic minorities.
- The use of persuasion, propaganda and repression, and why so few opposed the regime.

2.3 The experiences of Germans under the Nazis

● Economic changes: Employment and rearmament

FOCUS TASK

Part 1: The Nazis' economic policies

As you read through pages 81–83, you will come across a number of individuals, organisations and terms in bold type in the text, **like this**. You could add more of your own if you wish. Draw up a table containing definitions of the words, or explanations of their importance to the Nazis' economic policies. The completed table will help you with your revision. You could organise your table like this:

Key word/term/person	Definition/explanation

Hitler and the Nazis came to power because they promised to use radical methods to solve the country's two main problems – desperate unemployment and a crisis in German farming. In return for work and other benefits, the majority of the German people gave up their political freedom. Was it worth it?

At first, many Germans felt it was, particularly the 5 million who were unemployed in 1933. Hitler was fortunate in that by 1933 the worst of the Depression was over. Even so, there is no doubt that the Nazis acted with energy and commitment to solve some of the main problems. The brilliant economist **Dr Hjalmar Schacht** organised Germany's finances to fund a huge programme of work creation. The National Labour Service sent men on **public works projects** and conservation programmes, in particular to build a network of motorways or **autobahns**. Railways were extended or built from scratch. There were major house-building programmes and grandiose new public building projects such as the Reich Chancellery in Berlin.

SOURCE 1

A completed *autobahn*.

SOURCE 2

Previously unemployed men assemble for the building of a public works project, September 1933.

Other measures brought increasing prosperity. One of Hitler's most cherished plans was **rearmament**. In 1935 he reintroduced **conscription** for the German army. In 1936 he announced a **Four-Year Plan** under the control of **Goering** to get the German economy ready for war (it was one of the very few clear policy documents that Hitler ever wrote). The aim was to achieve self-sufficiency in as many aspects of the economy as possible.

Conscription reduced unemployment. The need for weapons, equipment and uniforms created jobs in the coal mines, steel industry and textile mills. Engineers and designers gained new opportunities, particularly when Hitler decreed that Germany would have a world-class air force (the *Luftwaffe*). As well as bringing economic recovery, these measures boosted Hitler's popularity because they boosted **national pride**. Germans began to feel that their country was finally emerging from the humiliation of the Great War and the Treaty of Versailles, and putting itself on an equal footing with the other GREAT POWERS.

FIGURE 3

Unemployment and government expenditure in Germany, 1932–38. Economic recovery was almost entirely funded by the state rather than from Germans investing their own savings. Despite this, unemployment fell steadily and Germany was actually running short of workers by 1939.

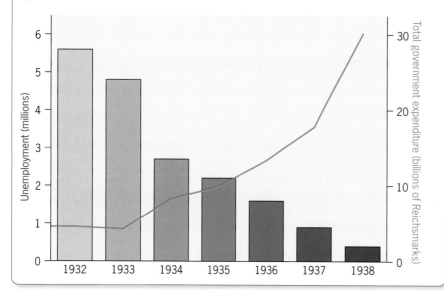

Economic change: Benefits and drawbacks

Hitler's economic miracle – as the Nazis saw it – provided initial advantages for many Germans. The disadvantages were either ignored or not appreciated. Later in the period, it was the drawbacks that came to the fore.

Industrial workers

Hitler promised (and delivered) lower unemployment which helped to ensure popularity among **industrial workers**. These workers were important to the Nazis: Hitler needed good workers to create the industries that would help to make Germany great and establish a new German empire in eastern Europe. This was an area containing essential raw materials and good farming land. The Slav people of eastern Europe were viewed as inferior to the Nazis, which provided a justification in itself.

It was very important for Hitler to keep the loyalty of industrial workers, particularly as he had abolished trade unions in stages from spring 1933.

Firstly, the Nazis took over trade union offices, confiscated their funds and arrested the leaders. The May Day parades, traditionally organised by the trade unions, were taken over by the Nazis as a new national holiday. Hitler went on to abolish all political parties other than the Nazis, thus removing the left-wing parties that many industrial workers supported.

In place of the unions, a new organisation was set up – the German Labour Front (DAF) – headed by **Dr Robert Ley**. The DAF kept strict control of workers. It was forbidden to strike for better pay and conditions and in some areas workers were prevented from moving to better paid jobs. Wages remained comparatively low, although prices were also strictly controlled. Even so, by the late 1930s, many workers were grumbling that their standard of living was still lower than it had been before the Depression.

With all these restrictions on workers, the Nazis had to work very hard to gain and maintain the loyalty of the working class, many of whom had voted Communist before Hitler became Chancellor. The DAF appealed to the patriotism of the workers. It was a national organisation, whereas the trade unions had represented sections of workers. The workers were referred to as a 'labour force' – the people who would work to make Germany great again after the disgrace of the Treaty of Versailles; the people who would rebuild Germany's reputation as a major world power.

Propaganda was extremely important in getting and maintaining support from this labour force. The message was clear: the re-building of Germany was in the hands of the workers; the nation was going to regain its greatness, at a time when other European countries were suffering from the consequences of the Great Depression. All the visual aspects of propaganda played on the emotions of the workers – the posters, the parades, the music, the films, helped by the Nazis' total control of the newspapers and radio.

Hitler also won the loyalty of industrial workers by a variety of initiatives:

- Schemes such as **Strength through Joy (KDF)** gave them cheap theatre and cinema tickets, and organised courses, trips and sports events. Workers were offered cut-price cruises on the latest luxury liners.
- Many thousands of workers saved five marks a week in the state scheme to buy the **Volkswagen Beetle**, the 'people's car'. It was designed by Ferdinand Porsche and became a symbol of the prosperous new Germany, even though no workers ever received a car because all car production was halted by the war in 1939.
- Another important scheme was the **Beauty of Labour** movement. This improved working conditions in factories. It introduced features not seen in many workplaces before, such as washing facilities and low-cost canteens.

Although some workers continued to grumble and to sympathise with Communist beliefs, most toed the Nazi line, as did other groups in society. By 1939 over 21 million workers were members of the German Labour Front. Hitler had his workforce, to build factories and roads and to re-arm the country for future war.

Farming communities

The farmers had been an important factor in the Nazis' rise to power. Hitler did not forget this and introduced a series of measures to help them. In September 1933 he introduced the **Reich Food Estate**. This set up central boards to buy agricultural produce from the farmers and distribute it to markets across Germany. It gave the peasant farmers a guaranteed market for their goods at guaranteed prices.

The second main measure was the **Reich Entailed Farm Law**. It gave peasants state protection for their farms: banks could not seize their land if they could not pay loans or mortgages. This ensured that peasants' farms stayed in their hands.

The Reich Entailed Farm Law also had a racial aim. Part of the Nazi philosophy was **'Blood and Soil'**, the belief that the peasant farmers were the basis of Germany's master race. They would be the backbone of the new German Empire in the east. As a result, their way of life had to be protected. As Source 4 shows, the measures were widely appreciated.

However, rather like the industrial workers, some peasants were not thrilled with the regime's measures. The Reich Food Estate meant that efficient, go-ahead farmers were held back by having to work through the same processes as less efficient farmers. Because of the Reich Entailed Farm Law, banks were unwilling to lend money to farmers. It also meant that only the eldest child inherited the farm. As a result, many children of farmers left the land to work for better pay in Germany's industries. **Rural depopulation** ran at about 3 per cent per year in the 1930s – the exact opposite of the Nazis' aims!

SOURCE 4

Lusse Essig's memories of harvest festivals in the 1930s. Lusse was a farm worker who went on to work for the Agriculture Ministry between 1937 and 1945.

Thousands of people came from all over Germany to the Harvest Festival celebrations … We all felt the same happiness and joy. Harvest festival was the thank you for us farmers having a future again. I believe no statesman has ever been as well loved as Adolf Hitler was at that time. Those were happy times.

Big business and the middle classes

The record of the Nazis with the **middle classes** was also mixed. Certainly many middle-class business people were grateful to the Nazis for eliminating the Communist threat to their businesses and properties. They also liked the way in which the Nazis seemed to be bringing order to Germany. For the owners of small businesses it was a mixed picture. If you owned a small engineering firm, you were likely to do well from government orders as rearmament spending grew in the 1930s. However, if you produced consumer goods or ran a small shop, you might well struggle. Despite Hitler's promises, the large department stores which were taking business away from local shops were not closed.

PRACTICE QUESTION

Which of the following groups benefited more from Nazi economic policy?

- Industrial workers
- The owners of big business.

Explain your answer with reference to both groups.

Part 2: How did the Nazis' economic policies affect German society?

Using your table that you created in the Focus Task on page 81, write two paragraphs to summarise how the Nazis' economic policies affected different groups in German society.

It was **big business** that really benefited from Nazi rule. The big companies no longer had to worry about troublesome trade unions and strikes. Companies such as the chemicals giant IG Farben gained huge government contracts to make explosives, fertilisers and even artificial oil from coal. Other household names today, such as Mercedes and Volkswagen, prospered from Nazi policies.

Impact of the war on the German economy and the people

Germans had no great enthusiasm for war. People still had memories of the First World War. But in war, as in peacetime, the Nazis used all methods available to make the German people support the regime.

Food rationing was introduced soon after war began in September 1939. Clothes rationing followed in November 1939. Even so, from 1939 to 1941 it was not difficult to keep up civilian morale because the war went spectacularly well for Germany. Hitler was in control of much of western and eastern Europe and supplies of luxury goods flowed into Germany from captured territories.

However, in 1941 Hitler took the massive gamble of invading the Soviet Union, and for the next three years his troops were engaged in an increasingly expensive war with Russian forces who 'tore the heart out of the German army', as the British war leader, Winston Churchill, put it. As the tide turned against the German armies, civilians found their lives increasingly disrupted. They had to cut back on heating, work longer hours and recycle their rubbish. Goebbels redoubled his censorship efforts. He tried to maintain people's support for the war by involving them in it through asking them to make sacrifices. They donated an estimated 1.5 million fur coats to help to clothe the German army in Russia.

1 Study Source 5. What are the clues that this is propaganda?
2 Why was it so important for the Nazis to produce propaganda like this two years after the start of the Second World War?

SOURCE 5

From the Nazi propaganda magazine *Signal*, 1941, showing life in Germany continuing as normal despite the war.

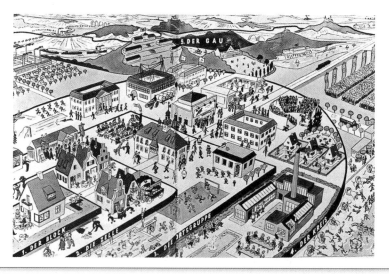

State control of the economy from 1942 onwards

From 1942, Albert Speer (as Minister of Armaments and War Production) began to direct Germany's war economy. All effort focused on the armament industries. Postal services were suspended and letter boxes were closed. All places of entertainment were closed, except cinemas – Goebbels needed these to show propaganda films. Women were drafted into the labour force in increasing numbers. Country areas had to take evacuees from the cities and refugees from eastern Europe.

These measures were increasingly carried out by the SS. In fact, the SS became virtually a state within the German state. This SS empire had its own armed forces, armaments industries and labour camps. It developed a business empire that was worth a fortune. However, even the SS could not win the war, let alone keep up German morale.

Bombing on German cities

British bombing on German cities began in 1942 when the north German city of Lubeck was virtually destroyed. Between 1943 and 1945, with American help, major bombing assaults were made on cities such as Hamburg and Dresden. Overall, it is estimated that about half a million German civilians died and three-quarters of a million were wounded, while 7.5 million German civilians were made homeless.

The loss of morale among German civilians

With defeat looming, support for the Nazis weakened. Germans stopped declaring food they had. They stayed away from Nazi rallies. They refused to give the 'Heil Hitler' salute when asked to do so. Himmler even contacted the Allies to ask about possible peace terms.

Refugees

By 1945 the German people were in a desperate state. As well as those made homeless by Allied bombings, refugees were fleeing the advancing Russian armies in the east. In eastern Germany over 3 million Germans were fleeing, but they got no help from the retreating German army. No transport was easily available as priority was given to retreating German troops and to moving equipment. Most of those fleeing were forced to walk hundreds of miles, with attendant cold, hunger and disease. Over half a million died on the journey. When the survivors reached western Germany they found cities devastated by bombing and chronic food shortages.

SOURCE 6

The text on this poster reads 'Hard times, hard tasks, hard hearts'.

SOURCE 7

A 1943 poster telling people to black out their windows: 'The enemy sees your light!'

FACTFILE

Germany and the Second World War

Sept 1939	German invasion of Poland
Spring 1940	German invasion of Holland, Belgium and France
Summer 1940	Start of the Battle of Britain
Spring 1941	German invasion of Balkans
June 1941	German invasion of the USSR
October 1942	German defeat at El Alamein in North Africa
February 1943	German army surrenders to Russians at Stalingrad
June 1944	Allied invasion of Europe (D-Day landings)
January 1945	Russian and Allied troops move in on Germany
May 1945	End of war in Europe; Hitler commits suicide.

PRACTICE QUESTIONS

1 Describe two problems faced by German civilians during the Second World War.
2 In what ways were the living standards of German civilians affected by the Second World War? Explain your answer.

THINK

What techniques do Sources 6 and 7 use to make them effective propaganda posters?

• Social policy and practice

Hitler wanted all Germans to think of themselves as part of a national community. Their first loyalty would be to Germany and the Führer, not to their regional area or group within society. They would be proud to belong to a great nation. Hitler's policies towards each group were designed to encourage this kind of loyalty to the Nazi state. In part, Hitler succeeded. The apparent benefits of Nazi rule made most Germans willing to accept some social control in the interests of making Germany great again.

SOURCE 8

A painting showing the Nazis' view of an ideal German family.

Effects on women

The Nazis were a very male-dominated organisation, and all the Nazi leaders were men. Hitler had a very traditional view of the role of the German woman as wife and mother. It is worth remembering that many women at the time agreed with him. In the traditional rural areas and small towns, many women felt that the proper role of a woman was to support her husband. There was also resentment towards working women in the early 1930s, since they were seen as keeping men out of jobs. It all created a lot of pressure on women to conform to what the Nazis called 'the traditional balance' between men and women. Women's role in society was summed up as 'Kinder, Küche, Kirche' ('Children, Cooking, Church').

Alarmed at the falling birth rate, Hitler offered tempting financial incentives for married couples to have at least four children. Women who had eight children received a 'Gold Cross', and were given a privileged seat at Nazi meetings. Posters, radio broadcasts and newsreels all celebrated the ideas of motherhood and homebuilding. The German Maidens' League reinforced these ideas, focusing on a combination of good physical health and housekeeping skills. This was reinforced at school (see Source 14 on page 88).

With all these encouragements the birth rate did increase from 15 per thousand in 1933 to 20 per thousand in 1939. There was also an increase in pregnancies outside marriage. These girls were looked after in state maternity hostels.

THINK

1. In what ways does Source 8 show typical Nazi values?
2. Using Source 9 and your contextual knowledge, why were camps such as the ones shown important in Nazi Germany in the 1930s?

SOURCE 9

Girls from the German Maidens' League camping. The League offered excitement and escape from boring duties in the home.

However, by 1939 there was a shortage of labour to work in factories. Many women were encouraged back into work – and this process accelerated during the early 1940s with the huge demands for war materials.

SOURCE 10

Leni Riefenstahl directing the shooting of her film of the 1936 Olympics.

SOURCE 11

Albert Speer, *Inside The Third Reich*, 1970. Speer was Minister of Armaments and War Production.

I went to Sauckel [the Nazi minister in charge of labour] with the proposition that we should recruit our labour from the ranks of German women. He replied brusquely that where to obtain which workers was his business. Moreover, he said, as Gauleiter [a regional governor] he was Hitler's subordinate and responsible to the Führer alone … Sauckel offered to put the question to Goering as Commissioner of the Four-Year Plan … but I was scarcely allowed to advance my arguments. Sauckel and Goering continually interrupted me. Sauckel laid great weight on the danger that factory work might inflict moral harm on German womanhood; not only might their 'psychic and emotional life' be affected but also their ability to bear children.

Goering totally concurred. But just to be absolutely sure, Sauckel went immediately to Hitler and had him confirm the decision. All my good arguments were therefore blown to the winds.

FOCUS TASK

How successful were the Nazi policies for women?

Read these two statements:

- 'Nazi policy for women was confused.'
- 'Nazi policy for women was a failure.'

For each statement explain whether you agree or disagree with it and use examples from the text to support your explanation.

Nazi policies towards young people and their impact

It was Hitler's aim to control every aspect of life in Germany, including the daily life of ordinary people. The Nazis had reorganised every aspect of the school curriculum to make children loyal to them.

Education policies and their impact

At school you would have learned about the history of Germany. You would have been outraged to find out how the German army was 'stabbed in the back' by the weak politicians who had made peace. You might well remember the hardships of the 1920s for yourself, but at school you would have been told how these were caused by Jews squeezing profits out of honest Germans. By the time you were a senior pupil, your studies in history would have made you confident that loyalty to the Führer was right and good. Your biology lessons would have informed you that you were special, as one of the Aryan race which was so superior in intelligence and strength to the *Untermenschen* or sub-human Jews and Slavs of eastern Europe. In maths you would have been set questions like the one in Source 13.

SOURCE 12

Dr Robert Ley, who was Chief of the Labour Front and in charge of making 'good citizens' out of the German people.

Our state is an educational state … It does not let a man go free from the cradle to the grave. We begin with the child when he is three years old. As soon as he begins to think, he is made to carry a little flag. Then follows school, the Hitler Youth, the storm troopers and military training. We don't let him go; and when all that is done, comes the Labour Front, which takes possession of him again, and does not let him go till he dies, even if he does not like it.

SOURCE 13

A question from a Nazi maths textbook, 1933.

The Jews are aliens in Germany. In 1933 there were 66,060,000 inhabitants of the German Reich of whom 499,862 were Jews. What is the percentage of aliens in Germany?

SOURCE 14

The daily timetable for a girls' school in Nazi Germany.

8.00	German (every day)
8.50	Geography, History or Singing (alternate days)
9.40	Race Studies and Ideology (every day)
10.25	Recess, Sports and Special Announcements (every day)
11.00	Domestic Science or Maths (alternate days)
12.10	Eugenics or Health Biology (alternate days)
1.00–6.00	Sport
Evenings	Sex education, Ideology or Domestic Science (one evening each)

SOURCE 15

A German newspaper, heavily controlled by the Nazis, approves of the curriculum in 1939.

All subjects – German language, History, Geography, Chemistry and Mathematics – must concentrate on military subjects, the glorification of military service and of German heroes and leaders and the strength of a rebuilt Germany. Chemistry will develop a knowledge of chemical warfare, explosives, etc., while Mathematics will help the young to understand artillery, calculations, ballistics.

As a member of the Hitler Youth (boys) or League of German Maidens (girls), you would have marched in exciting parades with loud bands. You would probably be physically fit. Your leisure time would also be devoted to Hitler and the Nazis. You would be a strong cross-country runner, and confident at reading maps. After years of summer camps, you would be comfortable camping out of doors and if you were a boy you would know how to clean a rifle and keep it in good condition.

Youth organisations

As a child in Nazi Germany, you might well feel slightly alienated (estranged) from your parents because they are not as keen on the Nazis as you are. They expect your first loyalty to be to your family, whereas your Hitler Youth leader makes it clear that your first loyalty is to Adolf Hitler. You find it hard to understand why your father grumbles about Nazi regulation of his working practices – surely the Führer (Hitler) is protecting him? Your parents find the idea of Nazi inspectors checking up on the teachers rather strange. For you it is normal.

THINK

1 Read Source 12. Do you think that the speaker is proud of what he is saying?
2 Do you think the real aim of the question in Source 13 is to improve mathematical skills?
3 Read Source 14. Eugenics is the study of how to produce perfect offspring by choosing ideal qualities in the parents. How would this help the Nazis?

SOURCE 16

A young German describes his feelings after a Hitler Youth rally.

Hitler looked over the stand, and I know he looked into my eyes, and he said: 'You my boys are the standard bearers, you will inherit what we have created.' From that moment there was not any doubt I was bound to Adolf Hitler until long after our defeat. Afterwards I told my friends how Hitler had looked into my eyes, but they all said: 'No! It was my eyes he was looking into.'

THINK

Study Sources 17 and 18. In what ways do they illustrate how the Nazis gained support for their policies?

SOURCE 17

Members of the Hitler Youth in the 1930s. From a very early age children were encouraged to join the Nazi youth organisations. It was not compulsory, but most young people did join.

SOURCE 18

Illustration from a Nazi children's book. The children are being taught to distrust Jews.

PRACTICE QUESTIONS

Read Interpretations A and B and then answer Questions 1–3.

Interpretation A An account of life in a Hitler Youth Camp in the 1930s. It is from *This is Germany* by C. W. Domville-Fife, a British writer, published in 1939. It was written to explain what the author had seen in a recent visit to a Hitler Youth Camp.

Life in the camp appeared to be one of healthy exercise in sports and games, but absolute discipline was maintained. By this I do not mean that it was harshly enforced. The boys were happy to accept it.

It seemed to me also that, although every boy was conscious of his approaching military service, there was little if any drill performed in the camp. The leader has, of course, served in the German army, and military enthusiasm is part of the healthy and cheerful pattern of the German Boy Scout movement.

Interpretation B A description of a Hitler Youth Camp in the 1930s. It comes from a book published in 1938, *Just Back from Germany* by J. A. Cole, a British writer.

It is claimed that the work of the Hitler Youth is in no way pre-military training. All the same, I should think it is a good preparation for the army. The children learn discipline. They march in ranks. They drill. When I attended a Hitler Youth Camp, I asked a boy what they had done last night. In the presence of several others and one of the leaders, he said pistol-shooting. Very good fun, and not necessarily a military pastime. However, it hardly justifies the claim that the youth movements have nothing to do with military training.

1 How does Interpretation B differ from Interpretation A about the Hitler Youth Camps?

   Explain your answer based on what it says in Interpretations A and B.

2 Why might the authors of Interpretations A and B have a different interpretation about Hitler Youth Camps?

   Explain your answer using Interpretations A and B and your contextual knowledge.

3 Which interpretation gives the more convincing opinion about the Hitler Youth Camps?

   Explain your answer based on your contextual knowledge and what it says in Interpretations A and B.

FOCUS TASK

How did young people react to the Nazi regime?

1 Young people were among the most fanatical supporters of the Nazi regime. Use pages 88–90 to write three paragraphs to explain why the Nazis were successful in winning them over. Include the following points:
   – Why the Nazis wanted to control young people.
   – How they set about doing it.
   – What the attractions of the youth movements were.
2 The Nazi regime was not successful in keeping the loyalty of all young people. Add a fourth paragraph to your essay to explain why some young people rejected the Nazi youth movements.

SOURCE 19

From a report by the Nazi youth leadership, 1942.

The formation of cliques, i.e. groupings of young people outside the Hitler Youth, has been on the increase before and particularly during the war to such a degree that one must speak of a serious risk of political, moral and criminal subversion of our youth.

SOURCE 20

The public hanging of twelve Edelweiss Pirates in Cologne in 1944.

Did all young people support the Nazis?

This is a difficult question to answer because many factors have to be taken into account. It depended on whether you were a young person from a working-class or middle-class background. It depended on you as a person of course. It also depended on when we ask that question. Levels of support for the Nazis differed at different times. Many young people were attracted to the Nazi youth movements by the leisure opportunities they offered. There were really no alternatives. All other youth organisations had been either absorbed or made illegal. Even so, only half of all German boys were members of the Hitler Youth in 1933 and only 15 per cent of girls were members of the League of German Maidens. As with all other sections of society, young people were monitored closely and the reports of the security services threw up some interesting groups, such as the 'Swing' youth movement and the Edelweiss Pirates. Neither of these groups had strong political views. They were not political opponents of the Nazis. But they resented and resisted Nazi control of their lives.

● **The 'Swing' youth:** This was made up mainly of middle-class teenagers. They went to parties where they listened to English and American music and sang English songs. They danced American dances such as the 'jitterbug' to jazz music which the Nazis had banned. They accepted Jews at their clubs. They talked about and enjoyed sex. They were deliberately 'slovenly'.

● **The Edelweiss Pirates:** The Edelweiss Pirates were working-class teenagers. They were not an organised movement, and groups in various cities took different names. The Pirates were mainly aged between 14 and 17 (Germans could leave school at fourteen, but they did not have to sign on for military service until they were seventeen). At the weekends, the Pirates went camping. They sang songs, just like the Hitler Youth, but they changed the lyrics of songs to mock Germany and when they spotted bands of Hitler Youth they taunted and sometimes attacked them. In contrast with the Hitler Youth, the Pirates included boys and girls.

The impact of the war

In 1939 membership of a Nazi youth movement was made compulsory. But by this time the youth movements were going through a crisis. Many of the experienced leaders had been drafted into the German army. Others, particularly those who had been leaders in the pre-Nazi days, had been replaced by keener Nazis. Many of the movements were now run by older teenagers who rigidly enforced Nazi rules. They even forbade other teenagers to meet informally with their friends.

As the war progressed, the activities of the youth movements focused increasingly on the war effort and military drill. The popularity of the movements decreased and indeed the popularity of anti-Hitler Youth movements increased. The Pirates' activities became increasingly serious during the war. In Cologne, for example, Pirates helped to shelter army deserters and escaped prisoners. They stole armaments and took part in an attack on the GESTAPO during which its chief was killed. The Nazi response was to round up the so-called 'ringleaders'. Twelve were publicly hanged in November 1944.

Control of Churches and religion

The relationship between the Churches and the Nazis was complicated. In the early stages of the Nazi regime, there was some co-operation between the Nazis and the Churches. Hitler signed a Concordat with the Catholic Church in 1933. This meant that Hitler agreed to leave the Catholic Church alone and allowed it to keep control of its schools. In return, the Church agreed to stay out of politics.

Hitler attempted to unify all of the Protestant Churches in one official Reich Church. The Reich Church was headed by the Protestant Bishop Ludwig Müller. However, many Germans still felt that their true loyalties lay with their original Churches in their local areas rather than with this state-approved Church.

In the 1930s at least most were totally ignorant about the intentions of Nazi policies towards the Jews and other minority groups. Many churchgoers either supported the Nazis or did little to oppose them. However, there were some very important exceptions. The Catholic Bishop Galen criticised the Nazis throughout the 1930s. In 1941 he led a popular protest against the Nazi policies of killing mentally ill and physically disabled people, forcing the Nazis temporarily to stop this policy. He had such strong support among his followers that the Nazis decided it was too risky to try to silence him because they did not want trouble while Germany was at war.

Protestant ministers also resisted the Nazis. Pastor Martin Niemöller was one of the most high-profile critics of the regime in the 1930s. Along with Dietrich Bonhoeffer, he formed an alternative Protestant Church to the official Reich Church. Niemöller spent the years 1938–45 in a concentration camp for resisting the Nazis. Dietrich Bonhoeffer preached against the Nazis until the Gestapo stopped him in 1937. He then became involved with members of the army's intelligence services who were secretly opposed to Hitler. He helped Jews to escape from Germany. Gradually he increased his activity and in 1942 he contacted the Allied commanders and asked what peace terms they would offer Germany if Hitler were overthrown. He was arrested in October 1942 and hanged shortly before the end of the war in April 1945.

SOURCE 21

British historian and journalist Charles Wheeler, writing in 1996.

Most post-war accounts have concentrated on the few German clerics who did behave bravely … But these were few. Most German church leaders were shamefully silent. As late as January 1945, the Catholic bishop of Würzburg was urging his flock to fight on for the Fatherland, saying that 'salvation lies in sacrifice'.

SOURCE 22

An extract from 'The Role of the Churches: Compliance and Confrontation', an article written by Victoria J. Barnett in 1998. The author is a researcher who specialises in the role of the Churches in Nazi Germany.

Reflecting on the failure of the Churches to challenge the Nazis should prompt us to ponder all the others – individuals, governments and institutions – that passively acquiesced to [slightly accepted] the Third Reich's tyranny. Even the wisest and most perceptive of them, it seems, failed to develop adequate moral and political responses to Nazi genocide [mass killing], failed to recognise that something new was demanded of them by the barbarism of Hitler's regime. Moreover, it has become abundantly clear that their failure to respond to the horrid events in Europe in the thirties and forties was not due to ignorance; they knew what was happening.

Ultimately, the Churches' lapses during the Nazi era were lapses of vision and determination. Protestant and Catholic religious leaders, loyal to creeds professing that love can withstand and conquer evil, were unable or unwilling to defy one of the great evils in human history. And so the Holocaust will continue to haunt the Christian Churches for a very, very long time to come.

FOCUS TASK

How did the Churches respond to the Nazis?

Sources 21 and 22 offer very harsh judgements about the role of the Churches in Nazi Germany.

1 Make a list of the most serious accusations which the authors make against the Churches.
2 Now find evidence and examples which support or contradict those accusations.
3 Now make a list of examples which either explain or justify the actions of the Churches. Remember there may be a big difference between something which explains and something which justifies the actions of the Churches.
4 There were other groups in Germany (with a few exceptional individuals) which either co-operated with the Nazis or failed to resist them, such as:
   – political parties
   – judges and lawyers
   – army commanders
   – industrialists.

Do you think it is fair that Sources 21 and 22 criticise the Churches more harshly than these other groups? Explain your answer in a paragraph.

Aryan ideas, racial policy and persecution

The Nazis believed in the superiority of the Aryan race. Through their 12 years in power they persecuted members of other races, and many minority groups such as Gypsies, homosexuals and mentally handicapped people. They persecuted any group that they thought challenged Nazi ideas: homosexuals were a threat to Nazi ideas on traditional family life; the mentally handicapped were a threat to Nazi ideas about Germans being a perfect master race; Gypsies were thought to be an inferior people.

The persecution of such minorities varied. In families where there were hereditary illnesses, sterilisation was enforced. Over 300,000 men and women were compulsorily sterilised between 1934 and 1945. A so-called 'euthanasia programme' was begun in 1939. At least 5,000 severely mentally handicapped babies and children were killed between 1939 and 1945 either by injection or by starvation. Between 1939 and 1941, 72,000 mentally ill patients were gassed before a public outcry in Germany itself brought this to an end. The extermination of the Gypsies, on the other hand, did not cause an outcry. Five out of every six Gypsies living in Germany in 1939 were killed by the Nazis. Similarly, there was little or no complaint about the treatment of so-called 'asocials' – homosexuals, alcoholics, the homeless, prostitutes, habitual criminals and beggars – who were rounded up off the streets and sent to concentration camps.

You are going to investigate this most disturbing aspect of Nazi Germany by tracing the story of Nazi treatment of the Jewish population in which anti-Semitism culminated in the dreadful slaughter of the 'FINAL SOLUTION'.

SOURCE 23

This text appeared on a poster published in 1920, directed at 'All German mothers'. It explains how many German Jews were killed fighting for their country in the First World War. It was produced by a Jewish soldiers' organisation, the Reich's Alliance of Jewish Frontline Soldiers.

To German mothers!

72000 Jewish soldiers died for the Fatherland on the field of honour.

Christian and Jewish heroes fought together and rest together in foreign lands.

120000 Jews fell in battle!

Blind rage for the Party will not stop before the graves of the dead.

Women of Germany, do not allow Jewish mothers to be mocked in their anguish.

SOURCE 24

SA and SS men enforcing the boycott of Jewish shops, April 1933.

SOURCE 25

From A. Bullock, *Hitler: A Study in Tyranny*, published in 1990.

To read the pages [of Hitler's Mein Kampf*] is to enter a world of the insane, a world peopled by hideous and distorted shadows. The Jew is no longer a human being, he has become a mythical figure, a grimacing leering devil invested with infernal powers, the incarnation of evil.*

THINK

1 What does Source 23 suggest about attitudes to Jews in 1920?
2 Why did Hitler hate the Jews?

Hitler and the Jews

Anti-Semitism means hatred of Jews. Throughout Europe, Jews had experienced discrimination for hundreds of years. They were often treated unjustly in courts or forced to live in GHETTOS. One reason for this persecution was religious, in that Jews were blamed for the death of Jesus Christ. Another reason was that they tended to be well educated and therefore held well-paid professional jobs or ran successful stores and businesses.

Hitler hated Jews insanely. In his years of poverty in Vienna, he became obsessed by the fact that Jews ran many of the most successful businesses, particularly the large department stores. This offended his idea of the superiority of Aryans. Hitler also blamed Jewish businessmen and bankers for Germany's defeat in the First World War. He thought they had forced the surrender of the German army.

As soon as Hitler took power in 1933 he began to mobilise the full powers of the state against the Jews. They were immediately banned from the civil service and a variety of public services such as broadcasting and teaching. At the same time, SA and later SS troopers organised boycotts of Jewish shops and businesses, which were marked with a Star of David.

In 1936 the pressure on Jews and other minorities relaxed a little. Some Jews saw this as a positive sign, and believed that the regime had gone as far as it was going to go to persecute them. The reality was that the persecution lapsed primarily because Germany was trying to present itself to the world in a positive light while the Olympics were being held in Berlin. During this respite many Jews took the opportunity to emigrate from Germany to any country which would take them.

Kristallnacht

In November 1938 a young Jew killed a German diplomat in Paris. The Nazi Propaganda Minister Joseph Goebbels turned this event into an opportunity for himself. He had recently fallen out of favour with Hitler and was desperate to regain his favoured status. Goebbels urged a wide-scale and brutal response to the event in Paris. Plain-clothes SS troopers were issued with pickaxes and hammers and the addresses of Jewish businesses. They ran riot, smashing up Jewish shops and workplaces. Ninety-one Jews were murdered. Hundreds of synagogues were burned. Twenty thousand Jews were taken to concentration camps and thousands more left the country. This event became known as *Kristallnacht* or 'The Night of Broken Glass'. Many Germans watched the events of *Kristallnacht* with alarm and concern. The Nazi-controlled press presented *Kristallnacht* as the spontaneous reaction of ordinary Germans against the Jews. Most Germans did not believe this. However, hardly anyone protested. The few who did were brutally murdered.

SOURCE 26

Anonymous letter from a German civil servant to the British consul, 1938.

I feel the urge to present to you a true report of the recent riots, plundering and destruction of Jewish property. Despite what the official Nazi account says, the German people have nothing whatever to do with these riots and burnings. The police supplied SS men with axes, house-breaking tools and ladders. A list of the addresses of all Jewish shops and flats was provided and the mob worked under the leadership of the SS men. The police had strict orders to remain neutral.

FOCUS TASK

How did Nazi policies towards minorities develop from the 1930s onwards?

Draw your own copy of the graph below. The aim is to show how Nazi policies towards minorities developed during the 1930s and beyond. Use the information and sources in this section, but refer to other sections of this chapter as well, especially the details on page 79.

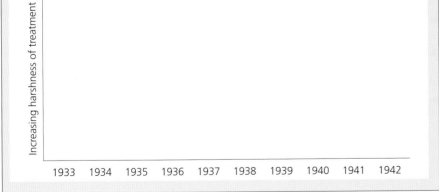

SOURCE 27

A cartoon from the Nazi newspaper *Der Stürmer*, 1935. Jews owned many shops and businesses. These were a constant target for Nazi attacks. This cartoon depicts stereotypically Jewish shopkeepers selling rats as meat. The caption reads 'Not quite kosher'.

SOURCE 28

Henrik Metelmann, member of the Hitler Youth, in 1938.

[The day after Kristallnacht] the teachers told us: don't worry about what you see, even if you see some nasty things which you may not understand. Hitler wants a better Germany, a clean Germany. Don't worry, everything will work out fine in the end.

SOURCE 29

Alfons Heck, member of the Hitler Youth in 1938, interviewed for a television programme in 1989.

Until Kristallnacht, many Germans believed Hitler was not engaged in mass murder. [The treatment of the Jews] seemed to be a minor form of harassment of a disliked minority. But after Kristallnacht no German could any longer be under any illusion. I believe it was the day that we lost our innocence. But it would be fair to point out that I myself never met even the most fanatic Nazi who wanted the extermination [mass murder] of the Jews. Certainly we wanted the Jews out of Germany, but we did not want them to be killed.

THINK

1 Read Sources 26, 28 and 29. How useful is each source to a historian looking at the German reaction to *Kristallnacht*?
2 Taken together, do they provide a clear picture of how Germans felt about *Kristallnacht*?

The Final Solution

The persecution of the Jews developed in intensity after the outbreak of war in 1939. After defeating Poland in 1939, the Nazis set about 'Germanising' western Poland. This meant transporting Poles from their homes and replacing them with German settlers. Almost one in five Poles died in the fighting and as a result of racial policies of 1939–45. Polish Jews were rounded up and transported to the major cities. Here they were herded into sealed areas, called ghettos. The able-bodied Jews were used for slave labour but the young, the old and the sick were simply left to die from hunger and disease.

The decision to go ahead with the systematic killing of all Jews was apparently taken in January 1942 at the Wannsee Conference on the outskirts of Berlin by senior Nazis. Himmler, the head of the SS and Gestapo, was put in charge of the programme of mass murder, which began on an industrial scale in camps such as those at Auschwitz and Treblinka in Poland.

Was the 'Final Solution' planned from the start?

Historians have debated intensely as to whether or not the 'Final Solution' was the result of a long-term plan of Hitler. Some historians (intentionalists) believe the whole dreadful process was planned. Other historians (structuralists) argue that there was no clear plan and that the policy of mass murder evolved during the war years. Part of the problem is the lack of evidence. Hitler made speeches in which he talked of the annihilation of the Jews, but he never signed any documents or made any recorded orders directly relating to the extermination of the Jews. The Nazis kept the killing programme as secret as they could, so there are relatively few documents.

Although historians disagree about whether there was a plan, they do generally agree that Hitler was ultimately responsible. However, they also point to others who bear some of the responsibility as well. The GENOCIDE would not have been possible without the following:

- The civil service bureaucracy – it collected and stored information about Jews.
- Police forces in Germany and the occupied lands – many victims of the Nazis, such as Anne Frank, were actually taken by the police rather than the Gestapo or SS.
- The SS – Adolf Eichmann devised a system of transporting Jews to collection points and then on to the death camps. He was also in charge of looting the possessions of the Jews. The SS Death's Head battalions and *Einsatzgruppen* also carried out many of the killings.
- The *Wehrmacht* (German armed forces) – the army leaders were fully aware of events.
- Industry – companies such as Volkswagen and Mercedes had their own slave labour camps. The chemicals giant IG Farben competed with other companies for the contract to make the Cyclon B gas which was used in the gas chambers.
- The German people – there was widespread support for anti-Semitism, even if these feelings did not include support for mass murder. Many Germans took part in some aspect of the HOLOCAUST, but closed their eyes to the full reality of what was happening (see Source 30).

SOURCE 30

American historian Gordon Craig, 1978.

The extermination of the Jews is the most dreadful chapter in German history, doubly so because the men who did it closed their senses to the reality of what they were doing by taking pride in the technical efficiency of their actions and, at moments when their conscience threatened to break in, telling themselves that they were doing their duty … others took refuge in the enormity of the operation, which lent it a convenient depersonalisation. When they ordered a hundred Jews to get on a train in Paris or Amsterdam, they considered their job accomplished and carefully closed their minds to the thought that eventually those passengers would arrive in front of the ovens of Treblinka.

● Nazi control

The Nazis under Hitler took control of the media and the Churches, restricted culture and dealt ruthlessly with any opposition. Thus, in theory, control over people's lives was total.

Goebbels and propaganda in Nazi Germany

Hitler appointed Dr Joseph Goebbels as Minister for Enlightenment and Propaganda. Goebbels passionately believed in Hitler as the saviour of Germany. His mission was to make sure that others believed this too. Throughout the twelve years of Nazi rule Goebbels constantly kept his finger on the pulse of public opinion and decided what the German public should and should not hear. He aimed to use every resource available to him to make people loyal to Hitler and the Nazis.

The Nuremberg rallies

Goebbels organised huge rallies, marches, torch-lit processions and meetings. Probably the best example was the Nuremberg rally which took place in the summer each year. There were bands, marches, flying displays and Hitler's brilliant speeches. The rallies brought some colour and excitement into people's lives. They gave them a sense of belonging to a great movement. The rallies also showed the German people the power of the state and convinced them that 'every other German' fully supported the Nazis. Goebbels also recognised that one of the Nazis' main attractions was that they created order out of chaos and so the whole rally was organised to emphasise this order.

> **PROFILE**
>
> ### Joseph Goebbels
> - From a humble background but very intelligent; university educated.
> - Small in stature and with a twisted right leg.
> - Joined Nazi Party in 1922; became one of Hitler's greatest supporters.
> - Created a Nazi newspaper in 1927, and soon became head of Nazi propaganda.
> - Became Minister for Public Enlightenment in 1933.
> - Promoted the Nazi message through films, radio, posters and the 1936 Olympic Games.
> - Encouraged burning of books that could be hostile to NAZISM. Bitterly anti-Jewish.
> - Skilful public speaker.
> - Committed suicide one day after Hitler in 1945.

> **THINK**
>
> Look at Source 31. How does the rally:
>
> a) make it clear who the leader is
> b) give people a sense of belonging
> c) provide colour and excitement
> d) show the power of the state
> e) show the Nazis' ability to create order out of chaos?

SOURCE 31

The annual rally at Nuremberg. The whole town was taken over and the rally dominated radio broadcasts and newsreels.

A Hitler speaks to the assembled Germans.

B A parade through the streets.

SOURCE 32

Poster advertising cheap Nazi-produced radios. The text reads 'All Germany hears the Führer on the People's Radio'. The radios had only a short range and were unable to pick up foreign stations.

SOURCE 33

A Nazi propaganda poster from the 1930s encouraging people to turn to Nazi-led community groups for help and advice.

Censorship and Nazi control of the media

Less spectacular than the rallies but possibly more important was Goebbels' control of the media. In contrast with the free expression of Weimar Germany, the Nazis controlled the media strictly. No books could be published without Goebbels' permission (not surprisingly the best-seller in Nazi Germany was *Mein Kampf*). In 1933 he organised a high-profile 'book-burning'. Nazi students came together publicly to burn any books that included ideas unacceptable to the Nazis.

Artists suffered the same kinds of restriction as writers. Only Nazi-approved painters could show their works. These were usually paintings or sculptures of heroic-looking Aryans, military figures or images of the ideal Aryan family.

Goebbels also controlled the newspapers closely. They were not allowed to print anti-Nazi ideas. Within months of the Nazi takeover, Jewish editors and journalists found themselves out of work and anti-Nazi newspapers were closed down. The German newspapers became very dull reading and Germans bought fewer newspapers as a result – circulation fell by about 10 per cent.

The cinema was also closely controlled. All films – factual or fictional, thrillers or comedies – had to carry a pro-Nazi message. Foreign films coming into Germany were censored by Goebbels. The newsreels which preceded feature films were full of the greatness of Hitler and the massive achievements of Nazi Germany. There is evidence that Germans avoided these productions by arriving late!

Goebbels plastered Germany with posters proclaiming the successes of Hitler and the Nazis and attacking their opponents. He banned jazz music (which had been popular in Germany) because it was 'black' music and black people were considered an inferior race.

Goebbels loved new technology and quickly saw the potential of radio broadcasting for spreading the Nazi message. He made cheap radios available so all Germans could buy one and he controlled all the radio stations. Listening to broadcasts from the BBC was punishable by death. Just in case people did not have a radio Goebbels placed loudspeakers in the streets and public bars. Hitler's speeches and those of other Nazi leaders were repeated on the radio over and over again until the ideas expressed in them – German expansion into eastern Europe, the inferiority of the Jews – came to be believed by the German people.

Throughout this period Goebbels was supported in his work by the SS and the Gestapo. When he wanted to close down an anti-Nazi newspaper, silence an anti-Nazi writer, or catch someone listening to a foreign radio station, they were there to do that work for him.

THINK

1   Look at Source 32 and explain why Goebbels wanted every German household to have a radio set.
2   Write your own ten-word definition of propaganda.
3   What does Source 33 tell you about the methods used in Nazi propaganda?

The police state

There was supposed to be no room for opposition of any kind in Nazi Germany. The aim was to create a totalitarian state. In a totalitarian state there can be no rival parties, no political debate. Ordinary CITIZENS must divert their whole energy into serving the state and to carrying out its leaders' orders.

The Nazis had a powerful range of organisations and weapons that they used to control Germany and terrorise Germans into submission.

PROFILE

Heinrich Himmler

- Had been a chicken farmer in Germany.
- Became head of the SS in 1929 when it was only a small organisation.
- By 1934 the SS had 52,000 members.
- Himmler was totally loyal to Hitler.
- He had the primary role of eliminating opposition to the Nazis, and carrying out Nazi racial policies.
- The Death's Head Units had the specific job of killing Jews and other undesirables.
- In May 1945 he was captured but committed suicide before his trial.

THE SS

SOURCE 34

SS guards after taking over the Berlin broadcasting station in 1933.

FIGURE 35

The elements of the SS during wartime.

Order police (Ordinary police)		Himmler (Reichsführer–SS and Head of Germany's police)		Race and resettlement office (Resettlement policy, especially in the occupied territories)
RHSA (Security head office for the Reich)	General–SS	Death's Head (Concentration camp units)	Waffen–SS (Military branch)	Office for the strengthening of Germanhood (Racial policy, especially in the occupied territories)

The SS was formed in 1925 from fanatics loyal to Hitler. After virtually destroying the SA in 1934, the SS grew into a huge organisation with many different responsibilities. It was led by Heinrich Himmler. SS men were of course Aryans, very highly trained and totally loyal to Hitler. Under Himmler, the SS had primary responsibility for destroying opposition to Nazism and carrying out the racial policies of the Nazis.

Two important sub-divisions of the SS were the Death's Head units and the Waffen-SS. The Death's Head units were responsible for the concentration camps and the slaughter of the Jews. The Waffen-SS were special SS armoured regiments which fought alongside the regular army.

The information on pages 97–98 gives the impression that Nazi Germany was run like a well-oiled machine: there to do the will of the Führer! Modern research suggests otherwise. It was, in fact, somewhat chaotic and disorganised. Hitler was not hard-working. He disliked paperwork and decision-making. He thought that most things sorted themselves out in time without his intervention. Officials competed with each other to get his approval for particular policies. The result was often a jumble of different government departments competing with each other and getting in each other's way.

THE GESTAPO

SOURCE 36

The Gestapo, the German secret state police, in action.

The Gestapo (secret state police) was the force that was perhaps most feared by the ordinary German citizen. Under the command of Reinhard Heydrich, Gestapo agents had sweeping powers. They could arrest citizens on suspicion and send them to concentration camps without trial or even explanation.

Modern research has shown that Germans thought the Gestapo were much more powerful than they actually were. As a result, many ordinary Germans informed on each other because they thought the Gestapo would find out anyway.

THE POLICE AND THE COURTS

SOURCE 37

German judges swearing their loyalty at the criminal courts in Berlin.

The police and courts also helped to prop up the Nazi dictatorship. Top jobs in local police forces were given to high-ranking Nazis reporting to Himmler. As a result, the police added political 'snooping' to their normal law and order role. They were, of course, under strict instructions to ignore crimes committed by Nazi agents. Similarly, the Nazis controlled magistrates, judges and the courts, which meant that opponents of Nazism rarely received a fair trial.

ACTIVITY

Summarise the information on pages 97–98 in a table with the following headings:

- Organisation
- Duties
- How it helped Hitler to make his position secure.

FOCUS TASK

Terror or propaganda – which was more important?

1 Work in pairs. Using the sources and information on pages 95–96, one of you should make notes on the techniques used by Goebbels to persuade people to support the Nazis. The other person should make notes using the sources and information on pages 97–98 on the work carried out by Himmler to ensure people supported the Nazis.

2 In your pairs discuss which of the following you most agree with:
   a) Goebbels' work was more important to Nazi success than that of Himmler (head of the SS).
   b) Himmler's work was more important to Nazi success than Goebbels'.
   c) The techniques of repression and propaganda go hand in hand – neither would work without the other.

CONCENTRATION CAMPS

SOURCE 38

Political prisoners at the Oranienburg concentration camp near Berlin.

Concentration camps were the Nazis' ultimate SANCTION against their own people. They were set up almost as soon as Hitler took power. The first concentration camps in 1933 were simply makeshift prisons in disused factories and warehouses. Soon these were purpose-built. These camps were usually in isolated rural areas, and run by SS Death's Head units. Prisoners were forced to do hard labour. Food was very limited and prisoners suffered harsh discipline, beatings and random executions. By the late 1930s, deaths in the camps became increasingly common and very few people emerged alive from them. Jews, socialists, Communists, trade unionists, churchmen and anyone else brave enough to criticise the Nazis ended up there.

Opposition and resistance in the Third Reich in the 1930s

The Nazis faced relatively little open opposition during their twelve years in power. In private, Germans complained about the regime and its actions. Some might refuse to give the Nazi salute. They might pass on anti-Nazi jokes and rude stories about senior Nazis. However, serious criticism was always in private, never in public. Historians have debated why this was so. The main answer they have come up with may seem obvious to you if you've read pages 97–98. It was terror! All the Nazis' main opponents had been killed, exiled or put in prison. The rest had been scared into submission. However, it won't surprise you to learn that historians think the answer is not quite as simple as that. Here is a summary of the important factors.

Nazi successes: 'It's all for the good of Germany'

Many Germans admired and trusted Hitler. They were prepared to tolerate rule by terror and to trade their rights in political freedom and free speech in return for work, foreign policy success and what they thought was strong government.

- Economic recovery was deeply appreciated.
- Many felt that the Nazis were bringing some much needed discipline back to Germany by restoring traditional values and clamping down on rowdy Communists.
- Between 1933 and 1938 Hitler's success in foreign affairs made Germans feel that their country was a great power again after the humiliations of the First World War and the Treaty of Versailles. For many Germans, the dubious methods of the Nazis may have been regrettable but necessary for the greater good of the country.

Economic fears: 'I don't want to lose my job'

German workers feared losing their jobs if they did express opposition (see Source 39). Germany had been hit so hard by the Depression that many were terrified by the prospect of being out of work again. It was a similar situation for the bosses. Businesses that did not contribute to Nazi Party funds risked losing Nazi business and going bankrupt, and so in self-defence they conformed as well. If you asked no questions and kept your head down, life in Nazi Germany could be comfortable. 'Keeping your head down' became a national obsession. The SS and its special security service, the SD, went to great lengths to find out what people were saying about the regime, often by listening in on conversations in cafés and bars. Your job could depend on silence.

> ## SOURCE 39
>
> A report by a socialist activist in Germany, February 1936.
>
> *The average worker is primarily interested in work and not in democracy. People who previously enthusiastically supported democracy showed no interest at all in politics. One must be clear about the fact that in the first instance men are fathers of families and have jobs, and that for them politics takes second place and even then only when they expect to get something out of it.*

Propaganda: 'Have you heard the good news?'

Underlying the whole regime was the propaganda machine. This ensured that many Germans found out very little about the bad things that were happening, or if they did they only heard them with a positive, pro-Nazi slant. You have studied the Nazi use of propaganda in detail on pages 95–96. Propaganda was particularly important in maintaining the image of Hitler. The evidence suggests that personal support for Hitler remained high throughout the 1930s.

FOCUS TASK

Why was there so little opposition in Nazi Germany?

1 Draw a spider diagram with the above question in the centre. Using pages 97–98 make notes around the centre under the following four headings:
  - Terror
  - Nazi successes
  - Economic fears
  - Propaganda.
2 Now use your notes to write two paragraphs to explain why there was so little opposition in Nazi Germany. Support your answer with evidence you have studied.

Opposition and resistance during the war

You might think that opinions would turn against the Nazis fairly soon during the Second World War. However, the Nazi propaganda machine helped to cover up defeats and most Germans only heard about successes. Hitler was still personally respected by most Germans right up to 1944 – when Germany was clearly losing the war.

The White Rose Group

Some groups did begin to act against Hitler as the war developed into a worldwide war in 1941. For example, a group of students at Munich University known as the White Rose Group gave out leaflets, put up posters and scrawled graffiti on walls in 1942 and early 1943. The six most prominent members were arrested, tortured and then beheaded. These students are now remembered as heroes in Germany for standing up to Nazi tyranny.

The Stauffenberg bomb plot, July 1944

Much more serious were the plots to end Hitler's rule. They had started in the late 1930s, including one to blow up Hitler in his plane that failed because the bomb did not go off. After various plans and plots that achieved nothing, in 1944 a group of army officers joined together to plan in meticulous detail. They could see that Germany was heading towards defeat and that Hitler was no longer capable of providing clear leadership. Claus von Stauffenberg was also disgusted at the brutality of the SS. The plan was to detonate a bomb under a table at a meeting that Hitler was attending. Army officers would then seize power in Berlin. However, someone moved the briefcase containing the bomb slightly further away from Hitler, and crucially to the other side of a heavy table leg. When the bomb went off, Hitler was only slightly injured, though four people were killed. All the plotters were rounded up and executed.

It was another ten months before the war in Europe ended. The Allies closed in on Berlin. Russian troops got to the city first. Hitler committed suicide on 30 April 1945, and Goebbels did the same the following day. Germany surrendered to the Allies without conditions.

KEY WORDS

Make sure you know what these words mean and are able to define them confidently:
- Autocracy
- Communist (Bolshevik)
- Concentration camps
- Democracy
- *Diktat*
- Final Solution
- *Freikorps*
- Gestapo
- Holocaust
- Imperial
- Hyperinflation
- Kaiser
- Nazism
- Parliamentary government
- Propaganda
- Proportional representation
- Putsch
- Rearmament
- Reichstag
- Reparations
- Republic
- Spartacists
- SA
- SS

TOPIC SUMMARY

The experiences of Germans under the Nazis
- Hitler had become Führer – leader – by summer 1934 and had established a dictatorship.
- Hitler created millions of jobs through public works schemes and expanding the size of the army.
- Many Germans were happy with the economic progress Germany appeared to be making.
- During the Second World War the German economy survived well at first, but there was much suffering by 1944.
- Hitler's policies had huge effects on women who assumed specific roles in society, especially as mothers.
- Many young people gained pride in their country and worshipped Hitler through the Hitler Youth.
- The Churches mostly supported Hitler. Dietrich Bonhoeffer was a notable exception to this.
- Non-German races were increasingly persecuted, from the Nuremberg Laws (1935) to *Kristallnacht* (1938) and the policy of the Final Solution adopted in 1942.
- Hitler maintained control through propaganda and censorship via the SS, the secret police and the courts.
- Opposition groups such as the White Rose Group began to campaign against Hitler during the war. One well-organised plot to assassinate Hitler failed in 1944.

ASSESSMENT FOCUS

KEY

Focus words

Command words

Interpretation/knowledge reminder words

Your exam will include six questions on this topic. The question types will be the same every year, but the questions could be on any content from the specification, so you need to know it all!

We have provided one example of each kind of question. For questions based on interpretations we have used interpretations that you have already come across in this chapter. We have analysed each of the questions to highlight what you are being asked to do and written a sample answer with comments on how it could be improved.

Read Interpretations A and B and then answer questions 1–3. Interpretation A is Interpretation A on page 89. Interpretation B is Interpretation B on page 89.

Q1 How does Interpretation B **differ** from Interpretation A about the Hitler Youth camps?

Explain your answer **based on what it says in Interpretations A and B**. (4 marks)

Sample answer

Interpretation A says that life in the camp included sports and games, but with discipline. Interpretation B focuses on the marching and military training.

Q2 Why might the authors of Interpretations A and B have a **different interpretation** about Hitler Youth camps?

Explain your answer using **Interpretations A and B** and your **contextual knowledge**. (4 marks)

Sample answer

The two authors might have visited different camps. We don't know how much they saw or which parts of Germany they visited.

Q3 Which interpretation gives the **more convincing opinion** about the Hitler Youth camps?

Explain your answer based on your **contextual knowledge** and what it says in **Interpretations A and B**. (8 marks)

Sample answer

We know that Hitler was using the Hitler Youth as a way of preparing German boys for future military conflict. Therefore, although the boys almost always seemed to be having a good time with games, sport and camps, the main purpose was to discipline them for army life and to give them basic training in weaponry. Therefore, I find Interpretation B more convincing. Interpretation A too easily accepts the public perception of Hitler Youth camps that the Nazis wanted to project.

Q4 Describe two political problems faced by the government of the Weimar Republic when it first met **in early 1920**. (4 marks)

Sample answer

The Weimar Republic had a constitution that included proportional representation. The existence of many political parties meant that it was impossible for any one party to get a majority vote.

There were many groups, some of them armed, who were opposed to the new democratic system of government. They wanted a return to what they remembered as the Kaiser's strong rule before the war.

- This answer provides a basic comparison between Interpretations A and B but it needs to provide more detailed evidence.
- For example, you need to be able to explain the differences in the content of the interpretations.
- *What extra evidence could you add to highlight the differences more completely?*

- This answer provides a good basis for development but it would benefit from more analysis of the provenance. For example, you could suggest that the author of Interpretation B had actually talked to boys to gain evidence. So make sure you think about how the writer has obtained the information.
- Also, many British people in the 1930s were applauding Hitler's achievements in Germany. Make sure you think about how the writers' personal attitudes affect their interpretations.
- *Write two sentences for each interpretation on the provenance of each. You should focus on the purpose and attitudes of the two authors.*

- This answer provides a basic analysis of the two interpretations through the use of some factual knowledge. You need to extend it further to argue in more depth.
- However, it is important that the knowledge is used as part of the analysis of the content of the interpretation, rather than being 'free-standing' as 'what I know about the topic'.
- *Think about the tone and language of each interpretation. What words and phrases could you use to describe them?*

- This brief answer introduces two problems, but they are only stated, and so need to be fully described.
- *List TWO details that you could add to EACH of the two short paragraphs in order to make the description more precise.*

Q5 In what ways were the lives of children affected by Nazi policies in the **1930s**?

Explain your answer. (8 marks)

Sample answer

At school in the 1930s the curriculum was changed to stress Nazi values and policies and through History children learnt how Germany would right the wrongs of the Treaty of Versailles and take its rightful place in the world as a leading Aryan nation.

Children were taught about Nazi racial theories, and, through the study of eugenics, how the German race could be improved further by selective breeding. They were taught to despise Jewish children who eventually were banned from attending school.

Out of school most German boys belonged to Hitler Youth and girls to the League of German Maidens. Here they learnt unquestioning obedience and were encouraged to be physically fit. Boys were taught how to use weapons; girls were taught how to cook and bring up children. Youth were also encouraged to spy on their parents and report any anti-Nazi talk.

Q6 Which of the following was the **more important reason** why Hitler became Chancellor in January 1933?
- The consequences of the Wall Street Crash
- The weak Weimar government

Explain your answer with reference to **both reasons**. (12 marks)

Sample answer

Hitler became Chancellor of Germany in January 1933. He controlled the largest party in the Reichstag with 37 per cent of the seats. Other Chancellors had failed to get Germany out of the depression into which it had sunk following the Wall Street Crash.

The Wall Street Crash affected German industry and trade very badly. The USA had loaned money following the Dawes Plan of 1924 (modified with the Young Plan of 1929). Germany had prospered in the late 1920s under Stresemann, but this prosperity was dangerously over-reliant on US dollars. Now with the withdrawal of US money and the collapse in world trade, many German businesses went bankrupt and laid off workers. By late 1932 there were 6 million unemployed, which for many led to destitution and homelessness.

In the midst of this, the Nazis' promises of overturning the Treaty of Versailles and making Germany great again were transmitted through sophisticated propaganda. These simple messages were very popular.

In the late 1920s, the Nazis had very few seats in the Reichstag – only 12 in the election of 1928 – far fewer than their rivals. But because of the effects of the Crash, the Nazis became the largest party in July 1932 with 230 seats.

However, Hitler and the Nazis were assisted by the weak Weimar government. The longest-serving Chancellor in the early 1930s was Brüning. His attempts to solve Germany's economic problems failed. A succession of Chancellors followed – Papen and Schliecher – while the government drifted. Neither of these two men could achieve much because they did not command enough support in the Reichstag. This led to Hindenburg in January 1933 being forced to call on Adolf Hitler, with Papen as his Vice-Chancellor.

The Wall Street Crash was the more important reason why Hitler came to power. The Weimar constitution's weaknesses were well known in the 1920s, but they did not stop the revival of the German economy and the achievement of stable government under Stresemann. The Crash enabled the Nazis to change from a weak national organisation to a popular party, widely supported by the middle classes. The weaknesses of the Weimar government were a contributory factor, which actually had more significance in the weeks and months after Hitler became Chancellor when he was able to destroy the Weimar constitution and create a Nazi dictatorship.

– This answer explains several aspects of how German children were affected by Nazi policies. It is wide-ranging and shows clear understanding. It could expand a little more on the developing nature of Nazi control during these years. Life for German youth in 1933 was very different from what it had become by 1939, with the background of foreign policy successes and actions against the Jews.

– *Write a list of points on Nazi policy in the later 1930s which could be added to this answer.*

– This answer evaluates both bullet points in turn. It reaches a sustained judgement based on precise arguments. The relationships between the two bullet points are explored and there is clarity on how the Nazi Party was able to manipulate public opinion in the context of the two named factors in the question.

– *Working backwards, read through the essay again and write out the plan that it must have been based on. You can then look at the plan and see why it was the starting point for this comprehensive answer.*

Now write your own answers to the questions on pages 101–102 using the teacher's feedback to help you.

Russia 1894–1945: Tsardom and Communism

3

This chapter focuses on the development of Russia during a turbulent half century of change. It was a period which saw the fall of the Tsar and the rise and consolidation of Communism.

You will be studying the development of Russia during this period, including the following:
- The political aspects of a society transformed from autocracy to Communism.
- The economic modernisation which took place.
- The social and cultural changes that accompanied Russia's transformation.
- The role of ideas in influencing change, such as the elimination of a culture based on religion.
- The role of key individuals such as Tsar Nicholas II, Lenin and Stalin in shaping change, and the impact the developments had on them.

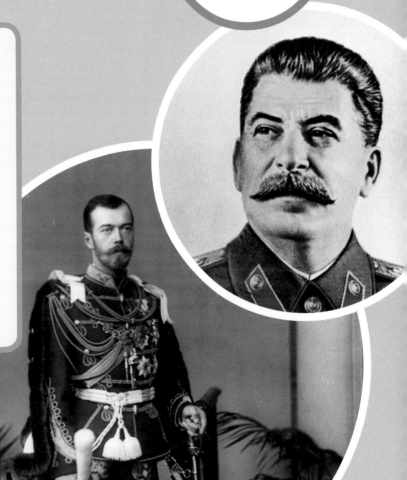

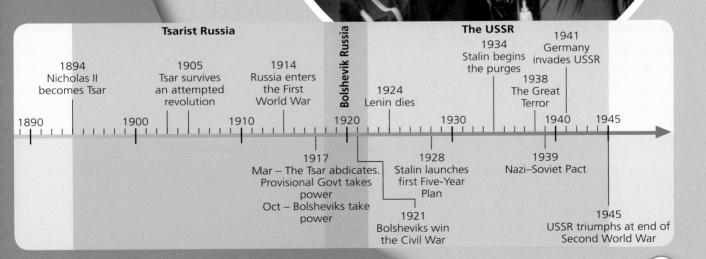

Tsarist Russia

Bolshevik Russia

The USSR

1894
Nicholas II becomes Tsar

1905
Tsar survives an attempted revolution

1914
Russia enters the First World War

1924
Lenin dies

1934
Stalin begins the purges

1941
Germany invades USSR

1938
The Great Terror

1890   1900   1910   1920   1930   1940   1945

1917
Mar – The Tsar abdicates. Provisional Govt takes power
Oct – Bolsheviks take power

1928
Stalin launches first Five-Year Plan

1939
Nazi–Soviet Pact

1921
Bolsheviks win the Civil War

1945
USSR triumphs at end of Second World War

Tsar Nicholas II

- Born 1868. Crowned as Tsar in 1896.
- Married to Alexandra of Hesse (a granddaughter of Queen Victoria).
- Believed in the Tsar as autocrat.
- Nicholas regularly rejected requests for reform.
- Led Russia into a disastrous war with Japan in 1904–05.
- He was not very effective as a ruler.
- By 1917 he had lost control of Russia and abdicated.
- In 1918 he and his family were shot by Bolsheviks during the Russian Civil War.

3.1 The end of Tsardom

FOCUS

This section is concerned with the situation in Russia during the reign of Tsar Nicholas II. Russia was developing economically and culturally, but the Tsar saw it as his religious duty to protect his own powers. As the First World War ensued, the Tsar was increasingly blamed for the political and economic chaos that developed.

In this part of the topic you will study the following:

- Russia's economy and society, and the effects of industrialisation.
- Nicholas II's autocracy and the court, and the extent to which Russia was well governed by 1914.
- The First World War, its effects on Tsardom and the Soviet people, and why the revolution of March 1917 was a success.

The new Tsar

When Nicholas II was crowned TSAR of Russia in 1894, the crowds flocked to St Petersburg to cheer. There were so many people that a police report said 1,200 people were crushed to death as the crowd surged forward to see the new Tsar, whom they called 'the Little Father of Russia'.

Twenty-three years later, he had been removed from power and he and his family were prisoners. They were held under armed guard in a lonely house at Ekaterinburg, far from the Tsar's luxurious palaces. Perhaps the Tsar might have asked himself how this had happened, but some commentators were predicting collapse long before 1917.

FIGURE 1

Russia in 1900.

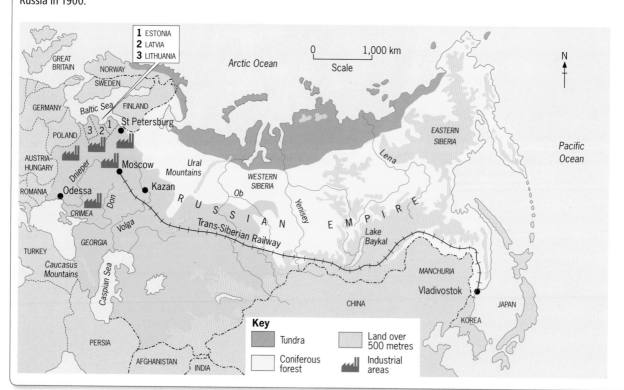

The Tsar's empire

Russia was a vast empire rather than a single country, and the Tsar was its supreme ruler. It was not an easy job.

The Tsar's empire included many different nationalities. Only 40 per cent of the Tsar's subjects spoke Russian as their first language. Some subjects, for example the Cossacks, were loyal to the Tsar. Others, for example the Poles and Finns, hated Russian rule. Jews often suffered racial prejudice and even vicious attacks, called pogroms, sponsored by the government.

● Russia's economy and society in 1894

Russian industrialisation and the cities

From the later nineteenth century, the Tsars had been keen to see Russia become an industrial power. The senior minister Sergei Witte introduced policies that led to rapid industrial growth. Oil and coal production trebled, while iron production quadrupled. Some peasants left the land to work in these newly developing industries. However, their living conditions hardly improved.

The greatest concentrations of these workers were in the capital, St Petersburg, and in Moscow. Here the population was growing fast as peasants arrived looking for a new way of life, or simply trying to earn some extra cash before returning for the harvest. Only a short walk away from the fabulous wealth of the Tsar's Winter Palace in St Petersburg, his subjects lived in filth and squalor. Overcrowding, terrible food, disease and alcoholism were everyday facts of life. The wretchedness of their living conditions was matched by the atrocious working conditions. Unlike every other European power, there were no government regulations on child labour, hours, safety or education. Trade unions were illegal. Low pay, 12–15 hour days, unguarded machinery and brutal discipline soon made the peasants realise that working in the factories was no better than working on the land.

As a result of industrialisation, a new class began to emerge in Russia – the CAPITALISTS. They were landowners, industrialists, bankers, traders and businessmen. Until this time, Russia had had only a small middle class which included people such as shopkeepers, lawyers and university lecturers. The capitalists increased the size of Russia's middle class, particularly in the towns. Their main concerns were the management of the economy, although the capitalists were also concerned about controlling their workforce. Clashes between workers and capitalists were to play an important role in Russia's history in the years up to 1917.

SOURCE 2

Workers' living conditions inside a dormitory. Urban workers made up about 4 per cent of the population in 1900.

Population of the Russian Empire, according to a census in 1897.			
Russians	55,650,000	Letts	1,400,000
Ukrainians	22,400,000	Georgians	1,350,000
Poles	7,900,000	Armenians	1,150,000
Byelorussians	5,900,000	Romanians	1,110,000
Jews	5,000,000	Caucasians	1,000,000
Kirghiz	4,000,000	Estonians	1,000,000
Tartars	3,700,000	Iranians	1,000,000
Finns	2,500,000	Other Asiatic peoples	5,750,000
Germans	1,800,000	Mongols	500,000
Lithuanians	1,650,000	Others	200,000

FIGURE 3

Graph showing the growth of St Petersburg.

Population in millions

	1863	1881	1897	1900	1914

Living and working conditions in villages

SOURCE **4**

A typical village in northern Russia.

Around 80 per cent of Russia's population were peasants who lived in communes. There were some prosperous peasant farmers called *kulaks*, but living and working conditions for most peasants were dreadful. Famine and starvation were common and in some regions the life expectancy of a peasant farmer was only 40 years of age.

Much of Russia's land was unsuitable for farming. As a result, land was in very short supply because, by the early 1900s, the population was growing rapidly. (It increased by 50 per cent between 1860 and 1897.) Russian peasants were still using ancient farming techniques. In most villages, the land was divided into large fields. Each family was allotted a strip of land in one of the fields. This subdivision of the fields was organised by peasant councils called *mir*. When a peasant had sons, the family plot was subdivided and shared between them.

There was no basic education in Russia and very few peasants could read or write. But, despite all their hardships, many peasants were loyal to the Tsar. This was partly because they were also religious. Every week, they would hear the priest say how wonderful the Tsar was and how they, as peasants, should be loyal subjects. However, not all peasants were loyal or religious. Many supported the opposition, the SOCIALIST REVOLUTIONARIES (see page 108). Their main discontent was over land – they resented the amount of land owned by the aristocracy, the Church and the Tsar.

> **THINK**
>
> Look at Sources 2 (page 105) and 4. Were workers in the town any better off than their cousins in the countryside? Explain your answer.

The aristocracy

The peasants' living conditions contrasted sharply with those of the aristocracy, who had vast estates, town and country houses and elegant lifestyles.

The aristocracy formed about 1.5 per cent of society but owned about 25 per cent of the land. They were a key part of the Tsar's government, often acting as local officials. In the countryside they dominated the local assemblies or *zemstva*. Most were loyal to the Tsar and wanted to keep Russian society as it was.

Many of the richer aristocrats lived not on their estates but in the glamorous cities. Some landlords were in financial trouble and had to sell their lands, a piece at a time. Perhaps the greatest fear of the aristocracy was that the peasants would rise up and take their lands.

FOCUS TASK

How did industrialisation affect Russian society during the reign of Nicholas II?

1 Copy and complete the following table and make notes to show how industrialisation affected each section of Russian society during the reign of Nicholas II.

2 Highlight all of the negative effects of industrialisation in one colour.

3 Highlight all of the positive effects of industrialisation in another colour.

4 Which group do you think was most affected by industrialisation during the reign of Nicholas II?

Section of Russian society	Effects of industrialisation
The peasants	
The workers	
The middle classes	
The aristocracy	
The Tsar	

● Nicholas II's autocracy and the court

The huge and diverse empire was ruled by an AUTOCRACY. One man, the Tsar, had absolute power to rule Russia. The Tsar believed that God had placed him in that position and the Russian Church supported him in this view. The Tsar could appoint or sack ministers or make any other decisions without consulting anyone else. By the early twentieth century most of the GREAT POWERS had given their people at least some say in how they were run, but Nicholas was utterly committed to the idea of autocracy and seemed to be obsessed with the great past of his family, the Romanovs. He had many good qualities, such as his loyalty to his family, his willingness to work hard and his attention to detail. However, he was not an able, forceful or imaginative monarch like his predecessors.

Nicholas avoided making important decisions, instead involving himself in day-to-day, insignificant tasks. In a country as vast as Russia, where tasks had to be delegated to officials, this was a major problem. He insisted on getting involved in the tiniest details of government. He personally answered letters from peasants and appointed provincial midwives. He even wrote out the instructions for the royal car to be brought round!

Nicholas also managed his officials poorly. He felt threatened by able and talented ministers, such as Count Witte and Peter Stolypin. He dismissed Witte in 1906 and was about to sack Stolypin when Stolypin was murdered in 1911. Nicholas refused to chair the Council of Ministers because he disliked confrontation. Instead, he insisted on seeing ministers in one-to-one meetings, which encouraged rivalry between them. This caused chaos, as different government departments refused to co-operate with each other.

He also appointed family members and friends from the court to important positions. Many of them were incompetent or even corrupt, making huge fortunes from bribes.

Control

Despite everything you have read so far, it is important to remember that the Tsar's regime was very strong in some ways. Resistance was limited. At the local level, most peasants had their lives controlled by the *mir*. The *mir* could be overruled by land captains. Land captains were usually minor landlords appointed by the Tsar as his officials in local areas. The *zemstva*, or local assemblies, also helped to control Russia. They were dominated by the landlords in the countryside and by professional people in the towns. Then there were local governors, appointed by the Tsar from the ranks of the aristocracy. In some areas, Russia was a police state, controlled by local governors. There were special emergency laws that allowed the local governors to:

- order the police to arrest suspected opponents of the regime
- ban individuals from serving in the *zemstva*, courts or any government organisation
- make suspects pay heavy fines
- introduce censorship of books, leaflets or newspapers.

Local governors controlled the police. The police had a special force with 10,000 officers whose job was to concentrate on political opponents of the regime. There was also the OKHRANA, the Tsar's secret police. Finally, if outright rebellion did erupt, there was the army, particularly the Tsar's loyal and terrifying Cossack regiments.

ACTIVITY

1 Draw up your own chart to summarise the Tsarist system of government.
2 Describe and explain at least two ways in which Nicholas II made Russia's government weak.

The growth of revolutionary opposition

The opposition came from three important groups. One was formed of middle-class reformers in the DUMA. Many middle-class people wanted greater DEMOCRACY in Russia and pointed out that Britain still had a king but also a powerful parliament. These people were called liberals or 'Cadets'.

Two other groups were more violently opposed to the Tsar. They believed that revolution was the answer to the people's troubles:

- The Socialist Revolutionaries (SRs) were a radical movement. Their main aim was to carve up the huge estates of the nobility and hand them over to the peasants. They believed in a violent struggle and were responsible for the ASSASSINATION of two government officials, as well as the murder of a large number of *Okhrana* (police) agents and spies. They had wide support in the towns and the countryside.
- The Social Democratic Party was a smaller but more disciplined party which followed the ideas of Karl Marx (see Factfile). In 1903 the party split itself into BOLSHEVIKS and MENSHEVIKS. The Bolsheviks (led by Lenin) believed it was the job of the party to create a revolution whereas the Mensheviks believed Russia was not ready for revolution. Both of these organisations were illegal and many of their members had been executed or sent in exile to Siberia. Many of the main Social Democrat leaders were forced to live abroad.

The 1905 Revolution and the October Manifesto

Despite the power of the Tsar's government, Nicholas faced increasing opposition. In 1905 Russia was almost overwhelmed by a wave of strikes and rebellions which turned into a full-scale revolution. In January 1905 about 200,000 peaceful protesters marched through the streets of St Petersburg towards the Winter Palace, led by a priest, Father Gapon. They wanted to hand in a petition asking for changes. The troops panicked and opened fire. At least a hundred were killed and several hundred more were injured in the event known as Bloody Sunday.

This led to a wave of strikes and protests in many cities. Many peasant rebellions broke out in the countryside. In June 1905 the crew of the battleship *Potemkin* mutinied in support of the striking workers.

The Tsar survived by issuing the October Manifesto. It offered concessions to the middle classes in the form of a *Duma* (an elected parliament), the right to free speech and the right to form political parties. These concessions divided his opponents and he was then able to crush the peasant rebellions in the countryside and the working-class rebels in the cities. For a short while it seemed that Russia was at peace, but this did not last. By 1914 there was still a great deal of discontent and unrest in Russia.

FIGURE 5

Statistics on strikes and strikers, compiled by the Tsar's Ministry of Trade and Industry.

Year	Strikes	Strikers
1905	13,995	2,863,173
1906	6,114	1,108,406
1907	3,573	740,074
1908	892	176,101
1909	340	64,166
1910	222	46,623
1911	466	105,110
1912	2,032	725,491
1913	2,404	887,096
1914	3,534	1,337,458

FACTFILE

Marxist theory

- Karl Marx was a German writer and political thinker. He believed that history was dominated by class struggle – conflict between the different classes in society.
- In MARXIST theory the first change brought about by the class struggle would be the middle classes taking control from the monarchy and aristocracy.
- There would then be a revolution in which the workers (the proletariat) would overthrow the middle classes.
- For a short while the Communist Party would rule on behalf of the people, but as selfish desires disappeared there would be no need for any government.
- All would live in a peaceful, Communist society.

SOURCE 6

Cartoon showing the Tsarist system. This was published in Switzerland by exiled opponents of the Tsar.

Look carefully at Source 6. It was drawn by opponents of the Tsar's regime who had been forced to live in Switzerland to avoid the Tsar's secret police. It is a representation of life in Russia under the rule of the Tsar. Discuss how far you think it is an accurate view of Russian society. Think about:

- ways in which its claims are supported by the information and sources in the text
- ways in which its claims are not supported by the information and sources in the text
- aspects of life in Russia that are not covered by the drawing.

FIGURE 7

Agricultural and industrial production, 1890–1913.

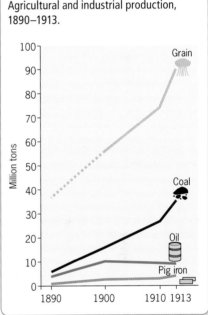

The *Dumas* and political stalemate

The *Duma* deputies who gathered for its first meeting in 1906 were hopeful that they could help to steer Russia on a new course. They were soon disappointed. The Tsar continued to rule without taking any serious notice of them. The first and second *Dumas* were very critical of the Tsar. They lasted less than a year before Nicholas sent them home. In 1907 Tsar Nicholas changed the voting rules so that his opponents were not elected to the *Duma*. This third *Duma* lasted until 1912, mainly because it was much less critical of the Tsar than the previous two. But by 1912 even this 'loyal' *Duma* was becoming critical of the Tsar's ministers and policies. However, it had no power to change the Tsar's policies and criticism alone was not a serious threat to the regime so the Tsar's rule continued.

FOCUS TASK

How well was Russia governed in 1914?

1 Here are five characteristics that you might expect of a good government:
   – Trying to improve the lives of all its people
   – Building up its agriculture and industry
   – Listening to and responding to its population
   – Running the country efficiently
   – Defending the country from enemies.

   On a scale of 1–5 (with 1 being the highest) say how well you think the Tsarist government did on each one up to 1914. Explain your reason for giving that score.

2 Now make a list of the successes and failures of the Tsarist government up to 1914.

3 Which of the following assessments do you most agree with?

   By 1913 the government was:

   – in crisis
   – strong but with some serious weaknesses
   – secure with only minor weaknesses.

PRACTICE QUESTIONS

1 Describe two events in the 1905 Revolution that made it a serious threat to the monarchy.
2 In what ways were Stolypin's policies able to change agriculture and industry in Russia?

Stolypin's policies – the use of oppression, land reform, and the expansion of industry

In 1906 the Tsar appointed a tough new Prime Minister – Peter Stolypin. Stolypin used a 'carrot and stick' approach to the problems of Russia.

- **The stick**: He came down hard on strikers, protesters and revolutionaries. Over 20,000 were exiled and over 1,000 hanged (the noose came to be known as 'Stolypin's necktie'). This brutal suppression effectively killed off opposition to the regime in the countryside until after 1914.

- **The carrot**: Stolypin also tried to win over the peasants with the 'carrot' they had always wanted – land. He allowed wealthier peasants, the *kulaks*, to opt out of the *mir* communes and buy up land. These *kulaks* prospered and in the process created larger and more efficient farms. Production did increase significantly. On the other hand, 90 per cent of land in the fertile west of Russia was still run by inefficient communes in 1916. Farm sizes remained small even in Ukraine, Russia's best farmland. Most peasants still lived in awful conditions.

Stolypin also tried to boost Russia's industries. There was impressive economic growth between 1908 and 1911 (see Figure 7 on page 109). But Russia was still far behind modern industrial powers such as Britain, Germany and the USA. Urban workers' wages stayed low and the cost of food and housing stayed high. Living and working conditions remained appalling.

The profits being made by industry were going to the capitalists, or they were being paid back to banks in France which had loaned the money to pay for much of Russia's industrial growth.

Stolypin was assassinated in 1911, but the Tsar was about to sack him anyway. He worried that Stolypin was trying to change Russia too much. Nicholas had already blocked some of Stolypin's plans for basic education for the people and regulations to protect factory workers. The Tsar was influenced by the landlords and members of the court. They saw Stolypin's reforms as a threat to the traditional Russian society in which everyone knew their place.

Relations between the Tsar and his people became steadily worse. The economy took a downturn in 1912, causing unemployment and hunger. The year 1913 saw huge celebrations for the 300th anniversary of the Romanovs' rule in Russia. The celebrations were meant to bring the country together, but enthusiasm was limited.

SOURCE 8

Tsar Nicholas at the 1913 celebrations of 300 years of Romanov rule. This was the first time since 1905 that the Tsar had appeared in public.

The First World War

In August 1914 Russia entered the First World War. Tensions in the country seemed to disappear. The Tsar seemed genuinely popular with his people and there was an instant display of patriotism. The Tsar's action was applauded. Workers, peasants and aristocrats all joined in the patriotic enthusiasm. Anti-government strikes and demonstrations were abandoned. The good feeling, however, was very short-lived. As the war continued, the Tsar began to lose the support of key sectors of Russian society.

The impact of military defeats on the Tsarist government

The Russian army was huge. At first, the soldiers were enthusiastic, as was the rest of society. Even so, many peasants felt that they were fighting to defend their country against the Germans rather than showing any loyalty to the Tsar. Russian soldiers fought bravely, but they stood little chance against the German army. Very early in the war they suffered major military defeats at Tannenburg and the Masurian Lakes. They were badly led and treated appallingly by their aristocrat officers. They were also poorly supported by the industries at home. They were short of rifles, ammunition, artillery and shells. Many did not even have boots.

The Tsar took command of the armed forces in September 1915. This made little difference to the war, since Nicholas was not a particularly able commander. However, it did mean that people held Nicholas personally responsible for the defeats and the blunders. The defeats and huge losses continued throughout 1916. It is not surprising that by 1917 there was deep discontent in the army and that many soldiers were supporters of the revolutionary Bolshevik Party.

Social and economic effects of the war on the countryside and the cities

It did not take long for the strain of war to alienate the peasants and the workers. The huge casualty figures took their toll. In August 1916, the local governor of the village of Grushevka reported that the war had killed 13 per cent of the population of the village. This left many widows and orphans needing state war pensions which they did not always receive.

By 1916 there was much discontent in the cities. War contracts created an extra 3.5 million industrial jobs between 1914 and 1916, but the workers received little in the way of extra wages. They also had to cope with even worse overcrowding than before the war. There were fuel and food shortages. What made it worse was that there was enough food and fuel, but it could not be transported to the cities. The rail network could not cope with the needs of the army, industry and the populations of the cities. As 1916 turned into 1917, many working men and women stood, shivering, in bread queues and cursed the Tsar.

The unpopularity of the Romanovs

The situation was so bad by late 1916 that the Council of the United Nobility was calling for the Tsar to step down. The junior officers in the army had suffered devastating losses in the war. Many of these officers were the future of the aristocrat class. The CONSCRIPTION of 13 million peasants also threatened aristocrats' livelihoods, because they had fewer workers for their estates. Most of all, many of the leading aristocrats were appalled by the influence of Rasputin (see page 112) over the government of Russia. When the Tsar left Petrograd (the new Russian version of the Germanic name St Petersburg) to take charge of the army, he left his wife in control of the country. The fact that she was German started rumours flying in the capital.

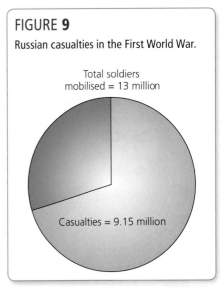

FIGURE 9

Russian casualties in the First World War.

Total soldiers mobilised = 13 million

Casualties = 9.15 million

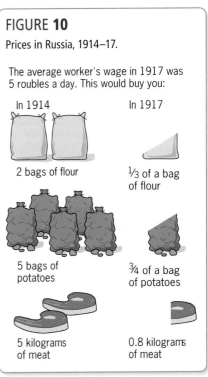

FIGURE 10

Prices in Russia, 1914–17.

The average worker's wage in 1917 was 5 roubles a day. This would buy you:

In 1914 — 2 bags of flour

In 1917 — ⅓ of a bag of flour

In 1914 — 5 bags of potatoes

In 1917 — ¾ of a bag of potatoes

In 1914 — 5 kilograms of meat

In 1917 — 0.8 kilograms of meat

SOURCE 11

A Russian cartoon. The caption reads: 'The Russian Tsars at home.'

THINK

Study Source 11. How does the cartoonist suggest that Rasputin is an evil influence on the Tsar and Tsarina?

Rasputin

Some of the Tsar's supporters were particularly alarmed about the influence of a strange and dangerous figure – Gregory Yefimovich, generally known as Rasputin. The Tsar's son Alexis was very ill with a blood disease called haemophilia. Through hypnosis, it appeared that Rasputin could control the disease. He was greeted as a miracle worker by the TSARINA (the Tsar's wife). Before long, Rasputin was also giving her and the Tsar advice on how to run the country. People in Russia were very suspicious of Rasputin. He was said to be a drinker and a womaniser. His name means 'disreputable'. The Tsar's opponents seized on Rasputin as a sign of the Tsar's weakness and unsuitability to rule Russia. The fact that the Tsar either didn't notice their concern or, worse still, didn't care, showed just how out of touch he was. There were also rumours of an affair between Alexandra and Rasputin. The concerns were so serious that a group of leading aristocrats murdered Rasputin in December 1916.

The Tsar's abdication

As 1917 dawned, few people had great hopes for the survival of the Tsar's regime. In January strikes broke out in some cities. In February the strikes spread. They were supported and even joined by members of the army. The Tsar's best troops lay dead on the battlefields. These soldiers were recent conscripts and had more in common with the strikers than their officers. On 7 March workers at the Putilov steelworks in Petrograd went on strike. They joined with thousands of women – it was International Women's Day – and other discontented workers demanding that the government provide bread. From 7 to 10 March the number of striking workers rose to 250,000. Industry came to a standstill. The *Duma* set up a Provisional Committee to take over the government. The Tsar ordered them to disband. The soldiers refused. On 12 March the Tsar ordered his army to put down the revolt by force. The soldiers refused. This was the decisive moment. Some soldiers even shot their own officers and joined the demonstrators. They marched to the *Duma* demanding that its members should take over the government. Reluctantly, the *Duma* leaders accepted – they had always wanted reform rather than revolution, but now there seemed no choice.

On the same day, revolutionaries set up the Petrograd Soviet again (as they had in 1905), and began taking control of food supplies to the city. They set up soldiers' committees, undermining the authority of the officers. It was not clear who was in charge of Russia, but it was obvious that the Tsar was not! On 15 March he issued a statement that he was ABDICATING. There was an initial plan for his brother Michael to take over, but Michael refused: Russia had finished with Tsars.

FIGURE 12

Peasant risings and strikes by factory workers, 1914–17.

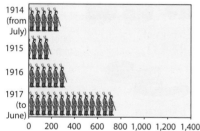
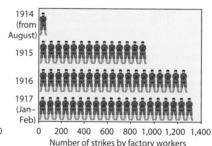

PRACTICE QUESTION

Which of the following was the more important reason why support for Tsar Nicholas II declined:
● military defeats in the First World War
● the actions of Rasputin?

Explain your answer with reference to both reasons.

FOCUS TASK

Why was the March 1917 revolution successful?

The Tsar faced a major revolution in 1905 but he survived. Why was 1917 different? Why was he not able to survive in 1917?

Stage 1

1 Study the following eight reasons why the Tsar was forced to abdicate in March 1917:
   - Failures in the war
   - Mutiny in the army
   - An alternative parliament – the *Duma*
   - Discontent in the countryside
   - Formation of soviets
   - Strikes
   - Food shortages
   - The Tsarina and Rasputin.

2 For each of the factors, write one or two sentences explaining how it contributed to the fall of the Tsar.

3 Draw lines between any of the factors that seem to be connected. Label your lines explaining what each link is.

Stage 2

4 In pairs or small groups, discuss the following points:
   a) Which factors were present in 1905?
   b) Were these same factors more or less serious than in 1905?
   c) Which factors were not present in 1905?
   d) Were the new factors decisive in making the March 1917 revolution successful?

PRACTICE QUESTIONS

Read Interpretations A and B, and then answer the questions that follow.

Interpretation A British diplomat George Buchanan writing in his memoirs in 1922. Buchanan had been Britain's representative to Russia during the First World War when Britain and Russia were allies against Germany. He is describing a meeting with Tsar Nicholas II in 1914.

I called His Majesty's attention to the attempts being made by the Germans, not only to create dissension between the Allies, but to estrange him from his own people. Their agents were everywhere at work. They were pulling the strings, and were using as their unconscious tools those who were in the habit of advising His Majesty as to the choice of his Ministers. They indirectly influenced the Empress through those in her entourage, with the result that, instead of being loved, as she ought to be, Her Majesty was discredited and accused of working in German interests. The Emperor once more drew himself up and said: "I choose my Ministers myself, and do not allow anyone to influence my choice."

Interpretation B An extract from *Always With Honour*, the memoirs of General Peter Wrangel, published in 1957. Wrangel served in the Russian Army under the Tsar and continued to serve after the revolution in 1917.

Those of us who loved our country and the Army were terribly anxious at the continual changes in the Ministry, the conflicts between the Government and the Duma, the ever-increasing number of petitions and appeals addressed to the Tsar by many influential organizations, each one demanding popular control, and, above all, by the alarming rumours concerning certain persons in the Tsar's entourage.

The patriots amongst the High Command suffered deeply as they watched the Tsar making fatal mistakes whilst the danger grew and came ever nearer.

1 How does Interpretation B differ from Interpretation A on opinions about Nicholas II and his government?

Explain your answer based on what it says in Interpretations A and B.

2 Why might the authors of Interpretations A and B have different opinions about Nicholas II and his government?

Explain your answer using Interpretations A and B and your contextual knowledge.

3 Which interpretation do you find more gives the more convincing opinion about Nicholas II and his government?

Explain your answer based on your contextual knowledge and what it says in Interpretations A and B.

TOPIC SUMMARY

The end of Tsardom

- Nicholas II became Tsar in 1894.
- His unpopularity was shown by the events of Bloody Sunday, 1905.
- The Tsar was forced to make concessions and the *Duma* first met in 1906.
- His chief minister, Stolypin, carried out reforms to modernise Russia, 1906–11.
- In 1913 the 300th anniversary of Romanov rule was celebrated.
- In 1914 the First World War started; Russia was quickly shown to be no match with Germany.
- By 1916 there was much economic and social discontent and starvation in the cities. The Tsar was extremely unpopular, not helped by the presence of Rasputin at court.
- In early 1917 demonstrations in the streets of Petrograd got out of control and the Tsar abdicated in March.

3.2 Lenin's new society

The abdication of the Tsar in March 1917 solved very little. Members of the *Duma* set up a temporary government which was then overthrown by the Bolsheviks led by Lenin later in the year. The Bolsheviks then set about creating a society that was based on totally different principles from the aristocratic rule that had existed for centuries.

In this section you will study the following:

- Why the Provisional Government failed to solve Russia's problems and why the Bolsheviks gained support and were able to take over government.
- The impact of Lenin's dictatorship and why the Bolsheviks were able to win the Civil War.
- Social and economic developments under Lenin and Trotsky, and how the Bolsheviks consolidated their rule.

SOURCE 1

A Provisional Government Minister explains why Russia should stay in the war, 1917.

The Provisional Government should do nothing now which would break our ties with the allies. The worst thing that could happen to us would be separate peace. It would be ruinous for the Russian revolution, ruinous for international democracy …

As to the land question, we regard it as our duty at the present to prepare the ground for a just solution of the problem by the Constituent Assembly.

THINK

Read Source 1. How popular do you think the Provisional Government's policies on:

a) the war
b) land

would be with the peasants and the soldiers?

• The Provisional Government: Social, economic and military problems

The *Duma*'s Provisional Committee took over the running of the government. It faced three overwhelmingly urgent decisions:

- to continue the war or make peace
- to distribute land to the peasants (who had already started taking it) or ask them to wait until elections had been held
- how best to get food to the starving workers in the cities.

The PROVISIONAL GOVERNMENT was a mixed group. While it included men such as the lawyer Alexander Kerensky – Justice Minister in the Provisional Government but also a respected member of the Petrograd Soviet – it also included angry revolutionaries who had no experience of government at all. The Provisional Government promised Russia's allies that it would continue the war, while trying to settle the situation in Russia. It also urged the peasants to be restrained and wait for elections before taking any land. The idea was that the Provisional Government could then stand down and allow free elections to take place to elect a new Constituent Assembly that would fairly and democratically represent the people of Russia. It was a very cautious message for a people who had just gone through a revolution.

However, the Provisional Government was not the only possible government. Most workers also paid close attention to the Petrograd Soviet. The Soviet had the support of workers in key industries such as coal mining and water, and the support of much of the army. During the crisis months of spring 1917, the Soviet and Provisional Government worked together.

Lenin and the growth of Bolshevik organisation

One man was determined to push the revolution further. He was Lenin, leader of the Bolsheviks (see page 117). When he heard of the March revolution he immediately returned to Russia from exile in Europe. The Germans even provided him with a special train, hoping that he might cause more chaos in Russia!

When Lenin arrived at the Finland Station in Petrograd, he set out the Bolshevik programme in his April Theses. He urged the people to support the Bolsheviks in a second revolution. Lenin's slogans, 'Peace, Land and Bread' and 'All Power to the Soviets', contrasted sharply with the cautious message of the Provisional Government. Support for the Bolsheviks increased quickly (see Figure 2), particularly in the soviets and in the army.

The Provisional Government's failure to deal with Russia's problems

In the second half of 1917, the Provisional Government's authority steadily collapsed:

- The war effort was failing. Soldiers had been deserting in thousands from the army. Kerensky became Minister for War and rallied the army for a great offensive in June. It was a disaster. The army began to fall apart in the face of a German counter-attack. The deserters decided to come home.
- Desertions were made worse because another element of the Provisional Government's policy had failed. The peasants ignored the orders of the government to wait. They were simply taking control of the countryside. The soldiers, who were mostly peasants, did not want to miss their turn when the land was shared out.

The Provisional Government's problems got worse in the summer. In July (the 'July Days'), Bolshevik-led protests against the war turned into a rebellion. However, when Kerensky produced evidence that Lenin had been helped by the Germans, support for the rebellion fell. Lenin, in disguise, fled to Finland. Kerensky used troops to crush the rebellion and took over the government.

Others were also fed up with the Provisional Government. In September 1917, the army leader Kornilov marched his troops towards Petrograd, intending to get rid of the Bolsheviks and the Provisional Government, and restore order. Kerensky was in an impossible situation. He had some troops who supported him but they were no match for Kornilov's. Kerensky turned to the only group which could save him: his Bolshevik opponents, who dominated the Petrograd Soviet. The Bolsheviks organised themselves into an army which they called the Red Guards. Kornilov's troops refused to fight members of the Soviet so Kornilov's plans collapsed.

However, it was hardly a victory for Kerensky. In fact, by October Kerensky's government was doomed. It had tried to carry on the war and failed. It had therefore lost the army's support. It had tried to stop the peasants from taking over the land and so lost their support too. Without peasant support it had failed to bring food into the towns and food prices had spiralled upwards. This had lost the government any support it had from the urban workers.

In contrast, the Bolsheviks were promising what the people wanted most (bread, peace, land). It was the Bolsheviks who had removed the threat of Kornilov. By the end of September 1917, there were Bolshevik majorities in the Petrograd and Moscow Soviets, and in most of Russia's other major towns and cities.

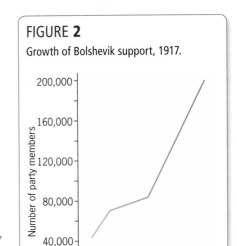

FIGURE 2

Growth of Bolshevik support, 1917.

SOURCE 3

A letter from Guchkov, Minister for War in the Provisional Government, to General Alekseyev, 22 March 1917.

The Provisional Government possesses no real power and its orders are executed only in so far as this is permitted by the Soviet of Workers' and Soldiers' Deputies, which holds in its hands the most important elements of actual power, such as troops, railroads, postal and telegraph service …

SOURCE 4

John Reed, an American writer who lived in Petrograd in 1917.

Week by week food became scarcer … one had to queue for long hours in the chill rain … Think of the poorly clad people standing on the streets of Petrograd for whole days in the Russian winter! I have listened in the bread-lines, hearing the bitter discontent which from time to time burst through the miraculous good nature of the Russian crowd.

THINK

Study Sources 3 and 4. Do you think that the Provisional Government was doomed to failure?

FOCUS TASK

Why did the Provisional Government fail to deal with Russia's problems?

1. Imagine you are Lenin addressing a crowd of Russians in 1917. Write a short speech to persuade your listeners that the Provisional Government has become a failure and that change is needed. Use the following headings to help you to structure your speech:
   - The Provisional Government's failures:
     - The war
     - Land distribution
     - Starving peasants.
   - The Bolsheviks' promises:
     - Bread, peace and land
     - All power to the soviets.
2. Lenin has reread the speech and has decided that it is too long. Choose the two most important points for him to make in the speech.

The October/November Revolution

You have seen how Bolshevik support increased throughout 1917. By the end of October 1917, Lenin was convinced that the time was right for the Bolsheviks to seize power. Lenin convinced his comrades to act swiftly. It was not easy – leading members like Bukharin felt that Russia was not ready, but neither he nor any other Bolsheviks could match Lenin in an argument.

Leon Trotsky, who had recently joined the Bolsheviks, was responsible for the organisation of the Red Guards in Petrograd (see Profile on page 118). During the night of 6 November, the Red Guards took control of post offices, bridges and the State Bank. On 7 November, Kerensky awoke to find the Bolsheviks were in control of most of Petrograd. Through the day, with almost no opposition, the Red Guards continued to take over railway stations and other important targets. On the evening of 7 November, they stormed the Winter Palace (again, without much opposition) and arrested the ministers of the Provisional Government. Kerensky managed to escape and tried to rally loyal troops. When this failed, he fled into exile. On 8 November an announcement was made to the Russian people (see Source 5).

THINK

When the Bolsheviks stormed the Winter Palace, they actually faced very little resistance. Why do you think the artist who painted Source 6 suggests that they did?

SOURCE 5

Proclamation of the Petrograd Soviet, 8 November 1917.

The Provisional Government has been overthrown. The cause for which the people have fought has been made safe: the immediate proposal of a democratic peace, the end of land owners' rights, workers' control over production, the creation of a Soviet government. Long live the revolution of workers, soldiers and peasants.

SOURCE 6

The Bolsheviks storm the Winter Palace. A painting from 1937 by the Soviet artist, Sokolov-Skalya, on the 20th anniversary of the Bolshevik takeover.

An analysis of the Bolshevik Revolution

Despite their claims, the Bolsheviks did not have the support of the majority of the Russian people. So how were they able to carry out their takeover in November 1917? The unpopularity of the Provisional Government was a critical factor – there were no massive demonstrations demanding the return of Kerensky!

A second factor was that the Bolsheviks were a disciplined party dedicated to revolution, even though not all the Bolshevik leaders believed this was the right way to change Russia. The Bolsheviks had some 800,000 members, and their supporters were also in the right places. At least half of the army supported them, as did the sailors at the important naval base at Kronstadt near Petrograd. (The Bolsheviks were still the only party demanding that Russia should pull out of the war.) The major industrial centres, and the Petrograd and Moscow Soviets especially, were also pro-Bolshevik. The Bolsheviks also had some outstanding personalities in their ranks, particularly Trotsky and their leader Lenin.

PRACTICE QUESTIONS

Read Interpretations A and B, and then answer Questions 1–6.

> **Interpretation A** The Bolshevik takeover of Petrograd in October 1917. From "The Russian Revolution, 1917 : A Personal Record" written by, Sukhanov, a leading Menshevik but supporter of the revolution. It was first published in 1922 but then suppressed under Stalin.
>
> *No resistance was shown. Beginning at 2 in the morning the stations, bridges, lighting installations, telegraphs and telegraphic agency were gradually occupied by small forces brought from the barracks. The decisive operations were quite bloodless; not one casualty was recorded. The city was absolutely calm. Both the centre and the suburbs were sunk in a deep sleep, not suspecting what was going on in the quiet of the cold autumn night.*

> **Interpretation B** An account of the October Revolution written by Alexandra Kollontai and published in 1924. The author was a member of the Bolshevik Party and held several important positions in the Party before the revolution and in the Bolshevik government after the revolution.
>
> *The women who took part in the Great October Revolution – who were they? Isolated individuals? No, there were hosts of them - tens, hundreds of thousands of nameless heroines who, marching side by side with the workers and peasants behind the Red Flag and the slogan of the Soviets, passed over the ruins of Tsarism into a new future. It is a clear and indisputable fact that, without the participation of women, the October Revolution could not have brought the Red Flag to victory. Glory to the working women who marched under that Red Banner during the October Revolution. Glory to the October Revolution!*

1 How does Interpretation A differ from Interpretation B about the October Revolution?

Explain your answer based on what it says in Interpretations A and B.

2 Why might these two historians have different interpretations about the October Revolution?

Explain your answer using Interpretations A and B and your contextual knowledge.

3 Which interpretation gives the more convincing opinion about the October Revolution? Explain your answer based on your contextual knowledge and what it says in Interpretations A and B.

4 Describe two problems faced by the Provisional Government when it was created in March 1917.

5 In what ways did the peasants and the city workers suffer under the Provisional Government? Explain your answer.

6 Which of the following was the more important reason why the Provisional Government was weakened during 1917:
   – The decision to continue fighting in the First World War
   – The growing power and influences of the soviets in Petrograd and other cities?

Explain your answer with reference to both reasons.

PROFILE

Leon Trotsky

- Born in 1879 into a respectable and prosperous Jewish farming family.
- Exceptionally bright at school and brilliant at university.
- Politically active – arrested in 1900 and deported to Siberia.
- Escaped to London in 1902 and met Lenin there.
- Joined the Social Democratic Party, but supported the Menshevik wing rather than the Bolsheviks.
- Played an important role in organising strikes in the 1905 revolution – imprisoned for his activities.
- Escaped in 1907 and became a Social Democrat activist in the years before the First World War, not belonging to either Mensheviks or Bolsheviks.

- Published newspapers, including *Pravda* when it was a revolutionary newspaper, before the name was taken over by Lenin and it became an official Bolshevik paper.
- In 1917 he returned to Russia and was increasingly in sympathy with Bolshevik aims for a second revolution.
- Trotsky became a full member of the Bolshevik Party in Sept/Oct 1917 when he was elected as chairman of the Petrograd Soviet on which the Bolsheviks had a majority.
- He played a key role in organising the actual Bolshevik takeover in Oct/Nov 1917.
- In 1918 he became the Commissar for War and led the Bolsheviks to victory in the CIVIL WAR which broke out in 1918.

PROFILE

Vladimir Ilich Lenin

- Born 1870 into a respectable Russian family.
- Brother hanged in 1887 for plotting against the Tsar.
- Graduated from St Petersburg University after being thrown out of Kazan University for his political beliefs.
- One of the largest *Okhrana* files was about him!
- Exiled to Siberia 1897–1900.
- In 1900–1905 lived in various countries writing the revolutionary newspaper *Iskra* ('The Spark').
- Took part in the 1905 revolution but was forced to flee.
- Returned to Russia after the first revolution in 1917.
- Led the Bolsheviks to power in November 1917.

Trotsky's role

SOURCE 7

Historian Orlando Figes, a leading international expert on the Russian Revolution, writing in 1996.

The Bolshevik party was greatly strengthened by Trotsky's entry into the party. No one else in the leadership came anywhere near him as a public speaker, and for much of the revolutionary period it was this that made Trotsky, perhaps even more so than Lenin, the best known Bolshevik leader in the country. Whereas Lenin remained the master strategist of the party, working mainly behind the scenes, Trotsky became its principal source of public inspiration. During the weeks leading up to the seizure of power he spoke almost every night before a packed house …

He was careful always to use examples and comparisons from the real life of the audience. This gave his speeches a familiarity and earned Trotsky the popular reputation of being 'one of us'. It was this that gave him the power to master the crowd, even sometimes when it was extremely hostile.

SOURCE 8

Mikhail Uritsky, 1917. Uritsky was a Bolshevik activist and went on to play an important role in Bolshevik governments after 1917.

Now that the great revolution has come, one feels that however intelligent Lenin may be he begins to fade beside the genius of Trotsky.

SOURCE 9

Historian Robert Service, writing in 1990.

The [November] Revolution has often and widely been held to have been mainly Lenin's revolution. But was it? Certainly Lenin had a heavier impact on the course [of events] than anyone else. The point is, however, that great historical changes are brought about not only by individuals. There were other mighty factors at work as well in Russia in 1917 … Lenin simply could not have done or even co-ordinated everything.

FOCUS TASK

Why were the Bolsheviks successful?

1. Read Source 9.
2. What do you think the writer had in mind when he said there were 'other mighty factors at work'? Make your own list of these factors.
3. Write two or more paragraphs to explain the importance of these factors.

The impact of Lenin's dictatorship

Lenin's Bolshevik government intended to establish COMMUNISM, but the Bolsheviks only had support from certain groups in society. While Lenin's supporters were full of enthusiasm for what was promised, others such as landowners and factory owners were alarmed at the prospect of the major changes to society that would result. Indeed, many hoped that Lenin's rule would be short-lived, with the government eventually returning to its traditional leadership.

Lenin and the Bolsheviks had promised the people bread, peace and land. Lenin knew that if he failed to deliver, he and the Bolsheviks would suffer the same fate as Kerensky and the Provisional Government.

Lenin immediately set up the Council of People's Commissars (the *Sovnarkom*). It issued its first decree on 8 November, announcing that Russia was asking for peace with Germany. There followed an enormous number of decrees from the new government that aimed to strengthen the Bolsheviks' hold on power (see Factfile). The peasants were given the Tsar's and the Church's lands. The factories and industries were put into the hands of the workers. The Bolsheviks were given power to deal ruthlessly with their opponents – and they did (see page 120).

The Constituent Assembly: the beginnings of dictatorship

Lenin had also promised free elections to the new Constituent Assembly. Elections were held in late 1917. As Lenin had feared, the Bolsheviks did not gain a majority in the elections. Their rivals, the peasant-based Socialist Revolutionaries, were the biggest party when the Assembly opened on 18 January 1918.

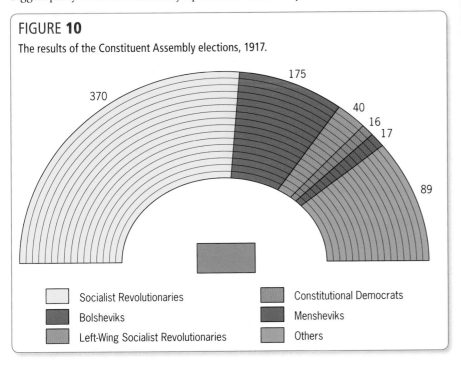

FIGURE 10
The results of the Constituent Assembly elections, 1917.

370   175   40   16   17   89

- Socialist Revolutionaries
- Bolsheviks
- Left-Wing Socialist Revolutionaries
- Constitutional Democrats
- Mensheviks
- Others

Lenin solved this problem in his typically direct style. He sent the Red Guards to close down the Assembly. After brief protests (again put down by the Red Guards) the Assembly was forgotten. Lenin instead used the Congress of Soviets to pass his laws as it did contain a Bolshevik majority.

Russia's DEMOCRATIC experiment therefore lasted less than 24 hours, but this did not trouble Lenin's conscience. He believed he was establishing a DICTATORSHIP of the proletariat which in time would give way to true Communism.

FACTFILE

Bolshevik decrees, 1917

8 November
- Land belonging to Tsar, Church and nobles handed over to peasants.
- Russia asked for peace with Germany.

12 November
- Working day limited to 8 hours; 48-hour week; rules made about overtime and holidays.

14 November
- Workers to be insured against illness or accident.

1 December
- All non-Bolshevik newspapers banned.

11 December
- The opposition Constitutional Democratic Party (Cadets) banned; its leaders arrested.

20 December
- *CHEKA* (secret police) set up to deal with 'spies and counter-revolutionaries'.

27 December
- Factories put under control of workers' committees.
- Banks put under Bolshevik government control.

31 December
- Marriages could take place without a priest if desired.
- Divorce made easier.

THINK

Study the Factfile. Which of the Bolshevik decrees would you say aimed to:

a) keep the peasants happy
b) keep the workers happy
c) increase Bolshevik control
d) improve personal freedom in Russia?

The Treaty of Brest-Litovsk, 1918.

From a letter written by Lenin in December 1917.

The bourgeoisie, landholders, and all wealthy classes are making desperate efforts to undermine the revolution which is aiming to safeguard the interests of the toiling and exploited masses … The partisans of the bourgeoisie, especially the higher officials, bank clerks, etc., are sabotaging and organising strikes in order to block the government's efforts to reconstruct the state on a socialistic basis. Sabotage has spread even to the food-supply organisations and millions of people are threatened with famine. Special measures must be taken to fight counter-revolution and sabotage.

The end of Russia's part in the First World War

The next promise that Lenin had to make good was for peace. He put Trotsky in charge of negotiating a peace treaty. He told Trotsky to try to spin out the peace negotiations as long as possible. He hoped that very soon a socialist revolution would break out in Germany as it had in Russia. By February of 1918, however, there was no revolution and the Germans began to advance again. Lenin had to accept their terms in the Treaty of Brest-Litovsk in March 1918.

The Treaty was a severe blow to Russia. You can see how much land was lost in Figure 11, but this was not the whole story. Russia's losses included 34 per cent of its population, 32 per cent of its agricultural land, 54 per cent of its industry, 26 per cent of its railways and 89 per cent of its coal mines. A final blow was the imposition of a fine of 300 million gold roubles. It was another example of Lenin's single-minded leadership. If this much had to be sacrificed to safeguard his revolution, then so be it. He may also have had the foresight to know that he would get it back when Germany lost.

The *Cheka*

Lenin's activities in 1917–18 were bound to make him enemies. In fact, in August 1918 he was shot three times by a Socialist Revolutionary agent but had a miraculous escape. In December 1917 he set up a secret police force called the CHEKA to crush his opponents.

The Tsars had used the *Okhrana* – secret police – to spy on anyone suspected of being disloyal. In December 1917 the 'All-Russian Emergency Commission for Combating Counter-Revolution and Sabotage', otherwise known as the *Cheka*, was established with much the same role. Within a year, agents whose purpose was to root out 'enemies of the state' could be found throughout Russia. These 'enemies' included army deserters, anyone who was suspected of hoarding food and political enemies.

The *Cheka* members were supposed to operate under a code of conduct, but in the chaotic situation after 1917 this was rapidly ignored. The *Cheka* was feared, and by 1921 there were at least 200,000 members. They were brutal and operated what became known as a Red Terror, leading to the killing of several thousand people (see page 122).

In 1922 the *Cheka* became the GPU – and later the NKVD, before becoming the KGB.

The Red Army

In October/November 1917 the Bolsheviks had a small body of disciplined Red Guards who led the actual takeover of Petrograd and Moscow. Lenin realised that he needed a much larger body, answerable to the new Bolshevik government, to enforce order and to deal with the many political opponents.

The Red Army was formed in January 1918, and all CITIZENS over the age of 18 were eligible. Some of its members came from the previous imperial army; some were new volunteers. Most of its members were peasants who were keen to protect the new government which represented the working classes.

Very soon in 1918 the newly formed Red Army was involved in a struggle to preserve the existence of the new Communist republic from all its political enemies in a civil war.

The causes of the Civil War

By the end of 1918 an unlikely collection of anti-Bolshevik elements had united in an attempt to crush the Bolsheviks. They became known as the Whites (in contrast to the Bolshevik Reds) and consisted of enemies of the Bolsheviks from inside and outside Russia (see Factfile).

The Bolsheviks' stronghold was in western Russia. Much of the rest of the country was more sympathetic to the Socialist Revolutionary Party.

In March 1918 the Czech Legion seized control of a large section of the Trans-Siberian Railway. Soon three separate White armies were marching on Bolshevik-controlled western Russia. Generals Yudenich and Denikin marched towards Petrograd and Moscow, while Admiral Kolchak marched on Moscow from central southern Russia.

FIGURE 13

The main developments of the Civil War.

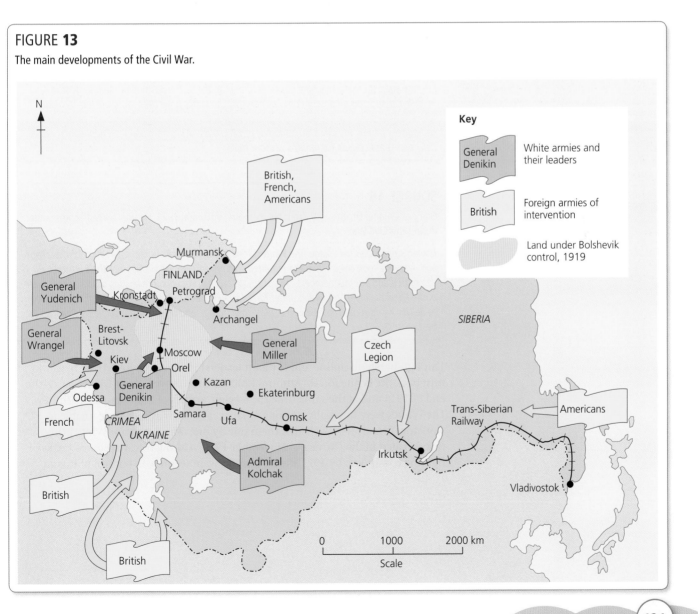

The nature of the Civil War

The reaction of the Bolsheviks was ruthless and determined. In an amazingly short time, Leon Trotsky created a new Red Army of over 300,000 men. They were led by former Tsarist officers. Trotsky made sure of their loyalty by holding their families hostage and by appointing political commissars to watch over them. The Cheka made sure that nobody in Bolshevik territories co-operated with the Whites. There were many beatings, hangings and shootings of opponents, or even suspected opponents, in what became known as the Red Terror.

Not even the Tsar escaped. In July 1918, White forces were approaching Ekaterinburg where the Tsar was being held. The Bolshevik commander ordered the execution of the Tsar and his family. Lenin could not risk the Tsar being rescued and returned as leader of the Whites.

The fighting was savage with both sides committing terrible acts of cruelty. The people who suffered most were the ordinary workers and above all the peasants in the areas where the fighting took place.

THINK

Using Sources 14 and 15, how effective do you think the harsh policies towards civilians were?

SOURCE 14

The Red Terror, observed by a British businessman in Russia in 1918.

In the villages the peasant will not give grain to the Bolsheviks because he hates them. Armed companies are sent to take grain from the peasant and every day, all over Russia, fights for grain are fought to a finish.

In the Red Army, for any military offence, there is only one punishment, death. If a regiment retreats against orders, machine guns are turned on them. The position of the bourgeoisie [middle class] defies all description. Payments by the banks have been stopped. It is forbidden to sell furniture. All owners and managers of works, offices and shops have been called up for compulsory labour. In Petrograd hundreds of people are dying from hunger. People are arrested daily and kept in prison for months without trial.

SOURCE 15

Diary of Colonel Drozdovsky, from his memoirs written in 1923. He was a White commander during the Civil War.

Having surrounded the village [the Whites] fired a couple of volleys in the direction of the village and everyone took cover. Then the mounted soldiers entered the village, met the Bolshevik committee and put the members to death … After the execution the houses of the culprits were burned and the male population under forty-five whipped … Then the population was ordered to deliver without pay the best cattle, pigs, fowl, forage and bread for the soldiers as well as the best horses.

Through harsh discipline and brilliant leadership, Trotsky's Red Army began to turn back the White forces. Admiral Kolchak's forces were destroyed towards the end of 1919 and at the same time the foreign 'armies of intervention' withdrew. The Whites were not really a strong alliance, and their armies were unable to work together. Trotsky defeated them one by one. The last major White army was defeated in the Crimea in November 1920. Although scattered outbreaks of fighting continued, by 1921 the Bolsheviks were securely in control of Russia.

Bolshevik propaganda

Both sides – the Reds and the Whites – used PROPAGANDA in the civil war. One reason why the Reds won was that theirs was probably more effective because the message was consistent – fight to protect the rights of the workers and fight to get rid of the foreign invaders who want to re-establish aristocratic rule.

Trotsky used the railway network, most of which was controlled by the Reds, to send out travelling cinemas which showed propaganda films to local people as well as the Red Army. Trotsky himself toured round, making frequent speeches, to raise morale. (See Sources 18 and 19 on pages 124–25.)

SOURCE 16

Red propaganda leaflet, 'Why Have You Come to Murmansk?'

For the first time in history the working people have got control of their country. The workers of all countries are striving to achieve this objective. We in Russia have succeeded. We have thrown off the rule of the Tsar, of landlords and of capitalists. But we still have tremendous difficulties to overcome. We cannot build a new society in a day. We ask you, are you going to crush us? To help give Russia back to the landlords, the capitalists and the Tsar?

THINK

1 Whom do you think Source 16 is aimed at?
2 Look at Source 17. Who is controlling the White forces?

SOURCE 17

Bolshevik propaganda cartoon, 1919. The dogs represent the White generals Denikin, Kolchak and Yudenich.

THINK

Study Sources 18 and 19.

How important do you think these trains were in the Civil War?

Why did the Bolsheviks win the Civil War?

The advantages of the Reds

The Red Army was no match for the armies that were still fighting on the Western Front in 1918. However, compared to the Whites, the Red Army was united and disciplined. It was also brilliantly led by Trotsky.

The Bolsheviks also kept strict control over their heartlands in western Russia:

- They made sure that the towns and armies were fed, by forcing peasants to hand over food and by rationing supplies.
- They took over the factories of Moscow and Petrograd so that they were able to supply their armies with equipment and ammunition.
- The Red Terror made sure that the population was kept under strict control.
- The Bolsheviks raised fears about the intentions of the foreign armies in league with the Whites. Effective propaganda also made good use of atrocities committed by the Whites and raised fears about the possible return of the Tsar and landlords.

Finally, the Reds had important territorial advantages. Their enemies were spread around the edge of Russia while they had internal lines of communication. This enabled them to move troops quickly and effectively by rail, while their enemies used less efficient methods.

SOURCE 18

Trotsky's war train. For most of the campaign he travelled on an enormous train, giving orders, rallying the troops or transporting essential supplies.

SOURCE 19

A Red Army propaganda train in the early 1920s. This is the cinema carriage. The Red Army spread Communist ideas across Russia.

The disadvantages of the Whites

The Whites, in contrast with the Bolsheviks, were not united. They were made up of many different groups, all with different aims. They were also widely spread so they were unable to co-ordinate their campaigns against the Reds. Trotsky was able to defeat them one by one.

They had limited support from the Russian population. Russian peasants did not especially like the Bolsheviks, but they preferred them to the Whites. If the Whites won, the peasants knew the landlords would return.

Both sides were guilty of atrocities, but the Whites in general caused more suffering to the peasants than the Reds.

SOURCE 20

R. Appignanesi, *Lenin for Beginners*, 1977.

The Civil War, 1918–1920, was a time of great chaos and estimates of Cheka executions vary from twelve to fifty thousands. But even the highest figure does not compare to the ferocity of the White Terror … for instance, in Finland alone, the number of workers executed by the Whites approaches 100,000.

FOCUS TASK

Why did the Bolsheviks win the Civil War?

Imagine it is the end of the war and you have been asked to make a poster for the Bolsheviks celebrating the victory and showing the main reasons for success.

Design your poster using the information in the text, then write an explanation of your poster to send to Lenin.

PRACTICE QUESTIONS

1 Describe *two* immediate problems faced by Lenin and the Bolsheviks when they had seized power in October/November 1917.
2 Which of the following was the more important reason for the Bolsheviks' victory in the Civil War (1918–21):
   ● The leadership of Trotsky
   ● Divisions among the Whites?

   Explain your answer with reference to both reasons.

SOURCE 21

Bolshevik poster, 1920. The sailor is welcoming the dawn of the revolution. The Kronstadt sailors played a key role in the Bolsheviks' original success in 1917–20.

• Social and economic developments, 1918–24

Lenin wanted to establish a Communist-style society and economy where everyone would be treated equally and fairly. However, he had to balance this against the situation he faced. The Bolsheviks inherited a country that had suffered enormously from the First World War and living conditions worsened during the Civil War that followed.

War Communism

WAR COMMUNISM was the name given to the harsh economic measures the Bolsheviks adopted during the Civil War. It had two main aims. The first aim was to put Communist theories into practice by redistributing (sharing out) wealth among the Russian people. The second aim was to help with the Civil War by keeping the towns and the Red Army supplied with food and weapons.

- All large factories were taken over by the government.
- Production was planned and organised by the government.
- Discipline for workers was strict and strikers could be shot.
- Peasants had to hand over surplus food to the government. If they didn't, they could be shot.
- Food was rationed.
- Free enterprise became illegal – all production and trade was controlled by the state.

War Communism achieved its aim of winning the war, but in doing so it caused terrible hardship. (Some historians believe that Lenin's ruthless determination to create a Communist society actually caused the war in the first place.) Peasants refused to co-operate in producing more food because the government simply took it away. This led to food shortages which, along with the bad weather in 1920 and 1921, caused a terrible famine. Some estimates suggest that 7 million Russian people died in this famine. There were even reports of cannibalism.

SOURCE 22

Children starving during the Russian famine of 1921.

The Kronstadt Rising

In February 1921 Bolshevik policies sparked a mutiny at Kronstadt naval base. Kronstadt was an important naval base on an island in the Gulf of Finland. It housed the Russian Baltic Fleet and guarded the approaches to Petrograd. Sailors on two of the leading battleships drew up a list of fifteen demands for the Bolsheviks. In response, Trotsky sent 60,000 troops to put down the uprising, killing more than a thousand of the Kronstadt sailors.

Soon afterwards Lenin abandoned the emergency policies of War Communism. Considering the chaos of the Civil War years, it may seem strange that this particular revolt had such a startling effect on Lenin. However, it did so because the Kronstadt sailors had been among the strongest supporters of Lenin and Bolshevism.

The New Economic Policy

After the Kronstadt revolt, Lenin recognised that changes were necessary. In March 1921, at the Party Congress, Lenin announced some startling new policies which he called the New Economic Policy (NEP). The NEP effectively brought back CAPITALISM for some sections of Russian society. Peasants were allowed to sell surplus grain for profit and would pay tax on what they produced rather than giving some of it up to the government.

FIGURE 23

How the NEP differed from War Communism.

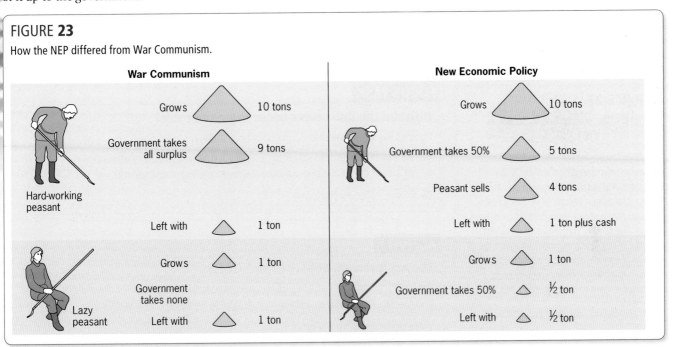

In the towns, small factories were handed back into private ownership and private trading of small goods was allowed.

Lenin made it clear that the NEP was temporary and that the vital heavy industries (coal, oil, iron and steel) would remain in state hands. Nevertheless, many Bolsheviks were horrified when the NEP was announced, seeing it as a betrayal of Communism. As always, Lenin won the argument and the NEP went into operation from 1921 onwards. By 1925 there seemed to be strong evidence that it was working, as food production in particular rose steeply. However, as Source 27 suggests (page 128), increases in production did not necessarily improve the situation of industrial workers.

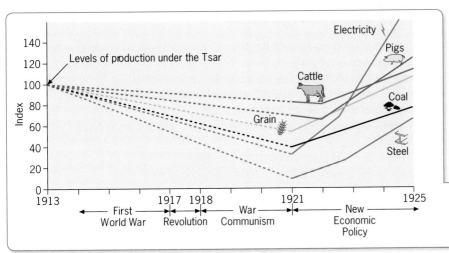

SOURCE 25

Lenin, introducing the NEP at the Party Congress, 1921.

Our poverty and ruin are so great that we cannot at one stroke restore large-scale socialist production … we must try to satisfy the demands of the peasants who are dissatisfied, discontented and cannot be otherwise … there must be a certain amount of freedom to trade, freedom for the small private owner. We are now retreating, but we are doing this so as to then run and leap forward more vigorously.

THINK

Explain what Figure 24 appears to show about the successes of NEP compared with the policy of War Communism.

FIGURE 24

Production under the New Economic Policy, 1921–25.

SOURCE 26

Bukharin, speaking in 1922. He was a leading Bolshevik and a strong supporter of the NEP.

Poor, starving old Russia, Russia of primitive lighting and the meal of a crust of black bread, is going to be covered by a network of electric power stations. The NEP will transform the Russian economy and rebuild a broken nation. The future is endless and beautiful.

SOURCE 27

Some problems identified by Soviet observers in the 1920s.

In 1925 the Soviet Commissar for Finance admitted that the pay of miners, metal workers and engine drivers was still lower than it had been before 1914. This in turn meant that workers' housing and food were poor. The factory committee of a cement works in Smolensk reported, for example, in 1929: 'Every day there are many complaints about apartments: many workers have families of six and seven people, and live in one room.'

SOURCE 28

The British historian A. J. P. Taylor writing in the 1960s.

Lenin did more than any other political leader to change the face of the twentieth-century world. The creation of Soviet Russia and its survival were due to him. He was a very great man and even, despite his faults, a very good man.

The death of Lenin and the creation of the USSR

Lenin did not live to see the recovery of the Russian economy. He suffered several strokes in 1922 and 1923 which left him paralysed and led to his death in January 1924. He was a remarkable man by any standards. He led Russia through revolution and civil war and even in 1923 he supervised the drawing up of a new constitution that turned the Russian Empire into the Union of Soviet Socialist Republics. Source 28 gives the opinion of a British historian.

We will never know what policies Lenin would have pursued if he had lived longer – he certainly left no clear plans about how long he wanted the NEP to last. He also left another big unanswered question behind him: who was to be the next leader of the USSR?

FOCUS TASK

How did the Bolsheviks consolidate their rule?

Look at the Topic Summary on Lenin's new society.

● At which moment do you think Bolshevik rule was most threatened?
● At which moment do you think Bolshevik rule was most secure?

Give reasons for your answers.

ACTIVITY

The achievements of Lenin and Trotsky

Go back through the narrative of this part (pages 114–128) and list the actions of Lenin and Trotsky from 1917 to 1924.

Were both equally important?

TOPIC SUMMARY

Lenin's new society
● The Provisional Government failed to solve Russia's huge economic and social problems, nor provide stable government.
● The Bolsheviks led by Lenin, with Trotsky heading up the military planning, seized control of Petrograd and overthrew the Provisional Government.
● The new Bolshevik government under Lenin passed decrees introducing a new society.
● One of the priorities was to end Russia's involvement in the First World War (March 1918).
● The Bolsheviks had many enemies inside and beyond Russia, leading to a civil war (1918–21).
● During this war Lenin imposed the policy of War Communism in order to ensure food supplies.
● Near the start of the Civil War the Romanovs were executed.
● In 1921 sailors at the Kronstadt naval base rebelled, forcing Lenin to make concessions to his policy of War Communism.
● The New Economic Policy was introduced in 1921, with less emphasis on Communist principles.
● In December 1922 Lenin suffered a major stroke.
● Lenin died in January 1924 with no clear successor agreed.

3.3 Stalin's USSR

FOCUS

By 1929 Stalin was sole ruler of the USSR. He proceeded to carry out a massive policy of modernisation which resulted in a total upheaval of society. This transformation also provided the military strength needed for defeating the German invasion in the Second World War.

In this section you will study the following:

- Stalin the dictator and the means he used to control the USSR.
- Stalin's modernisation of the USSR and:
  - the extent to which agriculture and industry were modernised
  - the effects the programme of modernisation had on different groups in Russian society.
- The impact of the Second World War, politically, economically and socially, and the importance of Stalin's leadership to Soviet victory.

● Stalin the dictator

When Lenin died in 1924 there were several leading Communists who were possible candidates to take his place. There would not be leadership elections. The Communist Party did not work that way. The leader would be the one who showed he had most power within the party. Among the contenders were Kamenev and Zinoviev, leading Bolsheviks who had played important parts in the Bolshevik Revolution of 1917. Bukharin was a more moderate member of the party who favoured the NEP and wanted to introduce Communism gradually to the USSR.

However, the real struggle to succeed Lenin was between two leading figures and bitter rivals in the Communist Party, Joseph Stalin and Leon Trotsky. The struggle between these two was long and hard and it was not until 1929 that Stalin made himself completely secure as the supreme leader of the USSR. Stalin achieved this through a combination of political scheming, the mistakes of his opponents and the clever way in which he built up his power base.

Stalin's struggle to succeed Lenin

SOURCE 1

Lenin's Testament. This is often used as evidence that Stalin was an outsider. However, the document contained many remarks critical of other leading Communists as well. It was never published in Russia, although, if it had been, it would certainly have damaged Stalin.

Comrade Stalin, having become Secretary General, has unlimited authority in his hands and I am not sure whether he will always be capable of using that authority with sufficient caution.

Comrade Trotsky, on the other hand, is distinguished not only by his outstanding ability. He is personally probably the most capable man in the present Central Committee, but he has displayed excessive self-assurance and preoccupation with the purely administrative side of the work.

Source 1 shows Lenin's opinions of Trotsky and Stalin. As Lenin lay dying in late 1923 few people in the USSR had any doubts that Trotsky would win. Trotsky was a brilliant speaker and writer, as well as, after Lenin, the party's best political thinker. He was also the man who had organised the Bolshevik Revolution and was the hero of the Civil War as leader of the Red Army (see pages 122–25). Finally, he was the man who negotiated peace for Russia with the Treaty of Brest-Litovsk.

So how did Trotsky lose this contest? Much of the blame lies with Trotsky himself. He was brilliant, but also arrogant. He often offended other senior party members. More importantly, he failed to take the opposition seriously. He made little effort to build up any support in the ranks of the party. And he seriously underestimated Stalin.

SOURCE 2

Historian I. Deutscher in *The Prophet Unarmed, Trotsky 1921–1929*, published in 1959.

Trotsky refrained from attacking Stalin because he felt secure. No contemporary, and he least of all, saw in the Stalin of 1923 the menacing and towering figure he was to become. It seemed to Trotsky almost a joke that Stalin, the wilful and sly but shabby and inarticulate man in the background, should be his rival.

In addition to his arrogance, Trotsky also frightened many people in the USSR. Trotsky argued that the future security of the USSR lay in trying to spread permanent revolution across the globe until the whole world was Communist. Many people were worried that Trotsky would involve the USSR in new conflicts.

FACTFILE

Stalin's steps to power

- **1923** Stalin the outsider – Lenin calls for him to be replaced. Trotsky calls him 'the party's most eminent mediocrity'.
- **1924** Lenin's death. Stalin attends funeral as chief mourner. Trotsky does not turn up (tricked by Stalin).
- **1924** Stalin, Kamenev and Zinoviev form the triumvirate (rule shared by three) that dominates the Politburo, the policy-making committee of the Communist Party. Working together, these three cut off their opponents (Trotsky and Bukharin) because between them they control the important posts in the party.
- **1925** Trotsky sacked as War Commissar. Stalin introduces his idea of 'Socialism in One Country'.
- **1926** Stalin turns against Kamenev and Zinoviev and allies himself with Bukharin.
- **1927** Kamenev, Zinoviev and Trotsky all expelled from the Communist Party.
- **1928** Trotsky exiled to Siberia. Stalin begins attacking Bukharin.
- **1929** Trotsky expelled from USSR and Bukharin expelled from the Communist Party.

SOURCE 3

Lenin and Stalin. Stalin made the most of any opportunity to appear close to Lenin. This photograph is a suspected fake.

ACTIVITY

1 Draw up a campaign poster or flyer listing Trotsky's qualities for the leadership of the party. Make use of Lenin's Testament (Source 1, page 129).

2 Draw up a campaign leaflet for Stalin. Remember to mention his strengths and the weaknesses of his opponent.

How did Stalin win?

As it often does in history, chance also played a part. Trotsky was unfortunate in falling ill late in 1923 with a malaria-like infection – just when Lenin was dying, and Trotsky needed to be at his most active.

He was also the victim of a trick by Stalin. Stalin cabled Trotsky to tell him that Lenin's funeral was to be on 26 January, when it was in fact going to be on the 27th. Trotsky was away in the south of Russia and would not have had time to get back for the 26th, although he could have got back for the 27th. As a result, Trotsky did not appear at the funeral whereas Stalin appeared as chief mourner and Lenin's closest friend.

We have already seen that Stalin was a clever politician and he planned his bid for power carefully. He made great efforts to associate himself with Lenin wherever possible and got off to an excellent start at Lenin's funeral.

He was also extremely clever in using his power within the Communist Party. He took on many boring but important jobs such as Commissar for Nationalities and, of course, General Secretary. He used these positions to put his own supporters into important posts and even to transfer supporters of his opponents to remote postings. He was also absolutely ruthless in picking off his rivals one by one. For example, he took Bukharin's side in the debate on the NEP in order to help get rid of Trotsky. Once he had got rid of Trotsky, he opposed Bukharin using exactly the same arguments as Trotsky had used before (see Factfile on Stalin's steps to power).

Stalin's policies also met with greater favour than Trotsky's. Stalin proposed that in future the party should try to establish 'Socialism in One Country' rather than try to spread revolution worldwide. Finally, Stalin appeared to be a straightforward Georgian peasant – much more a man of the people than his intellectual rivals. To a Soviet people weary of years of war and revolution, Stalin seemed to be the man who understood their feelings.

PROFILE

Joseph Stalin

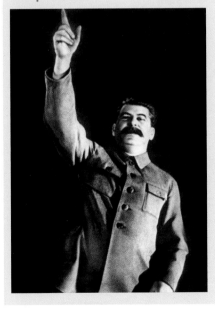

- Born in 1879 in Georgia. His father was a shoemaker and an alcoholic. He abandoned the family while Stalin was still a young child.
- Original name was Iosif Dzhugashvili but changed his name to Stalin (man of steel).
- Twice exiled to Siberia by the Tsarist secret police, he escaped each time.
- Made his name in violent bank raids to raise party funds.
- He was slow and steady, but very hard-working.
- He also held grudges and generally made his enemies suffer.
- Became a leading Communist after playing an important role in defending the Bolshevik city of Tsaritsyn (later Stalingrad) during the Civil War.
- Had become undisputed party leader by 1929.

PRACTICE QUESTIONS

1 Describe two claims that Trotsky had to succeed Lenin.
2 Which of the following was the more important reason for Stalin's success in becoming sole ruler by the end of the 1920s:
   - Trotsky's character
   - Stalin's character?

Explain your answer with reference to both reasons.

Alexander Solzhenitsyn, *Gulag Archipelago*, published in 1973. Solzhenitsyn lost his Soviet citizenship as a result of this book.

A tribute to Comrade Stalin was called for. Of course, everyone stood up ... for three minutes, four minutes, the 'stormy applause, rising to an ovation' continued ... Who would dare to be the first to stop? After all, NKVD [the state secret police organisation] men were standing in the hall waiting to see who quit first! After eleven minutes the director [of the factory] ... sat down ... To a man, everyone else stopped dead and sat down. They had been saved! ... That, however, was how they discovered who the independent people were. And that was how they eliminated them. The same night the factory director was arrested.

The purges and the terror of the 1930s

The control of the Communist Party over the government

For Stalin, it was not enough to be in power. He wanted to be in a position in which no one could possibly challenge him. The Constitution of 1936 appeared to provide basic freedoms and human rights, but in practice Stalin dominated everything through the Politburo (the equivalent of the British Cabinet). He was determined to crush anyone who opposed him or who might oppose him. He had seen how Lenin had used terror and force against potential opponents and he learned this lesson well.

Under Stalin the only legal political party was the Communist Party. Under Stalin an impressive army, armed with the latest weaponry and answerable only to Stalin, was in place. And under Stalin the secret police were watching those intent on opposition.

The purges

The really terrifying period in Stalin's rule, known as the PURGES, began in 1934 when Kirov, the leader of the Leningrad (the new name for Petrograd from 1924) Communist Party, was murdered. Stalin used this murder as an excuse to 'purge', or clear out, his opponents in the party. Historians strongly suspect that Stalin arranged for Kirov's murder to give him this excuse. In great 'SHOW TRIALS', loyal Bolsheviks, such as Kamenev (1936), Zinoviev (1936) and Bukharin (1938), confessed to being traitors to the state. It was not only leading figures who were purged. Estimates suggest that around 500,000 party members were arrested on charges of anti-Soviet activities and either executed or sent to labour camps (*gulags*). In 1940, Trotsky, who was in exile in Mexico, was murdered by Stalin's agents.

A cartoon published by Russian exiles in Paris in 1936. The title of the cartoon is 'The Stalinist Constitution' and the text at the bottom reads 'New seating arrangements in the Supreme Soviet'.

THINK

1 According to Source 4, what sort of people did Stalin want in the USSR?
2 Choose Source 5 or Source 6. Summarise the message of the cartoon in your own words. Refer to details from the cartoon to explain your answer.

The Great Terror

Even as the show trials were progressing, the purges began to hit other areas of the Communist Party. There are still mass graves all over the USSR today which mark the victims of the Great Terror, which lasted from 1936–38 but peaked in 1937. Stalin first turned his attention to the army, particularly the officers. Approximately 25,000 officers (around one in five) were removed, including the Supreme Commander of the Red Army, Marshal Tukhachevsky.

As the purges were extended, university lecturers and teachers, miners and engineers, factory managers and ordinary workers all disappeared. It is said that every family in the USSR lost someone in the purges. One of the most frightening aspects was the unpredictability. Arrests would take place in the middle of the night and victims were rarely told what they were accused of. Days of physical and psychological torture would gradually break the victims and they would confess to anything. If the torture failed, the NKVD would threaten the families of those arrested.

By 1937 an estimated 18 million people had been transported to labour camps and 10 million died. Stalin seriously weakened the USSR by removing so many able individuals. The army purges were nearly fatal. When Hitler invaded the USSR in 1941, one of the key problems of the Red Army was a lack of good-quality, experienced officers. Stalin had also succeeded in destroying any sense of independent thinking. Everyone who was spared knew that their lives depended on thinking exactly as Stalin did. In the population as a whole, the long-term impact of living with terror and distrust haunted the USSR for a generation.

SOURCE 7

Stalin shown holding a young child, Gelya Markizova, in 1936. Stalin had both of her parents killed. This did not stop him using this image on propaganda leaflets to show him as a kind, fatherly figure.

SOURCE 6

Russian exiles in France made this mock travel poster in the late 1930s. The text says: 'Visit the USSR's pyramids!'

What happened to the victims? The labour camps

A key part of Stalin's Terror was the network of labour camps which could be found all over the USSR but were mostly in remote, inaccessible regions. The regime in the labour camps was harsh – very hard physical labour in extremely cold conditions. By 1939 there were around 3 million people in the camps, or *gulags* as they were called. The prisoners produced most of the gold from the USSR's mines as well as timber and other resources. Prisoners also played an important role in the building of roads, railways and projects like the Belomor Canal. In fact some historians believe that one motive of the purges was to find labourers for the camps.

SOURCE 8

Extract from *One Day in the Life of Ivan Denisovitch*. This was a novel by the writer Alexander Solzhenitsyn who spent many years in a *gulag*.

Reveille was sounded, as always, at five a.m. – a hammer pounding on a rail outside camp HQ … Shukhov never slept through reveille but always got up at once. That gave him about an hour and a half to himself before the morning roll call, a time when anyone who knew what was what in the camps could always scrounge a little something on the side. He could sew someone a cover for his mittens out of a piece of old lining. He could bring one of the big gang bosses his dry felt boots while he still in his bunk, to save him the trouble of hanging around the pile of boots in his bare feet and trying to find his own. Or he could run around to one of the supply rooms where there might be a little job, sweeping or carrying something. Or he could go to the mess hall to pick up bowls from the tables and take piles of them to the dishwashers. That was another way of getting food, but there were always too many other people with the same idea. And the worst thing was that if there was something left in a bowl you started to lick it. You couldn't help it.

… Today was the big day for them. They'd heard a lot of talk of switching their gang (104) from putting up workshops to a new job, building a new 'Socialist Community Development'. But so far it was nothing more than bare fields covered with snowdrifts, and before anything could be done there, holes had to be dug, posts put in, and barbed wire put up – by the prisoners for the prisoners, so they couldn't get out. And then they could start building.

SOURCE 9

Prisoners at work building the Belomor Canal in 1933. This was drawn by a political prisoner, Sergie Korolkoff, and was published in 1953. It shows one prisoner being punished for working slowly by being forced to stand on a tree stump in freezing weather.

THINK

1. What does Source 9 reveal about work in the camps?
2. Does Source 9 support the impression of the camps given in Source 8? Explain your answer.
3. What reasons might historians have to be concerned about the reliability of each of Sources 8 and 9?

Propaganda and censorship

Through propaganda and censorship Stalin made it very clear to the Russian people which expressions of culture were permitted and which were not:

- Stalin wanted to be a part of people's daily lives. The Soviet people were deluged with portraits, photographs and statues of Stalin. Comrade Stalin appeared everywhere. Every Russian town had a Stalin Square or a Stalin Avenue and a large Stalin statue in the centre. In Moscow and other big cities huge building projects were undertaken, including the Palace of the Soviets (which was never finished because of war in 1941) and the awesome Moscow metro. Regular processions were organised through the streets of Russian towns and cities praising Stalin and all that he had achieved.

- Religious worship was banned. By 1939 only 1 in 40 churches were holding regular services and only seven bishops were active in the USSR. Monasteries were demolished (see Source 10). Muslim worship was also attacked. In 1917 there were 26,000 mosques in Russia but by 1939 there were 1,300.

- There were also smaller-scale projects. Around 70,000 libraries were built across the country and many towns gained excellent sports and leisure facilities.

All music and other arts in the USSR were carefully monitored by the NKVD. Poets and playwrights praised Stalin either directly or indirectly. Composers wrote music praising him. One of the most famous was Dmitri Shostakovich. He became a star of the Soviet system, but in 1936 an opera by Shostakovich met with disapproval from Stalin. He was attacked by the Soviet press and criticised by the Soviet Composers Union. Shostakovich scrapped his next piece of work and wrote his Fifth Symphony which he subtitled 'A Soviet Artist's Practical Creative Reply to Just Criticism'. Soviet artists and writers developed a style of art which became known as Socialist Realism. The aim of this style of art was to praise Stalin's rule. It usually involved heroic figures working hard in fields or factories.

SOURCE 10

A painting showing Soviet officials blowing up a monastery in 1930.

SOURCE 11

A Soviet writer describes how children in Soviet schools had to revise their school history books during the 1930s.

The teacher showed us her school textbooks where the portraits of Party leaders had thick pieces of paper pasted over them as one by one they fell into disgrace – this the children had to do on instructions from their teacher … with every new arrest, people went through their books and burned the works of disgraced leaders in their stoves.

THINK

1. Why did Stalin try to reduce the influence of religion?
2. What changes would ordinary Soviet citizens have noticed as they walked round their towns and cities?
3. What does the story of Shostakovich tell historians about life for musicians under Stalin? Try using the internet to look up other artists or writers such as Maxim Gorky.
4. Stalin wanted Socialist Realist art to send out very simple messages which everyone could understand. Do you think Source 10 achieves this aim?

SOURCE 12

Ode to Stalin on his 60th birthday by the composer, Prokofiev.

Never have our fertile fields such a harvest shown,
Never have our villages such contentment known.
Never life has been so far, spirits been so high,
Never to the present day grew so green the rye,
O'er the earth the rising sun sheds a warmer light,
Since it looked on Stalin's face it has grown more bright.
I am singing to my baby sleeping in my arms,
Grow like flowers in the meadow free from all alarm.
On your lips the name of Stalin will protect from harm.
You will learn the source of sunshine bathing all the land.
You will copy Stalin's portrait with your little hand.

The Cult of Personality

Today, Stalin's rule is looked back on as a time of great terror and oppression. However, if you had visited the USSR in the 1930s, you would have found that the average Soviet citizen admired Stalin. Ask about the purges and people would probably say that they were nothing to do with Stalin himself. For most Soviet citizens, Stalin was not a tyrant dominating an oppressed country. He and his style of government were popular. The Communist Party saw him as a winner and Soviet citizens saw him as a 'dictator of the people'. The Soviet people sincerely believed in Stalin and this belief was built up quite deliberately by Communist leaders and by Stalin himself. It developed into what is known as the Cult of Personality. The history of the Soviet Union was rewritten so that Lenin and Stalin were the only real heroes of the Bolshevik Revolution. The Soviet education system was geared to Stalinist propaganda and not to independent thinking. Schoolchildren were also expected to join the Young Pioneers.

FOCUS TASK

How did Stalin control the USSR?

1 Draw up a table like this one and fill it out as completely as you can. You may wish to add other subjects in the first column.

2 Discuss with a partner which of the methods you think was most important. Reorder your table so the methods are in order of importance.

3 Now use your table to create a presentation or a piece of extended writing on the question 'How did Stalin control the USSR?' Select the most important methods as headings for slides or paragraphs in your work.

Method	Example(s)
Propaganda	
Show trials	
Education	
Purges	
Control of the Communist Party	
The Constitution	
Loyal followers	
Cult of Personality	

SOURCE 13

The cover of *Ogonyok* magazine, December 1949, showing Stalin's godlike image projected into the sky, as part of the celebrations for his 70th birthday.

Stalin's modernisation of the USSR

Once in power, Stalin was determined to modernise the USSR as quickly as possible, and he had some powerful reasons:

- **To increase the USSR's military strength**: The First World War had shown that a country could only fight a modern war if it had the industries to produce the weapons and other equipment which were needed (see Source 14).
- **To rival the economies of the USA and other capitalist countries**: When Stalin took power much of Russia's industrial equipment had to be imported. Stalin wanted to make the USSR self-sufficient so that it could make everything it needed for itself. He also wanted to improve standards of living in Russia so that people would value Communist rule.
- **To increase food supplies**: Stalin wanted more workers in industries, towns and cities. He also wanted to sell grain abroad to raise cash and to buy industrial equipment. This meant fewer peasants had to produce more food and that farming would have to be reorganised.
- **To create a Communist society**: Communist theory said that most of the population had to be workers if Communism was going to work. In 1928 only about one in five Russians were industrial workers.
- **To establish his reputation**: Lenin had made big changes to Russia/the USSR. Stalin wanted to prove himself as a great leader by bringing about even greater changes.

Modernising agriculture: Collectivisation

For the enormous changes of the FIVE-YEAR PLAN to be successful, Stalin needed to modernise the USSR's agriculture. This was vital because the population of the industrial centres was growing rapidly and yet as early as 1928 the country was already 2 million tons short of the grain it needed to feed its workers. Stalin also wanted to try to raise money for his industrialisation programme by selling exports of surplus food abroad.

The problem was that farming was not organised to do this. Under the NEP, most peasants were either agricultural labourers (with no land) or *kulaks* – prosperous peasants who owned small farms. These farms were too small to make efficient use of tractors, fertilisers and other modern methods. In addition, most peasants had enough to eat and could see little point in increasing production to feed the towns. To get round these problems, Stalin set out his ideas for COLLECTIVISATION in 1929.

The government tried hard to sell these ideas to the peasants, offering free seed and other perks, but there were soon problems. The peasants, who had always been suspicious of government, whether it was the Tsar, Lenin or Stalin, were concerned about the speed of collectivisation. They disliked the fact that the farms were under the control of the local Communist leader. They were being asked to grow crops such as flax for Russia's industry rather than grain to feed themselves. In short, Stalin was asking the peasants to abandon a way of life that they and their ancestors had led for centuries.

Stalin had a difficult time convincing the peasants about collectivisation, but this was slight compared to the opposition of the *kulaks* who owned their own land. The *kulaks* simply refused outright to hand over their land and produce. Within a short time, collectivisation became a grim and bitter struggle. Soviet propaganda tried to turn the people against the *kulaks*. The war of words soon turned into violence. Requisition parties came and took the food required by the government, often leaving the peasants to starve. *Kulaks* were arrested and sent by the thousand to labour camps or were forced on to poor-quality land. In revenge, many *kulaks* burned their crops and slaughtered their animals so that the Communists could not have them.

SOURCE 14

Stalin speaking in 1931.

Throughout history Russia has been beaten again and again because she was backward … All have beaten her because of her military, industrial and agricultural backwardness. She was beaten because people have been able to get away with it. If you are backward and weak, then you are in the wrong and may be beaten and enslaved. But if you are powerful, people must beware of you.

It is sometimes asked whether it is not possible to slow down industrialisation a bit. No, comrades, it is not possible … To slacken would mean falling behind. And those who fall behind get beaten … That is why Lenin said during the October Revolution: 'Either perish, or overtake and outstrip the advanced capitalist countries.' We are 50 to 100 years behind the advanced countries. Either we make good the difference in 10 years or they crush us.

THINK

1. Why did Stalin feel it was compulsory to modernise Russia?
2. Study Source 14 carefully. In a paragraph, explain whether you think it provides all Stalin's reasons for wanting to modernise Russia.

FACTFILE

Collectivisation

- Peasants were to put their lands together to form large joint farms (*kolkhoz*) but could keep small plots for personal use.
- Animals and tools were to be pooled together.
- Motor Tractor Stations (MTS) provided by the government made tractors available.
- Ninety per cent of *kolkhoz* produce would be sold to the state and the profits shared out.
- The remaining 10 per cent of produce was to be used to feed the *kolkhoz*.

SOURCE 15

Historian E. Roberts, *Stalin, Man of Steel*, published in 1986.

Stalin, ignoring the great cost in human life and misery, claimed that collectivisation was a success; for, after the great famines caused at the time … no more famines came to haunt the Russian people. The collective farms, despite their inefficiencies, did grow more food than the tiny, privately owned holdings had done. For example, 30 to 40 million tons of grain were produced every year. Collectivisation also meant the introduction of machines into the countryside. Now two million previously backward peasants learned how to drive a tractor. New methods of farming were taught by agricultural experts. The countryside was transformed.

The countryside was in chaos. Even where collectivisation had been introduced successfully, peasants were unfamiliar with new ideas and methods. There was much bitterness as starving peasants watched Communist officials sending food for export.

Not surprisingly, food production fell under these conditions and there was a famine in 1932–33. Millions died in Kazakhstan and the Ukraine, Russia's richest agricultural region. When the Germans invaded the Ukraine in 1941, they were at first made welcome for driving out the Communists.

SOURCE 16

The *Manchester Guardian*, 1933.

'How are things with you?' I asked one old man. He looked around anxiously to see that no soldiers were about. 'We have nothing, absolutely nothing. They have taken everything away.' It was true. The famine is an organised one. Some of the food that has been taken away from them is being exported to foreign countries. It is literally true that whole villages have been exiled. I saw myself a group of some twenty peasants being marched off under escort. This is so common a sight that it no longer arouses even curiosity.

SOURCE 17

A painting from 1930 called *Day of Harvest and Collectivisation*.

THINK

1 According to Source 15, what advantages did collectivisation bring?
2 Do you agree that these advantages outweighed the human cost?
3 Explain why Stalin needed to change farming in the USSR.
4 Why did the peasants resist?
5 Read Source 16. Why do you think the only reports of the famine came from Western journalists?
6 Look at Source 17. Why do you think this was painted in 1930?

Despite the famine, Stalin did not ease off. By 1934 there were no *kulaks* left. By 1941 almost all agricultural land was organised under the collective system. Stalin had achieved his aim of collectivisation.

Modernising industry: The Five-Year Plans

Stalin ended Lenin's NEP and set about achieving modernisation through a series of Five-Year Plans. These plans were drawn up by GOSPLAN, the state planning organisation that Lenin set up in 1921. They set ambitious targets for production in the vital heavy industries (coal, iron, oil, electricity). The plans were very complex but they were set out in such a way that by 1929 every worker knew what he or she had to achieve.

GOSPLAN set overall targets for an industry.

▽

Each region was told its targets.

▽

The region set targets for each mine, factory, etc.

▽

The manager of each mine, factory, etc., set targets for each foreman.

▽

The foremen set targets for each shift and even for individual workers.

The first Five-Year Plan (1928–32) focused on the major industries and although most targets were not met, the achievements were still staggering. The USSR increased production and created a foundation on which to build the next Five-Year Plans. The USSR was rich in natural resources, but many of them were in remote places such as Siberia. So whole cities were built from nothing and workers taken out to the new industrial centres. Foreign observers marvelled as huge new steel mills appeared at Magnitogorsk in the Urals and Sverdlovsk in central Siberia. New dams and hydro-electric power fed industry's energy requirements. Russian 'experts' flooded into the Muslim republics of central Asia such as Uzbekistan and Kazakhstan, creating industry from scratch in previously undeveloped areas.

The second Five-Year Plan (1933–37) built on the achievements of the first. Heavy industry was still a priority, but other areas were also developed. Mining for lead, tin, zinc and other minerals intensified as Stalin further exploited Siberia's rich mineral resources. Transport and communications were also boosted, and new railways and canals were built. The most spectacular showpiece project was the Moscow underground railway.

Stalin also wanted industrialisation to help improve Russia's agriculture. The production of tractors and other farm machinery increased dramatically. In the third Five-Year Plan, which was begun in 1938, some factories were to switch to the production of consumer goods. However, this plan was disrupted by the Second World War.

FIGURE 18

The location of the new industrial centres.

FIGURE 19

The growth in the output of the USSR, 1913–40.

	1913	1928	1940
Gas (billion m³)	0.02	0.3	3.4
Fertilisers (million tons)	0.07	0.1	3.2
Plastics (million tons)	–	–	10.9
Tractors (thousand)	–	1.3	31.6

The extent of modernisation

There is much that could be and was criticised in the Five-Year Plans. Certainly there was a great deal of inefficiency, duplication of effort and waste, although the evidence shows that the Soviets did learn from their mistakes in the second and third Five-Year Plans. There was also an enormous human cost, as you will see on pages 141–43. But the fact remains that by 1937 the USSR was a modern state and it was this that saved it from defeat when Hitler invaded in 1941.

FIGURE 20

Graph showing share of world manufacturing output, 1929–38.

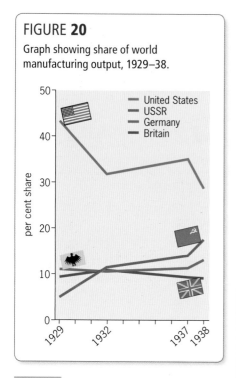

THINK

Look at Figures 20 and 21.

1 List the aspects of the statistics that indicate big successes.
2 List the aspects that indicate poor or disappointing progress.
3 Overall, could the Five-Year Plans be judged a success?

FIGURE 21

The achievements of the Five-Year Plans.

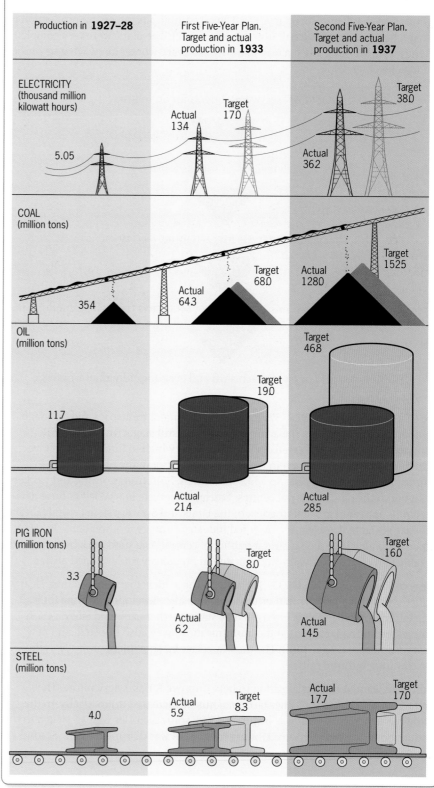

The Five-Year Plans were used very effectively for propaganda purposes. Stalin had wanted the Soviet Union to be a beacon of socialism and his publicity machine used the successes of industrialisation to further that objective.

Social and economic consequences for the Russian people

Throughout this period different groups in Russian society had to adapt and change in the face of huge social and economic shifts, while many others suffered as a consequence of the upheavals.

The *Kulaks*

As already explained on page 137, this group suffered badly. They were Stalin's chosen victims in his modernisation of agriculture.

Industrial workers

Any programme as extreme as Stalin's Five-Year Plans was bound to carry a cost. In the USSR this cost was paid by the workers. Many foreign experts and engineers were called in by Stalin to supervise the work and in their letters and reports they marvel at the toughness of the Russian people. The workers were constantly bombarded with propaganda, posters, slogans and radio broadcasts. They all had strict targets to meet and were fined if they did not meet them.

The most famous worker was Alexei Stakhanov. In 1935, with two helpers and an easy coal seam to work on, he managed to cut an amazing 102 tons of coal in one shift. This was fourteen times the average for a shift. Stakhanov became a 'Hero of Socialist Labour' and the propaganda machine encouraged all Soviet workers to be Stakhanovites.

Life was very harsh under Stalin. Factory discipline was strict and punishments were severe. Lateness or absences were punished by sacking, and that often meant losing your flat or house as well. To escape the hard work and hard discipline, some workers tried to move to other jobs, so the secret police introduced internal passports which prevented free movement of workers inside the USSR.

On the great engineering projects, such as dams and canals, many of the workers were prisoners who had been sentenced to hard labour for being political opponents, or suspected opponents, of Stalin, or for being *kulaks* (rich peasants) or Jews (who suffered much hatred in Russia as in many parts of Europe in the 1930s). Many other prisoners were simply unfortunate workers who had had accidents or made mistakes in their work but had been found guilty of 'sabotage'.

On these major projects conditions were appalling and there were many deaths and accidents. It is estimated that 100,000 workers died in the construction of the Belomor Canal (see Source 9 on page 134).

Women

The first Five-Year Plan revealed a shortage of workers, so from 1930 the government concentrated on drafting more women into industry. It set up thousands of new crèches and day-care centres so that mothers could work. By 1937 women made up 40 per cent of industrial workers (compared to 28 per cent in 1927), 21 per cent of building workers and 72 per cent of health workers. Four out of five new workers recruited between 1932 and 1937 were women.

THINK

What is the message of Source 22?

SOURCE 22

Soviet propaganda poster, 1933. In the top half, the hand is holding the first Five-Year Plan. The capitalist is saying (in 1928), 'Fantasy, Lies, Utopia.' The bottom half shows 1933.

FOCUS TASK

To what extent did Stalin modernise Russian agriculture and industry by 1941?

Work in pairs.

1 One of you make notes on Russian agriculture and the changes brought about by collectivisation (pages 137–38). The other should make notes on Russian industry and the changes brought about by the Five-Year Plans (pages 139–41).

2 Discuss your findings. To what extent did Stalin modernise Russian agriculture and industry by 1941?

THINK

1   Read Source 23. What impression do you get of women's attitudes towards their involvement in industrialisation?
2   Bearing in mind that when she was interviewed many other events had happened, how reliable do you think Tatyana Fyodorova's account is?

City dwellers

By the late 1930s many Soviet workers in the main cities had improved their conditions by acquiring well-paid skilled jobs and earning bonuses for meeting targets. Unemployment was almost non-existent. In 1940 the USSR had more doctors per head of population than Britain. Education became free and compulsory for all and Stalin invested huge sums in training schemes based in colleges and in the workplace. The influence of Stalin was everywhere, and many were proud to be living in a successful Communist regime.

The loyalty to Stalin was strong despite the relatively low living standards. Many items were hard to find in the shops and queuing became part of life. There were few consumer goods, such as radios and clothes for ordinary people to buy. Most housing was provided by the state, but overcrowding was a problem. Most families lived in flats and were crowded into two rooms which were used for living, sleeping and eating. Wages actually fell between 1928 and 1937. On the other hand, there were some positives. Health care improved enormously. Literacy became a high priority so education improved and public libraries became available. Most towns and cities got good sports facilities.

Professional workers

For some in society, life was even better. If you were ambitious, you could become one of the new class of foremen, supervisors, technicians or managers. Managers could also get items like clothing and luxuries in the official Communist Party shops. Although kept as secret as possible from the vast majority of the population, an elite of comparatively wealthy people was developing – totally against the theories of Communism and the wishes of Lenin.

FOCUS TASK

What were the social and economic consequences of Stalin's modernisation programme on Russian society?

Copy and complete the following spider diagram to summarise the effects of Stalin's programme of modernisation on different groups in Russian society.

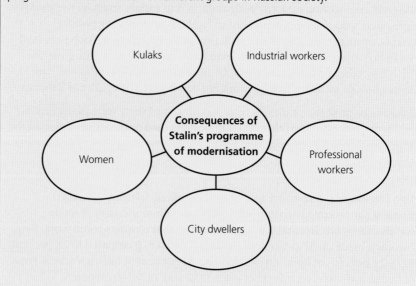

THINK

The two extracts below are historical interpretations of the Five Year Plans. From 1947 to 1989 the USSR and USA were generally hostile towards each other, in what was usually known as the Cold War. Many weapons were used in the Cold War, including history. Interpretation A has a particular purpose and audience. Interpretation B is more of an academic history textbook, but it is nonetheless an American perspective. Study both extracts and explain how the context, audience or purpose of each one has influenced the way the author has told the story.

Interpretation A The success of the Five-Year Plans. From *The Illustrated History of the USSR*, an official history published in Moscow in 1982.

The drive towards industrialisation was an heroic struggle by all the Soviet people. It showed their enthusiasm following the revolution of 1917 and victory in the Civil War. The Five-Year Plans gave a focus for the people's hopes and joy. The whole world watched closely to see the progress of industrialisation in the USSR and the success in getting rid of backwardness.

Interpretation B Another view of the Five-Year Plans. From *Stalin* by U. Alam. The book was published in the USA in 1973.

At tremendous human cost, the Soviet Union was pushed within a few years (1928–1934) into becoming an industrial country. To some, this is the greatest crime of modern history. To others, it is a huge feat of social control, ruthless and cruel in its effects on millions of human beings. Yet it laid the foundations of a richer economy and enabled Russia to withstand a foreign invasion and become a superpower.

PRACTICE QUESTIONS

Read Interpretations A and B and answer Questions 1–3

Interpretation A American journalist Eugen Lyons writing in 1937. Lyons was born in Russia but grew up in the USA. He worked as a reporter in the USSR from 1927 onwards

The period of the Five Year Plan has been called Russia's "Iron Age" by the best-informed and least sensational of my American colleagues in Moscow, William Henry Chamberlin. I can think of no more apt description. Iron symbolizes industrial construction and mechanization. Iron symbolizes no less the ruthlessness of the process, the bayonets, prison bars, rigid discipline and unfeeling determination of those who directed the period. It was a period that unrolled tumultuously, in a tempest of brutality. The Five Year Plan was publicized inside and outside Russia as no other economic project in modern history.

Interpretation B Official Soviet government report on the first Five Year Plan delivered to the Communist Party Central Committee in 1934

I have spoken of our successes in industry and agriculture, of the progress of industry and agriculture in the U.S.S.R. What are the results of these successes from the standpoint of improving the material conditions of the workers and peasants?

a) a doubling of the number of workers and other employees in large-scale industry compared with 1928;

b) an increase in the national income of 85 per cent over 1928;

c) an increase in the average annual wages of workers and other employees in large-scale industry by 67 per cent compared with 1928;

d) an increase in the social insurance fund by 292 per cent compared with 1928;

e) an increase in public catering facilities, now covering more than 70 per cent of the workers employed in the decisive industries.

1 How does Interpretation A differ from Interpretation B about the impact of the Five Year Plans?

Explain your answer based on what it says in Interpretations A and B.

2 Why might these two historians have a different interpretation of the impact of the Five Year Plans?

Explain your answer using Interpretations A and B and your own contextual knowledge.

3 Which interpretation gives the more convincing opinion about the Five Year Plans?

Explain your answer based on your contextual knowledge and what it says in Interpretations A and B.

What role did Stalin's wartime leadership play in the defeat of Germany in the Great Patriotic War?

Work in pairs.

1 Using the information on pages 144–46, one of you make notes on the role that Stalin played in the Soviet success in the Second World War. The other should make notes on other factors which ensured the Soviet victory.

2 Discuss your completed notes together.

3 Finally, write two paragraphs in answer to the following question:

How important was the role of Stalin in the defeat of Germany in the Great Patriotic War?

The impact of the Second World War

Stalin's wartime leadership

Hitler had not attacked the USSR in 1939 following the pact signed between two countries in August 1939. However, at dawn on 22 June 1941 over 2 million German troops invaded Russia. Hitler's Operation Barbarossa had been put into operation even though Britain had not been defeated. Stalin was totally taken by surprise, in spite of warnings from some of his colleagues. On the first day, 1,200 Russian aircraft were destroyed on the ground. There was much barbarity and cruelty on both sides as the Germans rapidly advanced into Russia towards the capital, Moscow.

By October the Germans sensed victory was soon to be achieved. However, as soldiers and civilians withdrew, Stalin ordered a 'scorched earth' policy. Over a thousand factories were taken to pieces to be reconstructed east of the Ural mountains out of the reach of the advancing Germans. Animals and crops were moved also – or else destroyed. The further the Germans advanced, the more difficult it became for them to get supplies from Germany.

Second, the Russian weather turned against the Germans. Initially, incessant rain in October turned the ground to mud and slowed the German advance. Then in November the temperature fell to well below freezing. The German soldiers were not dressed or equipped for such conditions. Vehicles ceased to work; men froze to death.

This gave Stalin time to act decisively. Hitler had unwisely decided to concentrate his attack on Stalingrad. Much of the city was destroyed, but with the onset of winter a huge Soviet army under Marshal Zhukov surrounded the Germans. Stalin held his nerve, and eventually what remained of the German army surrendered in February 1943. Similar events took place in Leningrad and Moscow.

Following the events of Stalingrad, the Soviet army was on the offensive. Zhukov had 1.3 million soldiers and 3,000 tanks at his command. Soviet forces advanced towards German soil, reaching Berlin in April 1945, before the American and British troops who were advancing from the West.

Rather like Churchill in his wartime role in Britain, Stalin was steadfastly at the helm in Russia and refused to accept that defeat was possible. He appealed to the patriotism of the Russian people, now invaded again by the hated Germans.

All the effects of Bolshevik propaganda and the Cult of Personality of the 1930s came to Stalin's aid. His speeches were broadcast on the radio. They were designed to appeal to patriotism; to show Russians that the sacrifices of the 1930s had been vital for producing the industrial revolution which was enabling the country to resist.

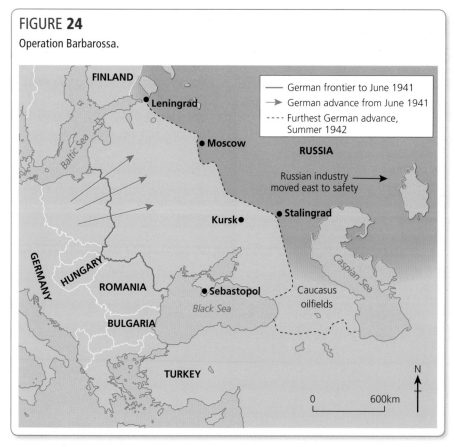

FIGURE 24

Operation Barbarossa.

German frontier to June 1941
German advance from June 1941
Furthest German advance, Summer 1942

SOURCE 25

Stalin's radio speech to the people of the USSR, 3 July 1941.

Comrades, citizens, brothers and sisters, men of our Army and Navy! It is to you that I am speaking, dear friends!

The perfidious [deceitful] attack by Hitlerite Germany on our Motherland, begun on 22 June, is continuing. In spite of the heroic resistance of the Red Army, and although the enemy's finest divisions and finest air force units have already been smashed and have found their graves on the field of battle, the enemy continues to push forward, hurling fresh forces to the front … Grave danger overhangs our country.

The Red Army, Red Navy and all citizens of the Soviet Union must defend every inch of Soviet soil, must fight to the last drop of blood for our towns and villages, must display the daring, initiative and mental alertness characteristic of our people.

SOURCE 26

A Soviet cartoon from 1941 showing the impending defeat of Hitler. The caption reads: 'Napoleon suffered defeat. So will the conceited Hitler!'

SOURCE 27

A Soviet poster from 1942: 'Bombs made beyond the Urals destroy the German army'.

THINK

1 What reaction were the Russian people likely to give to Stalin's speech (Source 25), and why?
2 How does the cartoonist in Source 26 convey his message that the defeat of Germany is imminent?
3 How does the poster shown in Source 27 aim to keep Russian citizens confident of victory, even at the height of the German invasion?
4 How does Source 28 reinforce the message of the cartoon shown in Source 26?
5 Bearing in mind the date of Source 28, what has happened to support what the author is arguing?

SOURCE 28

Soviet propaganda about Stalin's military triumph in 1945. It is taken from *The Great Victory* by V. Ryabov, published in 1975 by the official Press Agency of the USSR.

History has shown that any aggressive plans and the use of power politics against the Soviet Union entail disastrous consequences for the aggressor. Despite the great losses and damage sustained, the USSR emerged from the war even stronger and more experienced, capable of reliably defending its interests. Those fond of military ventures would do well to remember that piece of folk wisdom – look before you leap.

SOURCE 29

The Soviet victory in the Second World War, from *The Great Victory* by Major-General V. Ryabov, published in 1975 by the Novosti Press Agency, the official Soviet publisher in Moscow (pages 42–43).

The Soviet victory in the Battle of Stalingrad was of tremendous international significance. Marshal Zhukov writes, 'It marked the beginning of a turning point in the war in favour of the Soviet Union, and with it began the expulsion of the enemy troops from Soviet soil. It was a long-awaited joyous victory not only for the troops who fought in that battle, but for all Soviet people who worked hard day and night providing the army with everything it needed.'

The Nazi rout at Stalingrad gave great impetus to the national liberation struggle, and strengthened resistance against the invaders. The Soviet Union's prestige with the countries of the anti-Hitler alliance grew even more.

THINK

1 List the claims that are made in Source 29 about the achievements of the USSR in the Second World War.
2 For each claim, find evidence to agree or disagree.
3 How much has the provenance of the source influenced its content?

KEY WORDS

Make sure you know what these terms mean and are able to define them confidently:
- Autocracy
- Bolsheviks
- Capitalist
- *Cheka*
- Civil War
- Collectivisation
- Communist
- *Duma*
- Five-Year Plan
- Marxist
- Mensheviks
- NEP
- NKVD
- *Okhrana*
- Provisional Government
- Purges
- Show trials
- Social Democratic Party
- Socialist Revolutionaries
- USSR
- War Communism

Significance of Stalin's wartime leadership

The Soviet victory in the Second World War was a tremendous achievement. Much of the credit has to be given to the wartime leadership of Stalin. It was he who in 1941 had moved factories and raw materials to the Ural mountains and beyond as the Germans advanced. As a result of this, by 1944 Soviet industrial output had managed to recover to the levels of 1940. During the war the USSR managed to produce twice as many machine guns and rifles as Germany, and more of every major type of weapon.

Stalin had been responsible for the overall military strategy, together with the detailed planning of Marshal Zhukov and other generals. This made the best possible use of supplies and troops. It was Stalin who had provided the inspirational leadership focusing on patriotism during the war (as highlighted earlier on pages 144–45).

Political, economic and social problems caused by the Great Patriotic War to 1945

Politically, the war involved even more control by Stalin and his government. All aspects of life were subject to control, with the sole aim of ensuring that all resources were being used to gain military victory.

Therefore, economically and socially, the Great Patriotic War caused huge problems for the Soviet people. It was won at tremendous cost. Over 20 million Soviet citizens were killed – more than in the purges and the Terror of the 1930s. More Soviet people died defending Stalingrad than the USA lost in the whole war. Huge areas of farmland were devastated, including 100,000 collective farms. Nearly 2,000 towns and cities and 70,000 villages suffered major destruction. Six million houses were badly damaged or destroyed.

Some of the nationalities living within the USSR suffered particularly badly. Stalin suspected that some of those living in western Europe, for example those in the Ukraine, had pro-Nazi sympathies and thus might see the Nazis as liberating them from Soviet rule. Thus Stalin got his secret police to transport whole national groups, such as the Tartars, to the remoter parts of the USSR. Many thousands died during the journey or after arrival in an unhospitable climate.

TOPIC SUMMARY

Stalin's USSR
- Stalin used a variety of methods to defeat Trotsky and become sole ruler by 1929.
- Stalin used the purges to eliminate possible rivals, including show trials for important figures.
- The purges developed into full-scale terror resulting in millions of deaths in the late 1930s.
- Propaganda and censorship greatly facilitated Stalin's firm control.
- The Cult of Personality was apparently accepted by most, dazzled by the country's growing achievements.
- Economic modernisation was essential because the country was so backward.
- The policy of collectivisation led to huge areas being converted into collective farms.
- The Five-Year Plans brought industrialisation and big increases in production of basic industries such as coal, iron, electricity and tractors.
- Hitler's invasion in June 1941 was a major crisis which brought out the best qualities of Stalin's leadership. Defeat of the Nazis in 1945 cemented Stalin's heroic reputation.
- The costs of war were huge with over 20 million dead and large areas of land devastated.

ASSESSMENT FOCUS

KEY

Focus words

Command words

Interpretation/knowledge reminder words

Your exam will include six questions on this topic. The question types will be the same every year, but the questions could be on any content from the specification, so you need to know it all!

We have provided one example of each kind of question. For questions based on interpretations we have used interpretations that you have already come across in this chapter. We have analysed each of the questions to highlight what you are being asked to do and written a sample answer with comments on how it could be improved.

Read Interpretations A and B and then answer questions 1–3. Interpretation A is Interpretation A on page 113. Interpretation B is Interpretation B on page 113.

Q1 **How** does Interpretation B **differ** from Interpretation A on opinions about Nicholas II and his government?

Explain your answer **based on what it says in Interpretations A and B**. (4 marks)

Sample answer

Interpretation A says that German agents were infiltrating the court and influencing the Empress, but the Tsar still made the decisions. Interpretation B says that the Tsar made frequent mistakes when dealing with crises and worsened the country's problems.

- This answer provides a basic comparison between A and B, but it would benefit from more detailed evidence.
- You need to be able to explain the differences in the content of the interpretations.
- *What extra evidence could you add to highlight the differences more completely?*

Q2 **Why** might the authors of Interpretations A and B have **a different interpretation** on opinions about Nicholas II and his government?

Explain your answer using **Interpretations A and B** and your **contextual knowledge**. (4 marks)

Sample answer

Interpretation A comes from a British diplomat present at the time and who met the Tsar. Interpretation B reflects the anger of the Tsar's army leaders at their ruler's poor leadership.

- This answer provides a good basis for development, but ideally needs more analysis of the provenance. For example, you could explain more about the origins and dates of publication and how this would be likely to create differences. So make sure you think about how the writer has obtained the information.
- Also, think about the purpose of Interpretation B. Why is General Wrangel writing? Is he trying to protect his own reputation?
- *Write two sentences for each interpretation on the provenance of each. You should focus on the purpose and attitudes of the two authors.*

Q3 Which interpretation gives the **more convincing opinion** about Nicholas II and his government

Explain your answer based on your **contextual knowledge** and what it says in **Interpretations A and B**. (8 marks)

Sample answer

Interpretation A is reflecting what many thought was happening with rumours that Alexandra, a German princess, was in the pay of the Germans. In fact she was a Russian patriot and the rumours were mostly totally inaccurate. Interpretation B reflects the actual mistakes made by the Tsar including making himself Commander-in-Chief of the army, and listening to his wife's advice coming from Rasputin about changing government ministers frequently. Interpretation B is more convincing.

- This answer provides a basic analysis of the two interpretations through the use of some factual knowledge. You need to extend it further to argue in more depth.
- However, it is important that the knowledge is used as part of the analysis of the content of the interpretation, rather than being 'free-standing' as 'what I know about the topic'.
- *Think about the tone and language of each interpretation. What words and phrases could you use to describe them? Does one seem more objective than the other?*

Q4 **Describe** **two** political problems faced by the Provisional Government when it first met **in March 1917**. (4 marks)

Sample answer

The Provisional Government when it first met faced the problem of the First World War. Russia had been losing battles and millions of soldiers had died. Some were beginning to desert.

The Provisional Government also had to deal with huge economic problems with inflation and food shortages.

- This brief answer introduces two problems, but they are only stated, and so need to be more fully described.
- *List TWO details that you could add to EACH of the two short paragraphs above in order to make the description more precise.*

Q5 **In what ways** were the lives of Russian peasants affected by Stalin's policies **in the 1930s**?

Explain your answer. (8 marks)

Sample answer

Russian peasants suffered great changes in their lives in the 1930s. Under collectivisation they lost their individual bits of land and had to work on huge collectivised farms.

In the early 1930s millions starved as food was exported to help pay for the import of machinery.

The collectivised farms were given machinery to make farming more productive, but output only increased a little. Peasants resented losing their independence and some were forced to go and work in the new industrialised areas.

> – This answer mentions several aspects of how Russian peasants were affected. However, they could be presented with much more factual detail, rather than just a list.
>
> – *Write a list of evidence that could be included to support each of the sentences in the answer above.*

Q6 **Which** of the following was the **more important reason** why Stalin was able to increase his control over the USSR in the 1930s?
- Propaganda and censorship
- The purges

Explain your answer with reference to **both reasons**. (12 marks)

Sample answer

Stalin became dictator in the 1930s. He was sole ruler of the USSR, in control of law and order as well being able to manipulate the way people thought.

He used propaganda to put forward his cult of personality. The country was deluged with paintings, photographs and statues of Stalin. Streets were named after him. Posters showed Stalin with admiring crowds or supervising tremendous feats of engineering. Every success was said to be due to his great genius. The Moscow metro was a huge monument to the glories of his rule. Poems were written and published in his honour. Composers wrote patriotic music that emphasised Stalin's vision for a heroic Soviet state.

Censorship was an important weapon as well. In 1932, the Union of Soviet Writers was set up, dictating that novels had to celebrate Soviet heroes and stories had to have a happy ending. Famous writers such as Solzhenitsyn were sentenced to work in labour camps. The composer Shostakovich was lucky to escape with his life after Stalin criticised his musical style as not being positive enough in praising Soviet achievements. He had to apologise for his 'errors'. Religious worship was banned and most churches and mosques closed down. By 1939, there were only nine out of 163 Orthodox Christian bishops still functioning. Therefore, most Russians had little chance to express any opinion other than to agree, and most never heard any view that contradicted the greatness of their leader.

> – This answer evaluates both bullet points in turn. It reaches a judgement based on precise arguments. The relationships between the two bullet points are explored.
>
> – *Working backwards: Read through the essay again, and write out the plan that it must have been based on. You can then look at the plan and see why it was the starting point for this comprehensive answer.*

The purges were also an important mechanism of control. Anyone suspected of being critical of Stalin was either imprisoned or killed by the NVKD, his secret police under Yagoda. Russia had been used to strict rule under the Tsars, but Stalin's actions in the purges introduced a reign of uncontrolled terror. The NKVD could arrest and execute at will. At first, the main targets were party members – Stalin's rivals and their supporters. Leading members such as Kamenev and Zinoviev were arrested on false charges of terrorism. These and other important Bolsheviks were put on trial (the Show Trials) and made to admit their guilt. Many lesser party members were arrested and either shot or sent to labour camps.

The armed forces were also purged. Marshal Tukhachevsky and seven other generals were secretly tried and executed, followed by 75 out of 80 of the men on the Supreme Military Council. The purges continued through all the army ranks and six Admirals from the Navy were also shot. Through these purges Stalin eliminated opposition.

In one sense Stalin used both methods towards the same goal – the elimination of free speech and the establishment of total devotion to Stalin. The physical actions of the purges reinforced the effects of propaganda and censorship that already pervaded the USSR. Therefore it could be argued that the purges were the more important in ensuring that Stalin retained control until his death in 1953.

> Now write your own answers to the questions on pages 147–48 using the teacher's feedback to help you.

America, 1920–1973: Opportunity and Inequality

4

This period study focuses on the development of the USA during a turbulent half century of change. It was a period of opportunity and inequality – when some Americans lived the 'American Dream' while others grappled with the nightmare of discrimination and prejudice.

You will be studying this opportunity and inequality through:

- political developments as governments became more involved in the everyday lives of their citizens
- the economic aspects of a country that experienced the 'boom' of the 1920s, followed by the Depression of the 1930s, and the economic prosperity during and after the Second World War
- social inequalities and racial tension leading to the development of civil rights for African Americans by the 1960s
- developments in entertainment and popular culture such as new dances and styles of music
- the role of key individuals and groups in shaping change and the impact the developments had on them.

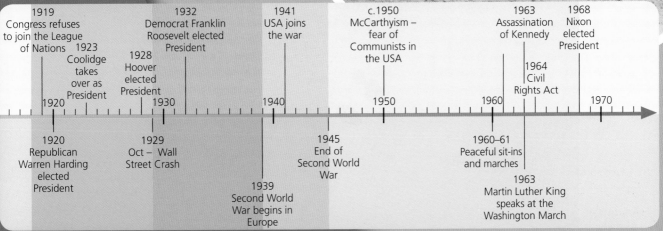

| 1919 Congress refuses to join the League of Nations | 1923 Coolidge takes over as President | 1928 Hoover elected President | 1932 Democrat Franklin Roosevelt elected President | 1941 USA joins the war | c.1950 McCarthyism – fear of Communists in the USA | 1963 Assassination of Kennedy | 1964 Civil Rights Act | 1968 Nixon elected President |

1920 — 1930 — 1940 — 1950 — 1960 — 1970

1920 Republican Warren Harding elected President

1929 Oct – Wall Street Crash

1939 Second World War begins in Europe

1945 End of Second World War

1960–61 Peaceful sit-ins and marches

1963 Martin Luther King speaks at the Washington March

4.1 The American people and the 'boom'

● The 'boom' and its benefits

The USA had grown in industrial strength before the First World War, using the nation's huge reserves of natural resources. By 1914 the USA was leading all other countries in most areas of industry.

The Americans tried hard to stay out of the fighting in the First World War. But throughout the war they lent money to the Allies, and sold arms and MUNITIONS to Britain and France. When they did finally enter the war in 1917 it wasn't for long enough to drain American resources the way it drained those in Europe. And after the war, when the USA decided not to join the League of Nations and to keep out of European political alliances, the country could take full advantage of its industrial strength. It could exploit its vast range of raw materials to produce steel, chemicals, glass and machinery.

FIGURE 1

The USA's main centres of population and main natural resources around 1920.

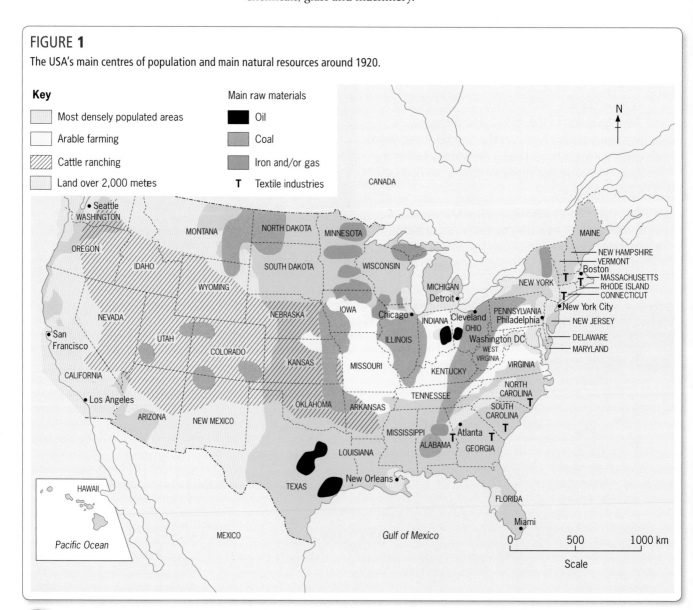

SOURCE 2

Skyscrapers being built in New York City. There was more building being done in the boom years of the 1920s than at any time in the history of the USA.

THINK

Study Source 2.

What does the source suggest about what life was like in New York City in the 1920s?

FIGURE 3

The growth of the US economy in the 1920s.

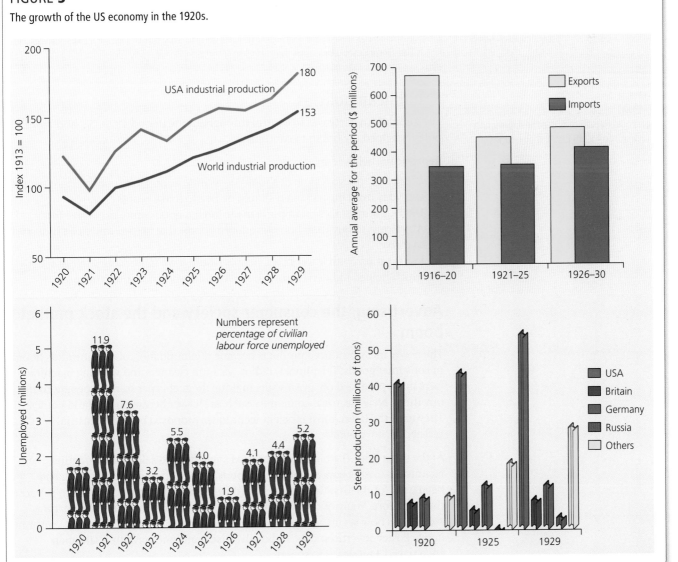

FIGURE 4

Sales of consumer goods, 1915–30. Overall the output of American industry doubled in the 1920s.

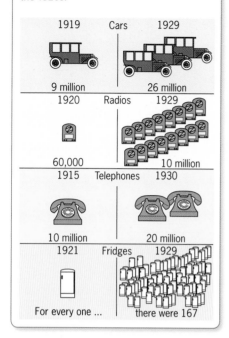

1919   Cars   1929

9 million   26 million

1920   Radios   1929

60,000   10 million

1915   Telephones   1930

10 million   20 million

1921   Fridges   1929

For every one ...   there were 167

THINK

How could Republicans use the information on pages 151–52 to justify their policies?

Republican policies

The Republican Party was in control throughout the period 1920–32, and its policies helped the boom to continue.

Republicans believed in:

- *laissez faire*: the government should do as little as possible to interfere in people's everyday lives; businessmen should be free to make profits
- TARIFFS: putting taxes on imports made foreign goods more expensive for Americans to buy than home-produced goods; that helped American industry to thrive
- low taxation: with lower taxes, people would have more money left to spend, which helped industrial growth; rich businessmen benefited the most.

Advertising, the consumer society and the stock market boom

The newly mass-produced products became the foundation of an enormous boom in consumer goods. Telephones, radios, vacuum cleaners and washing machines were mass-produced on a vast scale, making them cheaper so more people could buy them. New electrical companies such as Hoover became household names. They used the latest, most efficient techniques proposed by the 'Industrial Efficiency Movement'.

At the same time, the big industries used sophisticated sales and marketing techniques to get people to buy their goods. Mass nationwide advertising had been used for the first time in the USA during the war to get Americans to support the war effort. Many of the advertisers who had learned their skills in wartime PROPAGANDA now set up agencies to sell cars, cigarettes, clothing and other consumer items. Poster advertisements, radio advertisements and travelling salesmen encouraged Americans to spend.

Even if they did not have the money, people could borrow it easily. Or they could take advantage of the new 'Buy now, pay later' HIRE PURCHASE schemes. Eight out of ten radios and six out of ten cars were bought on CREDIT.

This confidence that prosperity would continue to grow encouraged the STOCK MARKET boom. Many people bought SHARES in companies (that is, they bought a part of a company) and gained a percentage of the profits in return. In the climate of the mid-1920s, many people wanted to buy shares, which put up their price, but also provided more money for the company to invest and expand. All this worked in favour of the investors and the companies until people started selling their shares for the large profits they could make.

Ford and the motor industry

The most important of these new booming industries was the motor car industry. The motor car had only been developed in the 1890s. The first cars were built by blacksmiths and other skilled craftsmen. They took a long time to make and were very expensive. In 1900 only 4,000 cars were made. Car production was revolutionised by Henry Ford. In 1913 he set up the first moving production line in the world, in a giant shed in Detroit. Each worker on the line had one or two small jobs to do as the skeleton of the car moved along. At the beginning of the line, a skeleton car went in; at the end of the line was a new car. The most famous of these was the Model T. More than 15 million were produced in this MASS PRODUCTION process between 1908 and 1925. In 1927 they came off the production line at a rate of one every ten seconds. In 1929, 4.8 million cars were made.

By the end of the 1920s the motor industry was the USA's biggest industry. As well as employing hundreds of thousands of workers directly, it also kept workers in other industries in employment. Glass, leather, steel and rubber were all required to build the new vehicles. Automobiles used up 75 per cent of US glass production in the 1920s! Petrol was needed to run them. And a massive army of labourers was busily building roads throughout the country for these cars to drive on. In fact, road construction was the biggest single employer in the 1920s.

Owning a car was not just a rich person's privilege, as it was in Europe. There was 1 car to 5 people in the USA compared with 1 to 43 in Britain, and 1 to 7,000 in Russia. The car made it possible for people to buy a house in the suburbs, which further boosted house-building. It also stimulated the growth of hundreds of other smaller businesses, ranging from hot dog stands and advertising bill boards to petrol stations and holiday resorts.

THINK

What do Sources 5 and 6 suggest about changing lifestyles for many in the USA in the 1920s?

PRACTICE QUESTIONS

1 Describe how the Ford motor industry affected the boom in the US economy in the 1920s.

2 Which of the following was the more important reason why the economic boom of the 1920s was sustained in the USA:
 ● hire purchase
 ● mass production?

 Explain your answer with reference to both factors.

FOCUS TASK

How did the 'boom' come about and how did car production help to encourage it?

1 Draw and cut out your own outline of one of Ford's Model Ts (see page 153).

2 On one side of your car, write down all the factors which enabled the 'boom' period in 1920s America.

3 On the other side, write down all the factors resulting from Ford's motor car industry which encouraged the continuation of the 'boom'.

4 Use your car to write a paragraph on the influence of the car industry on the 'boom' in 1920s America.

SOURCE 5

Labourers starting work on a new road. The new roads that were built encouraged a new truck industry. By 1929 there were 3.5 million trucks.

SOURCE 6

Model Ts in an American high street. In 1925 a Model T cost $290. This was almost three months' wages for an American factory worker.

American attitudes towards wealth in the 1920s

One thing that runs through all the factors you have looked at so far is an attitude or a state of mind. Most Americans believed that they had a right to 'prosperity'. For many it was a main aim in life to have a nice house, a good job and plenty to eat, and for their home to be filled with the latest consumer goods. Consuming more and more was seen as part of being American.

In earlier decades, thrift (being careful with money and saving 'for a rainy day') had been seen as a good quality. In the 1920s this was replaced by a belief that spending money was a better quality.

Inequalities of wealth

Throughout the decade there were plenty of Americans who were spending – billionaires such as the Rockefeller family and industrialists such as Henry Ford were reaping the rewards of this period of 'boom'. In contrast more than half the population, including most African Americans and recent immigrants, remained on the breadline. (For more details on African Americans and immigrants see pages 162–64.)

Farmers

Farmers were a very large group in American society and they did not share in the prosperity of the 1920s. Total farm income dropped from 22 billion dollars in 1919 to just 13 billion dollars in 1928, with the main problem being overproduction.

Workers in old industries

Workers in many older industries, such as coal, leather and textiles, did not benefit much either. Coal suffered from competition from new industries such as oil and electricity. Leather and textiles were protected from foreign competition, but not from domestic competition. They suffered from the development of new man-made materials. They also struggled to compete with cheap labour in the Southern states. Even if workers in these industries did get a pay rise, their wages did not increase on the same scale as company profits or dividends paid to shareholders (see Figure 8).

FIGURE 7

The distribution of income in 1925.

goes to the richest 5%

32%

10%

goes to the poorest 42%

FIGURE 8

A comparison of the growth of profits and the growth of average earnings.

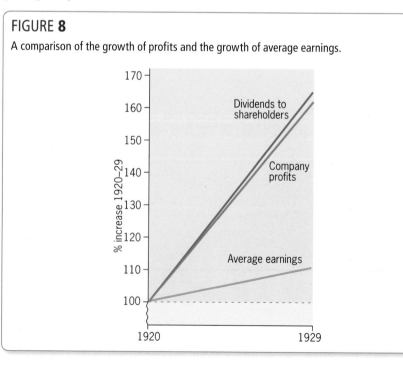

Dividends to shareholders

Company profits

Average earnings

% increase 1920–29

170
160
150
140
130
120
110
100

1920   1929

The unemployed and the poor

What's more, throughout this period unemployment remained a problem. The growth in industry in the 1920s did not create many new jobs. Industries were growing by electrifying or mechanising production. The same number of people (around 5 per cent) were unemployed at the peak of the boom in 1929 as in 1920. Yet the amount of goods produced had doubled. This group of millions of unemployed Americans included many poor whites, but an even greater proportion of African American and Hispanic people and other members of the USA's large immigrant communities.

The plight of the poor was desperate for the individuals concerned. But it was also damaging to American industry. The boom of the 1920s was a consumer-led boom, which means that it was led by ordinary families buying things for their home. But with so many families too poor to buy such goods, the demand for them was likely to begin to tail off. However, Republican policy remained not to interfere, and this included doing nothing about unemployment or poverty.

SOURCE 9

A cartoon showing the situation faced by American farmers in the 1920s.

THINK

Explain the message of Source 9.

SOURCE 10

A hunger march staged by workers in Washington in the 1920s.

FOCUS TASK

Why were there inequalities of wealth in 1920s America?

1 Using pages 154–55 and your own research, create a PowerPoint presentation on the two faces of the boom in 1920s America. On the first slide add the title: '1920s America: Wealth for all?'

2 Now choose three images to illustrate the boom. Add them to the next three slides, and include bullet points with each, to describe those who benefited from the boom.

3 Then choose three more images which show those who did not benefit from the boom. Add them to the following three slides and add bullet points to explain why certain people lost out.

4 Add a concluding slide to sum up why there were inequalities of wealth in 1920s America.

• Social and cultural developments

During the 1920s the USA rapidly developed a cultural style that was recognisable across the western world. More than half the population now lived in towns and cities, with skyscrapers punctuating the skyline. And with such huge changes came a cultural struggle between the traditional American way of life and the newer forces of modernity.

Entertainment

The 1920s in the USA are often called the ROARING TWENTIES. The name suggests a time of riotous fun, loud music and wild enjoyment when everyone was having a good time. Perhaps this was not true for all Americans, but it certainly seemed to be true for a lot of them. Important social changes, especially the growth of cities, changed the way many Americans lived. The growing prosperity gave many of them the spare time and money to go out and enjoy themselves. One of the most obvious examples of this new attitude was the growth of entertainment.

During the 1920s the entertainment industry blossomed. The average working week dropped from 47.4 to 44.2 hours so people had more leisure time. Average wages rose by 11 per cent (in real terms) so workers also had more disposable income. A lot of this spare time and money was channelled into entertainment.

Radio

Almost everyone in the USA listened to the radio. Most households had their own set. People who could not afford to buy one outright could purchase one in instalments. The choice of programmes grew quickly. In August 1921 there was only one licensed radio station in America. By the end of 1922 there were 508 of them. By 1929 the new network NBC was making $150 million a year.

Jazz

The radio gave much greater access to new music. Jazz music became an obsession among young people. African Americans who moved from the country to the cities had brought jazz and blues music with them. Blues music was particularly popular among the African American population, while jazz captured the imagination of young white and African Americans.

Such was the power of jazz music that the 1920s became known as the Jazz Age, with new dances such as the Charleston. The older generation saw jazz and everything associated with it as a corrupting influence on the young.

Sport

Sport was another boom area. Baseball became a big money sport with legendary teams like the New York Yankees and Boston Red Sox. Prominent figures such as Al Capone (see page 161) were baseball fans. Boxing was also a very popular sport, with heroes like world heavyweight champion Jack Dempsey.

Cinema

In a small suburb outside Los Angeles, called Hollywood, a major film industry was developing. All-year-round sunshine meant that the studios could produce large numbers of films or 'movies'. New stars like Charlie Chaplin and Buster Keaton made audiences roar with laughter, while Douglas Fairbanks thrilled them in daring adventure films. Until 1927 all movies were silent. In 1927 the first 'talkie' was made.

During the 1920s movies became a multi-billion dollar business and it was estimated that, by the end of the decade, a hundred million cinema tickets were being sold each week. That's as many as are sold in a year in Britain today.

SOURCE 11

King Oliver's Creole Jazz Band, 1920. Louis Armstrong is kneeling at the front.

PRACTICE QUESTIONS

1 Describe two ways in which the motor car encouraged social change.
2 In what ways did the development of jazz lead to changes in society?

FIGURE 12

The change in the USA's urban and rural populations, 1900–40.

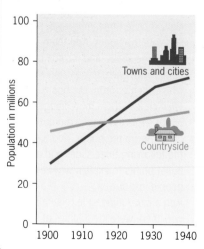

The car

The motor car was one of the major factors leading to change and made these other features possible. Cars helped the cities to grow by opening up the suburbs. They carried their owners to and from their entertainments and to an increasing range of sporting events, beach holidays, shopping trips, picnics in the country, or simply on visits to their family and friends, and boyfriends and girlfriends beyond the moral gaze of their parents.

The position of women in society

Women's lives changed considerably during the 1920s – but the changes were greater for some than others. Before the First World War middle-class women were expected to wear very restrictive clothes and behave politely. They were expected not to wear make-up. Their relationships with men were strictly controlled. They had to have a chaperone with them when they went out with a boyfriend. They were expected not to take part in sport or to smoke in public. In most states they could not vote. Most women were expected to be housewives. Very few paid jobs were open to women. Most working women were in lower-paid jobs such as cleaning, dressmaking and secretarial work.

In rural America there were particularly tight restrictions owing to the Churches' traditional attitude to the role of women. In the 1920s, many of these things began to change, especially for urban and middle-class women. When the USA joined the war in 1917, some women were taken into the war industries, giving them experience of skilled factory work for the first time. In 1920 they got the right to vote in all states. (Some states had introduced women voting before the First World War.) Through the 1920s they shared the liberating effects of the car, and their domestic work was made easier (in theory) by new electrical goods such as vacuum cleaners and washing machines.

For younger urban women many of the traditional rules of behaviour were eased as well. Women wore more daring clothes. They smoked in public and drank with men, in public. They went out with men, in cars, without a chaperone. They kissed in public. These new styles of behaviour were summed up in the image of the 'FLAPPER', a woman who wore short dresses and make-up and who smoked in public. One writer said that the ideal flapper was 'expensive and about nineteen'.

In urban areas more women took on jobs – particularly middle-class women. They typically took on jobs created by the new industries. There were 10 million women in jobs in 1929, 24 per cent more than in 1920.

Films and novels also exposed women to a much wider range of role models. Millions of women a week saw films with sexy or daring heroines, as well as other films that showed women in a more traditional role. The newspaper, magazine and film industries found that sex sold much better than anything else.

However, the changes were only partial. There was a strong conservative element in American society. A combination of traditional religion and old country values kept most American women in a much more restricted role than young

SOURCE 13

A schoolteacher in 1905.

SOURCE 14

Young flappers in the 1920s.

SOURCE 15

Gloria Swanson in *The Trespasser* (1929). Gloria Swanson was one of the most successful film stars of the 1920s and *The Trespasser* was her first 'talkie'.

urban women enjoyed. Take work, for example. Women were still paid less than men, even when they did the same job. In politics as well, women in no way achieved EQUALITY with men. They may have been given the vote but it did not give them access to political power. Political parties wanted women's votes, but they didn't particularly want women as political candidates as they considered them 'unelectable'. There was only a handful of women elected by 1929.

FOCUS TASK

How did life change for women in 1920s America?

1 Using the information and sources on pages 157–58 make notes on the changes to women's lives under two headings:
   – Employment and status
   – Culture and entertainment.

2 Using your notes, imagine you are a mother living in a city in 1920s America, who has an 18 year-old daughter who is a flapper. Write a letter home to your own mother describing how your daughter has changed, and your own views on her new-found 'freedom'.

SOURCE 16

The American radical feminist writer Doris E. Fleischman writing in her book *America as Americans See It*, published in 1932.

It is wholly confusing to read the advertisements in the magazines that feature the enticing qualities of vacuum cleaners, mechanical refrigerators and hundreds of other devices which should lighten the chores of women in the home. On the whole these large middle classes do their own housework with few of the mechanical aids.

Women who live on farms – and they form the largest group in the United States – do a great deal of work besides the labour of caring for their children, washing the clothes, caring for the home and cooking … thousands still labour in the fields … help milk the cows…

The other largest group of American women comprise the families of the labourers of the miners, the steel workers … the vast army of unskilled, semi-skilled and skilled workers. The wages of these men are on the whole so small [that] wives must do double duty – that is, caring for the children and the home and toil on the outside as wage earners.

THINK

Read Interpretations A and B and answer Questions 1–3.

Interpretation A Changes in society after the First World War. From the book, *The Perils of Prosperity* by W. E. Leuchtenberg, 1958. The author was an eminent historian who wrote many books and articles on American history.

There was never a time in American history when youth had such a special sense of importance as in the years after the First World War. There was a gulf between the generations. Young men who had fought in the trenches felt that they knew a reality their elders could not even imagine. Younger girls no longer consciously modelled themselves on their mothers, whose attitudes seemed irrelevant in the 1920s.

Interpretation B Another view of American society after the First World War. From the book, *America in the Twentieth Century*, by J. T. Patterson, 1988. Patterson was younger than Leuchtenberg and made a name for himself as a historian, questioning versions of US history which had been accepted by most people for many years.

Though a few young upper middle-class women in the cities talked about throwing off the older conventions – they were the flappers – most women stuck to more traditional attitudes concerning 'their place'. Most concentrated on managing the home. Their daughters were likely to prepare for careers as mothers and housewives.

1 Which of these two interpretations seems to agree most closely with the account of Source 16?

   Explain your answer.

2 Now explain why you think one agrees with Source 16 while the other one doesn't.

3 Discuss with a partner – could Source 16 be regarded as an interpretation rather than a source?

A divided society: The causes and consequences of tension

The USA was divided not just in terms of wealth and poverty, but also in attitudes – towards alcohol and the PROHIBITION laws, towards immigrants who spoke different languages and had different cultures and beliefs, and towards African Americans who were often regarded as an inferior race.

Prohibition

In the nineteenth century, in rural areas of the USA, there was a very strong 'temperance' movement. Members of temperance movements agreed not to drink alcohol and also campaigned to get others to give up alcohol. Most members of these movements were devout Christians who saw what damage alcohol did to family life. They wanted to stop that damage. By 1916, 21 states had banned saloons.

Supporters of Prohibition (the campaign to prohibit alcohol throughout the country) became known as 'dries'. The dries brought some powerful arguments to their case. They claimed that '3,000 infants are smothered yearly in bed, by drunken parents'. The USA's entry into the First World War in 1917 boosted the dries. Drinkers were accused of being unpatriotic cowards. Most of the big breweries were run by German immigrants who were portrayed as the enemy. Drink was linked to other evils as well. After the Russian Revolution, the dries claimed that BOLSHEVISM thrived on drink and that alcohol led to lawlessness in the cities, particularly in immigrant communities. Saloons were seen as dens of vice that destroyed family life. The campaign became one of country values against city values.

In 1917 the Eighteenth Amendment to the Constitution was passed. This 'prohibited the manufacture, sale or transportation of intoxicating liquors'. It became law in January 1920 and is known as the Volstead Act.

How was Prohibition enforced?

FIGURE 17

Activities of federal Prohibition agents.

	1921	1925	1929
Illegal distilleries seized	9,746	12,023	15,794
Gallons (US) of spirit seized	414,000	11,030,000	11,860,000
Arrests	34,175	62,747	66,878

Prohibition lasted from 1920 until 1933. It is often said that Prohibition was a total failure. This is not entirely correct. Levels of alcohol consumption fell by about 30 per cent in the early 1920s (see Figure 18). Prohibition gained widespread approval in some states, particularly the rural areas in the Midwest, although in urban states it was not popular (Maryland never even introduced Prohibition). The government ran information campaigns and Prohibition agents arrested offenders (see Figure 17). Two of the most famous agents were Isadore Einstein and his deputy Moe Smith (see Source 20, page 160). They made 4,392 arrests. Their raids were always low key. They would enter speakeasies (illegal bars) and simply order a drink. Einstein had a special flask hidden inside his waistcoat with a funnel attached. He preserved the evidence by pouring his drink down the funnel and the criminals were caught!

FIGURE 18

Average alcohol consumption (in US gallons) per year of Americans, 1905–40.

SOURCE 19

E. Mandeville, in *Outlook* magazine, 1925.

Statistics in the Detroit police court of 1924 show 7391 arrests for violations of the prohibition law, but only 458 convictions. Ten years ago a dishonest policeman was a rarity … Now the honest ones are pointed out as rarities … Their relationship with the bootleggers is perfectly friendly. They have to pinch two out of five once in a while, but they choose the ones who are least willing to pay bribes.

THINK

1 Read Source 19. How has Prohibition affected the police in Detroit?
2 Which of Figures 17 and 18 and Source 19 is the most useful to the historian investigating Prohibition?

What were the effects of Prohibition?

Despite the work of the agents, Prohibition proved impossible to enforce effectively in the cities. Enforcement was underfinanced. There were not enough agents – each agent was poorly paid and was responsible for a huge area. By far the biggest drawback was that millions of Americans, particularly in urban areas, were simply not prepared to obey this law. So bootleggers (suppliers of illegal alcohol) made vast fortunes. Al Capone (see page 161) made around $60 million a year from his speakeasies. His view was that 'Prohibition is a business. All I do is supply a public demand.' And the demand was huge. By 1925 there were more speakeasies in American cities than there had been saloons in 1919. Izzy Einstein filed a report to his superiors on how easy it was to find alcohol after arriving in a new city. Here are the results:

- Chicago: 21 minutes
- Atlanta: 17 minutes
- Pittsburgh: 11 minutes
- New Orleans: 35 seconds (he was offered a bottle of whisky by his taxi driver when he asked where he could get a drink!)

Illegal 'stills' (short for 'distilleries') sprang up all over the USA as people made their own illegal whisky – moonshine. The stills were a major fire hazard and the alcohol they produced was frequently poisonous. Agents seized over 280,000 of these stills, but we have no clear way of knowing how many were not seized. Most Americans had no need for their own still. They simply went to their favourite speakeasy. The speakeasies were well supplied by bootleggers. About two-thirds of the illegal alcohol came from Canada. The vast border between the USA and Canada was virtually impossible to patrol. Other bootleggers brought in alcohol by sea. They would simply wait in the waters outside US control until an opportunity to land their cargo presented itself. One of the most famous was Captain McCoy, who specialised in the finest Scotch whisky. This is where the phrase 'the real McCoy' comes from.

Corruption

Prohibition led to massive corruption. Many of the law enforcement officers were themselves involved with the liquor trade. Big breweries stayed in business throughout the Prohibition era. This is not an easy business to hide! But the breweries stayed in operation by bribing local government officials, Prohibition agents and the police to leave them alone.

In some cities, police officers were quite prepared to direct people to speakeasies. Even when arrests were made, it was difficult to get convictions because more senior officers or even judges were in the pay of the criminals. One in twelve Prohibition agents was dismissed for corruption. The New York FBI boss, Don Chaplin, once ordered his 200 agents: 'Put your hands on the table, both of them. Every son of a bitch wearing a diamond is fired.'

Organised crime

The most common image people have of the Prohibition era is the gangster. Estimates suggest that organised gangs made about $2 billion out of the sale of illegal alcohol.

The gangs fought viciously with each other to control the liquor trade and also the prostitution, gambling and protection rackets that were centred on the speakeasies. They made use of new technology, especially automobiles and the Thompson sub-machine gun, which was devastatingly powerful but could be carried around and hidden under an overcoat. In Chicago alone, there were 130 gangland murders in 1926 and 1927 and not one arrest. By the late 1920s fear and bribery made law enforcement ineffective.

The gangsters operated all over the USA, but they were most closely associated with Chicago. Perhaps the best example of the power of the gangsters is Chicago gangster boss Al Capone. He arrived in Chicago in 1919, on the run from a murder investigation in New York. He built up a huge network of corrupt officials among Chicago's police, local government workers, judges, lawyers and Prohibition agents. He even controlled Chicago's mayor, William Hale Thompson. Surprisingly, he was a high-profile and even popular figure in the city. He was a regular at baseball and American football games and was cheered by the crowd when he took his seat. He was well known for giving generous tips (over $100) to waiters and shop girls and spent $30,000 on a soup kitchen for the unemployed.

Capone was supported by a ruthless gang, hand-picked for their loyalty to him. By 1929 he had destroyed the power of the other Chicago gangs, committing at least 300 murders in the process. The peak of his violent reign came with the St Valentine's Day Massacre in 1929. Capone's men murdered seven of his rival Bugs Moran's gang, using a false police car and two gangsters in police uniform to put Moran's men off their guard.

Why was Prohibition ended?

The St Valentine's Day Massacre was a turning point. The papers screamed that the gangsters had graduated from murder to massacre. It seemed that Prohibition, often called 'The Noble Experiment', had failed. It had made the USA lawless, the police corrupt and the gangsters rich and powerful. When the WALL STREET CRASH was followed by the DEPRESSION in the early 1930s, there were sound economic arguments for getting rid of it. Legalising alcohol would create jobs, raise tax revenue and free up resources tied up in the impossible task of enforcing Prohibition. The Democrat President Franklin D. Roosevelt was elected in 1932 and Prohibition was repealed in December 1933.

SOURCE 21

Al Capone in 1930. Everyone knew of his activities, but it was impossible to convict him because of his control of the police.

FOCUS TASK

What was the impact of Prohibition?

1   Imagine you are an advisor to Franklin D. Roosevelt who is running in the presidential election in 1932. Create a dossier of evidence on the effects of Prohibition on American society. Use pages 159–61 and your own research to create your dossier.

2   Now, using evidence from your dossier, write a summary for Roosevelt to persuade him that Prohibition should be repealed if he becomes President.

PRACTICE QUESTION

Which of the following reasons was the more important for the ending of Prohibition in 1933?

● The failure of law enforcement against illegal speakeasies
● The violence of the gangsters controlling the illegal trade in alcohol.

Explain your answer with reference to both reasons.

The Ku Klux Klan

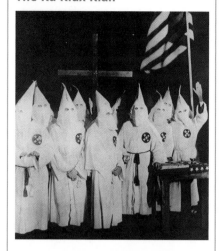

- Formed in the 1860s by former soldiers after the American Civil War with the aim of keeping whites in control.
- It used parades, beatings, lynchings and other violent methods to intimidate African Americans. It also attacked Jews, Catholics and foreign immigrants.
- It was strongest in the mid-west and rural south, where working-class whites competed with African Americans for unskilled jobs.
- It declined in the late nineteenth century but was started up again in 1915. It spread rapidly in the early 1920s, managing to get Klansmen elected into positions of political power.
- By 1924 it had 4.5 million members.
- Oregon and Oklahoma had governors who belonged to the Klan. The Klan was especially dominant in Indiana.
- The Klan declined after 1925. One of its leaders, Grand Wizard David Stephenson, was convicted of a vicious sexually motivated murder. He turned informer and the corruption of the Klan became common knowledge.

Racial tension

SLAVERY had been abolished in 1863, but despite this many African Americans, particularly those in the Southern states, were still suffering from prejudice and discrimination in the 1920s. Many still worked for PLANTATION owners on their land, or as servants in their homes. Most were denied access to higher education, good jobs and the right to vote.

Faced with such discrimination and poverty, many African Americans moved north. Through the 1920s the African-American population of both Chicago and New York doubled: New York's from 150,000 to 330,000 and Chicago's from 110,000 to 230,000.

In the North, African Americans had a better chance of getting good jobs and a good education.

However, many African Americans in the Northern cities lived in great poverty. In Harlem in New York they lived in poorer housing than whites, yet paid higher rents. They had poorer education and health services than whites.

In Chicago African Americans suffered great prejudice from longer-established white residents. If they attempted to move out of the African-American belt to adjacent neighbourhoods, they got a hostile reception (see Source 22).

SOURCE 22

From the *Chicago Property Owners' Journal*, 1920.

There is nothing in the make up of a negro, physically or mentally, that should induce anyone to welcome him as a neighbour. The best of them are unsanitary … ruin follows in their path. They are as proud as peacocks, but have nothing of the peacock's beauty … Niggers are undesirable neighbours and entirely irresponsible and vicious.

They got a similarly hostile reception from poor whites. In Chicago when African Americans attempted to use parks, playgrounds and beaches in the Irish and Polish districts, they were set upon by gangs of whites calling themselves 'athletic clubs'. The result was that African-American communities in Northern areas often became isolated GHETTOS.

The Ku Klux Klan

The KU KLUX KLAN was a white supremacy movement. It used violence to intimidate African Americans. It had been in decline, but was revived after the release of the film *The Birth of a Nation* in 1915. The film was set in the 1860s, just after the CIVIL WAR. It glorified the Klan as defenders of decent American values against renegade African Americans and corrupt white businessmen. President Wilson had it shown in the White House. He said: 'It is like writing history with lightning. And my only regret is that it is all so terribly true.' With such publicity from prominent figures, the Klan became a powerful political force in the early 1920s and subjected African Americans to vicious racist attacks.

Between 1919 and 1925 over 300 African Americans were murdered by lynching. Many reports describe appalling atrocities at which whole families, including young children, clapped and cheered. It is one of the most shameful aspects of the USA at this time.

The impact of immigration

The vast majority of Americans were either immigrants or descendants of recent immigrants.

IMMIGRATION to the USA was at an all-time high from 1901 to 1910. Immigrants were flooding in, particularly Jews from eastern Europe and Russia who were fleeing persecution, and people from Italy who were fleeing poverty. Many Italian immigrants did not intend to settle in the USA, but hoped to make money to take back to their families in Italy.

The United States had always prided itself on being a 'melting pot'. In theory, individual groups lost their ethnic identity and blended together with other groups to become just 'Americans'. In practice, however, this wasn't always the case. In the USA's big cities the more established immigrant groups – Irish Americans, French Canadians and German Americans – competed for the best jobs and the best available housing. These groups tended to look down on the more recent eastern European and Italian immigrants. These in turn had nothing but contempt for African Americans and Mexicans, who were almost at the bottom of the scale.

> ## SOURCE 23
>
> Maldwyn Jones argues in *Destination America* (published in 1985) that in many ways racist attitudes were more firmly entrenched in America than they had been in Europe.
>
> *Italians were reluctant to live alongside people with darker skins and tended to class Mexicans with Negroes. A social worker noted, however, that newly arrived Italians got on well with Mexicans; only after they had been in the United States for some time did they refuse to associate with them. 'In Italy', he said to one Italian, 'you would not be prejudiced against the Mexicans because of their colour.' The reply was 'No, but we are becoming Americanised.'*

The Red Scare

In the 1920s these racist attitudes towards immigrants were made worse by an increased fear of COMMUNISM. The USA watched with alarm as Russia became COMMUNIST after the Russian Revolution of 1917 (see Factfile on the right). In 1919 America was hit by a wave of strikes and riots. The main cause was economic hardship after men were laid off because wartime production levels fell. However, many Americans saw these disturbances as the work of Communists or other radical political groups such as anarchists. They feared that many of the more recent immigrants from eastern Europe and Russia were bringing similar radical ideas with them to the USA. This reaction was called the 'RED SCARE'.

Fear of Communism combined with prejudice against immigrants was a powerful mix, and the fears were not totally unjustified. Many immigrants in the USA did hold radical political beliefs. Anarchists published pamphlets and distributed them widely in American cities, calling for the overthrow of the government. In April 1919 a bomb planted in a church in Milwaukee killed ten people. In May, bombs were posted to 36 prominent Americans. In June more bombs went off in seven US cities, and one almost succeeded in killing Mitchell Palmer, the US Attorney General. The government reaction was quick and harsh. A young clerk called J. Edgar Hoover was appointed by Palmer and built up files on 60,000 suspects. In 1919–20 around 10,000 individuals were informed that they were to be deported from the USA. It later emerged that only 556 out of the thousands of cases brought by Hoover had any basis in fact.

> **FACTFILE**
>
> ## Russian Revolutions, 1917
>
> In Russia in 1917 there had been two revolutions. The first one in March ended the rule of the Tsar (Emperor). The second one in October/November brought the Communists under Lenin to power. Communists believed in equality, with state control rather than private ownership. Hence the possible spread of Communism to the USA was seen as a huge threat to American society.

The significance of the Sacco and Vanzetti Case

All those known to have radical political beliefs were rounded up. They were generally immigrants and the evidence against them was often flimsy. One particular pair, Nicola Sacco and Bartolomeo Vanzetti, became a long-running and notorious case. They were accused of two murders during an armed robbery at a shoe factory in Massachusetts. The case against them was very shaky. After the trial, the judge referred to the two as 'those anarchist bastards'. Sacco and Vanzetti were convicted on flimsy evidence. Explaining the verdict, a leading lawyer of the time said: 'Judge Thayer is narrow minded … unintelligent … full of prejudice. He has been carried away by fear of Reds which has captured about 90 per cent of the American people.' After six years of legal appeals, Sacco and Vanzetti were eventually executed in 1927, to a storm of protest around the world from both radicals and moderates who saw how unjustly the trial had been conducted. The case illustrates the extent to which some influential people in the USA had moved away from the open society of pre-1914.

Immigration quotas and the experiences of immigrants

By the time of the execution of Sacco and Vanzetti, government measures on immigration were already in place. In 1917 the government had introduced a literacy test for immigrants to check that they could read basic English. In 1921 the government brought in a system of immigration quotas, with further restrictions in 1924. These quotas reduced the number of immigrants to a maximum of 150,000 per year, compared with more than a million in the years before 1914. The restrictions also ensured that most immigrants came from north-west Europe rather than from areas where the language and culture were different from the dominant culture in US society.

Immigrants who did arrive were frequently disappointed that they did not share in the boom of the 1920s. Many lived in poor, over-crowded areas in cities such as New York. Many, if they found a job at all, were forced to accept low-paid menial tasks. Often, for friendship and reassurance, immigrant communities from a particular country lived close together. This had the unfortunate effect of them often continuing to be regarded as 'foreigners'.

FOCUS TASK

What was the impact of immigration on society?

1 It is 1921. Use pages 163–64 to make notes on the reasons why immigration quotas have been introduced in the USA.

2 Now put yourself in the position of a newspaper journalist from Italy or another country whose immigration quota has been reduced. Write an article to people back home explaining:
   - why the USA has brought in these measures
   - why you think people might have been disappointed if they had decided to emigrate to the USA.

TOPIC SUMMARY

American people and the 'boom'
- During the period of the boom the USA was the world's leading industrial nation.
- The Republican Party encouraged industry and trade through *laissez faire* policies.
- With the USA becoming a consumer society, the advertising industry became more important.
- There was a rapid growth in the use of motor cars due to Ford and the introduction of the moving production line.
- There were huge social inequalities between billionaires and the poor.
- Entertainment became more important based on radio, cinema, jazz and sport, and facilitated by car transport.
- Some women admired the flappers; others were much more socially conservative.
- Prohibition was introduced, but it led to the rise of organised crime.
- The number of immigrants was limited, reflecting growing racial intolerance.
- There were fears of Communism spreading to the USA from Russia, sparking a Red Scare.
- The KKK was feared by African Americans, with lynchings still occurring in the 1920s.

4.2 Bust – Americans' experiences of the Depression and New Deal

FOCUS

After the 'boom' of the 1920s, the Wall Street Crash of autumn 1929 led to a long period of depression. Millions of Americans suffered badly, and the government at first had no answer. A depression of this size had never happened before. While Presidents Hoover and, more successfully, Franklin D. Roosevelt grappled with attempts to alleviate the problems, it was only the demands of the Second World War that restored the US economy.

In this part of the topic you will study the following:

- American society during the Depression and why Roosevelt was elected president.
- The New Deal and the extent of its effectiveness on different groups in society.
- The impact of the Second World War:
  - Why it led to American economic recovery.
  - How it affected the lives of women and African Americans.

● American society during the Depression

In 1928 there was a presidential election. Herbert Hoover was the Republican candidate. Nobody doubted that the Republicans would win again. The US economy was still booming. After so much success, how could they lose?

Hoover did win, by a landslide, and all seemed well. One of his earliest statements as President was: 'We in America today are nearer to the final triumph over poverty than ever before … The poor man is vanishing from among us.' When Hoover formally became President in 1929 confidence was still there. He pointed out that Americans had more bathtubs, oil furnaces, silk stockings and bank accounts than any other country.

Six months later it was a very different picture. In October 1929 the Wall Street stock market crashed, the American economy collapsed, and the USA entered a long depression that destroyed much of the prosperity of the 1920s.

As a result of the Wall Street Crash millions of shares lost a lot of their value. At first, it was not clear what the impact of the Crash would be. In the short term, the rich large-scale investors – who had risked most money in the belief that the price of shares would continue to rise – lost most. As they had always been the main buyers of American goods, there was an immediate downturn in spending. Many others had borrowed money in order to buy shares that were now worthless. They were unable to pay back their loans to the banks and insurance companies, so they went bankrupt. Some banks themselves also went bankrupt.

SOURCE 1

A cartoon by American cartoonist John McCutcheon, 1932. The man on the bench has lost all his savings because of a bank failure.

THINK

Look at Source 1. Do you think the cartoonist is sympathetic or critical of the man on the bench? Explain your opinion.

SOURCE 2

Unemployed workers queuing for a cheap meal. For Americans used to prosperity and believing in self-help, needing charity was a hard blow to their pride.

FIGURE 3

Unemployment in the USA, 1929–33.

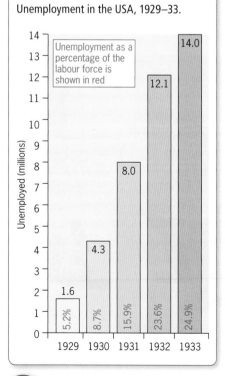

Unemployment as a percentage of the labour force is shown in red

Year	Unemployed (millions)	Percentage
1929	1.6	5.2%
1930	4.3	8.7%
1931	8.0	15.9%
1932	12.1	23.6%
1933	14.0	24.9%

Unemployment

While Hoover talked optimistically about the return of prosperity, the downward spiral in the economy was firmly established. Businesses cut production further and laid off more workers. They reduced the wages of those who still worked for them. Between 1928 and 1933, both industrial and farm production fell by 40 per cent, and average wages by 60 per cent.

As workers were laid off or were paid less, they bought even less. By 1932 the USA was in the grip of the most serious economic depression the world had ever seen. By 1933 there were 14 million unemployed, and 5,000 banks had gone bankrupt.

People in many towns suffered badly. For example, in 1932 in the steel city of Cleveland, 50 per cent of workers were now unemployed and in Toledo 80 per cent. At night the parks were full of the homeless and unemployed. In every city, workers who had contributed to the prosperity of the 1920s now queued for bread and soup dished out by charity workers. Every town had a so-called HOOVERVILLE. This was a shanty town of ramshackle huts where the migrants lived, while they searched for work. The rubbish tips were crowded with families hoping to scrape a meal from the leftovers of more fortunate people. Through 1931, 238 people were admitted to hospital in New York suffering from malnutrition or starvation. Forty-five of them died.

Farmers

Farm prices had fallen so low that the cost of transporting animals to market was higher than the price of the animals themselves. Total farm income had slipped to just $5 billion. The USA's international trade had also been drastically reduced, falling from $10 billion in 1929 to $3 billion in 1932.

People in agricultural areas were hardest hit by the Depression, because the 1920s had not been kind to them anyway. Huge numbers of farmers were unable to pay their mortgages. Some farmers organised themselves to resist banks seizing their homes. When sheriffs came to seize their property, bands of farmers holding pitch forks and hangman's nooses persuaded the sheriffs to retreat. Others barricaded highways. Most farmers, however, had no choice but to pack their belongings into their trucks and live on the road. They picked up work where they could.

To make matters worse for farmers, over-farming and drought in the central southern states turned millions of acres into a dust bowl and drove farmers off their land. Many of these ruined farmers headed to California looking for labouring work. Millions of people – entire families in many cases – were on the move desperately looking for work.

SOURCE 4

A dust bowl farm in Dallas, South Dakota. Over-farming, drought and poor conservation turned farmland into desert.

THINK

Study Sources 4 and 5.

1 In what ways do these sources show living conditions far removed from the usual image of the booming 1920s?

2 Why was there so much poverty in the 1920s for some Americans?

ACTIVITY

What impact did the Crash have on the American economy?

Draw a diagram to show how the following were connected to each other:

- The Wall Street Crash
- The banking crisis
- Reduced spending
- Unemployment.

SOURCE 5

A migrant family from Amarillo, Texas, outside their trailer home.

Businessmen

As the American stock market went into serious decline from late 1929 to 1932, businessmen were extremely badly affected. Many had expanded their operations in the late 1920s, fuelled by confidence in the economy, and had taken out loans that they could now not afford to repay. As a result of the crash, industries were producing far more goods than people could afford to buy – causing more businessmen to go bankrupt.

SOURCE 6

An attempt to make some cash after the Wall Street Crash of 1929.

Between 1929 and 1933, 10,000 banks closed and over 100,000 businesses went bankrupt. Some businessmen tried to survive by reducing their workforce and reducing their output levels. As a result, industrial production fell by 40 per cent in these years. US exports fell from $10 billion to $3 billion between 1929 and 1932. Banks, in a desperate situation themselves, tried to recover money by demanding the repayments of loans from businesses, but this meant that even more were forced to close.

Many businessmen tried new activities – such as selling newspapers or apples in the streets, or offering to polish shoes. For some, suicide was the only way out.

SOURCE 7

Written by a political commentator after the event.

Never before in this country has a government fallen to so low a place in popular estimation or been so universally an object of cynical contempt. Never before has [a President] given his name so freely to latrines and offal dumps, or had his face banished from the [cinema] screen to avoid the hoots and jeers of children.

SOURCE 8

President of the Farmers' Union of Wisconsin, A.N. Young, speaking to a Senate committee in 1932.

Farmers are just ready to do anything to get even with the situation. I almost hate to express it, but I honestly believe that if some of them could buy airplanes they would come down here to Washington to blow you fellows up … The farmer is a naturally conservative individual, but you cannot find a conservative farmer today. Any economic system that has in its power to set me and my wife in the streets, at my age what can I see but red?

Hoover's responses and unpopularity

In the 1932 election President Hoover paid the price for being unable to solve the problems of the Depression. It was partly his own fault. Until 1932 he refused to accept that there was a major problem. He insisted that 'prosperity is just around the corner'. This left him open to bitter criticisms such as those shown in Source 8. A famous banner carried in a demonstration of Iowa farmers said: 'In Hoover we trusted and now we are busted.'

Hoover was regarded as a 'do nothing' President. This was not entirely fair on Hoover. He tried to restart the economy in 1930 and 1931 by tax cuts. He tried to persuade business leaders not to cut wages. He set up the Reconstruction Finance Company, which propped up banks to stop them going bankrupt. He tried to protect US industries by introducing tariffs, but this simply strangled international trade and made the Depression worse.

To most observers these measures looked like mere tinkering. Hoover and most Republicans were very reluctant to change their basic policies. They believed that the main cause of the Depression had been economic problems in Europe, not weaknesses in the USA's economy. They said that business should be left alone to bring back prosperity. Government help was not needed. They argued that business went in cycles of boom and bust, and therefore prosperity would soon return.

Even more damaging to Hoover's personal reputation, however, was how little he tried to help people who were suffering because of the Depression. He believed that social security was not the responsibility of the government. Relief should be provided by local government or charities. The Republicans were afraid that if the government helped individuals, they would become less independent and less willing to work.

Hoover's reputation was particularly damaged by an event in June 1932. Thousands of servicemen who had fought in the First World War marched on Washington asking for their war bonuses (a kind of pension) to be paid early. The marchers camped peacefully outside the White House and sang patriotic songs. Hoover refused to meet them. He appointed General Douglas MacArthur to handle the situation. MacArthur convinced himself (with little or no evidence) that they were Communist agitators. He ignored Hoover's instructions to treat the marchers with respect. Troops and police used tear gas and burned the marchers' camps. Hoover would not admit he had failed to control MacArthur. He publicly thanked God that the USA still knew how to deal with a mob.

Roosevelt's election as president

There could be no greater contrast to Hoover than his opponent in the 1932 election, the Democrat candidate, Franklin D. Roosevelt. Roosevelt's main characteristics as a politician were:

- he was not a radical but believed in 'active government' to improve the lives of ordinary people, although only as a last resort if self-help and charity had failed
- he had plans to spend public money on getting people back to work; as Governor of New York, he had already started doing this in his own state
- he was not afraid to ask for advice on important issues from a wide range of experts, such as factory owners, union leaders and economists.

The election campaign

With such ill-feeling towards Hoover being expressed throughout the country, Roosevelt was confident of victory, but he took no chances. He went on a grand train tour of the USA in the weeks before the election and mercilessly attacked the attitude of Hoover and the Republicans.

Roosevelt's own plans were rather vague and general (see Source 10). But he realised people wanted action, whatever that action was. In a 20,800 km campaign trip he made 16 major speeches and another 60 from the back of his train. He promised the American people a 'New Deal'.

The election was a landslide victory for Roosevelt. He won by 7 million votes and the Democrats won a majority of seats in Congress. It was the worst defeat the Republicans had ever suffered.

SOURCE 9
Roosevelt's pre-election speech, 1932.

Millions of our citizens cherish the hope that their old standards of living have not gone forever. Those millions shall not hope in vain. I pledge you, I pledge myself, to a New Deal for the American people. This is more than a political campaign; it is a call to arms. Give me your help, not to win votes alone, but to win this crusade to restore America ... I am waging a war against Destruction, Delay, Deceit and Despair ...

SOURCE 10
Professor James Macgregor Burns, writing in November 2007. Burns is an expert on the methods used by political leaders.

Roosevelt, the only American President to win four terms in office ... saw the Democratic Party for what it was: an amorphous association [unclearly defined] representing a wide variety of competing interests. To win the Presidential nomination, he needed to keep on board an improbable mix of eastern liberals, western reformers, labour leaders, internationalists, Wall Street financiers and southern states' rights conservatives and white supremacists. So evasive was he that one columnist dubbed him 'the corkscrew candidate'.

FOCUS TASK

Why did Roosevelt win the 1932 election?

In many ways Roosevelt's victory needs no explanation. Indeed, it would have been very surprising if any President could have been re-elected after the sufferings of 1929–32. But it is important to recognise the range of factors that helped Roosevelt and damaged Hoover.

1 Write your own account of Roosevelt's success under the following headings:
   - The experiences of ordinary people
   - Actions taken by the Republicans
   - The policies of the Republicans
   - Roosevelt's election campaign.
2 Make a list of the differences between the views of Hoover and Roosevelt.
3 Explain why Hoover disliked Roosevelt's ideas.

● The effectiveness of the New Deal

During his election campaign Roosevelt had promised the American people a New Deal. It was not entirely clear what measures that might include. What was clear was that Franklin D. Roosevelt planned to use the full power of the government to get the USA out of depression. His priorities were:

● getting Americans back to work
● protecting their savings and property
● providing relief for the sick, old and unemployed
● getting American industry and agriculture back on their feet.

The Hundred Days

In the first hundred days of his presidency, Roosevelt worked round the clock with his advisers (who became known as the 'Brains Trust') to produce an enormous range of sweeping measures.

From his first day, Roosevelt went straight into action. One of the many problems affecting the USA was its loss of confidence in the banks. He immediately tackled this banking crisis.

The day after his inauguration Roosevelt ordered all of the banks to close and to remain closed until government officials had checked them over. A few days later 5,000 trustworthy banks were allowed to reopen. They were even supported by government money if necessary.

This gave the American people a taste of what the New Deal was to look like, but there was a lot more to come. In the Hundred Days, Roosevelt sent 15 proposals to Congress and all 15 were adopted. Just as importantly, he took time to explain to the American people what he was doing and why he was doing it. Every Sunday he would broadcast on radio to the nation. An estimated 60 million Americans tuned in to these 'fireside chats'. Nowadays, we are used to politicians doing this. At that time it was a new development.

Some of the key measures of the New Deal are as follows:

● The **Federal Emergency Relief Administration** set about meeting the urgent needs of the poor. A sum of $500 million was spent on soup kitchens, blankets, employment schemes and nursery schools.
● The **Civilian Conservation Corps** (CCC) was aimed at unemployed young men in particular. They could sign on for periods of six months, which could be renewed if they could still not find work. Most of the work done by the CCC was on environmental projects in national parks. The money earned generally went back to the men's families. Around 2.5 million young men were helped.
● The **Agricultural Adjustment Administration** (AAA) tried to take a long-term view of the problems facing farmers. It set quotas to reduce farm production in order to force prices gradually upwards. At the same time, the AAA helped farmers to modernise and to use farming methods that would conserve and protect the soil. In cases of extreme hardship, farmers could also receive help with their mortgages. The AAA certainly helped farmers, although modernisation had the unfortunate effect of putting more farm labourers out of work.

PROFILE

Franklin D. Roosevelt

● Born in 1882 into a rich New York family.
● In 1910 he entered politics as a Democratic senator for New York.
● In 1921 he was paralysed by polio and spent the rest of his life in a wheelchair.
● He became President in 1933.
● He was an excellent public speaker and a firm believer in the 'AMERICAN DREAM' – that anyone who worked hard enough could become rich.
● His policies of providing benefits for the unemployed, and employing men to work on massive state building projects (known as the 'New Deal') made him extremely popular.
● He was elected President four times.
● He led the USA through the Second World War until his death in 1945.

The **National Industrial Recovery Act** (NIRA) set up two important organisations:

- The **Public Works Administration** (PWA), which used government money to build schools, roads, dams, bridges and airports. These would be vital once the USA had recovered, and in the short term they created millions of jobs.
- The **National Recovery Administration** (NRA), which improved working conditions in industry and outlawed child labour. It also set out fair wages and sensible levels of production. The idea was to stimulate the economy by giving workers money to spend, without overproducing and causing a slump. It was voluntary, but firms which joined used the blue eagle as a symbol of presidential approval. Over 2 million employers joined the scheme.

The **Home Owners Loan Corporation** was established in June and began trading in August. It effectively took over the mortgages of many middle-income Americans who were struggling to pay their mortgages so that the banks did not REPOSSESS their homes. HOLC took over around 1 million mortgages at more favourable interest rates than banks were offering. Between 1933 and 1936, HOLC 'rescued' around 20 per cent of American homeowners and over 80 per cent of these successfully repaid the HOLC mortgage.

SOURCE 11

Roosevelt's inauguration speech, 1933.

This is the time to speak the truth frankly and boldly … So let me assert my firm belief that the only thing we have to fear is fear itself – nameless, unreasoning, unjustified terror which paralyses efforts to convert retreat into advance … This nation calls for action and action now … Our greatest primary task is to put people to work … We must act and act quickly.

THINK

1 Read Source 11. What do you think Roosevelt means by 'the only thing we have to fear is fear itself'?
2 Look carefully at Source 12. Put the message of each cartoon into your own words.

SOURCE 12

Two 1933 American cartoons.

A. President Roosevelt is shown throwing away the promises of the previous government.

B. The role of the NRA in the New Deal.

The Tennessee Valley Authority

The Tennessee Valley was a huge area that cut across seven states. The area had great physical problems. In the wet season, the Tennessee River would flood. In the dry it would reduce to a trickle. The farming land around the river was a dust bowl. The soil was eroding and turning the land into desert. The area also had great social problems. Within the valley people lived in poverty. The majority of households had no electricity. The problems of the Tennessee Valley were far too large for one state to deal with and it was very difficult for states to co-operate.

FIGURE 13

The Tennessee Valley and the work of the TVA.

Key
◗ Dams   ▨ Area covered by TVA

KENTUCKY
VIRGINIA
Mississippi river
T E N N E S S E E
Memphis
Cherokee Dam
Fontana Dam
Chickamauga Dam
Hiwassee Dam
NORTH CAROLINA
Chattanooga
SOUTH CAROLINA
Wilson Dam
MISSISSIPPI
GEORGIA
ALABAMA
0   100 km
Scale
N

SOURCE 14

Effects of erosion in the Tennessee Valley.

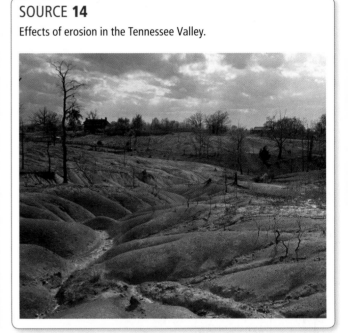

Roosevelt therefore set up an independent organisation called the TENNESSEE VALLEY AUTHORITY (TVA), which cut across the powers of the local state governments. The main focus of the TVA's work was to build a series of dams on the Tennessee River. They transformed the region. The dams made it possible to irrigate the dried-out lands. They also provided electricity for this underdeveloped area. Above all, building the dams created thousands of jobs in an area badly hit by the Depression.

More New Deal measures in 1935

Despite his achievements, by May 1935 Roosevelt was facing a barrage of criticism. Some critics (like Senator Huey Long, see page 174) complained that he was doing too little, others (mainly the wealthy business sector) too much. The USA was recovering less quickly than Europe from Depression. Business was losing its enthusiasm for the NRA (for example, Henry Ford had cut wages). Roosevelt was unsure what to do. He had hoped to transform the USA, but it didn't seem to be working.

Roosevelt met with a group of senators and close advisers who shared his views and aims. They persuaded him to take radical steps to achieve his vision and make the USA a fairer place for all Americans. The most significant aspects were as follows:

● The **Wagner Act**, which forced all employers to allow trade unions to operate in their companies and to let them negotiate with employers for better pay and conditions. The new Act made it illegal to sack workers for being in a union.

- The **Social Security Act**, which provided state pensions for the elderly and for widows. It also allowed state governments to work with the FEDERAL GOVERNMENT to provide help for the sick and the disabled. Most importantly, the Act set up a scheme for unemployment insurance. This meant that employers and workers made a small contribution to a special fund each week. If workers became unemployed, they would receive a small amount of benefit to help them out until they could find work.

- The **Works Progress Administration (WPA)**, later renamed the Works Project Administration, which brought together all the organisations whose aim was to create jobs. It also extended this work beyond building projects to create jobs for office workers and even unemployed actors, artists and photographers. Source 15 was produced by an artist working for the Federal Arts Project. The government paid artists to paint pictures to be displayed in the city or town they featured.

- The **Resettlement Administration (RA)**, which helped smallholders and tenant farmers who had not been helped by the AAA. This organisation moved over 500,000 families to better-quality land and housing. The **Farm Security Administration (FSA)** replaced the RA in 1937. It gave special loans to small farmers to help them buy their land. It also built camps to provide decent living conditions and work for migrant workers.

> **THINK**
>
> 1. What impression of the New Deal does Source 15 attempt to convey?
> 2. Why do you think Roosevelt wanted artists and photographers to be employed under the New Deal?

SOURCE 15

Steel Industry by Howard Cook, painted under the Federal Arts Project for the steel-making town of Pittsburgh, Pennsylvania.

Study Source 16.

Explain the message of this cartoon.

Successes and limitations of the New Deal

You have seen in the previous four pages how much the New Deal tried to do to help different groups in society. Yet economic recovery was slow. Unemployment remained stubbornly high, with all the misery that this entailed.

As a result, there were many critics of the New Deal.

SOURCE 16

A cartoon attacking the New Deal in the mid-1930s. Most newspaper owners were hostile to Roosevelt.

The Supreme Court

The Supreme Court had the power to overturn laws if it believed they were against the American Constitution. At the time of the New Deal the Court was dominated by Republicans, who declared certain aspects of the New Deal, such as the NRA, unconstitutional. They argued that these new laws extended the role of the federal government too far, and undermined the power of individual states. In response Roosevelt threatened to create six more Supreme Court judges who would support his policies in order to out-vote the Republican judges. However, after an outcry from the public (mostly wanting to leave the Court as it was but supporting Roosevelt's policies) the Supreme Court accepted the later measures of the New Deal.

Republicans

The Republicans, supported by most businesses, argued that the New Deal was doing too much. They believed that government should intervene as little as possible in business. They regarded Roosevelt as a dictator attempting to control too many aspects of Americans' lives. These Republicans wanted to return to the policies of the 1920s when business had thrived.

The experience of the New Deal on different groups in society

1 Using pages 170–74, make notes on how the New Deal helped:
  – the unemployed
  – banks
  – businesses
  – workers in industry
  – farmers
  – the homeless.
2 Can you think of any groups who appear *not* to be included in the help provided?

Radical politicians

Conversely, some Democrats argued that Roosevelt was not doing enough! They believed that more action was needed to aid disadvantaged groups. One such advocate was Senator Huey Long of Louisiana. He wanted to limit personal wealth to a maximum of $3 million in a scheme called 'Share our Wealth', in which government taxes would be shared between all Americans. Long had many radical supporters, but also enemies. He was ASSASSINATED in 1935.

However, in 1936 Roosevelt was re-elected with the highest margin of victory ever achieved by a US President. He was able to joke: 'Everyone is against the New Deal except the voters.'

Popular culture in the 1930s

People's lives – at least those who could afford it – changed substantially in the period between the wars, as leisure activities became more widespread.

Car ownership played a large role in enabling those who could afford it to travel to cinemas, sports venues and shopping centres. Even though many were suffering from the consequences of the Depression, their horizons were wider than those of their parents and grandparents simply because they were more mobile.

Horizons were also widened by the existence of radios with 28 million homes possessing one by 1939. Almost all the channels were commercial stations, relying on revenue from advertising goods that listeners were encouraged to buy. Many were local stations, but national broadcasting companies such as NBC and CBS also came into existence. The radio usually had a central place within the living room, and could act as a focus for the family to come together. Comedians such as Jack Benny became famous. Radio stations promoted soap operas, for example *Our Gal Sunday* told over many weeks the saga of a small-town girl who fell in love with a wealthy Englishman.

Watching sport was also a popular pastime, and huge numbers travelled to watch baseball teams. Some teams, such as the Harlem Globetrotters, became famous beyond the USA. Some stadiums gave free admission to women in a bid to boost interest within families. Those who couldn't travel could still listen to a match live on their radio sets.

However, the biggest single influence on American life, in the decade before television developed, was the cinema. During the 1920s silent movies had dominated the screens. Hollywood studios made huge profits in 1929 – the high point of the silent screen.

In the 1930s 'talkies' began to replace the silent movies. Many films reflected the conditions of the time – the Great Depression and the slow recovery under the New Deal – even if the tone was upbeat and confident. For example, *Swing Time* (1936), starred Fred Astaire and Ginger Rogers. One of the song-and-dance numbers included the words 'Pick yourself up, dust yourself off, and start all over again.' Many in the cinema audiences could empathise with those sentiments.

Films were becoming more expansive. John Steinbeck's novel, *The Grapes of Wrath* was made into a film in 1940. It is the most famous example of a film reflecting the hard times that millions suffered during the 1930s. The fictional Joad family and other 'Okies' evicted from their Oklahoma farm was a tale typical of the fate of many Americans.

SOURCE 17

Fred Astaire and Ginger Rogers dancing 'Pick Yourself Up'.

SOURCE 18

A still from the film *The Grapes of Wrath*.

```
 |——|——|——|——|——|——|——|——|——|——|
-5 -4 -3 -2 -1  0  1  2  3  4  5
```
Failure is –5. Success is +5

Below is a summary of the impact of the New Deal on various groups.

1 For each of the six aspects of the New Deal, decide where you would place it on the scale above. Explain your score and support it with evidence.

2 Compare your six 'marks' on the scale with those of someone else in your class.

3 Working together, try to come up with an agreed mark for the whole of the New Deal. You will have to think about the relative importance of different issues. For example, you might give more weight to a low mark in an important area than to a high mark in a less important area.

Was Roosevelt's New Deal a success?

In spite of all his critics and the partial failures of the New Deal, Roosevelt was still enormously popular with most ordinary Americans (he was elected again with a big majority in 1940). The problem was that the USA was no longer as united behind his New Deal as it had been in 1933. Indeed, by 1940 Roosevelt and most Americans were focusing more on the outbreak of war in Europe and on Japan's exploits in the Far East.

So was Roosevelt's New Deal a success? One of the reasons why this question is hard to answer is that you need to decide what Roosevelt was trying to achieve. We know that by 1940 unemployment was still high and the economy was certainly not booming. On the other hand, economic recovery was not Roosevelt's only aim. In fact it may not have been his main aim. Roosevelt and many of his advisers wanted to reform the USA's economy and society. So when you decide whether Roosevelt's policies were a success or not, you will have to decide what you think the aims of the New Deal were, as well as whether you think the aims were achieved.

Aspect 1: A new society?

- The New Deal restored the faith of the American people in their government.
- The New Deal was a huge social and economic programme. Government help on this scale would never have been possible before Roosevelt's time. It set the tone for future policies for government to help people.
- The New Deal divided the USA. Roosevelt and his officials were often accused of being Communists and of undermining American values. Ickes and Hopkins were both accused of being anti-business because they supported trade unions.
- The New Deal undermined local government.

Aspect 2: Industrial workers

- The New Deal measures strengthened the position of labour unions against the large American industrial giants.
- Roosevelt's government generally tried to support unions and make large corporations negotiate with them.
- Big business remained immensely powerful in the USA despite being challenged by the government.
- Unions were treated with suspicion by employers and many strikes were broken up with brutal violence in the 1930s.

Aspect 3: Unemployment and the economy

- The New Deal created millions of jobs.
- It stabilised the American banking system.
- It cut the number of business failures.
- Projects such as the TVA brought work and an improved standard of living to deprived parts of the USA, including schools, roads and power stations.
- The New Deal never solved the underlying economic problems.
- The US economy took longer to recover than that of most European countries.
- Confidence remained low – throughout the 1930s Americans only spent and invested about 75 per cent of what they had before 1929.
- There were 6 million unemployed in 1941 and only the USA's entry into the war brought an end to unemployment.

PRACTICE QUESTIONS

Read Interpretations A and B and answer Questions 1–6.

> **Interpretation A** An article 'The New Deal in Review' in the magazine, *The New Republic*, May 1940, looking at the impact of the New Deal.
>
> *The New Deal has clearly done far more for the general welfare of the country and its citizens than any administration [i.e. government] in the previous history of the nation. Its relief for the underprivileged in city and country has been indispensable. Without this relief an appalling amount of misery would have resulted … In addition, the New Deal has accomplished much of permanent benefit to the nation.*

> **Interpretation B** Senator Robert Taft speaking in the US Senate in October 1941. Taft was the leader of the Republicans from 1939-53 and a bitter critic of Roosevelt.
>
> *The New Deal was the great disaster which befell the American Republic in 1933, leading Americans away from their traditional liberties. The inefficiency and waste of many New Deal programs can only be condemned in the strongest terms. The New Deal held back and prevented private enterprise and businesses from restoring the nation's economy, relying instead upon government programs which only served to prolong it.*

1 How does Interpretation B differ from Interpretation A about the New Deal?

  Explain your answer based on what it says in Interpretations A and B.

2 Why might the authors of Interpretations A and B have a different interpretation about the New Deal?

  Explain your answer using Interpretations A and B and your contextual knowledge.

3 Which interpretation gives the more convincing opinion about the New Deal?

  Explain your answer based on your contextual knowledge and what it says in Interpretations A and B.

4 Describe two of the main policies of the New Deal that tried to reduce unemployment.

5 In what ways was the New Deal criticised in the 1930s? Explain your answer.

6 Which was the more important reason why the American economy was so weakened during the Great Depression of the early 1930s?
  - The collapse of the banks
  - The loss of faith in business and investment.

  Explain your answer with reference to both reasons.

Aspect 4: African Americans

- Around 200,000 African Americans gained benefits from the Civilian Conservation Corps and other New Deal agencies.
- Many African Americans benefited from New Deal slum clearance and housing projects.
- Many New Deal agencies discriminated against African Americans. They either got no work or received worse treatment or lower wages.
- Roosevelt failed to pass laws against the lynching of African Americans. He feared that Democrat senators in the Southern states would not support him.

Aspect 5: Women

- The New Deal saw some women achieve prominent positions. Eleanor Roosevelt became an important campaigner on social issues.
- Most of the New Deal programmes were aimed to help male manual workers rather than women (only about 8,000 women were involved in the CCC).

Aspect 6: Native Americans

- The Indian Reorganisation Act 1934 provided money to help Native Americans to buy and improve land.
- The Indian Reservation Act 1934 helped Native Americans to preserve and practise their traditions, laws and culture.
- Native Americans remained a poor and excluded section of society.

● The impact of the Second World War

As you have seen, despite all the efforts of Roosevelt, the New Deal was unable to bring complete economic recovery to America. What did bring it was war. When the Second World War broke out in Europe in 1939 the USA was not involved. Most Americans wanted to keep it that way. However, Roosevelt was worried by the rising power of Germany and Japan. For political reasons he was determined to support Hitler's main opponent, Britain. When Germany attacked the USSR in June 1941, Roosevelt supported Stalin's war effort as well.

Lend Lease

The main form of support was a programme called Lend Lease. It began in March 1941 with support to Britain but, by the end of the war, Lend Lease was sending arms, food, medicine and other equipment to the USSR, China, France and many other nations fighting against Japan or Germany. The basic principle of the Lend Lease programme was that the USA loaned war material to its allies on the understanding that it would be returned at the end of the war, but that it would not be charged for if it was destroyed. A total of $50.1 billion worth of materials were shipped. Although the USA received no payment for these materials during wartime, the vast majority of contracts for the materials were placed with US firms and as a result the programme stimulated the economy. When the USA entered the war itself in December 1941, the impact was even greater.

Wartime production

The achievements of the American war economy were staggering. By 1944, the USA was producing almost half of the weapons being made in the world – more than twice the production of Germany and Japan combined. How was this done?

Willing industrialists

The simple answer was that the will was there to do this. Throughout the New Deal years, many leading industrialists had opposed or mistrusted Roosevelt and his New Deal policies. Now, in the face of war, the industrialists rallied behind Roosevelt and co-operated fully with him. At the same time Roosevelt could effectively raise taxes and spend money at any level he wanted in order to win the war. This made for a powerful combination.

In January 1942, President Roosevelt set up the War Production Board under the industrialist William Knusden. He called in the USA's leading industrialists. He asked their advice about how to meet war production needs. Around 80 per cent of American contracts went to only 100 firms, although the work ended up with thousands of smaller firms which were subcontracted to supply tools, materials and equipment. These large firms wanted to help the war effort, but they also stood to make a lot of money out of it.

FIGURE 19

War production 1941–45.

War planes	296,429
Tanks	102,351
Artillery pieces	372,431
Trucks	2,445,964
Aircraft bombs	5,822,000
Small guns	20,086,061
Ammunition for small guns	44,000,000,000 rounds

Extra workers

The large-scale production required workers. Fourteen million worked in the factories. General Motors alone took on an extra 0.75 million workers during the war. Most of the manufacturing jobs were in the industrial north or on the Pacific coast. Around 4 million workers migrated from the rural south to these areas. This included a very significant number of African Americans. Nearly 0.75 million African Americans found work in the war industries. California saw an influx of 1.5 million new workers.

All available women

Before the war, there were already 12 million working women. During the war, 300,000 women joined the armed forces and another 7 million joined the workforce (for details see page 180).

Economic recovery

Of all the countries involved in fighting the Second World War, the USA was the only one that emerged economically stronger as a result.

- More than half a million new businesses started up during the war. Many became rich as a result of war contracts. Coca-Cola set up plants to follow the troops around the world (in the process, making Coca-Cola the most successful soft drink in the world). Wrigley took on the role of packaging rations for US forces (adding Wrigley's chewing gum to the rations, of course).
- The war effort ended unemployment – something that Roosevelt's New Deal had failed to do.
- Even American farmers, after almost 20 years of depressed prices and economic crisis, began to enjoy better times as the USA exported food to help its allies.
- As demand for workers increased so did wages, and the buying power of American workers stimulated new industries to meet their demands. It was similar to the boom of the 1920s, only this time the stimulus was war production, and spending was less extravagant. Many Americans invested their income in bonds. They effectively lent money to the government by buying war bonds, with a promise that the bonds would be paid back with interest at the end of the war. During the course of the war, Americans contributed $129 billion to the war effort by buying bonds. This gave the government money to spend on wartime production which continued to boost the economy.

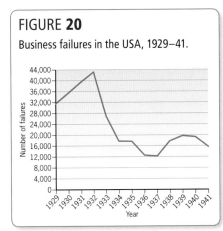

FIGURE 20

Business failures in the USA, 1929–41.

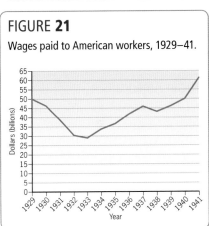

FIGURE 21

Wages paid to American workers, 1929–41.

FOCUS TASK

Why did the war bring about economic recovery?

1 Make your own copy of the diagram below and use the information on this page to show how war led to economic recovery.

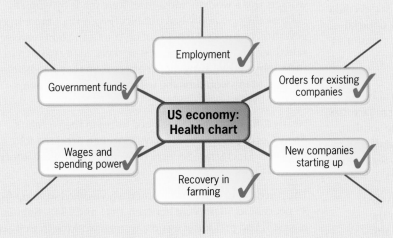

2 Discuss the following question with a partner: Why did war achieve complete recovery when the New Deal could not?
3 Try to come up with at least two possible explanations.
4 Discuss the possible explanations as a class and take a vote on which explanation you think is the most likely.

Social developments

Society became geared towards war production. There was comparatively little impact, however, on America domestically. There were very few shortages in the shops for basic goods, including food. The overproduction of cars and other goods in the 1930s allowed those industries to be directed by the War Production Board (WPB) to produce weapons, vehicles and other equipment for the armed forces.

Government expenditure rocketed – from $20 billion in 1941 to $97.2 billion in 1944. Taxes were increased; people were persuaded to save money in war bonds; and the national debt rose to six times what it had been in 1941. People in general accepted the larger role that the federal government had taken on. Once Japan had attacked Pearl Harbor in December 1941 and Germany had also declared war on the USA, most people saw little alternative to the USA ending its period of ISOLATIONISM.

African Americans

Changes took place for African Americans during the war which increased expectations of changes occurring after the conflict. As the USA was fighting to defeat racist Germany, more and more questions were asked about the racial segregation within its own borders.

Over 1 million African-American soldiers joined or were conscripted into the armed forces. Many of them were limited to menial tasks, but even then they were working alongside white Americans. This became noticeable, for example, when a sizeable proportion of the American troops stationed in Britain in 1943–44 were African Americans, and they were able to go into pubs and restaurants with white people. Many of the white American troops from the Southern states could not understand why Britain did not have a policy of racial segregation. But sometimes tensions in British communities ran high when African-American soldiers went out with white British girls.

African Americans also played an important role at home. By the end of 1944 about 2 million were working in factories producing war materials. Many migrated from the south to the more heavily industrialised north. And once again many more African Americans therefore saw that racial segregation was not the norm outside their local communities.

Thus expectations of changes occurring after the war rose. Membership of the National Association for the Advancement of Coloured People (NAACP) – the main organisation campaigning for equal rights – rose from 50,000 to nearly half a million. There was clearly going to be antagonism after the war between African Americans expecting social change and some groups of white Americans expecting life to return to pre-war 'normality' – just as there had been after the First World War.

African-American soldiers marching down the street in an English town during the war.

Changes for women

There were major changes to women's roles as a direct result of the USA's involvement in the Second World War.

As men went to fight, many women entered the workforce for the first time. One in three aircraft workers were women. Women were often given difficult welding jobs in awkward parts of aircraft bodies because they were smaller and more agile. In the munitions and electronics industries, one in two workers was a woman. Most fuses were made by women, because they generally had nimbler fingers than men. In a government survey, 60 per cent of American plant managers said that women were their best workers. Many women in these jobs were earning higher wages than they had before the war. Many would not be willing to go back to their pre-war lives.

Nearly 200,000 joined the armed forces in the Women's Army Corps (WACs) or the navy's Women Accepted for Volunteer Emergency Services (WAVES). Many more joined the Red Cross.

The percentage of married women who worked went up from 35 per cent to 50 per cent between 1941 and 1945. But many men still had prejudices against women working in well-paid jobs – especially married women. Returning soldiers often expected life to be as it had been and expected their wives to return to their domestic roles again. Thus society experienced many tensions in the years after 1945.

SOURCE 23

'She's a WOW'. This poster is encouraging women to work in a factory in order to support the men who had gone to fight.

SOURCE 24

'We can do it'. Rosie the Riveter became an important symbol of women taking over what had traditionally been men's work.

TOPIC SUMMARY

Americans' experiences of the Depression and New Deal

- The Wall Street Crash in 1929 led to economic depression in the 1930s.
- President Hoover failed to solve the problems created by the Crash.
- Roosevelt won the election in 1932 promising a New Deal.
- New Deal reforms tried to tackle Relief, Recovery and Reform.
- New Deal reforms had mixed success, e.g. unemployment fell but still millions were unemployed.
- Some groups received less help than others, e.g. farmers, African Americans.
- There was considerable opposition to the New Deal from Republicans and the Supreme Court.
- The Second World War revived the economy with millions of job opportunities in the armed forces and in industries.
- Women's roles changed significantly during the war.
- African Americans were much in demand during the war; but the expectations of African Americans that living conditions would improve after the war were mostly unfulfilled.

THINK

1. Why was the USA able to have such a dominant position in the manufacture of war materials for the Allies?
2. Who do you think was more affected socially by the experience of war – African Americans or white women?
3. Describe the role of women in the development of industry in the USA during the war.

FOCUS TASK

How did the Second World War affect women and African Americans?

Work in pairs.

1. One of you research the experience of women during the war, and make notes on the changes the war brought to their role and opportunities.
2. The other research the experience of African Americans during the war, and make notes on the changes the war brought to their experiences and opportunities.
3. Discuss your findings and write a sentence for each group to describe what you think their expectations will be in post-war America.

4.3 Post-war America

FOCUS

After the Second World War, Americans had to adjust to the fact that society had changed. The war had ended the Depression of the 1930s; it had left the USA as the most powerful country in the world; but it had also left major tensions within society.

In this part of the topic you will study the following:

- Life in post-war American society and its economy.
- Racial tension and developments in the 1950s and 1960s:
  - The extent of success for the Civil Rights campaign.
  - The effects of the Black Power movement.
- America and the 'Great Society':
  - How policies affected the role of government.
  - How women's lives changed.

● **American society and the economy after 1945**

In the period from 1945 to the early 1970s, American society changed tremendously. The economy grew rapidly. Much, though not all, of American society experienced a comfortable lifestyle of affluence. Popular culture and entertainment developed rapidly with the beginnings of pop music and television. Yet there were tensions over fears of Communist influence and over the inequalities suffered by many African Americans.

Consumerism and the causes of prosperity

Rapid economic growth provided most middle-class white Americans with a comfortable lifestyle. During the 1950s America was producing nearly half the world's goods. During the 1950s the GNP (the total value of all the goods and services produced) doubled. This economic boom arose from the conditions at the end of the Second World War, as you found out on pages 178–79. The USA had suffered no mainland bomb damage, unlike all her industrial competitors.

SOURCE 1

A refrigerator advertisement in 1949.

SOURCE 2

Watching television in the 1950s: a view of a typical American family.

The American Dream

Many wealthy white Americans moved out of the old city centres to new suburban areas, relying on the almost universal use of motor transport. Many modern conveniences became expected as the norm – refrigerators, washing machines and televisions.

It was assumed that the steadily increasing wealth, leading to more purchases of luxury goods and necessities, would ensure economic growth continued. And during the 1950s this certainly appeared to be true. In 1960 the living standard of the average American was three times that of the average British person. Spending rather than saving was accepted as normal. Shopping became a popular recreational activity. Advertising in magazines and newspapers was still important as well as television.

Hire purchase (that is, paying for something over months or years) became the normal way to buy as people got used to living on credit rather than saving up. The 1950s also marked the gradual acceptance that goods were only expected to last a few years until they would be replaced with a newer model. It was often difficult to get spare parts for old models, thus forcing people to give in to the temptations of the latest advertisements.

Compared with the 1920s the wealth was spread further down the social scale; but there were still many who felt excluded. In these circumstances it is not surprising that the majority of Americans aspired to be part of the American Dream.

SOURCE 4

A 1952 advertisement for Coca-Cola.

THINK

Describe two ways in which consumerism affected people's lives in the USA in the 1950s.

SOURCE 3

A suburban scene in the 1950s as a father arrives home from work.

SOURCE 5

From the film, *Oklahoma*.

SOURCE 6

Elvis Presley performing.

Popular culture

Popular culture became dominated by television, radio and cinema. Popular musicals were also made into films, such as *Oklahoma* in 1955. The films made during this period clearly defined the confidence and optimism of white America.

Teenagers

American youth of the 1940s and 1950s on average had more leisure time and more spending money than youth in previous generations. As a result, they began to assume their own styles and culture, and in the 1940s the term 'teenager' was used to describe this age group.

By the 1950s the term came to be associated with rebellion as youth were seen to act against parents and society by setting up their own alternative standards. Teenage rebels were also depicted on the silver screen by movie stars such as Marlon Brando and James Dean who were regarded by many parents as unsuitable role models for their offspring.

Rock and roll

Teenage discontent also presented itself in music. The new 'Beat music' of the 1940s soon transformed into the rock and roll music of the 1950s. As the popularity of this music spread, singers such as Elvis Presley took to the stage, and rocked the world. His gyrating hips and sexy persona shocked parents and wowed fans. He had at least 170 hit singles and over 80 top-selling albums.

Television

Television ownership developed rapidly. In fact, no other household technology has spread so rapidly:

- 1948: 0.4 per cent of households owned a television
- 1954: 55.7 per cent
- 1958: 83.2 per cent

Suddenly television replaced reading, listening to the radio or going to the cinema in many households – though the extent of viewing reduced when the initial phase of excitement had passed.

Television in the 1950s was dominated by commercial sponsors, all trying to encourage spending in the consumer society. Most of the programmes were game shows, sitcoms and soap operas, with little emphasis on more serious programming, except for TV news which became important as truly national networks developed. With so many children around in the 1950s (following the baby boom after the war), producers took the opportunity to also develop specific programmes for this new audience.

FOCUS TASK

What was life like in post-war American society?

Imagine you are a man or a woman living in post-war American society. Write a diary entry for one typical day in your life. Try to use as many of the following words and phrases in your entry as you can:

- suburbia
- advertisement
- hire purchase
- refrigerator
- television

- washing machine
- teenage rebels
- rock and roll
- cinema
- motor cars.

PRACTICE QUESTION

In what ways were American attitudes and lifestyles affected by television in the 1950s and 1960s? Explain your answer.

Yet television was powerful – controlling the aspirations of many Americans. Family purchases were often determined by what the neighbours purchased and what was heavily advertised on TV. With Americans watching the same programmes across the nation a new sense of national American culture developed.

McCarthyism

There was a dark side to American politics and society in the late 1940s and early 1950s. Hand in hand with the ideals of the 'American Dream' was the notion that the American values of DEMOCRACY and personal freedoms were under threat and must be protected. After the First World War American society had developed a fear of Communism spreading from Russia – the Red Scare (see page 163). After the Second World War those fears were heightened as Russia's control of eastern Europe was consolidated. In 1949 China also fell to the Communists, increasing the US fear of Communism spreading throughout the world.

These fears turned inwards, as Americans began to suspect anyone who did not display the so-called American virtues of patriotism, freedom and enterprise, of being Communist sympathisers. Fears were so great that the US Congress set up the House Committee of Un-American Activities to investigate Communist involvement in the government, education and the film industry. Those questioned were supposed to prove their loyalty to America, which was difficult. Many were sacked as 'security risks'. Many more started to name others, behaviour reminiscent of the witch-hunts of the seventeenth century.

Senator Joe McCarthy from Wisconsin started a campaign against possible Communists using half-truths, rumours, smears and lies. Fears against Communism were particularly potent around 1950 with the start of the Korean War. 'Reds under the beds' became the frantic cry. McCarthy claimed that many Communist sympathisers were working in the government. Many were put on trial and found guilty without much proof. He never uncovered any real evidence, but this did not stop anti-Communist headlines in newspapers and news reports on the radio and television. He then began to accuse some officers in the US army. At this point, for many Americans, McCarthy had gone too far.

A Senate sub-committee was set up to investigate. The hearings were televised, and they showed McCarthy to be an irresponsible bully. However, the damage had already been done to many people's lives – and to the USA's reputation across the world. Much effort was wasted on this at a time when other problems in American society could have been addressed.

One of McCarthy's staunch allies was J. Edgar Hoover, Director of the Federal Bureau of Investigation (FBI). He was a life-long opponent of anything that smacked of Communist influence. During the McCarthy period of the late 1940s and early 1950s, the FBI kept files on about 1 million suspects. Later Hoover's techniques, including phone tapping and other modern methods of surveillance, were used to investigate CIVIL RIGHTS leaders such as Martin Luther King. He remained as director of the FBI until his death in 1972, aged 77.

PRACTICE QUESTION

Which of the following was the more important reason why Senator McCarthy was so successful in encouraging the fear of Communism?
- The international situation c.1950
- The situation inside the USA c.1950.

Explain your answer with reference to both reasons.

SOURCE 7

Senator Joe McCarthy.

FACTFILE

Korean War

The Korean War was fought between North and South Korea. North Korea was Communist and supported by the USSR and China. The United Nations, led by the USA, supported South Korea in its fight against Communist takeover. See pages 337–38 for more details.

SOURCE 8

McCarthy announces that he has a list of known Communists, in a speech in January 1950.

While I cannot take the time to name all the men in the State Department who have been named as members of the Communist Party and members of a spy ring, I have here in my hand a list of 205 that are known to the Secretary of State as being members of the Communist Party and are still working and shaping the policy of the State Department.

SOURCE 9

President Truman denouncing what he called 'McCarthy's witch-hunt'.

Slander, lies, character assassination – these things are a threat to every single citizen everywhere in this country. When even one American – who has done nothing wrong – is forced by fear to shut his mind and close his mouth, then all Americans are in peril.

Racial tension and developments in the Civil Rights campaign in the 1950s and 1960s

Racial prejudice and violence had been common in the USA between the wars, especially in the Southern states. In spite of what many African Americans had contributed towards the American war effort, there was still ingrained prejudice in the 1950s and 1960s.

Segregation laws and racial prejudice

- Many Southern and border states enforced the so-called 'Jim Crow' laws, each one in slightly different ways and to different extents. These laws segregated use of everyday facilities such as parks, buses and schools.
- African Americans had officially been given the right to vote early in the century, but in some states various practices were used to prevent them from voting – most commonly, the threat of violence. In Mississippi, for example, African Americans who tried to register to vote faced intimidation or even lynching. Only 5 per cent of the African-American population in Mississippi was registered to vote.
- Law officers (police) not only failed to stop attacks on these people, they frequently took part in them. White juries almost always acquitted whites accused of killing African Americans.
- African Americans faced official and legal discrimination in areas such as employment and education. In the South, white teachers earned 30 per cent more than African American teachers.
- The best universities were closed to black people. In 1958, an African-American teacher called Clemson King was committed to a mental asylum for applying to the University of Mississippi.

Therefore in the 1950s and 1960s, although some whites believed in equality for African Americans, many were afraid of losing their privileged way of life.

The struggle for equal education: A legal challenge

For decades, it had been legal in the USA for states to have separate schools for black and white children. The states argued that separate education did not mean unequal if the schools for white children and the schools for African-American children were equally well equipped. However, the truth was that schools for African-American children were almost always less well equipped.

SOURCE 10

An American propaganda poster from 1943 entitled 'United we win'.

UNITED WE WIN

Brown v *Board of Education of Topeka*, 1954

The National Association for the Advancement of Coloured People (NAACP) brought a court case against the Board of Education in Topeka, Kansas. The case was about an African-American girl called Linda Brown who had to travel several kilometres and cross a dangerous rail track to get to school, rather than attend a whites-only school nearby. The civil rights campaigners chose it as a 'test case' to see whether the Supreme Court would allow states to continue to segregate schools. They knew that if they won this case, then the whole principle of 'separate but equal' would come tumbling down.

In May 1954 Chief Justice Earl Warren finally announced in favour of Brown and the NAACP. Warren stated that segregated education could not be considered equal. It created a feeling of inferiority for African-American students and that meant that all segregated school systems were unequal ones. He ordered the Southern states to set up integrated schools 'with all deliberate speed'.

Little Rock, Arkansas, 1957

Integration was met with bitter resistance in some states. Arkansas was one example. Three years after Justice Warren's decree, it had still failed to integrate its schools. In 1957 the Supreme Court ordered the Governor of Arkansas, Orval Faubus, to let nine African-American students attend a white high school in Little Rock. Faubus ordered his state troops to prevent the African-American students from attending school. He claimed that this was because he could not guarantee their safety. Faubus only backed down when President Eisenhower sent federal troops to protect the students and make sure that they could join the school. The troops stayed for six weeks.

THINK

Study Sources 10 and 11.

1 Compare the racial attitudes shown in the two sources.

2 Why do you think the attitudes are different?

SOURCE 11

One of the African-American students at Little Rock, 15-year-old Elizabeth Eckford, trying to ignore the abuse of the 1,000-strong crowd. Forty years later the woman yelling at Eckford publicly apologised for her actions.

Martin Luther King

- Born in January 1929, his father was a Baptist Minister in southern USA.
- Studied theology and went on to gain a doctorate from Boston University in 1955.
- Believed passionately in non-violence, but was willing to confront violent situations.
- He was a mesmerising speaker – most famous speech being 'I have a dream …'.
- In December 1964 he was awarded the Nobel Peace Prize.
- In 1968 he was assassinated.

SOURCE 12

From Martin Luther King's speech at Montgomery, Alabama, in 1955.

The great glory of American democracy is the right to protest for right. There will be no crosses burned at any bus stops in Montgomery. There will be no white persons pulled out of their homes and taken out on some distant road and murdered. There will be nobody among us who will stand up and defy the constitution of the Nation.

SOURCE 13

King writing to President Eisenhower in 1957 after the President expressed his view that laws cannot make people behave in a moral way.

A law may not make a man love me, but it can stop him from lynching me. It can also stop him from refusing to serve me in a restaurant.

Martin Luther King and peaceful protests

Martin Luther King is the person who stands out as the leader of the civil rights movement, but there were many other leaders at the time, and he was able to build on the work of organisations that had been active for decades, for example the NAACP.

Montgomery Bus Boycott, 1955–56

What we now call the civil rights movement is often said to have started with the actions of Rosa Parks from Montgomery, Alabama, in December 1955. Montgomery had a local law that African-American people were only allowed to sit in the middle and back seats of a bus and they had to give up those seats if white people wanted them.

Rosa Parks was a civil rights activist and she decided to make a stand against Montgomery's racially segregated bus service. She refused to give up her seat to a white man. She was promptly arrested and convicted of breaking the bus laws. The civil rights movement helped the African-American people of Montgomery to form the Montgomery Improvement Association (MIA). The MIA decided that the best way to protest and to generate publicity was to boycott the buses. On the first day of the boycott, the buses were empty and 10,000–15,000 people turned out to hear a speech from the newly elected MIA president, Martin Luther King. The boycott was a great success. The bus company lost 65 per cent of its income. The African-American community organised a car pool which carried about two-thirds of the passengers that the buses would have carried (the rest walked).

It was the first major example of the power of non-violent direct action – that is, challenging discrimination by refusing to co-operate with it. It showed how powerful people working together could be. At the same time, civil rights lawyers fought Rosa Parks' case in court. In December 1956, the Supreme Court declared Montgomery's bus laws to be illegal. This meant that all other such bus services were illegal and by implication that all segregation of public services was illegal.

Throughout the boycott, the MIA's leaders were subjected to massive intimidation. King was arrested twice. Local judges passed an injunction declaring the car pool to be illegal. Churches and homes were set on fire and racially integrated buses were shot at by snipers (seven bombers and snipers were charged, but all were acquitted).

SOURCE 14

A photo taken 21 December 1956. Rosa Parks sits at the front of the bus in what used to be whites only seats after the Supreme Court declared bus segregation to be illegal.

Direct action in late 1950s and early 1960s

After the success in Montgomery, the civil rights campaign took off in the late 1950s and early 1960s. A number of different groups began to organise similar direct action:

- King formed the Southern Christian Leadership Conference (SCLC). It ran conferences and trained civil rights activists in techniques of non-violent protest and how to handle the police, the law and the media.
- African-American and white American students were deeply moved by the civil rights movement and played a major role in it. They set up the Student Non-violent Coordinating Committee (SNCC).
- Another civil rights activist, James Farmer, formed the Congress of Racial Equality (CORE).

Together these groups staged many different protests.

Sit-ins

In 1960 in Greensboro, North Carolina, SNCC students began a campaign to end segregation in restaurants in the town. Their local branch of Woolworth's had a lunch counter which had chairs/stools only for whites, while African Americans had to stand and eat. Four black students sat on the whites only seats. They refused to leave the lunch counter when they were refused service. The next day 23 more students did the same; the next day there were 66 students. Within a week 400 African-American and white students were organising sit-ins at lunch counters in the town. With support from SNCC this non-violent tactic spread to other cities. By the end of 1960 lunch counters had been desegregated in 126 cities.

Similar protests were taking place in other towns and not just in restaurants. In February 1960, in Nashville, Tennessee, 500 students organised sit-ins in restaurants, libraries and churches. Their college expelled them, but then backed down when 400 teachers threatened to resign if the students were expelled. The students were attacked and abused but eventually Mayor Ben West was convinced by their actions. By May 1960 the town had been desegregated.

THINK

1 Study Sources 15 and 16. Make a list of the similarities and differences between the two scenes.
2 Which of these two sources would you choose as the image for the front cover of a book on the civil rights movement? Explain your answer.
3 Does it surprise you that Source 16 was published much more widely than Source 15? Explain your answer.

SOURCE 16

Black and white SNCC protesters in a sit-in at a segregated Woolworth's lunch counter in Jackson, Mississippi, June 1963, being abused by young white racists.

SOURCE 15

Freedom riders next to their burning bus near Anniston, Alabama. A mob of white people met the bus at the bus terminal, stoned it and slashed the tyres, then followed the bus out of town and set fire to it. They attacked the passengers as they fled the bus.

'Freedom rides'

In May 1961 CORE activists began a form of protest called 'freedom rides' (see Source 15, page 189). Many states were not obeying the order to desegregate bus services after the Montgomery ruling. The freedom riders deliberately rode on buses in the city of Birmingham, Alabama, to highlight this. They faced some of the worst violence of the civil rights campaigns. The SNCC then took up the freedom rides, with the same violent reaction as a result. Two hundred freedom riders were arrested and spent 40 days in jail.

The Governor of Alabama, John Patterson, did little to protect the riders until he was put under pressure from the new US President, John F. Kennedy, to do so. African Americans and their white supporters had shown that they were no longer prepared to be intimidated.

FOCUS TASK

How successful was the struggle for civil rights in the 1950s?

You are a member of the SNCC (the Student Non-violent Coordinating Committee) in June 1961. Someone asks you why you are part of the movement, suggesting that all that you and the other civil rights groups have achieved is a bus ride, getting beaten up and being arrested. Give an answer (either written or verbally) to this criticism. You could mention:

- the practical advances made since the late 1950s (for example, desegregation)
- the moral importance of these advances
- why you believe non-violence is the right tactic
- where you think your protests might go from here.

The March on Washington, 1963

The Civil Rights campaign had made substantial progress during the previous decade, ending segregation in education, shops and on transport. However, there was one issue that was increasingly seen as the most important – that is, for all African Americans to achieve the right to vote and thereby have a legal say in their own destiny. Figure 17 shows why the right to vote was a priority in the Southern states.

Meanwhile, the campaigners kept up the pressure for a civil rights bill. In August 1963, Martin Luther King staged his most high-profile event. Over 200,000 black people and 50,000 white people marched together to the federal capital, Washington. Their stated aim was to pressure President Kennedy to introduce a civil rights bill. There was no trouble at the march, not even any litter. At the rally, King gave his famous 'I have a dream' speech (Source 19). The event had a tremendous impact on American public opinion.

FIGURE 17

African Americans registered to vote in the Southern states of the USA, 1940–66.

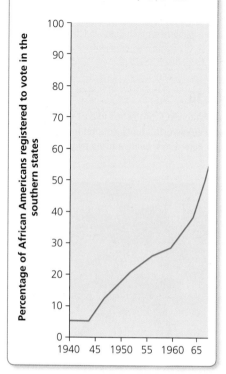

SOURCE 18

The march on Washington, 1963: thousands gather at the Lincoln Memorial.

SOURCE 19

From Martin Luther King's most famous speech, August 1963.

I have a dream that one day this nation will rise up and live out the true meaning of its creed: We hold these truths to be self-evident, that all men are created equal. I have a dream that one day on the red hills of Georgia the sons of former slaves and the sons of former slave owners will be able to sit together at the table of brotherhood. I have a dream that one day even the state of Mississippi, a state sweltering with the heat of injustice … and oppression will be transformed into an oasis of freedom and justice. I have a dream that my four little children will one day live in a nation where they will not be judged by the colour of their skin but the content of their character.

Malcolm X and the Black Power movement

Through the 1960s, at the same time as the campaign for voting rights was taking place, there were other developments within the black communities of the USA. Black nationalism was one. Most black nationalists rejected the non-violence of the civil rights movement. They felt that force was justified in order to achieve equality for African Americans. Others did not want equality so much as complete separation.

One movement that attracted many disillusioned African Americans was the Nation of Islam, headed by Elijah Muhammad. The Nation of Islam attracted figures such as boxer Cassius Clay (who changed his name to Muhammad Ali), who was an outspoken critic of racial discrimination. Another follower of the Nation of Islam was Malcolm Little, better known as Malcolm X. He was critical of Martin Luther King's methods, and believed that the civil rights movement held back black people. He wanted to see African Americans rise up and create their own separate black state in the USA, by force if necessary (see Source 21). Malcolm X was assassinated in 1965.

The SNCC itself became more radical when the black student Stokely Carmichael was elected chairman in 1966. He talked in terms of 'black power'. He set out a radical view of black power and in the process he was critical of Martin Luther King. Typical comments were: 'This nation [the USA] is racist from top to bottom, and does not function by morality, love and non-violence, but by power.'

Even more radical than Carmichael were the Black Panthers. They had around 2,000 members and were a political party but also a small private army. They believed African Americans should arm themselves and force the whites to give them equal rights. They clashed many times with police forces, killing nine police officers between 1967 and 1969.

Race riots from 1965 to 1967

American cities suffered a wave of race riots between 1965 and 1967. These were not the cities of the Southern states where African Americans faced the most obvious discrimination. These were cities in the north and west which had large African-American populations but which were officially free of racism. The cause of riots in most cases was poor relations between the police and African Americans. Most of the USA's cities were divided along race lines. Most of the police forces were white. Many black working-class people who lived in the inner cities felt that they did not get the same protection from crime as whites. They distrusted the police. The most serious of these riots were in the Watts area of Los Angeles in August 1965 and in Detroit in July 1967.

SOURCE 20

A highway patrolman stands guard over protesters after the Watts riots, Los Angeles, 1965. There were an estimated 30,000 rioters in this incident and 34 deaths.

PROFILE

Malcolm X

- Born in 1925 as Malcolm Little, son of a Baptist minister. His father was killed when he was 6.
- Lived in poverty, and became involved in drugs and crime. Imprisoned for burglary.
- Became a Black Muslim while in prison.
- He was keen to support African Americans in their desire for equality. He criticised Martin Luther King's non-violent methods, arguing a more violent approach would bring faster results.

SOURCE 21

Comments by Malcolm X.

The white man has taught the black people in this country to hate themselves as inferior, to hate each other, to be divided against each other. The brainwashed black man can never learn to stand on his own two feet until he is on his own. We must learn to become our own producers, manufacturers and traders; we must have industry of our own, to employ our own. The white man resists this because he wants to keep the black man under his thumb and jurisdiction in white society. He wants to keep the black man always dependent and begging – for jobs, food, clothes, shelter, education. The white man doesn't want to lose somebody to be supreme over.

SOURCE 22

Malcolm X's views on violence in the 1960s.

I am for violence if non-violence means we continue postponing a solution to the American black man's problems. If we must use violence to get the black man his human rights in this country then I am for violence.

What was the impact of Black Power?

There is no doubt that Black Power groups brought to national attention the disillusionment of many African Americans. But did this have a positive or a negative impact in the struggle for civil rights? There is much evidence from the time that the more radical elements of Black Power groups alarmed moderate opinion and alienated many white Americans who might otherwise have been sympathetic towards the civil rights movement. The BLACK POWER MOVEMENT was seen as at least partly responsible for race riots such as those shown in Source 20 on page 191. The Black Power movement was also criticised by some civil rights leaders such as Roy Wilkins because it gave law enforcement authorities the opportunity and the excuse to crack down on all African-American activists.

Not surprisingly the debate continues. As historians rethink and reinterpret the evidence they point out that:

- the Black Power movement has been misrepresented and was much more complex than it was portrayed at the time
- media coverage of Black Power at the time was very misinformed and based more on ignorance and fear than an attempt to understand the movement
- whereas Black Power and the civil rights movements are often portrayed by historians as two separate, divided movements, actually the two strands shared a lot of common ground. Stokely Carmichael and Martin Luther King were quite friendly and agreed on the need to fight poverty (Carmichael offered support for the 1968 Poor People's Campaign). Both were opposed to the Vietnam War. In 1967 King spoke at the SCLC Convention and told the audience to be proud of black pride and black culture.

Civil Rights Acts of the 1960s
The Civil Rights Act, 1964

By 1963 civil rights was without doubt a key national issue. Almost everyone in the USA had a view on it. In November 1963, President Kennedy was assassinated. President Johnson (1963–68) was just as committed to civil rights as Kennedy. On 2 July 1964 he signed the Civil Rights Act. The Act made it illegal for local government to discriminate in areas such as housing and employment.

With the momentum gained from the Civil Rights Act, King and the SCLC continued to encourage African Americans to register to vote. They were helped by young white people from the Northern states who came south in great numbers. In the 20 months that followed the Civil Rights Act, 430,000 African Americans registered to vote.

Selma

After the Civil Rights Act of 1964, King's priority was to get African Americans voting. He deliberately targeted areas where discrimination was worst. In early 1965 he organised a 'voting rights' march through Selma, Alabama. The population of Selma was 29,000 – 15,000 of whom were black adults old enough to vote yet only 335 (just 2.4 per cent) were registered to do so. The town was also notorious for its brutally racist sheriff, Jim Clark. The authorities banned the planned march. However, on 7 March, about 600 people went ahead with the march anyway (without King). They were brutally attacked. The media called it 'Bloody Sunday' and the TV pictures of the violence horrified America. King tried to keep the pressure on and rearranged the march. However, he compromised on 11 March by leading a token march. It turned back after a short distance.

FOCUS TASK

Did the Black Power groups harm the struggle for civil rights?

1 Study the information and sources about the Black Power groups:
   - What positive contributions of Black Power groups can you identify?
   - What examples of harm are mentioned?
2 Did the Black Power movement do more harm than good? Explain your answer.

SOURCE 23

Clayborne Carson, Professor of History at Stanford University, 1994.

Both civil rights and black power leaders were able to gain national prominence most readily by emphasising intangible goals – civil/human rights and increased group pride – rather than tangible, especially economic, goals … Black power proponents and black nationalist leaders challenged civil rights leaders to transform the living conditions of the black masses, but all black leaders found it easier to transform the status and esteem of African Americans than to change racial realities. As a result, the black consciousness movements of the 1960s and 1970s achieved psychological and cultural transformation without having much impact on the living conditions of poor and working-class blacks. The black masses acquired an ideological vocabulary to express their anger and frustration but still lacked the political awareness necessary for effective action.

THINK

In the light of Source 23 and your knowledge, which group do you think did more for the advancement of African Americans?

Voting Rights Act, 1965

King's compromise avoided more violence although it annoyed the more radical activists. However, his restraint probably helped President Johnson to force through a Voting Rights Bill in 1965. The Act allowed government agents to inspect voting procedures to make sure that they were taking place properly. It also ended the literacy tests that voters had previously had to complete before they voted. These had discriminated against poor African Americans in particular.

After 1965 five major cities, including Detroit, Atlanta and Cleveland, all had black mayors. In Selma, African Americans began to register to vote and in the next election Jim Clark lost his job.

The Civil Rights Act, 1968

This dealt with one other aspect of discrimination: housing could not be sold or rented on the basis of race, religion, national origin or sex.

The assassination of Martin Luther King, 1968

In 1968 Martin Luther King was assassinated, probably by a hired killer, although it has never been proven which of King's enemies employed the assassin. King's death marked the end of an era for the civil rights movement. During his life, King had helped to transform the movement from a Southern sideshow to a national movement. Major battles had been fought and won. Segregation was now illegal; the Civil Rights Act had enshrined black civil rights in law; African Americans in the South now held real political power.

But, at the same time, there was a feeling of insecurity and frustration among those who had watched these developments through the 1960s. The law might have changed, but had attitudes changed with it? And what did the future hold?

● America and the 'Great Society'

After eight years of Republican government under President Eisenhower, in 1961 John F. Kennedy was elected as a young Democrat promising changes in society. Even though his presidency was dominated by foreign affairs (the Berlin Wall, the Cuban Missile Crisis), he did initiate many domestic reforms.

After Kennedy's shock assassination in November 1963, Lyndon B. Johnson (LBJ) took over, and he was re-elected in his own right in 1964. Although Johnson lacked the charm of Kennedy, it was during Johnson's time in office that some of Kennedy's planned changes actually came into effect.

The social policies of Presidents Kennedy and Johnson

In 1960, when addressing the Democrat Party, Kennedy set out the idea of a new direction: 'We stand today on the edge of a new Frontier – the Frontier of the 1960s, the Frontier of unknown opportunities and perils …' As part of this new frontier Kennedy got a large number of reforms approved by Congress. These included:

- the extension of unemployment benefit
- more aid to poor cities to improve housing and transportation
- increases in social security benefits
- aid to economically distressed areas
- the expansion of rural electrification programmes providing help to rural farming.

President Johnson inherited what Kennedy had started. Johnson's Great Society laid out his grand ideas to tackle problems of unemployment, bad housing and inadequate medical care. Linked with these, but as a separate item on the agenda, was the question of civil rights (see pages 192–93).

PRACTICE QUESTIONS

1 Describe two ways in which the Civil Rights Acts of the 1960s helped to stop racial discrimination.
2 Which of the following was the more important reason why the civil rights movement made progress in the 1960s?
   - The policies and activities of Martin Luther King
   - The policies and activities of the Black Power movement.

Explain your answer with reference to both reasons.

SOURCE 24

President Johnson outlines his Great Society aims, in a speech in 1965.

I want to be the President who educated young children to the wonders of their world … who helped to feed the hungry and to prepare them to be taxpayers instead of tax-eaters … who helped the poor to find their own way and who protected the right of every citizen to vote in every election … who helped to end hatred among his fellow men and who promoted love among the people of all races and all regions and all parties … who helped to end war among the brothers of the earth.

THINK

Look at the speech in Source 24.

1 Republican politicians hated the state getting involved in people's lives rather than people working to sort out their own problems. Which parts of the speech would Republicans easily accept, and which would they try to oppose?

2 Using the information on this page, including Source 25, consider to what extent Johnson was able to fulfil his dream of the Great Society.

FOCUS TASK

How did the 'Great Society' affect the role of government?

1 Create a spider diagram on the measures passed as a result of the 'Great Society'. In the centre write the words 'The Great Society' and draw a box underneath. Then surround these words with all the measures of the Great Society reforms and their impact.

2 Now complete the box in the centre to describe how the role of government had changed as a result of the Democrats' policies.

Johnson was able to use his political skill to get various reforms through Congress:

- **The Economic Opportunity Act, 1964**: This provided training to disadvantaged youths aged 16–21, and recruited volunteers to work and teach in low-income slum areas.
- **Medicare and Medicaid, 1965**: This provided medical insurance for the over-65s and hospital care for the poor (most Americans have private health insurance).
- **The Development Act, 1964**: Money was provided for replacing inner-city slums with new homes.

There were schemes to help highway safety including compulsory safety measures for cars. There were laws to ensure clean water supplies and better air quality with less pollution.

Overall, however, there was much criticism of the reforms, especially from Republicans who hated the way in which they acted as a brake on people's freedoms. Many poor African Americans still lived in sub-standard housing. Unfortunately what was actually achieved was lost in the growing chorus of publicity about the Vietnam War, about which opinions were increasingly negative. When LBJ decided not to stand for re-election in 1968 he was at the time remembered almost entirely as the President who was responsible for the growing toll of deaths and injuries of American troops in Vietnam.

SOURCE 25

Continuing poverty and a divided society. Families in Harlem, New York, still waiting for their 'dream' in the early eighties.

The development and impact of feminist movements

Women had gained the right to vote after the First World War. The lives of many had been greatly changed during the Second World War with millions taking on new roles. However, in the 1950s it was still accepted by many families, especially in the expanding middle class living in suburbia, that a woman's place was in the home.

The 1960s was a decade for change in attitudes towards women, running parallel with the civil rights movement and protests against the Vietnam War. It is accepted that the symbolic starting point was the publication of *The Feminine Mystique* by Betty Friedan in 1963. She argued that for middle-class women the home had become a concentration camp and that most women wished to break out of this limited environment. The book became a best-seller. The phrase 'women's liberation' began to be used.

The National Organisation for Women, 1966

In 1966 a group of women including Friedan set up the National Organisation for Women (NOW). It adopted a Bill of Rights at its first national conference in 1967.

The fight for equal pay

During the later 1960s many women petitioned, threatened legal action and went on strike to persuade employers to provide equal opportunities and wages. An Equal Pay Act of 1963 had established the principle of equal pay for women doing the same job as men, but there were many exceptions. Some of these were removed in 1972 in the Equal Rights Amendment Act, but there was still agitation for more to be done in order to bring women's average pay above 70 per cent of that of men's.

Roe v *Wade*, 1973

This momentous Supreme Court decision made abortion legal. Abortion was declared to be a fundamental right for women under the US Constitution, but with limitations after the first trimester. This overturned the laws of individual states that had outlawed abortion or severely limited its use.

The Supreme Court decision sparked a huge debate between those in favour of and those opposed to abortion in any circumstances.

Supreme Court ruling on equal rights, 1972

The Supreme Court ruled in 1972 that contraception should be legally available to unmarried couples on the same terms as for married couples. This again caused a moral and religious debate within the nation.

Opposition to Equal Rights Amendment, 1972

The flurry of Acts passed by Congress and decisions made by the Supreme Court led to much debate within the USA (and, indeed, beyond!). So many issues had been imposed by law in areas where individual beliefs and practices could not suddenly change overnight.

Not all women agreed with these changes. Not all were pro-abortionists or in favour of measures which seemed to encourage pre-marital sex. Many women were happy with their status in society, especially if they enjoyed comfortable lifestyles. Many working-class women were not interested in feminism as such – just tangible aspects such as equal pay. Many religious groups, including both men and women, used the Bible to justify male domination in the home and elsewhere.

FACTFILE

The NOW Bill of Rights

1 Equal Rights Constitutional Amendment.
2 Enforce law banning sex discrimination in employment.
3 Maternity leave rights in employment and social security benefits.
4 Tax deduction for home and childcare expenses for working parents.
5 Child daycare centres.
6 Equal and unsegregated education.
7 Equal job training opportunities and allowances for women in poverty.
8 The right of women to control their reproductive lives.

FIGURE 26

Average wages per year, 1965. (Source: US Department of Labour.)

	Men	Women
Factory workers	$5,752	$3,282
Service industries	$4,886	$2,784
Sales staff	$7,083	$3,003
Clerical	$6,220	$4,237
Professional	$8,233	$5,573
Managers, executives	$8,658	$4,516

THINK

Compare the figures in Figure 26. The wages for women were not the same proportion as those for men in different categories of employment. Why do you think this was so?

Which of the following was the more important reason for changes in women's lifestyles in the decades after the Second World War?

- Modern technology in the home
- Changing attitudes towards women's rights.

Explain your answer with reference to both reasons.

FOCUS TASK

What was the impact of feminist movements in the 1960s and 1970s?

1 Look back to the Focus Task on page 181. Read the sentence that you wrote in answer to Question 3, about women's expectations in post-war America. Now read pages 195–96. Do you think these expectations have been met by the feminist movements of the 1960s and 1970s?

2 What new expectations do you think women might have as a result of these new developments?

KEY WORDS

Make sure you know what these words mean and are able to define them confidently:

- American Dream
- Black power movement
- Civil Rights
- Congress
- Depression
- Federal government
- Flappers
- Hire purchase
- Hooverville
- Ku Klux Klan (KKK)
- Mass production
- McCarthyism
- NAACP
- New Deal
- Prohibition
- Red Scare
- Roaring Twenties
- Shares
- Speculation
- Stock market
- Supreme Court
- Tariff

Women also protested against male sexism, which had been accepted as normal. Male institutions such as men's clubs were criticised and in some cases invaded by angry groups of women. Sexist magazines that exploited women were sometimes publically burnt. Some 'women's lib' supporters also criticised traditional women's magazines that were limited to cooking, child rearing and the home. There were well-publicised protests against American beauty contests.

The large protests died down in the 1970s, but there was much more general awareness and a gradual move towards a more equal society. Laws were gradually introduced – for example, in 1972 colleges were required to ensure that opportunities for women were equal to those of men.

SOURCE 27

Women's liberation movement protest, c.1970.

TOPIC SUMMARY

Post-war America

- The USA emerged from the Second World War by far the strongest world power.
- The 'sunny side' of American life in the 1950s focused on the American Dream and the pleasure of consumerism.
- Lifestyles, especially for the young, were changing with developments in popular culture, including pop music and rock and roll.
- Television had an impact in the homes of all those who could afford a set.
- McCarthyism uncovered the dark side of the USA – with witch-hunts carried out against suspected Communists.
- Racial tensions reached their peak in the 1950s and 1960s, with peaceful protests led by Martin Luther King.
- The Black Power movement argued that violence was needed to improve the lot of African Americans.
- African Americans gained basic rights in law with the Civil Rights Acts of the 1960s.
- The 'Great Society' promises of Kennedy and Johnson were partly overtaken by expenditure on the Vietnam War.
- Women gained more rights and the age of 'women's lib' was born.

ASSESSMENT FOCUS

Your exam will include six questions on this topic. The question types will be the same every year, but the questions could be on any content from the specification, so you need to know it all!

We have provided one example of each kind of question. For questions based on interpretations we have used interpretations that you have already come across in this chapter. We have analysed each of the questions to highlight what you are being asked to do and written a sample answer with comments on how it could be improved.

Read Interpretations A and B and then answer questions 1–3. Interpretation A is Interpretation A, page 177. Interpretation B is Interpretation B, page 177.

Q1 How does Interpretation B **differ** from Interpretation A about the New Deal?

Explain your answer **based on what it says in Interpretations A and B**. (4 marks)

Sample answer

Interpretation A claims that the New Deal was a huge success in providing relief for its poor citizens. Interpretation B argues that the New Deal wasted lots of money and reduced people's traditional liberties.

Q2 Why might the authors of Interpretations A and B have **a different interpretation** about the New Deal?

Explain your answer using **Interpretations A and B** and your **contextual knowledge**. (4 marks)

Sample answer

Interpretation A is taken from a magazine article which seeks to praise the New Deal for its achievements. On the other hand Interpretation B is written by an opponent of Roosevelt and is leading the Republican opposition in the Senate to New Deal policies.

Q3 Which interpretation gives the **more convincing opinion** about the New Deal?

Explain your answer based on your **contextual knowledge** and what it says in **Interpretations A and B**. (8 marks)

Sample answer

Interpretation A does highlight some positives about the New Deal. Relief was provided by the Federal Government via various agencies; jobs were provided via agencies such as the PWA and WPA. The Social Security Act promised state pensions for the elderly and widows. But the passage does not admit that the New Deal failed to solve unemployment which was still at 6 million in 1941.

Interpretation B gives no credit to the New Deal at all. It sees state intervention as stifling private enterprise and argues that this hindered the economy recovery. The Republican Party believed in laissez faire. Interpretation A has some merit, whereas Interpretation B only has merit if you believe in those Republican policies.

KEY

Focus words

Command words

Interpretation/knowledge reminder words

– This answer provides a basic comparison between A and B, but it needs to provide more detailed evidence.

– You need to be able to explain the differences in the content of the interpretations.

– *What extra evidence could you add to highlight the differences more completely?*

– This answer provides a good basis for development, but it needs more analysis of the provenance. For example, you could explain more about the implications of the title of each book. The authors will be writing from different perspectives. So make sure you think about how the writer has selected the information he has at his disposal.

– Also think about the time that each interpretation comes from. Neither could judge the New Deal with any perspective (1940 and 1941) before the USA was officially involved in the Second World War. The total recovery of the economy in the war allowed the New Deal's successes and failures to be seen in perspective.

– *Write two sentences for each interpretation on the provenance of each. You should focus on the purpose and attitudes of the two authors.*

– This answer provides a quite good analysis of the two interpretations through the use of some factual knowledge. You could usefully extend it further to argue in more depth.

– However, it is important that the knowledge is used as part of the analysis of the content of the interpretation, rather than being 'free-standing' as 'what I know about the topic'.

– *Think about the tone and language of each interpretation. What words and phrases could you use to describe them? Does one seem more objective than the other?*

– This brief answer introduces two problems, but they are only stated, and so need to be more fully described.

– List TWO details that you could add to EACH of the two short paragraphs above in order to make the description more precise.

Q4 Describe two problems faced by many American farmers during **the Depression of the 1930s**. (4 marks)

Sample answer

Because of the Depression many Americans could not afford to buy, so demand went down and so did prices.

Also some American farmers suffered the consequences of the dust bowl in the 1930s.

Q5 In what ways were the lives of American women affected by the development of feminist movements in **the 1960s and early 1970s**?

Explain your answer. (8 marks)

Sample answer

– This answer mentions several aspects of how American women were affected. However, they could be presented with more factual detail, rather than just short statements.

– Write a list of details that could be included to back up the main points in the answer.

In the 1960s and early 1970s American women were affected by substantial social changes. The period of the 1960s was one of protest and fights for equality, with the creation of the National Organization for Women. This organisation fought for women to be equal in pay, in employment, in education and training. There was the fight for women to have the right to contraception and abortion. Much of this was achieved in law with the Supreme Court ruling on equal rights. Not all women, however, agreed with these legal changes.

Q6 Which of the following was the **more important reason** for the ending of Prohibition in 1933?
- The failure of law enforcement against illegal speakeasies
- The violence of the gangsters controlling the illegal trade in alcohol

Explain your answer with reference to **both reasons**. (12 marks)

Sample answer

– The answer attempts to evaluate both bullet points in turn, and it does reach a judgement which is outlined clearly. It would be possible for the answer to include a little more substance on each bullet point and for the concluding paragraph to be more developed.

– Working backwards, read through the essay again and write out the plan that it must have been based on. You can then look at the plan and see why it was the starting point for this comprehensive answer.

Prohibition was introduced in 1920 with considerable support. After all, many states had voted for it before the First World War and Congress voted for it afterwards. Yet by the late 1920s there was increasing pressure, especially in urban areas, for 'the noble experiment' to be ended.

One reason was the failure of law enforcement. Bootleggers found it easy to smuggle alcohol into the country from Canada, Mexico and the Caribbean. People also set up illegal stills to manufacture whiskey, and these were difficult to detect. There were only a few hundred officers appointed by the Federal Government, and, although some worked really hard and adopted elaborate disguises (e.g. Izzy Einstein and Mo Smith), many others were easily bribed to turn a blind eye. In some areas police officers and judges were also corrupt and in the pay of the criminals. Even in the White House under President Harding alcohol was routinely drunk.

But people also saw the violence that prohibition encouraged. The illegal trade in alcohol was extremely profitable, and rival gangs vied to control the business in each large city. The worst city was Chicago with hundreds of gangland murders and no arrests. The most famous boss, Al Capone, built up a huge network of corrupt officials, including the city's mayor. The worst outbreak of violence came in 1929 when Al Capone's gang murdered seven of his rival Bugs Moran's gang.

Now write your own answers to the questions on pages 197–98 using the teacher's feedback to help you.

It was this event in 1929 that shocked people so much that calls quickly intensified for an end to prohibition, and therefore this was the more important reason. If there had been no violence, many Americans would have been content to carry on drinking in spite of the law.

Conflict and Tension, 1894–1918

5

This depth study focuses on the causes, nature and conclusion of the First World War. The war brought huge changes to society, to politics and to the economies of leading world powers. When the war started, no one had any idea how devastating it would be.

You will be studying the following:

- How and why the alliance systems developed before the war.
- How and why the crisis of the assassination of Archduke Franz Ferdinand led to war.
- The stalemate of the First World War and the key battles on the Western Front.
- The war on other fronts, including the war at sea and its importance.
- How and why the war came to an end in 1918.
- The abdication of the Kaiser and the armistice.

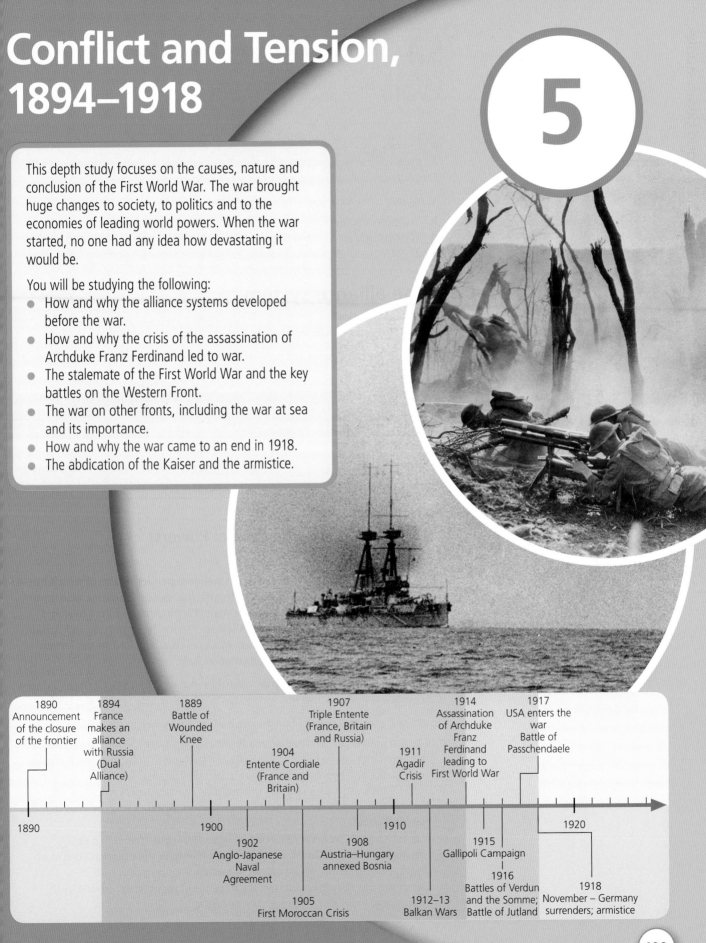

1890 Announcement of the closure of the frontier

1894 France makes an alliance with Russia (Dual Alliance)

1889 Battle of Wounded Knee

1904 Entente Cordiale (France and Britain)

1907 Triple Entente (France, Britain and Russia)

1911 Agadir Crisis

1914 Assassination of Archduke Franz Ferdinand leading to First World War

1917 USA enters the war Battle of Passchendaele

1890

1900

1902 Anglo-Japanese Naval Agreement

1908 Austria–Hungary annexed Bosnia

1910

1915 Gallipoli Campaign

1920

1916 Battles of Verdun and the Somme; Battle of Jutland

1905 First Moroccan Crisis

1912–13 Balkan Wars

1918 November – Germany surrenders; armistice

5.1 The causes of the First World War

FOCUS

No major war had engulfed Europe, let alone the world, since the Battle of Waterloo in 1815. The alliance systems which were designed to prevent war in fact did the exact opposite.

In this part of the topic you will study the following:

- The alliance systems and how they formed two rival camps by 1914.
- The development of Anglo-German rivalry and whether war was inevitable by 1914.
- The reasons for the outbreak of war, and the extent to which Germany was to blame.

● The alliance system

Nationalism, patriotism, jingoism, rivalries, suspicions and personal ambitions of rulers: all these and more explain the causes of the First World War.

By 1914 the six most powerful nations in Europe were divided into two opposing armed camps:

The Triple Alliance (Central Powers) Formed 1882	Triple Entente Formed 1907
Germany	Britain
Austria–Hungary	France
Italy	Russia

The Triple Alliance (the Central Powers)

Germany

Before 1870 Germany was a collection of small independent states of which Prussia was the most powerful. In 1870–71 the Prussian statesman Bismarck won a war against France, after which he united the many German states into a new and powerful German empire. Germany took from France the important industrial area of Alsace-Lorraine and, to guard against a revenge attack from the French, formed an alliance with Austria–Hungary and Italy.

The new Germany was especially successful in industry. By 1914 German industry had overtaken Britain's and was second in the world only to that of the USA.

However, Germany's leaders had greater ambitions, as well as concerns:

- The German KAISER felt that Germany should be a world power and should have overseas colonies and an empire just as France and Britain had. The Germans had established two colonies in Africa, but they wanted more.
- In the 1890s the Kaiser ordered the building of a large navy, which soon became the world's second most powerful fleet. Britain's was the largest and most powerful.
- German leaders were very worried by what they called 'encirclement'. Friendship between Russia to the east and France to the west was seen as an attempt to 'surround' and threaten Germany.
- Germany was also concerned by the huge build-up of arms, especially in Russia, and was itself building up a vast army.

FIGURE 1

The Triple Alliance and the Triple Entente, 1914.

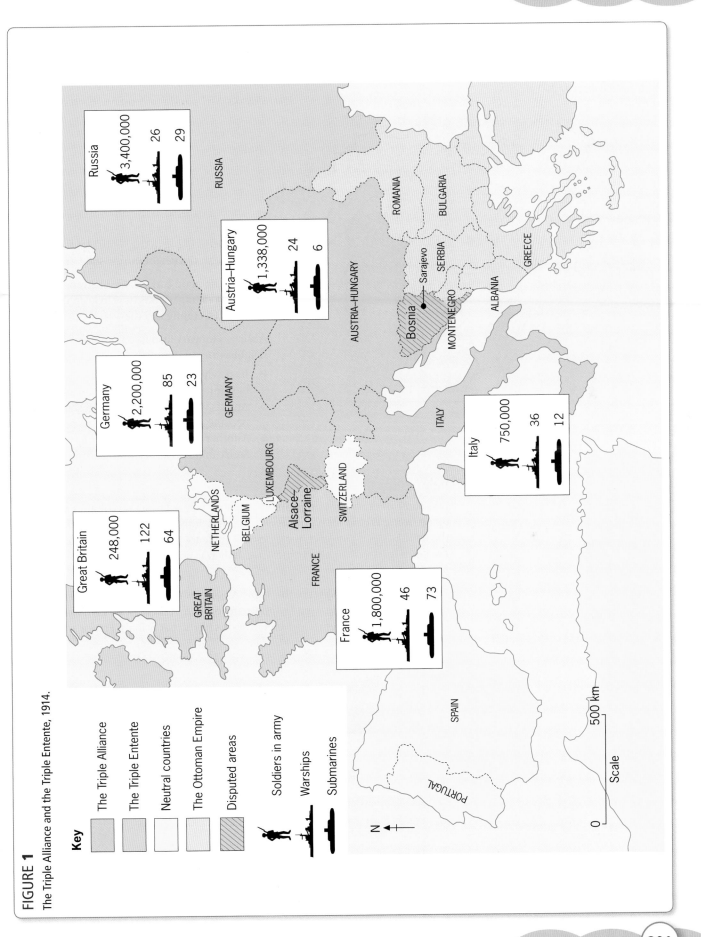

Key

- The Triple Alliance
- The Triple Entente
- Neutral countries
- The Ottoman Empire
- Disputed areas

- Soldiers in army
- Warships
- Submarines

Russia
3,400,000
26
29

Austria–Hungary
1,338,000
24
6

Germany
2,200,000
85
23

Great Britain
248,000
122
64

Italy
750,000
36
12

France
1,800,000
46
73

Scale
0   500 km

N

FIGURE 2

Austria–Hungary's empire, showing the many different nationalities it contained. The thick dotted line shows the division between the lands administered by the Austrians and those by the Hungarians.

Austria–Hungary

Austria–Hungary was a sprawling empire in central Europe. It was made up of people of different ethnic groups: Germans, Czechs, Slovaks, Serbs and many others. Each group had its own customs and language. Many of these groups wanted independence from Austria–Hungary:

- In the north the Czech people wanted to rule themselves.
- The Slav people in the south-west (especially the Croats) wanted their own state.
- The Serbs living in the south wanted to be joined to the neighbouring state of Serbia.

By 1914 the main concern of the Emperor of Austria–Hungary was how to keep this fragmented empire together.

Austria–Hungary also faced problems from neighbouring states:

- Its newly independent neighbour Serbia was becoming a powerful force in the Balkans. Austria was very anxious that it should not become any stronger.
- Another neighbour, Russia, supported the Serbs, and had a very strong army.

Italy

Like some of the other European powers, Italy wanted to set up colonies and build up an overseas empire. With this aim in mind, Italy joined Germany and Austria in the TRIPLE ALLIANCE. However, there is some evidence that Germany and Austria did not entirely trust their ally. In any case, Italy was not a strong industrial or military power.

The most important aspect of the Triple Alliance was an agreement that each member of the Alliance would support any other member if it was attacked. Although this agreement was secret, it seems likely that Britain, France and Russia knew about it by 1914.

ACTIVITY

1   Copy and complete the table below for these countries at the start of 1914.

	Strengths	Weaknesses
Germany		
Austria–Hungary		
Italy		

2   Do you think that preserving peace was a priority for these countries?

The Triple Entente

Britain

In the nineteenth century Britain had tried not to get involved in European politics. Its attitude became known as 'SPLENDID ISOLATION' as it concentrated on its huge overseas empire (see Figure 4 on page 204). For most of the nineteenth century, Britain had regarded France and Russia as its two most dangerous rivals. However, by the early 1900s the picture had begun to change.

There were three main reasons why Britain changed its attitude to Europe:

- France and Britain had reached a number of agreements about colonies in North Africa in 1904.
- Russia was defeated in a war against Japan in 1904–05. This weakened Russia so that Britain was less concerned about it.
- Above all, Britain was very worried about Germany. The German Kaiser had made it clear that he wanted Germany to have an empire and a strong navy, which Britain saw as a serious threat to its own empire and navy.

Britain began to co-operate more with France and signed an agreement with it in 1904. Britain signed another agreement with Russia in 1907. These agreements did not commit Britain to joining France and Russia if war broke out but it seemed unlikely that Britain would stay out of a war if it did happen.

France

France had been defeated by Germany in a short war in 1870–71. Since then, Germany had built up a powerful army and strong industries. It had an ambitious leader in Kaiser Wilhelm. France was worried about the growing power of Germany, so the French had also built up their industries and armies. France had also developed a strong and close friendship with Russia. As far back as 1892 Russia and France had established a secret military alliance. Each side promised to help the other if it was attacked by Germany.

The main concerns of France were:

- to protect itself against attack by Germany
- to get back the rich industrial region of Alsace-Lorraine which Germany had taken from it in 1871.

Russia

Russia was by far the largest of all the six powers, but was also the most backward. The country was almost entirely agricultural, although loans from France had helped Russia to develop some industries.

Russia shared France's worries about the growing power of Germany. It also had a long history of rivalry with Austria–Hungary. This was one reason why Russia was so friendly with Serbia. Another reason was that both Russians and Serbs were Slavs. Many other Slavs lived in Austria–Hungary's empire. Russia felt it should have influence over them.

Russia lost a war with Japan in 1905. There was then a revolution against the ruler, Tsar Nicholas II. He survived, but he knew Russia could not afford to lose in any other conflict. The Russians began to build up a large army in case of emergencies in the future.

ACTIVITY

1 Add Britain, France and Russia to your table on page 202. Complete the table for those countries in 1914.
2 Do you think that preserving peace was a priority for Britain, France or Russia?

FIGURE 3
European alliances in 1914.

FIGURE 4

The overseas empires of the European powers in 1914.

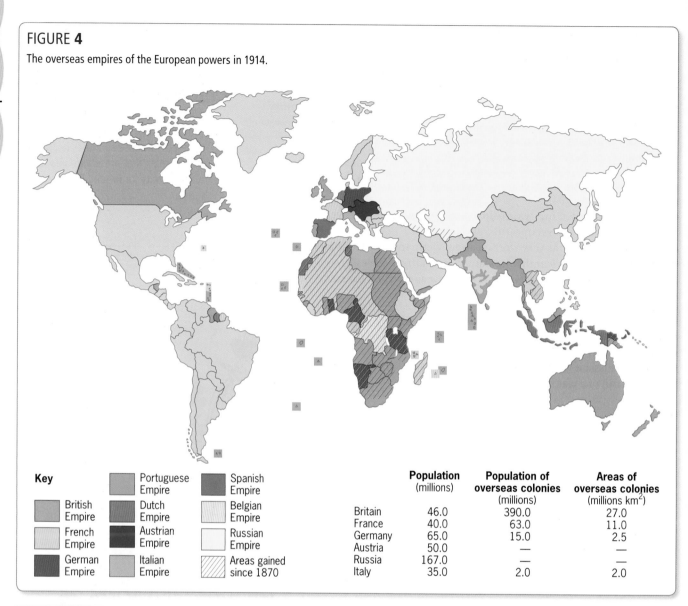

Key					Population (millions)	Population of overseas colonies (millions)	Areas of overseas colonies (millions km^2)
British Empire	Portuguese Empire	Spanish Empire	Britain		46.0	390.0	27.0
French Empire	Dutch Empire	Belgian Empire	France		40.0	63.0	11.0
German Empire	Austrian Empire	Russian Empire	Germany		65.0	15.0	2.5
Italian Empire	Areas gained since 1870		Austria		50.0	—	—
			Russia		167.0	—	—
			Italy		35.0	2.0	2.0

FOCUS TASK

Why was Europe divided into two armed camps by 1914?

Imagine it is 1914. An American visitor is staying with you. On the boat across the Atlantic he has been reading in the newspapers about the various alliances between the European powers. He is struggling to understand the alliances and generally thinks they are a bad idea. Your task is to explain to him how and why the alliances have come about and what they were trying to achieve. Work in stages:

1 Use the table below to gather your thoughts and ideas.

The Triple Alliance		
Members	**Main concerns**	**Why it made sense to be in this alliance**
Germany		
Austria–Hungary		
Italy		
The Triple Entente		
Members	**Main concerns**	**Why it made sense to be in this alliance**
Britain		
France		
Russia		

2 Now try to explain the alliances to your American visitor without looking at your table.

● Anglo-German rivalry

Britain increasingly saw Germany as the main threat to its position as the dominant power in the world and to its policy of Splendid Isolation. This meant that Britain had avoided international alliances which might have dragged the country into major wars. However, Germany's attempt to gain extra colonies around the world was bound to increase tensions between the two countries. A threat to British supremacy from Germany would cause tensions between the countries over trade – Germany was Britain's main trading partner in Europe – and over the monarchies, as Kaiser Wilhelm II was the nephew of King Edward VII (1901–10) and cousin of George V (1910–36).

Kaiser Wilhelm II's aims in foreign policy

You have already seen on page 200 that Germany's leader, Kaiser Wilhelm II, was determined that Germany should play an increasingly important role on the world stage. His policy of *weltpolitik* was designed to ensure that aggressive diplomacy would lead to the acquisition of more colonies, backed by the development of a large navy.

In the 1960s the German historian Fritz Fischer studied the Kaiser's letters and documents and concluded that he had wanted to replace Britain as the leading power in Europe and hoped to dominate Russia by building up a powerful alliance of countries in central Europe. Not all historians accept this view. Other historians point to the fact that the Kaiser felt Germany was encircled by enemies. However, most historians do agree that the Kaiser's unstable personality (see Profile) and actions increased tension in Europe in the period 1900–14.

> ### SOURCE 5
>
> Extract from *Germany's War Aims in the First World War* by the German historian Fritz Fischer, published in 1966.
>
> *Germany's foreign policy was based on a desire for growth. Sometimes it was friendly and based on reaching an agreement, at other times it was aggressive, but the final aim was always the expansion of German power and land.*

Anglo-German naval rivalry

One of the Kaiser's most significant actions was to announce his intention to build a powerful navy for Germany.

Britain felt very threatened by this. Germany's navy was much smaller than Britain's but the British navy was spread all over the world, protecting the British Empire. Germany didn't have much of an empire. Why did it need a navy? What was Germany going to do with all of these warships concentrated in the North Sea?

Not surprisingly, Germany did not see things the same way. The Kaiser and his admirals felt that Germany needed a navy to protect its growing trade. They felt that the British were over-reacting to the German naval plans.

Britain was not convinced by what the Germans said. In fact, in 1906 Britain raised the stakes in the naval race by launching HMS *Dreadnought*, the first of a new class of warships. Germany responded by building its own 'Dreadnoughts'. The naval race was well and truly on and both Britain and Germany spent millions on their new ships.

Kaiser Wilhelm II

- Born in 1861, with a badly withered left arm. Historians also think he suffered slight brain damage at birth, which affected both his hearing and his attention span.
- He did not have a loving family.
- He became Kaiser at the age of 27 when German industry was growing fast and Germany was becoming a world power.
- He was famous for his energy and enthusiasm, but he was also very unpredictable.
- He was keen on military parades and liked to be photographed wearing his military uniform. He appointed military people to most of the important positions in his government.
- He was very ambitious for Germany. He wanted Germany to be recognised as the greatest power in Europe by the older European states.
- He liked physical exercise and practical jokes.
- He was very closely involved in Germany's plans for war.
- When Germany was defeated in 1918 he fled into exile. He died in 1941.

SOURCE 6

Sir Edward Grey, British Foreign Secretary, in a speech to Parliament in 1909.

There is no comparison between the importance of the German navy to Germany, and the importance of our navy to us. Our navy is to us what their army is to them. To have a strong navy would increase Germany's prestige and influence, but it is not a matter of life and death to them as it is to us.

SOURCE 7

Kaiser Wilhelm, speaking in an interview with the *Daily Telegraph* in 1908. The Kaiser liked England and had friends there as well as being closely related to the English monarchy.

You English are like mad bulls; you see red everywhere! What on earth has come over you, that you should heap on such suspicion? What can I do more? I have always stood up as a friend of England.

SOURCE 8

HMS *Barham*, a British 'Dreadnought', with the British fleet in Scapa Flow.

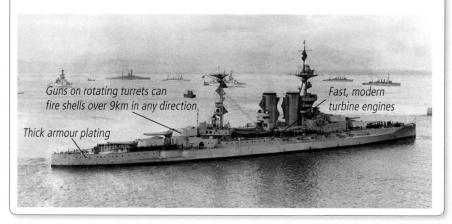

Guns on rotating turrets can fire shells over 9km in any direction

Fast, modern turbine engines

Thick armour plating

SOURCE 9

James Joll, *Origins of the First World War*, 1992. Joll is a well-respected British historian with expert knowledge of this topic.

The arms race in which all the major powers were involved contributed to the sense that war was bound to come, and soon. Financing it caused serious financial difficulties for all the governments involved in the race; and yet they were convinced there was no way of stopping it.

Although publicly the arms race was justified to prevent war, no government had in fact been deterred from arming by the programmes of their rivals, but rather increased the pace of their own armament production.

FIGURE 10

Number of 'Dreadnoughts' built by Britain and Germany, 1906–14.

Year		
1906	⛴	
1907	⛴ ⛴ ⛴	
1908	⛴ ⛴	⛴ ⛴ ⛴ ⛴
1909	⛴	⛴ ⛴ ⛴
1910	⛴ ⛴ ⛴	⛴
1911	⛴ ⛴ ⛴ ⛴	⛴ ⛴
1912	⛴	⛴ ⛴
1913	⛴ ⛴ ⛴ ⛴ ⛴	⛴ ⛴
1914	⛴ ⛴	⛴

Britain — Total built by 1914: 29   Germany — Total built by 1914: 17

SOURCE 11

From the diary of Admiral von Muller, head of the Kaiser's naval cabinet, December 1912.

General von Moltke said: I believe war is unavoidable; war the sooner the better. But we ought to do more through the press to prepare the population for a war against Russia … the enemies are arming more strongly than we are.

In Germany, in particular, war and militarism were glorified. The Kaiser surrounded himself with military advisers. He staged military rallies and processions. He loved to be photographed in military uniforms. He involved himself closely in Germany's military planning.

THINK

1 Why was Britain concerned by Germany's naval plans?
2 How did Germany react to Britain's concerns?
3 Do you think that either country was acting unreasonably? Give your reasons.

PRACTICE QUESTIONS

1 Study Source 11.
   Source 11 says that Germany will have to fight a war. How do you know?
   Explain your answer by using Source 11 and your contextual knowledge.

2 Study Sources 6 and 8.
   How useful are Sources 6 and 8 for studying the naval ARMS RACE between Britain and Germany?
   Explain your answer by using Sources 6 and 8 and your contextual knowledge.

European rearmament

Around Europe, countries were building up the size of their armies. It was argued that this was for defence in case of attack by members of the opposing alliance. In fact, countries were afraid that war was bound to happen at some point and therefore it was important to be prepared.

Germany

Germany's army was not the biggest army in Europe but most people agreed it was the best trained and the most powerful.

The problem facing the German commanders was that if a war broke out they would probably have to fight against Russia and France at the same time. The Germans came up with the SCHLIEFFEN PLAN. Under this plan they would quickly attack and defeat France, then turn their forces on Russia which (the Germans were sure) would be slow to get its troops ready for war.

Austria–Hungary

Austria–Hungary knew it needed the help of Germany to hold back Russia. It too relied on the success of the Schlieffen Plan so that Germany could help it to defeat Russia.

Russia

The Russian army was badly equipped, but it was huge. Given enough time, Russia could eventually put millions of soldiers into the field. The Russian plan was to overwhelm Germany's and Austria's armies by sheer weight of numbers.

France

France had a large and well-equipped army. Its main plan of attack was known as Plan 17. French troops would charge across the frontier and attack deep into Germany, forcing surrender.

Britain

Britain's military planners had been closely but secretly involved in collaboration with French commanders. This led to Britain setting up the British Expeditionary Force (BEF), consisting of 150,000 highly trained and well-equipped professional soldiers. The BEF could go to France and fight alongside the French at short notice.

What unites all of these plans was the assumption that a war, if it came, would be quick. No one planned for the war dragging on. It was assumed that none of the powers would be able to keep up a long, drawn-out war. The sheer cost of a war would lead to economic collapse (of the enemy only, of course) and so the war would be over in a matter of weeks or months.

With so much talk of war, you might think, as many at the time did, that war was inevitable.

SOURCE 12

From *Howard's End*, a widely read novel by E. M. Forster, published in 1910.

The remark 'England and Germany are bound to fight' makes war a little more likely each time it is made, and is therefore made more often by the gutter press of each nation.

FIGURE 13

Military personnel of the powers, 1900–14 (excluding reserves). While Britain and Germany built up their navies, the major powers on mainland Europe were also building up their armies.

	1900	1910	1914
France	0.7m	0.8m	0.9m
Britain	0.6m	1.3m	0.5m
Russia	1.1m	1.3m	0.8m
Austria–Hungary	0.25m	0.3m	0.35m
Germany	0.5m	0.7m	1.5m
Italy	0.25m	0.3m	0.35m

SOURCE 14

Written by Gottlieb von Jagow, the German Foreign Secretary, May 1914. He was writing this from memory, soon after the end of the war.

In Moltke's opinion there was no alternative to making preventive war in order to defeat the enemy while we still had a chance of victory … I pointed out that the Kaiser … would only agree to fight if our enemies forced war upon us…

THINK

1   Read Source 14. What do you think the writer means by 'preventive war'?
2   Does either Source 11 or 14 suggest that people in Germany wanted a war?
3   Source 12 comes from a novel. In what ways is it useful as evidence about the mood in Britain before the First World War?

Pre-war crises and their effects on international relations

Morocco, 1905 and 1911

In 1905 and 1911, two crises in Morocco raised the temperature in Europe.

In 1905 the Kaiser visited Morocco in North Africa. Germany was building up its own African empire and had colonies in central and southern Africa (see Figure 4 on page 204). The Kaiser was now keen to show that Germany was an important power in North Africa as well. The French had plans to take control of Morocco so the Kaiser made a speech saying he supported independence for Morocco. The French were furious at his interfering in their affairs. An international conference was held in Algeciras in 1906. But the conference did not cool things down. In fact, it did the opposite: at the conference the Kaiser was humiliated. He had wanted to be seen as a major power in Africa. Instead his views were rejected. He was treated as if he had no right to speak on such matters. This made him bitter. He was also alarmed by the way that Britain and France stuck together at the conference to oppose him. These old rivals now seemed very close.

In 1907, in the wake of the Moroccan crisis, Britain and France formed an alliance with Russia, the Triple Entente (see page 203). The ENTENTE POWERS saw their alliance as security against German aggression. The Kaiser saw a threatening policy of encirclement, with hostile powers surrounding Germany.

In 1911 Morocco saw another crisis. The French tried to take over Morocco again. They said they were prepared to compensate Germany if its trade suffered as a result. However, the Kaiser's response was to send a gunboat (the *Panther*) to Agadir. The British feared that the Kaiser wanted to set up a naval base in Agadir, and they did not want German ships in the Mediterranean. Another conference was called. The British and French again stood firm against Germany. France took control of Morocco. Germany was given land in central Africa as compensation. Behind the scenes, Britain and France reached an agreement that the French should patrol the Mediterranean and the Royal Navy should defend France's Atlantic and North Sea coasts.

The Balkans: Bosnia, 1908

The Balkans were a very unstable area. The area had been ruled by Turkey for many centuries, with many different nationalities mixed together. Turkish power was now in decline. The new governments which had been set up in place of Turkish rule were regularly in dispute with each other. To make matters more serious, Russia and Austria bordered the countries in this region. Both wanted to control this area because it gave them access to the Mediterranean.

The first Balkan crisis came in 1908. Austria took over the provinces of Bosnia and Herzegovina. Russia and Serbia protested, but they backed down when Germany made it clear that it supported Austria. Neither Russia nor Serbia was prepared to risk war with Germany over this issue. However, there were some serious consequences in 1914.

THINK

1   How did the actions of the Kaiser in the Moroccan crises affect the policies of Britain, France and Russia?
2   How did the actions of Britain, France and Russia over Morocco affect the Kaiser?

PRACTICE QUESTION

Write an account of how events in Morocco in 1911 became an international crisis.

FOCUS TASK

At the beginning of 1914 was major European conflict inevitable?

Imagine you are an American journalist who has started work for an English newspaper. It is early 1914.

1   Using pages 205–08, make *brief* notes on the developments that have taken place in Europe between 1900 and early 1914.
2   Use your notes to write an article explaining whether or not you think that the alliance systems that are now in place are likely to lead to a major war involving all the European powers. Your article must be no longer than 250 words.

● The outbreak of war

The assassination of Archduke Franz Ferdinand and its consequences

SOURCE 15

Adapted from *Britain at War* by Craig Mair, 1982.

Sunday 28 June 1914 was a bright and sunny day in Sarajevo. Sarajevo in Bosnia was preparing for a royal visit from Archduke Franz Ferdinand of Austria [see Source 16]. Crowds lined the streets and waited for the procession of cars to appear. Hidden among the crowds, however, were six teenage [Bosnian Serb] terrorists sworn to kill the Archduke. They hated him and they hated Austria. They were stationed at intervals along the riverside route which the cars would follow on their way to the Town Hall. They all had bombs and pistols in their pockets, and phials of poison which they had promised to swallow if they were caught, so that they would not give the others away. It seemed as if the plan could not fail.

Finally, the cavalcade of four large cars came into sight. The Archduke was in a green open-topped car. He looked every inch a duke, wearing a pale blue uniform, a row of glittering medals and a military hat decorated with green ostrich feathers. Beside him sat his wife Sophie, looking beautiful in a white dress and a broad hat and waving politely to the crowd.

At 10.15 the cars passed Mehmedbasic, the first in line of the waiting killers. He took fright, did nothing, and then escaped. The next assassin, Cabriolvic, also lost his nerve and did nothing. But then as the cars passed the Cumurja Bridge, Cabrinovic threw his bomb, swallowed his poison, and jumped into the river. The Archduke saw the bomb coming and threw it off his car, but it exploded under the car behind, injuring several people. Now there was total confusion as the procession accelerated away, fearing more bombs. Meanwhile the police dragged Cabrinovic out of the river. His cyanide was old and had not worked.

The Archduke was driven to the Town Hall, where he demanded to be taken to visit the bomb victims in hospital. Fearing more terrorists, the officials decided to take a new route to avoid the crowds, but this was not properly explained to the driver of the Archduke's car. Moreover, no police guard went with the procession.

Meanwhile the other assassins, on hearing the bomb explode, assumed the Archduke was dead and left – all except Princip, who soon discovered the truth. Miserably he wandered across the street towards Schiller's delicatessen and café.

Princip was standing outside the café when, at 10.45, the Archduke's car suddenly appeared beside him and turned into Franz Josef Street. This was a mistake, for according to the new plan the procession should have continued straight along the Appel Quay. As the driver realised he had taken a wrong turn he stopped and started to reverse. Princip could hardly believe his luck. Pulling an automatic pistol from the right-hand pocket of his coat, he fired two shots at a range of just 3 or 4 metres. He could not miss. One bullet pierced the Archduke's neck and the other ricocheted off the car into Sophie's stomach. Fifteen minutes later she died and the Archduke followed soon after.

Princip was immediately seized. He managed to swallow his poison, but it did not work and he was taken off to prison. All the plotters except Mehmedbasic were eventually caught, but only the organiser, Ilic, was hanged, for the others were too young for the death penalty. Princip died in an Austrian jail, however, in April 1918, aged 23.

SOURCE 16

The Archduke Franz Ferdinand and his wife Sophie arrive in Sarajevo. The Archduke was heir to the throne of Austria, whose powerful empire covered much of central Europe (see page 202).

> **THINK**
>
> There were many moments during 28 June 1914 when events could have turned out differently. Study the account of the murders in Source 15 and list any moments at which a different decision might have saved the lives of the Archduke and his wife.

At his trial, Princip said: 'I am not a criminal, for I destroyed a bad man. I thought I was right.' Two years later he said that if he had known what was to follow he would never have fired the two fatal shots – but his regret was too late. Within six weeks of the Archduke's ASSASSINATION, almost all of Europe had been dragged into the bloodiest war in history.

Slav nationalism and the effect on relations between Serbia and Austria–Hungary

Most people in Europe assumed that the terrible assassination was just a local issue involving Austria–Hungary and Serbia. However, following the successful takeover of Bosnia in 1908, Austria now felt confident that Germany would support it in future disputes. Some historians think that this made Austria too confident, and encouraged Austria to make trouble with Serbia and Russia. Russia resented being faced down in 1909. It quickened its arms build-up. It was determined not to back down again. From 1912 to 1913 there was a series of local wars. Serbia emerged from these as the most powerful country in the Balkans. This was very serious for Austria. Serbia had a strong army and it was a close ally of Russia.

An extra dimension in this unstable area was nationalism. Serbia, like Russia, was predominantly Slav in its nationality. The strong nationalist beliefs within Austria assumed that Slav culture was inferior. Austria believed that the hugely diverse Austrian-Hungarian Empire, containing many different languages, ethnic groups and cultures, was destined to stay intact and dominate central and south-eastern Europe.

Austria decided that Serbia would have to be dealt with. By 1914 Austria was looking for a good excuse to crush Serbia. Some of the politicians in Austria–Hungary were determined to make an example of Serbia. This feeling was encouraged by the news that Germany promised to support Austria–Hungary. Serbia did not want war; the country was recovering from the Balkan Wars of the previous two years.

The July Crisis

On 23 July Austria–Hungary sent a ten-point ultimatum to Serbia. Serbia, keen to avoid war, accepted nine of the points, but could not accept the remaining one without losing control of its justice system. Serbia even offered to refer that point to the International Court at The Hague, thinking this would certainly be sufficient to placate Austria–Hungary.

However, the Austrians, with the promise of German support, felt confident in acting against Serbia. War was declared on 28 July.

This declaration of war triggered off the alliances. Russia was determined to support Serbia, and on 30 July began to mobilise (get its forces ready for war) against Austria–Hungary and Germany. Germany then declared war on Russia on 1 August.

At this crucial stage, only eastern Europe was involved. However, the Schlieffen Plan was responsible for it spreading to the west.

The Schlieffen Plan and Belgium

When France and Russia had signed an alliance in the 1890s, Germany became concerned about the possibility of war on two fronts – east and west. In 1905 the head of the army, von Schlieffen, decided that the best way to solve the problem was to attack the French first and defeat them within six weeks. The attack would go through neutral Belgium and Holland (where the French would not expect it) rather than Alsace-Lorraine. In fact, the plan was revised to only go through Belgium. Russia would take a long time to mobilise, so there would be plenty of time to move German troops to the east before the Russians could launch a major attack. The whole plan relied on the swift defeat of France.

FIGURE 17

The intended route of the Schlieffen Plan.

HOLLAND
BRITAIN
BELGIUM
GERMANY
LUXEMBOURG
● Paris
French Fortress Towns
FRANCE
SWITZERLAND

SOURCE 18

Winston Churchill later described the scene in London as war was declared. From his book, *The World Crisis*, published in 1923.

It was eleven o'clock at night – twelve by German time – when the ultimatum expired. The windows of the Admiralty were thrown wide open in the warm night air. Under the roof from which Nelson had received his orders were gathered a small group of admirals and captains and a cluster of clerks, pencils in hand, waiting. Along the Mall from the direction of the Palace the sound of an immense concourse singing 'God save the King' flouted [flooded] in. On this deep wave there broke the chimes of Big Ben; and, as the first stroke of the hour boomed out, a rustle of movement swept across the room. The war telegram, which meant, 'Commence hostilities against Germany', was flashed to the ships and establishments under the White Ensign all over the world. I walked across the Horse Guards Parade to the Cabinet room and reported to the Prime Minister and the Ministers who were assembled there that the deed was done.

Britain's position

Britain had no intention of joining the war in support of Russia against Austria–Hungary. Britain, though rivals with Germany, was primarily concerned with its own security. It did not want a strong country in west Europe – and this included France and the Low Countries (Holland and Belgium).

The Treaty of London, signed by all the main European powers in 1839, had declared that Belgium was a neutral country and that all the countries signing it should make sure that this was respected. The Schlieffen Plan involved breaking this treaty. Because Belgian neutrality was important to British interests, including European trade, the British government decided to take a stand on this issue.

When German troops entered Belgium on 3 August, Britain gave Germany an ultimatum – withdraw or Britain would declare war. War was declared on 4 August.

Churchill seemed to indicate that there was a general expectation for war in Britain (see Source 18). Although some members of the German government were worried about international law, the German public was also enthusiastic about the prospect of war.

Austria declared war on Russia two days later on 6 August. The system of alliances designed to keep the peace had failed in a situation that had spiralled out of control.

FOCUS TASK

Reasons for the outbreak of war in 1914

The atmosphere in Europe between 1900 and 1914 has been likened to a bonfire waiting to be lit.

1   Make your own simple copy of this bonfire diagram. Don't worry about the detail! Add labels to suggest factors that made war possible.
2   Put major factors on big sticks, less important factors on smaller sticks.
3   Add more sticks to the fire if you wish to show more factors.
4   Why do you think the Sarajevo murders 'lit the fire' when previous events such as the Moroccan crisis in 1905 had not? Mention these points in your answer:
  a) Austria's worries about Serbia
  b) The build-up of international problems
  c) The way the alliances worked.

Was Germany responsible for the war?

> ## SOURCE 19
>
> The 'war guilt' clause from the Treaty of Versailles, 1919.
>
> *The Allied governments affirm, and Germany accepts, the responsibility of Germany and her allies for causing all the loss and damage to which the Allied governments and their peoples have been subjected as a result of the war.*

After the war, the victorious Allies forced the defeated Germany to sign the 'WAR GUILT' clause (Source 19). Germany had to accept that it was responsible both for starting the war and for all the damage caused by it. However, as the state 'on trial', Germany refused to accept the sole blame. Historians have argued about this issue ever since. Some have continued to blame Germany. Others have reached different verdicts.

FOCUS TASK

Was Germany to blame for the war?

What do you think? Was Germany to blame?

Your task is to look over the evidence and hold your own retrial, looking back from today. You will study evidence and hear from witnesses. You must then reach one of four verdicts:

Verdict 1: Germany was rightly blamed for starting the war.

Verdict 2: Germany was mainly responsible for starting the war, but the other powers should accept some of the blame.

Verdict 3: All of the major powers helped to start the war. They should share the blame.

Verdict 4: No one was to blame. The powers were swept along towards an inevitable war. It could not be stopped.

This is how to run the trial. You can work on your own, or in groups.

1 Draw up a table like the one below:

Witness	Which verdict does the witness support?	What evidence does the witness give to support the viewpoint?	Can I trust the witness?

2 Read all nine witnesses' statements on page 213–14. Complete columns 1 and 2.
3 In column 3, note what evidence the witness gives to support his/her viewpoint.
4 In column 4, note what might make the witness reliable or unreliable.

Think about:

— the date and origin of each source
— whether the witness was involved in the events of the time
— the value and reliability of each witness.

5 Look through the other information in this chapter to see if there are other witnesses you should consider.
6 Choose your verdict from verdicts 1–4.
7 Once you have chosen a verdict, you should sum up the evidence for it in a short explanation. Remember to explain why you have chosen your verdict, but also explain why you have rejected the others.
8 Use your table and explanation for a class debate.

WITNESS 1

German militarism, which is the crime of the last fifty years, had been working for this for twenty-five years. It is the logical result of their doctrine. It had to come.

Walter Hines Page, US Ambassador in London, 1914. The USA was an ally of Britain and France during the war, and fought against Germany from 1917 to 1918.

WITNESS 2

Bethmann stood in the centre of the room … There was a look of anguish in his eyes … For an instant neither of us spoke. At last I said to him: 'Well, tell me, at least, how it all happened.' He raised his arms to heaven and answered, 'Oh – if only I knew!'

Prince von Bülow, speaking in 1918, remembers calling on the German Chancellor Bethmann-Hollweg in August 1914.

WITNESS 3

None of the rulers of the Great Powers really knew what they were fighting about in August 1914 … the crisis gathered pace and the calculations of statesmen were overwhelmed by the rapid succession of events, the tide of emotion in the various capitals, and the demands of military planning.

The Origins of the First World War by British historian L. C. F. Turner, 1983.

WITNESS 4

The Schlieffen Plan must rank as one of the supreme idiocies of modern times … It restricted the actions of the German government disastrously. In July 1914 they had just two choices; either to abandon the only plan they had to win the next war, or to go to war immediately.

Historian D. E. Marshall in *The Great War: Myth and Reality*, 1988.

WITNESS 5

The World War was directly started by certain officials of the Russian General Staff. But their conduct was caused by the criminal activity of an Austrian Foreign Minister, and this in turn was aided by criminal negligence at Berlin … But they would have been quite unable to start any war, had they not been equally with millions of common people … willing agents of forces moving the world towards war …

From the *Encyclopaedia Britannica*, 1926.

WITNESS 6

We are being forced to admit that we alone are to blame for the war: such an admission on my lips would be a lie. We are not seeking to absolve [pardon] Germany from all responsibility for this World War, and for the way in which it was fought. However, we do strongly deny that Germany, whose people felt they were fighting a war of defence, should be forced to accept sole responsibility.

Count Brockdorff-Rantzau, head of the German delegates at Versailles, 1919.

WITNESS 7

The greatest war of modern times, and perhaps in the whole history of the human race, was begun by Germany using the crime of a schoolboy as an excuse … Austria had regarded the growing power of Serbia with concern for many years … The situation in Europe seemed to encourage the German peoples in this adventure. England, it was thought, could do nothing … with the threats of CIVIL WAR in Ireland. Russia was in the midst of the reorganisation of her army … As for France, Germany believed herself quite competent to deal with her, and sought an opportunity of doing so.

From *The Great War: The Standard History of the All-Europe Conflict*, 1914 (Vol IV). This was a patriotic weekly journal written and published in Britain, describing the war 'as it happened'.

WITNESS 8

German: I wonder what history will make of all of this?

Clemenceau: History will not say that Belgium invaded Germany!

From a conversation between French Prime Minister Clemenceau and a German representative at the peace conference after the war. Clemenceau was a hard-line anti-German.

WITNESS 9

…the Kaiser authorised me to inform our gracious majesty that we might, in this case as in all others, rely upon Germany's full support … it was the Kaiser's opinion that this action must not be delayed … Russia was in no way prepared for war and would think twice before it appealed to arms … If we had really recognised the necessity of warlike action against Serbia, the Kaiser would regret if we did not make use of the present moment which is all in our favour.

Count Szogyeny, the Austrian ambassador in Berlin, reporting a famous conversation with the Kaiser, July 1914. Historians are divided as to whether the Kaiser was making a planned policy statement or was simply giving reassurance on the spur of the moment.

PRACTICE QUESTION

'The main reason for the outbreak of war in 1914 was the German invasion of neutral Belgium.'

How far do you agree with this statement?
Explain your answer.

TOPIC SUMMARY

The causes of the First World War

- In the late nineteenth century the major countries of Europe had started to form defensive alliances. The alliance of France and Russia was set against the alliance of Germany, Austria–Hungary and Italy.
- Britain became involved through the Entente Cordiale with France and then the Triple Entente which also included Russia.
- Britain and Germany were rivals at sea and Germany was competing to gain more colonies.
- The Anglo-German naval race was a visible sign of competition.
- The assassination of Archduke Franz Ferdinand set in motion the events that spiralled out of control and led to war.
- The Schlieffen Plan, designed to allow a quick German victory over France, had the effect of Britain declaring war on Germany.

5.2 The First World War: Stalemate

FOCUS

With the failure of the Schlieffen Plan, the quick war that had been hoped for soon turned to stalemate. Rapid troop movements had by autumn 1914 become entrenched positions. At sea the two powerful navies were each trying to outmanoeuvre the other.

In this part of the topic you will study the following:

● How and why the stalemate developed as the Schlieffen Plan failed.
● The Western Front:
    – What was life like on the Front?
    – How important was the development of weaponry?
● The war on other fronts:
    – Why the Gallipoli campaign failed.
    – How significant was the war at sea?

● The Schlieffen Plan

As soon as war was declared the German army put its Schlieffen Plan into operation. The Schlieffen Plan was simple but risky. The idea was to send German forces through Belgium and to quickly knock France out of the war. The theory was that Russia would take a long time to mobilise. It was an all-or-nothing gamble. The Germans had to try to get to Paris and defeat France within six weeks, so that they could then send all their troops to fight against Russia. However, as Figure 1 shows, neither the Belgians nor the Russians did what the Schlieffen Plan expected them to do.

At first, it looked as though the Germans could succeed. The German army invaded Belgium on 4 August. The Belgians put up a heroic resistance from their frontier forts but it did not stop the crushing German advance. Massive German artillery bombardments destroyed the Belgian forts and soon enormous numbers of well-equipped and well-trained German infantry and cavalry were moving ominously towards the French border. Even so, the Belgian resistance won them many friends and bought time for British and French troops to mobilise.

FIGURE 1

Why the Schlieffen Plan failed.

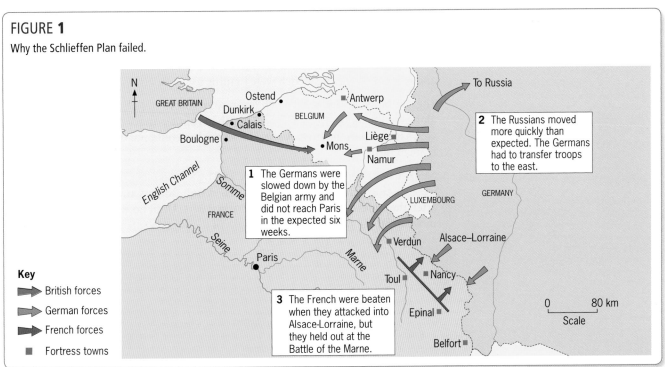

1 The Germans were slowed down by the Belgian army and did not reach Paris in the expected six weeks.

2 The Russians moved more quickly than expected. The Germans had to transfer troops to the east.

3 The French were beaten when they attacked into Alsace-Lorraine, but they held out at the Battle of the Marne.

Key
➤ British forces
➤ German forces
➤ French forces
■ Fortress towns

0   80 km
Scale

The British Expeditionary Force (BEF), led by Sir John French, landed in France and met the advancing Germans at Mons on 23 August. This small but well-trained force of professional soldiers gave the Germans a nasty shock. The troops at Mons were well led by Lieutenant-General Douglas Haig and were using Lee Enfield .303 bolt action rifles which could fire quickly and accurately. German reports from the time showed that they thought they were up against machine-gun fire. Haig went on to be heavily criticised for the loss of life incurred with his tactics, but eventually he played an important part in the Allied victory in 1918.

Despite their early success, the British were hugely outnumbered. In fact, the best they could do was to organise an orderly retreat. They did slow the Germans down, but only the French had enough forces in the field to stop the German advance. However, the French were facing their own problems.

When war broke out, the French launched a direct attack on Germany through Alsace-Lorraine. The French lost over 200,000 men in 12 days. They now regrouped their forces to defend Paris from the advancing Germans.

THINK

In Source 2, how important do you think the reason given is for the failure of the Schlieffen Plan?

> ### SOURCE 2
>
> Written by General von Kluck, a German army commander, after the Battle of the Marne.
>
> *That [French soldiers] who have retreated for ten days, sleeping on the ground and half dead with fatigue, should be able to take up their rifles when the bugle sounds is a thing which we never expected.*

The Battle of the Marne

The French may have been on the defensive in September 1914, but by this stage things were not going entirely well for the Germans either. The German Supreme Commander Moltke had to pull 100,000 troops out of the army advancing on Paris because the Russians had mobilised far more quickly than expected and had already invaded Germany. The Germans were also struggling to keep their troops supplied with food and equipment.

Von Kluck, the German commander, decided he could not swing round Paris according to the original plan, so he advanced straight towards it. While the Germans advanced on foot, the French diverted troops to Paris by rail, and then on to the front, transporting some of them there by taxi! The German army was weary and overstretched. The French were fighting to save their country.

The combined British and French forces were able to stop the German advance along the line of the River Marne. They then counter-attacked and pushed the Germans back to the River Aisne. However, they could not drive them out of France entirely.

Neither side could make any progress, and by 8 September troops on both sides were digging trenches to protect themselves from snipers and shell fire. Soon after, they added machine guns and barbed wire. Until now, it had been a war of movement, but these were the first signs of the STALEMATE that was to come.

The race to the sea

The Battle of the Marne was a turning point. The German generals realised that they could not break through the enemy lines. They decided to try to outflank (get round the end of) the enemy's lines. The charge began on 12 October. It became known as 'the race to the sea'.

As the Germans charged west towards the sea, the British and French moved troops (usually by rail) to block them whenever it seemed that the Germans were about to break through.

FIGURE 3

The Battle of the Marne, 1914.

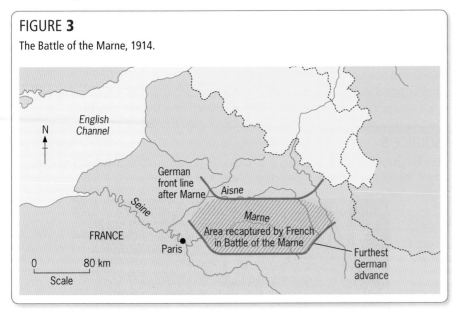

FIGURE 4

The race to the sea.

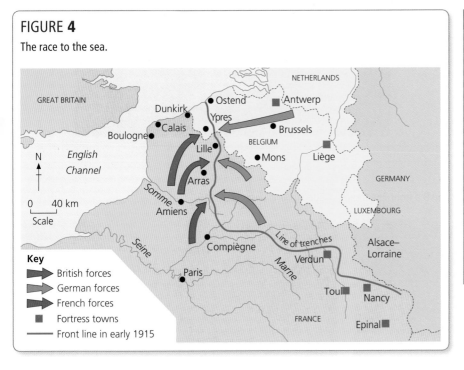

Key
- ▶ British forces
- ▶ German forces
- ▶ French forces
- ■ Fortress towns
- —— Front line in early 1915

FOCUS TASK

Why did the war become a stalemate?

It is late in 1914. You have been asked by a newspaper to write an article explaining why the war has become a stalemate. You could include some of these points:

- Why the German advance failed and how British forces contributed.
- Why the casualties are so high and what lessons are being learned.
- What you think will happen in 1915.

Try to keep your article to around 200 words.

● The Western Front

By November 1914 it was a deadlock. The BEF had been decimated. The French had already suffered around 1 million dead or wounded in just ten weeks. Despite this, the French army tried to break through the German lines in Artois and Champagne in December, but they were beaten back with heavy losses. As 1914 ended, the fighting had reached a stalemate which was to last until 1918. Millions of troops were dug into a line of trenches that stretched from the sea in the west to the Alps in the east. It became known as the 'Western Front'.

Trench warfare

As the war of movement ended late in 1914, the First World War developed into a stalemate based on trenches. Source 5 shows you a small section of the trench system and Sources 6A and 6B give a sense of what it was like to be in the different types of trenches at different times. Front-line trenches like 6B were supported by much stronger reserve trenches and linked by communication trenches.

ACTIVITY

1 Study Source 5 carefully. Decide where you think each of the following would be found:
   – Front-line trenches
   – Support trenches
   – No man's land (the area between front-line trenches).
2 Explain why you think the trenches are arranged as zig-zag lines, not straight lines.
3 How would you get from your headquarters behind the lines (marked X) to the front-line position (marked Y)?
4 Make a list of the differences between Sources 6A and 6B. What reasons can you think of to explain these differences?
5 Sources 5 and 6 are different types of evidence – aerial and ground photographs. Is it possible to say one is more useful than the other to a historian studying the trenches?

SOURCE 5

The trench system. This is an aerial photograph taken by British planes. The British trenches are in the right-hand corner. The main trench area is German.

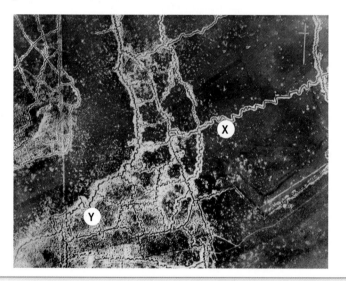

SOURCE 6

A A reserve trench in the Somme area, July 1916 and B a front-line trench in Guedecourt, December 1916.

Conditions in the trenches

Trenches offered the best protection from snipers, shellfire, mines and other dangers for the soldiers who fought in them. But clearly the troops did not hide in the trenches for the whole length of the war. This was where the infantry came in. Before the war, the theory was that an attack on the enemy would be led by a cavalry charge. The infantry's job was to follow the cavalry and take charge of the captured positions. They then had to defend the position against counter-attack. TRENCH WARFARE changed the role of the infantry dramatically. The cavalry charge was replaced by the 'infantry charge', which became the main tactic used in the war.

'Over the top'

A major assault would usually proceed like the diagram on the left. The infantry charge was the only attacking strategy the generals had. They thought that if they did it often enough, with enough men, eventually it would wear down the enemy, and they could break through. However, the traditional view that the generals simply threw away lives is not supported by the evidence. As the war continued, the generals tried different ways to make the infantry charge more effective and they introduced new tactics, weapons and equipment. Steel helmets giving some protection against shrapnel from enemy shelling became standard equipment in 1916. New camouflage techniques were used to protect troops and guns. Artillery and infantry attacks were better synchronised. Troops were given gas masks.

In the front line

The soldiers did not spend all their time charging the enemy trenches. Far from it. Most of the infantry's work was more routine. Infantry soldiers spent much of their time digging new trenches or repairing old ones. They carted supplies and equipment up and down communications trenches. They spent long hours on sentry duty or in secret-listening posts near to enemy trenches. There were also specialist infantry called sappers. Sappers were usually ex-miners who dug tunnels below enemy trenches and placed huge mines there. The infantry also made patrols into no man's land or raided enemy trenches – to capture prisoners or particular positions. Prisoners provided priceless information. If a new enemy unit was in your sector, you could soon be facing an attack.

All of these activities, plus the possibility that death could arrive in the form of a shell at any moment, put inevitable strains on the troops and sometimes generated bitter feelings towards their commanders.

Millions of men and thousands of horses lived close together. In the summer the smell of the trenches was appalling owing to a combination of rotting corpses, sewage and unwashed soldiers. The soldiers were also infested with lice, or 'chats' as they called them.

In summer the trenches were hot, dusty and smelly. In wet weather soldiers spent much time up to their ankles or knees in water. Many thousands suffered from 'trench foot', caused by standing in water for hours or days. In winter the trenches offered little protection from the cold. Many soldiers got frostbite.

To add to all of these unpleasant problems, the trenches were infested by rats. Many soldiers on all sides described the huge, fat 'corpse rats' which thrived on the dead bodies and the rubbish created by the armies. Some accounts even speak of cats and dogs killed by rats in overwhelming numbers.

1

The attacking side's artillery bombarded the front-line trenches of the enemy. This was called a 'barrage'.

2

As soon as the barrage stopped, attacking troops would go 'over the top' – that is, climb out of their trenches. It was now a race between them and the defenders, who had to emerge from their shelters and set up their machine guns before the attackers got over the barbed wire of no man's land.

3

The defenders usually had the advantage. They swept the advancing attackers with machine-gun fire, sometimes setting up a cross-fire.

4

If the attackers did capture forward positions, they then had to hold them. This generally proved impossible and they were usually forced back to their original position.

PRACTICE QUESTION

Study Sources 6 (page 218) and 7.

How useful are the two sources in studying conditions in the trenches?
Explain your answer using both sources and your contextual knowledge.

So why did the soldiers put up with the conditions?

When people study the First World War they often wonder why British soldiers put up with the conditions they had to endure. Part of the reason for this is that most books and TV programmes only cover the worst aspects of life in the trenches. It probably will not surprise you to know that when we look at a bigger picture a different story emerges about life in the trenches. The diagram below summarises this bigger, less commonly told story.

SOURCE 7

Memories of the Somme. A British soldier interviewed by the *Sunday Times* for an article published in 1986 – the 70th anniversary of the Battle of the Somme.

It was just as dangerous to go back as it was to go on. There were machine gun bullets spraying to and fro all the time … When I reached our trenches I missed my footing and fell on the floor, stunned. When I got up I saw an officer standing on the fire step looking through binoculars at No Man's Land. As I walked down the trench towards the dressing station he stood in my way with a pistol in his hand. He never said a word, but then he just stepped aside and let me pass. When I got to the dressing station I asked someone 'What's that officer doing back there with the gun in his hand?', and they said that his job was to shoot anyone who came back not wounded. I thought to myself, what kind of a job is that? Anyone could have lost his nerve that day.

A soldier's life

Adventure

Travel: Most soldiers were ordinary working-class men. They had not travelled much before the war. The fighting took them to France and Belgium, the Middle East and Africa – places they would not otherwise have visited.

Excitement: Some men actually enjoyed the risk and the thrill of war.

Challenge: Most people like a challenge. War was the ultimate challenge. In wartime, many soldiers achieved things they would never have dreamt possible. It may have been an act of bravery or simply putting up with pain or hardship.

Discipline

Soldiers who disobeyed orders, fell asleep on sentry duty or deserted were court-martialled and could be executed. A total of 3,080 British soldiers were condemned to death by the army and 346 actually had the sentence carried out.

Leisure time

The officers worked very hard to organise tours of duty so that the troops got a chance to rest and recuperate. On average a battalion could expect to spend around ten days a month in the trenches, but this included time in the reserve trenches which could be a mile from the front line. Troops would usually spend about three days in the most dangerous sections of the front line before being relieved. However, during a major assault, such as the Battle of the Somme, soldiers could be in the front line for much longer. We also need to remember that soldiers spent about 60 per cent of their time out of the trenches. Many of them took up correspondence courses. Many went sightseeing in France. There were football and other sports teams. There was usually a concert party every week.

Humour

We should not underestimate the importance of the British sense of humour in keeping up morale. Soldiers produced many humorous news sheets, and other publications, often poking fun at the commanders. This Bairnsfather cartoon is called 'The things that matter'. It shows GHQ on the phone enquiring about the number of tins of raspberry jam issued the previous week.

FOCUS TASK

Life in the trenches

Work in pairs.

1 Each of you write a letter home from the trenches describing exactly what it is like in as much detail as you can. Use all of the information and sources on these two pages to help you. You could even include sketches.

2 Now swap your letters over. Each of you act as censor on the other one's letter and edit out anything which you think is too horrific or which reflects badly on the army.

You may be able to use word processing or email for this task. Make sure you keep a copy of the original.

Comradeship

Old friends: Many battalions were made up of close friends who all joined the army together. Soldiers relied on each other totally. They did not want to let each other down. After the war, many soldiers said they greatly missed the sense of comradeship they had experienced during the war.

New friends: Allied soldiers came from all over the world. British soldiers met Canadian, Australian, South African, New Zealand, Indian, West African and Caribbean soldiers. They also met many other British people.

Patriotism

The soldiers on all sides were generally patriotic. Whatever the horrors of war, most believed they were there to do a job for their country and that the job was worth doing well.

Comforts

Care: Remember this was at a time when civilian life was very hard indeed. Life expectancy was the early 40s for a working-class man. Death and disease were common. So were poverty, hunger, illness and accidents at work. The army looked after its soldiers as well as it could. British forces suffered less from disease than any other army.

Rations: For British troops, food rations were generally good. Soldiers complained about always having tinned beef and jam, but they knew they were better off than French soldiers, and even French civilians, and they were much better fed than the Germans. In fact an average working-class soldier put on around 10 kilos in weight when he joined the army because he was better fed there!

Letters: Soldiers received regular letters and parcels from home. The postal service was very efficient and this was a major factor in keeping morale high.

Luxuries: They also received lots of luxuries such as chocolate, cigarettes and alcohol.

Respect

Soldiers had respect for their leaders. There is a widespread modern myth that the generals wined and dined in the officers' mess while the men lived and died in the squalor of the trenches. In fact officers went over the top with their men and suffered higher death rates (around 17 per cent) than the ordinary troops (around 12 per cent). Among senior commanders 78 officers above the rank of brigadier-general from Britain and the British Empire died on active service and 146 were wounded. This is evidence that British generals were often close enough to the front line to be in danger of losing their lives.

The technology of war: New developments

You have seen how the war became bogged down in a stalemate of trench warfare by the end of 1914. There is a traditional view of the war which says that the stalemate continued because the commanders were too incompetent and inflexible to try out any new weapons, technology or ideas. In fact, this idea is quite wrong. All the armies on the Western Front constantly improvised new weapons and tried out new tactics, but these measures often cancelled each other out. In this section we are going to look at some of the main developments in warfare on the Western Front.

Artillery

The First World War was an artillery war. Many people think that machine guns caused the most casualties in the war but this is wrong. Artillery bombardments by large heavy guns fired from a distance caused more casualties than any other weapon. The artillery had two main jobs – to destroy enemy positions and defences so they could be captured and to destroy enemy guns.

At the beginning of the war the guns were not very accurate. Firing from well behind their own lines, artillery often bombarded their own forward trenches before they got their range right. By the end of the war, artillery was much more powerful, and it was also more accurate. By 1918 artillery tactics were extremely sophisticated as well (see Source 14 on page 225). Artillery was the key weapon of the Great War. Throughout the war a vast part of European industry was given over to making shells for the artillery. British performance in the war became more effective after 1916 because British industry was supplying enough guns and shells and British forces were using these weapons effectively.

SOURCE 8

The bodies of two German soldiers in a trench hit by British artillery at the Battle of the Somme, July 1916.

SOURCE 9

An extract from the poem 'The Voice of the Guns' by Gilbert Frankau. Frankau was an officer in the Royal Artillery.

We are the guns, and your masters! Saw ye our flashes?
Heard ye the scream of our shells in the night, and the shuddering crashes?
Saw ye our work by the roadside, the shrouded things lying,
Moaning to God that He made them – the maimed and the dying?
Husbands or sons,
Fathers or lovers, we break them. We are the guns!

Machine guns

This weapon is the one which most people associate with the appalling casualties of the First World War, even though machine guns did not cause the most casualties. Once the war became a stalemate the infantryman became the backbone of the British army. The job of the infantry was to try to capture enemy positions (and hold on to them) or to defend positions they already held.

This is where the machine gun came into its own. Machine guns at the start of the war were very large and heavy so they were not very useful in an attack on an enemy trench. However, they were devastatingly effective as defensive weapons. A machine gun could fire eight bullets a second or more, and each trench would have a number of machine guns. During an infantry charge it could cut down a whole brigade in minutes. The machine gun made it inevitable that any charge on an enemy trench would cost many lives. Machine guns proved to be devastating against British forces in the Battle of the Somme (see pages 225–27). After the war British commanders were often criticised for underestimating the machine gun, and Sir Douglas Haig is said to have believed that it was overrated. However, some

THINK

Study Source 9. What is the attitude of the poet towards the war?

officers did have faith in it. At the start of the war British troops had the same ratio of machine guns to troops as the Germans and the British army established its first dedicated Machine Gun Corps in 1915. By 1918 most platoons had their own machine guns and troops even had lightweight sub-machine guns. These guns proved very effective in actions like the capture of the St Quentin Canal in 1918 (see page 234 – the Hundred Days).

SOURCE 10

British machine gun crew in 1916.

SOURCE 11

'Dulce Et Decorum Est' ('How right and good it is to die for your country'), by Wilfred Owen. Owen was an officer in the British army. He was killed in 1918, not long before the end of the war.

GAS! GAS! Quick, boys! – An ecstasy of fumbling.
Fitting the clumsy helmets just in time;
But someone still was yelling out and stumbling
And flound'ring like a man in fire or lime…
Dim, through the misty panes and thick green light,
As under a green sea, I saw him drowning.

In all my dreams, before my helpless sight,
He plunges at me, guttering, choking, drowning.

If in some smothering dreams you too could pace
Behind the wagon that we flung him in,
And watch the white eyes writhing in his face,
His hanging face, like a devil's sick of sin;
If you could hear, at every jolt, the blood
Come gargling from the froth-corrupted lungs,
Obscene as cancer, bitter as the cud
Of vile, incurable sores on innocent tongues, –
My friend, you would not tell with such high zest
To children ardent for some desperate glory,
The old Lie: Dulce et decorum est
Pro patria mori.

Poison gas

The first poison gas attack was in April 1915. The Germans released chlorine which wafted on the wind across no man's land into the British trenches. There was panic there as the soldiers coughed, retched and struggled to breathe.

From that time on, gas attacks by both sides became a regular feature of the war. To start with, the aim of a gas attack was to disable enemy troops so that your own infantry charge would be successful. Later, scientists on both sides began to perfect new and more lethal gases such as mustard gas, which had a perfumed smell but which burned, blinded or slowly killed the victims over four to five weeks.

However, scientists also developed very effective gas masks. Soldiers in the trenches would carry their gas masks with them all the time. At the alert they would put them on. As a result only 3,000 British troops died from gas in the whole war. The main significance of gas was its psychological impact. Soldiers who could bear a long bombardment by artillery often lived in fear of a gas attack.

THINK

1 How does Source 10 help to explain why the machine gun was primarily a defensive weapon?
2 Is Source 10 more useful as a source on how the machine gun was used or on how effective it was?
3 Study Source 11. How does the poet convey the horrors of war?

PRACTICE QUESTION

Write an account of how the use of gas influenced trench warfare on the Western Front.

SOURCE 12

The text below appeared on a poster produced by the government to encourage people to support the building of tanks by buying war bonds and saving scrap metal.

The tank is a travelling fortress that clears the way for our soldiers.

It cuts through wire – under fire

It saves lives

*It is **our** War discovery*

It is a matter of pride to help build tanks

Tanks

The tank was a British invention. Early in the war inventors took the idea of a tank to the army leaders but it was rejected as impractical. However, Winston Churchill, head of the navy, thought that the idea had potential and his department funded its development.

Two years later, the tanks were used for the first time at the Battle of the Somme. They advanced ahead of the infantry, crushing barbed-wire defences and spraying the enemy with machine-gun fire. They caused alarm among the Germans and raised the morale of the British troops. Surely this was the weapon that could achieve a breakthrough!

However, these first machines only moved at walking pace. They were not very manoeuvrable and were very unreliable – more than half of them broke down before they got to the German trenches. It was not until a year later, in November 1917 at Cambrai, that tanks actually achieved great success. Unfortunately they were too successful. They blasted through enemy lines so quickly that the infantry could not keep up.

By 1918, German forces were using armour-piercing machine-gun bullets to deadly effect. They had also learned how to adapt field guns to fire at tanks. Tanks were virtually impossible to miss because they were so large and slow. However, the tank offered a significant boost to British morale.

PRACTICE QUESTION

Study Source 12.

Source 12 is supporting the British war effort. How do you know?
Explain your answer by using Source 12 and your contextual knowledge.

SOURCE 13

A still of a 'dogfight' (aerial combat). Such battles were often shown in films.

Aircraft

One of the few aspects of the fighting in the First World War which gained a glamorous reputation was the war in the air. All countries had brilliant pilots and the thrill of heroic flying in up-to-date machines is easy to understand. The newspapers and journals began to pick up on the story of 'flying aces' from an early stage in the war and moviemakers glamorised them after the war. But were they really important?

In 1914 aeroplanes were extremely primitive. They were also very unreliable and highly dangerous. Losses were very high indeed, especially among new pilots. At the start of the war, planes did the same job as observation balloons.

Soon their speed and mobility meant that commanders used them for detailed reconnaissance work over enemy trenches. The photographs they took were very valuable.

Enemy aircraft would be sent to shoot down reconnaissance flights and soon the 'dogfight' had emerged. In these early battles in the air, the pilots used pistols and rifles. It was not until April 1915 that planes were successfully fitted with machine guns. By 1918 spectacular aerial battles were common over the Western Front. Planes also played a part in slowing down the German advance in 1918 and in the Allied advances of the Hundred Days (see page 234).

In four years aircraft had changed from simple flying machines to quite advanced pieces of military equipment. In four years the Royal Naval Air Service and Royal Flying Corps had gone from having 37 aeroplanes to 23,000. Even so, aircraft were really only a side show to the land war. Air power was, if anything, more valuable at sea where the aircraft could observe and attack shipping.

Putting it all together

It is important to remember that all of these weapons and developments took place as the war was being fought. They were often the result of ordinary soldiers trying out ideas which officers then recommended for wider use. There was a constant exchange of information and discussion between troops, front-line officers and senior commanders. All of this meant that the British army became increasingly professional as the war went on and that between 1914 and 1918 the way the war was fought was transformed.

SOURCE 14

An extract from *Tommy: The British Soldier on the Western Front* by the British military historian Professor Richard Holmes (2004).

Look at a photograph of a group of British infantrymen in 1914 … Then look at a photograph from October 1918. The shape and silhouette are different, for the infantryman now resembles not the gamekeeper but the industrial worker. The faces are different, for the average age of senior officers has dropped by about ten years … Half the infantrymen in France are eighteen years old, although all too often young faces frame old eyes. They now wear steel helmet and leather jerkin. It is far more difficult to make out the officers. Even those who are wearing officer-style uniforms have moved their badges of rank to their shoulders instead of their chests.

By 1918 some wholly new weapons are in evidence. Pouches bulge with hand grenades and respirators are always handy, for both sides now use gas as a matter of course.

… And the infantry now has its own artillery. Trench mortars are attached to each infantry brigade … In 1914 most artillery was close behind the firing line … In 1918 artillery was tucked into folds of ground behind the infantry, there were far more heavy guns, lurking unseen over the horizon, with a power and range that the men of 1914 could never have dreamt of. Forward observation parties abounded, along with signallers. There were wireless sets at all main headquarters. Even some aircraft were now fitted with wireless to enable them to control the fire of the heavy guns … By 1918 the air was very busy: one artillery officer reckoned that he could often see fifty aircraft in the sky at any one time.

The key battles on the Western Front and their significance

In 1915 the French, British and Germans all tried and failed to break the deadlock. Early in 1915 the French lost many thousands in an unsuccessful offensive in Champagne (arrow 1 in Figure 15, page 226). The British gained some ground at Neuve Chapelle in March but at a heavy cost. The Germans were driven back from Ypres in April (arrow 2) with heavy losses.

1916: The year of attrition – Verdun

In February 1916 the Germans began a determined battle to capture strategic French forts surrounding Verdun (arrow 3). The Germans recognised that the French were leading the Allied effort at this stage of the war. The German commander, Falkenhayn, came up with a strategy of ATTRITION – that is, to wear down the enemy's strength until resistance was no longer possible. His tactic was to 'bleed France white'. The tactic failed, in that both sides suffered roughly equal losses. For six months both sides poured men and resources into this battle. Attacks were followed by counter-attacks and by July 1916 some 700,000 men had fallen. The French, led by General Pétain, held out, but by the summer of 1916 they were close to breaking. The huge losses had weakened both sides, but the Germans had greater resources. The French army was near breaking point.

FOCUS TASK

How important were new developments in warfare?

You have been approached by a company designing a new computer game which is set in the First World War. You have been asked to create profiles of some of the weapons and developments which emerged during the war which game players can use for reference. Take all of the developments on pages 222–24 and rate each weapon's significance in terms of:

- why it was developed and how it was used
- examples of this weapon in action
- whether the weapon developed further during the course of the war
- the impact of the weapon (for example, the casualties caused, the psychological impact)
- the reputation of the weapon (think about different groups of people such as the general public, troops, commanders and also the reputation of the weapon at different times)
- how each weapon worked with other weapons
- your view of its overall significance on a scale of 1–10 (where 10 is high).

You could present these profiles as written reports, presentations or in a format such as Top Trumps cards. You may be able to research these developments further using the internet, or research other weapons and developments such as camouflage or transport.

The Somme

To relieve the pressure, the British led by Field Marshal Douglas Haig launched their long-planned offensive at the Somme (arrow 4). After a week-long artillery bombardment of German trenches, British troops advanced. On the first day there were 57,000 British casualties. The fighting continued until November 1916 with the loss of 1.25 million men.

Back in Britain, politicians and the general public were horrified at the losses. But to the military leaders the nature of the exercise was clear. The war was a contest to see which side could last out the long and dreadful war of attrition. Douglas Haig briefed the government that 'the nation must be taught to bear losses'. The nation did accept them and in doing so played a key role in victory.

Battle of Passchendaele, 1917

The Battle of Passchendaele is also known as the Third Battle of Ypres. It started in July 1917, and illustrates how new technology could become hopelessly outmanoeuvred by weather conditions.

The British detonated huge mines at Messines which destroyed the German artillery positions and killed 10,000 German soldiers at a stroke. However, the infantry advance which followed became hopelessly bogged down when heavy rain created nightmare conditions, particularly around the ruined village of Passchendaele.

Even when tanks were used at Cambrai in November 1917 it was the same story: 350 tanks made good progress but were unable to hold the ground they had captured.

The casualty figures for this battle are disputed, but there were nearly a quarter of a million casualties on the Allied side, and even more on the German side.

PRACTICE QUESTIONS

1 Write an account of how the Battles of Verdun and the Somme became important in the long struggle on the Western Front.
2 'Mud was the main enemy on the Western Front.'

   How far do you agree with this statement? Explain your answer.

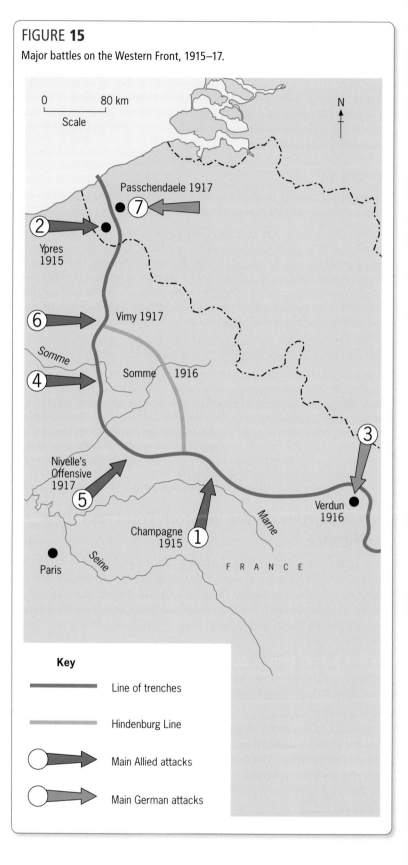

FIGURE **15**

Major battles on the Western Front, 1915–17.

Key

────────	Line of trenches
────────	Hindenburg Line
⬤➡	Main Allied attacks
⬤➡	Main German attacks

An investigation: The Battle of the Somme

The Battle of the Somme has been the most controversial battle of the First World War. With such huge casualties, were the generals and the British government incompetent? Or were such losses an essential part in the road towards eventual victory? You can imagine that by the end of 1916 many military personnel and onlookers might have believed the first alternative. After victory in 1918, many came to believe that the battle was a regrettable necessity. That was certainly the view that General Haig wanted to portray in his memoirs, written in the 1920s.

The Somme stands out as the battle most associated with a war of attrition – wearing down the other side to see which could continue fighting the longest.

Compare Sources 16, 17 and 18 on the opening days of the Battle of the Somme.

SOURCE 16

An extract from *The First Day of the Somme* by D. M. Middlebrook (1971).

After three or four days continuous shelling, most of the targets should have been destroyed. Of these targets the wire, a vital one for the infantry, was the only one where the damage could be easily assessed … The reports were inconsistent: in some places the wire was well cut, in others there were a few gaps; but in several places the wire was still intact. The Germans spotted some of the gaps in the wire and their machine guns turned those narrow alleys into death-traps.

SOURCE 17

From a report by Haig on the first day of the attack, 1 July 1916.

Very successful attack this morning … All went like clockwork … The battle is going very well for us and already the Germans are surrendering freely. The enemy is so short of men that he is collecting them from all parts of the line. Our troops are in wonderful spirits and full of confidence.

SOURCE 18

Another historian, N. Jones, made these comments in *The War Walk*, 1983.

But all this immense shell-fire had not fatally destroyed the enemy as the Allied Commanders had fondly hoped. Far from it – their defences consisted of a vast network of dug-outs, trenches, dormitories dug to a depth of 40 feet [12 metres]. This fundamental failure by the British Command to realise the strength of the enemy defences, coupled with the imperfectly cut wire and the rigid parade-ground manner in which the infantry attacked, were the main reasons for the horrible failure of the attack.

The battle continued from July until November. Having had a disastrous start, should the battle have been allowed to continue for so long? Opinions varied at the time. As the battle drew to a close in November Lord Lansdowne, an ex-Cabinet minister, wrote a letter to the *Daily Telegraph*, in which he argued, 'We are slowly but surely killing off the best of the male population of these islands. Can we afford to go on paying the same sort of price for the same sort of gain?'

However, some recent historians have tried to assess which tactics worked and which did not – and why some commanders adapted to them and others did not (see Source 19).

SOURCE 19

Gary Sheffield, Professor of War Studies at the University of Birmingham, writing in the *BBC History Magazine* in July 2011.

On July 1st 1916 the British army had too few heavy guns for the job it was given – that of destroying the enemy positions. What's more, the available guns were given too many targets to bombard, catastrophically reducing the concentration of firepower. Moreover infantry tactics were often crude. But even in the midst of disaster there were signs of hope, of some units using methods that worked.

One of the formations on the right of the British line was the 18th Division. Its commander, Major-General Maxse, had a reputation as one of the best trainers in the British army and before the battle his men had thoroughly rehearsed its assault. The artillery fired a creeping barrage, by which a curtain of shells moved steadily ahead of the infantry and helped the 18th Division take all of its objectives.

ACTIVITY

Read the sources on this page and carry out your own research on the Battle of the Somme and the contrasting attitudes towards it among historians.

Debate whether:

- the British generals should be blamed for wasting so many lives
- the battle served any purpose by continuing for so long.

FIGURE 20

The Dardanelles strait and the Gallipoli campaign.

● The war on other fronts

The war was not just limited to the Western Front. Huge casualties were being suffered in the east where Russia was trying to defend itself against Germany and Austria–Hungary. Fighting was also taking place in the Middle East where 700,000 Indian troops were supporting the British against the Turks. But one campaign has become particularly famous – the Gallipoli campaign.

Gallipoli and its failure

As casualties mounted on the Western Front, and with no prospect of ending the stalemate, ministers looked for alternatives. Winston Churchill, First Lord of the Admiralty, persuaded the British government that an attack should be mounted on the Dardanelles Strait, a narrow stretch of water linking the Aegean Sea and the Sea of Marmara, which then gave access to the Black Sea. This was an attack on the Turks, and would also enable supplies to get through to help Russia in their campaigns (see Figure 20).

As Britain had the most powerful navy, the plan seemed attractive. In March 1915 the warships began their assault, and bombarded the strong forts that lined the strait (see Figure 20). But as they entered the strait a combination of mines and shell fire from the forts on the shore doomed the attack. The Allied commanders decided that they would have to launch a land assault to capture the peninsula before the naval operation could succeed.

Land attacks

In April a hastily assembled force of British, French and ANZAC (Australian and New Zealand) troops attacked the Helles Beach. The Turks, supported by German troops, had strengthened the defences and had dug trenches on the hills overlooking the beaches where the Allies were likely to land. The Allied troops fought bravely, and did capture a few trenches, but it quickly became clear that they would not be able to remove the Turks from the peninsula.

The Allied troops also dug in, but conditions for both sides were dreadful. In the blistering summer heat, and with decaying corpses strewn along the front line on both sides, disease was rampant. Neither side could break the deadlock, even with more troops. Another landing was made at Suvla Bay, but that also failed to break through the defences of the Turks.

SOURCE 21

Memories from 2nd Lieutenant G. D. Horridge of conditions in summer 1915 at Gallipoli.

The land in between the trenches was covered with dead … Because of this and the hot sun, the flies bred there until their number was horrendous … They attacked our food remorselessly. Any bit of food uncovered was blotted out by flies in a couple of seconds. The contamination made everybody ill. Typhoid and dysentery were rife. Those that didn't get either had very unpleasant tummy trouble and were continually on the trot.

Only one part of the Allies' campaign was successful – submarines got through the minefields of the strait to attack Constantinople harbour and sank many Turkish ships. But the main fleet never attempted to get through.

Withdrawal

By November there was a new problem for the Allies – frostbite. The troops were extremely ill-equipped for the harsh winter. By December it was clear that there was no prospect of success. The decision was taken to pull out. The withdrawal was well-organised, but the campaign was seen as a failure, and Churchill was humiliated.

SOURCE 22

From *Gallipoli* by Michael Hickey, 1995.

There was a lack of up to date knowledge about Turkish troop positions. The instructions were vague. Kitchener had only a hazy idea of what was needed … [British Army Commander] Hamilton's only intelligence consisted of a 1912 manual on the Turkish army, some old (and very inaccurate) maps, a tourist guide book and what little could be found out from the Turkish desk at the Foreign Office … Hamilton had no idea of what had been done to establish a supply base. Above all, he was given no hint as to the relationship between himself and the naval commander with whom he was required to work.

SOURCE 23

An Australian trench in the front line at Gallipoli. The Turkish trenches were only a few metres away. A sniper is using a clamped rifle and a sniperscope. Behind him another soldier is using a periscope to spot enemy soldiers.

FOCUS TASK

Why did the Gallipoli campaign fail?

1 Having read the information on pages 228–229 and studied the sources, write a list of the reasons why the Gallipoli campaign failed in its objective.
2 Then decide which you think was the most important factor and give reasons for your choice.

The events and significance of the war at sea

There were no decisive battles at sea during the First World War, but the events that took place there were vitally important for both sides. For example, Britain and Germany both needed crucial supplies to be brought in by sea. Before the war, the build-up of arms had anticipated the importance of the navies. During the war torpedoes were developed so that they could be launched from ships, submarines or from the air. Improvements in radio meant that ships could keep in better contact with each other and with the shore. Crucially, submarines were new to warfare. Both sides had them, but the Germans were quick to use them more effectively than the British.

Blockade

The British navy's main activity was to mount a BLOCKADE on German ports (see Source 24 and Figure 25). The aim was to stop essential supplies of food and war materials reaching Germany. Many German ships were blocked in their own ports. As the war went on the blockade hit harder. By 1918 many Germans were starving and there was a mutiny in the German navy. Indeed, the blockade was one of the factors which led to the German surrender in November 1918.

SOURCE 24

From *The British Experience of Enforcing Blockade* by Chris Page, 1996.

To some, the performance of the Royal Navy was disappointing: the hoped-for and expected Trafalgar-like encounter with the German High Seas Fleet did not take place, and the results of the only major Fleet action, off Jutland, in May 1916, seem to support the feeling of disappointment. Too little tends to be made of the major successes. These include maintaining sea communications with Britain's friends, enabling Britain to feed her people and import the materials necessary to carry on with the war. This involved a great struggle to defeat the U-boats. The navy transported millions of troops with tiny losses. But perhaps the navy's prime achievement was the enforcement of the naval blockade. There is little doubt that it was a vital factor in the defeat of Germany.

FIGURE 25

Map showing the British blockade.

🚢 Battle	**Note**
×××× British mines	As part of their blockade, the British laid mines to stop the Germans getting into the North Sea.
○○○○ German mines	
▲ Naval base	
▲ Convoy port	The Germans laid mines off the British coast, as well as around their own bases.

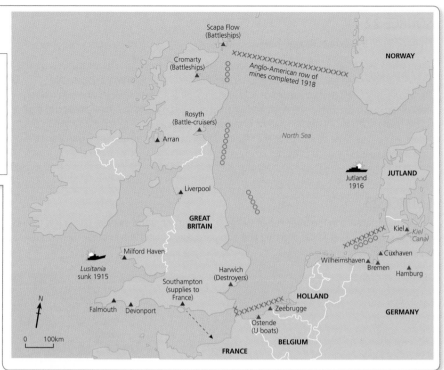

SOURCE 26

British destroyer escorting a convoy of ships.

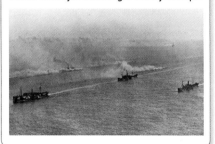

FIGURE 27

Losses of Allied shipping, 1914–18.

The U-boat campaign: the USA joins the war

The Germans fought back using U-boats (underwater boats). They sank ships that were bringing supplies to Britain from the British Empire and from the USA. In 1915 a British liner, the *Lusitania*, was sunk after being hit by torpedoes from a German U-boat, killing 1,198 passengers, including 128 US CITIZENS. Angry protests from the USA, still officially neutral, led the Kaiser to order the German navy to stop attacking American ships. He did not want the USA to enter on the Allied side!

However, in early 1917 the Germans were so desperate that they started attacking American ships again. The plan nearly worked. By May 1917 Britain was left with only six weeks' supply of some basic goods. However, in April 1917 President Woodrow Wilson was able to persuade CONGRESS to declare war on Germany.

Convoys

The British began to defend their ships against U-boats by introducing the convoy system. Slow-moving merchant ships sailed in groups, protected by fast-moving destroyers. Soon the amount of shipping destroyed by U-boats began to fall. The British also began to use massive underwater anti-submarine nets and laid minefields.

The Battle of Jutland

In the North Sea on 31 May 1916 the only major sea battle of the war began. The German fleet, led by Admiral Scheer, had the initial advantage with powerful guns. The British battle cruiser squadron under Vice-Admiral Beatty was under great pressure and in danger of defeat. However, the other part of the Grand Fleet under Admiral Jellicoe arrived just in time. The fighting continued during the night, but by morning the German fleet had gone back to the safety of port.

The British had lost 14 ships and 6,000 sailors. The Germans had lost 13 ships and 2,500 sailors.

The Germans had done better in the sense that the British ships lost were larger and more important than the German ones. However, after Jutland the Germans never came out to fight again. The fleet remained trapped in port and the British controlled the sea for the rest of the war.

FIGURE 28

Map to show the Battle of Jutland.

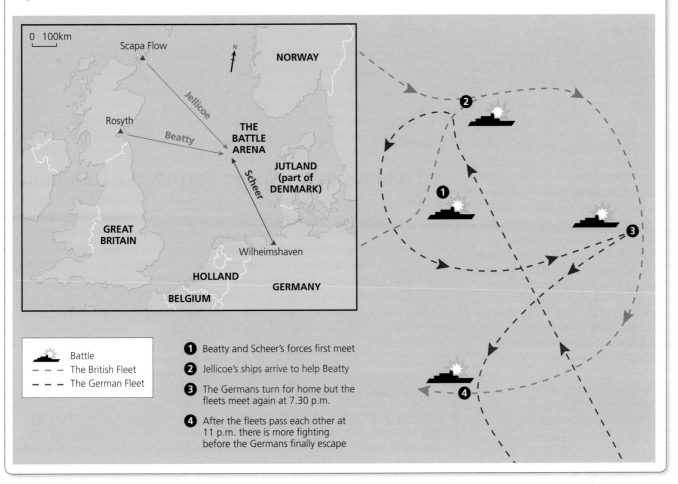

- **1** Beatty and Scheer's forces first meet
- **2** Jellicoe's ships arrive to help Beatty
- **3** The Germans turn for home but the fleets meet again at 7.30 p.m.
- **4** After the fleets pass each other at 11 p.m. there is more fighting before the Germans finally escape

Legend:
- Battle
- – – – The British Fleet
- – – – The German Fleet

TOPIC SUMMARY

The First World War: Stalemate

- The war began unexpectedly as Germany were unable to defeat France quickly and the Schlieffen Plan failed.
- The British Expeditionary Force went to help the French, and Russia attacked Germany.
- There was no quick war. Stalemate developed.
- Trenches were dug, and tactics were developed for this unexpected form of warfare.
- New technologies were developed throughout the conflict, such as gas, the tank and airplanes.
- Key battles involved enormous losses on both sides – Verdun, the Somme, Passchendaele.
- The Gallipoli campaign was meant to be a way of breaking the deadlock on the Western Front, but it was not successful.
- The war at sea was vital for maintaining essential supplies from abroad.
- Britain blockaded German ports.
- U-boats tried to disrupt goods reaching Britain, but the convoy system was developed in 1917 to protect Allied merchant ships.
- The Battle of Jutland was won by neither side, but Britain benefited more from its results.

FOCUS TASK

How significant was the war at sea?

1 Make a list of the reasons why the war at sea often seemed of minimal significance during the war on one side of your page, and the reasons why the war at sea was of great significance on the other side.

2 Using pages 229–31, add evidence to your lists.

3 Write a concluding paragraph to summarise how significant you think the war at sea was during the First World War.

5.3 Ending the war

FOCUS

This section deals with the reasons for the Allied victory in 1918 following the German surrender. In this part of the topic you will study the following:

- Changes in the Allied forces, why the USA entered the war, and the impact of these developments on the Allies' chances of victory.
- Military developments in 1918 and their contribution to Germany's defeat.
- The German surrender and why Germany asked for an armistice.

● Changes in the Allied Forces: the USA joins

For the first few years of the war, the USA was officially neutral. However, the DEMOCRAT government of Woodrow Wilson was supplying loans and equipment to the Allies. In 1915 Germany, angered by US help to the Allies, started a policy of attacking shipping in the Atlantic that was thought to be carrying war materials to Europe. As a result of this tactic, in May 1915 a German U-boat sunk the passenger liner, the *Lusitania*, which was travelling from New York to Liverpool, with the loss of over 1,000 lives, including 128 Americans. Although the Germans were breaking accepted international codes of practice by attacking a passenger ship, the Allies were also in the wrong – the ship was indeed carrying much war cargo, which is why a second internal explosion was responsible for sinking the ship in 18 minutes. The British denied that the ship was carrying illegal cargo, and the Germans wanted to avoid war with the USA, so from then on the policy of attacking shipping was strictly controlled.

However, in February 1917, when the situation for the Germans was desperate, they restarted their campaign of unrestricted submarine warfare, attacking and destroying many American ships which they suspected of carrying supplies to the Allies. This, coupled with the discovery that Germany hoped to ally with Mexico against them, was the final straw. The USA declared war on Germany on 6 April 1917.

Germany was dismayed; psychologically it was a big blow. The US navy was the third largest in the world after Britain and Germany. Its destroyers could be used on convoy duty to protect merchant shipping routes in the Atlantic. This would help Britain's critical shortage of food. The US government was also willing to lend Britain money to buy war materials. But in the short term, the US contribution was minimal. American troops had to be trained; equipment had to be manufactured and assembled. It was not until summer 1918 that America was able to make a decisive contribution in Europe, when about 1 million troops landed in France.

The Russian Revolution

Meanwhile, there were problems in Russia. In March 1917 the Tsar was forced to give up his throne. A temporary (Provisional) government took over. Although its policy was to keep Russia in the war, its armies became less and less effective.

Then, in November 1917, a second revolution in Russia brought in a COMMUNIST government under Lenin. It immediately declared that it was not going to fight and opened negotiations, which led to a peace with Germany in March 1918. The terms of the Treaty of Brest-Litovsk were harsh, with Russia being forced to lose substantial areas of territory which provided food and raw materials for industry. In addition, the Germans could now transfer hundreds of thousands of troops back to the Western Front. The German armies had the opportunity to attack on the Western Front before American troops and equipment had arrived in any decisive numbers.

● Military developments in 1918

Things may have looked bad for the Allies but the German situation was also desperate in early 1918. Despite the good news of the Russian surrender, the Allies' blockade of German ports had starved the economy of raw materials and the population (including the soldiers) of food. Worse still, the USA was sending tanks and heavy guns to France and was moving troops there at a rate of 50,000 per month. The Allies had increasing numbers of tanks that were able to deal with the terrain more effectively, and the military tactics had developed from 1916 onwards, replacing a rigid trench warfare mentality with more attacking and innovative tactics, utilising the latest technology.

For example, German aircraft could no longer attack targets in England with impunity, as the government ordered better searchlights, anti-aircraft guns and planes. The ensuing success over land encouraged the navy to use aircraft against enemy submarines. By October 1918 there had been a huge increase in the size of the Royal Flying Corps (RFC) which had over 20,000 aircraft.

Above all, the German army was not the quality fighting machine it had been. Germany needed a quick victory and the surrender of Russia gave the Germans one last opportunity to achieve a military breakthrough and end the stalemate.

Ludendorff and the German Spring Offensive, 1918

In March 1918 the German Commander Ludendorff launched the great gamble to win the war. It started with the typical huge bombardment and gas attacks. However, instead of the usual 'wave' of infantry, he followed up with attacks by smaller bands of specially trained and lightly equipped 'storm troops' who struck during a heavy fog along the entire front line. The idea was to stop the Allies massing their defence in a single place. The Germans broke through the Allied lines in many places, advanced 64 km and Paris was now in range of heavy gunfire.

The 'Ludendorff Offensive' had so far gone very well. A German victory seemed to be a real possibility. However, the German army lost 400,000 men in making this breakthrough and they had no reserves to call on. The troops of 1918 did not compare well with those of 1914. Their discipline was poor and they were badly fed and supplied. Many of the planned German advances were held up as troops stopped to loot food and supplies from captured trenches or villages. They also came up against well-led and well-equipped Allied forces.

General Ludendorff (1865–1937)

- Born 1865; entered the army in 1885 and enjoyed a long, distinguished career.
- From 1905 onwards contributed to the details of the Schlieffen Plan.
- Appointed Deputy Chief of Staff to the German Second Army in August 1914; active in defeat of Belgium, and then on Eastern Front against Russia.
- Joint head of German army with Hindenburg, 1916–18.
- In March 1918 he planned and led the offensive against the Allies.
- Dismayed when Allied counter-attack began August 1918; knew that Germany was defeated, and tried to get favourable terms for a surrender from the Americans.
- Dismissed from office by the Kaiser in October 1918.
- After the war constantly blamed Germany's government, including the Kaiser, for letting the military down and causing German defeat. He was a leading proponent of the 'stab in the back' theory.
- Died in 1937.

FIGURE 2

A map of the last stages of the Western Front, 1918.

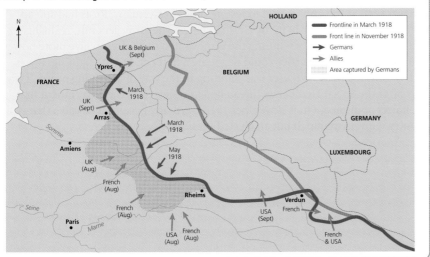

FOCUS TASK

Reasons for the Allied advance

1. Use pages 232–34 and your own research to draw up a list of reasons why the Allies were becoming increasingly confident of victory during 1918.
2. Now imagine it is summer, 1918. Create your own poster to be displayed throughout the cities in England, with the heading 'Success is Ours'. On your poster include images and up to four bullet points to reassure the British public and to indicate why victory for the Allies is imminent.

The Allied advance during the Hundred Days

Between May and August the Germans made no further progress and it was clear that they had run out of time and resources. The Germans had ended trench warfare but it was the Allies who eventually gained the benefit. By now, they had large numbers of well-fed and well-equipped troops, much of the equipment and manpower coming from the USA. These troops were supported by tanks, aircraft and improved artillery. By 1918 the big guns were capable of hitting targets with impressive accuracy as well as laying down smokescreens or giving covering fire for attackers.

On 8 August the Allies counter-attacked along much of the Western Front. This later became known as the German army's 'Black Day'. It was now just a matter of time before the Allies defeated Germany. By late September they had reached the Hindenburg Line. By October the Germans were in full retreat. This period has become known as the 'Hundred Days'.

• Germany surrenders: The impact of the blockade

By November 1918 Germany's allies were surrendering. In the northern ports German sailors mutinied. In Berlin crowds marched through the streets.

SOURCE 3

A member of the German government, October 1918.

We have no meat, potatoes cannot be delivered because we are short of 4,000 trucks a day. Fat is unobtainable. The shortage is so great it is a mystery to me what the people of Berlin live on. The workers say 'Better a horrible end than an endless horror'.

SOURCE 4

A letter from General Hindenburg to the German government, early November 1918.

The supreme commander [i.e. Hindenburg] demands an immediate dispatch of a peace offer to our enemies. There no longer exists any hope of forcing peace on our enemies. The enemy can bring in new and fresh reserves. The German army holds fast and repulses all attacks with success. But we must stop fighting to save the German people from further useless sacrifices.

PRACTICE QUESTION

Study Sources 3 and 4.

Which source is more useful for understanding why the German government decided that it had to end the fighting?
Explain your answer using both sources and your contextual knowledge.

FIGURE 5

German civilian deaths as a result of poor diet.

Year	Number of deaths
1915	88,000
1916	120,000
1917	260,000
1918	294,000

The abdication of the Kaiser

It was not easy for the Kaiser to agree to ABDICATE. However, by November 1918 this was seen as the only option to restore order in Germany. Riots had spread from the Kiel naval base to many German cities. The army generals, realising that there was no hope of winning the war, wanted the Kaiser to give more power to the politicians so that they could negotiate a fairer end to the fighting. It was widely believed that the Kaiser was standing in the way of achieving peace. It was only after the Social Democrats threatened to resign from the government that the Kaiser abdicated. On 9 November 1918 Germany became a REPUBLIC, that is, a country with no monarch but an elected President.

The armistice

Negotiations about a ceasefire, or ARMISTICE, had been going on for the previous few weeks. The German government expressed a willingness to proceed on the basis of President Wilson's Fourteen Points. These listed in general terms the possible ingredients of a peace settlement; they were drawn up in January 1918 – well before the outcome of the war was certain. Wilson had tried to look at the situation from the point of view of fairness, principles and the needs of millions of displaced and starving people in several European countries. For example, his Fourteen Points stated that people should rule themselves, and not be part of huge multi-national empires.

However, after the abdication of the Kaiser, the situation was critical. Friedrich Ebert, a Social Democrat, became Chancellor. German delegates were driven across the front line to Marshal Foch's private train parked in a railway siding. The Germans were given a list of the Allied demands. There was to be no negotiation, and the list did not fully reflect Wilson's fair-minded Fourteen Points. The Allied demands included money to pay for the costs incurred in the war (REPARATIONS payments) and a severe reduction in Germany's army and navy. There were many practical demands that were designed to ensure that Germany could not re-start the war:

- All territory occupied by Germany in France, Belgium, Luxemburg and Alsace-Lorraine was to be evacuated in a fortnight, and everything up to the Rhine within a month.
- It stipulated that 5,000 guns, 25,000 machine guns and 1,700 planes were handed over, as well as 5,000 lorries, 5,000 railway engines and 150,000 trucks.
- All Allied prisoners were to be released.
- Most of the German navy (including all submarines) had to be surrendered.
- In the east all German troops were to be withdrawn from occupied territory.

The armistice was signed at 5 a.m. on 11 November, to come into effect at 11 a.m. Paris time (12 noon German time). Those signing the armistice were later accused of stabbing Germany in the back. They had no choice, but the army generals did not necessarily view it in this way.

Across Europe, in both victorious and defeated nations, there was relief that the fighting was over. In Britain and France there was naturally much rejoicing.

Discussions started in January 1919 at Paris about a detailed peace settlement, leading to the signing of the Treaty of Versailles in June 1919.

SOURCE 6

Crowds celebrating the armistice in London. Sights such as this were common.

SOURCE 7

In his book, *The World Crisis*, Winston Churchill looked back to 11 a.m. on 11 November, 1918.

And then suddenly the first stroke of the chime. I looked again at the broad street beneath me. It was deserted. From the portals of one of the large hotels … darted the slight figure of a girl clerk … Then from all sides men and women came scurrying into the street. The bells of London began to clash. Northumberland Avenue was now crowded with people in hundreds, nay, thousands rushing hither and thither in a frantic manner, shouting and screaming with joy … Flags appeared as if by magic … the strict, war-straitened, regulated streets of London had become a triumphant pandemonium.

PRACTICE QUESTION

Study Sources 6 and 7.

How useful are Sources 6 and 7 to a historian studying reactions to the armistice on 11 November 1918? Explain your answer using Sources 6 and 7 and your contextual knowledge.

FOCUS TASK

Why did Germany ask for an armistice in 1918?

The following factors all played a role in forcing Germany to ask for an armistice in 1918. At the moment they are in alphabetical order. Rearrange them in order of importance, with an explanation of your decision:

- Ability of British and American industry to supply the resources the Allied armies needed
- Arrival of the USA into the war
- British naval blockade
- Failure of Ludendorff Offensive
- German losses in 1916 and 1917
- Increasing improvements in the effectiveness of the British army, 1917–18 (see also pages 222–24 and 233–34.

ACTIVITY

Carry out your own further research on the contributions of Foch and Haig.

Write an article arguing who you think made the greater contribution towards Allied success in the First World War.

PRACTICE QUESTION

'Germany lost the First World War because of the British naval blockade.'

How far do you agree with this statement?
Explain your answer.

How important were individuals in the Allied victory? The roles of Sir Douglas Haig and Marshal Foch

PROFILE

Marshal Foch, 1851–1929

- Born 1851.
- Distinguished military career before 1914.
- One of the leading French generals in the early years of the war.
- Late 1916, after the failure of the Allied offensives, he was removed from his position as the French commander of Army Group North.
- In 1917 he was recalled to become Chief of the General Staff.
- Spring 1918, appointed as Commander-in-Chief of all the Allied armies. Spearheaded the planning that halted the German Offensive at that time.
- Summer 1918, given the title of Marshal Foch, and planned with Haig the grand offensive against Germany from August 1918 onwards.
- His exact contribution has been a matter of debate, and the evidence made less clear because of disputes during the war involving the French government and other military leaders.
- After the war he received many decorations and honours from Allied countries.
- Died in 1929 aged 77.

PROFILE

Sir Douglas Haig, 1861–1928

- Born 1861.
- Military career before the First World War.
- Commanded British armies from 1915 to the end of the war.
- His reputation was adversely affected by the huge casualties at the Somme in 1916.
- Overall strategy proved successful in 1918.
- Actively promoted new strategies and technologies which helped the Allied victory.
- Spring 1918, led determined resistance against the German Offensive.
- In August 1918, working under the overall control of Marshal Foch, led the British army against the main German armies.
- Captured nearly 200,000 prisoners and nearly 3,000 guns.
- In spite of huge British casualties (greater per day than at the Somme), Haig was decorated after the war, and seen as a war hero.
- Died in 1928 aged 66.

KEY WORDS

Make sure you know what these words mean and are able to define them confidently:

- Abdication
- Armistice
- Assassination
- Attrition
- Blockade at sea
- Entente powers
- Kaiser
- Parliamentary government
- Rearmament
- Reichstag
- Schlieffen Plan
- Splendid Isolation
- Stalemate
- Trench warfare
- Triple Alliance
- *Weltpolitik*

TOPIC SUMMARY

Ending the war

- In 1917 Russia ceased to be an effective ally of France and Britain after the Tsar abdicated.
- After the Communists came to power in November 1917, Russia withdrew from the fighting and signed a peace treaty with Germany.
- In April 1917 the USA entered the war after Germany had resumed unrestricted U-boat warfare.
- The USA's military contribution was not large until the last months of the war, but Germany was scared of the potential effect of the USA.
- In March 1918 the Germans tried one last offensive on the Western Front, achieving some success.
- In August 1918 the Allies were able to counter-attack and also made substantial progress.
- In October 1918 negotiations started about a ceasefire.
- In early November riots across German cities caused a crisis for the German government.
- Kaiser Wilhelm II abdicated on 9 November and Germany became a republic.
- The armistice came into effect on 11 November with Germany given no choice about the terms of surrender.

ASSESSMENT FOCUS

Your exam will include four questions on this topic. The question types will be the same every year, but the questions could be on any content from the specification, so you need to know it all!

We have provided one example of each kind of question. For questions based on sources we have used sources that you have already come across in this chapter. We have analysed each of the questions to highlight what you are being asked to do and written a sample answer with comments on how it could be improved.

Source A is Source 10, page 223.

Q1 Study Source A. Source A **suggests** that the machine gun was primarily a defensive weapon. **How do you know?**

Explain your answer by using **Source A** and your **contextual knowledge**.

(4 marks)

Sample answer

The men in the photo are wearing gas masks. That suggests they fear a gas attack. The machine gun is also positioned on the ground, thus suggesting that it is not primarily a mobile weapon.

Source B is Source 6 on page 218. Source C is Source 7 on page 220.

Q2 Study Sources B and C. **How useful** are these **two sources** to a historian studying trenches on the Western Front in the First World War?

Explain your answer using **Sources B and C** and your **contextual knowledge**.

(12 marks)

Sample answer

Source B consists of two photographs of trenches. They show that lots of digging had taken pace so that the men could move around without being seen at ground level. Steps had been built as well as primitive shelters for the soldiers.

Source C is from a British soldier who was present at the Battle of the Somme. He describes what it was like and how scared some of the men were of going over the top. This is useful because it was a first-hand account from someone at the time, who was interviewed for a newspaper article.

Q3 Write an account of how aerial warfare in the First World War **influenced** the outcome of the war. (8 marks)

Sample answer

Aerial warfare became important, especially towards the end of the war. This was surprising really as planes were so primitive in 1914. Pilots took photographs from the air and these could identify buildings, troop movements and conditions on the ground. 'Dogfights' took place, although at first the planes did not actually carry any fitted weapons. By 1918, planes were fighting important battles over the Western Front.

— This answer shows a clear understanding of what the photo is showing, but it should include some knowledge to support its statements. For example, you could explain about the use of gas – what happened if gas masks were not worn. You could also use contextual knowledge to support the idea of the machine gun being a defensive weapon.

— *Study Source 7 from page 220. Attempt this similar question, using that source: This source shows that aerial combat would have been dangerous for the airmen. How do you know?*

— The answer provides some basic comments on each of the two sources, but it needs more in-depth analysis of the content and some examination of the provenance. There is very little contextual knowledge shown. This could be improved substantially.

— *For each of the two sources, make a list of what you know (and don't know!) about the provenance, and whether or not you think this makes the source more or less reliable.*

— *Then think about the context of the period in which the sources were created. What might the photographs have been taken to show? Why was the ex-soldier interviewed in 1986, and how might that affect the emphasis of his account?*

— *Now look at the content of each source. Using your knowledge, think about how useful the content is for studying conditions in the trenches.*

— The answer provides an outline of what happened – it could usefully include more precise details of what actually happened, together with developments in the planes themselves.

— The end of the answer mentions 'importance', but does not really explain the effect of aerial warfare on the overall result.

— *List two main reasons why aerial warfare was important. To help you, think about:*
  — *what the planes could see and report back*
  — *what planes could achieve in the air and on the ground, once they had been equipped with machine guns.*

Q4 'The main reason for the German decision to surrender in November 1918 was the **entry of the USA into the war**.' **How far** do you agree with this statement?

Explain your answer.

(16 marks)

Sample answer

The USA joined the First World War in April 1917 (even though assistance had been provided to the Allies before then). In November 1918, Germany surrendered for a variety of reasons. How important was the role of the USA for Germany to be forced into surrender?

When the USA entered the war it was a huge morale booster for the Allies and seen by Germany as a potential disaster. Immediately, the USA was able to help the Allied effort at sea with protection against the German U-boat warfare that had proved so devastating to Allied shipping. This meant that a larger proportion of the essential war and food supplies needed in Western Europe was reaching safe harbours, while the food situation in Germany was becoming desperate following the success of the Allied blockade on German ports.

On the Western Front there was no immediate help from America. Indeed, there were fewer than 100,000 American soldiers in France by the end of 1917. America had no actual military impact in that year. Yet Germany knew that it had to win quickly before a wave of fresh American troops arrived. It was this that pushed Germany into an all-out attempt for a quick win on the Western Front in early 1918 (made possible because of the withdrawal of Russia from the war).

However, once this offensive, which started in March 1918, ran out of steam by August some way short of its targets in France, the Allies were able to counter-attack with the aid of over 1 million American personnel. The German army was exhausted. Reserves due to have been called up in 1919 had already been used. With more and more Americans arriving in Europe, the German government was forced to face reality – against the wishes of some of the leading army commanders. The Kaiser fled and Germany asked for an armistice. This suggests that the potential strength of the USA could be the decisive factor.

However, there were other factors. While Britain's allies (apart from Russia) remained strong, Germany's allies were crumbling – Austria-Hungary, Bulgaria and Turkey were all on the verge of collapse. There was widespread near-starvation in many areas and crucial decisions had to be made before the next winter set in. The Allied blockade of German ports had had a major impact on food supplies.

The Allies had, overall, made better use of new weapons as the war progressed. The old image of Douglas Haig sticking to old methods does not stand up to close scrutiny. In the Allied counter-attack in August 1918 tanks were increasingly important in forcing German armies to retreat.

The German government also decided to surrender – on the basis of Wilson's Fourteen Points – because it was thought that Germany would be able to gain a less harsh settlement than if they carried on fighting until they were totally defeated. With this in mind, the Kaiser fled to Holland, leaving 'new politicians' to approach the Allies.

Therefore there were several reasons for German surrender. It was the potential of the USA's contribution in 1919 that precipitated the decision to surrender in November 1918.

- This is a clearly argued answer. It develops an explanation of the stated factor and puts this alongside other factors.
- It demonstrates a range of accurate knowledge and understanding, and the answer is organised in a way that is totally focused on the question.
- However, although the 'named factor' (the USA) is dealt with in detail, the other factors could benefit from more precise information.
- The answer contains accurate spelling and punctuation, the meaning is clearly expressed and a range of specialist terms are used to explain arguments.
- *Can you add more details of evidence to this answer, especially in relation to the 'other factors'?*

Now write your own answers to the questions on pages 237–38 using the teacher's feedback to help you.

Conflict and Tension, 1918–1939

6

This wider world study is concerned with understanding the complex and diverse interests of different individuals and states. It focuses on the peace settlements after the First World War, the optimistic hopes of the 1920s, and then the slide towards war in the 1930s. In its focus on the Second World War you will be studying how and why conflict occurred and why it proved difficult to resolve the issues which caused it. You will also be considering the role of key individuals and groups as well as how they were affected by and influenced international relations.

The topic is divided into three sections:
- Peacemaking, 1919 – the aims of the leaders, the terms of the Treaty of Versailles and the reactions to it.
- The formation of the League of Nations, its structure and membership. The peace of the 1920s, followed by the difficulties of the 1930s and the ultimate collapse of the League.
- The origins and outbreak of the Second World War.

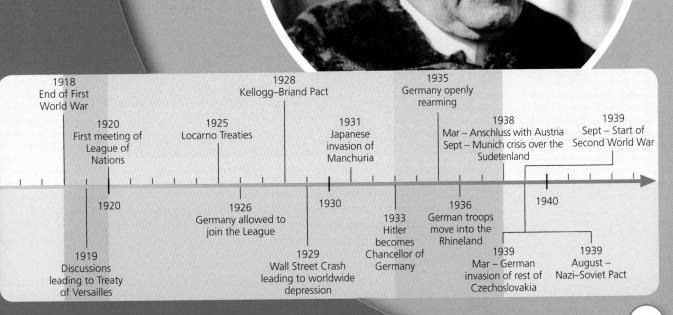

1918
End of First World War

1919
Discussions leading to Treaty of Versailles

1920
First meeting of League of Nations

1920

1925
Locarno Treaties

1926
Germany allowed to join the League

1928
Kellogg–Briand Pact

1929
Wall Street Crash leading to worldwide depression

1930

1931
Japanese invasion of Manchuria

1933
Hitler becomes Chancellor of Germany

1935
Germany openly rearming

1936
German troops move into the Rhineland

1938
Mar – Anschluss with Austria
Sept – Munich crisis over the Sudetenland

1939
Mar – German invasion of rest of Czechoslovakia

1940

1939
August – Nazi–Soviet Pact

1939
Sept – Start of Second World War

6.1 Peacemaking, 1919

● **The armistice**

FOCUS

This section explores the peace settlement made at the end of the First World War. It explains how the leaders of the victorious countries came together to sort out how to deal with Germany and its allies. Germany had no say in the terms that the German representatives had to sign at Versailles.

In this section, you will be studying the following:

● The ARMISTICE and the aims of the Big Three.
● The nature and extent of the Versailles Settlement and the extent to which it satisfied the Big Three.
● The impact of the treaty and why Germans reacted so angrily towards it.

SOURCE **1**

Allied soldiers and officials watch the signing of the Treaty of Versailles.

Source 1 was taken at the signing of the Treaty of Versailles at the Paris Peace Conference. It was a spectacular occasion and a momentous event. Months of hard negotiation, argument and compromise ended when the two German representatives who had been summoned to sign the Treaty did so on 28 June 1919.

When the treaty terms were announced the Germans complained that it was unfair. Many historians have criticised it since. To understand this, we need to look at the mood in 1919.

The aims of the peacemakers in 1919

When the leaders of Britain (Lloyd George), France (Clemenceau) and the USA (Wilson) arrived in Paris in January 1919 to draw up a treaty, they were already under pressure to deal severely with Germany. The people of the victorious countries, particularly in France and Britain, felt strongly that Germany was responsible for the war and should be punished.

There was also a strong feeling that Germany should pay for all the damage and destruction caused by the war. Apart from the USA, all of the countries that had fought in the war were exhausted. Their economies and their industries were in a bad state. Millions of young men had been killed or injured on both sides. Total British and French casualties, killed or injured, probably amounted to over 9 million. Ordinary civilians had faced shortages of food and medicine. Villages and towns in large areas of Belgium and France had been devastated. Illness and disease was commonplace.

As soon as the Paris Peace Conference began, there was disagreement about what the Conference was aiming to do:

- Some felt that the aim was to punish Germany.
- Others felt that the aim was to cripple Germany so that it could not start another war.
- Many felt that the point of the Conference was to reward the winning countries.
- Others believed that the aim of the Conference should be to establish a just and lasting peace.

President Wilson (USA)

Wilson has often been seen as an IDEALIST whose aim was to build a better and more peaceful world from the ruins of the Great War. This is partially true, but Wilson was not a politician who could be pushed around. He refused to cancel the debts owed to the USA by Britain and its Allies so that he could put pressure on them to accept his ideas. Wilson did believe that Germany should be punished. However, he also believed that the treaty with Germany should not be too harsh. His view was that if Germany was treated harshly, some day it would recover and want revenge. Wilson's main aim was to strengthen DEMOCRACY in the defeated nation so that its people would not let its leaders cause another war.

He believed that nations should co-operate to achieve world peace. In January 1918 he published his Fourteen Points to help achieve this. The most important for Wilson was the fourteenth. In this he proposed the setting up of an international body called the LEAGUE OF NATIONS.

He also believed in SELF-DETERMINATION (the idea that nations should rule themselves rather than be ruled by others). He wanted the different peoples of eastern Europe (for example, Poles, Czechs and Slovaks) to rule themselves rather than be part of Austria–Hungary's empire.

FACTFILE

The Paris Peace Conference, 1919–20

- The Conference took place in the Palace of Versailles (a short distance from Paris).
- Thirty-two nations were supposed to be represented, but no one from the defeated countries was invited.
- Five treaties were drawn up at the Conference. The main one was the Treaty of Versailles which dealt with Germany. The other treaties dealt with Germany's allies.
- The important decisions on Germany's fate were taken by the 'Big Three': Clemenceau, Lloyd George and Wilson.
- The Big Three were supported by many diplomats and expert advisers, but they often ignored their advice.
- The Big Three got on badly from the start and relations between them got worse throughout the Conference.

SOURCE 2

President Wilson in 1918.

Sometimes people call me an idealist. Well that is the way I know I am an American … America is the only idealist nation in the world.

THE FOURTEEN POINTS

1. No secret treaties.
2. Free access to the seas in peacetime or wartime.
3. Free trade between countries.
4. All countries to work towards DISARMAMENT.
5. Colonies to have a say in their own future.
6. German troops to leave Russia.
7. Independence for Belgium.
8. France to regain Alsace-Lorraine.
9. Frontier between Austria and Italy to be adjusted.
10. SELF-DETERMINATION for the peoples of eastern Europe (i.e. they should rule themselves).
11. Serbia to have access to the sea.
12. Self-determination for the people in the Turkish Empire.
13. Poland to become an independent state with access to the sea.
14. League of Nations to be set up.

Woodrow Wilson (President of the USA)

Character

An idealist, and a reformer. As president, he had campaigned against corruption in politics and business. However, he had a poor record with regard to the rights of African Americans. He concentrated on keeping the USA out of the war. Once the USA had joined the war, he drew up the Fourteen Points as the basis for ending the war fairly, so that future wars could be avoided. Once he made up his mind on an issue he was almost impossible to shift. This irritated Clemenceau and Lloyd George. So did the fact that Wilson felt the USA was morally superior to the European powers.

Background

- Born in 1856.
- Became a university professor.
- First entered politics in 1910.
- Became president in 1912 and was re-elected in 1916.

Many people in France and Britain did not agree with the ideas contained in Wilson's Fourteen Points. They seemed impractical. Take self-determination, for example. It would be very difficult to give the peoples of eastern Europe the chance to rule themselves because they were scattered across many countries. For example, 25 per cent of the population of the new state of Czechoslovakia were neither Czechs nor Slovaks. Some people were bound to end up being ruled by people from another group with different customs and a different language. Some historians have pointed out that, while Wilson talked a great deal about eastern and central Europe, he did not actually know very much about the area.

Georges Clemenceau (France)

France had suffered enormous damage to its land, industry, people – and self-confidence. Over two-thirds of the men who had served in the French army had been killed or injured. The war affected almost an entire generation. By comparison, Germany seemed to many French people as powerful and threatening as ever.

Ever since 1870, France had felt threatened by its increasingly powerful neighbour, Germany. The war increased this feeling. German land and industry had not been as badly damaged as France's. France's population (around 40 million) was in decline compared to Germany's (around 75 million). Clemenceau and other French leaders saw the treaty as an opportunity to cripple Germany so that it could not attack France again. The French President (Poincaré) even wanted Germany broken up into a collection of smaller states, but Clemenceau knew that the British and Americans would not agree to this. Clemenceau was a REALIST and knew he would probably be forced to compromise on some issues. However, he had to show he was aware of public opinion in France. He demanded a treaty that would weaken Germany as much as possible.

Georges Clemenceau (Prime Minister of France)

Background

- Born in 1841 (he was aged 77 when the Paris Conference began).
- First entered French politics in 1871.
- Was Prime Minister from 1906 to 1909. From 1914 to 1917 he was very critical of the French war leaders. In November 1917 he was himself elected to lead France through the last years of the war.

Character

A hard, tough politician with a reputation for being uncompromising. He had seen his country invaded twice by the Germans, in 1870 and in 1914. He was determined not to allow such devastation ever again.

FIGURE 3

Proportion of forces killed or wounded.

	% dead	% wounded	% unhurt
Britain	12	27	59
France	14	53	29

SOURCE 4

Georges Clemenceau, speech at the Paris Peace Conference (16 June 1919).

The war which began on 1 August 1914, was the greatest crime against humanity and the freedom of peoples that any nation, calling itself civilised, has ever consciously committed. For many years the rulers of Germany, true to the Prussian tradition, strove for a position of dominance in Europe. They were not satisfied with that growing prosperity and influence to which Germany was entitled, and which all other nations were willing to accord her, in the society of free and equal peoples. They required that they should be able to dictate and tyrannize to a subservient Europe, as they dictated and tyrannized over a subservient Germany. Germany's responsibility, however, is not confined to having planned and started the war. She is no less responsible for the savage and inhuman manner in which it was conducted.

The conduct of Germany is almost unexampled in human history. The terrible responsibility which lies at her doors can be seen in the fact that not less than seven million dead lie buried in Europe, while more than twenty million others carry upon them the evidence of wounds and sufferings, because Germany saw fit to gratify her lust for tyranny by resort to war.

Justice, therefore, is the only possible basis for the settlement of the accounts of this terrible war.

THINK

1 In your own words, what were Clemenceau's arguments, as set out in Source 4?
2 What evidence do you have to support Clemenceau's claims?

David Lloyd George (Britain)

At the peace talks Lloyd George was often in the middle ground between Clemenceau and Wilson. He wanted Germany to be justly punished but not too harshly. He wanted Germany to lose its navy and its colonies because Britain thought they threatened the British Empire. However, like Wilson, he did not want Germany to seek revenge in the future and possibly start another war. He was also keen for Britain and Germany to begin trading with each other again. Before the war, Germany had been Britain's second largest trading partner. British people might not like it, but the fact was that trade with Germany meant jobs for them.

Like Clemenceau, Lloyd George had real problems with public pressures at home for a harsh treaty. Even his own MPs did not always agree with him and he had just won the 1918 election in Britain by promising to 'make Germany pay', even though he realised the dangers of this course of action.

PROFILE

David Lloyd George (Prime Minister of Britain)

Background

● Born in 1863.
● First entered politics in 1890. A very able politician who became prime minister in 1916 and remained in power until 1922.

Character

A realist. As an experienced politician, he knew there would have to be compromise. Thus he occupied the middle ground between the views of Wilson and those of Clemenceau.

FOCUS TASK

Part 1: What were the aims of the Big Three at the Paris Peace Conference?

Using the information and sources on pages 240–43, draw up a chart like the one below summarising the aims of the three leaders at the Paris Peace Conference.

N.B. Leave the fifth column blank. You will need it for a later task.

Leader	Country	Attitude towards Germany	Main aim	

SOURCE 5

Lloyd George speaking to the House of Commons, before the Peace Conference.

We want a peace which will be just, but not vindictive. We want a stern peace because the occasion demands it, but the severity must be designed, not for vengeance, but for justice. Above all, we want to protect the future against a repetition of the horrors of this war.

SOURCE 6

A cartoon from *Punch* magazine, 1919. The original title was, 'Giving him rope?', with the caption: '*German criminal (to Allied police)*: "Here, I say, stop! You're hurting me!" *[Aside]* "If I only whine enough I may be able to wriggle out of this yet."'

PUNCH, OR THE LONDON CHARIVARI.—February 19, 1919.

GIVING HIM ROPE?

German Criminal (*to Allied Police*). "HERE, I SAY, STOP! YOU'RE HURTING ME! [*Aside*]
IF I ONLY WHINE ENOUGH I MAY BE ABLE TO WRIGGLE OUT OF THIS YET."

Disagreements and compromises

As the talks at Versailles went on, it became clear that the very different objectives of the three leaders could not all be met. Clemenceau clashed with Wilson over many issues. The USA had not suffered nearly as badly as France in the war. Clemenceau resented Wilson's more generous attitude to Germany. They disagreed over what to do about Germany's Rhineland and coalfields in the Saar. In the end, Wilson had to give way on these issues. In return, Clemenceau and Lloyd George did give Wilson what he wanted in eastern Europe, despite their reservations about his idea of self-determination. However, this mainly affected the other four treaties, not the Treaty of Versailles.

Clemenceau also clashed with Lloyd George, particularly over Lloyd George's desire not to treat Germany too harshly. For example, Clemenceau said: '… if the British are so anxious to appease Germany they should look overseas and make colonial, naval or commercial concessions'. Clemenceau felt that the British were quite happy to treat Germany fairly in Europe, where France rather than Britain was most under threat. However, they were less happy to allow Germany to keep its navy and colonies, which would be more of a threat to Britain.

Wilson and Lloyd George did not always agree either. Lloyd George was particularly unhappy with point 2 of the Fourteen Points, allowing all nations access to the seas. Similarly, Wilson's views on people ruling themselves were somewhat threatening to the British government, for the British Empire ruled millions of people all across the world from London.

THINK

Study Source 6.

1   According to the cartoonist, what is the German trying to achieve?
2   What is the message of the cartoon?

ACTIVITY

1   Work in groups. Draw up a table to show what views:
    – Clemenceau
    – Lloyd George
    would have expressed on points 2, 4, 5, 8, 10 and 14 of President Wilson's Fourteen Points. You can find them on page 241.

2   On your own, write a letter from one of the two leaders to Wilson summarising your view of the Fourteen Points.

3   Copy the following diagram and use it to summarise the attitudes of the three leaders to each other.

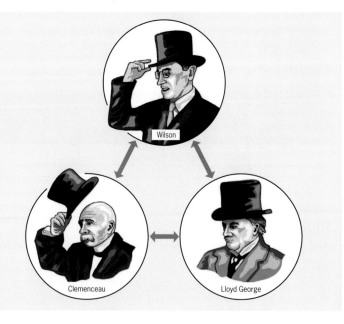

Wilson

Clemenceau

Lloyd George

● The Versailles Settlement, 1919

The Treaty of Versailles involved compromises on the part of the Big Three. But it also was a '*DIKTAT*' – Germany had no say in the negotiations. If the German representatives had not signed the treaty, the Allies promised to re-start the war.

Territorial changes

As a result of the treaty, Germany's overseas empire was taken away (see Figure 9, page 246). This had been one of the causes of bad relations between Britain and Germany before the war. As a result of the treaty, former German colonies became MANDATES controlled by the League of Nations. This meant that the League was given power to rule them. In practice, the League delegated responsibility to its leading members, which effectively meant that France and Britain controlled them.

Germany's European borders were very extensive, and the section dealing with former German territories was a complicated part of the treaty (see Figure 7). In addition to these changes, the treaty also forbade Germany to join together with its former ally Austria.

FIGURE 7

The impact of the Treaty of Versailles on the borders of Europe.

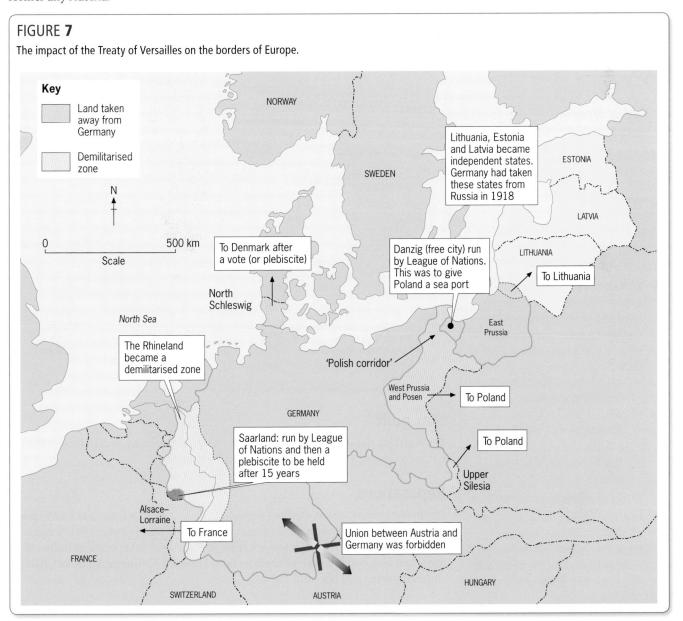

Military restrictions

The size and power of the German army was a major concern of all the powers, especially France. The treaty therefore restricted German armed forces to a level well below what they had been before the war.

● The army was limited to 100,000 men.
● CONSCRIPTION was banned – soldiers had to be volunteers.
● Germany was not allowed armoured vehicles, submarines or aircraft.
● The navy could build only six battleships.
● The Rhineland became a DEMILITARISED ZONE. This meant that no German troops were allowed into that area. The Rhineland was important because it was the border area between Germany and France (see Figure 7).

SOURCE 8

The 'War Guilt' clause from the Treaty of Versailles, 1919.

The Allied governments affirm, and Germany accepts, the responsibility of Germany and her allies for causing all the loss and damage to which the Allied governments and their peoples have been subjected as a result of the war.

FOCUS TASK

Part 2: What were the views of the Big Three on the Treaty of Versailles?

1 Work in threes. Look back at the profiles of Clemenceau, Wilson and Lloyd George on pages 241–43. Choose one each. Study the terms of the treaty on pages 245–46. Think about:
    – which terms of the treaty would please your chosen person and why
    – which terms would displease him and why
    – how far he seemed to have achieved his aims.
    Report your findings to your partners.

2 Look back at the chart you compiled on page 243. There should be a blank fifth column. Put the heading 'How they felt about the treaty' and fill it in for each leader with a one-sentence summary.

FIGURE 9

What happened to Germany's overseas empire as a result of the Treaty of Versailles.

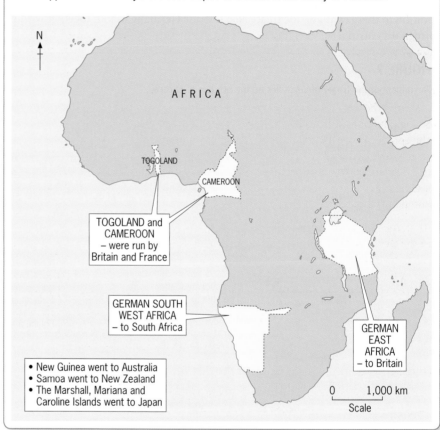

TOGOLAND

CAMEROON

AFRICA

TOGOLAND and CAMEROON – were run by Britain and France

GERMAN SOUTH WEST AFRICA – to South Africa

GERMAN EAST AFRICA – to Britain

• New Guinea went to Australia
• Samoa went to New Zealand
• The Marshall, Mariana and Caroline Islands went to Japan

0   1,000 km
Scale

War guilt

The WAR GUILT clause was simple but was seen by the Germans as extremely harsh. Germany had to accept the blame for starting the war.

Reparations

The major powers agreed, without consulting Germany, that Germany had to pay REPARATIONS to the Allies for the damage caused by the war. The exact figure was not agreed until 1921 when it was set at £6,600 million – an enormous figure. If the terms of the payments had not later been changed, Germany would not have finished paying this bill until 1984.

The impact of the Treaty of Versailles

After the First World War, all of the defeated nations were assigned their own peace treaties, comprising reparations terms. The Austro-Hungarian Empire was split up, with new nations created, such as Czechoslovakia, and separate treaties were imposed on Austria, Hungary, Bulgaria and Turkey. However, it was the Treaty of Versailles, presented to Germany, which was to shape the course of events in Europe in the coming decades.

German objections to the treaty

The terms of the treaty were announced on 7 May to a horrified German nation. Germany was to lose:

- 10 per cent of its land
- all of its overseas colonies
- 12.5 per cent of its population
- 16 per cent of its coalfields and almost half of its iron and steel industry.

Its army was reduced to 100,000 men. It could have no air force, and only a tiny navy. Worst of all, Germany had to accept the blame for starting the war and would therefore pay reparations.

The overall reaction of Germans was one of outrage. They certainly did not feel they had started the war. They did not even feel they had lost the war. In 1919 many Germans did not really understand how bad Germany's military situation had been at the end of the conflict. They believed that the German government had simply agreed to a ceasefire, and that therefore Germany should have been at the Paris Peace Conference to negotiate peace. They were angry that their government was not represented at the talks and that they were being forced to accept a harsh treaty without any choice.

At first, the new government refused to sign the treaty and the German navy sank its own ships in protest. At one point, it looked as though war might break out again. But what could the German leader Ebert do? He consulted the army commander, Hindenburg, who made it clear that Germany could not possibly win, but indicated that as a soldier he would prefer to die fighting.

Ebert was in an impossible position. How could he inflict war and certain defeat on his people? Reluctantly, he agreed to accept the terms of the treaty and it was signed on 28 June 1919.

War guilt and reparations

The 'war guilt' clause was particularly hated. Germans felt at the very least that blame should be shared. What made matters worse, however, was that because Germany was forced to accept blame for the war, it was also expected to pay for all the damage caused by it. The German economy was already in tatters. People had very little food. They feared that the reparations payments would cripple them. As Source 12 shows, there was little sympathy for them among their former enemies.

When Germany failed to pay its reparations in 1922–23, French and Belgian troops took over the Ruhr, Germany's main industrial area. This was completely legal under the treaty (see Chapter 2 on Germany, pages 60–1 for more details).

SOURCE 10

From *Deutsche Zeitung* (*German News*), on the day the treaty was signed.

Today in the Hall of Mirrors the disgraceful Treaty is being signed. Do not forget it! The German people will, with unceasing labour, press forward to reconquer the place among the nations to which it is entitled.

SOURCE 11

From *Peacemakers*, by Professor Margaret Macmillan of the University of Toronto, published in 2001.

The mistake the Allies made, and it did not become clear until much later, was that, as a result of the armistice terms, the great majority of Germans never experienced their country's defeat at first hand. Except in the Rhineland, they did not see occupying troops. The Allies did not march in triumph to Berlin, as the Germans had done in Paris in 1871. In 1918 German soldiers marched home in good order, with crowds cheering their way; in Berlin, Friedrich Ebert, the new president, greeted them with 'No enemy has conquered you'!

SOURCE 12

Headlines and article from the British newspaper the *People*, 25 May 1919.

ALLIES STERN REPLY TO HUNS.
Terms of Peace Treaty Better Than Germany Deserves.
WAR-MAKERS MUST BE MADE TO SUFFER

The Allies have made a stern and uncompromising reply to Rantzau's pleas that German industry will be ruined and her population rendered destitute by the economic terms of the Peace Treaty.

The reply points out that the terms have been determined by Germany's capacity to pay, not by her guilt; and the Huns are reminded that as they were responsible for the war they must suffer the consequences as well as other nations.

The German Delegation has left for Spa to consult with their Government, probably with the idea of arranging a means for 'saving their face', as it is now believed they will sign the Treaty.

THINK

1 How would you describe the tone of Source 10?
2 How does Source 11 help to explain the attitude shown in Source 10?

PRACTICE QUESTION 1

Source 13 is criticising Germany's complaints about the Treaty of Versailles. How do you know?

Explain your answer by using Source 13 and your contextual knowledge.

SOURCE 13

A cartoon from *Punch* magazine, 1919.

THE RECKONING.

Pan-German. "Monstrous, I call it. Why, it's fully a quarter of what we should have made *them* pay, if we'd won."

Disarmament

The disarmament terms upset Germans. An army of 100,000 was very small for a country of Germany's size and the army was a symbol of German pride. Despite Wilson's Fourteen Points calling for disarmament, none of the Allies disarmed to the extent that Germany was disarmed in the 1920s. It is no great surprise that Adolf Hitler received widespread approval for his actions when he rebuilt Germany's armed forces in 1935.

German territories

Germany certainly lost a lot of territory. This was a major blow to German pride, and to its economy. Both the Saar and Upper Silesia were important industrial areas. Meanwhile, as Germany was losing land, the British and French were increasing their empires by taking control of German and Turkish territories in Africa and the Middle East.

The Fourteen Points were not reflected in the treaty

To most Germans, the treatment of Germany was not in keeping with Wilson's Fourteen Points. For example, while self-determination was given to countries such as Estonia, Latvia and Lithuania, German-speaking peoples were being divided by the terms forbidding ANSCHLUSS with Austria or hived off into new countries such as Czechoslovakia to be ruled by non-Germans.

Germany felt further insulted by not being invited to join the League of Nations, an organisation which had been set out in the last of the Fourteen Points.

PRACTICE QUESTION 2

Write an account of how land lost by Germany in 1919 caused anger among Germans.

'Double standards'?

German complaints about the treaty fell on deaf ears. In particular, many people felt that the Germans were themselves operating a double standard. Their call for fairer treatment did not square with the harsh way they had treated Russia in the Treaty of Brest-Litovsk in 1918. Versailles was much less harsh a treaty than Brest-Litovsk.

There was also the fact that Germany's economic problems, although real, were partly self-inflicted. Other states had raised taxes to pay for the war. The KAISER's government planned to pay war debts by extracting reparations from the defeated states.

Reactions of the Allies: Strengths and weaknesses of the settlement

The Treaty of Versailles is one of history's most controversial events. As you have seen, it was bitterly criticised by most Germans in 1919. The treaty was blamed for all of the major problems that Germany faced over the next few years: a revolution; strikes; an invasion; HYPERINFLATION, you name it!

But it was not just the Germans who disliked the treaty. There were plenty of critics in Britain as well.

Even the Big Three who drew up the treaty were not satisfied with it:

- Clemenceau's problem was that it was not harsh enough to satisfy many French people, and in 1920 he was voted out in a general election.
- Lloyd George received a hero's welcome when he returned to Britain. However, at a later date he described the treaty as 'a great pity' and indicated that he believed another war would happen because of it.
- Wilson was very disappointed with the treaty. He said that if he were a German he would not have signed it. In a letter to his wife he said, 'Well, it is finished, and, as no one is satisfied, it makes me hope that we have made a just peace; but it is all in the lap of the gods'. The American CONGRESS later refused to approve the treaty.

So … could the treaty be justified?

It's a very difficult question and one of the difficulties is to distinguish between criticisms from the time and criticisms made with hindsight. History has shown how the treaty helped to create a cruel regime in Germany (the Nazis) and eventually a second world war. This will always affect modern attitudes to the treaty. It has certainly affected historians' judgements. They have tended to side with critics of the treaty. At the time, however, the majority of people outside of Germany thought that it was fair. Some indeed thought that it was not harsh enough. A more generous treaty would have been totally unacceptable to public opinion in Britain or France. Today historians are more likely to point out how hard a task it was to agree the peace settlement. They suggest that the treaty was the best that could be hoped for in the circumstances. Study Sources 14–18 and see what you think.

SOURCE 14

British historian W. Carr, *A History of Germany*, 1972.

Severe as the Treaty seemed to many Germans, it should be remembered that Germany might easily have fared much worse. If Clemenceau had had his way … the Rhineland would have become an independent state, the Saar would have been annexed [joined] to France and Danzig would have become a part of Poland …

FOCUS TASK

Why did Germans react so angrily to the Treaty of Versailles?

Imagine you are in an exam and you have to answer this question. You only have time to explain two of the points below to answer the question of why Germany reacted so angrily to the treaty. Decide which two you would choose and then hold a class vote to see if the rest of your group agrees with you.

1. Germans were not aware of the situation in 1919
2. War guilt and reparations
3. Disarmament
4. German territories
5. Fourteen Points and the League of Nations
6. Double standards.

SOURCE 15

Extract from *Peacemakers* by Professor Margaret Macmillan of the University of Toronto, published in 2001.

The peacemakers of 1919 made mistakes, of course. By their offhand treatment of the non-European world they stirred up resentments for which the West is still paying today. They took pains over the borders in Europe, even if they did not draw them to everyone's satisfaction, but in Africa they carried on the old practice of handing out territory to suit the imperialist powers. In the Middle East they threw together peoples, in Iraq most notably, who still have not managed to cohere into a civil society. If they could have done better, they certainly could have done much worse. They tried, even cynical old Clemenceau, to build a better order. They could not foresee the future and they certainly could not control it. That was up to their successors. When war came in 1939, it was a result of twenty years of decisions taken or not taken, not of arrangements made in 1919.

SOURCE 16

Winston Churchill, speaking in 1919. He had been a member of the government and a serving officer during the war.

… a fair judgment upon the settlement, a simple explanation of how it arose, cannot leave the authors of the new map of Europe under serious reproach. To an overwhelming extent the wishes of the various populations prevailed.

SOURCE 17

An extract from the diary of Edward House, one of Wilson's top officials, 29 June 1919.

Looking at the conference in retrospect there is much to approve and much to regret. It is easy to say what should have been done, but more difficult to have found a way for doing it.

To those who are saying that the Treaty is bad and should never have been made and that it will involve Europe in infinite difficulties in its enforcement, I feel like admitting it. But I would also say in reply that empires cannot be shattered and new states raised upon their ruins without disturbance. To create new boundaries is always to create new troubles. The one follows the other. While I should have preferred a different peace, I doubt whether it could have been made, for the ingredients for such a peace as I would have had were lacking at Paris.

THINK

1 Who is the 'Tiger' referred to in Source 18?
2 Explain the message of the cartoon.

PRACTICE QUESTIONS

Study Sources 17 and 18.

1 How useful are the two sources for studying reactions to the Treaty of Versailles?
  Explain your answer using both sources and your contextual knowledge.

2 'The main cause of German dissatisfaction with the peace settlement was reparations payments.'
  How far do you agree with this statement?
  Explain your answer.

SOURCE 18

A cartoon by the artist Will Dyson, first published in the *Daily Herald*, 13 May 1919. The '1940 class' represents the children born in the 1920s who might die in a future war resulting from the treaty.

PEACE AND FUTURE CANNON FODDER

The Tiger: "Curious! I seem to hear a child weeping!"

TOPIC SUMMARY

Peacemaking

- Wilson intended the peace settlement to be based on his Fourteen Points.
- Clemenceau wanted a much tougher treaty comprising punishment and guarantees that Germany would not invade France again.
- Lloyd George had to reflect British public opinion, wanting revenge, whereas he knew that Germany needed to recover to continue to be one of Britain's main trading partners.
- The Versailles Settlement was a *Diktat* – the German representatives had to sign.
- Germany lost territory and had restrictions placed on her armed forces.
- Germany was forced to accept war guilt and as a result had to pay reparations.
- Germans hated the terms of the treaty. The Allies were not united in their praise either.
- The settlement left bitterness which festered throughout the 1930s.

6.2 The League of Nations and international peace

FOCUS

After the First World War the overriding concern was to avoid repeating conflict on a global scale. A League of Nations was therefore created, intent on solving international problems. But by 1939 the League had collapsed and the world faced yet another conflict of even greater proportions.

In this part of the topic you will study the following:

● The League of Nations, its make-up and impact, weaknesses and strengths.
● Diplomacy outside the League in the 1920s and the reasons for optimism over a peaceful Europe.
● How the League declined in the 1930s and its failure to prevent war in 1939.

● The formation and Covenant of the League of Nations

SOURCE 1

The front page of the *Daily Express*, 27 December 1918. Following the Allied victory in the First World War, President Woodrow Wilson was given a rapturous reception by ordinary people wherever he went in western Europe.

Although there was agreement on a League being formed in 1918, there was disagreement about what kind of organisation it should be. President Wilson wanted the League of Nations to be like a world parliament where representatives of all nations could meet regularly to decide on any matters that affected them all. Many British leaders thought the best League would be a simple organisation that would just get together in emergencies. France proposed a strong League with its own army.

PRACTICE QUESTION

Source 3 is very doubtful about whether the League of Nations will succeed in keeping the peace. How do you know?

Explain your answer by using the source and your contextual knowledge.

It was President Wilson who won. He insisted that discussions about a League should be a major part of the peace treaties and in 1919 he took personal charge of drawing up plans for the League. By February he had drafted a very ambitious plan:

- All the major nations would join the League.
- They would disarm.
- If they had a dispute with another country, they would take it to the League. They promised to accept the decision made by the League.
- They also promised to protect one another if they were invaded. This was called the Covenant, and all countries joining the League had to sign this.
- If any member did break the Covenant and go to war, other members promised to stop trading with that country and to send troops if necessary to force it to stop fighting.

Wilson's hope was that CITIZENS of all countries would be so much against another conflict that this would prevent their leaders from going to war. Many politicians had grave doubts about Wilson's plans, and Wilson's own arrogant style did not help matters. He acted as if only he knew the solutions to Europe's problems.

Even so, most people in Europe were prepared to give Wilson's suggestions a try. They hoped that no country would dare invade another if they knew that the USA and other powerful nations of the world would stop trading with them or send their armies to stop them. In 1919 hopes were high that the League, with the United States in the driving seat, could be a powerful peacemaker.

Membership of the League and how it changed

Absence of the USA

Of course the USA could only be in the driving seat of the League if it belonged to it. Back in the USA, Wilson was facing major problems. He needed the approval of Congress to join the League and in the USA this idea was not popular. The USA did not want what they referred to as 'European entanglements'. European countries should now sort out their own problems.

Wilson toured the USA to put his arguments to the people, but when Congress voted in 1919 he was defeated. Despite serious illness he continued to press for the USA to join the League. He took the proposal back to Congress again in March 1920 but was defeated again. When the League opened for business in January 1920 the American chair was empty. The USA never joined. It was a bitter disappointment to Wilson and a body blow to the League.

Who was in the League and how was the League supposed to work?

In the absence of the USA, Britain and France were the most powerful countries in the League. Italy and Japan were also permanent members of the Council, but throughout the 1920s and 1930s it was Britain and France who usually guided policy. Any action by the League needed their support.

SOURCE 3

A cartoon from the magazine *Punch*, March 1919. *Punch* was famous for its political cartoons.

OVERWEIGHTED.

President Wilson. "HERE'S YOUR OLIVE BRANCH. NOW GET BUSY."
Dove of Peace. "OF COURSE I WANT TO PLEASE EVERYBODY; BUT ISN'T THIS A BIT THICK?"

However, both countries were poorly placed to take on this role. Both had been weakened by the First World War. Neither country was quite the major power it had once been. Neither of them had the resources to fill the gap left by the USA. Indeed, some British politicians said that, had they foreseen the American decision, they would not have voted to join the League either. They felt that the Americans were the only nation with the resources or influence to make the League work. In particular, they felt that TRADE SANCTIONS would only work if the Americans applied them.

For the leaders of Britain and France, the League posed a real problem. They were the ones who had to make it work, yet even at the start they doubted how effective it could be.

SOURCE 4

A *Punch* cartoon from 10 December 1919. The figure in the white top hat represents the USA.

THE GAP IN THE BRIDGE.

SOURCE 5

Arthur Balfour, chief British representative at the League of Nations, speaking in 1920.

The League of Nations is not set up to deal with a world in chaos, or with any part of the world which is in chaos. The League of Nations may give assistance but it is not, and cannot be, a complete instrument for bringing order out of chaos.

Both countries had other priorities. British politicians, for example, were more interested in rebuilding British trade and looking after the British Empire than in being an international police force.

France's main concern was still Germany. It was worried that without an army of its own the League was too weak to protect France from its powerful neighbour. It did not think Britain was likely to send an army to help it. This made France quite prepared to bypass the League if necessary in order to strengthen its position against Germany.

FIGURE 6

Membership of the League of Nations. This chart shows only the most powerful nations. More than 50 other countries were also members.

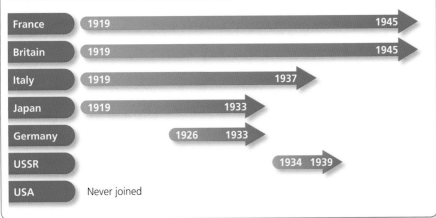

France	1919 — 1945
Britain	1919 — 1945
Italy	1919 — 1937
Japan	1919 — 1933
Germany	1926 — 1933
USSR	1934 — 1939
USA	Never joined

THINK

1 Look at Source 4. Explain what the cartoonist was trying to say:
   – about the USA
   – about the League of Nations.

2 Look back at Source 3. Does Source 4 agree with Source 3 about the chances of the League of Nations' success?

3 List the strengths and weaknesses of Britain and France as leaders of the League of Nations.

4 France proposed that the League should have an army of its own. Why do you think most people opposed this?

5 Think back to Wilson's ideas for the League. What problems would be caused by the fact that:
   a) the USA
   b) Germany
   were not members of the League?

The organisation and powers of the League

The Covenant laid out the League's structure and the rules for each of the bodies within it – see Figure 7 below.

FIGURE 7

The League of Nations Agencies.

The Assembly

The Assembly was the League's Parliament. Every country in the League sent a representative to the Assembly. The Assembly could recommend action to the Council and could vote on:

- admitting new members to the League
- appointing temporary members of the Council
- the budget of the League
- other ideas put forward by the Council.

The Assembly only met once a year. Decisions made by the Assembly had to be unanimous – they had to be agreed by all members of the Assembly.

The Council

The Council was a smaller group which met more often, usually about five times a year and in case of emergency. It included:

- permanent members. In 1920 these were Britain, France, Italy and Japan.
- temporary members. They were elected by the Assembly for three-year periods. The number of temporary members varied between four and nine at different times in the League's history.

Each of the permanent members of the Council had a veto. This meant that one permanent member could stop the Council acting even if all other members agreed. The main idea behind the Council was that if any disputes arose between members, the members brought the problem to the Council and it was sorted out through discussion before matters got out of hand. However, if this did not work, the Council could use a range of powers:

- Moral condemnation: they could decide which country was 'the aggressor', i.e. which country was to blame for the trouble. They could condemn the aggressor's action and tell it to stop what it was doing.
- Economic and financial sanctions: members of the League could refuse to trade with the aggressor.
- Military force: the armed forces of member countries could be used against an aggressor.

The Permanent Court of International Justice

This was meant to be a key part of the League's job of settling disputes between countries peacefully. The Court was based at The Hague in the Netherlands and was made up of judges from the member countries.

If it was asked, the Court would give a decision on a border dispute between two countries. It also gave legal advice to the Assembly or Council.

However, the Court was not like the courts which carried out the law within member countries. It had no way of making sure that countries followed its rulings.

The Secretariat

The Secretariat was a sort of civil service. It kept records of League meetings and prepared reports for the different agencies of the League. The Secretariat had specialist sections covering areas such as health, disarmament and economic matters.

The International Labour Organisation (ILO)

The ILO brought together employers, governments and workers' representatives once a year. Its aim was to improve the conditions of working people throughout the world. It collected statistics and information about working conditions and it tried to persuade member countries to adopt its suggestions.

FACTFILE

The League of Nations

- The League's home was in Geneva in Switzerland.
- Despite being the brainchild of the US President, the USA was never a member of the League.
- The League was based on a Covenant. This included a set of 26 Articles or rules which all members of the League agreed to follow.
- Probably the most important Article was Article 10: 'The Members of the League undertake to respect and preserve as against external aggression the territorial integrity and existing political independence of all Members of the League. In case of any such aggression or in case of any threat or danger of such aggression the Council [of the League] shall advise upon the means by which this obligation shall be fulfilled.'
- Article 10 really meant COLLECTIVE SECURITY. By acting together (collectively), the members of the League could prevent war by defending the lands and interests of all nations, large or small.
- One of the jobs of the League was to uphold and enforce the Treaty of Versailles.
- Forty-two countries joined the League at the start. By the 1930s it had 59 members.

ACTIVITY

1 Consider each part of the League of Nations. In your own table, list the strengths and weaknesses of each part:
   - The ASSEMBLY
   - The COUNCIL
   - The SECRETARIAT
   - The Permanent Court of International Justice
   - The International Labour Organisation.

2 Choose three of the League of Nations Agencies outlined on these pages. For each write a sentence about what they did. Then say why you think these Agencies could only have limited success.

The League of Nations Commissions

As well as dealing with disputes between its members, the League also attempted to tackle other major problems. This was done through commissions or committees such as:

The Mandates Commission
The First World War had led to many former colonies of Germany and her allies ending up as League of Nations mandates ruled by Britain and France on behalf of the League. The Mandates Commission made sure that Britain or France acted in the interests of the people of that territory, not in its own interests.

The Refugees Committee
This helped to return refugees to their original homes after the end of the First World War.

The Slavery Commission
This worked to abolish SLAVERY around the world.

The Health Committee
The Health Committee attempted to deal with the problem of dangerous diseases and to educate people about health and sanitation.

FOCUS TASK

Were there weaknesses in the League's organisation?

Here is a conversation which might have taken place between two diplomats in 1920.

> Peace at last! The League of Nations will keep large and small nations secure.

> I'm not sure. It might look impressive but I think there are weaknesses in the League.

Work in pairs.

Choose one statement each and write out the reasons each diplomat might give for his opinion.

In your answer make sure you refer to:
- the membership of the League
- what the main bodies within the League can do
- how each body will make decisions
- how the League will enforce its decisions.

The contribution of the League to peace in the 1920s

Throughout the 1920s the League of Nations was called upon to help sort out international disputes. In 1921, for example, the League helped to solve a dispute between Poland and Germany over the territory of Upper Silesia. League troops took temporary control of the area and the League organised a vote of the people who lived there to decide which state they wanted to be part of. The industrial areas voted mainly for Germany, rural areas for Poland. The League divided the region along these lines, with safeguards for co-operation over power and water supplies in the border areas. Both Poland and Germany accepted the final result of the vote.

Similarly, in 1920, both Sweden and Finland claimed the right to the Aaland Islands. The League investigated the issue and the territory was given to Finland. Sweden accepted the decision. And in 1925 Greece invaded Bulgaria. The League of Nations ordered the Greeks to withdraw, and they did.

In addition, some of the League's agencies did extremely important humanitarian work, as described in Figure 7 on pages 254–255. For example, hundreds of thousands of refugees and prisoners of war were returned to their home countries.

Indeed, the later 1920s seemed a time of promise in world affairs. In 1925 Germany signed the Locarno Treaties and appeared to accept the Treaty of Versailles (the Locarno agreements sought to clarify the European borders and gave France some guarantee of border security). Germany was invited to join the League of Nations in 1926. In 1928 most of the world's major powers signed the Kellogg–Briand Pact, agreeing not to use force as a way of settling international disputes. There was much to be optimistic about.

However, when in 1920 Poland invaded Vilna, the capital of Lithuania, the League's protestations were ignored. This illustrated the limited nature of the League's actual powers to enforce its decisions, even when these decisions involved smaller nations. But the success of the League was always going to be measured by how well it stood up to a major power acting aggressively. In 1923 Benito Mussolini, the leader of Italy, invaded the Greek island of Corfu as part of a dispute with Greece. Mussolini was clearly the aggressor, but the League sided with him. The Greeks even had to pay Italy compensation. Cracks in the League's strengths were beginning to show.

FOCUS TASK

How successful was the League in the 1920s?

Look back to the Focus Task on page 255.

1 Using the information on this page, write one speech bubble for each of the two diplomats to explain how they would feel about the League of Nations by the end of the 1920s.
2 Add a speech bubble for each diplomat to explain their views on the future of the League.

● Diplomacy outside the League of Nations in the 1920s

During the 1920s not all international diplomacy took place as a result of the League of Nations. There were some key treaties and alliances agreed outside the League.

The Locarno treaties

A whole series of Treaties were drawn up at Locarno in Switzerland in autumn 1925 and then signed in London in December of that year. These treaties involved leading European countries, including Germany and the USSR who were not in the League of Nations at that time.

Some of the treaties were agreements to settle disputes peacefully. However, the main treaty involved France, Belgium and Germany who promised not to invade each other, and Germany agreed to keep its troops out of the Rhineland. In other words, Germany was accepting the territorial terms of the Treaty of Versailles on her western front. However, there was no similar firm promise on her eastern front.

The Kellogg–Briand Pact, 1928

On the initiative of US Secretary of State, Frank B. Kellogg, and the French foreign minister, Aristide Briand, 61 countries signed the Kellogg–Briand Pact. Each country promised not to use war as a way of solving international disputes. It seemed like a triumph of pacifism and common sense. However, in retrospect it could be seen as a weakening of the League of Nations whose apparent strength lay in the belief in COLLECTIVE SECURITY. No sanctions were agreed upon against countries which ignored the agreement in the future.

Thus in the late 1920s there was an air of optimism surrounding European diplomacy. However, very soon in the 1930s all this changed as DICTATORSHIPS tore up agreements and treaties.

THINK

1 Why do you think the Locarno Treaties were drawn up in Switzerland?
2 Why do you think the agreements at Locarno about western Europe were reached so easily?
3 Why were no promises made about eastern Europe?
4 Explain how the Kellogg–Briand Pact can be seen as:
   a) a success for world peace
   b) an indication that future world peace might not be secure.

FOCUS TASK

Why was there optimism over peace in Europe by the end of the 1920s?

Work in small groups and use your findings on pages 255–56 to discuss the following.

From an American point of view in early 1929, European peace looked secure. To what extent was this due to the Locarno Treaties and Kellogg Pact, and to what extent was this due to the existence and work of the League of Nations?

FOCUS TASK

The decline of the League, Part 1

Study Figure 8, which shows the League's declining influence.

Some teachers and students have told us that the shape of the decline is wrong. They think the slope should be softer in some places and steeper in others. As you work through the rest of the chapter, see if you agree. You could make your own copy of the diagram to suggest a better shape for the slope.

● The collapse of the League in the 1930s

The historian Piers Brendon has called the 1930s the 'Dark Valley', because it was a period of tension and mistrust which paved the way for the devastation of the Second World War.

What went wrong? Why did the League fail to keep the peace? Figure 8 summarises the three main problems which the League dealt with in the 1930s. You are going to investigate two of these issues in the rest of this chapter.

How did the Depression affect international relations?

As Figure 8 shows, the 1930s saw a steady decline in the influence of the League. Historians are still debating exactly why this happened. Some argue that the key factor was the effect of the worldwide ECONOMIC DEPRESSION of the 1930s. The DEPRESSION began when the US economy crashed in 1929. Everyone traded with the USA. Most countries also borrowed money from American banks. As a result of this trade, most countries were getting richer in the 1920s and this reduced international tension. When the US economy crashed it led to poverty, unemployment and misery in many other countries. This in turn created major political problems, as you can see in Figure 9.

FIGURE 8

The failure of the League of Nations in the 1930s.

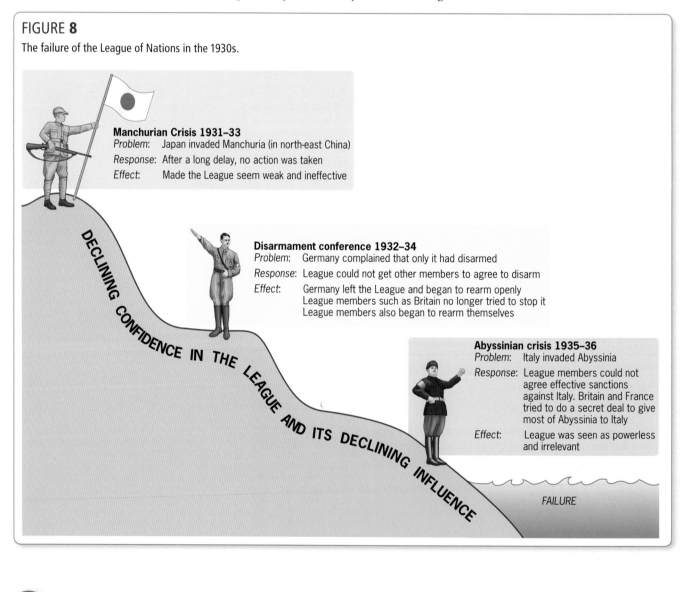

Manchurian Crisis 1931–33
Problem: Japan invaded Manchuria (in north-east China)
Response: After a long delay, no action was taken
Effect: Made the League seem weak and ineffective

Disarmament conference 1932–34
Problem: Germany complained that only it had disarmed
Response: League could not get other members to agree to disarm
Effect: Germany left the League and began to rearm openly
League members such as Britain no longer tried to stop it
League members also began to rearm themselves

Abyssinian crisis 1935–36
Problem: Italy invaded Abyssinia
Response: League members could not agree effective sanctions against Italy. Britain and France tried to do a secret deal to give most of Abyssinia to Italy
Effect: League was seen as powerless and irrelevant

DECLINING CONFIDENCE IN THE LEAGUE AND ITS DECLINING INFLUENCE

FAILURE

There were also problems in Asia. Since 1900, Japan's economy and population had been growing rapidly. By the 1920s Japan was a major power:

- It had a very powerful army and navy – army leaders often dictated government policy.
- It had a strong industry, exporting goods to the USA and China in particular.
- It had a growing empire which included the Korean peninsula (see Figure 10 on page 260).

The Depression hit Japan badly. Both China and the USA put up TARIFFS (trade barriers) against Japanese goods. The collapse of the American market put the Japanese economy in crisis. Without this trade Japan could not feed its people. Army leaders in Japan were in no doubt about the solution to Japan's problems – they wanted to build up a Japanese empire by force.

So the question historians discuss is how far the economic depression and the problems it caused were responsible for the failure of the League. In the rest of this chapter you are going to examine two of the developments shown in Figure 9 and judge for yourself.

FOCUS TASK

How did the Depression affect the League of Nations?

Look back at the Focus Task on page 256.

1 Using the information on pages 258–59, add another speech bubble for each of the two diplomats to sum up their views of the League now that the world has been affected by the Depression.

2 Add a speech bubble for each diplomat to explain their views on the future of the League.

FIGURE 9

How the Depression affected various countries' attitudes to international relations.

The USA
One way that the League of Nations could stop one country invading another was to use economic sanctions. But the Depression made the USA unwilling to help in this because economic sanctions would make its own economy even worse.

Top priority – sort out US economy. Low priority – help sort out international disputes.

Britain
Britain was one of the leaders of the League of Nations. But, like the USA, it was unwilling to help sort out international disputes while its economy was bad. For example, when Japan invaded Manchuria it did nothing – it did not support economic sanctions against Japan and did not send troops to protect Manchuria.

Top priority – sort out British economy. Low priority – help sort out international disputes.

Germany
The Depression hit Germany badly. There was unemployment, poverty and chaos. Germany's weak leaders seemed unable to do anything. As a result, Germans elected Adolf Hitler to lead them. He was not good news for international peace. He openly planned to invade Germany's neighbours and to win back land that Germany had lost in the Great War.

He'll make Germany great again.

Japan
The Depression threatened to bankrupt Japan. Its main export was silk to the USA, but the USA was buying less silk. So Japan had less money to buy food and raw materials. Its leaders were all army generals. They decided to build an empire by taking over weaker countries that had the raw materials Japan needed. They started by invading Manchuria (part of China) in 1931.

Plans for Japanese empire

Italy
In Italy economic problems encouraged Mussolini to try and build an overseas empire to distract people's attention from the difficulties the government faced.

The Manchurian Crisis, 1931–33

FIGURE 10

The railways and natural resources of Manchuria.

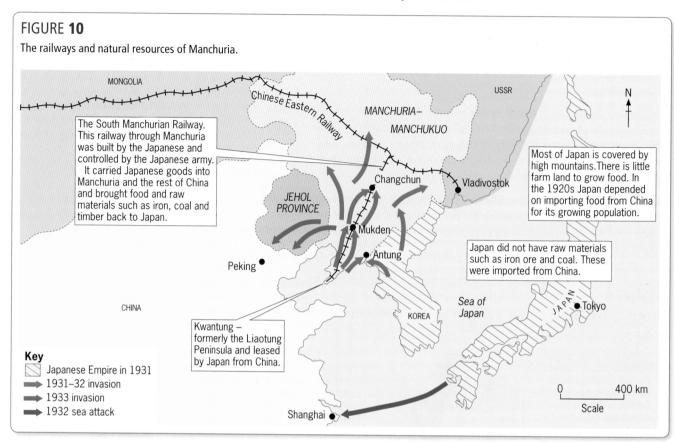

The South Manchurian Railway. This railway through Manchuria was built by the Japanese and controlled by the Japanese army. It carried Japanese goods into Manchuria and the rest of China and brought food and raw materials such as iron, coal and timber back to Japan.

Most of Japan is covered by high mountains. There is little farm land to grow food. In the 1920s Japan depended on importing food from China for its growing population.

Japan did not have raw materials such as iron ore and coal. These were imported from China.

Kwantung – formerly the Liaotung Peninsula and leased by Japan from China.

Key
- Japanese Empire in 1931
- 1931–32 invasion
- 1933 invasion
- 1932 sea attack

0   400 km
Scale

SOURCE 11

Japanese troops in action in Manchuria.

In 1931 an incident in Manchuria gave Japan the opportunity it had been looking for to expand the Japanese Empire. As you can see from Figure 10, the Japanese army controlled the South Manchurian Railway. In September 1931 they claimed that Chinese soldiers had sabotaged the railway. In retaliation they overran Manchuria and threw out all Chinese forces. In February 1932 Japan set up a PUPPET GOVERNMENT in Manchuria, which did exactly what the Japanese army told it to do. The Japanese renamed the province Manchukuo. Later in 1932 Japanese aeroplanes and gunships bombed Shanghai. The civilian government in Japan told the Japanese army to withdraw, but its instructions were ignored. It was clear that it was the army and not the government that was in control of Japanese foreign policy.

China appealed to the League of Nations. Japan claimed it was not invading as an aggressor, but simply settling a local difficulty. The Japanese argued that China was in such a state of anarchy that they had to invade in self-defence to keep peace in the area. For the League of Nations this was a serious test. Japan was a leading member of the League. It needed careful handling. What should the League do?

There was now a long and frustrating delay. The League's officials sailed round the world to assess the situation in Manchuria for themselves. It was September 1932 – a full year after the invasion – before they presented their report. It was detailed and balanced, but the judgement was very clear. Japan had acted unlawfully. Manchuria should be returned to the Chinese.

However, in February 1933, instead of withdrawing from Manchuria, the Japanese announced that they intended to invade more of China. They still argued that this was necessary in self-defence. On 24 February 1933 the report from the League's officials was approved by 42 votes to 1 in the Assembly. Only Japan voted against. Smarting at the insult, Japan resigned from the League on 27 March 1933. The next week it invaded Jehol (see Figure 10).

The League was powerless. It discussed economic sanctions, but without the USA, Japan's main trading partner, they would be meaningless. Besides, Britain seemed more interested in keeping up good relationships with Japan than in agreeing to sanctions. The League also discussed banning arms sales to Japan, but the member countries could not even agree about that. They were worried that Japan would retaliate and the war would escalate.

There was no prospect at all of Britain and France risking their navies or armies in a war with Japan. Only the USA and the USSR would have had the resources to remove the Japanese from Manchuria by force and they were not even members of the League.

SOURCE 12

A cartoon by David Low, 1933. Low was one of the most famous cartoonists of the 1930s. He regularly criticised both the actions of dictators around the world and the ineffectiveness of the League of Nations. The paper next to the woman's body is labelled 'Honour of Nations' and the box beside the man is labelled 'Face-saving outfit'.

All sorts of excuses were offered for the failure of the League. Japan was so far away. Japan was a special case. Japan did have a point when it said that China was itself in the grip of anarchy. However, the significance of the Manchurian Crisis was obvious. As many of its critics had predicted, the League was powerless if a strong nation decided to pursue an aggressive policy and invade its neighbours. Japan had committed blatant aggression and got away with it. Back in Europe, both Hitler and Mussolini looked on with interest. Within three years they would both follow Japan's example.

THINK

1 Why did it take so long for the League to make a decision over Manchuria?
2 Look at Source 12. What criticisms is the cartoonist making of:
   a) Japan
   b) the League?
3 Did the League fail in this incident because of the way it worked or because of the attitude of its members?

PRACTICE QUESTION

Study Sources 12 and 13.

How useful are Sources 12 and 13 to a historian studying the Manchurian Crisis, 1931–33?
Explain your answer using Sources 12 and 13 and your contextual knowledge.

SOURCE 13

The British elder statesman Sir Austen Chamberlain visited the League of Nations late in 1932 in the middle of the Manchurian Crisis. This is an adapted extract from his letters.

I was sad to find everyone [at the League] so dejected. The Assembly was a dead thing. The Council was without confidence in itself. Beneš [the Czechoslovak leader], who is not given to hysterics, said [about the people at the League] 'They are too frightened. I tell them we are not going to have war now; we have five years before us, perhaps six. We must make the most of them.'

The Abyssinian crisis and its consequences

The fatal blow to the League came when the Italian dictator Mussolini invaded Abyssinia (now Ethiopia) in 1935. There were both similarities with and differences from the Japanese invasion of Manchuria. Like Japan, Italy was a leading member of the League. Like Japan, Italy wanted to expand its empire by invading another country. However, unlike Manchuria, this dispute was on the League's doorstep. Italy was a European power. It even had a border with France. Abyssinia bordered on the Anglo-Egyptian territory of Sudan and the British colonies of Kenya and British Somaliland.

Unlike events in Manchuria, the League could not claim that this problem was in an inaccessible part of the world. Some argued that Manchuria had been a special case. Would the League do any better in this Abyssinian crisis?

FIGURE 14

British, French and Italian possessions in eastern Africa.

N

ITALY

Supplies via the Suez Canal

LIBYA

EGYPT

FRENCH EMPIRE IN AFRICA

SUDAN

ERITREA

Addis Ababa

BRITISH SOMALILAND

Wal-Wal

ABYSSINIA

ITALIAN SOMALILAND

UGANDA

KENYA

TANGANYIKA

0   500 km
Scale

Key

→ Italian advance

Italian territory

French territory

British territory or strong British influence

SOURCE 15

A cartoon from *Punch*, 1935. *Punch* was usually very patriotic towards Britain. It seldom criticised British politicians over foreign policy.

THE AWFUL WARNING.

FRANCE AND ENGLAND (*together ?*).

"WE DON'T WANT YOU TO FIGHT,
BUT, BY JINGO, IF YOU DO,
WE SHALL PROBABLY ISSUE A JOINT MEMORANDUM
SUGGESTING A MILD DISAPPROVAL OF YOU."

Background

The origins of this crisis lay back in the previous century. In 1896 Italian troops had tried to invade Abyssinia but had been defeated by a poorly equipped army of tribesmen. Mussolini wanted revenge for this humiliating defeat. He also had his eye on the fertile lands and mineral wealth of Abyssinia. However, most importantly, he wanted glory and conquest. His style of leadership needed military victories and he had often talked of restoring the glory of the Roman Empire.

In December 1934 there was a dispute between Italian and Ethiopian soldiers at the Wal-Wal oasis – 80 km inside Abyssinia. Mussolini took this as his cue and claimed this was actually Italian territory. He demanded an apology and began preparing the Italian army for an invasion of Abyssinia. The Abyssinian emperor Haile Selassie appealed to the League for help.

Phase 1 – January 1935 to October 1935: The League plays for time

In this period Mussolini was supposedly negotiating with the League to settle the dispute, while at the same time he was shipping his vast army to Africa and whipping up war fever among the Italian people – he was preparing for a full-scale invasion of Abyssinia.

To start with, the British and the French failed to take the situation seriously. They played for time. They were desperate to keep good relations with Mussolini, who seemed to be their strongest ally against Hitler. Early in 1935 they signed an agreement with him known as the Stresa Pact which formalised a protest at German REARMAMENT and a commitment to stand united against Germany. At the meeting to discuss this, they did not even raise the question of Abyssinia. Some historians suggest that Mussolini believed that Britain and France had promised to turn a blind eye to his exploits in Abyssinia in return for his joining them in the Stresa Pact.

However, as the year wore on, there was a public outcry against Italy's behaviour. A ballot was taken by the League of Nations Union in Britain in 1934–35. It showed that a majority of British people supported the use of military force to defend Abyssinia if necessary. Facing an autumn election at home, British politicians now began to 'get tough'. At an assembly of the League, the British Foreign Secretary, Sir Samuel Hoare, made a grand speech about the value of collective security, to the delight of the League's members and all the smaller nations. There was much talking and negotiating. However, the League never actually did anything to discourage Mussolini.

On 4 September, after eight months' deliberation, a committee reported to the League that neither side could be held responsible for the Wal-Wal incident. The League put forward a plan that would give Mussolini some of Abyssinia. Mussolini rejected it.

ACTIVITY

Draw a timeline, from December 1934 to May 1936, down the middle of a piece of paper and use the text to mark the key events on it. On one side put the actions of Mussolini or Hitler, on the other the actions of Britain, France and the League.

Phase 2 – October 1935 to March 1936: Sanctions or not?

In October 1935 Mussolini's army was ready. He launched a full-scale invasion of Abyssinia. Despite brave resistance, the Abyssinians were no match for the modern Italian army equipped with tanks, aeroplanes and poison gas.

This was a clear-cut case of a large, powerful state attacking a smaller one. The League was designed for just such disputes and, unlike in the Manchurian Crisis, it was ideally placed to act.

Why the League of Nations failed over Abyssinia

There was no doubting the seriousness of the issue either. The Covenant (see Factfile, page 255) made it clear that sanctions must be introduced against the aggressor. A committee was immediately set up to agree what sanctions to impose.

SOURCE 16

British statesman Philip Noel Baker speaking at the very last session of the League in April 1946.

Yes, we know that World War began in Manchuria fifteen years ago. We know that four years later we could easily have stopped Mussolini if we had taken the sanctions against Mussolini that were obviously required, if we had closed the Suez Canal to the aggressor and stopped his oil.

Sanctions would only work if they were imposed quickly and decisively. Each week a decision was delayed would allow Mussolini to build up his stockpile of raw materials. The League imposed an immediate ban on arms sales to Italy while allowing them to Abyssinia. It banned all loans to Italy. It banned all imports from Italy. It banned the export to Italy of rubber, tin and metals.

However, the League delayed a decision for two months over whether to ban oil exports to Italy. It feared the Americans would not support the sanctions. It also feared that its members' economic interests would be further damaged. In Britain, the Cabinet was informed that 30,000 British coal miners were about to lose their jobs because of the ban on coal exports to Italy.

More important still, the Suez Canal, which was owned by Britain and France, was not closed to Mussolini's supply ships. The canal was the Italians' main supply route to Abyssinia and closing it could have ended the Abyssinian campaign very quickly. Both Britain and France were afraid that closing the canal could have resulted in war with Italy. This failure was fatal for Abyssinia.

Equally damaging to the League was the secret dealing between the British and the French that was going on behind the scenes. In December 1935, while sanctions discussions were still taking place, the British and French Foreign Ministers, Hoare and Laval, were hatching a plan. This aimed to give Mussolini two-thirds of Abyssinia in return for his calling off his invasion! Laval even proposed to put the plan to Mussolini before they showed it to either the League of Nations or Haile Selassie. Laval told the British that if they did not agree to the plan, then the French would no longer support sanctions against Italy.

However, details of the plan were leaked to the French press. It proved quite disastrous for the League. Haile Selassie demanded an immediate League debate about it. In both Britain and France it was seen as a blatant act of treachery against the League. Hoare and Laval were both sacked. But the real damage was to the sanctions discussions, which lost all momentum. The question about whether to ban oil sales was further delayed. In February 1936 the committee concluded that if they did stop oil sales to Italy, the Italians' supplies would be exhausted in two months, even if the Americans kept on selling oil to them. But by then it was all too late. Mussolini had already taken over large parts of Abyssinia. And the Americans were even more disgusted with the ditherings of the French and the British than they had been before and so blocked a move to support the League's sanctions. American oil producers actually stepped up their exports to Italy.

Mussolini 'obtains' Abyssinia

On 7 March 1936 the fatal blow was delivered. Hitler, timing his move to perfection, marched his troops into the Rhineland, an act prohibited by the Treaty of Versailles (see page 246). If there had been any hope of getting the French to support sanctions against Italy, it was now dead. The French were desperate to gain the support of Italy and were now prepared to pay the price of giving Abyssinia to Mussolini.

Italy continued to defy the League's orders and by May 1936 had taken the capital of Abyssinia, Addis Ababa. On 2 May, Haile Selassie was forced into exile. On 9 May, Mussolini formally annexed the entire country. The League watched helplessly. Collective security had been shown up as an empty promise. The League of Nations had failed.

If the British and French had hoped that their handling of the Abyssinian crisis would help strengthen their position against Hitler, they were soon proved very wrong. In November 1936 Mussolini and Hitler signed an agreement of their own called the Rome-Berlin Axis.

PRACTICE QUESTION

Write an account of how events in Abyssinia in 1935–36 became an international crisis.

A disaster for the League and for the world

Historians often disagree about how to interpret important events. However, one of the most striking things about the events of 1935 and 1936 is that most historians seem to agree about the Abyssinian crisis: it was a disaster for the League of Nations and had serious consequences for world peace. When Europe was on the brink of war in 1939 the League of Nations had no power and no credibility left.

THINK

1 Explain in your own words:
 a) why the Hoare–Laval deal caused such outrage
 b) how it affected attitudes to the League
 c) how the USA undermined the League.
2 Look at Source 17. What event is the cartoonist referring to in 'the matter has been settled elsewhere'?
3 From Sources 18–22, make a list of ways in which the Abyssinian crisis damaged the League.

SOURCE 17

A German cartoon from the front cover of the pro-Nazi magazine *Simplicissimus*, 1936. The warrior is delivering a message to the League of Nations: 'I am sorry to disturb your sleep but I just wanted to tell you that you should no longer bother yourselves about this Abyssinian business. The matter has been settled elsewhere.'

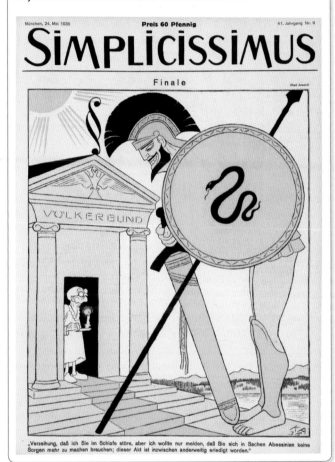

München, 24. Mai 1936 — Preis 60 Pfennig — 41. Jahrgang Nr. 9

SIMPLICISSIMUS
Finale

VÖLKERBUND

„Verzeihung, daß ich Sie im Schlafe störe, aber ich wollte nur melden, daß Sie sich in Sachen Abessinien keine Sorgen mehr zu machen brauchen; dieser Akt ist inzwischen anderweitig erledigt worden."

SOURCE 18

Written by historian J. R. Western in 1971.

The crises of 1935–6 were fatal to the League, which was not taken seriously again … it was too late to save the League. Instead, it began the emotional preparation among the democracies for the Second World War …

SOURCE 19

Written by historian T. A. Morris in 1995.

The implications of the conquest of Abyssinia were not confined to East Africa. Although victory cemented Mussolini's personal prestige at home, Italy gained little or nothing from it in material terms. The damage done, meanwhile, to the prestige of Britain, France and the League of Nations was irreversible. The only winner in the whole sorry episode was Adolf Hitler.

SOURCE 20

Written by historian James Joll in 1976.

After seeing what happened first in Manchuria then in Abyssinia, most people drew the conclusion that it was no longer much use placing their hopes in the League …

SOURCE 21

Written by historian A. J. P. Taylor in 1966.

The real death of the League was in 1935. One day it was a powerful body imposing sanctions, the next day it was an empty sham, everyone scuttling from it as quickly as possible. Hitler watched.

SOURCE 22

An extract from 'Back to the League of Nations' by Susan Pedersen, Professor of History at Columbia University, 2007.

If new accounts by historians show that statesmen were able to use the League to ease tension and win time in the 1920s, no such case appears possible for the 1930s. Indeed, the League's processes may have played a role in that deterioration. Diplomacy requires leaders who can speak for their states; it requires secrecy; and it requires the ability to make the credible threats. The Covenant's security arrangements met none of those criteria.

SOURCE 23

Two cartoons from *Punch*, 1938. The doctors in **A** represent Britain and France.

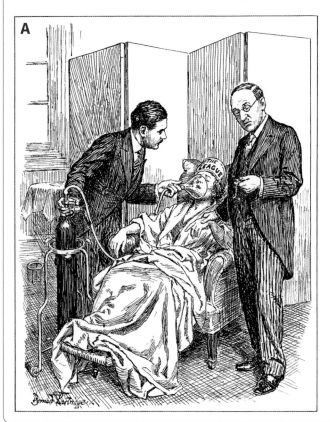

ACTIVITY

Work in pairs. Write a caption for one of the two cartoons in Source 23, showing people's feelings about the League after the Abyssinian crisis.

FOCUS TASK

The decline of the League, Part 2

Now that you have completed your diagram from the Focus Task on page 258, get together in small groups to discuss your findings. Discuss any similarities and differences. Which crisis do you think damaged the League of Nations the most?

PRACTICE QUESTION

'The main reason for the failure of the League of Nations was the absence of the United States.'

How far do you agree with this statement?
Explain your answer.

TOPIC SUMMARY

The League of Nations and international peace

- The League of Nations was created in 1919–20 with high hopes of maintaining world peace.
- The USA voted not to join – and this was a fatal weakness.
- The structure was flawed, with the Assembly and the Council having little real power to act with no standing army.
- Only victorious countries were at first allowed to join.
- Even in the 1920s some initiatives occurred outside the League such as the Locarno Treaties.
- The Depression affected leading trading countries, including Japan.
- In 1931 the Japanese invaded Manchuria; the League was slow to meet and act.
- In 1935 the Italians invaded Abyssinia.
- The League acted with limited sanctions over Abyssinia and was shown to be weak.
- Hitler saw the weaknesses of the League and knew that he could act with little real opposition.

6.3 The origins and outbreak of the Second World War

FOCUS

International tension rose dramatically in the 1930s. The single biggest cause was Adolf Hitler. Other European leaders worked hard to try to prevent the rising tension leading to war. They failed when war broke out in September 1939.

In this part of the topic you will study the following:

● The development of tension between Hitler and the Allies including:
  – Hitler's aims
  – the extent to which Hitler had achieved his aims by 1936.
● Reasons for the escalation of tension and the failure of appeasement, and how Hitler undermined the Treaty of Versailles.
● The outbreak of war and who held most responsibility for it.

● The development of tension

SOURCE 1

Adolf Hitler (right) during the First World War.

SOURCE 2

Adolf Hitler is welcomed by a crowd of Nazi supporters in 1933.

SOURCE 3

British historian Professor Richard Overy, writing in 1996.

Any account of the origins and course of the Second World War must give Hitler the leading part. Without him a major war in the early 1940s between all the world's great powers was unthinkable.

Fewer than 20 years separate Sources 1 and 2. Between 1918 and 1933, Adolf Hitler rose from being an obscure and demoralised member of the defeated German army to become the all-powerful Führer, dictator of Germany, with almost unlimited power and an overwhelming ambition to make Germany great once again. His is an astonishing story which you can read about in detail in Chapter 2 on pages 66–80. Here you will be concentrating on just one intriguing and controversial question: how far was Hitler responsible for the outbreak of the Second World War? Is Source 3 right?

SOURCE 4

From Hitler's *Mein Kampf*, 1923–24.

We demand equality of rights for the German people in its dealings with other nations, and abolition of the Peace Treaties of Versailles and St Germain. [The Treaty of St Germain was Austria's equivalent of the Treaty of Versailles.]

SOURCE 5

From Hitler's *Mein Kampf*.

We turn our eyes towards the lands of the east … When we speak of new territory in Europe today, we must principally think of Russia and the border states subject to her. Destiny itself seems to wish to point out the way for us here.

Colonisation of the eastern frontiers is of extreme importance. It will be the duty of Germany's foreign policy to provide large spaces for the nourishment and settlement of the growing population of Germany.

SOURCE 6

From Hitler's *Mein Kampf*.

We must not forget that the Bolsheviks are blood-stained. That they overran a great state [Russia], and in a fury of massacre wiped out millions of their most intelligent fellow-countrymen and now for ten years have been conducting the most tyrannous regime of all time. We must not forget that many of them belong to a race which combines a rare mixture of bestial cruelty and vast skill in lies, and considers itself specially called now to gather the whole world under its bloody oppression.

The menace which Russia suffered under is one which perpetually hangs over Germany. Germany is the next great objective of Bolshevism. All our strength is needed to raise up our nation once more and rescue it from the embrace of the international python … The first essential is the expulsion of the Marxist poison from the body of our nation.

Hitler's aims and Allied reactions

Hitler was never secretive about his plans for Germany. As early as 1924 he had laid out in his book *Mein Kampf* what he would do if the Nazis ever achieved power in Germany. His three main aims are described below.

Abolish the Treaty of Versailles!

Like many Germans, Hitler believed that the Treaty of Versailles was unjust. He hated the Treaty and called the German leaders who had signed it 'The November Criminals'. The treaty was a constant reminder to Germans of their defeat in the First World War and their humiliation by the Allies. Hitler promised that if he became leader of Germany he would reverse it.

By the time he came to power in Germany, some of the terms had already been changed. For example, Germany had stopped making reparations payments altogether. However, most points were still in place. The table in the Focus Task on page 249 shows the terms of the treaty that most angered Hitler.

Expand German territory!

The Treaty of Versailles had taken away territory from Germany. Hitler wanted to get that territory back. He wanted Germany to unite with Austria. He wanted German minorities in other countries such as Czechoslovakia to rejoin Germany. But he also wanted to carve out an empire in eastern Europe to give extra LEBENSRAUM or 'living space' for Germans.

Defeat Communism!

A German empire carved out of the Soviet Union would also help Hitler in one of his other objectives – the defeat of COMMUNISM or BOLSHEVISM. Hitler was anti-Communist. He believed that Bolsheviks had helped to bring about the defeat of Germany in the First World War. He also believed that the Bolsheviks wanted to take over Germany.

FOCUS TASK

What were Hitler's aims for Germany by 1933?

It is 1933. Write a briefing paper for the British government on Hitler's plans for Germany. Use Sources 4–6 to help you.

Conclude with your own assessment on whether the government should be worried about Hitler and his plans.

In your conclusion, remember these facts about the British government:

● Britain is a leading member of the League of Nations and is supposed to uphold the Treaty of Versailles, by force if necessary
● The British government does not trust the Communists and thinks that a strong Germany could help to stop the Communist threat.

Hitler's actions

The timeline on the right shows how, between 1933 and 1939, Hitler turned his plans into actions.

When you see events leading up to the war laid out this way, it makes it seem as if Hitler planned it all step by step. In fact, this view of events was widely accepted by historians until the 1960s. In the 1960s, however, the British historian A. J. P. Taylor came up with a new interpretation. His view was that Hitler was a gambler rather than a planner. Hitler simply took the logical next step to see what he could get away with. He was bold. He kept his nerve. As other countries gave into him and allowed him to get away with each gamble, so he became bolder and risked more. In Taylor's interpretation it is Britain, the Allies and the League of Nations who are to blame for letting Hitler get away with it – by not standing up to him. As you examine Hitler's actions in more detail, you will see that both interpretations are possible. You can make up your own mind which you agree with. You will also need to understand why Britain and her allies appeared to give in to Hitler's demands so easily on each occasion until the beginning of 1939.

The Dollfuss Affair, 1934

Austria had been a separate country ever since the Austro-Hungarian Empire had been broken up after the First World War. However, many people harked back to what they saw as the glorious Austrian Empire with Vienna as one of the major capital cities of Europe.

Dollfuss became the Chancellor of Austria in 1932. He was the head of the Christian Social Party, which held, in spite of its title, nationalist and conservative beliefs, which encouraged thoughts of previous Austrian glories. Austria had been suffering from the effects of a harsh peace treaty in 1919 just like Germany, and the effects of the Depression were keenly felt. With outbreaks of violence occurring in various parts of the country, Dollfuss established a dictatorship in 1933. He outlawed all other political parties, including the Nazi Party. In fact, the Austrian Nazi Party had been founded before Hitler's, but with Hitler in power in Germany the Austrian Nazis looked to Hitler for support.

As fighting continued and increased between different rival factions, a state of CIVIL WAR developed. In the spring of 1934 Dollfuss declared a new constitution which removed the last traces of democracy. He expressed his admiration for Mussolini's government and his dictatorship continued amidst the fighting.

In July 1934 Dollfuss was ASSASSINATED by ten Austrian Nazis. Hitler considered an invasion in support of the Austrian Nazis, but Mussolini was at that time keen to promote his friendship with Austria. He threatened war in the event of a German invasion. The Austrian Nazis were soon weakened in the civil war and Hitler found it convenient to pretend that he had not been supporting the Austrian Nazis – aware that he could not afford to risk war with Italy at this point. But as a result he realised he urgently needed to rearm, and he needed to gain Mussolini's support in any expansionist plans.

1933

DATE	ACTION
1933	Took Germany out of the League of Nations
	Began rearming Germany
1934	Tried to take over Austria but was prevented by Mussolini
1935	Held massive rearmament rally in Germany
	Reintroduced CONSCRIPTION in Germany
1936	Sent German troops into the Rhineland
	Made an anti-Communist alliance with Japan
1937	Tried out Germany's new weapons in the Spanish Civil War
	Made an anti-Communist alliance with Italy
1938	Took over Austria
	Took over the Sudetenland area of Czechoslovakia
1939	Invaded the rest of Czechoslovakia
	Invaded Poland

1939 WAR

The Saar, 1935

The Saar region of Germany had been run by the League of Nations since 1920. In 1935 the League of Nations held the promised plebiscite for people to vote on whether their region should return to German rule. The vote was an overwhelming success for Hitler. Around 90 per cent of the population voted to return to German rule. This was entirely legal and within the terms of the Treaty of Versailles. It was also a real morale booster for Hitler.

SOURCE 7

Following the plebiscite in 1935, people and police express their joy at returning to the German Reich by giving the Nazi salute.

German rearmament and conscription

Hitler came to power in Germany in 1933. One of his first steps was to increase Germany's armed forces. Thousands of unemployed workers were drafted into the army. This helped him to reduce unemployment, which was one of the biggest problems he faced in Germany. But it also helped him to deliver on his promise to make Germany strong again and to challenge the terms of the Treaty of Versailles.

Hitler knew that German people supported rearmament and bitterly resented the limits on German forces which the treaty had put on Germany (see page 246). But Hitler also knew rearmament would cause alarm in other countries. He handled it cleverly. His first step was to make a clear statement at the League of Nations Disarmament Conference in Geneva, which ran from 1932 to 1934. He pointed out that no other countries had disarmed during the 1920s and made the other states as uncomfortable as possible on this issue. In May 1933 Hitler promised not to rearm Germany if 'in five years all other nations destroyed their arms'. In June 1933 Britain produced an ambitious disarmament plan but it was rejected by the Conference. In October 1933 Hitler withdrew from the Disarmament Conference, and soon after took Germany out of the League altogether.

FIGURE 8

The proportion of German spending that went into armaments, 1935–40.

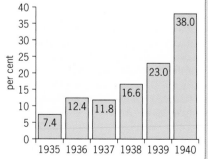

SOURCE 9

German soldiers and armaments on show at the Proclamation of Freedom to Rearm Rally in 1935.

FIGURE 10

German armed forces in 1932 and 1939.

	1932	1939
Warships	30	95
Aircraft	36	8,250
Soldiers	100,000	950,000

ACTIVITY

1 Design a Nazi poster to present the information in Figure 10 to the German people.
2 What factors allowed Hitler to get away with rearming Germany?

Rearmament began in secret. In 1934 Hitler signed a Non-Aggression Pact with his eastern neighbour Poland. Each side agreed not to use force in settling disputes. This agreement strengthened Hitler's position because it gave him time and space to rearm and it also weakened the alliance between Poland and Germany's enemy, France. In 1935 Hitler openly paraded his 2,000 aircraft in the Luftwaffe.

Hitler reintroduced conscription to the army in March 1935. It included all able-bodied boys over the age of 19. By 1939 the army had grown from 100,000 to 1 million. Hitler was breaking the terms of the Treaty of Versailles, but he guessed correctly that he would get away with rearmament. In 1935 many other countries were using rearmament as a way to fight unemployment. The final collapse of the League of Nations Disarmament Conference in 1934 had shown that other nations were not prepared to disarm. He even staged a massive military rally celebrating the German armed forces (see Source 9).

Rearmament was a very popular move in Germany. It boosted Nazi support. Hitler also knew that Britain had some sympathy with Germany on this issue. Britain believed that the limits put on Germany's armed forces by the Treaty of Versailles were too tight. The permitted forces were not enough to defend Germany from attack. Britain also thought that a strong Germany would be a good buffer against Communism.

The Stresa Front, April 1935

In response to Hitler openly flouting the terms of the Treaty of Versailles, in 1935 Italy, Britain and France agreed upon the Stresa Front. This was a mutual agreement to uphold their territorial boundaries and to stop Germany from further undermining the Treaty of Versailles.

In reality, the agreement had little impact. Britain went on to allow Germany a larger navy (see below), and in October of the same year, Italy invaded Abyssinia.

The Anglo-German Naval Agreement, June 1935

Later in the same year Britain helped to dismantle the Treaty of Versailles by signing a naval agreement with Hitler, allowing Germany to increase its navy to up to 35 per cent of the size of the British navy. The French were angry with Britain about this, but there was little they could do. This again showed Hitler that Britain would compromise over the exact terms of the 1919 peace settlement.

FOCUS TASK

To what extent did Hitler achieve his aims by 1935?

Hitler's main aims for Germany were to:

- abolish the Treaty of Versailles
- expand German territory
- defeat Communism.

1 Using the sources and information on pages 269–71, make notes using these headings on the actions Hitler took to achieve his aims.
2 Write a paragraph to explain how far Hitler had achieved his aims by 1935.

FIGURE 11

The Rhineland.

North Sea

NETHERLANDS

GERMANY

•Cologne

BELGIUM

LUXEMBOURG

FRANCE

Rhine

SWITZERLAND

ITALY

0   100 km
Scale

N

Key

January 1935: Saar returned to Germany after a plebiscite

March 1936: German forces re-enter the Rhineland

The escalation of tension, 1936–38

A sequence of events escalated tension while Hitler used his opportunities to destroy aspects of the Treaty of Versailles. As you go through this section, pay close attention to *why* Hitler was able to succeed and why Britain and France followed a policy of APPEASEMENT – that is, giving in to many of what seemed at the time to be Hitler's reasonable demands.

The remilitarisation of the Rhineland

In March 1936, Hitler took his first really big risk by moving troops into the Rhineland area of Germany.

The DEMILITARISATION of the Rhineland was one of the terms of the Treaty of Versailles. It had also been accepted by Germany in the Locarno Treaties of 1925. Hitler was taking a huge gamble. If he had been forced to withdraw, he would have faced humiliation and would have lost the support of the German army (many of the generals were unsure about him, anyway). Hitler knew the risks, but he had chosen the time and place well.

France had just signed a treaty with the USSR to protect each other against attack from Germany (see Source 13). Hitler used the agreement to claim that Germany was under threat. He argued that in the face of such a threat he should be allowed to place troops on his own frontier.

Hitler knew that many people in Britain felt that he had a right to REMILITARISE the Rhineland and he was fairly confident that Britain would not intervene. His gamble was over France. Would France let him get away with it?

SOURCE 12

Hitler looks back on his gamble over the Rhineland some years after the event.

At that time we had no army worth mentioning … If the French had taken any action we would have been easily defeated; our resistance would have been over in a few days. And the Air Force we had then was ridiculous – a few Junkers 52s from Lufthansa and not even enough bombs for them …

SOURCE 13

An American cartoon published in March 1936 showing the encirclement of Germany by France and the USSR.

Ring-Around-the-Nazi!

RUSSIA

MUTUAL

ASSISTANCE PACT

FRANCE

SOURCE 14

German troops marching through the city of Cologne in March 1936. This style of marching with high steps was known as goose-stepping.

As the troops moved into the Rhineland, Hitler and his generals sweated nervously. They had orders to pull out if the French acted against them. Despite the rearmament programme, Germany's army was no match for the French army. It lacked essential equipment and air support. In the end, however, Hitler's luck held.

The attention of the League of Nations was on the Abyssinian crisis which was happening at exactly the same time (see pages 262–66). The League condemned Hitler's action but had no power to do anything else. Even the French, who were most directly threatened by the move, were divided over what to do. They were about to hold an election and none of the French leaders was prepared to take responsibility for plunging France into a war. Of course, they did not know how weak the German army was. In the end, France refused to act without British support and so Hitler's big gamble paid off. Maybe next time he would risk more!

SOURCE 15

A British cartoon about the reoccupation of the Rhineland, 1936. *Pax Germanica* is Latin and means 'Peace, German style'.

THE GOOSE-STEP

"GOOSEY GOOSEY GANDER,
WHITHER DOST THOU WANDER?"
"ONLY THROUGH THE RHINELAND—
PRAY EXCUSE MY BLUNDER!"

SOURCE 16

Written by William Shirer in 1936. He was an American journalist in Germany during the 1930s. He was a critic of the Nazi regime and had to flee from Germany in 1940.

Hitler has got away with it. France is not marching. No wonder the faces of Göring and Blomberg [Nazi leaders] were all smiles.

Oh, the stupidity (or is it the paralysis?) of the French. I learnt today that the German troops had orders to beat a hasty retreat if the French army opposed them in any way.

THINK

1 Does Source 13 support or contradict Hitler's argument that Germany was under threat? Explain your answer.
2 Study Sources 12 and 16. Do they agree or disagree with one another?
3 Would you regard reoccupation of the Rhineland as a success for Hitler or as a failure for the French and the British? Explain your answer by referring to the sources.
4 Why has the cartoonist in Source 15 shown Germany as a goose?
5 Look at the equipment being carried by the goose. What does this tell you about how the cartoonist saw the new Germany?

PRACTICE QUESTION

Write an account of how Hitler's remilitarisation of the Rhineland in March 1936 became a success for his foreign policy.

The Spanish Civil War

These early successes seemed to give Hitler confidence. In 1936 a civil war broke out in Spain between Communists, who were supporters of the Republican government, and right-wing rebels under General Franco. Hitler saw this as an opportunity to fight against Communism and at the same time to try out his new armed forces.

In 1937, as the League of Nations looked on helplessly, German aircraft made devastating bombing raids on civilian populations in various Spanish cities. The destruction at Guernica was terrible. The world looked on in horror at the suffering that modern weapons could cause.

Mussolini, the Anti-Comintern Pact, 1936–37 and the Axis

The Italian leader Mussolini was also heavily involved in the Spanish Civil War. Hitler and Mussolini saw that they had much in common also with the military dictatorship in Japan. In 1936, Germany and Japan signed an Anti-Comintern Pact. In 1937, Italy also signed it. Anti-Comintern means 'Anti-Communist International'. The aim of the pact was to limit Communist influence around the world. It was particularly aimed at the USSR. The new alliance was called the Axis alliance.

SOURCE 17

A postcard published in France to mark the bombing of Guernica in 1937. The text reads 'The Basque people murdered by German planes. Guernica martyred 26 April 1937'.

Anschluss with Austria, March 1938

With the successes of 1936 and 1937 to boost him, Hitler turned his attention to his homeland of Austria. The Austrian people were mainly German, and in *Mein Kampf* Hitler had made it clear that he felt that the two states belonged together as one German nation. Many in Austria supported the idea of union with Germany, since their country was so economically weak. Hitler was confident that he could bring them together into a 'greater Germany'. In fact, he had tried to take over Austria in 1934, but on that occasion Mussolini had stopped him. Four years later, in 1938, the situation was different. Hitler and Mussolini were now allies.

There was a strong Nazi Party in Austria. Hitler encouraged the Nazis to stir up trouble for the government. They staged demonstrations calling for union with Germany. They caused riots. Hitler then told the Austrian Chancellor Schuschnigg that only ANSCHLUSS (political union) could sort out these problems. He pressurised Schuschnigg to agree to *Anschluss*. Schuschnigg asked for help from France and Britain but was refused it. So he called a plebiscite (a referendum), to see what the Austrian people wanted. Hitler was not prepared to risk this – he might lose! He sent his troops into Austria in March 1938, supposedly to guarantee a trouble-free plebiscite. Under the watchful eye of the Nazi troops, 99.75 per cent voted for *Anschluss*. *Anschluss* was completed without any military confrontation with France and Britain. Chamberlain, the British Prime Minister, felt that Austrians and Germans had a right to be united and that the Treaty of Versailles was wrong to separate them. Britain's Lord Halifax had even suggested to Hitler before the *Anschluss* that Britain would not resist Germany uniting with Austria.

> **THINK**
>
> Explain what each of the cartoons in Source 18 is saying about the *Anschluss*.

SOURCE 18

Two cartoons commenting on the *Anschluss*, 1938. **A** is from *Punch*. **B** is a Soviet cartoon showing Hitler catching Austria.

GOOD HUNTING

Mussolini. "All right, Adolf—I never heard a shot"

Once again, Hitler's risky but decisive action had reaped a rich reward – Austria's soldiers, weapons and its rich deposits of gold and iron ore were added to Germany's increasingly strong army and industry. Hitler was breaking yet another condition of the Treaty of Versailles, but the pattern was becoming clear. The treaty itself was seen as suspect. Britain and France were not prepared to go to war to defend a flawed treaty. Where would Hitler go next and how would Britain and France react?

Appeasement

Britain signed a naval agreement with Germany in 1935. For the next three years, Britain followed a policy of giving Hitler what he wanted – a policy that became known as 'APPEASEMENT'. Neville Chamberlain is the man most associated with this policy (see Profile, page 279), although he did not become Prime Minister until 1937. Many other British people, including many politicians, were also in favour of this policy. See Figure 19 for their reasons.

Reasons for the policy of appeasement

FIGURE **19**

At least Hitler is standing up to Communism
Hitler was not the only concern of Britain and its allies. He was not even their main worry. They were more concerned about the spread of Communism and particularly about the dangers to world peace posed by Stalin, the new leader in the USSR. Many saw Hitler as the buffer to the threat of spreading Communism.

The attitude of Britain's Empire
It was not at all certain that British Empire and Commonwealth states (e.g. Canada) would support a war against Germany.

We must not repeat the horrors of the Great War
Both British and French leaders vividly remembered the horrific experiences of the First World War. They wished to avoid another war at almost any cost.

Arguments for appeasement

The USA will not support us if we stand up to Hitler
American leaders were determined not to be dragged into another war. Could Britain and her allies face up to Germany without the guarantee of American support?

Hitler is right – the Treaty of Versailles is unfair
Many felt that the Treaty of Versailles was unfair to Germany. They assumed that once these wrongs were put right then Germany would become a peaceful nation again.

Britain is not ready for war
The British government believed that the armed forces were not ready for war against Hitler.

Our own economic problems are a higher priority
Britain and France were still suffering from the effects of the Depression. They had large debts and huge unemployment.

What was wrong with appeasement?

Britain's leaders may have felt that they had no option but to appease Hitler, but there were obvious risks to such a policy. Some of these were stated at the time (see Sources 21 and 22). Others became obvious with hindsight (Figure 20).

FIGURE **20**

It encouraged Hitler to be aggressive
With hindsight, you can see that each gamble he got away with encouraged him to take a bigger risk.

It put too much trust in Hitler's promises
With hindsight, you can see that Hitler often went back on his promises. Appeasement was based on the mistaken idea that Hitler was trustworthy.

Arguments against appeasement

It allowed Germany to grow too strong
With hindsight, you can see that Germany was not only recovering lost ground: it was also becoming much more powerful than Britain or France.

It scared the USSR
With hindsight, you can see how the policy alarmed the USSR. Hitler made no secret of his plans to expand eastwards. Appeasement sent the message to the Soviet Union that Britain and France would not stand in Hitler's way.

SOURCE 21

A cartoon by David Low from the London *Evening Standard*, 1936. This was a popular newspaper with a large readership in Britain. In this image the stepping stones are labelled from bottom right to top left: Rearmament; Rhineland fortification; Danzig; ?; ??; !!; !!!; Boss of the Universe.

STEPPING STONES TO GLORY.

SOURCE 22

A cartoon from *Punch*, November 1937. *Punch* was deeply critical of the British government's policies that allowed Hitler to achieve what he wanted in the 1930s. The magazine was an important influence on public opinion, particularly among educated and influential people. It had a circulation of about 120,000 copies per week during the 1930s.

THE BLESSINGS OF PEACE
or
MR. EVERYMAN'S IDEAL HOME

1 Look at Source 21. What does the cartoonist think appeasement will lead to?
2 Most people in Britain supported appeasement. Write a letter to the London *Evening Standard* justifying appeasement and pointing out why the cartoonist in Source 21 is mistaken. Use the points given in Figure 19.

ACTIVITY

Why appeasement?

1 Read the explanations in Figure 19 of why Britain followed a policy of appeasement.
2 Make notes under the following headings to summarise why Britain followed a policy of appeasement:
  – Military reasons
  – Economic reasons
  – Fear
  – Public opinion
  – Other.
3 Use your notes to help you to write a paragraph to explain in your own words how each of these reasons influenced the policy of appeasement.

The Sudeten crisis, September 1938

After the Austrian *Anschluss,* Hitler was beginning to feel that he could not put a foot wrong. But his growing confidence was putting the peace of Europe in increasing danger.

FIGURE 23

Central Europe after the *Anschluss.*

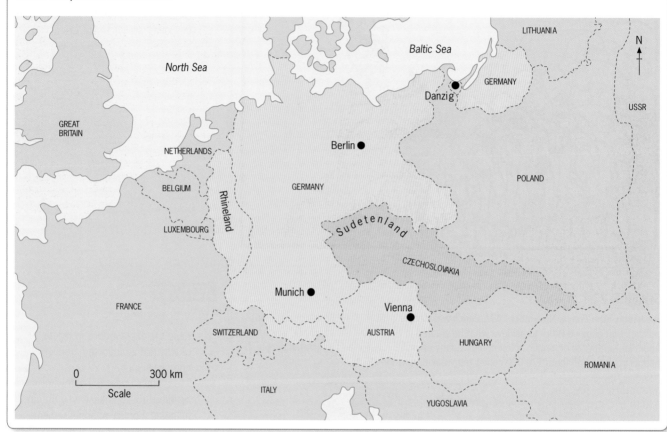

SOURCE 24

Hitler speaking to Chamberlain in 1938.

I give you my word of honour that Czechoslovakia has nothing to fear from the Reich.

SOURCE 25

From a radio broadcast by Neville Chamberlain, September 1938.

How horrible, fantastic, incredible it is that we should be digging trenches and trying on gas masks here because of a quarrel in a far away country between people of whom we know nothing. I am myself a man of peace to the depths of my soul.

Unlike the leaders of Britain and France, Edward Beneš, the leader of Czechoslovakia, was horrified by the *Anschluss.* He realised that Czechoslovakia would be the next country on Hitler's list for takeover. It seemed that Britain and France were not prepared to stand up to Hitler. Beneš sought guarantees from the British and French that they would honour their commitment to defend Czechoslovakia if Hitler invaded. The French were bound by a treaty and reluctantly said they would. The British felt bound to support the French. However, Chamberlain asked Hitler whether he had designs on Czechoslovakia and was reassured by Hitler's promise (Source 24).

Despite what he said to Chamberlain, Hitler did have designs on Czechoslovakia. This new state, created by the peace treaties after the First World War, included a large number of Germans – former subjects of Austria–Hungary's empire – in the Sudetenland area. Henlein, who was the leader of the Nazis in the Sudetenland, stirred up trouble among the Sudetenland Germans and they demanded to be part of Germany. In May 1938, Hitler made it clear that he intended to fight Czechoslovakia if necessary. Historians disagree as to whether Hitler really meant what he said. There is considerable evidence that the German army was not at all ready for war. Even so the news put Europe on full war alert.

Unlike Austria, Czechoslovakia would be no walk-over for Hitler. Britain, France and the USSR had all promised to support Czechoslovakia if it came to war. The Czechs themselves had a modern army. The Czechoslovak leader, Beneš, was prepared to fight. He knew that without the Sudetenland and its forts, railways and industries, Czechoslovakia would be defenceless.

All through the summer the tension rose in Europe. If there was a war, people expected that it would bring heavy bombing of civilians as had happened in the Spanish Civil War, and in cities around Britain councils began digging air raid shelters. Magazines carried advertisements for air raid protection and gas masks.

SOURCE 26

Digging air raid defences in London, September 1938.

In September the problem reached crisis point. In a last-ditch effort to avert war, Chamberlain flew to meet Hitler on 15 September. The meeting appeared to go well. Hitler moderated his demands, saying he was only interested in parts of the Sudetenland – and then only if a plebiscite showed that the Sudeten Germans wanted to join Germany. Chamberlain thought this was reasonable. He felt it was yet another of the restrictions imposed on Germany after the First World War that needed to be addressed. Chamberlain seemed convinced that, if Hitler got what he wanted, he would at last be satisfied.

On 19 September Chamberlain and the French leader Edward Daladier put to the Czechs their plans to give Hitler the parts of the Sudetenland that he wanted. However, three days later at a second meeting, Hitler increased his demands. He said he 'regretted' that the previously arranged terms were not enough. He wanted all the Sudetenland.

SOURCE 27

Hitler speaking in Berlin, September 1938.

The Sudetenland is the last problem that must be solved and it will be solved. It is the last territorial claim which I have to make in Europe.

The aims of our foreign policy are not unlimited … They are grounded on the determination to save the German people alone … Ten million Germans found themselves beyond the frontiers of the Reich … Germans who wished to return to the Reich as their homeland.

To justify his demands, he claimed that the Czech government was mistreating the Germans in the Sudetenland and that he intended to 'rescue' them by 1 October. Chamberlain told Hitler that his demands were unreasonable. The British navy was mobilised. War seemed imminent.

The Munich Agreement, September 1938

With Mussolini's help, a final meeting was held in Munich on 29 September. While Europe held its breath, the leaders of Britain, Germany, France and Italy decided on the fate of Czechoslovakia. On 29 September they decided to give Hitler what he wanted. They announced that Czechoslovakia was to lose the Sudetenland. They did not consult the Czechs, nor did they consult the USSR. This is known as the Munich Agreement. The following morning Chamberlain and Hitler published a joint declaration (Source 28) which Chamberlain said would bring 'peace for our time'.

SOURCE 28

The joint declaration of Chamberlain and Hitler, 30 September 1938.

We regard the Agreement signed last night … as symbolic of the desire of our two peoples never to go to war with one another again. We are resolved that we shall use consultation to deal with any other questions that may concern our two countries, and we are determined to continue our efforts to assure the peace of Europe.

SOURCE 29

The *Daily Express* comments on the Munich Agreement, 30 September 1938.

People of Britain, your children are safe. Your husbands and your sons will not march to war. Peace is a victory for all mankind. If we must have a victor, let us choose Chamberlain, for the Prime Minister's conquests are mighty and enduring – millions of happy homes and hearts relieved of their burden.

Hitler had gambled that the British would not risk war. He spoke of the Munich Agreement as 'an undreamt-of triumph, so great that you can scarcely imagine it'. The prize of the Sudetenland had been given to him without a shot being fired. On 1 October German troops marched into the Sudetenland. At the same time, Hungary and Poland helped themselves to Czech territory where Hungarians and Poles were living.

The Czechs had been betrayed. Beneš resigned. But the rest of Europe breathed a sigh of relief. Chamberlain received a hero's welcome back in Britain, when he returned with the 'piece of paper' – the agreement – signed by Hitler.

What do you think of the Munich Agreement? Was it a good move or a poor one? Most people in Britain were relieved that it had averted war, but many were now openly questioning the whole policy of appeasement. Even the public relief may have been overstated. Opinion polls in September 1938 show that the British people did not think appeasement would stop Hitler. It simply delayed a war, rather than preventing it. Even while Chamberlain was signing the Munich Agreement, he was approving a massive increase in arms spending in preparation for war.

ACTIVITY

Write extracts from the diaries of some of the main parties affected by the Sudetenland crisis, e.g. Chamberlain, Hitler, Beneš or one of the diplomats who was involved in making the agreement, or of an ordinary Briton or an ordinary Czech.

SOURCE 30

The *Yorkshire Post*, December 1938.

By repeatedly surrendering to force, Chamberlain has encouraged aggression … our central contention, therefore, is that Mr Chamberlain's policy has throughout been based on a fatal misunderstanding of the psychology of dictatorship.

SOURCE 31

Winston Churchill speaking in October 1938. He felt that Britain should resist the demands of Hitler. However, he was an isolated figure in the 1930s.

We have suffered a total defeat … I think you will find that in a period of time Czechoslovakia will be engulfed in the Nazi regime. We have passed an awful milestone in our history. This is only the beginning of the reckoning.

THINK

1 Study Sources 28–33. Sort them into the following categories:
    – Those that support the Munich Agreement
    – Those that criticise the Munich Agreement.
2 List the reasons why each source supports or criticises the agreement.

SOURCE 32

A British cartoon by David Low, 18 July 1938. The caption on the cartoon reads 'What's Czechoslovakia to me anyway?' The rocks poised to fall read: Anglo-French security; French Alliances; Rumania; Poland; Czecho.

SOURCE 33

The front page of the *Daily Sketch*, 1 October 1938.

FOCUS TASK

Hitler and the Treaty of Versailles

1   Draw up a table like this one to show some of the terms of the Treaty of Versailles that affected Germany.

Terms of the Treaty of Versailles	What Hitler did and when	The reasons Hitler gave for his action	The response from Britain and France
Germany's armed forces to be severely limited			
Saar to be run by the League of Nations for 15 years			
The Rhineland to be a demilitarised zone			
Germany forbidden to unite with Austria			
The Sudetenland taken into the new state of Czechoslovakia			
The Polish Corridor given to Poland			

2   Now you have studied Hitler's foreign policy to 1938, look back at the events and complete the chart – except for the row on Poland which you can complete later.

PRACTICE QUESTIONS

1   Study Sources 29 (page 282) and 32. How useful are Sources 29 and 32 for understanding attitudes towards the policy of appeasement?
Explain your answer using Sources 29 and 32 and your contextual knowledge.

2   Study Source 33. Source 33 supports the British policy of appeasement in September to October 1938.
How do you know?
Explain your answer by using Source 33 and your contextual knowledge.

• The outbreak of war

It was only from the end of 1938 and during the early part of 1939 that more and more people realised that war would be difficult to avoid. It was Hitler's actions over Czechoslovakia in March 1939 that confirmed that Hitler could not be trusted and would not keep his promises.

The occupation of Czechoslovakia, March 1939

Although the British people welcomed the Munich Agreement, they did not trust Hitler. In an opinion poll in October 1938, 93 per cent said they did not believe him when he said he had no more territorial ambitions in Europe. In March 1939 they were proved right. On 15 March, with Czechoslovakia in chaos, German troops took over the rest of the country.

FIGURE **34**

The takeover of Czechoslovakia by 1939.

Key

October 1938
Teschen taken by
Poland

November 1938 to
March 1939
Slovak border areas
and Ruthenia taken
by Hungary

October 1938
Sudetenland region
given to Germany in
the Munich Agreement

March 1939
Remainder of
Czechoslovakia taken
under German control

—— German border
in 1939

There was no resistance from the Czechs. Nor did Britain and France do anything about the situation. However, it was now clear that Hitler could not be trusted. For Chamberlain it was a step too far. Hitler had no excuse to send troops into Czechoslovakia. This was an invasion. If Hitler continued unchecked, his next target was likely to be Poland. Britain and France told Hitler that if he invaded Poland they would declare war on Germany. The policy of appeasement was ended. However, after years of appeasement, Hitler did not actually believe that Britain and France would risk war by resisting him.

The Nazi–Soviet Pact, August 1939

As Hitler was gradually retaking land lost at Versailles, logically his next target was the strip of former German land in Poland known as the Polish Corridor (see Figure 34). He had convinced himself that Britain and France would not risk war over this, but he was less sure about Stalin and the USSR.

Background

Stalin had been very worried about the German threat to the Soviet Union ever since Hitler came to power in 1933. Hitler had openly stated his interest in conquering Russian land. He had denounced Communism and imprisoned and killed Communists in Germany. Even so, Stalin could not reach any kind of lasting agreement with Britain and France in the 1930s. From Stalin's point of view, it was not for want of trying. In 1934 he had joined the League of Nations, hoping the League would guarantee his security against the threat from Germany. However, all he saw at the League was its powerlessness when Mussolini successfully invaded Abyssinia, and when both Mussolini and Hitler intervened in the Spanish Civil War. Politicians in Britain and France had not resisted German rearmament in the 1930s. Indeed, some in Britain seemed even to welcome a stronger Germany as a force to fight Communism, which they saw as a bigger threat to British interests than Hitler (see page 276).

Stalin's fears and suspicions grew in the mid-1930s. He signed a treaty with France in 1935 that said that France would help the USSR if Germany invaded the Soviet Union. But Stalin was not sure he could trust the French to stick to it, particularly when they failed even to stop Hitler moving into the Rhineland, which was right on their own border.

The Munich Agreement in 1938 increased Stalin's concerns. He was not consulted about it. Stalin concluded from the agreement that France and Britain were powerless to stop Hitler or, even worse, that they were happy for Hitler to take over eastern Europe and then the USSR.

SOURCE 35

Stalin, in a speech in 1941.

It will be asked how it was possible that the Soviet government signed a non-aggression pact with so deceitful a nation, with such criminals as Hitler and Ribbentrop … We secured peace for our country for eighteen months, which enabled us to make military preparations.

Despite his misgivings, Stalin was still prepared to talk with Britain and France about an alliance against Hitler. The three countries met in March 1939, but Chamberlain was reluctant to commit Britain. From Stalin's point of view, France and Britain then made things worse by giving Poland a guarantee that they would defend it if it was invaded. Chamberlain meant the guarantee as a warning to Hitler. Stalin saw it as support for one of the USSR's potential enemies.

Negotiations between Britain, France and the USSR continued through the spring and summer of 1939. However, Stalin also received visits from the Nazi foreign minister Ribbentrop. They discussed a rather different deal, a Nazi–Soviet Pact.

In August, Stalin made his decision. On 23 August 1939, Hitler and Stalin, the two arch enemies, signed the Nazi–Soviet Pact and announced the terms to the world. They agreed not to attack one another. Privately, they also agreed to divide Poland between them.

SOURCE 36

A British cartoon from 1939 by David Low.

SOMEONE IS TAKING SOMEONE FOR A WALK

SOURCE 37

From *The Modern World since 1870*, a school textbook by L. E. Snellgrove, published in 1980.

Hitler regarded the Pact as his master stroke. Although he had promised the Russians eastern Poland, Finland, Estonia and Latvia, he never intended to allow them to keep these territories.

Stalin did not expect Hitler to keep his word either. He was sure he could only gain from a long war in which Britain, France and Germany exhausted themselves. Seldom have two countries entered an alliance so dishonestly.

SOURCE 38

Soviet historian Kukushkin, writing in 1981.

Why did Britain and France help Hitler to achieve his aims? By rejecting the idea of a united front proposed by the USSR, they played into the hands of Germany. They hoped to appease Hitler by giving him some Czech territory. They wanted to direct German aggression eastward against the USSR and the disgraceful Munich deal achieved this.

[In 1939] the USSR stood alone in the face of the growing Fascist threat. The USSR had to make a treaty of non-aggression with Germany. Some British historians tried to prove that this treaty helped to start the Second World War. The truth is it gave the USSR time to strengthen its defences.

Why did Stalin sign? It was probably a combination of factors that led to the Pact:

- Stalin was not convinced that Britain and France would be strong and reliable enough as allies against Hitler.
- He also had designs on large sections of eastern Poland and wanted to take over the Baltic states, which had been part of Russia in the Tsar's day.
- He did not believe Hitler would keep his word, but he hoped for time to build up his forces against the attack he knew would come.

SOURCE 39

A Soviet cartoon from 1939. CCCP is Russian for USSR. Daladier (France) and Chamberlain (Britain) are directing Hitler away from western Europe and towards the USSR.

THINK

1 Look at Source 36. What point is the cartoonist making about the Nazi–Soviet Pact?
2 Do you agree with his view of the Pact?
3 What do Sources 37, 38 and 39 agree about?
4 What do they disagree about?
5 What does Source 38 reveal about Soviet attitudes to Britain and France?
6 How might a British politician justify the Munich Agreement to Stalin?

The invasion of Poland and the outbreak of war, September 1939

The Pact cleared the way for Germany's invasion of Poland.

On 1 September 1939 the German army invaded Poland from the west. On 17 September Soviet forces invaded Poland from the east. Poland soon fell.

If Hitler was planning ahead at all, then in his mind the next move would surely be an attack against his temporary ally, the USSR. He was certain that Britain and France would not go to war over Poland. But Hitler's triumph was spoilt by a nasty surprise. Britain and France did keep their pledge. On 3 September they declared war on Germany.

Hitler had started a war, but it was not the war he had in mind. It was too soon and against the wrong opponents. Hitler had taken one gamble too many.

Responsibility for the outbreak of war

On page 287 you will read about the views of the historian A. J. P. Taylor in the 1960s. He argued that at least some of the responsibility for the war belonged to leaders like Chamberlain who encouraged Hitler. Today, most historians believe that the primary responsibility for the outbreak of the Second World War was Hitler's (see Source 3 on page 267).

On the other hand, Stalin also bore some of the responsibility. First his Communist policies were seen as a threat to countries in western Europe, and therefore some politicians were keen to see a strong Germany that could act as a buffer against Communist expansion. Stalin had only brought the USSR into the League of Nations in 1934. Then in August 1939 he signed a Pact with Hitler which virtually guaranteed that Poland would be attacked jointly by the two countries. Stalin cynically signed the Pact because he knew that it would ensure that, after Poland, Hitler would look west, not east. The USSR would be safe from attack – at least in the short term.

How far was Chamberlain responsible for the outbreak of war?

Chamberlain certainly believed in appeasement and this encouraged Hitler in his expansionist policies. On page 276 you studied the main reasons why Chamberlain followed this policy and the reasons why people opposed him. However, remember that Chamberlain was not on his own. There were many more politicians who supported him in 1938 than opposed him.

Yet when Hitler broke his promises and the policy did not stop war, the supporters of appeasement quickly turned against the policy, some claiming they had been opposed to it all along. And historians since then have judged Chamberlain very harshly. Appeasers are portrayed as naïve, foolish or weak – Source 36 on page 284 is one of hundreds of examples one could choose which parody the policy and the people who pursued it. Chamberlain's 'Peace for our time' speech is presented as self-deception and a betrayal.

On the other hand the opponents of appeasement such as Winston Churchill are portrayed as realists who were far-sighted and brave. This has not been helped by the fact that the most influential writer about this period is Winston Churchill himself. Churchill himself once remarked to President Roosevelt 'History will judge us kindly because I shall write the history.'

SOURCE 40

Dr Ruth Henig of Lancaster University, 1997.

There is now general agreement among historians that the chief responsibility for unleashing war in Europe, in 1939, rests on Hitler and the Nazis ... Taylor's argument that the outbreak of war owed as much to 'the faults and failures of European statesmen' as it did to Hitler's ambitions, has been firmly rejected. The consensus now is that it was Hitler's determination to transform the basis of European society which brought war to Europe in 1939. It was not necessarily the war he was planning for; the evidence suggests that Hitler was aiming to prepare Germany for a massive conflict with Russia in the early 1940s. Unquestionably, however, it was a war provoked by his relentless pursuit of policies based on 'race' and on 'space'.

ACTIVITY

Study Source 40 carefully.

Look back over pages 268–85 and find three or four examples which support Dr Henig's view that Hitler's policies were based on 'race' and 'space'.

THINK

1 What is Source 41 trying to say about the supporters of appeasement?
2 Make a list of the reasons why appeasement has generally been seen as a major cause of the Second World War.

SOURCE 41

A cartoon by the American artist Dr Seuss published on 13 August 1941 (before the USA entered the Second World War).

'Remember . . . One More Lollypop, and Then You All Go Home!'

SOURCE 42

Professor John Charmley of the University of East Anglia writing about Churchill's account of the 1930s called *The Gathering Storm*.

The Gathering Storm *has been one of the most influential books of our time. It is no exaggeration to claim that it has strongly influenced the behaviour of Western politicians from Harry S. Truman to George W. Bush.*

...It is a good tale, told by a master story-teller, who did, after all, win the Nobel Prize for Literature; but would a prize for fiction have been more appropriate?

It really has been a very one-sided debate. Yet this debate matters because the failure of appeasement to stop Hitler has had a profound influence on British and American foreign policy ever since. It is now seen as the 'right thing' to stand up to dictators. It influenced the USA and Britain in their policy towards Saddam Hussein's regime in Iraq. This is a lesson people have learned from history – and that is why people study history, isn't it: to avoid making the same mistakes again! Or is it? Were Britain and France ready to stand up to Hitler in 1938? Or were politicians walking a tightrope?

SOURCE 43

A British cartoon commenting on the Sudetenland crisis of 1938.

Did appeasement buy time for Chamberlain to rearm Britain?

One of the strongest arguments for appeasement was that in 1938 Britain simply was not equipped to fight a war with Germany. So did appeasement allow Britain to catch up?

In the 1960s, British historian A. J. P. Taylor argued that Chamberlain had an exaggerated view of Germany's strength. Taylor believed that German forces were only 45 per cent of what British intelligence reports said they were.

But Taylor was writing in 1965 – not much help to Chamberlain in the 1930s. Britain had run down its forces in the peaceful years of the 1920s. The government had talked about rearmament since 1935 but Britain only really started rearming when Chamberlain became Prime Minister in 1937. Chamberlain certainly thought that Britain's armed forces were not ready for war in 1938. His own military advisers and his intelligence services told him this.

So did appeasement allow Britain the time it needed to rearm? Figure 44 will help you to decide.

FIGURE 44

The armaments build-up in the 1930s.

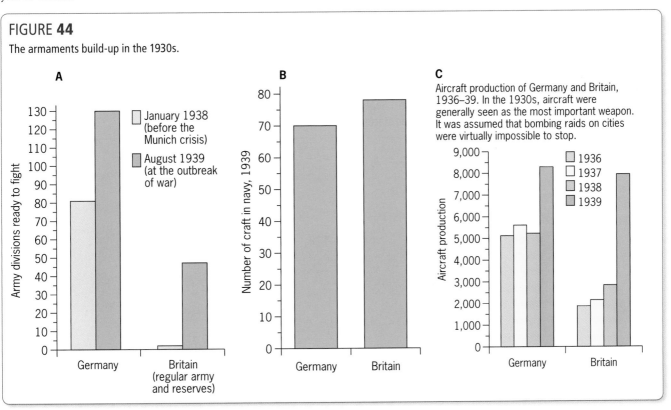

A – Army divisions ready to fight
■ January 1938 (before the Munich crisis)
■ August 1939 (at the outbreak of war)
Germany; Britain (regular army and reserves)

B – Number of craft in navy, 1939
Germany; Britain

C – Aircraft production of Germany and Britain, 1936–39. In the 1930s, aircraft were generally seen as the most important weapon. It was assumed that bombing raids on cities were virtually impossible to stop.
■ 1936 ■ 1937 ■ 1938 ■ 1939
Germany; Britain

PRACTICE QUESTION

'The failure of the policy of appeasement was the main reason why the Second World War occurred.'

How far do you agree with this statement?
Explain your answer.

KEY WORDS

Make sure you know what these words mean and are able to define them confidently.

- *Anschluss*
- Appeasement
- Assembly of League of Nations
- Collective security
- Conscription
- Council of League of Nations
- Covenant of League of Nations
- Demilitarisation
- Depression
- Disarmament
- Hyperinflation
- Idealist
- Isolationism
- *Lebensraum*
- Mandates
- Realist
- Remilitarisation
- Reparations
- Sanctions
- Secretariat of League of Nations
- Self-determination
- Trade sanctions
- Wall Street Crash
- War guilt

FOCUS TASK

Who held most responsibility for the start of the Second World War?

Work in three groups. Use the information given here and further information found by researching on the internet.

1 Each of you take one of the following people, and write a speech which argues that person was responsible for the outbreak of war in September 1939:
  – Hitler
  – Chamberlain
  – Stalin.

  Present your findings to the class.

2 Now discuss as a class whether any factors which helped cause the war have not been covered and need to be added to the debate.

3 As a class decide which leader held most responsibility for the start of the Second World War.

TOPIC SUMMARY

The origins and outbreak of the Second World War

- Hitler had clear aims about changing the terms of the Treaty of Versailles.
- He tried to benefit from the chaos in Austria in 1934 after the assassination of Dollfuss, but failed.
- Germany regained the Saarland 1935 after a plebiscite.
- Germany began rearmament in earnest in 1935, and also gained a naval agreement with Britain. All this meant a disregard for the terms of the Treaty of Versailles.
- In 1936 German troops marched into the Rhineland.
- Hitler achieved alliances with Italy and Japan.
- In March 1938 Germany took over Austria (the *Anschluss*).
- In September 1938 the crisis over the Sudetenland led to the Munich Agreement.
- Appeasement ended when Hitler took over the rest of Czechoslovakia in March 1939.
- Britain and France promised to protect Poland if it was attacked by Germany.
- In August 1939 the Nazi–Soviet Pact was signed. Germany was free to attack Poland and then western Europe.
- On 1 September 1939 German troops invaded Poland. The Second World War had started.

ASSESSMENT FOCUS

Your exam will include four questions on this topic. The question types will be the same every year, but the questions could be on any content from the specification, so you need to know it all!

We have provided one example of each kind of question. For questions based on sources we have used sources that you have already come across in this chapter. We have analysed each of the questions to highlight what you are being asked to do and written a sample answer with comments on how it could be improved.

Study Source A. Source A is Source 3, page 252.

Q1 **Study** Source 3. Source 3 is **very doubtful** about whether the League of Nations will succeed in keeping the peace. **How do you know**?

Explain your answer by using **Source A** and your **contextual knowledge**.

(4 marks)

Sample answer

The dove of peace is being given a huge olive branch to hold – much too large for it to succeed. This suggests that the League that is being created is being asked to take on too big a task in maintaining world peace.

Source B is Source 12, page 261. Source C is Source 13, page 261.

Q2 **Study** Sources B and C. **How useful** are these **two sources** to a historian studying the crisis in Manchuria, **1931–1933**?

Explain your answer using **Sources B and C** and your **contextual knowledge**.

(12 marks)

Sample answer

Source B is a cartoon showing the Japanese walking all over the League of Nations who is lying there lifeless. It is showing that the Manchurian Crisis was a disaster for the League. The cartoonist, David Low, is biased in showing how weak the League was and ignores its achievements in earlier years.

Source C is from a British politician. He is saying, from first-hand evidence, that people at the League of Nations were dejected. They thought that the League was in a hopeless mess. This is useful because it was a first-hand account from someone at the time, and written in a letter.

Q3 Write an account of how the German reoccupation of the Rhineland in March 1936 **increased** international tension. (8 marks)

Sample answer

In March 1936, Hitler gambled. It was his first big step since starting rearmament. The Treaty of Versailles had said that German troops should not be stationed in the Rhineland area of Germany – the area that bordered France. This was so that France could feel more secure from German invasion in the future. Hitler argued that it was fine for him to put troops in his own territory in order to protect Germany from a possible invasion in the future by France.

Hitler was very nervous. He told his commanders to withdraw the troops if the French made any move against them. In France, the French were more concerned about an election that was about to take place, and the League was busy dealing with Abyssinia.

The move by Hitler showed European leaders that he meant business in getting Germany back as a powerful country.

– This answer shows a clear understanding of the cartoon's intention, but it should include some knowledge to support its statements. For example, you could explain who Wilson was. You can also look at the source to explain any other features of the cartoon, for example, look at President Wilson's face.

– *Study Source 4 on page 253. Attempt the same question with that source.*

– The answer provides some basic comments on each of the two sources, but it needs more in-depth analysis of the content and some examination of the provenance. There is very little contextual knowledge shown. This could be improved substantially.

– *For each of the two sources, make a list of what you know about the provenance, and whether or not you think this makes the source more or less reliable.*

– *Then think about the context of the period in which the sources were created. What were people's attitudes in general at that time? What was the League doing?*

– *Now look at the content of each source. Using your knowledge, think how useful the content is for studying the crisis in Manchuria.*

– The answer provides some details of the event – it needs more precise details such as the troops crossing into the Rhineland and the reactions of those living there.

– The end of the answer mentions why France and the League did nothing, but it could then go on to explain how this increased international tension.

– *List two main reasons why this action by Hitler over the Rhineland was important. To help you:*

– *think about what the event had shown Hitler*

– *think what Hitler would be able to assume about the League in the future.*

Q4 'The **main reason** for the failure of the League of Nations was the **rise of Hitler'**. **How far** do you agree with this statement?

Explain your answer. (16 marks)

Sample answer

- This is a clearly argued answer. It develops an explanation of the stated factor and puts this alongside other factors.

- It demonstrates a range of accurate knowledge and understanding, and the answer is organised in a way that is totally focused on the question.

- The answer contains accurate spelling and punctuation, the meaning is clearly expressed and a range of specialist terms are used to explain arguments.

- *Are there any more details of evidence that you would add to this answer?*

The League of Nations was set up with high hopes in 1919. Unfortunately these hopes were dashed with the start of the Second World War in 1939, and the League having been shown to be useless several years before.

Hitler was partly to blame. It was he who tested the League's determination to uphold the Treaty of Versailles. The Covenant of the League, which all members signed, stated that they were bound to do this. Hitler started rearmament, firstly in secret and then openly, including reintroducing conscription. He even got Britain to sign a Naval Agreement in 1935 which said Germany could increase the size of its fleet. In 1936, he put troops in the Rhineland – and again the League did nothing. He ignored the Treaty of Versailles when he annexed Austria in March 1938. By then the League was totally weak and useless.

However, it was not just Hitler who had caused this. He had merely utilised existing weaknesses and situations to Germany's advantage. The League had fundamental flaws in its make-up. It had little power; it relied on moral persuasion; it had no standing army; the world's most powerful country, the USA, had opted not to join.

Other countries contributed to the failure of the League, including two of the original permanent members of the Council. Japan had invaded Manchuria in 1931, and when the League voted in support of China, Japan simply continued to occupy Manchuria and left the League. Italy invaded Abyssinia in 1935, and ignored the League's wish, backed up by weak sanctions, for a withdrawal. Italy, too, left the League after this.

In the atmosphere of the Depression of the 1930s Britain and France, the two remaining powerful member states, bear some responsibility as well. Neither was prepared to provide an army or armaments to enforce the decisions of the League. They weakly gave in to Hitler's demands – as seen in 1938 in Munich. Both countries were far more concerned with the huge numbers of unemployed and the problems of providing benefits for them.

Therefore, the League of Nations failed for many reasons. However, it was the weaknesses and inaction of the League in the early and mid-1930s that convinced Hitler he could act without fear of conflict. The League had become useless politically long before its official death.

Now write your own answers to the questions on pages 289–90 using the teacher's feedback to help you.

Conflict and Tension between East and West, 1945–1972

7

This wider world depth study focuses on the complex and diverse interests of different states and individuals and the ideologies that they represented. The focus is on the causes and development of the Cold War in the quarter-century after the Second World War, and why it proved difficult to end the hostile situation. You will also be looking at the role of key individuals and groups in shaping change, and how they were both influenced and affected by international relations and events.

You will be studying the following in three sections:
- The origins of the Cold War, in the East–West tensions which arose from the Second World War.
- The development of the Cold War in the 1950s, which saw the spread of Communism and the escalation of the arms race.
- The transformation of the Cold War after the global threat of the Cuban Missile Crisis turned to a gradual easing of tensions.

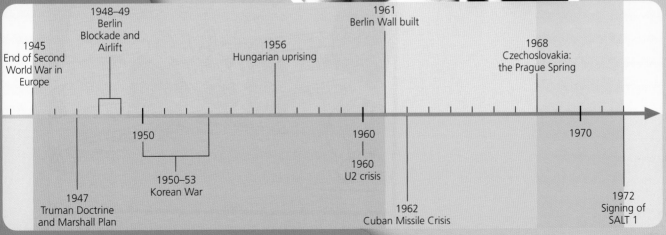

1945
End of Second World War in Europe

1947
Truman Doctrine and Marshall Plan

1948–49
Berlin Blockade and Airlift

1950

1950–53
Korean War

1956
Hungarian uprising

1960

1960
U2 crisis

1961
Berlin Wall built

1962
Cuban Missile Crisis

1968
Czechoslovakia: the Prague Spring

1970

1972
Signing of SALT 1

7.1 The origins of the Cold War

FOCUS

The years immediately after the end of the Second World War were full of unexpected events. Communist USSR was always likely to see capitalist USA as a major threat, and vice versa; but the way tensions developed into events in the late 1940s took the world by surprise at a time when the main focus was on recovering and rebuilding after the war. This all had a huge effect on world politics and called into question some of the details of the post-war settlement.

In this part of the topic, you will study:

● The end of the Second World War and the reasons why the Allied leaders began to fall out.
● The Iron Curtain and the evolution of East–West rivalry:
– Soviet responses to US policies.
– Who was to blame for the start of the Cold War conflict?

● The end of the Second World War

The wartime alliance which held together Britain, the USA and the USSR was not a strong bond of brotherhood, as Source 1 shows. It was based purely on the fact that all three countries had a common enemy – Hitler's Germany. Before the war brought them together relations between the USA and the USSR had long been hostile and suspicious. The Soviet leader Stalin was leader of the Communist Party which ruled the USSR. Soon after the COMMUNISTS took power in 1917, they faced a CIVIL WAR. During this civil war troops from Britain and the USA helped the enemies of the Communists. In the 1920s the US government deported thousands of suspected Communists from their country and in the 1930s Britain's policy of APPEASEMENT (see page 276) convinced Stalin that Britain was happy to see Germany grow in power so that Hitler could attack the USSR. So in many ways it is not that surprising that the wartime alliance broke down when the war ended. Perhaps it is more surprising that this did not happen before.

THINK

What is Source 1 saying about the wartime alliance of the Allies?

SOURCE 1

A British cartoon from 1941, with the caption 'Love conquers all'. Hitler is shown on the left, and seated on the bench are, from left to right, Roosevelt, Stalin and Churchill.

Contrasting attitudes and ideologies

What lay behind these fears and suspicions? The simple answer is that there was a clash of ideologies. The USSR was a Communist state, and the majority of important politicians, business leaders and other important figures in Britain and the USA hated and feared Communist ideas. You can see a summary of the two ideologies in the Factfiles below.

FACTFILE

The USA: A capitalist society

- American society was based on two key ideas: DEMOCRACY and CAPITALISM.
- Democracy meant that the American president and CONGRESS were elected in free elections and they could be voted out.
- Capitalism meant that property and businesses were owned by private individuals and companies.
- The USA was the world's richest country, but there were extremes of wealth and poverty.
- For Americans, the rights and freedoms of individual Americans (for example, free speech) were more important than everyone being equal.
- The majority of Americans believed passionately in the American way. They felt that COMMUNISM threatened their way of life.

FACTFILE

The USSR: A Communist society

- Soviet society was based on Communist ideas. It was a one-party state. There were elections, but Soviet people could only elect Communists.
- Industry was organised and run by the state. Unemployment and extreme poverty were rare, but the standard of living for most Soviet CITIZENS was lower than for the average American.
- Communists believed that the rights of individuals were less important than the good of society as a whole. As a result, there were many restrictions on the individual's freedom.
- The state kept close control over the press, radio, film and art. Communism was also hostile to organised religion.
- Soviet leaders believed that other countries should be run in the Communist way.
- Many people in the USSR were bitterly opposed to capitalism.

ACTIVITY

Work in small groups.

1 One half of your group has been asked to write a script or storyboard for a propaganda film, explaining why Communism is such a good system and why US capitalism is bad.
2 The other half has been asked to write a script or storyboard for a propaganda film, explaining why US capitalism is such a good system and why Communism is bad.
3 Each group can then make a presentation to the other, and both groups can list the differences between the two systems.

The differing beliefs of the USA and the USSR go some way to explain why the COLD WAR developed, but not all the way. After all, the two countries had the same ideologies in the 1930s, but they had largely ignored each other then. There were some important differences between the 1930s and the 1940s. The USA and the USSR had emerged from the war as the two 'SUPERPOWERS'. In the 1930s, other countries such as Britain and France had been as important in international affairs. However, the war had finally demoted Britain and France to a second division. They were not big enough, rich enough or strong enough to exercise real international leadership. Only the USA and the USSR were able to do this. They were the superpowers, and each superpower was determined that it would not be pushed around by the other one. In the next few years this would become very clear.

The Yalta Conference, February 1945

The general public in 1945 would have seen few signs of the tensions which you have just read about. In February 1945 the Allied leaders met at Yalta in Ukraine to plan what would happen to Europe after the war ended. The Yalta Conference went well. Despite their differences, the Big Three – Stalin, Roosevelt and Churchill – agreed on some important matters:

- Stalin agreed to enter the war against Japan once Germany had surrendered.
- They agreed that Germany would be divided into four zones: American, French, British and Soviet. Since the German capital, Berlin, was deep in the Soviet zone, it was agreed that Berlin itself would also be divided into four zones.
- As Allied soldiers advanced through Germany, they saw the horrors of the Nazi CONCENTRATION CAMPS. The Big Three agreed to hunt down and punish war criminals who were responsible for the GENOCIDE.
- They agreed that, as countries were liberated from occupation by the German army, they would be allowed to hold free elections to choose the government they wanted.
- The Big Three all agreed to join the new United Nations Organisation, which would aim to keep peace after the war.
- The Soviet Union had suffered terribly in the war. An estimated 20 million Soviet people had died. Stalin was therefore concerned about the future security of the USSR. The Big Three agreed that eastern Europe should be seen as 'a Soviet sphere of influence'.

SOURCE 2

A publicity photograph of the Big Three at the Yalta Conference, February 1945.

- The only real disagreement was about Poland. Stalin wanted the border of the USSR to move westwards into Poland. He argued that Poland, in turn, could move its border westwards into German territory. Churchill did not approve of Stalin's plans for Poland, but he also knew that there was not very much that he could do about it because Stalin's Red Army was in total control of both Poland and eastern Germany. Roosevelt was also unhappy about Stalin's plan, but Churchill persuaded Roosevelt to accept it, as long as the USSR agreed not to interfere in Greece where the British were attempting to prevent the Communists taking over. Stalin accepted this.

It seemed that, although they could not all agree, they were still able to negotiate and do business with one another. But was this a misleading impression?

Investigating Yalta

Look at the sources below which are about the Yalta Conference.

SOURCE 3

An extract from President Roosevelt's report to the US Congress on the Yalta Conference.

We argued freely and frankly across the table. But at the end on every point unanimous agreement was reached … We know, of course, that it was Hitler's hope and the German war lords' hope that we would not agree – that some slight crack might appear in the solid wall of allied unity … But Hitler has failed. Never before have the major allies been more closely united – not only in their war aims but also in their peace aims.

SOURCE 4

Stalin speaking to a fellow Communist, Milovan Djilas, in 1945. Djilas was a supporter of Stalin.

Perhaps you think that just because we are the allies of the English we have forgotten who they are and who Churchill is. There's nothing they like better than to trick their allies. During the First World War they constantly tricked the Russians and the French. And Churchill? Churchill is the kind of man who will pick your pocket of a kopeck! [A kopeck is a low value Soviet coin.] And Roosevelt? Roosevelt is not like that. He dips in his hand only for bigger coins. But Churchill? He will do it for a kopeck.

SOURCE 5

A Soviet cartoon. Churchill is shown with two flags, the first proclaiming that 'Anglo-Saxons must rule the world' and the other threatening an 'IRON CURTAIN'.

SOURCE 6

Stalin, proposing a toast at a dinner at the Yalta Conference, 1945.

I want to drink to our alliance, that it should not lose its … intimacy, its free expression of views … I know of no such close alliance of three Great Powers as this … May it be strong and stable, may we be as frank as possible.

SOURCE 7

Churchill writing to Roosevelt shortly after the Yalta Conference.

The Soviet Union has become a danger to the free world. A new front must be created against her onward sweep. This front should be as far east as possible. A settlement must be reached on all major issues between West and East in Europe before the armies of democracy melt.

ACTIVITY

1 Imagine you are describing the scene in Source 2 for a radio audience in 1945. You can use the internet to find examples of radio broadcasts from the period. Describe for the listeners:
   – the obvious points (such as the people that you can see)
   – the less obvious points (such as the mood of the scene).

2 Source 2 presents a friendly, positive scene. Look through the information on the Yalta Conference and list facts, points and evidence which support this view of the Conference.

3 Now list any facts, points and evidence which support the view that the Conference was not as friendly and positive as it first appears.

4 Suggest a new caption for Source 2 which tells readers a little more about Yalta.

SOURCE 9

Stalin speaking soon after the end of the Second World War about the takeover of eastern Europe.

This war is not as in the past; whoever occupies a territory also imposes on it his own social system. Everyone imposes his own system as far as his army has power to do so. It cannot be otherwise.

SOURCE 10

Stalin, replying to Allied leaders about his plans for Poland in April 1945. Britain had helped to prop up an anti-Communist government in Greece (see page 301).

Poland has borders with the Soviet Union which is not the case with Great Britain or the USA. I do not know whether a truly representative government has been established in Greece. The Soviet Union was not consulted when this government was being formed, nor did it claim the right to interfere because it realises how important Greece is to the security of Great Britain.

The Potsdam Conference, July–August 1945

In May 1945, three months after the Yalta Conference, Allied troops reached Berlin. Hitler committed suicide. Germany surrendered. The war in Europe was won.

A second conference of the Allied leaders was arranged for July 1945 in the Berlin suburb of Potsdam. However, in the five months since Yalta a number of changes had taken place which would greatly affect relationships between the leaders.

1 Stalin's armies were occupying most of eastern Europe

Soviet troops had liberated country after country in eastern Europe, but instead of withdrawing his troops Stalin had left them there. By July, Stalin's troops effectively controlled the Baltic states, Finland, Poland, Czechoslovakia, Hungary, Bulgaria and Romania, and refugees were fleeing these countries fearing a Communist takeover. Stalin had set up a Communist government in Poland, ignoring the wishes of the majority of Poles. Britain and the USA protested, but Stalin defended his action (see Source 9). He insisted that his control of eastern Europe was a defensive measure against possible future attacks.

2 America had a new president

On 12 April 1945, President Roosevelt died. He was replaced by his Vice-President, Harry Truman. Truman was a very different man from Roosevelt. He was much more anti-Communist than Roosevelt and was very suspicious of Stalin. Truman and his advisers saw Soviet actions in eastern Europe as preparations for a Soviet takeover of the rest of Europe.

3 The USA had developed an atomic bomb

The Americans had developed and successfully tested a new weapon of tremendous and terrible power, and it would affect the future of relations between the superpowers (see page 297).

Disagreements at Potsdam

The Potsdam Conference finally got underway on 17 July 1945. Not surprisingly, it did not go as smoothly as Yalta. In July there was an election in Britain. Churchill was defeated, so halfway through the conference he was replaced by a new Prime Minister, Clement Attlee. In the absence of Churchill, the conference was dominated by rivalry and suspicion between Stalin and Truman. A number of issues arose on which neither side seemed able to appreciate the other's point of view:

- **They disagreed over what to do about Germany**: Although they agreed about dividing Germany into four zones, Stalin wanted to cripple Germany completely to protect the USSR against future threats. Truman did not want to repeat the mistake of the Treaty of Versailles.
- **They disagreed over REPARATIONS**: 20 million Russians had died in the war and the Soviet Union had been devastated. Stalin demanded $10 billion compensation from Germany. Truman, however, was once again determined not to repeat the mistakes made at the end of the First World War and create a bitter, unstable Germany. He resisted this demand.
- **They disagreed over Soviet policy in eastern Europe**: At Yalta, Stalin had won agreement from the Allies that he could set up pro-Soviet governments in eastern Europe. He said, 'If the Slav [the majority of east European] people are united, no one will dare move a finger against them.' Stalin saw this as a way to protect the USSR from future attack. Truman saw it as evidence that Stalin wanted to build up a Soviet empire in Europe. He adopted a 'get tough' attitude towards Stalin.

Effect of the atomic bomb

As the Potsdam Conference approached, the USA was close to developing an effective ATOMIC BOMB. In fact, the first successful test took place on 16 July, the day before the Conference officially opened. The story of the bomb shows the mistrust which was developing between the two sides. The atom bomb had been developed in complete secrecy. However, once Truman knew he had a weapon which worked, he took Stalin to one side and told him about it.

In fact, Stalin knew about the project to develop the atom bomb all along – his spies had been keeping him informed since 1942! The A-bomb continued to be a source of tension after Truman's announcement. Japan refused to consider a surrender to the USA. Therefore, on 6 August 1945 the USA dropped the first weapon on the Japanese city of Hiroshima, followed by a second atomic attack on Nagasaki on 9 August. The devastation showed the horrific power of this new weapon (see Source 11).

SOURCE 11

The aftermath of the Hiroshima bomb, August 1945. At least 75,000 were killed instantly. Thousands more died from radiation poisoning in the years that followed.

Some historians believe that Truman authorised the use of the bomb as a warning to Stalin. Ever since 1945 there has, of course, been a debate over whether the USA was justified in using the bomb at that time.

ACTIVITY

Look back at what you have studied on pages 292–97 and copy and complete the following table to consider the aims of the international leaders in 1945, and how far they had fulfilled them.

	Aims for their country in 1945	Were these aims achieved completely, partly or not at all?
Stalin		
Churchill		
Roosevelt		
Attlee		
Truman		

FOCUS TASK

Why did the Allies begin to fall out in 1945?

1 Under the following headings, make notes to summarise why the Allies began to fall out in 1945:
   - Personalities
   - Actions by the USA
   - Actions by the USSR
   - Misunderstandings.
2 Which do you think was the most important factor in causing the falling out?

The Iron Curtain and the evolution of East–West rivalry

By 1946 there was a clear division between eastern Europe, with countries falling under the control of Stalin, and western Europe, with governments fearful of further Communist advance.

The Potsdam Conference ended without complete agreement on major issues like eastern Europe, but Stalin did not wait to implement his plans. Over the next nine months, Stalin achieved the domination of eastern Europe that he was seeking. By 1946 Poland, Hungary, Romania, Bulgaria and Albania all had Communist governments which owed their loyalty to Stalin. Churchill described the border between Soviet-controlled countries and the West as an 'Iron Curtain' (see Source 12). The name stuck, and so did Stalin's control (see page 299).

SOURCE 12

Winston Churchill speaking in the USA, in the presence of President Truman, 5 March 1946.

A shadow has fallen upon the scenes so lately lighted by the Allied victory. From Stettin on the Baltic to Trieste on the Adriatic, an Iron Curtain has descended. Behind that line lie all the states of central and eastern Europe. The Communist parties have been raised to power far beyond their numbers and are seeking everywhere to obtain totalitarian control. This is certainly not the liberated Europe we fought to build. Nor is it one which allows permanent peace.

SOURCE 13

Stalin, replying to Churchill's speech (Source 12).

The following circumstances should not be forgotten. The Germans made their invasion of the USSR through Finland, Poland and Romania. The Germans were able to make their invasion through these countries because, at the time, governments hostile to the Soviet Union existed in these countries. What can there be surprising about the fact that the Soviet Union, anxious for its future safety, is trying to see to it that governments loyal in their attitude to the Soviet Union should exist in these countries?

THINK

1 How do Sources 12 and 13 differ in their interpretation of Stalin's actions?
2 Explain why they see things so differently.

PRACTICE QUESTION 1

Source 14 shows that Churchill was worried about what was happening behind what he termed 'the Iron Curtain'. How do you know?
Explain your answer by using Source 14 and your contextual knowledge.

SOURCE 14

A British cartoon commenting on Churchill's 'Iron Curtain' speech, in the *Daily Mail*, 6 March 1946.

PRACTICE QUESTION 2

'The main reason for the development of the Cold War 1945–46 was the dropping of the atomic bombs on Japanese cities.'

How far do you agree with this statement?
Explain your answer.

Soviet expansion in eastern Europe

FIGURE 15

The Communists in eastern Europe, 1945–48.

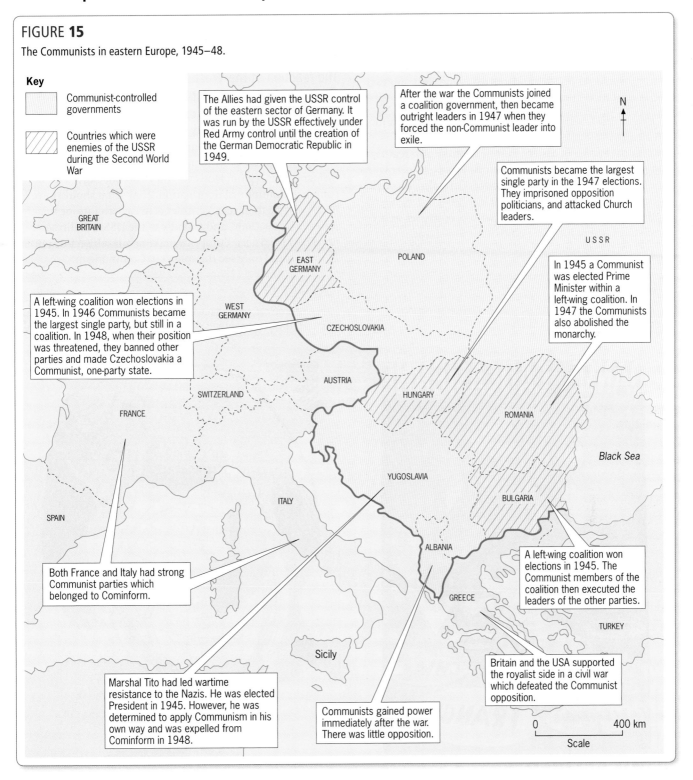

Key

☐ Communist-controlled governments

▨ Countries which were enemies of the USSR during the Second World War

The Allies had given the USSR control of the eastern sector of Germany. It was run by the USSR effectively under Red Army control until the creation of the German Democratic Republic in 1949.

After the war the Communists joined a coalition government, then became outright leaders in 1947 when they forced the non-Communist leader into exile.

Communists became the largest single party in the 1947 elections. They imprisoned opposition politicians, and attacked Church leaders.

In 1945 a Communist was elected Prime Minister within a left-wing coalition. In 1947 the Communists also abolished the monarchy.

A left-wing coalition won elections in 1945. In 1946 Communists became the largest single party, but still in a coalition. In 1948, when their position was threatened, they banned other parties and made Czechoslovakia a Communist, one-party state.

Both France and Italy had strong Communist parties which belonged to Cominform.

A left-wing coalition won elections in 1945. The Communist members of the coalition then executed the leaders of the other parties.

Marshal Tito had led wartime resistance to the Nazis. He was elected President in 1945. However, he was determined to apply Communism in his own way and was expelled from Cominform in 1948.

Communists gained power immediately after the war. There was little opposition.

Britain and the USA supported the royalist side in a civil war which defeated the Communist opposition.

ACTIVITY

Study Figure 15 and summarise how the Communists gained control of each country in eastern Europe.

Soviet and American policies

Stalin tightens his control

With Communist governments established throughout eastern Europe, Stalin gradually tightened his control in each country. The secret police imprisoned anyone who opposed Communist rule, or might oppose it at a later date.

In October 1947, Stalin set up the Communist Information Bureau, or COMINFORM, to co-ordinate the work of the Communist Parties of eastern Europe. Cominform regularly brought the leaders of each Communist Party to Moscow to be briefed by Stalin and his ministers. This also allowed Stalin to keep a close eye on them. He spotted independent-minded leaders and replaced them with people who were completely loyal to him. The only Communist leader who escaped this close control was Tito in Yugoslavia. He resented being controlled by Cominform and was expelled for his hostility in 1948.

The reaction of the West

The Western powers were alarmed by Stalin's takeover of eastern Europe. Roosevelt, Churchill and their successors had accepted that Soviet security needed friendly governments in eastern Europe. They had agreed that eastern Europe would be a Soviet 'sphere of influence' and that Stalin would heavily influence this region. However, they had not expected such complete Communist domination. They felt it should have been possible to have governments in eastern Europe that were both DEMOCRATIC and friendly to the USSR. Stalin saw his policy in eastern Europe as making himself secure, but Truman could only see the spread of Communism.

SOURCE 16

A French cartoon commenting on Stalin's takeover of eastern Europe. The dancing figure is Stalin.

SOURCE 17

An American cartoon commenting on Stalin's takeover of eastern Europe. The bear represents the USSR.

THINK

1   Do Sources 16 and 17 have the same message? Explain your answer.
2   Which one is more useful for studying the start of the Cold War?

PRACTICE QUESTION

Write an account of how Stalin's takeover of eastern Europe affected the development of the Cold War.

American and Soviet policies in Greece and Turkey

By 1948, Greece and Czechoslovakia were the only eastern European countries not controlled by Communist governments. It seemed to the Americans that not only Greece and Czechoslovakia but even Italy and France were vulnerable to a Communist takeover. Events in two of these countries were to have a decisive effect on America's policy towards Europe.

Greece and Turkey

Truman's first concerns were with Greece and Turkey.

- **Greece**: When the Nazis were driven out of Greece in 1944, two rival groups wanted to rule the country. The Communists wanted Greece to be a Soviet REPUBLIC. The monarchists wanted the return of the king of Greece. Churchill sent British troops to Greece in 1945 supposedly to help restore order and supervise free elections. In fact, the British supported the monarchists and the king was returned to power. In 1946 a CIVIL WAR broke out between the two sides. The British did not have the resources to control the situation and announced their withdrawal on 24 February 1947. Truman faced the prospect of yet another European country falling to Communism.
- **Turkey**: Stalin was trying to gain influence in Turkey. He wanted to get access to the Mediterranean for Soviet ships through the Black Sea Straits. Truman was concerned that if Turkey became an ally of the USSR then Stalin might use Turkey as a stepping stone to spread Communist influence into the Middle East. This area was important to the USA because of its oil reserves.

Truman wanted to resist what he saw as the Communist threat. His problem was that he still had to convince the American public and the US Congress. They did not entirely accept Truman's belief that the USA had to take a role in world affairs and they were also concerned about what this role might cost. To convince them, Truman talked up the scale of the threat in Greece and Turkey to a greater level than it actually was. Congress agreed to pass the Greece and Turkey Aid Bill in March 1947. This was a package of $400 million in aid to Greece and Turkey. It secured Turkey as a US ally and propped up the monarchist government in Greece. On the other hand, by talking up the threat of the USSR, Truman probably made relations between himself and Stalin even worse. Stalin had actually kept his promise to Churchill in 1945 that he would not help the Communists in Greece.

The Truman Doctrine, March 1947

American intervention in Greece and Turkey marked a new era in the USA's attitude to world politics, which became known as 'the TRUMAN DOCTRINE'.

Under the Truman Doctrine, the USA was prepared to send money, equipment and advice to any country which was, in the American view, threatened by a Communist takeover. Truman accepted that eastern Europe was now Communist. His aim was to stop Communism from spreading any further. This policy became known as CONTAINMENT.

Others thought containment should mean something firmer. They said that it must be made clear to the Soviet Union that expansion beyond a given limit would be met with military force.

> ### SOURCE 18
> President Truman, writing to his Secretary of State in January 1946.
>
> *Unless Russia is faced with an iron fist and strong language another war is in the making. Only one language do they understand – 'how many [army] divisions have you got?' ... I'm tired of babying the Soviets.*

> ### SOURCE 19
> Senator Arthur Vandenberg of the US Senate's International Relations Committee, April 1946.
>
> *I am more than ever convinced that Communism is on the march on a worldwide scale, and only the USA can stop it.*

> **THINK**
>
> Explain why Truman acted the way he did over Greece and Turkey.

> ### SOURCE 20
> President Truman speaking on 12 March 1947, explaining his decision to help Greece.
>
> *I believe that it must be the policy of the United States to support free peoples who are resisting attempted subjugation by armed minorities or by outside pressures ... The free peoples of the world look to us for support in maintaining those freedoms. If we falter in our leadership, we may endanger the peace of the world.*

The Marshall Plan

Truman believed that Communism succeeded when people faced poverty and hardship. He sent the American Secretary of State and former army general George Marshall to assess the economic state of Europe. What he found was a ruined economy. The countries of Europe owed $11.5 billion to the USA. There were extreme shortages of all goods. Most countries were still rationing bread. There was such a coal shortage in the hard winter of 1947 that in Britain all electricity was turned off for a period each day. Churchill described Europe as 'a rubble heap, a breeding ground of hate'.

THINK

1 Which of the problems shown in Figure 21 do you think would be the most urgent for the Marshall Plan to tackle? Explain your choice.

FIGURE 21

Problems in post-war Europe.

Homeless people

Refugees

Shortage of food and clothing

Cost of rebuilding damaged homes

Damage caused by war to infrastructure (roads, bridges, etc.)

Debts from cost of war effort

Shortage of fuel

SOURCE 22

An American cartoon from 1949.

I LOVE THE GUY, BUT SOMETIMES I THINK HE'S TOO GOOD!

U.S. TAXPAYER

TO ALL PARTS OF THE WORLD

Marshall suggested that about $17 billion of aid would be needed to rebuild Europe's prosperity. 'Our policy', he said, 'is directed against hunger, poverty, desperation and chaos.'

In December 1947, Truman put his plan to Congress. For a short time, the American Congress refused to grant this money. Many Americans were becoming concerned by Truman's involvement in foreign affairs. Besides, $17 billion was a lot of money!

THINK

2 Does Source 22 support or criticise the Marshall Plan?

Stalin's reaction to the Marshall Plan

American attitudes changed when the Communists took over the government of Czechoslovakia in 1948.

Czechoslovakia had been ruled by a coalition government which, although it included Communists, had been trying to pursue policies independent of Moscow. The Communists came down hard in March 1948. Anti-Soviet leaders were purged. One pro-American Minister, Jan Masaryk, was found dead below his open window. The Communists said he had jumped. The Americans suspected he'd been pushed. Immediately, Congress accepted the MARSHALL PLAN and made $17 billion available over a period of four years.

On the one hand, Marshall Aid was an extremely generous act by the American people. On the other hand, it was also motivated by American self-interest. They wanted to create new markets for American goods. The Americans remembered the disastrous effects of the DEPRESSION of the 1930s and Truman wanted to do all he could to prevent another worldwide slump.

Stalin viewed the Marshall Plan with suspicion. After expressing some initial interest, he refused to have anything more to do with it. He forbade any of the eastern European states to apply for Marshall Aid. He also tightened his grip on the eastern European states by setting up two new organisations, COMECON and Cominform (see Factfiles). Stalin's view was that the anti-Communist aims behind Marshall Aid would weaken his hold on eastern Europe. He also felt that the USA was trying to dominate as many states as possible by making them dependent on dollars.

Yugoslavia

All of the Communist governments in eastern Europe followed Stalin's directions except Marshal Tito in Yugoslavia. In this and other areas, Yugoslavia was the only Communist state to resist domination by Stalin. The Soviet Union kept up a propaganda battle against Tito, but took no military action.

FACTFILE

Comecon

- Comecon stands for the Council for Mutual Economic Assistance.
- It was set up in 1949 to co-ordinate the industries and trade of eastern European countries.
- The idea was that members of Comecon traded mostly with one another, rather than trading with the West.
- Comecon favoured the USSR far more than any of its other members. It provided the USSR with a market to sell its goods. It also guaranteed it a cheap supply of raw materials. For example, Poland was forced to sell its coal to the USSR at one-tenth of the price that it could have got selling it on the open market.
- It set up a bank for socialist countries in 1964.

THINK

1   Explain how events in Czechoslovakia affected American policy in Europe.
2   Look back at Figure 15 on page 299. How does the geographical position of Yugoslavia help to explain why Stalin did not take any direct action against Tito whereas Stalin did act against Czechoslovakia?

FACTFILE

Cominform

- Cominform stands for the Communist Information Bureau.
- Stalin set up Cominform in 1947 as an organisation to co-ordinate the various Communist governments in eastern Europe.
- The office was originally based in Belgrade in Yugoslavia but moved to Bucharest in Romania in 1948 after Yugoslavia was expelled by Stalin because it would not do what the Soviet Union told it to do.
- Cominform ran meetings and sent out instructions to Communist governments about what the Soviet Union wanted them to do.

FOCUS TASK

How did the USSR react to US policy?

You are an adviser to Stalin. Write a briefing paper on the USA's plans for Europe. Your report should mention:

- President Truman's plans for Europe
- the methods being used by Truman to resist the spread of Communism
- how the USSR has reacted to these plans
- whether you think the USSR should be worried.

The Berlin Blockade and Airlift

Despite all the threatening talk of the early years of the Cold War, the two sides had never actually fired on one another. But in 1948 they came dangerously close to war.

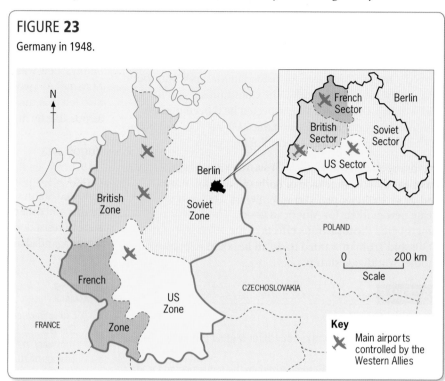

FIGURE 23

Germany in 1948.

As stated on page 294, at the Yalta Conference in early 1945 it was agreed that Germany should be divided into four zones and that the city of Berlin should be divided into four sectors, as shown on the map (Figure 23).

Germany had become a real headache for the Western Allies. After the destruction of war, their zones were in economic chaos. Stalin feared a recovering Germany and wanted to keep it crippled. But it was clear to the Allies that Germany would not be able to feed its people if it was not allowed to rebuild its industries. Although they themselves were wary of rebuilding Germany too quickly, Britain, France and the USA combined their zones in 1948 to form one zone (which became known in 1949 as West Germany; see page 306). In 1948 they reformed the currency and within months there were signs that Germany was recovering.

Stalin felt that the USA's handling of western Germany was provocative. He could do nothing about the reorganisation of the western zones, or the new currency, but he felt that he could stamp his authority on Berlin. It was deep in the Soviet zone and was linked to the western zones of Germany by vital roads, railways and canals. In June 1948, Stalin blocked all these supply lines, cutting off the 2-million strong population of West Berlin from Western help. Stalin believed that this BLOCKADE would force the Allies out of Berlin and make Berlin entirely dependent on the USSR.

THINK

1 Read Source 24. What reasons did the Soviet Union give for cutting off West Berlin?

2 Why do you think the USA did not believe these were genuine reasons?

SOURCE 24

US government report, June 1948.

On 23 June the Soviet authorities suspended all traffic into Berlin because of alleged technical difficulties … They also stopped barge traffic on similar grounds. Shortly before midnight, the Soviet authorities issued orders to … disrupt electric power from Soviet power plants to the Western sectors. Shortage of coal was given as a reason for this measure.

It was a clever plan. If US tanks did try to ram the roadblocks or railway blocks, Stalin would see it as an act of war. However, the Americans were not prepared to give up. They saw West Berlin as a test case. If they gave in to Stalin on this issue, the western zones of Germany might be next. Truman wanted to show that he was serious about his policy of containment. He wanted Berlin to be a symbol of freedom behind the Iron Curtain.

The only way into Berlin was by air. So in June 1948 the Allies decided to AIRLIFT supplies. As the first planes took off from their bases in western Germany, everyone feared that the Soviets would shoot them down, which would have been an act of war. People waited anxiously as the planes flew over Soviet territory, but no shots were fired. The planes got through and for the next ten months West Berlin was supplied by a constant stream of aeroplanes bringing in everything from food and clothing to oil and building materials, although there were enormous shortages and many Berliners decided to leave the city altogether. By May 1949, however, it was clear that the blockade of Berlin would not make the Western Allies give up Berlin, so Stalin reopened communications.

THINK

1. How do Sources 26 and 27 differ in their interpretation of the blockade and airlift?
2. Which do you think is the more useful source for a historian studying the Berlin Blockade and airlift?
3. Which source do you think gives the more reliable view of the blockade and airlift?

SOURCE 26

President Truman, speaking in 1949.

We refused to be forced out of the city of Berlin. We demonstrated to the people of Europe that we would act, and act resolutely, when their freedom was threatened. Politically it brought the people of Western Europe closer to us. The Berlin Blockade was a move to test our ability and our will to resist.

SOURCE 27

A Soviet commentary on the crisis, quoted in P. Fisher, *The Great Power Conflict*, a textbook published in 1985.

The crisis was planned in Washington, behind a smokescreen of anti-Soviet propaganda. In 1948 there was danger of war. The conduct of the Western powers risked bloody incidents. The self-blockade of the Western powers hit the West Berlin population with harshness. The people were freezing and starving. In the Spring of 1949 the USA was forced to yield … their war plans had come to nothing, because of the conduct of the USSR.

SOURCE 25

Coal being unloaded from a plane at Berlin airport, 1948. For ten months, planes landed every three minutes throughout the day and night.

FOCUS TASK

Who was to blame for the Cold War?

Work in small groups. Five people per group would be ideal.

You are going to investigate who was to blame for the Cold War. The possible verdicts you might reach are as follows:

A   The USA was most to blame.

B   The USSR was most to blame.

C   Both sides were equally to blame.

D   No one was to blame. The Cold War was inevitable.

This is our suggested way of working.

1   Start by discussing the verdicts together. Is one more popular than another in your group?

2   **a)** Each member of the group should research how one of the following factors helped to lead to the Cold War. You can start with the page numbers given. You can introduce your own research from other books or the internet if you wish.

  – The situation before the Second World War (page 292).
  – The personal relationships between the various leaders (pages 294–303).
  – The conflicting beliefs of the superpowers (page 293).
  – The war damage suffered by the USSR (pages 294 and 296).
  – Stalin's takeover of eastern Europe (pages 298–299).
  – The Marshall Plan (page 302).
  – Stalin's response to the Marshall Plan (page 303).

  b) Present your evidence to your group and explain which, if any, of the verdicts A–D your evidence most supports.

3   As a group, discuss which of the verdicts now seems most sensible.

4   Write a balanced essay on who was to blame, explaining why each verdict is a possibility but reaching your own conclusion about which is best.

The significance of the blockade and airlift for the Cold War

As a result of the Berlin Blockade, Germany was firmly divided into two nations. In May 1949, the British, French and American zones became the Federal Republic of Germany (known as West Germany). The Communist eastern zone was formed into the German Democratic Republic (or East Germany) in October 1949.

Germany would stay a divided country for 41 years. Throughout that time Berlin would remain a powerful symbol of Cold War tensions.

Berlin was more than a symbol, however. It was also a potential flashpoint. As you study the story of the Cold War, you will find that the USA's and the USSR's worries about what might happen in Berlin affected their policies in other areas of the world. You will pick up the story of Berlin again on pages 320–22.

Most importantly, the Berlin Blockade set out a pattern for Cold War confrontations. On the one hand, the two superpowers and their allies had shown how suspicious they were of each other; how they would obstruct each other in almost any way they could; how they would bombard each other with propaganda. On the other hand, each had shown that it was not willing to go to war with the other. The Berlin Blockade established a sort of tense balance between the superpowers that was to characterise much of the Cold War period.

TOPIC SUMMARY

The origins of the Cold War

- At the Yalta and Potsdam Conferences the wartime allies tried to reach agreements about the peace settlement, including the division of Germany into four zones.
- Some disagreements remained, fuelled by mutual suspicions.
- Soviet fears of the USA escalated after the USA dropped atomic bombs on Japan.
- The USSR took over eastern European countries, 1945–48.
- The Truman Doctrine (1947) and Marshall Plan (1947) made the USA's intentions clear.
- The USSR set up Cominform and Comecon to control Communist eastern Europe.
- The Berlin Blockade and Airlift (1948–49) showed how serious and dangerous the Cold War had become.

7.2 The development of the Cold War, 1949–60

• The significance of events in Asia for superpower relations

The focus of the Cold War was very clearly centred on Europe. However, events in Asia had a huge influence on attitudes and intensified the existing situation still further.

China becomes Communist, 1949

A civil war had been going on in China since the 1920s. Because world attention had been focused on Europe in the 1930s and then on the Second World War, the progress made by the Communists under Mao Zedong had not been appreciated. US foreign policy had certainly largely ignored what was happening – though it is fair to say that little was known about the events outside China.

In October 1949 Mao took complete control of the most populous nation on earth. It was correctly assumed in the West that the USSR would support its new Communist neighbour. In February 1950, the Soviet Union and Communist China agreed the Treaty of Friendship, Alliance and Mutual Assistance. After the details had been decided Mao went to the Soviet Union to sign the treaty, one of only two times that he left China. This alliance changed the balance of power between East and West. In America the fear of Communist expansion had reached fever pitch. American foreign policy was intent on stopping the spread of Communism, but although containment had enjoyed some success in Europe, it had failed in Asia.

The Korean War, 1950–53

Korea had been controlled by the Japanese since 1910. At the end of the Second World War, the Japanese forces had surrendered to the USSR in the north of Korea and to American forces in the south. The temporary dividing line was the 38th Parallel. Free elections were to be held, but in fact by 1948 two separate countries had been created, each claiming control of the whole. North Korea was ruled by a Communist DICTATORSHIP; South Korea was anti-Communist, but it was not very democratic either.

The war started when North Korea invaded South Korea. Most of the South was quickly overrun. The South appealed to the United Nations, which had been created in 1945 to replace the League of Nations.

The UN had recently failed to recognise the new Communist government of China, and had decided to continue supporting the nationalist side led by Chiang Kai-Shek, now in exile on the island of Formosa (Taiwan). In protest, the USSR had boycotted the meetings of the UN Security Council. This allowed an American proposal to help South Korea to be passed unopposed. As a result, the Americans, helped by other nations including Britain, fought in Korea against Communist North Korea (for details of the war, see Chapter 8, pages 334–41). They all fought as UN troops rather than for their individual countries. However, the majority of troops were American and the overall commander was General MacArthur, a leading US commander from the Second World War.

FOCUS

In the 1950s the Cold War intensified. The Korean War and escalation of both the arms and space race illustrated the growing hostility felt between the USA and the USSR.

In this part of the topic you will study the following:

● The significance of events in Asia for superpower relations.
● Military rivalries fought in the arms race and the space race and how the Cold War escalated.
● Events in Hungary, Khrushchev's rule and the extent to which there was a 'thaw' in Cold War relations.

PRACTICE QUESTION

Write an account of how events in China in 1949 became a reason for the worsening of the Cold War.

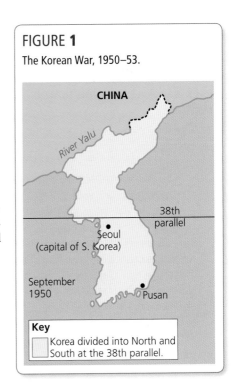

FIGURE 1

The Korean War, 1950–53.

FOCUS TASK

What was the significance of events in Asia for superpower relations?

1 Take three pieces of card, and write the following headings in the centre of them:
   – Events in China 1949–50
   – The Korean War 1950–53
   – Events in Vietnam in the 1950s.

2 Using the information on pages 307–08 and 342–44, write notes in the middle of each card outlining the events that took place.

3 Now around the outside of each card, write down the significance of each of these events in terms of the relationship between the superpowers.

4 Write a paragraph to summarise your view on the significance of events in Asia for superpower relations.

The significance of the Korean War for superpower relations

The Korean War played out the divisions between East and West in a global conflict. As each side used the conflict to test out new and deadly weapons, they became increasingly polarised in their views against each other. And as STALEMATE ensued, until an armistice was agreed in 1953, the divisions between both sides were deeply entrenched and there was no peace treaty.

The UN had proved that it could act – albeit only in the absence of the USSR. However, the UN had failed to unite Korea.

The USSR quickly resumed its seat on the Security Council, and has never again made the same mistake of being absent for an important vote.

The situation in Vietnam

At the same time there was a parallel situation in Vietnam. Vietnam was still ruled by the French, but the Communist Vietminh were fighting a civil war against France and, in effect, the USA who was providing financial aid. The Vietnam War, which was underway by the 1960s, developed the situation a stage further, with the North being supported by Communist China and the USSR and the South by the USA (see Chapter 8, page 333 onwards). Again the war had a huge effect on US–USSR relations during the continuing Cold War.

SOURCE 2

A refugee in Korea walks along the road, with everything he owns on his back.

● Military rivalries

The physical signs of a developing Cold War were seen in the development of international alliances and the stockpiling of weapons.

The formation of NATO, 1949

During the Berlin Blockade, war between the USSR and the USA seemed a real possibility. At the height of the crisis, the Western powers met in Washington and signed an agreement to work together. The new organisation they formed in April 1949 was known as NATO (North Atlantic Treaty Organisation).

You can see the main terms of the NATO alliance in Source 3. The main motive for the alliance for President Truman was that NATO countries could provide US forces with secure bases in Europe. Truman was aware that Stalin's forces were well positioned to invade western Europe if he chose to. US forces would have to cross the Atlantic before they could meet the Soviets. With the signing of the NATO treaty, US forces could resist any advance which Stalin might make. US allies such as Britain were happy to have US forces in western Europe as it guaranteed their protection from a possible Soviet attack. Not surprisingly, the Soviet Union did not see the alliance in the same way. Source 4 shows how NATO was viewed from the Soviet side of the Iron Curtain.

The Warsaw Pact

The WARSAW PACT came into existence in 1955. By this time Stalin had died, and a new leader, Khrushchev, had emerged. In some ways he acted differently from Stalin, but he still saw it as essential for the USSR to maintain the security of Communist eastern Europe. For example, he wanted to improve living standards in order to benefit the Soviet people but also to show that Communism could deliver the same benefits for its people as the USA could deliver for its people.

One aspect of Stalin's policy did not change. His aim in eastern Europe had always been to create a buffer against attack from the West. Khrushchev continued this policy. In May 1955 the Western Allies signed a series of agreements in Paris which made West Germany a member of NATO and allowed the country to have its own armed forces again. There were strict limits on the new German army, but to the Soviet Union the sight of the USA rearming the enemy which had caused so much misery during the Second World War was worrying. In response, Khrushchev created the Warsaw Pact. This was a military alliance similar to NATO (see page 308). The members would defend each other if one was attacked. The Warsaw Pact included all the Communist countries of eastern Europe except Yugoslavia, but it was dominated by the Soviet Union.

The arms race

Another area of superpower rivalry was in science and technology, particularly the deadly technology of nuclear weapons. When the USA dropped the first atomic bomb on Japan in August 1945 (see page 297), Stalin realised the USSR had to catch up with its rivals. He made atomic research his top priority.

Massive amounts of money were poured into research and development. Entire towns like Arzamas-16 were created to house the scientists and engineers. The hard work paid off and by 1949 the Soviets had their own atomic bomb. It was the beginning of a deadly ARMS RACE.

The USA takes the lead	The USSR takes the lead
	Aug 1949 USSR detonates its first atomic bomb. This causes great concern in the USA. US Intelligence had predicted that the USSR would not be able to develop a bomb until 1953.
1951 US Strategic Air Command (SAC) develops policy of constant readiness. SAC Commander Curtis Le May identifies 6,000 targets in the USSR to be hit in event of war.	
Nov 1952 USA detonates the first hydrogen bomb. The H-bomb is 1,000 times more powerful than the atom bomb.	
	Aug 1953 USSR detonates its own H-bomb.
Mar 1954 USA develops an H-bomb small enough to be dropped from a bomber.	
	Sept 1954 USSR drops a test H-bomb from a bomber.

SOURCE 3

Extracts from the NATO Charter.

Article 3: To achieve the aims of this Treaty, the Parties will keep up their individual and collective capacity to resist armed attack.

Article 5: The Parties agree that an armed attack against one or more of them in Europe or North America shall be considered an attack against them all.

SOURCE 4

Stalin commenting on the formation of NATO, 1949.

The Soviet government did everything it could to prevent the world from being split into two military blocks. The Soviet Union issued a special statement analysing the grave consequences affecting the entire international situation that would follow from the establishment of a military alliance of the Western powers. All these warnings failed, however, and the North Atlantic Alliance came into being.

THINK

1 Look at Source 3. What did NATO members agree to do?
2 The members of NATO argued that this was a defensive alliance. Explain why Stalin was not convinced about this.

SOURCE 5

Extracts from the Warsaw Pact Treaty, 1955.

Because the recent Paris agreements have created a remilitarised Western Germany and entered it into the North Atlantic bloc, which increases the threat of another war and creates a menace to the national security of the peace-loving states and … Convinced that, under these circumstances, the peace loving states of Europe should take the necessary measures for safeguarding their security … The peace-loving states of Europe have resolved to conclude this Treaty of Friendship, Co-operation and Mutual Assistance…

Article 4. In the event of an armed attack in Europe on one or several states that are signatories of the treaty by any state or group of states, each state that is a party to this treaty shall … render the state or states so attacked immediate assistance.

The USA allocated 40 per cent of its defence spending to its air force, particularly the Strategic Air Command bombing force. This level of funding continued throughout the Cold War. Money was also pumped into developing stockpiles of nuclear weapons. There was a further concern in the USA when the Soviets developed the Bison jet bomber and the long range TU-95 bomber. These aircraft could hit American cities with nuclear weapons and this triggered off a panic known as a 'Bomber Gap'. The new US President Eisenhower ordered new B-52 bombers to close the gap with the USSR. In reality, there never was a bomber gap – the USA always had more nuclear bombers than the USSR – but, in the paranoid atmosphere of the time, threats were exaggerated rather than investigated.

There was debate in the USA about the nuclear build-up. In December 1953 Eisenhower put forward a plan to the United Nations to share nuclear research and technology, but this was strongly opposed by many of his own supporters and the US military. Despite having been a general in the US army in the Second World War, Eisenhower had misgivings about what was called the military–industrial complex. Some commentators claimed that American industries and the top US military commanders were in league. The military wanted huge spending on weapons and other developments, while big business benefited from huge government contracts for the military. It is a debate which still continues today, and it was deeply controversial then.

The significance of the arms race

SOURCE 6

An extract from *Arsenals of Folly: The Making of the Nuclear Arms Race* by American journalist and historian Richard Rhodes, published in 2008.

Paul Nitze, the principal author of the 1950 NSC report, intentionally exaggerated Soviet nuclear capacities and minimized those of the US in order to 'bludgeon the mass mind of "government"' – as Nitze's superior, Secretary of State Dean Acheson, admitted years later. Although the Soviet Union had lost at least 25 million people and half its industry in World War II, Nitze portrayed the USSR as a fanatical enemy that, within a few years, would threaten America with an estimated 200 nuclear weapons. According to his report, the then American stockpile of 1,400 weapons would be insufficient to counter such a threat. Nitze's report came at a time when international events, including the Korean War, seemed to validate this dark vision. In response, Truman quadrupled the defence budget and began a strategic programme that would increase the US nuclear arsenal to some 20,000 thermonuclear bombs by 1960 and 32,000 by 1966.

SOURCE 7

An extract from an American National Security Council Report from April 1950, which is often referred to as 'NSC-68'. This document was an analysis by government officials of the threat posed by the USSR to the USA. This section looked at nuclear weapons.

A MILITARY EVALUATION OF US AND USSR ATOMIC CAPABILITIES

1. The United States now has an atomic capability, including both numbers and deliverability, estimated to be adequate, if effectively utilised, to deliver a serious blow against the war-making capacity of the USSR. It is doubted whether such a blow, even if it resulted in the complete destruction of the contemplated target systems, would cause the USSR to sue for terms or prevent Soviet forces from occupying western Europe …

2. As the atomic capability of the USSR increases, it will have an increased ability to hit at our atomic bases and installations and thus seriously hamper the ability of the United States to carry out an attack such as that outlined above. It is quite possible that in the near future the USSR will have a sufficient number of atomic bombs and a sufficient deliverability to raise a question whether Britain with its present inadequate air defence could be relied upon as an advance base from which a major portion of the US attack could be launched.

It is estimated that, within the next four years, the USSR will attain the capability of seriously damaging vital centres of the United States …

Effective opposition to this Soviet capability will require among other measures greatly increased air warning systems, air defences, and vigorous development and implementation of a civilian defence program …

THINK

1. Study Source 7. According to this source, how serious was the Soviet nuclear threat?
2. What measures is Source 7 calling for?
3. How would you describe the tone of Source 7? Use examples of words and phrases in the text to support your answer.
4. Study Source 6. What criticisms are made of Source 7?
5. Do you think the author of Source 7 wanted to increase tension and the risk of war? If not, what were his motives?
6. Do the criticisms in Source 6 mean that Source 7 is not a useful historical source? Explain your answer.

The space race

One of the most spectacular forms of rivalry between the USA and USSR was illustrated by the space race.

During the Second World War, German scientists had developed powerful rockets like the V-2. The Soviets and the Americans used this technology and developed it to see if they could break free of earth and reach space. US President Eisenhower announced a programme in 1955 to develop a man-made satellite. However, in October 1957 the Soviets shocked the Americans by sending one of their rockets into space and launching the first ever man-made satellite, called *Sputnik*. They rubbed salt in the wound in November 1957 when they launched *Sputnik II*. This satellite was larger than *Sputnik I* and it carried a dog called Laika.

The Americans responded by pouring money into space research. The government funded existing programmes, and set up new ones. The government also set up a new project called Explorer. It was run by the US army. By 1958 the US investment was beginning to pay off. In January the Americans launched the *Explorer I* satellite. In July the US Congress approved the formation of the National Aeronautics and Space Administration (NASA), whose original role was to encourage and co-ordinate research into the peaceful application of space science.

It seemed that the USA was edging ahead in the space race but in 1961 the Soviets gave the Americans another shock. On 12 April the Soviet's Vostok Rocket programme sent Major Yuri Gagarin of the Red Army to become the first human in space. When he returned safely he was celebrated as a hero in the USSR and became an instant worldwide celebrity. President Kennedy of the USA responded with the Apollo manned space programme which ran from 1961 to 1975. The primary aim of this programme was to put a man on the Moon. It was a long, difficult and massively expensive process but in July 1969 *Apollo 11* landed Commander Neil Armstrong on the surface of the Moon. The Soviets were also developing their space programme at the same time, including plans to send cosmonauts around the far side of the Moon.

PRACTICE QUESTIONS

1 Study Source 8.
Source 8 supports the USSR. How do you know?
Explain your answer by using Source 8 and your contextual knowledge.

2 Study Sources 9 and 10 (page 312).
How useful are these sources to a historian studying American attitudes towards the space race at the beginning of the 1960s?
Explain your answer by using Sources 9 and 10 and your contextual knowledge.

SOURCE 8

A poster celebrating Yuri Gagarin and the Vostok Space Programme in 1961. The dates on the leaves of the branch are important stages in the Soviet space programme.

SOURCE 9

The logo of the US Apollo 11 mission.

THINK

Read Source 10 carefully. Does Kennedy explain all of his motives for supporting the Apollo programme in this extract? Explain your answer.

SOURCE 10

Extracts from a speech by US President John F. Kennedy. Kennedy became President in January 1961.

First, I believe that this nation should commit itself to achieving the goal, before this decade is out, of landing a man on the Moon and returning him safely to the Earth. No single space project in this period will be more impressive to mankind, or more important in the long-range exploration of space; and none will be so difficult or expensive to accomplish.

SOURCE 11

Boris Chertok, a Soviet rocket designer, interviewed in 1998.

Sputnik came as a shock overseas. The American military and others realised that the period when they were out of reach had ended. A new era had begun when instead of a Sputnik, a nuclear weapon could not merely circle the earth, but land where it was ordered to.

SOURCE 12

Oleg Troyanovski, an adviser to Khrushchev in the 1950s.

Khrushchev, around that period, came to the conclusion that missiles were the weapons of the future, and that warships were getting obsolete, bombers were getting obsolete. That we should concentrate everything on missiles, and as he said somewhere that, 'We are on the point of producing missiles like sausages.'

The importance of the space race and arms race

Why did the superpowers invest so much effort and money into their space programmes? At one level it was simple Cold War rivalry – the best political system should have the best technology. The space programme was also a powerful propaganda tool. Space caught the imagination of people all over the world. Soviet and American achievements in space technology were reported in all of the world's media. However, there was one slightly sinister element to the space race. A key reason why both superpowers were interested in space technology was that the same technology could be used to build missiles which could carry nuclear weapons (see Source 11).

The Soviet leader Khrushchev was quick to recognise that space technology would soon make missiles the most important weapons. Engineers from all over the Soviet Union were brought together in a remote location in Kazakhstan to build the top-secret rocket base of Baykonyr. On 15 May 1957, they began testing the world's first INTERCONTINENTAL BALLISTIC MISSILE, an ICBM. This technology gave the Soviets the capability to launch a missile into space and then bring it down on a target in the USA.

It was not long before the USA caught up again. In 1959 the Americans developed their own ICBM systems. Atlas and Minuteman missiles would be able to reach the USSR as quickly and as accurately as Soviet missiles could reach the USA. A further American technological development was the introduction of Polaris missiles. These could be fired from submarines which were virtually undetectable.

As the 1950s ended and the 1960s began, America was beginning to pull ahead in the nuclear arms race. However, if you had lived in the USA at the time you probably would not have believed this. The American public was alarmed by the fear that the USSR had many more nuclear missiles than the USA. US President Eisenhower knew this was not the case. He began to worry about the spiralling cost of US defence spending and called for 'reasonable control'. He also criticised what he saw as hysterical reporting in some of the media, such as the *Life* magazine article in 1959 which talked of the threat of the missile gap between the USA and the USSR. Part of Eisenhower's problem was that he knew there was no missile gap, but he could not really tell the world how he knew (see page 316–17 on spying missions).

FOCUS TASK

How did the Cold War escalate?

Work in groups of three. Each of you should choose one of the three areas in which Cold War rivalry developed:

● International organisations
● The arms race
● The space race.

1 Using the information and sources on pages 308–12 and your own research, make notes on the ways in which the Cold War escalated in your area.
2 Use your notes to create two PowerPoint slides summarising the ways in which the Cold War developed in the area you are researching.
3 As a group, combine your PowerPoint slides to create a whole presentation.
4 Together, add a concluding slide summing up the situation between the USSR and the USA by the end of the 1950s.

● Khrushchev and the 'thaw'

PROFILE

Nikita Khrushchev

- Born in 1894, the son of a coal miner.
- Fought in the Red Army during the Civil War.
- Afterwards worked for the Communist Party in Moscow. Was awarded the Order of Lenin for his work building the Moscow underground railway in the 1930s.
- In 1949 he was appointed by the Communist Party to run Soviet agriculture.
- There was a power struggle after Stalin's death over who would succeed him. Khrushchev had come out on top by 1955 and by 1956 he felt secure enough in his position to attack Stalin's reputation.
- Became Prime Minister in 1958.
- Took his country close to nuclear war with the USA during the Cuban Missile Crisis in 1962 (see pages 323–27).
- Was forced into retirement in 1964.
- Died in 1971.

SOURCE 13

Nikita Khrushchev speaking in 1955.

We must produce more grain. The more grain there is, the more meat, lard and fruit there will be. Our tables will be better covered. Marxist theory helped us win power and consolidate it. Having done this we must help the people eat well, dress well and live well. If after forty years of Communism, a person cannot have a glass of milk or a pair of shoes, he will not believe Communism is a good thing, whatever you tell him.

THINK

Write your own definition of 'de-Stalinisation'. Make sure you include:

- at least two examples
- an explanation of why it was radical.

Death of Stalin, 1953

The Korean War inevitably raised tensions between the superpowers, but the temperature of the Cold War was about to change. In March 1953 Stalin died. Stalin was a hero to millions of people in the USSR. He had defeated Hitler and given the USSR an empire in eastern Europe. He made the USSR a nuclear superpower. When he died in 1953, amid the grief and mourning, many minds turned to the question of who would succeed Stalin as Soviet leader. The man who had emerged by 1955 was Nikita Khrushchev.

Khrushchev's policies

Khrushchev seemed very different from Stalin. He ended the USSR's long feuds with China and with Yugoslavia. His new approach also seemed to bring about a thaw in the frosty Cold War relations between the superpowers. He talked of peaceful CO-EXISTENCE with the West. He made plans to reduce expenditure on arms. He attended the first post-war summit between the USSR, the USA, France and Britain in July 1955.

Khrushchev also relaxed the iron control of the Soviet Union on eastern Europe. He agreed to pull Soviet troops out of Austria (they had been posted there since the end of

the Second World War). He seemed to be signalling to the countries of eastern Europe that they would be allowed much greater independence to control their own affairs.

De-Stalinisation

At the Communist Party International Conference in 1956, Khrushchev made an astonishing attack on Stalin. He dredged up the gory evidence of Stalin's PURGES (Chapter 3, pages 132–34) and denounced him as a wicked tyrant who was an enemy of the people and kept all power to himself. Khrushchev went on to say much worse things about Stalin and began a programme of 'DE-STALINISATION':

- He released more political prisoners.
- He closed down Cominform as part of his policy of reconciliation with Yugoslavia.
- He invited Marshal Tito to Moscow.
- He dismissed Stalin's former Foreign Minister, Molotov.

Khrushchev also said that he wanted to improve the living standards of ordinary Soviet citizens and those of eastern Europe (see Source 13).

Hungary and the reforms of Nagy

Hungary was led by a hard-line Communist called Mátyás Rákosi. Hungarians hated the restrictions which Rákosi's Communism imposed on them. Most Hungarians felt bitter about losing their freedom of speech. They lived in fear of the secret police. They resented the presence of thousands of Soviet troops and officials in their country. Some areas of Hungary even had Russian street signs, Russian schools and Russian shops. Worst of all, Hungarians had to pay for Soviet forces to be in Hungary.

In June 1956 a group within the Communist Party in Hungary opposed Rákosi. He appealed to Moscow for help. He wanted to arrest 400 leading opponents. Moscow would not back him. Rákosi's assistant said sarcastically: 'Might I suggest that mass arrests are not reconcilable with our new brand of socialist legality.' The Kremlin ordered Rákosi to be retired 'for health reasons'.

However, the new leader, Ernö Gerö, was no more acceptable to the Hungarian people. Discontent came to a head with a huge student demonstration on 23 October, when the giant statue of Stalin in Budapest was pulled down. The USSR allowed a new government to be formed under the well-respected Imre Nagy. Soviet troops and tanks stationed in Hungary since the war began to withdraw. Hungarians created thousands of local councils to replace Soviet power. Several thousand Hungarian soldiers defected from the army to the rebel cause, taking their weapons with them.

Nagy's government began to make plans. It would hold free elections, create impartial courts, restore farmland to private ownership. It wanted the total withdrawal of the Soviet army from Hungary. It also planned to leave the Warsaw Pact and declare Hungary neutral in the Cold War struggle between East and West. There was widespread optimism that the American President, Eisenhower, who had been the wartime supreme commander of all Allied forces in western Europe, would support the new independent Hungary.

SOURCE 14

A Hungarian student describes the mood in 1953.

Living standards were declining and yet the papers and radio kept saying that we had never had it so good. Why? Why these lies? Everybody knew the state was spending the money on armaments. Why could they not admit that we were worse off because of the war effort and the need to build new factories? … I finally arrived at the realisation that the system was wrong and stupid.

SOURCE 15

Written by László Beke, a student who helped lead the Hungarian uprising in 1956.

Wearing western clothes was considered dangerous. To cite a small example: my colleague John showed up at lectures one day in a new suit, a striped shirt and necktie from the United States. His shoes were smooth suede and would have cost one month's wages in Hungary. After classes John was summoned by the party officer. He received a tongue-lashing and was expelled.

Soviet fears and reaction

Khrushchev at first seemed ready to accept some of the reforms. However, he could not accept Hungary leaving the Warsaw Pact. In November 1956 thousands of Soviet troops and tanks moved into Budapest. Unlike in Poland, the Hungarians did not give in. Two weeks of bitter fighting followed. Some estimates put the number of Hungarians killed at 30,000. However, the latest research suggests about 3,000 Hungarians and 7,000–8,000 Russians were killed. Another 200,000 Hungarians fled across the border into Austria to escape the Communist forces. Imre Nagy and his fellow leaders were imprisoned and then executed.

SOURCE 16

From a report in a Yugoslav newspaper. Yugoslavia, although Communist, did not approve of Soviet policies.

In Hungary thousands of people have obtained arms by disarming soldiers and militia men … Soldiers have been making friends with the embittered and dissatisfied masses … The authorities are paralysed, unable to stop the bloody events.

SOURCE 17

Written by László Beke, a Hungarian student.

October 27, 1956. On my way home I saw a little girl propped up against the doorway of a building with a machine gun clutched in her hands. When I tried to move her, I saw she was dead. She could not have been more than eleven or twelve years old. There was a neatly folded note in her pocket she had evidently meant to pass on to her parents. In childish scrawl it read: 'Dear Mama, Brother is dead. He asked me to take care of his gun. I am all right, and I'm going with friends now. I kiss you. Kati.'

SOURCE 18

The effects of the uprising in Budapest, showing the scene of destruction outside the Kilian Barracks, where heavy fighting was experienced.

The Hungarian resistance was crushed in two weeks. The Western powers protested to the USSR but sent no help; they were too preoccupied with the Suez crisis in the Middle East (see page 316 for details on this).

Khrushchev put János Kádár in place as leader. Kádár took several months to crush all resistance. Around 35,000 anti-Communist activists were arrested and 300 were executed. Kádár cautiously introduced some of the reforms being demanded by the Hungarian people. However, he did not waver on the central issue – membership of the Warsaw Pact.

SOURCE 19

A telex message sent by the Hungarian rebels fighting the Communists. Quoted in George Mikes, *The Hungarian Revolution*, 1957.

We have almost no weapons, no heavy guns of any kind. People are running up to the tanks, throwing in hand grenades and closing the drivers' windows. The Hungarian people are not afraid of death. It is only a pity that we cannot last longer. Now the firing is starting again. The tanks are coming nearer and nearer. You can't let people attack tanks with their bare hands. What is the United Nations doing?

THINK

1 How do Sources 16 and 19 differ in the impression they give of the Hungarian uprising?
2 Why do you think they differ?
3 Does the photo in Source 18 give the same impression as either Source 16 or Source 19?
4 Look back at Source 14. Why do you think Hungary's membership of the Warsaw Pact was so important to the Soviet Union?
5 Why do you think the Hungarians received no support from the West?

ACTIVITY

Explain which of these statements you most agree with:

- 'The severity of the Red Army in dealing with Hungary in 1956 shows how fragile the Soviet hold on Hungary really was.'
- 'The speed at which the Red Army crushed resistance in Hungary shows how completely the Soviet Union controlled Hungary.'

How did events in Hungary affect Cold War relations?

The Soviet actions in Hungary led to bitter condemnation from the USA and its allies but the only serious action against the USSR came in the form of harsh words in the United Nations and in the newspapers and TV programmes of Western states. There were two main reasons why the West did little to help:

● At almost exactly the same time as the Hungarian revolt, the USA, Britain and France were deeply distracted by a crisis concerning the Suez Canal in Egypt. The British and French invaded Egypt to take back the canal without consulting the Americans. The USA and the USSR both condemned British actions and there was furious debate in the United Nations, eventually forcing the British to pull out. In these circumstances it was almost impossible to react to events in Hungary.
● Hungary was simply too close to the USSR. It would have been impossible for the West to help the rebels without sending massive forces across Europe and this would have run the risk of triggering a major war. The American President Eisenhower was simply not prepared to do this.

The lesson which emerged from the Hungarian revolt was that Khrushchev was not going to let Hungary pull out of the Warsaw Pact. It is possible that he would have allowed some of the reforms to take place but total independence was out of the question. In the months which followed, the Soviet invasion resulted in a new government which disbanded most of the Hungarian army and began a programme of political education in the remaining units to ensure their loyalty to the USSR.

In addition, Khrushchev increased the number of Soviet divisions in Hungary from two to four and made the Hungarian government accept the presence of these troops for the protection of Hungary. Hungary also had to pay for these troops to be stationed there. It was clear that Communist control in Hungary could only be maintained if it was propped up by the presence of the Red Army, and Khrushchev was quite prepared to do that.

The U-2 crisis and the Paris Peace Summit

For some years the USA had been illegally flying spying missions over the USSR, and so President Eisenhower knew all about the USSR's nuclear capability. The flights had begun in 1950, without permission from President Truman, when US Strategic Air Command began spy flights over the USSR. When he found out, Truman banned them because they violated Soviet air space.

In 1956 the flights began again, with the agreement of President Eisenhower. This time they used a brand new spy plane called the U-2. This flew so high that it could not be shot down by Soviet fighters or by anti-aircraft missiles, but it carried sophisticated listening devices and such powerful cameras that it could read a newspaper on the ground from 23,000 metres. U-2 spying flights kept the Americans fully informed about Soviet weapons technology through the late 1950s.

Khrushchev was furious about the flights. He said that each flight 'spat in the face of the Soviet people'. His problem was that he could not complain about the flights because he had no proof and he did not want to have to admit that the Soviets did not have the technology to shoot down the U-2s.

PRACTICE QUESTIONS

1 Write an account of how the events in Hungary in 1956 increased tensions in the Cold War.
2 'The main reason for increasing tensions in the Cold War in the mid-1950s was the developing arms race.'

 How far do you agree with this statement?
 Explain your answer.

In May 1960 events suddenly turned in his favour. He was preparing for the Four Power Summit with France, Britain and the USA, which was to be held in Paris. On 1 May he received the news that the USSR's new S-75 anti-aircraft missiles had shot down a U-2. The pilot, Gary Powers, parachuted to safety but was arrested by Soviet soldiers. The USSR paraded Powers on television and accused the USA of spying. The USA at first denied Powers was on a spying mission, but then admitted he was. However, President Eisenhower refused to apologise or to promise there would be no more flights. Without an apology, Khrushchev refused to attend the summit and pulled out. As a result, in the short term the U-2 crisis worsened relations between the USA and the USSR.

SOURCE 20

A 1960 Soviet cartoon commenting on the uses of the U-2 spy plane.

SOURCE 21

Nikita Khrushchev, Summit Conference Statement, 16 May 1960.

As is generally known, a provocative act by the American air force against the Soviet Union has recently taken place. It consisted in the fact that on 1 May of this year a US military reconnaissance plane intruded into the USSR on a definite espionage mission of gathering intelligence about military and industrial installations on Soviet territory. After the aggressive purpose of the plane's flight became clear, it was shot down by a Soviet rocket unit. Unfortunately, this is not the only instance of aggressive and espionage actions by the US air force against the Soviet Union.

Naturally, the Soviet government was obliged to describe these actions by their proper name and show their perfidious [deceitful] character, inconsistent with the elementary requirements of normal peacetime relations between states, to say nothing of their conflicting grossly with the aim of reducing international tension and creating the conditions needed for fruitful work at the Summit conference …

Gary Powers was sentenced to ten years in a Soviet prison, but was exchanged for a captured Soviet spy (Rudolf Abel) in February 1962. Eisenhower and his REPUBLICAN PARTY were criticised abroad for the U-2 flights. At home, they were criticised for being too soft with the Soviets. The rival Democratic Party had a young and seemingly brilliant new leader, called John F. Kennedy, who exploited this feeling very effectively. In the presidential elections of 1960 he talked up the threat of the missile gap between the USSR and the USA even though he almost certainly knew there was no such gap. Kennedy won the elections and became President in January 1961. After eight years of Eisenhower as President, Kennedy could make it clear that his approach would be different – even though in reality his options were limited.

THINK

1 Look at Source 20. What is the Soviet cartoon saying about the U-2 plane?

2 Read Source 21. Explain why the USSR was so angry about the US spy flights.

3 How would the USA justify this violation of Soviet territory?

4 Explain how Kennedy exploited the U-2 crisis of 1960.

Living in the shadow of the bomb: Kennedy and Khrushchev

Kennedy therefore inherited a tense situation which soon became worse with the building of the Berlin Wall and the Cuban Missile Crisis.

By 1961, both of the superpowers had hundreds of missiles pointed at each other. The USA had more than the USSR, but the advantage did not really matter because both sides had enough to destroy each other many times over. On each side the theory was that such weapons made them more secure. The enemy would not dare attack first, because it knew that, if it did, the other would strike back before its bombs had even landed and it too would be destroyed. It would be suicidal. So having nuclear weapons deterred the other side from attacking first. This policy also became known as MAD (Mutually Assured Destruction). Surely no side would dare strike first when it knew the attack would destroy itself too!

FIGURE 22

The location of American missiles trained on the USSR. Short-range missiles could hit the USSR in minutes. Long-range ones from the USA would take 30 minutes.

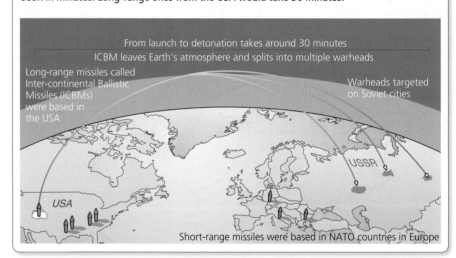

'Duck and Cover'

Leaders might regard their nuclear weapons as a deterrent, but others worried that the world was moving into a very dangerous time. Both sides developed their weapons and prepared their pilots and missile crews.

The situation was not eased in October 1961 when the USSR carried out a test explosion of the largest bomb ever exploded. The single blast exceeded the power of all the explosives used in the Second World War. The Americans responded with their own programme of nuclear tests until even the two superpowers began to have some concerns about the environmental damage the tests were causing.

All of these developments were taking place against a long-term background of concern which had been going on since the 1950s. Fear of 'the bomb' was a common feature of life in 1950s and 1960s USA. The arms race was a topic of everyday conversation. Throughout the 1950s Americans had been warned of the terrible dangers of nuclear attack. Americans, young and old, had also been through drills like the one in Source 24. Bert the Turtle had warned children to 'Duck and Cover'. On a slightly less serious note, films like *The War of the Worlds* painted a picture of a world where America and all it stood for was under attack.

SOURCE 23

Herbert York, US nuclear physicist.

It became obvious that there was no containing the Russians. They were shooting not just this big bomb, but lots and lots of them and we essentially did the same thing. We went and, you know, we got bombs from wherever we could find 'em and took 'em to Nevada and shot them just in order to respond to these Russian tests. It was a crazy period.

SOURCE 24

Extracts from *Duck and Cover*, a very well-known and widely broadcast information programme
designed to warn children about what to do in a possible nuclear attack.

A The opening song from the film.

There was a turtle by the name of Bert
And Bert the Turtle was very alert
When danger threatened him he never got hurt
He knew just what to do.
He'd Duck and Cover, Duck and Cover
He did what we all must learn to do
Me and you and you and you –
Duck and Cover.

B Bert The Turtle.

C Children following Bert's advice to 'Duck and Cover'.

FOCUS TASK

To what extent was there a 'thaw' in Cold War relations by the end of the 1950s?

1 Use the sources and information on pages 313–19 to make two lists.
   One list of evidence that there was a 'thaw' in Cold War relations, and the other of evidence of worsening Cold War relations.

2 Use your lists to write an answer of no more than two paragraphs to the following question:

   'To what extent was there a 'thaw' in Cold War relations by the end of the 1950s?'

TOPIC SUMMARY

The development of the Cold War

- China became Communist in 1949 and allied with the USSR – a huge threat to the USA.
- The Korean War was fought by the USA and her allies to prevent the spread of Communism.
- The war showed how dangerous the international situation was.
- The West set up NATO (1949) and Khrushchev responded in 1955 with the Warsaw Pact – two international organisations that were ranged against each other.
- The arms race, together with the beginnings of the space race, further heightened tensions in the Cold War.
- Khrushchev, succeeding Stalin, promised a thaw and made some concessions.
- However, in 1956 he ordered troops into Hungary to stop the reforms taking place that would have weakened Communist control.
- The U-2 spy plane and its pilot Gary Powers were shot down over Soviet territory.
- The USA was forced to admit spying activities on the USSR, and this wrecked the Paris Peace Summit of 1960.
- The effects of this further encouraged the proliferation of weapons of destruction.

7.3 Transformation of the Cold War

THINK

Study Source 1. What is the aim of this cartoon?

FOCUS

The decade of the 1960s started with events that have become famous (Berlin Wall, Cuban Missile Crisis) and then saw developments later on under Brezhnev and the gradual realisation that trying to reach an agreement on armaments was essential in order to lessen international tension.

In this part of the topic you will study the following:

- The Berlin Wall – why it was constructed in 1961 and Kennedy's response.
- Tensions over Cuba, the USA's response to Castro and Khrushchev, and the dangers and results of the Cuban Missile Crisis.
- The Prague Spring, its effect on East–West relations and to what extent the Cold War had developed during the 1960s.
- Détente and the individuals involved in the easing of tension.

● **The Berlin Wall**

You have already seen how important Berlin was as a battleground of the Cold War in the late 1940s (see pages 304–06). In 1961 it also became the focus of the Soviet Union's latest attempt to maintain control of its eastern European satellite countries.

The crushing of the Hungarian uprising had confirmed for many people in eastern Europe that it was impossible to fight the Communists. For many, it seemed that the only way of escaping the repression was to leave altogether. Some wished to leave eastern Europe for political reasons – they hated the Communists – while many more wished to leave for economic reasons. As standards of living in eastern Europe fell further and further behind the West, the attraction of going to live in a CAPITALIST state was very great.

The contrast was particularly apparent in the divided city of Berlin. Living standards were tolerable in the East, but just a few hundred metres away in West Berlin, East Germans could see some of the prize exhibits of capitalist West Germany – shops full of goods, great freedom, great wealth and great variety. East Germans could also watch West German television. This had been deliberately done by the Western powers. They had poured massive investment into Berlin.

In the 1950s East Germans were still able to travel freely into West Berlin (see Figure 3, page 321). From there they could travel on into West Germany. It was very tempting to leave East Germany, with its harsh Communist regime and its hard-line leader, Walter Ulbricht. By the late 1950s thousands were leaving and never coming back.

Those who were defecting were very often highly skilled workers or well-qualified managers. The Communist government could not afford to lose these high-quality people. More importantly, from Khrushchev's point of view, the sight of thousands of Germans fleeing Communist rule for a better life under capitalism undermined Communism generally.

In 1961 the USA had a new President, the young and inexperienced John F. Kennedy. Khrushchev thought he could bully Kennedy and chose to pick a fight over Berlin. He insisted that Kennedy withdraw US troops from the city. He was certain that Kennedy would back down. Kennedy refused. However, all eyes were now on Berlin. What would happen next?

SOURCE 2

President Kennedy speaking in 1960, before he became President.

West Berlin ... has many roles. It is more than a showcase of liberty, an island of freedom in a Communist sea. It is more than a link with the free world, a beacon of hope behind the iron curtain, an escape hatch for refugees. Above all, it has become the resting place of Western courage and will ... We cannot and will not permit the Communists to drive us out of Berlin.

FIGURE 3

The number of people crossing from East to West Germany, 1950–64.

Y-axis: Defectors (thousands) — 0, 50, 100, 150, 200, 250, 300. X-axis: 1950, 51, 52, 53, 54, 55, 56, 57, 58, 59, 1960, 61, 62, 63, 64.

The building of the Berlin Wall

At two o'clock in the morning on Sunday 13 August 1961, East German soldiers erected a barbed-wire barrier along the entire frontier between East and West Berlin, ending all free movement from East to West. It was quickly replaced by a concrete wall. All the crossing points from East to West Berlin were sealed to foreigners and allied soldiers, except for one. This became known as Checkpoint Charlie.

Families were divided. Berliners were unable to go to work, chaos and confusion followed. Border guards kept a constant look-out for anyone trying to cross the wall. They had orders to shoot people trying to defect. Hundreds were killed over the next three decades.

SOURCE 4

Stages in the building of the Berlin Wall. On the sign in **B**, which has been superimposed by a photographer wanting to make a point, Ulbricht assures the world that 'no one has any intention of building a wall'.

SOURCE 5

East German security guards recover the body of a man shot attempting to cross the wall in 1962.

SOURCE 6

Colonel Jim Atwood, who was part of the US Military Mission in Berlin in 1961.

Instructions were given to our tank commander that he was to roll up and confront the Soviet tank, which was at the identical distance across from Checkpoint Charlie. The tension escalated very rapidly for the one reason that this was Americans confronting Russians. It wasn't East Germans. There was live ammunition in both tanks of the Russians and the Americans. It was an unexpected, sudden confrontation that in my opinion was the closest that the Russians and the Allies came to going to war in the entire Cold War period.

The effects of the Berlin Wall on the Cold War

SOURCE 7

Extracts from a speech by President Kennedy in June 1963, soon after visiting Berlin.

Today, in the world of freedom, the proudest boast is 'Ich bin ein Berliner'.

There are many people in the world who really don't understand, or say they don't, what is the great issue between the free world and the Communist world. Let them come to Berlin. There are some who say that Communism is the wave of the future. Let them come to Berlin. And there are some who say in Europe and elsewhere we can work with the Communists. Let them come to Berlin. And there are even a few who say that it is true that Communism is an evil system, but it permits us to make economic progress. Let them come to Berlin. Freedom has many difficulties and democracy is not perfect, but we have never had to put a wall up to keep our people in, to prevent them from leaving us.

SOURCE 8

The Soviet explanation for the building of the wall, 1961.

The Western powers in Berlin use it as a centre of subversive activity against the GDR [the initial letters of the German name for East Germany]. In no other part of the world are so many espionage centres to be found. These centres smuggle their agents into the GDR for all kinds of subversion: recruiting spies; sabotage; provoking disturbances.

The government presents all working people of the GDR with a proposal that will securely block subversive activity so that reliable safeguards and effective control will be established around West Berlin, including its border with democratic Berlin.

For a while, the wall created a major crisis. Access to East Berlin had been guaranteed to the Allies since 1945. In October 1961 US diplomats and troops crossed regularly into East Berlin to find out how the Soviets would react.

On 27 October Soviet tanks pulled up to Checkpoint Charlie and refused to allow any further access to the East. All day, US and Soviet tanks, fully armed, faced each other in a tense stand-off. Then, after 18 hours, one by one, five metres at a time, the tanks pulled back. Another crisis, another retreat.

The international reaction was relief. Khrushchev ordered Ulbricht to avoid any actions that would increase tension. Kennedy said, 'It's not a very nice solution, but a wall is a hell of a lot better than a war.' So the wall stayed, and over the following years became the symbol of division – the division of Germany, the division of Europe, the division of Communist East and democratic West. The Communists presented the wall as a protective shell around East Berlin. The West presented it as a prison wall.

FOCUS TASK

Why was the Berlin Wall built in 1961?

Work in pairs. Make a poster or notice to be stuck on the Berlin Wall explaining the purpose of the wall. One of you make a poster for the East German side and the other make a poster for the West German side. You can use pictures and quotations from the sources in this chapter or use your own research.

Make sure you explain in your poster the reasons why the wall was built and what the results of building the wall will be.

• The Cuban Missile Crisis

This episode is the most famous crisis in the Cold War. The significant fact is that worldwide destruction was averted because neither side was willing to risk war or its consequences.

Cuba: The background

Cuba is a large island just 160 km from Florida in the southern USA. It had long been a playground for the benefit of wealthy Americans who enjoyed its sun and bars in the midst of the poverty of its people. Americans owned most of the businesses on the island and they had a huge naval base there.

The Americans also provided the Cuban ruler, General Batista, with economic and military support. Batista was a dictator. His rule was corrupt and unpopular. The Americans supported Batista primarily because he was just as opposed to Communism as they were.

However, there was plenty of opposition to Batista in Cuba. From 1956 onwards Fidel Castro was building up support in the Sierra Maestra mountains. In July 1958 Batista's army was sent there but it was defeated. This gave Castro the confidence to move from the mountains, relying on much support from ordinary people. Batista panicked and fled abroad. Castro entered the capital, Havana, on 8 January 1959. He was charming and clever, but also ruthless. He quickly killed, arrested or exiled many political opponents. With his vision for a better Cuba, he quickly won over the majority of Cubans.

The response of the USA to Castro's rule

The USA was taken by surprise at first and decided to recognise Castro as the new leader of Cuba. However, within a short period of time relations between the two countries grew worse. Their governments were very different in philosophy, the capitalist USA contrasting with the Communist-leaning Cuba under Castro. In particular two important practical issues emerged by 1961:

- There were thousands of Cuban exiles in the USA who had fled from Castro's rule. They formed powerful pressure groups demanding action against Castro.
- Castro took over some American-owned businesses in Cuba, particularly the agricultural businesses. He took their land and distributed it to his supporters among Cuba's peasant farmer population.

As early as June 1960, US President Eisenhower authorised the US Central Intelligence Agency (CIA) to investigate ways of overthrowing Castro. The CIA provided support and funds to Cuban exiles. They also investigated ways to disrupt the Cuban economy, such as damaging sugar PLANTATIONS. American companies working in Cuba refused to co-operate with any Cuban businesses which used oil or other materials that had been imported from the USSR. The American media also broadcast a relentless stream of criticism of Castro and his regime.

Castro responded to US hostility with a mixed approach. He assured Americans living in Cuba that they were safe and he allowed the USA to keep its naval base. He said he simply wanted to run Cuba without interference. However, by the summer of 1960 he had allied Cuba with the Soviet Union. Soviet leader Khrushchev signed a trade agreement giving Cuba $100 million in economic aid. Castro also began receiving arms from the Soviet Union, and American spies knew this.

Fidel Castro

- Born 1926, the son of a wealthy farmer.
- Studied law at Havana University and then practised as a lawyer helping poor Cubans.
- His left-wing political beliefs focused on abolishing the US imperialist domination of Cuba and overthrowing the dictator Batista.
- He believed in social justice and political freedom.
- By the early 1950s he was more and more influenced by MARXIST teachings.
- His 1953 plan to overthrow Batista failed and he was imprisoned for a year.
- From 1954 onwards he led a guerrilla war against Batista from the Sierra Maestra mountains.
- In 1959 he overthrew Batista and became Prime Minister.
- He nationalised US businesses without compensation and accepted economic help from the USSR.
- He defeated America's invasion attempt at the Bay of Pigs in 1961.
- Cuban Missile Crisis, 1962 – Castro emerged stronger.
- In 1976, instead of being Prime Minister, he became the President (until 2008).

SOURCE 9

A 1960 Soviet cartoon. The notice held by the US Secretary of State says to Castro in Cuba: 'I forbid you to make friends with the Soviet Union'.

SOURCE 10

Kennedy speaking after a meeting with Khrushchev in 1961 in which Khrushchev had been very aggressive towards Kennedy.

I think he [Khrushchev] did it [was so aggressive] because of the Bay of Pigs. He thought that anyone who was so young and inexperienced as to get into that mess could be beaten; and anyone who got into it and didn't see it through had no guts. So he just beat the hell out of me.

If he thinks I'm inexperienced and have no guts, until we remove those ideas we won't get anywhere with him.

The Bay of Pigs, 1961

In January 1961 the USA's new President, John F. Kennedy, broke off diplomatic relations with Cuba. Castro thought that the USA was preparing to invade his country. In fact, the USA was not preparing an actual invasion, at least, not directly. But the USA was no longer prepared to tolerate a Soviet satellite in its own 'sphere of influence' and the plans to overthrow Castro which were begun under Eisenhower began to take shape.

Rather than a direct invasion President Kennedy instead supplied arms, equipment and transport for 1,400 anti-Castro exiles to invade Cuba and overthrow him. In April 1961 the exiles landed at the Bay of Pigs. They were met by 20,000 Cuban troops armed with tanks and modern weapons. The invasion failed disastrously. Castro captured or killed them all within days.

The results of the invasion

The half-hearted invasion suggested to Cuba and the Soviet Union that, despite its opposition to Communism in Cuba, the USA was unwilling to get directly involved in Cuba. Khrushchev was scornful of Kennedy's pathetic attempt to oust Communism from Cuba.

Historians also argue that the Bay of Pigs fiasco further encouraged the spread of Communism. On the one hand, it suggested to the USSR that Kennedy was weak. On the other hand, it made Castro and Khrushchev very suspicious of US policy.

FOCUS TASK

How did the USA respond to the Cuban revolution?

1 Here are some possible ways that the USA could have dealt with Cuba:

> Invade! | Influence! | Ignore! | Pressurise! | Destabilise! | Send aid! | Disrupt! | Discredit!

Record examples of the USA doing any of these things. If you find examples of American actions that are not covered by these words, record them too.

2 Place these actions on a scale like this:

Friendly   Neutral   Hostile

3 Write a paragraph to summarise the American response to Castro taking over Cuba.

Khrushchev sending arms and missiles to Cuba and the US response

After the Bay of Pigs fiasco, Soviet arms flooded into Cuba. In May 1962 the Soviet Union announced publicly for the first time that it was supplying Cuba with arms. By July 1962 Cuba had the best-equipped army in Latin America. By September it had thousands of Soviet missiles, plus patrol boats, tanks, radar vans, missile erectors, jet bombers, jet fighters and 5,000 Soviet technicians to help to maintain the weapons.

The Americans watched all this with great alarm. They seemed ready to tolerate conventional arms being supplied to Cuba, but the big question was whether the Soviet Union would dare to put nuclear missiles there. In September Kennedy's own Intelligence Department said that it did not believe the USSR would send nuclear weapons to Cuba. The USSR had not taken this step with any of its satellite states before and the US Intelligence Department believed that the USSR would consider it too risky to do it in Cuba. On 11 September, Kennedy warned the USSR that he would prevent 'by whatever means might be necessary' Cuba's becoming an offensive military base – by which, everyone knew, he meant a nuclear missile base. The same day the USSR assured the USA that it had no need to put nuclear missiles on Cuba and no intention of doing so.

The crisis: October 1962

On Sunday, 14 October 1962, an American spy plane flew over Cuba. It took amazingly detailed photographs of missile sites in Cuba. To the military experts two things were obvious – that these were nuclear missile sites, and that they were being built by the USSR.

More photo reconnaissance followed over the next two days. This confirmed that some sites were nearly finished but others were still being built. Some were already supplied with missiles, others were awaiting them. The experts said that the most developed of the sites could be ready to launch missiles in just seven days. American spy planes also reported that 20 Soviet ships were currently on the way to Cuba carrying missiles.

SOURCE 11

Map showing the location of Cuba and the range of the Cuban missiles.

SOURCE 12

President Kennedy's brother, Robert Kennedy, describing events on Thursday 18 October in the book he wrote about the crisis, *Thirteen Days*.

[Estimates were that the] missiles had an atomic warhead [power] of about half the current missile capacity of the entire Soviet Union. The photographs indicated that missiles were directed at certain American cities. The estimate was that within a few minutes of their being fired 80 million Americans would be dead.

Kennedy's decision to act

On Tuesday 16 October, President Kennedy was informed of the discovery. He formed a special team of advisers called Ex Comm. They came up with several choices.

ACTIVITY

Work in groups. You are advisers to the President over the situation in Cuba. You have to reduce the five options below to just two for the President to choose between.

When you have made your decision, explain why you have rejected the other three.

1 Do nothing
2 Surgical air attack
3 Invasion
4 Diplomatic pressures
5 Blockade

The events of the crisis

Tues 16 October	**President Kennedy is informed** of the missile build-up. Ex Comm formed.
Sat 20 October	**Kennedy decides** on a blockade of Cuba.
Mon 22 October	**Kennedy announces** the blockade and calls on the Soviet Union to withdraw its missiles. 'I call on Chairman Khrushchev to halt and eliminate this reckless and provocative threat to world peace … He has the opportunity now to move the world back from the abyss of destruction … withdrawing these weapons from Cuba.'
Tues 23 October	**Kennedy receives a letter** from Khrushchev saying that Soviet ships will not observe the blockade. Khrushchev does not admit the presence of nuclear missiles on Cuba.
Wed 24 October	**The blockade begins.** The first missile-carrying ships, accompanied by a Soviet submarine, approach the 500-mile (800 km) blockade zone. Then suddenly, at 10.32 a.m., the 20 Soviet ships which are closest to the zone stop or turn around.
Thurs 25 October	**Despite this,** intensive aerial photography reveals that work on the missile bases in Cuba is proceeding rapidly.
Fri 26 October	**Kennedy receives a long personal letter from Khrushchev.** The letter claims that the missiles on Cuba are purely defensive, but goes on: 'If assurances were given that the USA would not participate in an attack on Cuba and the blockade was lifted, then the question of the removal or the destruction of the missile sites would be an entirely different question.' This is the first time Khrushchev has admitted the presence of the missiles.
Sat 27 October a.m.	**Khrushchev sends a second letter** – revising his proposals – saying that the condition for removing the missiles from Cuba is that the USA withdraw its missiles from Turkey.
	An American U-2 plane is shot down over Cuba. The pilot is killed. The President is advised to launch an immediate reprisal attack on Cuba.
Sat 27 October p.m.	**Kennedy decides to delay** an attack. He also decides to ignore the second Khrushchev letter, but accepts the terms suggested by Khrushchev on 26 October. He says that if the Soviet Union does not withdraw, an attack will follow.
Sun 28 October	**Khrushchev replies to Kennedy:** 'In order to eliminate as rapidly as possible the conflict which endangers the cause of peace … the Soviet government has given a new order to dismantle the arms which you described as offensive and to crate and return them to the Soviet Union.'
Sun 28 October	**Kennedy** announces the end of the crisis.

The results of the crisis

- Cuba stayed Communist and highly armed. However, the nuclear missiles were withdrawn under United Nations supervision.
- Both leaders emerged with something from the crisis. Kennedy came out of the crisis with a greatly improved reputation in his own country and throughout the West. He had stood up to Khrushchev and had made him back down.
- Khrushchev was also able to claim a personal triumph. Cuba remained a useful ally in 'Uncle Sam's backyard'. The fact that Khrushchev had been forced to back down was quickly forgotten in Soviet circles. Instead, his role as a responsible peacemaker, willing to take the first move towards compromise, was highlighted.
- Historians agree that the Cuban Missile Crisis helped to thaw Cold War relations between the USA and the USSR. Both leaders had seen how their game of brinkmanship had nearly ended in nuclear war. Now they were more prepared to take steps to reduce the risk of nuclear war. A permanent 'hot line' phone link direct from the White House to the Kremlin was set up in 1963. In the same year they signed a Nuclear Test Ban Treaty. It did not stop the development of weapons, but it limited tests and was an important step forward.
- Within the USA, the crisis had an effect on anti-Communist opinion. Hardliners had wanted the USA to invade Cuba – to turn back Communism. However, the Cuban Crisis highlighted the weakness of their case. Such intervention was not worth the high risk. A Communist Cuba was an inconvenience to the USA. A nuclear war would be the end of civilisation.

SOURCE 13

A cartoon by Vicky (Victor Weisz) from the London *Evening Standard*, 24 October 1962.

"INTOLERABLE HAVING YOUR ROCKETS ON _MY_ DOORSTEP!"

British Cartoon Archive, University of Kent
© Solo Syndication/Associated Newspapers Ltd.

SOURCE 14

Richard Crockatt, Senior Lecturer in American History at the University of East Anglia, writing in 2000.

Much of the evidence tends to support the view that, despite the many unpredictable elements in the decision making process, in crucial instances the leaders on both sides chose courses of action which were both non-provocative and allowed room for retreat from exposed positions …

THINK

1. Source 13 is a British cartoon. Pretend you did not know this and explain why it is unlikely to be an American or Soviet cartoon.
2. What are the strengths and weaknesses of Source 13 for understanding the issues in the Cuban Missile Crisis?

SOURCE 15

Khrushchev was forced from power in 1964. This extract comes from his memoirs written in 1971.

[In 1961] we increased our military aid to Cuba. We were sure the Americans would never agree to the existence of Castro's Cuba. They feared, and we hoped, that a socialist Cuba might become a magnet that would attract other Latin American countries to socialism. We had to find an effective deterrent to American interference in the Caribbean.

The Caribbean Crisis was a triumph of Soviet foreign policy and a personal triumph in my own career. Today Cuba exists as an independent socialist country right in front of America. Cuba's very existence is good propaganda.

We behaved with dignity and forced the United States to demobilise and to recognise Cuba.

PRACTICE QUESTIONS

1. Study Sources 13 and 15.
   How useful are these sources to a historian for understanding the Cuban Missile Crisis?
   Explain your answer using both sources and your contextual knowledge.
2. Write an account of how the ending of the Cuban Missile Crisis when the Soviet ships turned around affected the reputations of the USA and the USSR.
3. 'The main person to benefit in the Cuban Missile Crisis was Castro, not Kennedy or Khrushchev.'
   How far do you agree with this statement?
   Explain your answer.

SOURCE 16

From a speech given by Ludvik Vaculik, a leading figure in the reform movement, in March 1968.

In Czechoslovakia the people who were trusted [by the Communist government] were the obedient ones, those who did not cause any trouble, who didn't ask questions. It was the mediocre man who came off best.

In twenty years not one human problem has been solved in our country, from primary needs like flats, schools, to the more subtle needs such as fulfilling oneself … the need for people to trust one another … development of education.

I feel that our Republic has lost its good reputation.

SOURCE 17

A Soviet news agency report, 21 August 1968.

The party and government leaders of the Czechoslovak Socialist Republic have asked the Soviet Union and other allies to give the Czechoslovak people urgent assistance, including assistance with armed forces. This request was brought about … by the threat from counter revolutionary forces … working with foreign forces hostile to socialism.

SOURCE 18

A Prague radio report, 21 August 1968.

Yesterday troops from the Soviet Union, Poland, East Germany, Hungary and Bulgaria crossed the frontier of Czechoslovakia … The Czechoslovak Communist Party Central Committee regard this act as contrary to the basic principles of good relations between socialist states.

THINK

Explain how and why Sources 17 and 18 differ in their interpretation of the Soviet intervention.

Czechoslovakia and the Prague Spring, 1968

Twelve years after the brutal suppression of the Hungarians (see pages 314–15), Czechoslovakia posed a similar challenge to Soviet domination of eastern Europe. Khrushchev had by now been ousted from power in the USSR. A new leader, Leonid Brezhnev, had replaced him.

Why was there opposition in Czechoslovakia?

In the 1960s a new mood developed in Czechoslovakia. People examined what had been happening in 20 years of Communist control and they did not like what they saw. In 1967 the old Stalinist leader was forced to resign. Alexander Dubček became the leader of the Czech Communist Party. He proposed a policy of 'socialism with a human face': less censorship, more freedom of speech and a reduction in the activities of the secret police. Dubček was a committed Communist, but he believed that Communism did not have to be as restrictive as it had been before he came to power. He had learned the lessons of the Hungarian uprising and reassured Brezhnev that Czechoslovakia had no plans to pull out of the Warsaw Pact or Comecon.

The Czech opposition was led by intellectuals who felt that the Communists had failed to lead the country forward. As censorship had been eased, they were able to launch attacks on the Communist leadership, pointing out how corrupt and useless they were. Communist government ministers were 'grilled' on live television and radio about how they were running the country and about events before 1968. This period became known as the 'Prague Spring' because of all the new ideas that seemed to be appearing everywhere.

By the summer even more radical ideas were emerging. There was even talk of allowing another political party, the Social Democratic Party, to be set up as a rival to the Communist Party.

How did the Soviet Union respond?

The Soviet Union was very suspicious of the changes taking place in Czechoslovakia. Czechoslovakia was one of the most important countries in the Warsaw Pact. It was centrally placed, and had the strongest industry. The Soviets were worried that the new ideas in Czechoslovakia might spread to other countries in eastern Europe. Brezhnev came under pressure from the East German leader, Walter Ulbricht, and the Polish leader, Gomulka, to restrain reform in Czechoslovakia.

The USSR tried various methods in response. To start with, it tried to slow Dubček down. It argued with him. Soviet, Polish and East German troops performed very public training exercises right on the Czech border. It thought about imposing economic SANCTIONS – for example, cancelling wheat exports to Czechoslovakia – but didn't because it thought that the Czechs would ask for help from the West.

In July the USSR had a summit conference with the Czechs. Dubček agreed not to allow a new Social Democratic Party. However, he insisted on keeping most of his reforms. The tension seemed to ease. Early in August, a conference of all the other Warsaw Pact countries produced a vague declaration simply calling on Czechoslovakia to maintain political stability.

Then 17 days later, on 20 August 1968, to the stunned amazement of the Czechs and the outside world, Soviet tanks moved into Czechoslovakia.

There was little violent resistance, although many Czechs refused to co-operate with the Soviet troops. Dubček was removed from power. His experiment in socialism with a human face had not failed; it had simply proved unacceptable to the other Communist countries.

SOURCE 19

A street cartoon in Prague.

The Prague Spring once again poisoned East–West relations. The USSR had shown the West that it could not tolerate losing any part of its control over eastern Europe. Members of the Warsaw Pact saw that trying to move away from official Soviet policies would not be tolerated.

FOCUS TASK

How far did the Cold War develop during the 1960s?

1 Compare the two rebellions in Hungary in 1956 and Czechoslovakia in 1968.

For each rebellion consider:
- the aims of the rebels
- attitude towards Communism
- attitude towards democracy
- attitude to the USSR
- attitude to the West
- why the Soviet Union intervened
- how each state responded to Soviet intervention.

Now discuss:
a) which is the biggest difference?
b) which is the biggest similarity?

2 In pairs, discuss how far the Cold War developed during the 1960s. Each write a paragraph to summarise your conclusions.

The Brezhnev Doctrine

The Prague Spring gave rise to the BREZHNEV DOCTRINE. The essentials of Communism were defined as:

- a one-party system
- to remain a member of the Warsaw Pact.

Unlike Nagy in Hungary, Dubček was not executed. But he was gradually downgraded. First he was sent to be ambassador to Turkey, then expelled from the Communist Party altogether. Photographs showing him as leader were 'censored'.

Before the Soviet invasion, Czechoslovakia's mood had been one of optimism. After, it was despair. A country that had been pro-Soviet now became resentful of the Soviet connection. Ideas that could have reformed Communism were silenced.

Twenty years later, Mikhail Gorbachev, the leader of the USSR, questioned the invasion, and was himself spreading the ideas of the Prague Spring that the Soviet Union had crushed in 1968.

PRACTICE QUESTION

Study Source 20.
Source 20 opposes the Soviet Union.
How do you know?
Explain your answer by using Source 20 and your contextual knowledge.

SOURCE 20

Czechs burning Soviet tanks in Prague, August 1968.

SOURCE 21

The Brezhnev Doctrine.

When internal and external forces hostile to socialism attempt to turn the development of any socialist country in the direction of the capitalist system, when a threat arises to the cause of socialism in that country, a threat to the socialist commonwealth as a whole – it becomes not only a problem for the people of that country but also a general problem, the concern of all socialist countries

ACTIVITY

Carry out your own research on the background of SALT 1. Who was more important in the negotiations – Nixon or Brezhnev?

KEY WORDS

Make sure you know what these words mean and are able to define them confidently:
- Airlift (Berlin)
- Atomic bomb
- Blockade (Berlin)
- Brezhnev Doctrine
- Capitalism
- Co-existence
- Cold War
- Comecon
- Cominform
- Communism
- Containment
- Democracy
- De-Stalinisation
- Détente
- Dictatorship
- Intercontinental Ballistic Missile (ICBM)
- Iron Curtain
- Isolationism
- Marshall Plan
- NATO
- Nuclear deterrent
- SALT 1
- Superpower
- Truman Doctrine
- Warsaw Pact

● The easing of tension: Détente and SALT 1

In the late 1960s and early 1970s the word 'DÉTENTE' came to be used to signify the relaxing of tension in the Cold War. The USA and the USSR were not friends, but were less hostile. The Cuban Missile Crisis had shown how dangerous the Cold War was. Both countries had come to accept each other's areas of influence in the world. However, the West still held fears that the Communist world would expand, particularly in Asia. In Vietnam the USA was assisting the South in its fight against the Communist North. But even here, it was becoming obvious by the end of the 1960s that this battle was not only costly but futile.

Various factors encouraged détente:

- Rising INFLATION and huge costs over the Vietnam War were crippling the American economy. The USSR needed to expand its world trade in order to improve living standards.
- Both sides had stockpiles of weapons that could destroy the Earth many times over.
- Both were worried about conflicts in the Middle East that would disrupt oil supplies.
- Both were worried about the growing power of China.
- President Nixon, taking office in 1969, was keen to talk with Brezhnev, and Brezhnev was keen to extend Khrushchev's policy of peaceful CO-EXISTENCE.

There had been agreements in the 1960s over nuclear weapons. In 1968 the USA, the USSR and Britain signed the Nuclear Non-Proliferation Treaty, aimed at stopping the spread of nuclear weapons.

SALT 1, 1972

After three years of talks the Strategic Arms Limitations Talks (SALT) agreement was reached in 1972. This agreement:

- limited the number of INTERCONTINENTAL BALLISTIC MISSILES (ICBMs) and Anti-Ballistic Missiles (ABMs) on both sides
- allowed each side to use spy satellites to check on the other side.

The signing of the agreement, to last for five years, was seen as a huge achievement at the time.

TOPIC SUMMARY

Transformation of the Cold War
- The Berlin Wall became a symbol of the division between East and West in the Cold War.
- Castro became the ruler of Cuba, which held American financial and military interests.
- Khrushchev was keen to assist Cuba – in return for placing missiles on the island.
- The crisis in October 1962 could have led to world destruction.
- Eventually, both sides backed down in order to avoid further escalation.
- The Czechs wanted to loosen the hold of Communism on the country.
- The USSR sent in troops to end the Prague Spring in 1968.
- In spite of all the crises in international relations, tensions began to ease at the end of the 1960s under Nixon and Brezhnev, with both having solid reasons for doing so.
- The result in 1972 was SALT 1 which was a step towards limiting nuclear weapons.

ASSESSMENT FOCUS

KEY

Focus words

Command words

Source/knowledge reminder words

Your exam will include four questions on this topic. The question types will be the same every year, but the questions could be on any content from the specification, so you need to know it all!

We have provided one example of each kind of question. For questions based on sources we have used sources that you have already come across in this chapter. We have analysed each of the questions to highlight what you are being asked to do and written a sample answer with comments on how it could be improved.

Source A is Source 8, page 311.

Q1 **Study** Source A. Source A **supports** the USSR. **How do you know**?

Explain your answer by using **Source A** and your **contextual knowledge**.

(4 marks)

Sample answer

The way the poster is drawn shows that the USSR is proud of Gagarin's achievements in space. He is shown with a confident face and in a commanding position in relation to the globe and to space. He is being praised for what he has achieved, putting the USSR ahead of the USA in the space race.

Source B is Source 9, page 311. Source C is Source 11, page 312.

Q2 **Study** Sources B and C. **How useful** are these **two sources** to a historian studying American attitudes towards the space race at the beginning of the 1960s?

Explain your answer using **Sources B and C** and your **contextual knowledge**.

(12 marks)

Sample answer

Source B is a logo for the US space mission programme involving a landing on the Moon. Showing an eagle landing on the Moon shows the strength and ambitions of the USA. It shows the image that the USA was trying to project with the purpose of showing confidence and dominance.

Source C is from a speech by Kennedy when he became President of the USA in 1961. The speech is useful for showing Kennedy's ambitions to land a man on the Moon. The language he uses is intended to impress the listener. He sounds confident and wants to impress the American nation.

Q3 Write an account of how events in Hungary in 1956 **affected** the Cold War.

(8 marks)

Sample answer

Hungary was in the part of Eastern Europe that was controlled by the USSR. The Communist government under Rákosi was criticised by many Hungarians, especially because of his use of the secret police (the AVH). Widespread protests developed into riots in Budapest. There was street fighting for several days. Rákosi was forced to resign and Nagy took over. Hungarians thought they had won, but when Nagy demanded that Hungary withdraw from the Warsaw Pact, Russian tanks moved into the city and crushed the uprising. A new pro-Russian government was set up under Kádár. Hungary was firmly under Soviet control.

— This answer shows a clear understanding of the cartoon's intention, but ideally it should include some knowledge to support its statements. For example, you could explain what Gagarin achieved and why it was important at that particular moment in the space race.

— *Study Source 1 from page 320. Attempt the same question, using that source.*

— The answer provides some basic comments on each of the two sources, but it could usefully include more in-depth analysis of the content and some examination of the provenance. There is very little contextual knowledge shown. This could be improved substantially.

— *For each of the two sources, make a list of what you know about the provenance, and whether or not you think this makes the source more or less reliable.*

— *Then think about the context of the period in which the sources were created. What were people's attitudes in general at that time? What was the situation in the space race in the 1960s?*

— *Now look at the content of each source. Use your knowledge to put the content of the sources into context.*

— The answer provides some details of the events, including the names of key Hungarians. It could contain more factual details, such as the number of tanks or the number of deaths, etc.

— The end of the answer mentions that Hungary was defeated, but it does not develop anything on how events increased international tension.

— *List two main reasons why these events were important in the developing international tensions in the Cold War. To help you, think about:*
  — *how the USSR had behaved towards Hungary.*
  — *how the countries of Western Europe and the USA would react to the news from Hungary, and how this would affect the Cold War at a time when there had been hopes of a thaw.*

Q4 'The **main reason** for the development of the Cold War, 1945–1948, was the **occupation of Eastern Europe by the USSR**.'

How far do you agree with this statement? **Explain** your answer. (16 marks)

Sample answer

- This is a clearly argued answer. It develops an explanation of the stated factor and puts this alongside other factors.

- It demonstrates a range of accurate knowledge and understanding, and the answer is organised in a way that is totally focused on the question. It could, however, have slightly more factual detail in places, and it could introduce additional arguments (though three well developed ones should be sufficient).

- The answer contains accurate spelling and punctuation, the meaning is clearly expressed and a range of specialist terms are used to explain arguments.

- *Are there any more details of evidence that you would add to this answer?*

By 1948 the Cold War was well established, though it had only gained its name the previous year, and the year before that Churchill had coined the phrase, 'the iron curtain'. So whose fault was this situation?

It is easy to blame the Soviet Union. In 1945–46 the USSR had occupied and set up governments that were friendly to Communism in the key countries of Eastern Europe. The countries had been 'liberated' from Nazism only to gain a new dictatorship. These included Hungary, Czechoslovakia, Romania and parts of Germany. Stalin was convinced that the USSR needed a barrier from attack – having suffered twice in 1914 and in 1941. He needed a barrier against the aggressive attitudes of the capitalist West.

However, the USA was also to blame for the Cold War. It was terrified of the spread of Communism.

Therefore the USA acted to 'protect' Western Europe through the Truman Doctrine (the USA would act against armed aggression) and Marshall Aid (funding rebuilding projects in an effort to eliminate terrible living conditions which might encourage support for Communism).

The USA was also to blame for exploding the first atomic bomb at Hiroshima in 1945. The USSR was rightly frightened – and retaliated with its own research so that the USSR possessed atomic power by 1949. This was really one of the spurs to the development of the Cold War which led to the arms race and then the space race. It could be argued that this, indeed, was the main reason.

The distrust was increasingly obvious in the closing stages of the war. Agreements at Yalta and Potsdam reflected compromises and decisions that were bound to lead to acute tension after the surrender of Germany. At the heart of these tensions was the fate of Germany itself. This could suggest that the development of the Cold War was the fault of both sides. Two contrasting ideologies were on a collision course once they had defeated the common enemy of Fascism.

Now write your own answers to the questions on pages 331–32 using the teacher's feedback to help you.

Conflict and Tension in Asia, 1950–1975

8

This wider world depth study focuses on the complex and diverse interests of different states and individuals and the ideologies they represented. You will be studying the causes and events of the Cold War in Asia and learning how and why conflict occurred and why it proved difficult to resolve. You will also be looking at the role of key individuals and groups in shaping change, and how they both influenced and were affected by international relations and events.

You will be studying this in three sections:
- The Korean War, 1950–53, and its impact on international relations.
- The escalation of conflict in Vietnam in the 1950s and 1960s.
- Opposition to the Vietnam War in America, and the ending of the conflict.

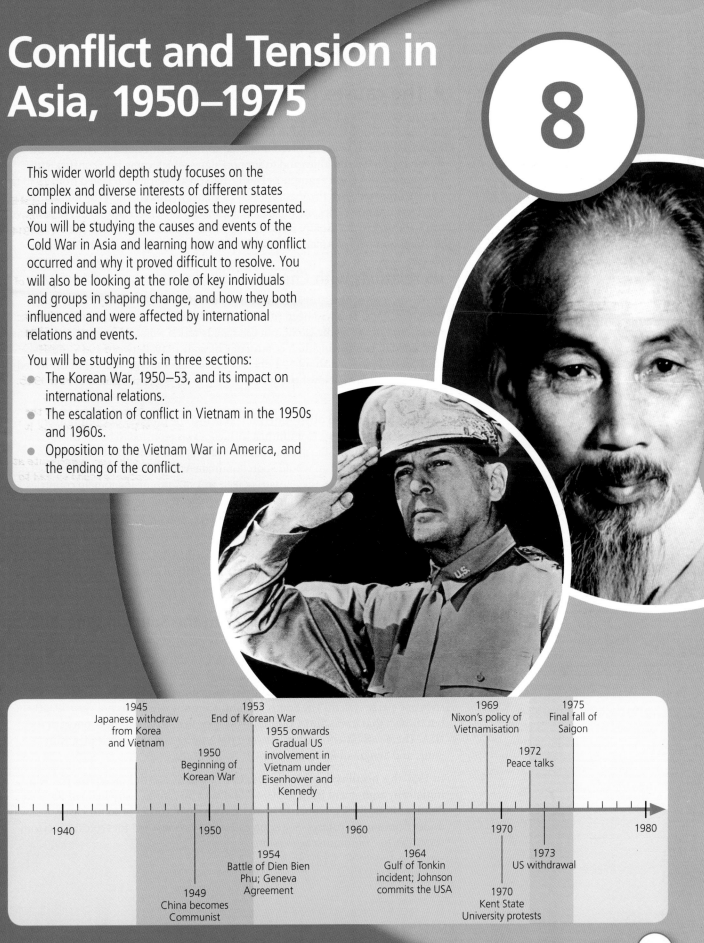

1945 Japanese withdraw from Korea and Vietnam

1953 End of Korean War

1955 onwards Gradual US involvement in Vietnam under Eisenhower and Kennedy

1969 Nixon's policy of Vietnamisation

1975 Final fall of Saigon

1950 Beginning of Korean War

1972 Peace talks

1940

1950

1960

1970

1980

1954 Battle of Dien Bien Phu; Geneva Agreement

1964 Gulf of Tonkin incident; Johnson commits the USA

1973 US withdrawal

1949 China becomes Communist

1970 Kent State University protests

The conflict in Korea started five years after the end of the Second World War. It was an early example of how the Cold War could break out into violence between the West and the Communist world, which by 1950 included China. The struggle was savage, but it never gained the notoriety of the Vietnam War, partly because technology had not advanced sufficiently in the early 1950s for all events to be filmed in colour.

In this part of the topic you will study the following:

- The causes of the Korean War.
- The development of the Korean War.
- The end of the Korean War and its significance for Cold War relations.

8.1 Conflict in Korea

• The causes of the Korean War

During the 1950s an ARMS RACE was being played out between America and the USSR. Against the background of this developing nuclear rivalry, both SUPERPOWERS were anxious not to get involved in a head-to-head confrontation. However, they were happy to recruit allies and to support states which came into conflict with their enemies. A good example of this is the Korean War which lasted from 1950 to 1953. Compared with the Vietnam War (see later in this chapter) the Korean War is relatively unknown, despite the fact that it was an extremely brutal and destructive war with very high casualty rates. In fact, in the Korean War the rate (rather than the total number) of American casualties was actually higher than in Vietnam.

US relations with China

There was a lot of anti-COMMUNIST feeling in the USA, which reached its height in the early 1950s. This had been fuelled by what was seen as a Communist takeover of eastern Europe by the USSR, but then made much worse when the Communists succeeded in completing their control of China in 1949. Between 1946 and 1949 the USA had pumped about $2 billion of aid to help the Nationalists in China led by Chiang Kai-Shek. Now he had been forced to retreat to the island of Formosa (Taiwan).

President Truman and other Americans watched the progress of Communism with increasing anxiety. Communist influence was reported to be on the increase in Malaya, Indonesia, Burma and the Philippines as well as Korea. Americans feared that Communism would soon dominate Asia. President Truman had set out what became known as the TRUMAN DOCTRINE in 1947, promising to help countries threatened by unwelcome Communist takeovers. At the time he was primarily thinking of Stalin's threat to countries in Europe, but the doctrine was equally applicable in Asia.

In the short term, the USA refused to recognise the new Communist government of China led by Mao Zedong, and maintained official diplomatic channels through the Nationalist government in exile.

Reasons why the North invaded the South in June 1950

Korea had been ruled by Japan until 1945. At the end of the Second World War the northern half was liberated by Soviet troops and the southern half by Americans (see Figure 1). When the war ended, the North remained Communist-controlled, with a Communist leader who had been trained in the USSR, and with a Soviet-style one-party system. The South was anti-Communist. It was not very DEMOCRATIC, but the fact that it was anti-Communist was enough to win it the support of the USA. There was bitter hostility between the North's Communist leader, Kim Il Sung, and Syngman Rhee, President of South Korea.

In 1950 this hostility spilled over into open warfare. North Korean troops, helped initially by equipment from the USSR and later by China, overwhelmed the South's forces. By September 1950 all except a small corner of south-east Korea was under Communist control. See Sources 2 and 3 on page 335 for typical American responses to Communist aggression.

FIGURE 1

A map of Korea.

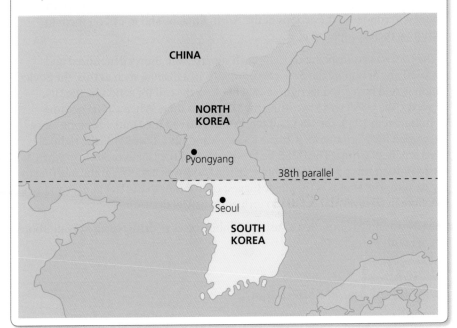

SOURCE 2

American Senator Tom Connally speaking in 1950. He was a REPUBLICAN and strongly anti-Communist.

If the UN is ever going to do anything, this is the time, and if the UN cannot bring the crisis in Korea to an end then we might as well just wash up the United Nations and forget it.

SOURCE 3

The US State Department, 1950.

Korea is a symbol to the watching world. If we allow Korea to fall within the Soviet orbit, the world will feel we have lost another round in our match with the Soviet Union, and our prestige and the hopes of those who place their faith in us will suffer accordingly.

PROFILE

Kim Il Sung, Supreme Leader of North Korea 1948–94

- Born in 1912 – not much is certain about his childhood.
- In 1931 he joined the Communist Party, and in the 1930s became involved in anti-Japanese activities in China and Korea and was recognised as an excellent military leader.
- He was a major in the Soviet Red Army fighting against Japan, 1941–45.
- In 1945 he assumed control in North Korea which had been liberated from the Japanese.
- In 1948 he failed to hold all-Korean elections, and instead pronounced North Korea as a separate Communist REPUBLIC.
- He authorised the invasion of South Korea in 1950.
- He died in 1994.

PROFILE

Syngman Rhee, President of South Korea 1948–60

- Born in 1875. He was well educated, learnt English and studied in the USA. Gained a PhD.
- In the period 1910–40 he campaigned tirelessly against the Japanese who had imposed their rule over Korea. He was in exile, mostly in the USA, and became well known to government figures there. During the Second World War he campaigned for the creation of an independent Korea.
- He returned to Korea in 1945 and set up a provisional government. He won elections in South Korea in 1948.
- In 1950 the USA supported him in South Korea despite his dictatorial anti-democratic style of government.
- He lost power in 1960, and died in Hawaii in 1965.

THINK

Explain how the Communist victory in China helped the USA to get the UN to intervene in North Korea.

UN and US responses

President Truman immediately sent advisers, supplies and warships to the waters around Korea. At the same time, he put enormous pressure on the UN Security Council to condemn the actions of the North Koreans and to call on them to withdraw their troops.

In the COLD WAR atmosphere of 1950, each superpower always denounced and opposed any action by the other. So normally, in a dispute such as this, the Soviet Union would have used its right of VETO to block the call for action by the UN. However, the USSR was boycotting the UN at this time. When China became Communist in 1949, the USA had blocked its entry to the United Nations, since it regarded the Nationalists (Chiang Kai-shek and his followers) as the rightful government of China. The USSR had walked out of the UN in protest. So when the resolution was passed (see Source 4), the USSR was not even at the meeting to use its veto. The USA was the single biggest contributor to the UN budget and was therefore in a powerful position to influence the UN decision.

The UN was now committed to using member forces to drive North Korean troops out of South Korea.

FOCUS TASK

Why did the war in Korea begin?

There have been many different reasons given for the start of the war in Korea. The table here shows some of the main suggestions.

Reason for conflict in Korea	Explanation
A show of Russian strength towards the Americans – part of the Cold War (see pages 298–300)?	To get their own back after the climb-down over Berlin (see pages 304–06).
A show of Russian strength towards the Chinese?	Stalin showing Mao that he was the leader of Communism in Asia.
A North Korean attack planned in Moscow and backed by Beijing?	It would strengthen Russia's defences in the Pacific. (America thought this was the reason.)
An independent attack by North Korea, without Russian or Chinese backing?	Because America had not included Korea in her defence plans for the Pacific?
An attack provoked by South Korea?	To regain American help against Communism. (North Korea claimed that South Korean troops had attacked first.)

1 Work in groups of four. In order to carry out this task you will need some background knowledge on:
   - the Cold War crisis in Europe – see pages 298–306
   - relations between Russia and China – see page 307.
   Use these page references and your own research to help you make notes.

2 Now each of you take one of the reasons given in the table above and carry out your own research on it.

3 Each of you report back to your group on your findings.

4 Discuss each reason and decide which one you think is the most likely reason for the outbreak of conflict in Korea.

• The development of the Korean War

Eighteen states (including Britain) provided troops or support of some kind, but the overwhelming part of the UN force that was sent to Korea was American. The commander, General MacArthur, was also an American.

SOURCE 5

General MacArthur writing to President Truman in 1950.

I have received your announcement of your appointment of me as United Nations Commander. I can only repeat the pledge of my complete personal loyalty to you as well as an absolute devotion to your monumental struggle for peace and goodwill throughout the world. I hope I will not fail you.

The UN campaign in South and North Korea: The Inchon landings

United Nations forces stormed ashore at Inchon in September 1950. At the same time, other UN forces and South Korean troops advanced from Pusan. For the first time the North Koreans had been outmanoeuvred. They were driven back beyond their original border (the 38th Parallel) within weeks. MacArthur had quickly achieved the original UN objective of removing North Korean troops from South Korea. By the end of September MacArthur had been able to retake Seoul.

But the Americans did not stop. Despite warnings from China's leader, Mao Zedong, that pressing on would mean China joining the war, the UN approved a plan to advance into North Korea. By October, US forces, on behalf of the UN, had reached the Yalu river and the border with China (see Figure 6). The nature of the war had now changed. It was clear that MacArthur and Truman were striving for a bigger prize – to remove Communism from Korea entirely.

ACTIVITY

1 As you work through pages 337–41, make brief notes on the events of the Korean War.
2 Look back at your notes and explain why the fighting turned to a stalemate.

FIGURE 6
The Korean War, 1950–53.

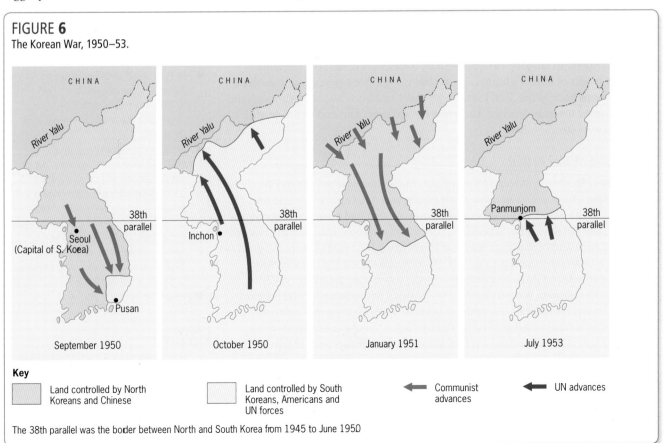

September 1950   October 1950   January 1951   July 1953

Key

Land controlled by North Koreans and Chinese

Land controlled by South Koreans, Americans and UN forces

← Communist advances

← UN advances

The 38th parallel was the border between North and South Korea from 1945 to June 1950

SOURCE 7

The Inchon landings.

General Douglas MacArthur

- Born in 1880. His father was a successful army leader.
- Trained at West Point, the top American military academy.
- Fought in the First World War. He got thirteen medals for bravery and became the youngest commander in the American army in France.
- Became chief of staff in the army in 1930.
- During the Second World War he was the commander of the war against the Japanese. He devised the successful island-hopping strategy that allowed the Americans to drive out the Japanese from their island strongholds.
- In 1945 he personally accepted the Japanese surrender, and from 1945 to 1951 he virtually controlled Japan, helping the shattered country get back on its feet.
- His bullying, no-nonsense style enabled him to get things done, but he sometimes annoyed political leaders back in Washington by following his own policies.
- In 1950, at the age of 70, he was given command of the UN forces in Korea.
- He was relieved of his duties in Korea in 1951. He tried unsuccessfully to be elected as a presidential candidate in 1952.
- He died in 1964.

Intervention of Chinese troops, October 1950

MacArthur underestimated the power of the Chinese. Late in October 1950, 200,000 Chinese troops (calling themselves 'People's Volunteers') joined the North Koreans. They launched a blistering attack. They had soldiers who were strongly committed to Communism and had been taught by their leader to hate the Americans. They had modern tanks and planes supplied by the Soviet Union. The United Nations forces were pushed back by the sheer size of the Chinese force into South Korea. In January 1951 the US/UN forces were driven out of Seoul. Only after weeks of bitter fighting were the UN troops able to recover and push the Chinese troops back to the 38th Parallel. STALEMATE had been reached. Although the tide had turned towards America, there was no real sign of an end to the deadlock. Casualties were steadily rising.

The sacking of MacArthur

At this point, Truman and MacArthur fell out. MacArthur wanted to carry on the war, invading China and even using nuclear weapons if necessary. Truman felt that saving South Korea was good enough. After all, that had been the original aim of the UN-led forces. His allies in the UN force convinced him that the risks of attacking China and of starting a war that might bring in the USSR were too great, and so an attack on China was ruled out. However, in March 1951 MacArthur blatantly ignored the UN instruction and openly threatened an attack on China. In April Truman removed MacArthur from his position as commander and brought him back home. He rejected MacArthur's aggressive policy towards Communism. CONTAINMENT was underlined as the American policy. One of the American army leaders, General Omar Bradley, said that MacArthur's approach would have 'involved America in the wrong war, in the wrong place, at the wrong time, and with the wrong enemy'.

1 Use Source 5 to write an extra sentence for the profile of General MacArthur describing his personality and beliefs.

2 Why did the Americans not support MacArthur in continuing the war and attacking China?

● The end of the Korean War
Peace talks and the armistice

Stalemate had been reached by early 1951. Peace talks between North and South Korea began in June 1951, but made no progress because of a major dispute over exchange of prisoners. Talks began again in 1952 but bitter fighting continued.

In the November 1952 presidential elections Truman was replaced by President Eisenhower who wanted to end the war. He promised to bring the war to 'an early and honourable end'. Stalin's death in March 1953 made the Chinese and North Koreans less confident, as there was no immediate successor and future USSR policy might change. An ARMISTICE was finally signed at Panmunjom in July 1953.

SOURCE 8

Photographs from the Korean War. Conditions were some of the worst the American forces had known, with treacherous cold and blinding snowstorms in the winter of 1950–51. The Chinese forces were more familiar with fighting in the jagged mountains, forested ravines and treacherous swamps – as the landscape was similar to many areas of China. Many civilians suffered as a result of the war and there were also reports of prisoners of war being treated very badly.

The impact of the Korean War

SOURCE 9

The signing of the peace agreement, 1953.

The Korean War: A balance sheet

	Gains	Losses
UN	Gained respect by taking prompt direct action. Used combined force to stop aggression. Achieved joint action – therefore more effective than League of Nations.	Over 30,000 casualties, most of whom were US troops. Only able to act because of USSR's absence from Security Council and therefore unable to exercise its veto.
USA	Saved South Korea from Communism. Containment policy seen to work in Asia.	30,000 casualties. Defence spending increased from 12 to 60 billion dollars. Failed to liberate North Korea.
USSR	Achieved close friendship with Communist China. Conflict between China and USA was to Russia's advantage.	Forced into expensive arms race with the USA.
China	Gained respect of Communist supporters in Asia. Saved North Korea from American control. Had received much financial and military help from the USSR. Had secured North Korea as a buffer state on its own borders.	Over half a million casualties. Failed to win South Korea for Communism. Increased US protection and help for Chiang Kai-Shek on Formosa. Suffered loss of potential trade with USA.
Korea	None as the border remained along the 38th Parallel.	Huge casualties – 1.3 million – almost equal numbers from the North and the South, and including many civilians as well as military personnel. One in ten civilians had died. Much industry destroyed. Agriculture ruined. Millions of refugees. Neither North nor South gained the united Korea they had fought for.

The Cold War was no longer confined to Europe. Relationships between the USA, the USSR and China were bound to be complicated – especially with the existence of Nationalist China on the island of Formosa, which was recognised as the official Chinese government by both the USA and the UN.

In 1954 SEATO was founded – the South East Asia Treaty Organisation – a copy of NATO, and designed to contain Communism in the Far East. This further heightened mistrust between the USA and the USSR.

From the USSR's perspective it appeared that the USA was forging powerful alliances in both Europe and Asia against all Communist states.

FOCUS TASK

Korea 1950–53: The Cold War reaches a new level

The Korean War is over. You have been asked to write a newspaper article assessing the significance of the Korean War. Your aim is to explain to readers how the Korean War took the Cold War to a new level of intensity. Your article should refer to:

- the USA's concerns about developments in Asia
- how the UN became involved and whether you think a similar event might happen again
- how and why the conflict escalated to involve China
- whether you think there was a real danger that the conflict might have spread further
- the military and civilian cost of the war.

Finally, add a conclusion to your article which:

- argues EITHER that the Korean War shows the need for the USA to continue its aggressive stance towards Communism OR that the USA should try to improve relations with the USSR and China
- AND states whether you think the new US President Eisenhower will follow your advice.

PRACTICE QUESTIONS

1 'The main reason why the Korean War ended in stalemate was the contribution of the Chinese.'
  How far do you agree with this statement?
  Explain your answer.

2 Write an account of how negotiations over the ending of the Korean War affected US–USSR relations afterwards.

TOPIC SUMMARY

Conflict in Korea
- After the Second World War, Korea had been divided into North (Communist) and South (anti-Communist) along the line of the 38th Parallel.
- The USA's policy of containment was bolstered by the Truman Doctrine in 1947.
- The USA's fears of Communism spreading in Asia were justified when the Communists won the long civil war in China in 1949.
- In 1950 North Korea invaded South Korea.
- The United Nations were able to act because the USSR was absent from the Security Council. The UN sent joint military forces to help South Korea.
- Eighteen countries sent troops, but the USA took the leading role.
- Rapid advances by the North into the South were halted when UN forces landed at Inchon.
- General MacArthur wanted to invade China and was dismissed by President Truman.
- Peace talks dragged on into 1953 when Eisenhower had become President and Stalin had died.
- Truce signed at Panmunjom in July 1953. South Korea had remained non-Communist.

FOCUS

After the stalemate of the Korean War, there were other areas in Asia where Communism seemed (from the point of view of the West!) to be a threat. The area that came into prominence, partly because of its instability following the withdrawal of the French, was Vietnam. The war casts a huge shadow over American history in the later twentieth century.

In this part of the topic you will study:

- The end of French colonial rule and the emergence of the Viet Cong.
- The nature of and reasons for US involvement in Vietnam.
- President Johnson's escalation of the war and:
  - tactics used by both sides
  - why the Tet Offensive was a turning point in the conflict.

8.2 Escalation of conflict in Vietnam

● The end of French colonial rule

Before the Second World War, Vietnam (or Indochina as it was called then) was ruled by France. During the war the region was conquered by the Japanese. They ruled the area brutally and treated the Vietnamese people savagely. As a result, a strong anti-Japanese resistance movement (the VIET MINH) emerged under the leadership of Communist Ho Chi Minh. Ho was a remarkable individual. He had lived in the USA, Britain and France. In the 1920s he had studied Communism in the USSR. He had learnt about techniques of GUERRILLA WARFARE. In 1930 he had founded the Indochinese Communist Party. He inspired the Vietnamese people to fight for an independent Vietnam. When the Second World War ended, the Viet Minh controlled the north of the country and were determined to take control of the whole country. The Viet Minh entered the city of Hanoi in 1945 and declared Vietnamese independence.

The French had other ideas. In 1945 they wanted to rule Vietnam again but Ho was not prepared to let this happen. Another nine years of war followed between the Viet Minh and the French. Ho was supported by China, which became a Communist state in 1949 under Mao Zedong. The Americans saw the Viet Minh as the puppets of Mao and the Chinese Communists so they helped the French by pouring $500 million a year into the French war effort. Despite this the French were unable to hold on to the country. They underestimated the strength of the Viet Minh, who were bolstered by Russian and Chinese military support.

Dien Bien Phu, 1954, and its consequences

In 1954 the French suffered a major defeat. At the Battle of Dien Bien Phu, 8,000 French troops were killed, in addition to the 73,000 killed during the previous decade. France surrendered. A small nation had defeated a major European power.

Geneva Agreement, 1954

After the Battle of Dien Bien Phu, in May 1954 Britain, France, China, the USSR, the USA and Vietnam met in Geneva, Switzerland. Their task was to decide the future of Vietnam and to reach a settlement for the whole of what had been Indo-China. They agreed on a withdrawal of French troops, the creation of a ceasefire and a new territorial settlement. The new countries of Laos and Cambodia were formed. North Vietnam (Communist) and South Vietnam (non-Communist) were also created on what was intended to be a temporary basis. The dividing line was the 17th Parallel, with a demilitarised zone at that point. It was intended that there would be elections across the whole of Vietnam in 1956 to decide on the future government.

Civil war in South Vietnam and opposition to Diem's government

After the Geneva agreement of 1954 a non-Communist government was set up in South Vietnam under President Diem. However, his rule was harsh, corrupt, and unpopular. Enemies were imprisoned. Money was wasted or spent on defence. Diem himself was a Catholic in a largely Buddhist country, and the government persecuted the Buddhist majority. Monks protested about the lack of religious toleration, in extreme cases by setting fire to themselves. In spite of this, Diem received the support of the US government – simply because he was anti-Communist.

The Viet Cong – aims, support, leadership and guerrilla tactics

Meanwhile in North Vietnam Ho Chi Minh was a popular leader. Had there been elections in 1956 as intended he would almost certainly have won. His mission was to unify Vietnam. In 1960 the National Liberation Front (NLF) was formed, with the support of Ho Chi Minh, with the specific task of unifying the country. Diem reacted to the formation of the NLF with scorn, calling its members the Vietnamese Communists (VIET CONG). The NLF demanded the removal of Diem and started a campaign of guerrilla warfare. By 1961 there were over 20,000 Viet Cong guerrillas in South Vietnam. It would have to defeat not only the government of South Vietnam but also its allies – principally the USA.

The NLF was a guerrilla movement, trained in the art of conducting ambushes, and it had much support in North Vietnam and a considerable amount in the South. The Viet Cong were trained in surprise attacks, laying traps and using the cover of the jungle. The Ho Chi Minh trail was created in 1959 to carry supplies from the North to the South. This 'trail' was in fact hundreds of interlocking trails that all led from North to South, many passing through neutral Laos and Cambodia in order to avoid US air strikes. Extending along hundreds of miles, walking along it with supplies could take up to two months.

In South Vietnam the Viet Cong set out to win more support by working with the local populations, treating them well, and winning their respect. With over 100,000 active troops, the Viet Cong controlled substantial parts of South Vietnam by the early 1960s.

Meanwhile, Diem was becoming increasingly unpopular, and in 1963 was overthrown and killed by his own troops. The country had ten different governments in the next two years – just at the time that the USA was committing itself to a major war.

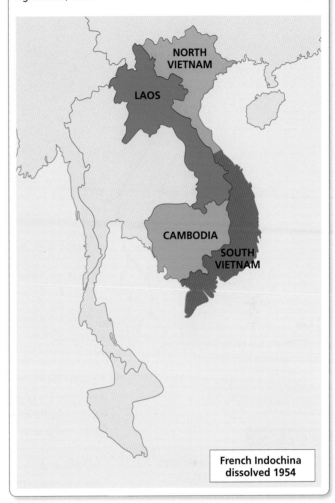

FIGURE 1

The division of French Indochina as a result of the Geneva Agreement, 1954.

NORTH VIETNAM

LAOS

CAMBODIA

SOUTH VIETNAM

French Indochina dissolved 1954

PROFILE

Ho Chi Minh, 1890–1969

- Born in Vietnam in 1890; provided with traditional education as a boy.
- In 1908–17 he spent time in France, the USA and many other countries, and became firmly Communist in his beliefs.
- In 1917–41, after the Communists came to power in Russia, he lived in Russia, China, Thailand and elsewhere, working with Communist groups.
- Returned to Vietnam in 1941 and founded the Viet Minh independence movement to fight against the Japanese and French.
- In 1945 he established the Communist-ruled Democratic Republic of Vietnam (though he did not control the whole country, with the French still claiming the territory).
- His forces defeated the French at Dien Bien Phu in 1954.
- Vietnam was divided, with Ho Chi Minh leader of the Communist government of North Vietnam.
- He stepped down because of poor health in 1965 – but continued to support the Viet Cong in the war.
- He died in 1969.

FIGURE 2

Vietnam.

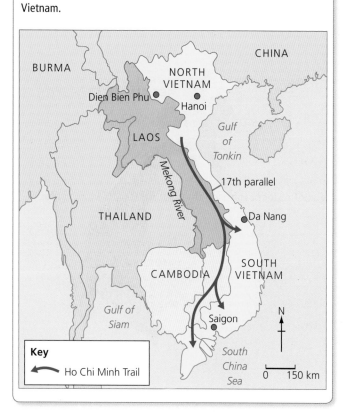

The US involvement: The Domino Theory

The USA was not prepared to see Vietnam fall to Communism. President Eisenhower and his Secretary of State J. F. Dulles were convinced that China and the USSR were planning to spread Communism throughout Asia (the DOMINO THEORY). If Vietnam fell to Communism, then Laos, Cambodia, Thailand, Burma, and possibly even India might also fall – just like a row of dominoes.

Intervention under Eisenhower and Kennedy

Under Eisenhower the USA continued to provide aid to South Vietnam; $1.6 billion between 1954 and 1960. Military advisers were sent to help the South Vietnamese army. By 1962 there were 11,000 there providing training. With hindsight we can see that the Americans became involved in Vietnam without clear aims or a clear plan. American firepower and technology were superior but winning over hearts and minds was just as important. Most US servicemen were unaware that the government they were supporting had lost the support of the majority of Vietnamese people.

For example, in the early 1960s the South Vietnam government had been pursuing the Strategic Hamlets programme. This moved peasant villages from Viet Cong controlled areas to areas controlled by the South Vietnam government. The Americans supplied building materials, money and food for the villagers to build new improved farms and homes but this put the US troops in a difficult position (Source 4).

FOCUS TASK

What was the nature of and the reasons for the USA's involvement in Vietnam?

1 The direction of the US war campaign in Vietnam changed as the war progressed. Start to make notes on what approaches the US forces used and how effective they were.

2 Separately make a list of the reasons why the USA was involved in Vietnam initially, and why it continued to be involved.

3 Add to your notes as you work through the chapter.

SOURCE 3

Philip Caputo, a US Marine in Vietnam.

We were all kind of hot to go, hot to get into something, do something that was other than train and drill and, um, there was a kind of a feeling, I don't know if anybody ever said this – a sort of feeling that being US Marines, our mere presence in Vietnam was going to terrify the enemy into quitting.

SOURCE 4

An extract from *Vietnam – A History* by S. Kamow, published in 1994.

In reality, the strategic hamlet programme often converted peasants into Viet Cong sympathisers. In many places they resented working without pay to dig moats, plant bamboo stakes and erect fences against an enemy that did not threaten them. Many were angered by corrupt officials, who pocketed the money which was meant for seed, fertiliser and irrigation, as well as medical care, education and other social benefits.

Timeline: Vietnam War

DATE	ACTION
1954	Vietnam is divided into North and South Vietnam.
1959	The North Vietnamese army creates the Ho Chi Minh trail to carry supplies down to South Vietnam.
1960	North Vietnam creates the National Liberation Front of South Vietnam (usually called the Viet Cong).
1961	Around 16,000 American 'advisers' help to organise the South Vietnamese army.
1962–63	The Viet Cong use guerrilla tactics against South Vietnam's army and government. More American advisers and equipment arrive.
1964	North Vietnamese patrol boats fire on American warships in the Gulf of Tonkin. The American CONGRESS gives President Johnson the authority to do whatever he thinks is necessary.
1965	
February	Operation Rolling Thunder – a gigantic bombing campaign against North Vietnam. Factories and army bases are bombed, as well as the Ho Chi Minh trail and the capital of North Vietnam, Hanoi.
March	The first American combat troops (3,500 marines) come ashore at Da Nang.
June–September	A major Viet Cong offensive.
November	Battle in La Dreng Valley. The Communists suffer heavy losses.
1966	American forces build heavily armed camps. They control towns. The Viet Cong largely control the countryside.
1967	Continual running battles between American and Communist forces around the North–South Vietnam border. The Communists are unable to force out American troops.
1968	
January	The Tet Offensive: a large-scale Communist attack on over a hundred major towns and cities in South Vietnam. Even the American embassy in Saigon is attacked. Some of the fiercest fighting of the war takes place. The city of Hué is almost flattened by intense fighting. Tet is a defeat for the Communists but is also a major shock to the American military and public who thought the war was almost won. Intense fighting continues throughout 1968. Casualties on both sides mount.
October	Operation Rolling Thunder finishes after three and a half years. More bombs have been dropped on North Vietnam than all the bombs dropped on Germany and Japan during the Second World War.
1969	The USA begins its policy of 'VIETNAMISATION'. This means building up the South Vietnamese army and withdrawing American combat troops. American air power continues to bomb North Vietnam. Intense fighting continues throughout the year. This includes the Battle for Hamburger Hill in May.
1970–71	The fighting spreads to Cambodia. US Secretary of State Kissinger and North Vietnam leader Le Duc begin secret peace talks.
1972	Most American forces are now out of Vietnam. A major Communist offensive in March captures much ground. Most land is recaptured by the South Vietnam army by the end of the year. American heavy bombers bomb Hanoi and Haiphong.
1973	Ceasefire signed in Paris. The last US troops leave Vietnam.
1974	Major North Vietnamese army offensive against South Vietnam.
1975	South Vietnam capital Saigon falls to Communists; US officials are evacuated by helicopter.

● Johnson's war

US involvement in the war reached its peak under President Johnson – and so did opposition within the USA to all the brutalities, as they became evident on TV screens and in news reports.

The Gulf of Tonkin, 1964, and the US response

President Kennedy had been sending military personnel (he always called them 'advisers') to fight the Viet Cong. After his ASSASSINATION in November 1963, his successor, Lyndon Johnson, was more prepared than Kennedy to commit the USA to a full-scale conflict in Vietnam to prevent the spread of Communism.

In August 1964, North Vietnamese patrol boats opened fire on US ships in the Gulf of Tonkin (see Figure 2, page 344). In a furious reaction, the US Congress passed the Tonkin Gulf Resolution. The Resolution gave Lyndon Johnson the power to 'take all necessary measures to prevent further aggression and achieve peace and security'. It effectively meant that he could take the USA into a full-scale war if he felt it was necessary, and very soon that was the case.

After more Viet Cong attacks in 1965, Johnson approved a massive bombing campaign in February against North Vietnam called Operation Rolling Thunder. On 8 March 1965, 3,500 US marines (combat troops rather than advisers) came ashore at Da Nang. It was an end to the policy of supplying other forces with money or equipment. America was at war in Vietnam and intended to use its own troops to defeat the Communists.

Viet Cong tactics, 1964–68

In early 1965 the Viet Cong and North Vietnamese army (NVA) had about 170,000 soldiers. They were well supplied with weapons and equipment from China and the USSR, but they were heavily outnumbered and outgunned by the South Vietnamese forces and their US allies. The Communist forces were no match for the US and South Vietnamese forces in open warfare. In November 1965 in the La Dreng Valley, US forces killed 2,000 Viet Cong for the loss of 300 troops. This did not daunt Ho Chi Minh. He believed that superior forces could be defeated by guerrilla tactics. He had been in China and seen Mao Zedong use guerrilla warfare to achieve a Communist victory there. Ho had also used these guerrilla tactics himself against the Japanese and the French. The principles were simple: retreat when the enemy attacks; raid while the enemy camps; attack when the enemy tires; pursue when the enemy retreats.

Guerrilla warfare was a nightmare for the US army. Guerrillas did not wear uniform. They had no known base camp or headquarters. They worked in small groups with limited weapons. They were hard to tell apart from the peasants in the villages. They attacked and then disappeared into the jungle, into the villages or into their tunnels (see Figure 5).

PRACTICE QUESTION

Write an account of how the Gulf of Tonkin incident (1964) became of major importance in the development of US involvement in Vietnam.

The aim of guerrilla attacks was to wear down the enemy soldiers and wreck their morale. This was very effective. US soldiers lived in constant fear of ambushes or booby traps. Booby traps could be simple devices such as tripwires or pits filled with sharpened bamboo staves. Weapons like these were cheap and easy to make and very effective in disrupting US patrols. One of the most unpopular duties in a patrol was going 'on point'. This meant leading the patrol, checking for traps. There were other more sophisticated traps such as the Bouncing Betty land mine. This would be thrown into the air when triggered and would then explode causing terrible injuries to the stomach or groin. Booby traps caused about 11 per cent of US casualties. Another 51 per cent were caused by small arms fire in ambushes or 'firefights'. The Viet Cong and NVA quickly learned to fear American air power, so when they did attack they tried to make sure it was close-quarter fighting. This meant that US air power or artillery could not be used because of the danger of hitting their own troops. This tactic was sometimes known as 'hanging on to American belts'.

FIGURE 5

A Viet Cong tunnel complex. To avoid the worst effects of American air power, the Viet Cong used a vast network of underground tunnels, probably around 240 km of them.

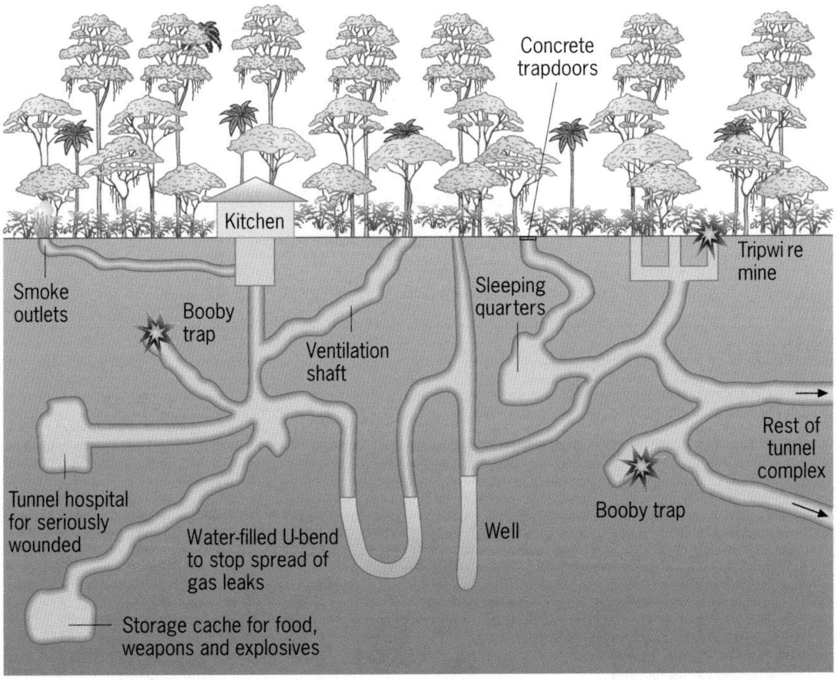

Ho Chi Minh knew how important it was to keep the population on his side. The Viet Cong fighters were expected to be courteous and respectful to the Vietnamese peasants. They often helped the peasants in the fields during busy periods. However, the Viet Cong could be ruthless – they were quite prepared to kill peasants who opposed them or who co-operated with their enemies. They also conducted a campaign of terror against the police, tax collectors, teachers and any other employees of the South Vietnamese government. Between 1966 and 1971 the Viet Cong killed an estimated 27,000 civilians.

FOCUS TASK

Who were the Viet Cong?

1 Use the information and sources on pages 343, 346–47 to make notes on the Viet Cong under the following headings:
   – Aims
   – Leadership
   – Tactics
   – Success.
2 Using your notes, decide upon the most important points and create your own Factfile on the Viet Cong.

Viet Cong resilience

The greatest strength of the Viet Cong fighters was that they simply refused to give in. The Viet Cong depended on supplies from North Vietnam that came along the Ho Chi Minh trail. US and South Vietnamese planes bombed this constantly, but 40,000 Vietnamese worked to keep it open whatever the cost. The total of Viet Cong and North Vietnamese dead in the war has been estimated at 1 million – far higher than US losses. However, this was a price that Ho Chi Minh was prepared to pay. Whatever the casualties, there were replacement troops available.

FIGURE 6

A Spike Trap Pit

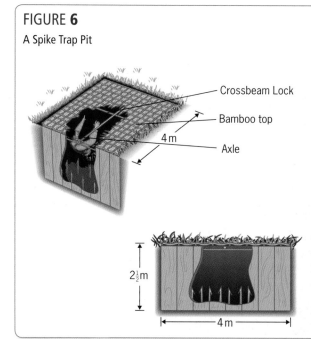

Crossbeam Lock

Bamboo top

4 m

Axle

2½ m

4 m

A diagram showing one type of booby trap. A trap pit is a large trap box with a bamboo top. Stakes are made of sharpened bamboo or barbed spikes and used to line the box. When a man steps on the trap he will fall into the pit. The top turns on an axle; therefore, the trap does not need to be reset to work again. The pit is often prepared as a defensive obstacle and then made safe by locking it in place with a crossbeam (so it can be crossed safely by the enemy) until the desired time of use.

SOURCE 7

A Viet Cong poster from the 1960s.

THINK

1 Choose one piece of evidence from pages 346–48 to show that the Viet Cong had the support of the Vietnamese people.
2 Choose one piece of evidence from pages 346–48 that suggests that they did not.

PRACTICE QUESTION

Study Source 7.

Source 7 supports the Viet Cong. How do you know?
Explain your answer by using Source 7 and your contextual knowledge.

SOURCE 8

A Chinese poster commenting on the Vietnam War. The caption reads: 'US imperialism – Get out of South Vietnam!'

SOURCE 9

Extracts from a letter written in 1965 by Le Duan, Secretary of the North Vietnamese Communist Party and one of Ho Chi Minh's closest associates. The letter was explaining how North Vietnam was planning to react to the large-scale arrival of US forces in 1965.

We need to use the methods most suited for destroying the American troops – guerrilla forces encircling the American troops' bases …

This upcoming spring and summer, we are aiming for killing about 10,000 Americans as already planned and for the next few years, we should at least kill 40,000 to 50,000 Americans. This is a new goal which will determine our victory. Along with trying to lessen the Americans' strength, we should try to cause great loss of American aircraft, at the same time, curb their activities.

We must not neglect the political war. Even though the US brings in more troops to Vietnam, they will fail to weaken our political power. In fact, our political power is likely to be enhanced and the US will be isolated and fail miserably … The more troops the US brings in, the more military bases it builds, the larger area it occupies, the more sophisticated weapons it uses, the more B-52 bombs it drops, the more chemical poisons it uses, the worse the conflict between our people and them becomes, the more our people hate them.

PRACTICE QUESTIONS

1   Study Sources 8 and 9.
    How useful are Sources 8 and 9 for studying attitudes towards the invading US armies?
    Explain your answer using Sources 8 and 9 and your contextual knowledge.
2   'The main reason that the USA became involved in Vietnam in the late 1950s and early 1960s was the policy of containment.'
    How far do you agree with this statement?
    Explain your answer.

FOCUS TASK

How effective were the Viet Cong as a fighting force?

The table below sets out some of the qualities of an effective army. Use the information and sources on pages 346–48 to copy and complete the table for the Viet Cong. You will complete the rest of the table later.

Qualities of a successful army	Did this apply to the Viet Cong?	Did this apply to the US army?	Who had the advantage – Viet Cong or US army?
Well-trained soldiers			
The right technology			
Reliable supplies and equipment			
Effective tactics			
Support from the local population			
Motivated and committed soldiers			
Effective leadership			
Other			

ACTIVITY

Discussion

Sources 10–13 are all American sources which reveal something about Viet Cong tactics. Do you think they are more or less useful than Figures 5 and 6 and Sources 7–9 on pages 347–49? You might want to consider:

- what each source reveals about Viet Cong tactics
- what each source reveals about the impact of Viet Cong tactics.

FOCUS TASK

Look back at your work from the Focus Task on page 349. Add any extra points or examples to the table which have emerged from Sources 10–13.

SOURCE 13

Philip Caputo, US Marine.

How do you distinguish a civilian from a Viet Cong? Well of course he shoots at you or he's armed. But how about what happens after a firefight and you find bodies out there, but no weapons? And we were told this … well, if it's dead and Vietnamese, it's VC. Those were the exact words.

The US response to Viet Cong tactics

SOURCE 10

Philip Caputo, a lieutenant in the Marine Corps in Vietnam in 1965–66, speaking in 1997.

I remember sitting at this wretched little outpost one day with a couple of my sergeants. We'd been manning this thing for three weeks and running patrols off it. We were grungy and sore with jungle rot and we'd suffered about nine or ten casualties on a recent patrol. This one sergeant of mine said, 'You know, Lieutenant, I don't see how we're ever going to win this.' And I said, 'Well, Sarge, I'm not supposed to say this to you as your officer – but I don't either.' So there was this sense that we just couldn't see what could be done to defeat these people.

SOURCE 11

General William Westmoreland, commander, US forces, Vietnam.

The attitude of the enemy was not comparable to what our attitude would have been under the circumstances. He was ready, willing and able to pay a far greater price than I would say we would.

SOURCE 12

Lieutenant George Forrest, US army, commenting on one battle with Viet Cong fighters.

My casualties in my company were relatively light and I say relatively light. I lost seventeen killed and about 43 wounded so the unit was almost combat ineffective with those kind of casualties, but fortunately we were able to weather that particular piece of the battle.

The mass bombing campaign

On 7 February 1965 the USA launched Operation Rolling Thunder. Rolling Thunder involved extensive bombing raids on military and industrial targets in North Vietnam. It was the beginning of an air offensive that was to last until 1972. The list of targets was soon expanded to include towns and cities in North and South Vietnam. The list also included sites in Laos and Cambodia along the Ho Chi Minh trail.

To some extent bombing was effective:

- It certainly damaged North Vietnam's war effort and it disrupted supply routes.
- It enabled the USA to strike at Communist forces even when it was reducing US ground forces in Vietnam after 1969.
- From 1970 to 1972, intense bombing campaigns against Hanoi (North Vietnam's capital) and the port of Haiphong forced the North Vietnamese to the negotiating table.

However, US air power could not defeat the Communists – it could only slow them down. The Viet Cong continued to operate its supply lines. Even after major air raids on North Vietnam in 1972, the Communists were still able to launch a major assault on the South.

The financial cost of the air war was horrendous. The Communists shot down 14,000 US and South Vietnamese aircraft. In 1967 the American *Life* magazine calculated that it cost the USA $400,000 to kill one Viet Cong fighter, a figure that included 75 bombs and 400 artillery shells.

SOURCE 14

People in the South Vietnamese city of Hué sort through the wreckage of their homes after a US bombing raid in 1968. Two-thirds of US bombs were dropped on targets in South Vietnam.

SOURCE 15

A ten-year-old Vietnamese girl runs naked after tearing her burning clothes from her body following a napalm attack. This photograph became one of the most enduring images of the war.

THINK

1 Study Source 14. Why do you think so much of the bombing by the USA was concentrated on South Vietnam?

Chemical weapons

The USA also developed other weapons. One such powerful chemical weapon was called AGENT ORANGE. It was a sort of highly toxic 'weedkiller'. It was used to destroy the jungle where the Viet Cong hid. The Americans used 82 million litres of Agent Orange. They dropped a total of 100 million pounds of defoliants in 30,000 missions. This wiped out 4 million acres of forests and farms and affected 1.3 million people.

NAPALM was another widely used chemical weapon. It destroyed jungles where guerrillas might hide. It also burned through skin to the bone. Around 20,000 tons of napalm were dropped between 1965 and 1973. Many civilians and soldiers were also killed by these chemical weapons.

THINK

2 'Mixed results.' Is this a fair summary of the effectiveness of bombing in the Vietnam War? Explain your answer.

3 Would you say the US ground forces in Vietnam were more or less effective than the air forces? Explain your answer.

SOURCE 16

Lieutenant Colonel George Forrest, US army.

You would go out, you would secure a piece of terrain during the daylight hours and you'd surrender that – and I mean literally surrender, not be forced off, well maybe surrender's probably not a good word, but … but you'd give it up, because you … the helicopters would come in and pick you up at night and fly you back to the security of your base camp.

Search and destroy

Bombing could not defeat a guerrilla army. The US commander General Westmoreland developed a policy of SEARCH AND DESTROY. He established secure and heavily defended US bases in the south of the country and near to the coasts. From here, US and South Vietnamese forces launched search and destroy raids from helicopters. They would descend on a village and destroy any Viet Cong forces they found. Soldiers had to send back reports of body counts.

Search and destroy missions did kill Viet Cong soldiers, but there were problems:

- The raids were often based on inadequate information.
- Inexperienced US troops often walked into traps.
- Innocent villages were mistaken for Viet Cong strongholds.
- Civilian casualties were extremely high in these raids. For every Viet Cong weapon captured by search and destroy, there was a body count of six. Many of these were innocent civilians.
- Search and destroy tactics made the US and South Vietnamese forces very unpopular with the peasants. It pushed them towards supporting the Viet Cong.

THINK

What impressions of the war would Source 17 have caused with the American public?

SOURCE 17

US troops on a search and destroy mission in Vietnam. These were sometimes called Zippo raids, named after the Zippo cigarette lighters they used to set fire to villages.

Problems facing the Americans

Political problems

Although the Americans had huge advantages in technology and firepower, they were limited in one respect. Political considerations meant that they could not send their forces into North Vietnam or neighbouring Cambodia and Laos. This gave the NVA and Viet Cong a huge advantage. They were able to retreat to these other countries and reinforce their losses and get new equipment, ammunition, etc. As you have seen in Figure 2 on page 344, they also used these countries to supply their forces along the Ho Chi Minh trail. In fact, the Americans did send unofficial missions into these neighbouring countries and did bomb the Ho Chi Minh trail and other targets. However, they were never able to officially enter these countries with their full force.

SOURCE 18

A first aid station in Vietnam in 1966.

SOURCE 19

From *Four Hours in My Lai* by Michael Bilton, 1992. The average age of US combat troops in Vietnam was only 19. Many recruits had just left school. This was their first experience of war.

An increasing number of recruits scored so low on the standardised intelligence tests that they would have been excluded from the normal peacetime army. The tour of duty in Vietnam was one year. Soldiers were most likely to die in their first month. The large majority of deaths took place in the first six months. Just as a soldier began gaining experience, he was sent home. A rookie army which constantly rotated inexperienced men was pitted against experienced guerrillas on their home ground.

Troops and their officers

In the early stages of the war the majority of US troops were professional soldiers who had volunteered for the forces as a career. Generally their morale was good and they stood up well to the conditions. However, after 1967 an increasing number of troops in Vietnam had been drafted. Many of these were very young men who had never been in the military before. They often cared little for democracy or Communism and just wanted to get home alive. In theory, they came from all walks of life. In reality, the majority of the infantry who fought on the ground were from poor and immigrant backgrounds because those privileged enough to be going to university could delay the draft and many were able to use their influence to avoid the draft altogether.

As the war went on, the quality of recruits declined further (see Source 19). There were widespread attempts to dodge the draft. There were over 500,000 incidents of desertion (although this figure included a single individual who might desert several times). When we consider the fact that 60 per cent of the 56,000 Americans killed in Vietnam were aged 17–21 it is easy to see why they felt a limited commitment to the cause they were fighting for. There were also tensions between officers and troops. Many officers were professional soldiers. They wanted to gain promotion. In Vietnam this meant gaining as many kills as possible. Most soldiers just wanted to stay alive and there is some evidence of 'fragging' – troops killing their own officers.

Hearts and minds

Poor quality troops, low morale and Viet Cong tactics could create situations which could sometimes result in atrocities against civilians. From a relatively early stage in the war President Johnson began to speak of the importance of winning hearts and minds in Vietnam. He first mentioned the phrase in 1964 and between 1964 and 1968 he discussed the importance of winning hearts and minds in 28 speeches. The trouble was that US tactics were based on ATTRITION – killing large numbers of the enemy. This inevitably led to large numbers of civilian casualties. This in turn led to the Vietnamese people supporting the Viet Cong and began to cause concern to many people back in the USA.

THINK

How does Source 19 help to explain the poor morale among US troops?

My Lai

This issue came to a head with one particularly famous and gruesome event – the My Lai massacre of 1968. American soldiers on a search and destroy mission killed nearly 400 civilians in the village of My Lai. Most were women, children and old men.

News of the massacre was kept quiet. Officially, the operation at My Lai had been a success, with US troops killing 90 VC fighters. The Americans had one casualty – shot in the foot. It was later claimed by the victim that he had done this to himself to get out of the killing rage that was going on around him.

Eventually in November 1969 – 18 months later – the American press, after hearing rumours, got hold of the story. The trial and conviction of one of these officers who led the raid, Lieutenant William Calley, deeply shocked the American public. He was sentenced to life imprisonment for personally killing 22 villagers. It was the clearest evidence that the war had gone wrong. Many people in the USA at first refused to believe the story or believed that the killings had been justified because of the alleged presence of Viet Cong troops in the village. In November 1969, almost 700,000 anti-war protestors demonstrated in Washington DC. It was the largest political protest in American history. (For details of the anti-war movement, see pages 360–64.)

(For details of the anti-war movement, see pages 360–64.)

PRACTICE QUESTION

Write an account of how the My Lai massacre affected American attitudes towards the Vietnam War.

FOCUS TASK

Viet Cong or US forces – which side had the advantage?

1   Look back to the table you created on page 349. Use the information and sources on pages 352–53 to complete the third row of your table for the American forces and their allies.

Qualities of a successful army	Did this apply to the Viet Cong?	Did this apply to the US forces and allies?	Who had the advantage – Viet Cong or US forces?
Well-trained soldiers			
The right technology			
Reliable supplies and equipment			
Effective tactics			
Support from the local population			
Motivated and committed soldiers			
Effective leadership			
Other			

2   Now use the final column in the table to say whether you think the Viet Cong or the Americans had the advantage in this particular area.

3   Now think about the overall picture – how the strengths and weaknesses work together.
   a) Were the armies finely balanced or was the balance strongly weighted to one side or the other?
   b) Which quality was most important in determining who won the war? Was one feature so important that being ahead in that area meant that other advantages or disadvantages did not matter?

4   Now write up your answer. You could use this structure:
   a) Describe how the failure of the US army was a combination of its own weaknesses and Viet Cong strengths.
   b) Give balanced examples of US successes and failures.
   c) Give balanced examples of Viet Cong successes and failures.
   d) Choose one American weakness and one Viet Cong strength that you think were absolutely vital in preventing the USA from beating the Viet Cong and explain the significance of the points you have chosen.

The Tet Offensive and its impact

From 1965 to 1967, the official view of the war was that it was going reasonably well. The US and South Vietnamese forces were killing large numbers of Viet Cong. Although they were struggling against guerrilla tactics (see pages 346–49) they were confident that the enemy was being worn down.

This confidence was shattered early in 1968. During the Tet New Year holiday, Viet Cong fighters attacked over 100 cities and other military targets. One Viet Cong commando unit tried to capture the US embassy in Saigon. US forces had to fight to regain control room by room. Around 4,500 fighters tied down a much larger US and South Vietnamese force in Saigon for two days.

In many ways the Tet Offensive was a disaster for the Communists. They hoped that the people of South Vietnam would rise up and join them. They didn't. The Viet Cong lost around 10,000 experienced fighters and were badly weakened by it. However, the Tet Offensive proved to be a turning point in the war because it raised hard questions about the war in the USA.

- There were nearly 500,000 troops in Vietnam and the USA was spending $20 billion a year on the war. So why had the Communists been able to launch a major offensive that took US forces completely by surprise?
- US and South Vietnamese forces quickly retook the towns captured in the offensive, but in the process they used enormous amounts of artillery and air power. Many civilians were killed. The ancient city of Hué was destroyed. Was this right?
- Until this point media coverage of the war was generally positive, although some journalists were beginning to ask difficult questions in 1967. During the Tet Offensive the gloves came off. CBS journalist Walter Cronkite asked 'What the hell is going on? I thought we were winning this war.' Don Oberdorfer of the *Washington Post* later wrote (in 1971) that as a result of the Tet Offensive 'the American people and most of their leaders reached the conclusion that the Vietnam War would require greater effort over a far longer period of time than it was worth'.

SOURCE 20

US Marines pinned down by Viet Cong snipers in the city of Hué during the Tet Offensive, January 1968.

SOURCE 21

An extract from *The Tet Offensive: Intelligence Failure in War* by James Wirtz.

The Tet Offensive was the decisive battle of the Vietnam War because of its profound impact on American attitudes about involvement in Southeast Asia. In the aftermath of Tet, many Americans became disillusioned … To the American public and even to members of the administration, the offensive demonstrated that US intervention … had produced a negligible effect on the will and capability of the Viet Cong and North Vietnamese.

SOURCE 22

Wounded US Marines in Saigon during the Tet Offensive.

SOURCE 23

Devastation in Saigon towards the end of the Tet Offensive, 1968. Most of the damage was caused by US artillery or aircraft.

FIGURE 24

Map showing attacks by the Viet Cong during the Tet Offensive of 1968.

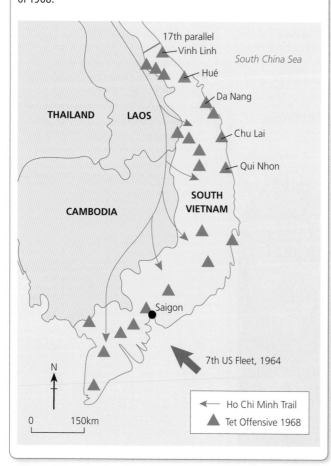

FOCUS TASK

Study Sources 20–23 carefully. Choose two sources which you think would improve your presentation in the Focus Task on page 355. Write a short paragraph explaining this choice.

TOPIC SUMMARY

The escalation of conflict in Vietnam

- French colonial rule collapsed, and ended at the Battle of Dien Bien Phu in 1954.
- The Geneva Agreement divided Vietnam into North (Communist) and South (anti-Communist).
- The Viet Cong, led by Ho Chi Minh, developed support to unify Vietnam.
- The USA became involved. They had been helping the French. Now the policy of containment and the Domino Theory meant South Vietnam had to be kept non-Communist.
- The Gulf of Tonkin incident was used by Johnson as a reason to escalate the war.
- Viet Cong guerrilla techniques made fighting difficult for the American troops.
- US tactics to win the war – mass bombing, search and destroy missions – increased opposition.
- The My Lai massacre in 1968 was kept quiet, but publicised 18 months later to great criticism.
- The Tet Offensive in 1968 was actually a US success, but portrayed in the media as a disaster.
- The war was increasingly seen by Americans as unwinnable, putting pressure on the US government.

8.3 The ending of conflict in Vietnam

FOCUS

In this section you will be studying the events and analysing the reasons for the war ending in Vietnam – primarily the decision of the USA to withdraw and what led to this decision.

In this part of the topic you will study the following:

● The war under President Nixon and how he tried to de-escalate US involvement.
● Opposition to war and the reasons why the media coverage of the conflict is so controversial.
● The end of the war and the reasons why the USA lost the conflict.

● Nixon's war

Nixon was campaigning to become President in 1968 at a time when the war was increasingly unpopular in the USA. This influenced his policy towards Vietnam.

'Vietnamisation'

Nixon was elected President in November 1968, promising that the war would continue until 'peace with honour' could be achieved. In fact, peace talks had already started in Paris in May 1968. No progress had been made with no compromise from either side. The USA could not agree to anything that would see a united Vietnam, whereas the North would only agree to a peace which reunited the two parts. In addition, the USA insisted that all North Vietnamese and US troops should leave South Vietnam before an election took place.

Nixon adopted the policy of 'Vietnamisation' – the idea that gradually American troops would leave Vietnam with the South Vietnamese army taking more of the responsibility for the fighting, but the USA would continue to support the government of Saigon.

This policy was bound to fail as the South Vietnamese army was no match for the army in the North which was receiving support from the Chinese and the USSR. The new President of South Vietnam, Nguyen Van Thieu, was also justifiably suspicious of the US policy.

In September 1969, the USA started direct secret peace talks with the North, leaving Thieu out of the discussions. Meanwhile Nixon started to withdraw the half-million American troops from Vietnam; 25,000 were withdrawn in June and another 35,000 in September.

SOURCE 1

From President Nixon's television speech, 3 November 1969

My fellow Americans … we have only two choices if we want to end this war.

I can order an immediate withdrawal of all US troops without regard to the effects of their action. Or we can persist in our search for a just peace through a negotiated settlement, if possible through the continued implementation of our plan for Vietnamisation.

I have chosen the second course. It is not the easy way. It is the right way. It is a plan which will end the war and serve the course of peace. And so tonight, the great silent majority of my fellow Americans, I ask for your support.

THINK

Study Source 1.

1 Which issues is Nixon addressing in the speech?
2 Which issues and problems is Nixon ignoring?
3 In the speech, how does Nixon try to appeal to Americans?

Relations with China under Nixon

The policies of Nixon and his Secretary of State, Henry Kissinger, have to be viewed in the wider context of the Cold War. After the major crises of the earlier 1960s (Berlin Wall, Cuban Missile Crisis), relations between the USA and the USSR had gradually been improving. The word 'DÉTENTE' was beginning to be used to define the new tentative situation – that is, a situation where differences were not forgotten but constructive discussions could take place over disagreements.

At the same time, American diplomats were keen to improve relations with Communist China. Mao Zedong was still in control, though he was now in his eighties. Also, relations between China and the USSR had worsened, with shots being fired across the border. Nixon took advantage of this situation by visiting China in February 1972 and the Soviet Union in May 1972. He knew that in this climate it would be easier for the USA to negotiate a ceasefire.

SOURCE 2

A cartoon commenting on Nixon's war policy, c.1970.

"...AND, VOILA, WE HAUL OUT A DOVE...A DOVE...I'LL HAVE TO ASK YOU TO IMAGINE THIS IS A DOVE!"

PRACTICE QUESTION

Study Source 2.
Source 2 is opposed to Nixon's foreign policy. How do you know?
Explain your answer by using Source 2 and your contextual knowledge.

FIGURE 3

US strategies to extricate US troops from involvement in Vietnam.

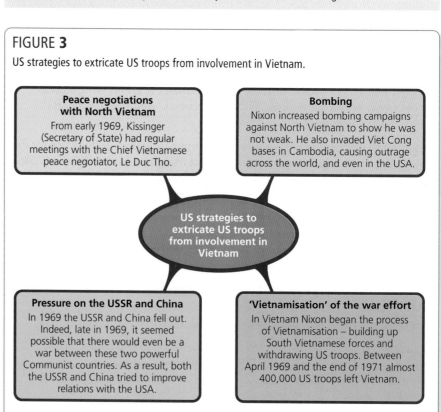

Peace negotiations with North Vietnam
From early 1969, Kissinger (Secretary of State) had regular meetings with the Chief Vietnamese peace negotiator, Le Duc Tho.

Bombing
Nixon increased bombing campaigns against North Vietnam to show he was not weak. He also invaded Viet Cong bases in Cambodia, causing outrage across the world, and even in the USA.

US strategies to extricate US troops from involvement in Vietnam

Pressure on the USSR and China
In 1969 the USSR and China fell out. Indeed, late in 1969, it seemed possible that there would even be a war between these two powerful Communist countries. As a result, both the USSR and China tried to improve relations with the USA.

'Vietnamisation' of the war effort
In Vietnam Nixon began the process of Vietnamisation – building up South Vietnamese forces and withdrawing US troops. Between April 1969 and the end of 1971 almost 400,000 US troops left Vietnam.

The invasion of Cambodia and Laos, 1970–71

Meanwhile, to step up pressure on North Vietnam, the USA invaded Cambodia – allegedly to destroy Viet Cong bases there. Nixon hoped that this would encourage Hanoi to be more willing to negotiate. In fact, it achieved the opposite – the North Vietnamese government boycotted all talks, both the secret ones and the ones in Paris, until American troops were withdrawn.

In 1971 the USA backed a South Vietnamese invasion of Laos to block the Ho Chi Minh trail. The USA provided bombing raids as a back-up. However, the invasion was a failure. After six weeks the troops withdrew, with half of them killed or wounded. Meanwhile, the number of American troops continued to drop. By the end of 1971 there were just 140,000 left; 400,000 had been withdrawn in three years. American troops had mostly lost all enthusiasm. The number of deserters and soldiers absent without leave also rose sharply. Many soldiers resorted to alcohol and drug abuse – habits that were formed in Vietnam and proved hard to break once home.

SOURCE 4

From a speech by President Nixon, 30 April 1970, explaining his decision to send troops to Cambodia.

The action I have taken is completely necessary for the success of the withdrawal programme from Vietnam. A majority of the American troops want to keep the casualties of our brave men in Vietnam at an absolute minimum. The invasion of Cambodia is essential if we are to achieve that goal. We take this action for the purpose of ending this war.

SOURCE 5

From an article in the newspaper *St Louis Post-Dispatch*, 3 May 1970.

In asking the American people to support the expansion of the Vietnam War to Cambodia, they are asked to seek peace by making war; seek withdrawal of our troops by enlarging the arena of combat; and to diminish US casualties by sending more young men to their death.

FOCUS TASK

How did Nixon try to de-escalate US involvement in Vietnam?

Study the information and sources on pages 357–59.

1 List the ways in which Nixon tried to de-escalate US involvement in the war.
2 Why was he able to carry out this de-escalation with so little opposition?

FIGURE 6

Map to show Communist influence in South East Asia.

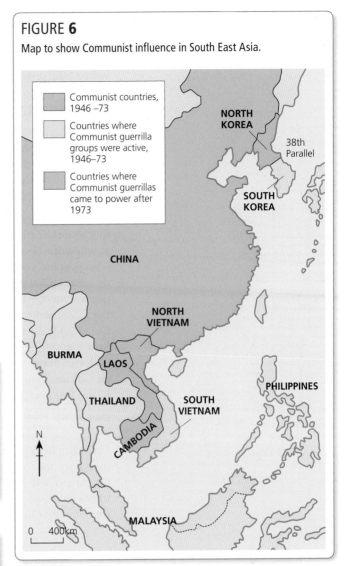

- Communist countries, 1946–73
- Countries where Communist guerrilla groups were active, 1946–73
- Countries where Communist guerrillas came to power after 1973

NORTH KOREA
38th Parallel
SOUTH KOREA
CHINA
NORTH VIETNAM
BURMA
LAOS
THAILAND
SOUTH VIETNAM
PHILIPPINES
CAMBODIA
MALAYSIA

N
0   400km

Renewed bombing of the North, 1972

In March 1972 the North Vietnamese invaded the South, led by 100 Soviet tanks. An easy victory was expected as most of the US troops had left. Nixon knew he had to respond to maintain any credibility and to put pressure on the North. In April 1972 he ordered the air force to bomb the North. The bombing offensive was codenamed Operation Linebacker, and it destroyed North Vietnamese roads, bridges, lorries, tanks, railway lines, storage depots, and the port of Haiphong. Smart bombs, guided by lasers, were used for precision bombing. Nixon hoped to persuade the North to give up on its invasion – for example, by cutting off supplies of fuel.

The renewed bombing campaign was greeted with a storm of protest in the USA and across the world.

• Opposition to the Vietnam War

Attitudes to the war had been changing during the 1960s. As events unfolded more concerns were raised about the way the war was being fought, and more people voiced total opposition.

The importance of the media

The Vietnam War was covered extensively by the American and world media, probably in more detail than any other war. Of course, newspaper and radio journalists were there on the scene, but as the war went on it was television which really brought the war into American homes and made the American public aware of what was happening.

In the early stages of the war the newspapers, radio and TV journalists largely followed the official line of policy. There were some small disagreements such as when one US army spokesman snapped 'Get on team!' (meaning 'Get on side – support us!') to an American journalist when several US helicopters were shot down at Ap Bac in 1963. However, even when the war escalated and US forces were directly involved, the relationship between the US military and government and the media was relatively good. The US army created MACV (Military Assistance Command, Vietnam) to liaise with journalists. Journalists could be accredited by MACV and they would then get transport to war areas, interviews and briefings with commanders and regular reports. In return they were expected not to reveal any information which would help the enemy. Between 1964 and 1968 only three journalists had their accreditation removed.

Back in the USA editors rarely wanted to publish bad news stories about Vietnam. On the one hand they did not want to be accused of undermining the war effort. For example, Seymour Hersh, the journalist who broke the story of the My Lai massacre, had to try several newspapers before he could find one willing to publish the story. There were also commercial considerations. TV networks were reluctant to broadcast off-putting scenes of violence and destruction during peak viewing times because they were worried viewers would switch channels.

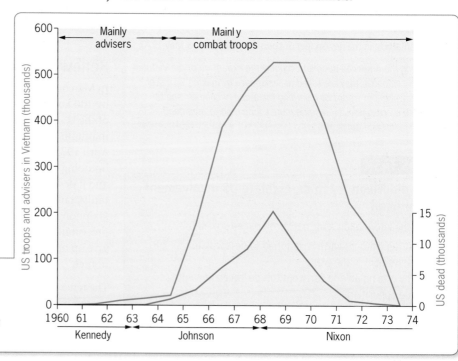

FIGURE 7

US troops and deaths in Vietnam, 1960–74. US troops were not the only foreign soldiers in the war. About 46,000 Australian and New Zealand troops fought too.

SOURCE 8

A Viet Cong suspect is executed in the street by South Vietnamese police chief Colonel Nguyen Ngoc Loan in February 1968. Televisions beamed this scene into the living rooms of the USA. It deeply shocked the American people.

Between 1967 and 1968, however, the tone of reporting on Vietnam was beginning to change. At the same time, television was taking over as the most important source of news for most Americans. As early as 1965 the US TV network CBS showed US Marines using Zippo lighters to set fire to Vietnamese villagers' homes. During the Tet Offensive of 1968 (see pages 355–56) TV viewers saw South Vietnamese police chief Colonel Nguyen Ngoc Loan executing a Viet Cong suspect (see Source 8). Improving technology meant that TV crews could bring lightweight cameras very close to the conflict zones. One of the most famous reporters was CBS' Walter Cronkite. He reported throughout the Tet Offensive as US forces devastated large areas of the South Vietnam city of Hué in their efforts to destroy Viet Cong and NVA fighters. It was during the Tet Offensive that Cronkite declared that he thought the war was unwinnable. As the war progressed the media continued to report on the conflict, with journalists reporting from the front line and powerful images beamed into American living rooms.

SOURCE 9

Text of a TV report by a journalist on patrol with US Marines in the Mekong Delta in 1969.

The Marines who carry out patrols like this in the Mekong Delta are convinced they are winning their war against the VC. They point out as evidence of their success the number of VC dead and the number of VC defectors. But to do this they have needed the support of thousands of well-trained troops, of barrack ships, helicopter gunships, air support and the river marine force to contain and destroy what amounts to scattered handfuls of Viet Cong in these parts.

SOURCE 10

CBS News journalist Walter Cronkite broadcasting from Vietnam in February 1968. He was regarded as the most trusted reporter in America.

PRACTICE QUESTION

Study Sources 8 and 9.
How useful are Sources 8 and 9 to a historian studying why American attitudes turned against the Vietnam War in the late 1960s?
Explain your answer using Sources 8 and 9 and your contextual knowledge.

THINK

1   Would you regard the tone of Source 9 as controversial or critical, or fairly neutral? Explain your answer.
2   Do you think the scene in Source 8 would have been more shocking as a photograph or shown as it happened on TV? Explain your answer.

What was the impact of the media coverage?

The issue of the media coverage during the Vietnam War has been the subject of intense debate, as you can see from Source 11.

SOURCE 11

Daniel Hallin, Professor of Communications at the University of California, writing on the Museum of TV website.

What was the effect of television on the development and outcome of the war? The conventional wisdom has generally been that for better or for worse it was an anti-war influence. It brought the 'horror of war' night after night into people's living rooms and eventually inspired revulsion and exhaustion. The argument has often been made that any war reported in an unrestricted way by television would eventually lose public support. Researchers, however, have quite consistently told another story.

SOURCE 12

An extract from a blog called the 'Warbird's Forum'. The author was the daughter of a Vietnam veteran.

The horrors of war entered the living rooms of Americans for the first time during the Vietnam War. For almost a decade in between school, work, and dinners, the American public could watch villages being destroyed, Vietnamese children burning to death, and American body bags being sent home. Though initial coverage generally supported US involvement in the war, television news dramatically changed its frame of the war after the Tet Offensive. Images of the US-led massacre at My Lai dominated the television, yet the daily atrocities committed by North Vietnam and the Viet Cong rarely made the evening news. Moreover, the anti-war movement at home gained increasing media attention while the US soldier was forgotten in Vietnam. Coverage of the war and its resulting impact on public opinion has been debated for decades by many intelligent media scholars and journalists, yet they are not the most qualified individuals to do so: the veterans are.

THINK

Study Source 12. Do you agree that veterans are the people most qualified to comment on the impact of the media?

President Johnson remarked that if he had lost the support of Cronkite he had lost the support of Middle America. US Admiral Grant Sharp and General Westmoreland both claimed the media undermined the war effort. Plenty of other commentators have put forward the view that the media crippled the war effort in Vietnam. Opponents of this view have also put forward their arguments:

- American attitudes were turning against the Vietnam War by 1967 anyway. The media reflected the changing views rather than creating them.
- Casualties (see Figure 7 on page 360) and war weariness were the reasons why support for the war dropped – not the media.
- Shocking scenes were very rare on the TV screens. Less than 25 per cent of reports showed dead or wounded, and usually not in any detail.
- Research shows that, from 1965 to 1970, only 76 out of 2,300 TV reports showed heavy fighting. In a sample of almost 800 broadcasts of the time, only 16 per cent of criticisms of government policy came from journalists. The majority of critical comments came from officials or the general public.
- If the journalists were lying, why was Walter Cronkite regarded as the most trustworthy man in America?

FOCUS TASK

Why is the role of the media in Vietnam a controversial issue?

Study the information and sources on these pages and prepare a presentation on this question. You will need to explain:

- how the attitude of the reporting changed
- the importance and influence of television
- the case that the media did undermine the war effort
- the case against this view.

If you are feeling very brave you could decide which side of the debate you stand on! You could also research this issue on the internet, as there is a great deal of debate still going on.

The anti-war protest movement

For many Americans, 1968 meant more than the war in Vietnam. The year 1968 saw protests in the USA on a wide range of issues such as the right to free speech in universities, CIVIL RIGHTS for African Americans and the condition of the poorest people in the USA.

These factors were all connected of course. When President Johnson was elected in 1964 he promised to create a 'Great Society'. By this he meant better living standards, health care and other benefits for all Americans. He did manage to deliver on some of his promises but the horrendous cost of the Vietnam War undermined his most ambitious plans. So in this respect the Vietnam War became linked to the issue of poverty and welfare. In 1968 the African American civil rights leader Martin Luther King began to widen his campaigning for civil rights to include issues of poverty. He also criticised the war itself and the way it was being fought.

SOURCE 13

Civil rights leader Martin Luther King speaking in the USA in April 1968.

This confused war has played havoc with our domestic destinies. Despite feeble protestations to the contrary, the promises of the great society have been shot down on the battlefields of Vietnam. The pursuit of this widened war has narrowed the promised dimensions of the domestic welfare programs, making the poor – white and Negro – bear the heaviest burdens both at the front and at home.

The war has put us in the position of protecting a corrupt government that is stacked against the poor. We are spending $500,000 to kill every Viet Cong soldier while we spend only $53 for every person considered to be in poverty in the USA. It has put us in a position of appearing to the world as an arrogant nation. Here we are 10,000 miles away from home fighting for the so-called freedom of the Vietnamese people when we have so much to do in our own country.

Vietnam also became linked to the issue of race. There were relatively few African Americans in college in the USA, which meant that fewer of them could escape the draft. As a result, 30 per cent of African Americans were drafted compared to only 19 per cent of white Americans. African Americans also pointed out that 22 per cent of US casualties were African American, even though this group made up only 11 per cent of the total US forces. One high-profile African-American athlete, the boxer Muhammad Ali, made his own stand by refusing to obey the draft on the grounds of his Muslim faith. He was stripped of his world title and had his passport taken. Ali was a follower of the radical Black Power group, Nation of Islam. These groups all opposed the draft when African Americans were discriminated against at home. As some of them pointed out, 'the Viet Cong never called us nigger'.

SOURCE 14

An American cartoon from 1967.

"There's Money Enough To Support Both Of You — Now, Doesn't That Make You Feel Better?"

Student protests

One of the most powerful sources of opposition to the war was the American student movement. Many young Americans did not want to be drafted to fight in a war they did not believe in, or even thought was morally wrong. They had seen the media reports from the front line, especially the massacre at My Lai in 1968. Instead of Vietnam being a symbol of a US crusade against Communism, to these students Vietnam had become a symbol of defeat, confusion and moral corruption (see Source 15). Students taunted the American President Lyndon B. Johnson with the chant 'Hey, Hey LBJ, how many kids did you kill today?' Thousands began to 'draft dodge' – refusing to serve in Vietnam when they were called up. The anti-war protests reached their height between 1968 and 1970.

SOURCE 15

An American comments on US policy failure in Vietnam.

One does not use napalm on villages and hamlets sheltering civilians if one is attempting to persuade these people of the rightness of one's cause. One does not defoliate [destroy the vegetation of] the country and deform its people with chemicals if one is attempting to persuade them of the foe's evil nature.

In the first half of 1968, there were over a hundred demonstrations against the Vietnam War involving 40,000 students. Frequently, the protest would involve burning the American flag – a criminal offence in the USA and a powerful symbol of the students' rejection of American values.

Kent State University, 1970

Anti-war demonstrations often ended in violent clashes with the police. At Berkeley, Yale and Stanford universities, bombs were set off. The worst incident by far came in 1970. At Kent State University in Ohio, students organised a demonstration against President Nixon's decision to invade Vietnam's neighbour, Cambodia. Panicked National Guard troopers opened fire on the demonstrators. Four students were killed and eleven others were injured. The press in the USA and abroad were horrified. Some 400 colleges were closed as 2 million students went on strike in protest at the action.

PRACTICE QUESTION

'The main reason for Nixon's policy of Vietnamisation was the cost of the war.'

How far do you agree with this statement?
Explain your answer.

SOURCE 16

The Kent State University demonstrations in Ohio, 4 May 1970.

The Watergate affair

By 1972 Nixon's main priority was to get re-elected. Policies in Vietnam and in Asia in general were directed at this. However, at home he faced another problem – Watergate.

The Watergate complex is a large office building in Washington DC. In 1972 the Democratic Party had their campaign headquarters there. In June 1972 five men were caught by policemen inside the Democratic Party Offices. They had forced their way in, and were attempting to place bugging devices. The arrested men were Republicans working for CREEP (the Campaign to Re-Elect the President). The Democratic leadership protested; the Republicans said they knew nothing about it. Nixon went on to win the presidential election by a landslide.

However, evidence began to emerge that implicated the President's office, if not the President himself. Newspapers and television began to dig out the facts, while Nixon used his presidential powers to obstruct everything as much as possible. It then emerged that Nixon had been secretly recording every conversation in his Oval Office – with the intention of the content providing details for his memoirs. Nixon at first refused to hand over the tapes, and then when he was forced to do so by the SUPREME COURT it was discovered that there were sections missing. Experts decided that the erasure was deliberate, not accidental. Nixon was threatened with IMPEACHMENT (that is, a vote to remove him from office). Faced with this, he resigned in August 1974.

All this was going on as the last stages of the saga in Vietnam were unfolding.

SOURCE 17

A cartoon by Garland from the British newspaper the *Daily Telegraph*, 11 January 1967.

"... AND IN VIETNAM MY PRIMARY OBJECTIVE IS TO WIN THE HEARTS AND MINDS OF THE PEOPLE—OF THE U.S.A."

ACTIVITY

Source 17 is one of a series of cartoons which is to be presented in an online exhibition. Your task is to write a caption for the cartoon which explains the point being made in it. Your caption needs to be in two sections:

- A brief 20-word caption explaining the cartoon.
- A more detailed caption which internet users can select if they want to know more. This should be about 150 words.

You can refer to later events, even though this cartoon was published in 1967.

● The end of the war

While attention was focused in the USA on Watergate, and on developments in the Cold War, including the signing of the agreement at the end of the SALT talks in 1972 (see page 330), the last phases of the war in Vietnam were quickly happening.

The Paris Peace talks

As early as 1969 the new President, Nixon, authorised his National Security Adviser, Henry Kissinger, to open secret negotiations with North Vietnam. But the talks made little progress, especially as the North Vietnamese government was demanding the immediate withdrawal of all US troops, and was supported in this by the Viet Cong in South Vietnam. Meanwhile US public opinion was turning strongly against the war, and the North Vietnamese could afford to take a firm stance on the expectation that pressure at home would force the USA to withdraw its troops anyway.

The world situation dramatically changed in 1972. The North Vietnamese launched a major offensive but were unable to conquer South Vietnam. Meanwhile President Nixon made historic visits to both China and the Soviet Union, exploiting rivalry and distrust between the two. Brezhnev and his advisers agreed to act as intermediaries between North Vietnam and the USA. A provisional agreement was reached in October 1972, as a result of much work. The American delegation was led by Kissinger.

In Paris in January 1973 the peace agreement was signed by North Vietnam, South Vietnam and the USA. Nixon described it as 'peace with honour'. Others disagreed, but it opened the door for Nixon to pull out all US troops. By the end of March 1973 all American forces had left Vietnam.

> ### SOURCE 20
>
> A headline in the *Los Angeles Times*, 24 January 1973.
>
> ***History of Viet Conflict – Murky Start, Uncertain End***

The fall of Saigon

It is not clear whether Nixon really believed he had secured a lasting peace settlement. But within two years it was meaningless and South Vietnam had fallen to the Communists.

Nixon had promised continuing financial aid and military support to Vietnam, but Congress refused to allow it. They did not want to waste American money. The evidence was that the South Vietnamese regime was corrupt and lacked the support of the majority of the population. Even more importantly, Nixon himself was in big political trouble with the Watergate scandal. In 1974 Nixon was forced to resign over Watergate, but the new President, Gerald Ford, also failed to get the backing of Congress over Vietnam.

Without US air power or military back-up, and without the support of the majority of the population, the South Vietnamese government could not survive for long. In December 1974 the North Vietnamese launched a major military offensive against South Vietnam. The capital, Saigon, fell to Communist forces in April 1975.

One of the bleakest symbols of American failure in Vietnam was the televised news images of desperate Vietnamese men, women and children trying to clamber aboard American helicopters taking off from the US embassy. All around them Communist forces swarmed through Saigon. After 30 years of constant conflict, the struggle for control of Vietnam had finally been settled and the Communists had won.

> ### SOURCE 18
>
> The main points of the peace agreement of January 1973.
>
> 1 *Immediate ceasefire.*
> 2 *Release of all prisoners of war within 60 days.*
> 3 *Withdrawal of all US forces and bases.*
> 4 *Full accounting of missing in action.*
> 5 *Self-determination for South Vietnam.*

> ### SOURCE 19
>
> Reaction to the agreement of January 1973 in the American magazine *Newsweek*, 5 February 1973.
>
> #### *For Whom the Bell Tolls*
>
> *… The nation began at last to extricate itself from a quicksandy war that had plagued four Presidents and driven one from office, that had sundered the country more deeply than any event since the Civil War, that in the end came to be seen by a great majority of Americans as having been a tragic mistake.*
>
> *… but its more grievous toll was paid at home – a wound to the spirit so sore that news of peace stirred only the relief that comes with an end to pain. A war that produced no famous victories, no national heroes and no strong patriotic songs, produced no memorable armistice day celebrations either. America was too exhausted by the war and too chary [cautious] of peace to celebrate.*

THINK

Study Source 19. Do you think the views expressed would be common to most Americans?

SOURCE 21

A scene from the American embassy in Saigon, April 1975. An embassy official is punching a man in the face to make him let go of the helicopter.

SOURCE 22

US personnel and selected South Vietnamese boarding the last helicopter out of Saigon, 30 April 1975.

SOURCE 23

An extract from a website, 'Vietnam War Statistics', by an American ex-serviceman.

The American military was not defeated in Vietnam – *The American military did not lose a battle of any consequence. From a military standpoint, it was almost an unprecedented performance. This included Tet 68, which was a major military defeat for the VC and NVA.*

The United States did not lose the war in Vietnam, the South Vietnamese did – *The fall of Saigon happened 30 April 1975, two years after the American military left Vietnam. The last American troops departed in their entirety 29 March 1973. How could we lose a war we had already stopped fighting? We fought to an agreed stalemate.*

The fall of Saigon – *The 140,000 evacuees in April 1975 during the fall of Saigon consisted almost entirely of civilians and Vietnamese military, not American military running for their lives. There were almost twice as many casualties in Southeast Asia (primarily Cambodia) the first two years after the fall of Saigon in 1975 than there were during the ten years the US was involved in Vietnam.*

THINK

Study Sources 21 and 22. What would be the reactions to these photographs in the USA?

FOCUS TASK

Why did the USA lose the Vietnam War?

Look back at your answers to the Focus Tasks on pages 359 and 362. You will find them very useful for this summary activity.

The Americans did not lose purely for military reasons. There were other factors as well.

1 In the centre of a large sheet of paper put the question: 'Why did the USA lose the Vietnam War?'
2 Around the question, draw six boxes. In five boxes write an explanation or paste a source which shows the importance of the following factors:
   – US military tactics in Vietnam
   – The unpopularity of the South Vietnamese regime
   – The experience of the Viet Cong and the inexperience of the American soldiers
   – Opposition to the war in the USA
   – Chinese and Soviet support for the Viet Cong.
3 In the sixth box write: 'But did they really lose?' and summarise the argument put forward in Source 23, and your view on it.
4 Add other boxes if you think there are other factors you should consider.
5 Add lines to connect the factors and write an explanation of each connection.

The price of conflict: Problems of Vietnam in 1975

Effects on Vietnamese CITIZENS

- Chemical warfare meant that South Vietnamese citizens had in their bodies levels of dioxin (a powerful poison used in Agent Orange) three times as high as US citizens.
- Large numbers of unexploded mines and bombs caused death and injury to adults and children for years to come.
- Napalm caused horrific burns which killed or disfigured victims, often civilians caught in crossfire.

Effects on the environment

Chemical warfare

- Damaged crops, which led to food shortages.
- Destroyed 5.4 million acres of forest areas and the animals and plants living there.
- Poisoned streams and rivers.

Effects on US troops

- **Drug addiction**: Hard drugs were available easily and cheaply in Vietnam from neighbouring Laos and Cambodia – official US army estimates put heroin use by American troops at 30 per cent.
- **Confusion and bitterness**: US forces were not welcomed home in the same way as victorious troops in the Second World War. Many found it difficult to adjust to civilian life.
- **Stress**: Strains of war led to post-traumatic stress.
- **Cancer**: Some troops who handled Agent Orange contracted cancer.

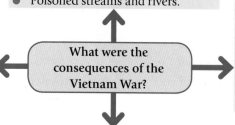

What were the consequences of the Vietnam War?

Effects on Vietnamese society

Morals:

- Fighting drove thousands of peasants into shanty towns near US bases – poverty, prostitution and drug abuse were common.
- US forces were supplied with vast amounts of luxuries as well as military supplies – this created a huge black market with corrupt South Vietnamese government officials.
- Buddhist priests protested about the effects of the American presence in Vietnam in the late 1960s.

Refugees:

- Around 5 million South Vietnamese were displaced from their homes. Towns and villages in North and South Vietnam were devastated by bombing and ground fighting.
- Vietnam took well over 20 years to start recovering from the war. Poverty, Communist policies and the hope of a better life led thousands of Vietnamese to become 'boat people' in the late 1970s onwards. They tried to sail to Malaysia and Hong Kong in makeshift boats. Around 1 million refugees escaped to the West (mainly USA). At least 50,000 were drowned or murdered by pirates. In the mid-1990s the USA finally ended its trade ban with Vietnam and the World Bank was allowed to invest there, even though it remained a Communist country.

KEY WORDS

Make sure you know what these words mean and are able to define them confidently.

- Agent Orange
- Armistice (Korea)
- Arms race
- Atomic bomb
- Capitalism
- Cold War
- Communism
- Containment
- Domino Theory
- Guerrilla warfare
- Mass bombing
- Napalm
- Search and destroy
- SEATO
- United Nations (UN)
- Viet Cong
- Viet Minh
- Vietnamisation

TOPIC SUMMARY

The ending of conflict in Vietnam

- Nixon was elected with the promise of ending the war in Vietnam.
- He saw Vietnam in the wider context of the Cold War, especially relations with China.
- After peace talks initially made no progress, the war was escalated into Cambodia and Laos and with intensive bombing of North Vietnam.
- At home there was increasing opposition to the war, as reflected in the media.
- Demonstrations and student protests gained much publicity, including the one at Kent State University.
- Peace talks resumed in Paris with an agreement in 1973.
- All US troops were withdrawn from South Vietnam in 1973.
- North Vietnamese troops completed the conquest of the South in 1975.
- The last American advisers and government officials left Saigon by helicopter in April 1975.
- Substantial problems remained for Vietnam (damage, injuries, etc.) and for the USA (e.g. huge loss of pride).

ASSESSMENT FOCUS

KEY

Focus words

Command words

Source/knowledge reminder words

Your exam will include four questions on this topic. The question types will be the same every year, but the questions could be on any content from the specification, so you need to know it all!

We have provided one example of each kind of question. For questions based on sources we have used sources that you have already come across in this chapter. We have analysed each of the questions to highlight what you are being asked to do and written a sample answer with comments on how it could be improved.

Source A is Source 7, page 348.

Q1 Study Source A. Source A **supports** the Viet Cong. **How do you know**?

Explain your answer by using **Source A** and your **contextual knowledge**.

(4 marks)

Sample answer

The poster shows American soldiers surrounded by Viet Cong soldiers hiding in the jungle. This is how the Viet Cong fought using guerrilla tactics.

– This answer shows a clear understanding of the poster's intention, but ideally it should include some knowledge to support its statements. For example, you could explain about the significance of guerrilla warfare. You can also look at the source to comment on the way the American and Viet Cong soldiers are shown.

– *Study Source 15 on page 351. Attempt the same question with that source.*

Source B is Source 8, page 349. Source C is Source 9, page 349.

Q2 Study Sources B and C. **How useful** are **Sources B and C** to a historian studying attitudes towards the invading US armies in Vietnam?

Explain your answer using **Sources B and C** and your **contextual knowledge**.

(12 marks)

Sample answer

Source B is a poster telling the USA to get out of Vietnam. The Americans are being accused of being imperialists. This means that they are trying to build an empire. The poster is clearly anti-American. The people in the poster look determined and angry. Therefore the poster is useful for showing attitudes against the US soldiers.

Source C is from a letter written by an important person in the North Vietnamese Communist Party. It says that the Vietnamese must get rid of the Americans, but it does acknowledge that the more misery the Americans inflict the more they will be hated. Therefore the source is useful for showing the attitudes towards the American invading armies.

– The answer provides some basic comments on each of the two sources, but it could usefully include more in-depth analysis of the content and some examination of the provenance. There is very little contextual knowledge shown. This could be improved substantially.

– *For each of the two sources, make a list of what you know about the provenance and whether or not you think this makes the source more or less reliable.*

– *Then think about the context of the period in which the sources were created. What were people's attitudes in general at that time – in Vietnam and in the USA?*

– *Now look at the content of each source. Using your knowledge, think how useful the content is for studying attitudes towards the invading US armies.*

Q3 Write an account of how the Tet Offensive of 1968 **influenced** American attitudes towards the war in Vietnam.

(8 marks)

Sample answer

The Tet Offensive by the North Vietnamese occurred in 1968. Viet Cong fighters attacked over 100 cities and some military targets. The US embassy in Saigon was temporarily captured. US troops fought back and the Viet Cong had very heavy casualties, probably about 10,000 dead. The Viet Cong had not received sufficient support from the people of South Vietnam.

However, the attack was reported differently in the USA. Media coverage, which had been generally favourable in America to what was happening in Vietnam, changed dramatically. The temporary loss of the US embassy was seen as a disgrace – especially when the USA had half a million troops in Vietnam. More Americans joined the calls for the withdrawal of troops from Vietnam.

– The answer provides some details of the event – it could have more precise details of the attacks.

– The end of the answer mentions the consequences of the Tet Offensive in the context of the war.

– *List two main reasons why the Tet Offensive was important in the context of the war. To help you, think about:*

– *what the event had shown the American public (and politicians)*

– *what the American public's view would be about whether the war was winnable.*

Q4 'The **main reason** why the Korean War ended in stalemate was **the reluctance of the USA to escalate the war beyond North Korea into China.**' **How far** do you agree with this statement?

Explain your answer.

(16 marks)

Sample answer

The Korean War lasted from 1950 to 1953. It started when North Korean troops invaded South Korea. Well before the end of the war stalemate had been reached. Why was this?

The USA was eager to show its power in Korea in 1950. President Truman was alarmed at the spread of Communism in the East – China had become Communist in late 1949 and Communist North Korea wanted to take over South Korea as well. The USA managed to get the UN Security Council to pass a resolution to intervene to protect South Korea. (This was possible because the USSR had walked out over Communist China not being admitted to the UN instead of Nationalist China.)

However, the American government was well aware of how dangerous it would be if the war escalated too much. The USSR possessed atomic bombs as well as the USA. The USSR and China had massive reserves of manpower to aid North Korea if the war spread outside the borders of Korea. Hence General MacArthur's unapproved foray into Chinese territory was swiftly ended by President Truman and MacArthur was sent back home.

However, there were other major reasons for the war ending in stalemate. The North Koreans were increasingly getting support (officially in secret) from both China and the USSR – both manpower and weapons. This meant that however many troops America and other countries sent (including the British), they were going to be matched or outnumbered by the Communists.

Another was the terrain. Just like Vietnam fifteen years later, the UN troops found progress around the country difficult. Indeed, General MacArthur had used the sea to land at Inchon in order to surprise the North Koreans. Troops found the weather bitterly cold in the mountains in the winter and had no possibility of controlling the area, where local knowledge was essential for controlling the mountain passes.

Another reason for stalemate was the condition of the South Korean government. The President of South Korea, Syngman Rhee, was anti-Communist. But his government was corrupt and not really democratic. American politicians found it increasingly difficult to support Rhee with enthusiasm.

Therefore, it could be argued that the USA was wise not to escalate the war and settle for a stalemate because of the other factors explained above.

- This is a clearly argued answer. It develops an explanation of the stated factor and puts this alongside other factors.

- It demonstrates some accurate knowledge and understanding, and the answer is organised in a way that is totally focused on the question.

- However, in several of the aspects identified it lacks precise details.

- The answer contains accurate spelling and punctuation, the meaning is clearly expressed and a range of specialist terms are used to explain arguments.

- *What additional details of evidence could you add to the latter paragraphs to improve this answer?*

Now write your own answers to the questions on pages 369–70 using the teacher's feedback to help you.

GLOSSARY

ABDICATION   The act of giving up the throne.

ABOLITIONIST   Movement devoted to abolishing slavery.

AGENT ORANGE   Defoliant chemical used by the USA in the Vietnam War.

AIRLIFT (BERLIN)   Food and other supplies brought in to Western Berlin following Russian blockade.

AMERICAN DREAM   An American ideal in which equal opportunity is available to all.

ANSCHLUSS   Incorporating Austria into Nazi Germany in 1938.

APPEASEMENT   The policy of giving in to what are regarded at the time as reasonable demands in order to avoid a worse solution.

ARMISTICE   An end to the fighting in a war so that discussions can begin which then lead to a peace treaty.

ARMS RACE   Competition between nations to develop the most superior weapons.

ASSASSINATED   Killed for political or religious reasons.

ASSASSINATION   The murder of an important person (e.g. head of state) in a surprise attack.

ASSEMBLY OF LEAGUE OF NATIONS   The part of the League where all member states were represented equally.

ATOMIC BOMB   Violent explosive, powered by rapid release of nuclear energy.

ATTRITION   Wearing down the opposition through continuous sustained pressure.

AUTHORITARIANISM   Accepting that some people have authority over others. Personal freedoms are therefore limited.

AUTOBAHN High speed motorways built by the Nazis in Germany in the 1930s to create jobs.

AUTOCRACY   A system of government where complete authority is in the hands of one person who can make all important decisions.

BLACK POWER MOVEMENT   African-American movement emphasising racial pride and equality.

BLOCKADE (BERLIN)   Attempt by Soviet Union to prevent supplies reaching western Berlin.

BLOCKADE AT SEA   Enemy warships stopping people and supplies from getting in or out.

BOLSHEVIKS/BOLSHEVISM   Russian political movement led by Lenin and following Communist ideas developed by Karl Marx and further developed by Lenin.

BREZHNEV DOCTRINE   The right claimed by Soviet Russia to intervene in the politics of other Communist countries.

CAPITALISM/CAPITALIST   Political, social and economic system centred on democracy and individual freedoms such as free speech, political beliefs and freedom to do business.

CARICATURED   Depiction of a person in which certain features are exaggerated for comic effect.

CHEKA   Name of the State secret police under Lenin.

CITIZENS   The people of a country or place.

CIVIL RIGHTS   The right of citizens to political and social freedom and equality.

CIVIL WAR   War between two sides within the same nation or group. An example is in Russia between 1918 and 1921.

CLAIM   A plot of land or a stake in a mine.

CO-EXISTENCE   To live peacefully with other nations in spite of differences.

COLD WAR   Non-violent conflict between USA and USSR from 1945. The term gained currency when used by an American newspaper writer, Walter Lippmann, in spring 1947.

COLLECTIVE SECURITY   Co-operation between allies to strengthen security for each of them.

COLLECTIVISATION   Policy to modernise agriculture in the USSR 1928-40. Succeeded in modernising farming to some extent but with terrible human cost.

COMECON   Association of Communist countries in Eastern Europe to help trade and development.

COMINFORM   Communist Information Bureau, founded in 1947.

COMMUNISM/COMMUNIST   Political, economic and social system involving state control of economy and less emphasis on individual rights than Capitalism.

CONCENTRATION CAMPS Camps used by Nazis to hold political opponents in Germany.

CONGRESS   In the USA, the federal (i.e. national) law-making body, composed of the Senate and the House of Representatives.

CONSCRIPTION   A system whereby people are forced to join the army or navy.

CONTAINMENT   The Western policy during the Cold War designed to control the spread of Communism.

COUP   A brave action such as touching a live enemy in battle.

COVENANT OF LEAGUE OF NATIONS   Document which all members had to sign guaranteeing to carry out the League's purposes.

CREDIT   Gaining goods and services with an agreement to pay later, usually in instalments.

DAWES ACT   A law to turn Native Americans into farmers by giving them parcels of land, rather than tribes having large reservations.

DEMILITARISATION   Establishing an area that would have no armed troops or weapons.

DEMOBILISED   Released from the army.

DEMOCRACY Political system in which population votes for its government in elections held on a regular basis.

DEMOCRATIC   Giving more rights to the people, e.g. instead of the Kaiser or the Tsar.

DEPRESSION   Long period of financial problems in the economy involving lower living standards.

DESERT   Waterless area of land with little or no vegetation typically covered with sand.

DE-STALINISATION Reforms that took place after the death of Stalin.

DÉTENTE Easing of strained relations between East and West, e.g. in 1970s.

DICTATORSHIP A government where one person (or a small group) makes all the decisions.

DIKTAT Term used in Germany to describe the Treaty of Versailles because Germany had no say in the terms of the Treaty.

DISARMAMENT Getting rid of military forces and weapons.

DOMINO THEORY The theory that political events in one country could cause similar events in neighbouring countries.

DUMA Russian Parliament established after 1905 revolution in Russia and a source of opposition to Tsar 1905-17.

ENTENTE POWERS Agreement between two or more countries to work together; not a binding alliance, e.g. the Triple Entente of Britain, France and Russia.

EXODUSTERS Movement of Black Americans to Kansas in the late nineteenth century.

FEDERAL System of government where several states come together to form one country but remain independent in their internal affairs.

FINAL SOLUTION Nazi plan to exterminate the Jews and other races in Europe. Generally thought to have begun in 1942.

FIVE-YEAR PLAN Programme of economic development in the USSR from 1928 onwards. Achieved considerable progress in industry but with heavy human cost.

FLAPPERS Young women in the USA in 1920s who did not behave as traditional society expected.

FORT LARAMIE TREATY Agreement to bring peace between the whites and the Sioux Indians, 1851.

FORTY-NINER Someone looking for gold in California gold rush of 1849.

FREE-SOILER An opponent of slavery being permitted in new American states.

FREIKORPS Ex-soldiers in Germany after WW1.

GATLING GUNS Early type of machine gun with revolving barrels.

GENOCIDE The deliberate attempt to wipe out the people of a nation or ethnic group.

GENTILE What Mormons called anyone who was not a Mormon.

GESTAPO Secret police in Nazi Germany.

GHETTOS Part of a city, especially a slum area, occupied by a minority or persecuted group, usually in crowded and insanitary conditions.

GREAT POWERS A term used to describe the most powerful countries at the time – principally, Britain, France, Germany and the USA.

GUERRILLA WARFARE Hit and run tactics used instead of an 'open' battle.

HIRE PURCHASE Method to buy goods and pay in regular instalments.

HOLOCAUST The mass murder of Jews and other racial groups by the Nazis in WW2.

HOMESTEADER A settler who acquired free land on which they farmed and built their home.

HOOVERVILLE Slum area of makeshift shacks where unemployed workers lived in 1930s in USA.

HYPERINFLATION Where prices increased very rapidly and out of control, e.g. Germany 1923.

IDEALIST A person guided by hope and abstract plans rather than practical considerations.

IMMIGRATION People arriving at a foreign country to live there permanently.

IMPEACHMENT Process by which a President could be removed from office.

IMPERIAL Related to having an empire ruled by an emperor (in Germany a Kaiser; in Russia a Tsar).

INFLATION Rising prices.

INTER-CONTINENTAL BALLISTIC MISSILE (ICBM) Missile containing nuclear weapons with a range of at least 5500 km.

IRON CURTAIN Boundary between East and West Europe after 1945. Term first used by Winston Churchill in 1946.

IRRIGATION The supply of water to land and crops by a series of channels.

ISOLATIONISM Staying apart from the political affairs of other countries, e.g. USA in 1920s.

KAISER Title of ruler of Germany from 1871 to 1918; Emperor.

KU KLUX KLAN White American group using violence against Black Americans and other minority groups. Founded 1866.

LEBENSRAUM Additional territory believed to be necessary by a country for its natural development, e.g. Germany in the 1930s.

MANDATES Authority given by League of Nations to one of its members to rule a territory on behalf of the League.

MANIFEST DESTINY Belief that the expansion of the USA throughout the American continents was justified.

MARSHALL PLAN American scheme, 1947, giving money to European countries to help with rebuilding after the Second World War. It lasted for four years.

MARXIST Person who follows ideas of Karl Marx, a political commentator who believed that societies would eventually become Communist as workers overthrew bosses and took control of wealth and power.

MASS PRODUCTION Production of large quantities of goods, especially using assembly lines.

MCCARTHYISM Extreme opposition in the USA to Communism in the 1940s and 1950s, led by Senator Joe McCarthy.

MEDICINE MAN An Indian holy man who was believed to have healing powers.

MENSHEVIKS Opposition party in Russia in early 1900s, part of the Social Democratic Party before it split into Bolsheviks and Mensheviks.

MILITIA Military force raised from the civilian population to supplement a regular army in an emergency.

MORMONS Members of the Church of Jesus Christ of Latter-Day Saints founded in 1830 by Joseph Smith.

MUNITIONS   The equipment and ammunition of an army and navy.

MUTILATION   Damage done to a dead enemy's body such as cutting off parts.

NAACP   A civil rights organisation in the USA – National Association for the Advancement of Coloured People.

NAPALM   Substance containing petrol that burns strongly; used in some bombing in Vietnam.

NATION   Large group of people united through a common history and culture and usually under one government.

NATO   Formed in 1949 – North Atlantic Treaty Organisation – to protect North America and western Europe against perceived Communist threat.

NAVAL RACE   Competition between two countries to build the best navy, e.g. before 1914.

NAZISM   National Socialism, the political belief of Adolf Hitler and the Nazi Party based on aggressive expansion of German lands and the superiority of the Aryan race.

NEP   New Economic Policy put in place by Lenin in Russia in 1921.

NEW DEAL   Name given to F. D. Roosevelt's policies to help the USA recover from the Great Depression.

NKVD   Secret police within department responsible for internal security; powerful under Stalin in 1930s.

NOMADIC   Moving in search of animals to hunt or grass to feed your horses.

NUCLEAR DETERRENT   Theory that if a country has nuclear weapons it will prevent an attack from a hostile country.

OKHRANA   Secret police force of the Russian Tsars.

PARAMILITARY   Group of civilians organised in a military fashion to assist or to act in place of the regular army.

PARLIAMENTARY GOVERNMENT   Elected representatives having responsibility for policies and law-making.

PERPETUAL EMIGRATING FUND   Created by Mormon Church to help Mormon refugees migrate to Utah.

PLANTATION   Large estate on which crops were grown using slave labour.

POLYGAMY   Having more than one wife at a time.

PRESIDENT   Title given to someone who is head of state – usually as the result of elections.

PROHIBITION   Law banning the production and sale of alcohol in the USA between 1920 and 1933.

PROPAGANDA   Information given in a biased or misleading way, usually intended to support a specific political view. Also used in wartime to raise morale.

PROPORTIONAL REPRESENTATION   System where political parties get seats according to how many votes they get in the country as a whole.

PROVISIONAL GOVERNMENT   Government which took control of Russia after the March 1917 revolution which ended rule by Tsars.

PUPPET GOVERNMENT   One where a government appears to have power, but is in fact controlled by a stronger power.

PURGES   Policy pursued by Stalin in USSR in 1930s to remove potential opponents. Involved arrests, torture, show trials, deportations to labour camps and executions.

PUTSCH   Revolt designed to overthrow the existing government, most commonly associated with Kapp Putsch in 1920 and Nazis' attempted Putsch in Munich in 1923.

RANCHES   Large farms where cattle were raised.

RAWHIDE   Untanned buffalo or cattle hide.

REALIST   Someone who looks at things as they are and deals with them in a practical manner.

REARMAMENT   Building up arms and armed forces, used as a means to fight unemployment by many states in the 1930s, including Nazi Germany and Britain.

RECONSTRUCTION   The transformation of the southern states in the USA in the decade after the Civil War.

RED SCARE   A fear of Communism promoted by a group or a government, e.g. USA in early 1920s.

REICHSTAG   German word for Parliament under the Kaiser and then the Weimar Republic.

REMILITARISATION   Assembling troops and weapons in readiness for war.

REPARATIONS   Compensation to be paid by Germany to France, Belgium, Britain and other states as a result of the First World War.

REPOSSESS   To retake possession of a property when the owner can no longer make the repayments on their debts.

REPUBLIC   A country with no hereditary ruler; power is held by the people and those they elect.

REPUDIATE   To refuse to accept or be associated with or pay.

RESERVATIONS   Areas of land set aside by the US government for the Indian Nations to live on.

ROARING TWENTIES   Decade of wealth and excitement for many Americans, associated with new styles of dance and dress and new entertainments.

SA   The Brownshirts – stormtroopers of the Nazi Party.

SALT 1   The agreements reached in 1972 following Strategic Arms Limitations Talks.

SANCTIONS   Penalties for disobeying a law or regulation. Often used when a country has disobeyed international agreements and is punished.

SCALP   The scalp with the hair cut away from an enemy's head as a war trophy.

SCAPEGOATS   Groups made to take the blame for others.

SCHLIEFFEN PLAN   Plan drawn up in 1905 for possible rapid invasion of France. Used in 1914.

SEARCH AND DESTROY   Military strategy used in Vietnam, putting ground troops into enemy territory to seek out and destroy them.

SEATO   Southeast Asia Treaty Organisation, created for collective defence in Southeast Asia.

SECRETARIAT OF LEAGUE OF NATIONS   The huge number of clerical workers at all levels who were tasked with the job of maintaining the machinery of government of the League.

SELF-DETERMINATION   Where the people decide their own political future.

SETTLER   Person who goes to live in a new country or new area, e.g. on the Great Plains of the USA in nineteenth century.

SHARES   Shares in a company are bought and sold providing part-ownership.

SHOW TRIALS   Trials of political opponents which were given great publicity – most prominent in the USSR under Stalin in the 1930s.

SIEGE   When an army settles down around a fort or city to capture it and stops anyone from going in or out.

SLAVERY   Where one person is owned as property by another.

SOCIAL DEMOCRATIC PARTY   A left-wing political party, for example, the popular party in Germany in the 1920s.

SOCIALIST REVOLUTIONARIES   Opposition group in Tsarist Russia, the most well supported group as they had the support of the peasants.

SOD HOUSE   A house made using strips of turf.

SOVEREIGN NATION   A large independent group of people united by their common descent, culture and language.

SPARTACISTS   Communists in Germany in 1919 who wanted a revolution in Germany similar to the 1917 revolution in Russia

SPECULATION   Investing money in the hope of gain, but also risking loss.

SPLENDID ISOLATION   A country choosing to stand alone and have no involvement in the affairs of other countries, e.g. Britain in the pre-World War One era.

SS   Organisation within the Nazi Party which began as Hitler's bodyguard but expanded to become a state within a state.

STALEMATE   Deadlock; an unresolved situation where no-one seems able to win, e.g. trenches in First World War.

STATE (RELATING TO THE USA)   Once a territory reached a certain population size and had its own working government it could apply to become a state of the United States.

STOCK MARKET   A place where shares are bought and sold.

SUBSIDY   A sum of money paid from government funds.

SUFFRAGE   The right to vote.

SUPERPOWER   A country with lots of influence and power, e.g. USA and USSR after Second World War.

SUPREME COURT   Highest court in a country or state, e.g. Supreme Court of USA with its nine judges.

TARIFF   A tax to pay on imported goods or services.

TENNESSEE VALLEY AUTHORITY (TVA)   Created in the 1930s to promote economic development of the Tennessee river area across seven states.

TERRITORY (RELATING TO THE USA)   Administrative area set up in the West by the US government as it was settled.

TIPI   Also known as a lodge or a *tepee*, this was a portable home made of buffalo skins stretched over a framework of wooden poles.

TOTAL WAR   Full-scale war where any weapons can be used and where usual rules of war are ignored.

TRADE SANCTIONS   Penalties imposed as a punishment by one or more nations on another to harm trade.

TRANSCONTINENTAL   Crossing the North American continent from the Atlantic to the Pacific or crossing Russia from the West to the Pacific at Vladivostok.

TRENCH WARFARE   Combat in war where each side fights from a system of protective trenches.

TRIPLE ALLIANCE   An agreement between three countries to protect each other if attacked, e.g. Triple Alliance of 1882.

TRUMAN DOCTRINE   President Truman's policy of providing help for countries threatened by Communism.

TSAR   Ruler of Russia up until revolution in 1917.

TSARINA   Wife of Tsar.

UNO   United Nations Organisation, set up in 1945.

USSR   The former Russian Empire after it became a Communist state in the 1920s.

VETO   A president's constitutional right to reject a decision made by by law-making body, e.g. Congress in the USA.

VIET CONG   Communist-led guerrilla force of South Vietnam.

VIET MINH   Vietnamese group who fought for independence from French rule.

VIETNAMISATION   Policy of US withdrawal and handing over government to South Vietnam.

VIGILANTE   Someone who takes the law into their own hands and takes it upon themselves to punish wrongdoers.

WAGON TRAIN   Collection of as many as a hundred horse- or ox-drawn covered wagons travelling together across the Great Plains.

WALL STREET CRASH   The 1929 slump on the stock market in New York. People lost a lot of money and it led to the Great Depression of the 1930s.

WAR COMMUNISM   Policy pursued by Communist leader Lenin 1918-21 to try to build Communist society in Russia and also fight against his opponents. Caused major hardships and had to be temporarily replaced with New Economic Policy.

WAR GUILT   Clause 231 of Treaty of Versailles which blamed Germany and her allies for the First World War.

WARRIOR   A fighter.

WARSAW PACT   Alliance of Communist countries in E Europe, set up in 1955 as a reaction against NATO.

WELTPOLITIK   Germany's aggressive foreign policy before the First World War, intended to increase Germany's influence.

INDEX